Early Thame: Archaeological Investigations at Oxford Road Thame, Oxfordshire 2015

Volume 2: The Roman and Saxon Periods

Early Thame: Archaeological Investigations at Oxford Road, Thame, Oxfordshire 2015
Volume 2: The Roman and Saxon Periods

by

Chris Ellis and Alex Davies

with contributions by

Leigh Allen, Paul Booth, Lee G. Broderick, Seren Griffiths, Martin Henig, Lynne Keys, Louise Loe
Lauren McIntyre, E.R. McSloy, Julia Meen, Rebecca F. Nicholson, Cynthia Poole, Alice Rose
Ruth Shaffrey and Sarah F. Wyles

Illustrations by

Ken Lymer, Helena Munoz-Mojado, Aleksandra Osinska, Charlie Patman, Charles Rousseaux
Li Sou, Magdalena Wachnik and Amy Wright

Oxford Cotswold Archaeology Monograph No. 2
2024

Oxford Cotswold Archaeology Monograph No. 2

Published by Oxford Cotswold Archaeology

Copyright © Oxford Cotswold Archaeology 2024

Cotswold Archaeology, Building 11, Cotswold Business Park, Cirencester, Gloucestershire GL7 6BQ

Oxford Archaeology, Janus House, Osney Mead, Oxford, OX2 0ES

Oxford Cotswold Archaeology is an unincorporated Joint Venture comprising Oxford Archaeology and Cotswold Archaeology

All rights reserved. No part of this publication may be reproduced, stored in a retrieval system, or transmitted in any form or by any means, electronic, photocopying, recording or otherwise, without the prior permission of the copyright owner.

ISBN 978-1-9998222-7-9

British Library Cataloguing in Publication Data
A catalogue record of this book is available from the British Library

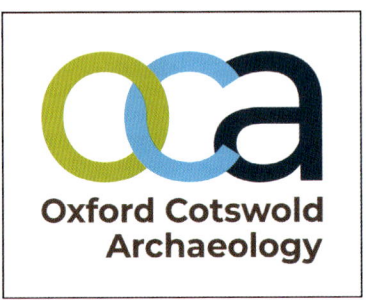

Front cover: Saxon loomweights within a sunken featured building
Back cover: Roman pottery beaker with white paint overslip decoration

Cover design by: Oxford Cotswold Archaeology
Produced by Past Historic, Kings Stanley, Gloucestershire
Printed by Henry Ling Ltd, Dorchester

CONTENTS

List of Figures	ix
List of Tables	xi
Acknowledgements	xiii
Abstract	xiv

Chapter 1   Introduction *by Chris Ellis* — 1
- Introduction and the structure of this publication — 1
- Archaeological background — 1
  - The wider picture — 1
  - The local picture — 5
  - Project aims — 5
- Previous work on the site — 5
- Site location, topography and geology — 5
  - The lie of the land — 6
  - The geology — 8
- The approach to excavation — 9
- General sequence and chronology — 10
  - Radiocarbon dating and Bayesian modelling — 10
  - Chronological summary — 11

Chapter 2   The Late Iron Age and Romano-British Period *by Alex Davies* — 13
- Late Iron Age/Early Roman (Period 3a; *c.* 25 BC–AD 100) — 13
  - Late Iron Age (Period 3ai; *c.* 25 BC–AD 50) — 13
  - Late Iron Age/Early Roman transition (Period 3aii; *c.* AD 50–70) — 16
  - Early Roman 1 (Period 3aiii; *c.* AD 70–100) — 18
  - Late Iron Age/Early Roman (Period 3a; unphased) — 20
- Early and Middle Roman (Period 3b; *c.* AD 100–240) — 23
  - Early Roman 2 (Period 3bi; *c.* AD 100–150) — 23
  - Middle Roman (Period 3bii; c. AD 150–240) — 32
- Late Roman (Period 3c; *c.* AD 240–410) — 32
  - Late Roman 1 (Period 3ci; *c.* AD 240–325) — 32
  - Late Roman 2 (Period 3cii; *c.* AD 325–350) — 36
  - Late Roman 3 (Period 3ciii; *c.* AD 350–410) — 36
- Roman (Period 3d; AD 43–410) — 40

Chapter 3   The Late Iron Age and Romano-British Finds and Environmental Remains — 41
- Late Iron Age and Roman pottery, *by Paul Booth* — 41
  - Fabrics/wares — 41
  - Vessel types — 48
  - Phasing and dates — 61
  - Use, reuse and repair — 66
  - Chronology — 67
  - General discussion — 69
  - Catalogue of illustrated vessels — 73

Roman metal finds, *by E.R. McSloy (with a contribution from Dr Martin Henig)*	75
Objects of personal adornment/dress	76
Household utensils – Copper alloy	78
Weights and measures – Lead	78
Tools – Copper alloy	80
Tools – Iron	80
Agricultural – Iron	80
Weaponry – Iron	80
Objects of uncertain function – Copper alloy	80
Objects of uncertain function – Iron	82
Roman coins, *by E.R. McSloy*	82
Coin list	82
Worked stone, *by Ruth Shaffrey*	83
The querns and millstones	83
Catalogue of querns and millstones	83
Other worked stone	85
Catalogue of other worked stone	85
Discussion	86
Fired clay, *by Cynthia Poole*	87
Fabrics	87
Structural fired clay	87
Portable furniture	89
Miscellaneous furniture	92
Structures	94
Discussion	95
Catalogue of illustrated fired clay	96
Roman ceramic building material, *by Cynthia Poole*	96
Fabrics	96
Forms	97
Markings	97
Discussion	97
Industrial residues, *by Lynne Keys*	98
Human remains, *by Lauren McIntyre and Alice Rose, with Louise Loe*	98
Period 3a – Late Iron Age/Early Roman (*c.* 25 BC–AD 100)	98
Period 3b – Early and Middle Roman (*c.* AD 100–240)	101
Period 2a–3d – Iron Age–Roman (*c.* 700 BC– AD 410)	105
Discussion, *by Lauren McIntyre*	106
Animal bone, *by Lee G. Broderick*	107
Fish bones, *by Rebecca A. Nicholson*	109
Charcoal, *by Julia Meen*	109
Period 3a – Late Iron Age/Early Roman (*c.* 25 BC–AD 100)	109
Period 3b – Early and Middle Roman (*c.* AD 100–240)	111
Period 3d – Roman (AD 43–410)	111
Period 3c – Late Roman (*c.* AD 240–410)	111
Woodland in the Romano-British period	112
Plant macrofossils, *by Sarah F. Wyles*	112
Period 3a – Late Iron Age/Early Romano-British (*c.* 25 BC–AD 100)	112
Period 3b – Early and Middle Romano-British (*c.* AD 100–240)	112
Period 3c – Late Romano-British (*c.* AD 240–410)	118
Period 3d – Romano-British (AD 43–410)	118
Discussion	119
Chapter 4 The Saxon Period *by Chris Ellis*	121
Post-Roman/Early Saxon burials	121
Sunken-featured buildings	121
Structure 33	129
Structure 35	131

Structure 36	133
Ditches/Gullies	135
Ditch/gully – phase 1	135
Ditch – phase 2	135
Ditch/gully – phase 3	135
Ditch/gully – phase 4	135
Late Saxon ovens and associated features	136
Oven 1	136
Oven 2	136
Oven 3	136
Oven 4	139
Stakeholes group 8046 and postholes 6993, 6981	139
The Late Saxon enclosure	139
The radiocarbon dates from the post-Roman features, *by Seren Griffiths*	142

Chapter 5 Saxon Finds and Environmental Remains — 143

Saxon pottery, *by Paul Booth*	143
Early–Mid Saxon	143
Later Saxon/Early medieval	147
Discussion	151
Catalogue of illustrated vessels	154
Metal finds, *by E.R. McSloy*	155
Select catalogue	155
Grave catalogue	155
Worked stone, *by Ruth Shaffrey*	157
Catalogue	157
Discussion	157
Loomweights and spindle whorls, *by Ruth Shaffrey*	158
Loomweights	158
Spindle whorls	161
Catalogue	161
Discussion	162
Fired clay, *by Cynthia Poole*	162
Fabrics	163
Form and function	163
Discussion	164
Illustrated fired clay	165
Medieval and post-medieval ceramic building material, *by Cynthia Poole*	165
Roof tile	165
Bricks	165
Discussion	165
Industrial residues, *by Lynne Keys*	165
Worked bone, *by Leigh Allen*	165
Catalogue	167
Human remains, *by Lauren McIntyre and Alice Rose, with Louise Loe*	167
Discussion *by Lauren McIntyre*	168
Animal bone, *by Lee G. Broderick with Rebecca A. Nicholson*	168
Taphonomy and spatial distribution	169
Age and sex	170
Element representation	172
Butchery	172
Pathology	173
Associated Bone Group	173
Discussion	173
Fish bones, *by Rebecca A. Nicholson*	176
Charcoal, *by Julia Meen*	176
Sunken-featured buildings	176

Ovens	176
Discussion	178
Plant macrofossils, *by Sarah F. Wyles*	182
Period 4a/b Saxon	182
Discussion	187

Chapter 6 Discussion *by Alex Davies and Chris Ellis* — 189

The Late Iron Age and Roman periods, *by Alex Davies*	189
The Late Iron Age/Early Romano-British period	189
The Early and Middle Roman period	190
The Middle Roman period	191
The Late Roman period	191
The development of Late Iron Age and Roman occupation at Thame in context	192
The Late Iron Age to Early Roman transformation	192
The Middle Roman decline and transformation: from settlement to agricultural production	193
Late Roman agricultural intensification	194
The post-Roman and Saxon period, *by Chris Ellis*	196
The post-Roman period	196
The Early–Mid Saxon settlement	197
The Late Saxon settlement	201
The Saxon settlements in context	202

Appendix   Methods Employed in Analysis — 205

Radiocarbon dates methodology, *by Seren Griffiths and Alex Davies*	205
Fired clay methodology, *by Cynthia Poole*	205
Ceramic building material methodology, *by Cynthia Poole*	205
The industrial residues methodology, *by Lynne Keys*	206
The human remains methodology, *by Lauren McIntyre and Alice Rose, with Louise Loe*	206
Charcoal methodology, *by Julia Meen*	207
Plant macrofossils methodology, *by Sarah F. Wyles*	207

References — 209

Index — 221

List of Figures

Chapter 1
1.1 Site location — 2
1.2 Archaeological sites in the immediate area — 4
1.3 Archaeological features and LiDAR and geophysical survey — 6
1.4 Site topography — 7
1.5 Site geology — 8
1.6 Site Areas — 9

Chapter 2
2.1 Late Iron Age period 3ai: plan — 14
2.2 Late Iron Age/Early Roman ditches: sections — 15
2.3 Late Iron Age/Early Roman period 3aii: plan — 17
2.4 Early Roman 1 period 3aiii: plan — 19
2.5 Late Iron Age/Early Roman inhumations: photographs — 21
2.6 Late Iron Age/Early Roman unphased: plan — 22
2.7 Late Iron Age/Early Roman unphased pits: plans and sections — 24
2.8 Early Roman 2 period 3bi: plan — 25
2.9 Results of Thame Site F1 Excavation and Site F2 Geophysical survey, showing Roman enclosure and droveway system — 27
2.10 Early Roman 2 period 3bi, corndrier 25: plan, sections and photograph — 28
2.11 Early Roman 2 period 3bi, corndriers 24 and 46: plans, sections and photograph — 30
2.12 Early Roman 2 (period 3bi) and Middle Roman (period 3bii) well 23: plan, section and photographs — 31
2.13 Late Roman 1 period 3ci: plan — 33
2.14 Late Roman 1 period 3ci, corndrier 29: plan and sections — 35
2.15 Late Roman 2 period 3cii: plan — 37
2.16 Late Roman 2 period 3ciii and unphased: plan — 38
2.17 Late Roman 3 corndrier 26 and Late Roman possible corndrier 27: plan, sections and photographs — 39

Chapter 3
3.1 Roman pottery, nos 1–17 — 49
3.2 Roman pottery, nos 18–31 — 50
3.3 Roman pottery, nos 32–48 — 51
3.4 Roman pottery, nos 49–60 — 52
3.5 Roman pottery, nos 61–77 — 53
3.6 Roman pottery, nos 78–101 — 54
3.7 Roman pottery, nos 102–124 — 55
3.8 Roman pottery, nos 125–144 — 56
3.9 Roman metal objects, nos 1–11 — 77
3.10 Roman metal objects, nos 12–19 — 79
3.11 Roman metal objects, nos 20–27 — 81
3.12 Worked stone, nos 1–2 — 84
3.13 Fired clay from wattle-supported structure, nos 1–2 — 88
3.14 Fired clay decorated plate *in situ*, no. 3 — 89
3.15 Fired clay, complete disc *in situ*, no. 4 — 90
3.16 Fired clay, nos 5–7 — 92
3.17 Fired clay, nos 8–11 — 93
3.18 Charcoal taxa, by sample, period 3 — 109

Chapter 4
4.1 Saxon phase plan — 122
4.2 Grave 16417 (SK. 1501) and grave 16629 (SK. 1502): plan and photographs — 123
4.3 SFB structure 33: plans with the location of finds within the feature, sections and photograph — 130
4.4 SFB structure 35: plans with the location of finds within feature and sections — 132
4.5 SFB structure 35: photographs — 133
4.6 SFB structure 36: plans with the location of finds within the feature, sections and photograph — 134
4.7 Late Saxon ovens (structure 44): plan and sections — 137
4.8 Late Saxon ovens (structure 44): photographs — 138
4.9 Late Saxon enclosure: plan, sections and photographs — 140
4.10 Post-Roman and Saxon features – modelled dates — 141

Chapter 5
5.1 Saxon pottery, nos 1–4 — 148
5.2 Saxon pottery, nos 5–14 — 149
5.3 Saxon pottery, nos 15–20 — 150

5.4	Late Saxon pottery, nos 21–23	151	5.12	Animal bone species proportions by NISP for each SFB with >20 NISP from hand-collected material 170
5.5	Post-Roman metal objects	156	5.13	Charcoal taxa, by sample 178
5.6	Saxon worked stone	158	5.14	Charcoal growth rings and diameter 182
5.7	Saxon loomweights, nos 1–3	159		
5.8	Saxon loomweights, nos 4–7	160		
5.9	Saxon fired clay	163		
5.10	Saxon worked bone	166		

Chapter 6

6.1	Anglo-Saxon sites in the Thames Valley	198
6.2	Early Anglo-Saxon cemeteries in the Upper Thames Valley	198

5.11 Proportions of identified animal bone fragments by condition category from the SFBs 169

List of Tables

Chapter 1
1.1 Radiocarbon dates: Roman and Saxon   10

Chapter 3
3.1 Late Iron Age and Roman pottery fabric codes and descriptions   42
3.2 Late Iron Age and Roman fabric quantification by sherd count, weight and rim equivalents (REs)   46
3.3 Samian ware stamps   48
3.4 Description and overall quantification of Late Iron Age and Roman vessel classes by rim equivalents (REs)   57
3.5 Quantification of vessel classes by fabric (rim equivalents) (row percent)   59
3.6 Fabric by phase (number of sherds – column percent)   62
3.7 Vessel type by phase (rim equivalents – column percent)   64
3.8 Broad chronological profiles of quantified Roman assemblages in Bicester area   70
3.9 Broad chronological profiles of quantified Roman assemblages from selected Buckinghamshire sites   70
3.10 Proportions of principal vessel functional groupings by main periods   73
3.11 Summary of metal finds according to period and functional category   75
3.12 Coins summary   82
3.13 Human remains. Period 3a: Late Iron Age/Roman (*c.* 25 BC–AD 100)   99
3.14 Human remains. Period 3a: Late Iron Age/Roman, summary of bone weights (Weight (% of total weight))   100
3.15 Period 3a: Late Iron Age/Roman cremated human bone, summary of fragmentation   100
3.16 Cremated bone: 2–0.5mm fraction prop ortional bone content (all contexts)   101
3.17 Human remains. Period 3b: Early Roman (*c.* AD 100–240)   102
3.18 Human remains. Period 3b: Early Roman, summary of bone weights (Weight (% of total weight))   103
3.19 Period 3b: Early Roman cremated human bone, summary of fragmentation   104
3.20 Human remains. Period 2a–3d: Iron Age to Roman (*c.* 700 BC–AD 410)   105
3.21 Human remains, undated, summary of bone weights (weight (% of total weight))   106
3.22 Undated cremated human bone, summary of fragmentation   106
3.23 Measurements taken from the Roman Associated Bone Groups (in mm)   107
3.24 Charcoal from period 3a, 3b, 3c and 3d features   110
3.25 Charred plant remains from period 3a and 3b features   113
3.26 Charred plant remains from period 3c and 3d features   115

Chapter 4
4.1 Summary of SFBs   124

Chapter 5
5.1 Quantification of Early–Mid Saxon pottery fabrics   144
5.2 Quantification of Late Saxon pottery fabrics   145
5.3 Summary of Saxon pottery from SFBs   146
5.4 Summary of selected Early–Mid Saxon assemblages from the Oxford region   152
5.5 Human remains. Period 4a: Saxon   168
5.6 Saxon animal bone. Number of Identified Specimens (NISP) and Number of Specimens (NSP)   169
5.7 Saxon animal bone. NISP values per SFB   171
5.8 Butchery marks recorded from the Saxon animal bone specimens   172
5.9 Measurements taken from the bones recorded from the Saxon period (in mm)   174
5.10 Charcoal identifications from Saxon samples   177
5.11 Wood taxa from spatial samples in SFB structure 35   179
5.12 Additional measurements of hazel roundwood from oven 3, layer 7386   181
5.13 Charred plant remains from period 4a/b features   183

Acknowledgements

Oxford Archaeology (OA) and Cotswold Archaeology (CA) formed a joint venture (Oxford Cotswold Archaeology (OCA)) to carry out required archaeological works at the request of Nexus Heritage, on behalf of Bloor Homes. OCA extends thanks to them for their input throughout the project and to Gerry Wait, the project consultant at Nexus Heritage (latterly GW Heritage). Thanks are also due to Richard Oram, archaeological advisor Oxfordshire Historic and Natural Environment Team (OHaNET), the archaeological advisors to the local planning authority (LPA), South Oxfordshire District Council.

The fieldwork Project Manager was Ken Welsh and Project Supervisors were Chris Ellis, John Boothroyd and Stuart Joyce. John Dillon was OCA manager at CA. Post-excavation management was carried out by Chris Hayden (OA), Karen Walker (CA), and latterly Clare Randall (CA). Rebecca Nicholson (OA) and Sarah Cobain (CA) were environmental managers. John Bennett (CA) and Matt Bradley (OA) were geomatics managers and Magda Wachnik (OA) was graphics manager/senior illustrator. Charlotte Patman and Amy Wright (CA) provided illustrations. Artefact drawings were prepared by Charles Rousseaux (OA) Aleksandra Osinska, Helena Munoz-Mojado and Li Sou (all CA) and the other finds photography by Magdalena Wachnik (OA), and the figures were prepared for publication by Charlie Patman, Amy Wright and Ken Lymer (all CA). The archive has been prepared for deposition with Oxfordshire Museums Service by Hazel O'Neill (CA) supported by volunteers.

We are grateful to the many field staff from OA and CA who carried out the excavation and our reviewer who provided extremely helpful advice in refining the text.

Abstract

Excavations at Site F, Oxford Road, Thame during 2015 revealed activity from the Late Iron Age and throughout the Roman and Saxon periods. This succeeded a Neolithic causewayed enclosure and Early Iron Age settlement which are described in a companion volume.

From the Late Iron Age and throughout the Roman period, landscape division was the predominant indicator of activity, with the use of the agricultural landscape underlined by the presence of corndriers and other pyrotechnical features in numerous sub-periods. The initial Late Iron Age field enclosure system was replaced, in a clear re-orientation, by a single settlement enclosure around the period of the Roman conquest. This offers relatively rare evidence in the region of discontinuity in rural settlement and landscape use during this period. The establishment of land enclosure however cannot be directly related to the political upheavals related to the conquest. Nevertheless, once established, the orientation of the land division was maintained, and a more significant enclosure system developed during the Early Roman period. Millstones attest to industrial-level activities during the early 2nd century, but there is only indirect evidence of a nearby settlement from pottery and other cultural material. Interestingly, activity greatly reduced during the Middle Roman period. The enclosures remained visible as some were recut in the Late Roman period. If settlement and associated agricultural processing activity moved away from the area during the Middle Roman period, the land probably remained in agricultural use, albeit at lower intensity. More visible activity resumed in the Late Roman period with more recutting of enclosure ditches and an increase in cultural material, suggesting that a settlement had reappeared nearby.

Either at the very end of the Roman period or in the post-Roman period two inhumation burials were made. At least one was associated with the final phases of Roman land division, suggesting that it occurred at least whilst the field boundaries were still visible. After a possible hiatus a settlement which comprised 13 sunken-featured buildings, arranged in a loose group, was established. These appear to have dated to the 6th–7th centuries. Several of the pits of these buildings contained evidence of weaving equipment in the form of loomweights, whilst one had burned down, or more likely had been dismantled and part of the structure burned, preserving important information about the structure and materials which had been used in its construction. After what appears to have been a further hiatus in settlement, a sequence of ovens was established in the 9th–10th centuries, suggesting that the area was again used for agricultural processing; evidence for both crop drying and malting was present. Adjacent to these ovens, a partial ditched enclosure was also created during the Late Saxon period, although it is unclear if its creation overlapped with the use of the ovens. The fills provided a date in the 10th–11th centuries, and whilst it contained no evidence of a building, it did possibly reference what may have been a prehistoric mound.

Chapter 1
Introduction

by Chris Ellis

The excavation of a large and complex multi-period site at Oxford Road, Thame, Oxfordshire covered an area of 3.9ha overlooking the River Thame. It was 1.5km to the north-west of the centre of the modern town of Thame, which is located roughly midway between Oxford and Aylesbury, amid the rolling hills of the tributaries of the Upper Thames catchment. Use of the area started in the Early Neolithic and continued to the later 1st millennium AD. A nationally important complex of monuments comprised a triple-ditched Early Neolithic causewayed enclosure, clusters of pits, and penannular monument. A Neolithic ring ditch and Middle Bronze Age cremation burial were succeeded in the Early Iron Age by a settlement which included a D-shaped enclosure, an extensive spread of pits, and burials. The prehistoric activity is presented in Volume 1. Late Iron Age and Romano-British field systems, a Saxon settlement and a Late Saxon enclosure are covered here in Volume 2.

Introduction and the structure of this publication

This volume presents reports on discoveries resulting from excavations undertaken from February to September 2015, on land at Oxford Road, Thame (Fig. 1.1). The archaeological features and deposits post-dating the prehistoric period include an extensive complex of field boundaries and ditches dating from the Late Iron Age/Early Romano-British period and throughout the Roman period. There were a number of burials made throughout the area in a number of periods. The Roman period could be divided into a number of phases, but the majority of the activity occurred during the Early Roman period. Post-Roman activity was indicated by burials dated to the 5th or 6th century, and this activity was superseded by the establishment of a Middle Saxon settlement. An enclosure associated with ovens was created during the Late Saxon period.

This publication presents an account of the archaeological features, deposits and finds relating to the Late Iron Age/Early Romano-British, Roman and Saxon periods of use. Earlier periods are dealt with in Volume 1. After introducing the project and its archaeological background (this chapter), Volume 2 is divided into two main chronological sections: the Late Iron Age/Early Romano-British and Roman periods (Chapters 2 and 3), and the Saxon period (Chapters 4 and 5), which describe the archaeological features and deposits and include reports on the artefactual and environmental/biological material within them. The volume is concluded with a discussion (Chapter 6) of the development and significance of the site within its broader regional context during these periods. Further information is included in the Appendix and in the site archive. This publication and the reports which it contains has been prepared by the Oxford Cotswold Archaeology Joint Venture (OCA) at the request of Nexus Heritage (later for GW Heritage), on behalf of Bloor Homes. The work was funded by Bloor Homes.

Archaeological background

The wider region in which the site at Thame is located has been relatively well studied, so this section seeks to outline the background which pertained prior to the project described in this volume. The ways in which this site contributes to further understanding are picked up in Chapter 6.

The wider picture

Against the backdrop of a well-settled landscape of the Thames Valley in the Middle Iron Age, there had been various developments during the Late Iron Age.

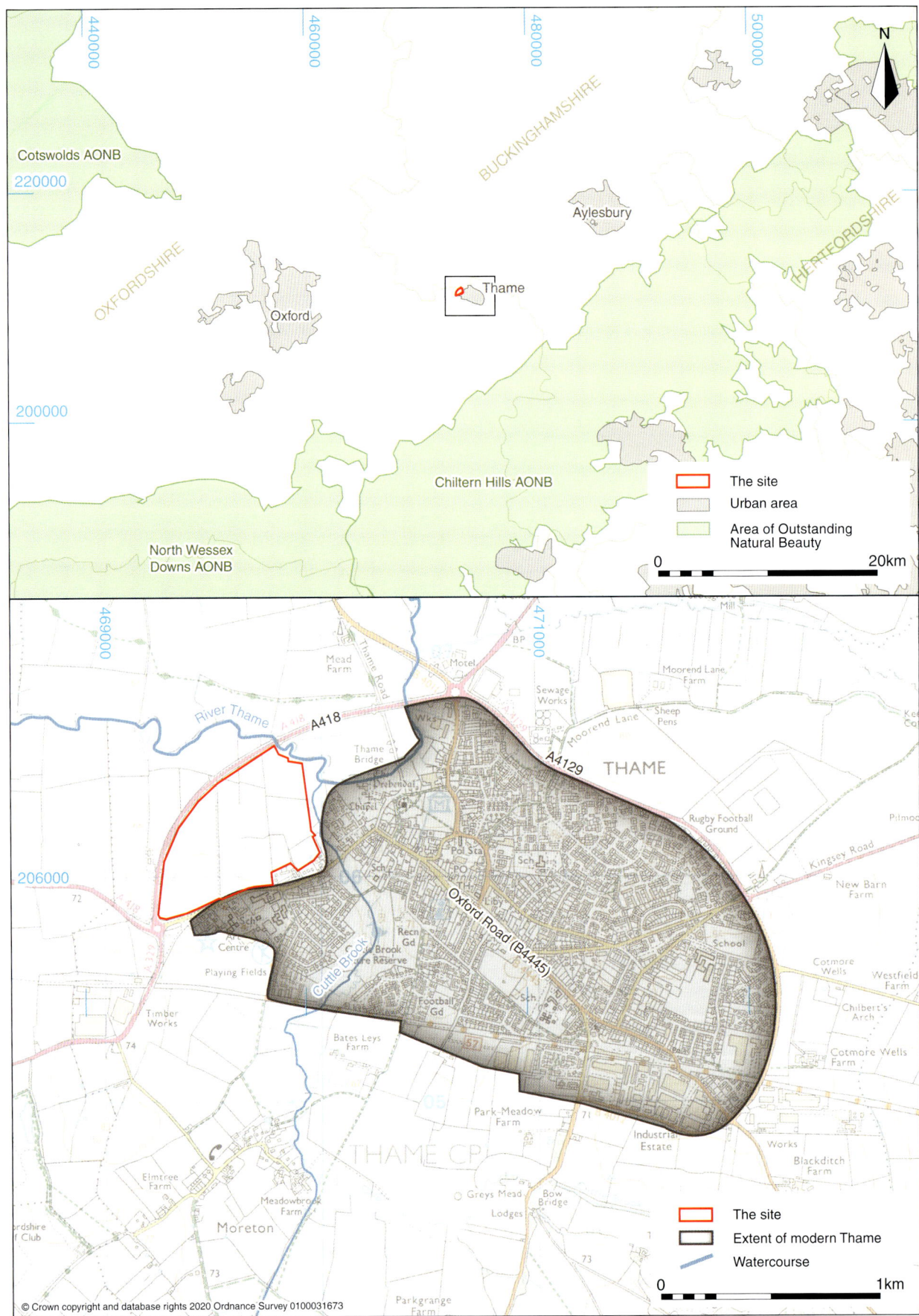

Fig. 1.1   Site location

Widespread changes to the building tradition occurred, with fewer roundhouses and a reduction in the digging of pits (Booth *et al.* 2007, 35). There does not appear, however, to have been a great deal of disruption of Late Iron Age field systems in the 1st century (Henig and Booth 2000, 106), and there is widespread evidence of continuity on settlements into the Early Roman period, with indications of change in the 2nd century.

The Roman period of the region saw the creation of a road network linking new urban centres, many of which grew up on locations of early military activity such as Alchester and Dorchester-on-Thames (Henig and Booth 2000), which would have been the largest centres near to the site at Thame. Other roadside settlements appeared, with the countryside populated by scattered small-scale rural settlements, some of which developed into villas during the Roman period. Associated fields and tracks occur throughout the region although these are not well understood and often not closely dated. Fields appear to be less commonly known to the north of the Thames (ibid., 99), although extensive systems are known which relate to other settlements, such as field systems around Alchester and associated with some villas, such as small rectangular enclosures around Ditchley (ibid., 101). Nucleated settlements started to come into existence during the first half of the 2nd century AD, and the general patterns of settlement appear to have continued into the 4th century once established (ibid., 109–10). The process of abandonment, creation and re-organisation of settlements went on throughout the 3rd and 4th centuries (Booth *et al.* 2007, 43, 75). Small rural cemeteries with various burial practices represented also occur (ibid., 227) along with dispersed 'backland' (Esmonde Cleary 2000) burials.

The Early Roman period has limited evidence for burial practice, with scattered inhumation burials and cremation graves a feature of many rural areas, although in some cases this was elaborated by the use of small defined enclosures. However, the number of burials known increased considerably in the Late Roman period, particularly in the Upper Thames Valley, although the focus for much of this was the extramural cemeteries associated with major towns (Booth *et al.* 2007, 224–5).

The original early medieval settlement at Thame dated to at least the 7th century (VCH 1962a, 170), and its location was close to the River Thame, in an area called 'Priestend'. This was at the junction of a north-west/south-east road from London to Oxford, the north-east/south-west road between Aylesbury and the royal vill at Quarrendon and Dorchester-on-Thames and a river crossing. This fits with a well-understood distribution of Saxon sites alongside the Thames and at its confluences with its tributaries (Hawkes 1986), used for exchange, movement and communication (Hamerow *et al.* 2013). This is highlighted by the creation of numerous minsters and other churches from the late 7th century within the Thames Valley, all within 4.8km of the river (Blair 1996, 5–6). The Mercian king Wulfhere swore an oath in AD 675 on the altar of the church at Thame, and this was most likely a minster church (Blair 1988; VCH 1962a, 163–5, 170–2; VCH 1962b, 199–200). Thame was one of three Hundredal Manors and an episcopalian vill, endowed to the bishops of Dorchester-on-Thames by Wulfhere, and was one of the most important settlements in east Oxfordshire up to the Domesday Survey of AD 1086 (Blair 1988, 50).

Some degree of continuity from the Late Roman period has been noted in the region. Mid to late 5th-century evidence overlay Late Roman occupation at Barton Court Farm villa (Miles 1986) and Yarnton (Hey 2004). Cemetery and settlement evidence of the Early and Mid Saxon period occurs throughout the Upper Thames Valley particularly along the Abingdon to Dorchester-on-Thames stretch, showing increasing influence and perhaps population of Germanic peoples in the later 5th and 6th centuries (Blair 1988, fig. 33; Booth *et al.* 2007, 380). Single burials or isolated/metal-detector finds likely to derive from burials are recorded quite regularly (Dickinson 1976; Blair 2018; Hamerow *et al.* 2013) in the region. A small concentration of 5th–6th-century burials and burial artefacts was recorded by Dickinson in the Upper Thame Valley around 10km from Thame (at Dinton, Winchendon, Bishopstone and Kingsey), south-west of Aylesbury.

Increasing social stratification and complexity are attested by later 6th-century and early 7th-century cemeteries at Berinsfield, burials and buildings at Long Wittenham, and settlement evidence at Sutton Courtenay (Dickinson 1976; Hawkes 1986; Brennan and Hamerow 2015; Hamerow *et al.* 2007; McBride *et al.* 2022). Settlements are characterised by earthfast timber halls and sunken-featured buildings showing little variation in status or indeed design (Booth *et al.* 2007, 83). In the majority of 5th–6th-century settlements, there is little evidence of planned layout (Reynolds 2003; Hamerow 2012).

The Mid Saxon period saw changes in the layout of settlement. The 8th and 9th-century phase at Yarnton comprised a series of enclosures along a track, the only building seen being a smithy (Hey 2004). This continued into the Late Saxon period with the emergence of towns throughout the region, of which Thame was one. It was also the period of the most evident origins of what would become a system of manorial holdings. There was a proliferation of small estates during this period, but knowledge of them is often dependent on documentary sources (Booth *et al.* 2007, 116–17). Archaeological evidence of Mid to Late Saxon settlement is relatively limited. At Lake End Road, Dorney, pottery suggested occupation from the 10th century, but a rectilinear enclosure appears to have only appeared in the 11th century; boundary ditches of the 10th century occurred at nearby Lot's Hole (Foreman *et al.* 2002, 73). Other

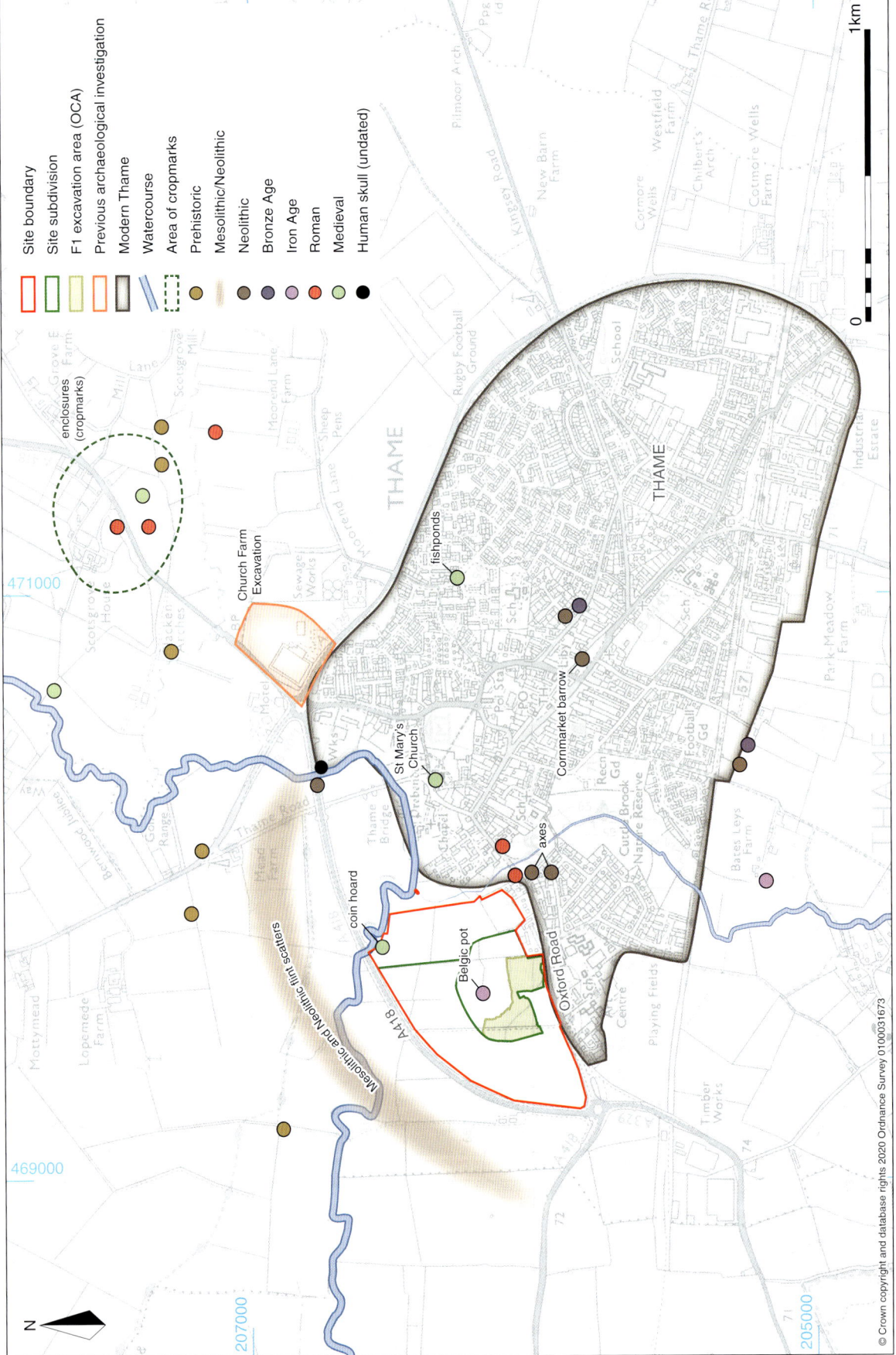

Fig. 1.2   *Archaeological sites in the immediate area*

excavations close to later village centres have also yielded features of this period, such as ditched enclosures at Wraysbury (Astill *et al.* 1989), and Manor Farm, Drayton (Booth *et al.* 2007, 120).

The local picture

Prior to the programme of archaeological investigation on the site and in its immediate surroundings, there was a limited indication of prehistoric and later activity. Mesolithic and Neolithic/Bronze Age flint scatters were reported in low to moderate density to the north, on both sides of the Thame Valley, as well as to the north-east of Thame. Two Neolithic flint axes were recorded about 200m south-east of the Oxford Road site (JMHS 2010). The most significant previous nearby archaeological investigation was that at Church Farm, Thame 1.3km to the north-east. Excavation revealed a rich archaeological sequence which included Late Neolithic, Early Bronze Age, Iron Age, Roman and post-medieval activity (Taylor 2012).

The prehistoric sites in the areas are summarised in Volume 1. A range of Late Iron Age, Romano-British and later material has also been noted in the immediate area of the site (Fig. 1.2). A 'Belgic' jar was recovered from the current site in the early 1960s and may have been an ancillary vessel from an unidentified burial. The description implies a Late Iron Age or transitional date.

As well as occasional isolated finds such as coins, Roman pottery has been found in low to moderate quantities from fieldwalking surveys in the Thame area, particularly on the north side of the Thame Valley, to the north and north-east of Thame approximately 2km to the north-east of the site. A Roman grey-ware vessel and part of an undated human cranium were recovered from the River Thame in 1978, on the Buckinghamshire side of the river. Ephemeral Roman and post-medieval activity was also present at Church Farm (Taylor 2012, 153).

Saxon finds in the immediate area had been limited, comprising a pottery assemblage from a ditch at Crendon Industrial Estate, about 2.5km to the north-east of the site. However, records show that Thame was a place of importance in the Early Saxon period. Records suggest that the Mercian king, Wulfhere, signed a charter there in AD 675 (Kemble, cited in VCH 1962c). A new town of Thame was laid out to the east of the earlier settlement at some point in the Late Saxon or early medieval period, and there are records of its physical and mercantile development, from the 12th and 13th centuries (VCH 1962c). A medieval hoard, of ten silver coins and five rings of 14th to 15th-century date, was recovered on the south bank of the River Thame in 1940 north of the site, during dredging operations (Evans *et al.* 1941). There are also a number of medieval finds scatters to the north-east of Thame.

Project aims

The aims of the project were, against the archaeological backdrop outlined above, to:
- record any evidence of past settlement or other land use;
- recover artefactual and other material evidence to date past settlement and activity;
- understand the nature of human burial practice on the site over time;
- determine the continuity (or otherwise) or settlement and other activity over time from prehistory into the medieval period and to understand the changing pattern of land use over those millennia;
- sample and analyse environmental remains to create a better understanding of past land use and economy.

Previous work on the site

A programme of archaeological work was required as part of planning consent relating to residential development on the land off Oxford Road (Fig. 1.3). A heritage desk-based assessment (JMHS 2010) identified that the site was in an area where a range of archaeological finds and observations had been made. A watching brief was therefore undertaken during site geotechnical investigations (Ground Investigation Services 2011; Hydrock 2014). Ground investigation test pits were dug including six which were within the development area. Archaeological remains were identified in two of the test pits as well as deposits associated with springs which arose on the site. Tile fragments dating to the Roman and post-medieval periods were recovered from one test pit and in another an undated ditch on an east/west alignment was recorded. Another test pit recorded two ditches on north/south and east/west alignments which contained artefacts appearing to indicate an Iron Age presence. Subsequently an archaeological trial trench evaluation was carried out across the site (JMHS 2014), consisting of 46 trenches. This identified a rich archaeological landscape with remains and artefacts dating from the 'Mesolithic/Neolithic' to the post-medieval periods focused around an area of natural springs (JMHS 2014). Further residential development is planned at Oxford Road. A geophysical survey (Bartlett-Clark Consultancy 2015) and archaeological evaluation (OCA 2016) have taken place on land surrounding the area discussed in these two volumes.

Site location, topography and geology

The site designated 'Site F1' is part of a 9.7ha area of land at Oxford Road, Thame, Oxfordshire (centred at NGR: SP 6965 0615). It lies on the north-western side of Thame, to the north of Oxford Road and Town

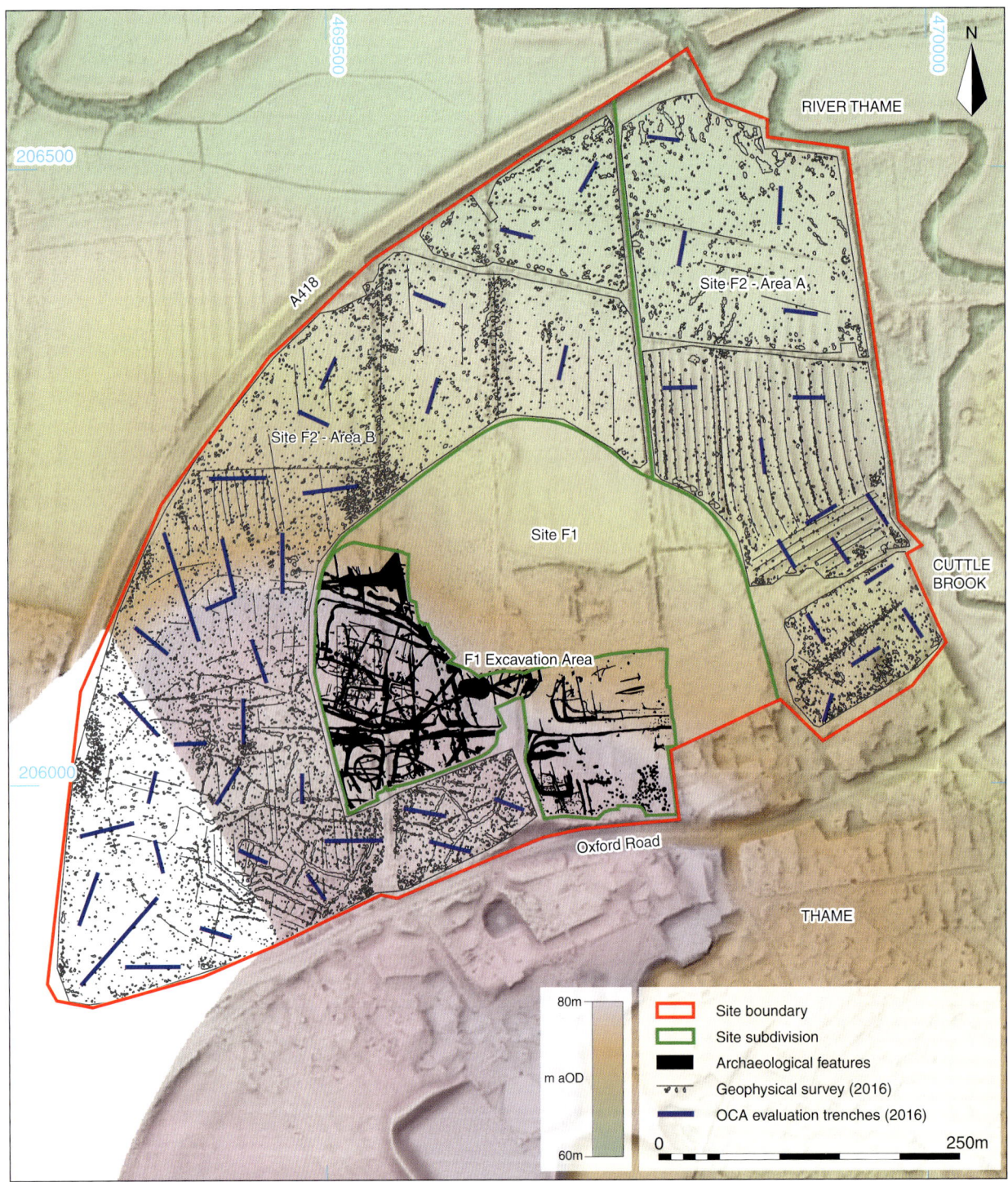

Fig. 1.3   Archaeological features and LiDAR and geophysical survey

Farm Close, east of the A418, in a gently undulating landscape (Fig. 1.4). The town of Thame lies in a well-protected position on the bend of the navigable River Thame and it had good communications routes such as the Icknield Way and London Way close by in the past (VCH 1962c).

The lie of the land

The land on which the site lies has been known locally as 'the pigfields' from the prevalence of pig farming on the site over many years, and at the time of the excavation was in arable agricultural use. It lies on the southern side of the River Thame Valley, and the watercourse runs only

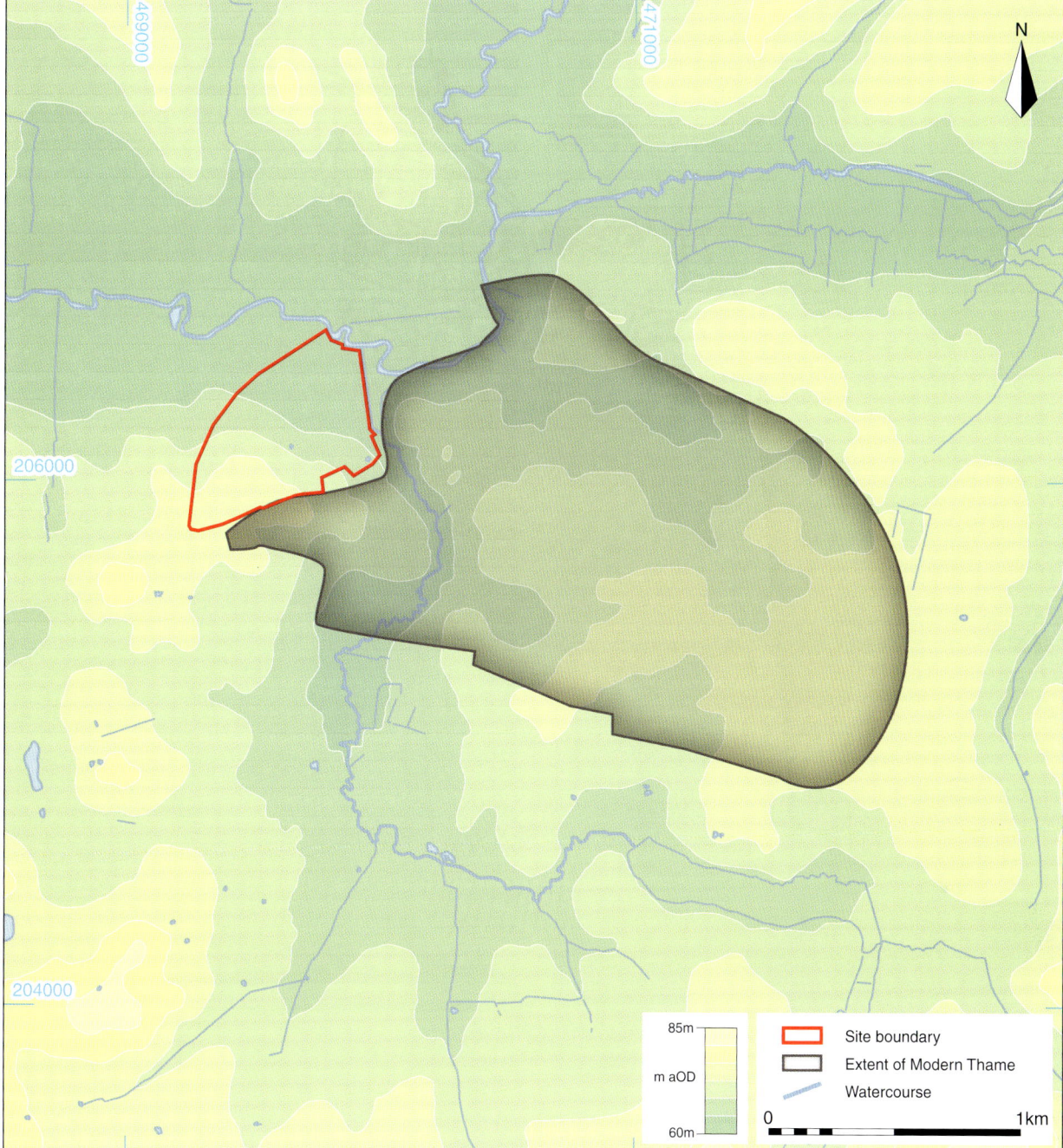

Fig. 1.4   Site topography

around 500m to the north. The Cuttle Brook, a tributary of the River Thame, is situated some 250m to the east.

The site lies on the top of, and along the northern slope of, a north-north-east-facing plateau, at a maximum height of 77m above Ordnance Datum (aOD) at the south-western extent, gently dipping down to the north and the east to 65m aOD as it drops towards the river. The eastern and western parts of the site were divided by a north-east/south-west-aligned, approximately 60m-wide, curvilinear 'coombe' or shallow, dry valley which ran up onto the ridge from the River Thame floodplain. The coombe was 1.4m deep with gentle, concave sides and base and was filled by a homogenous colluvial deposit, very similar in character to the overlying subsoil on the site. The 'coombe', as well as the general topography of the site and surrounding area, seems to have had a significant effect on the positions and layout of archaeological monuments, features and landscape organisation over thousands of years.

Archaeological features and deposits occurred across

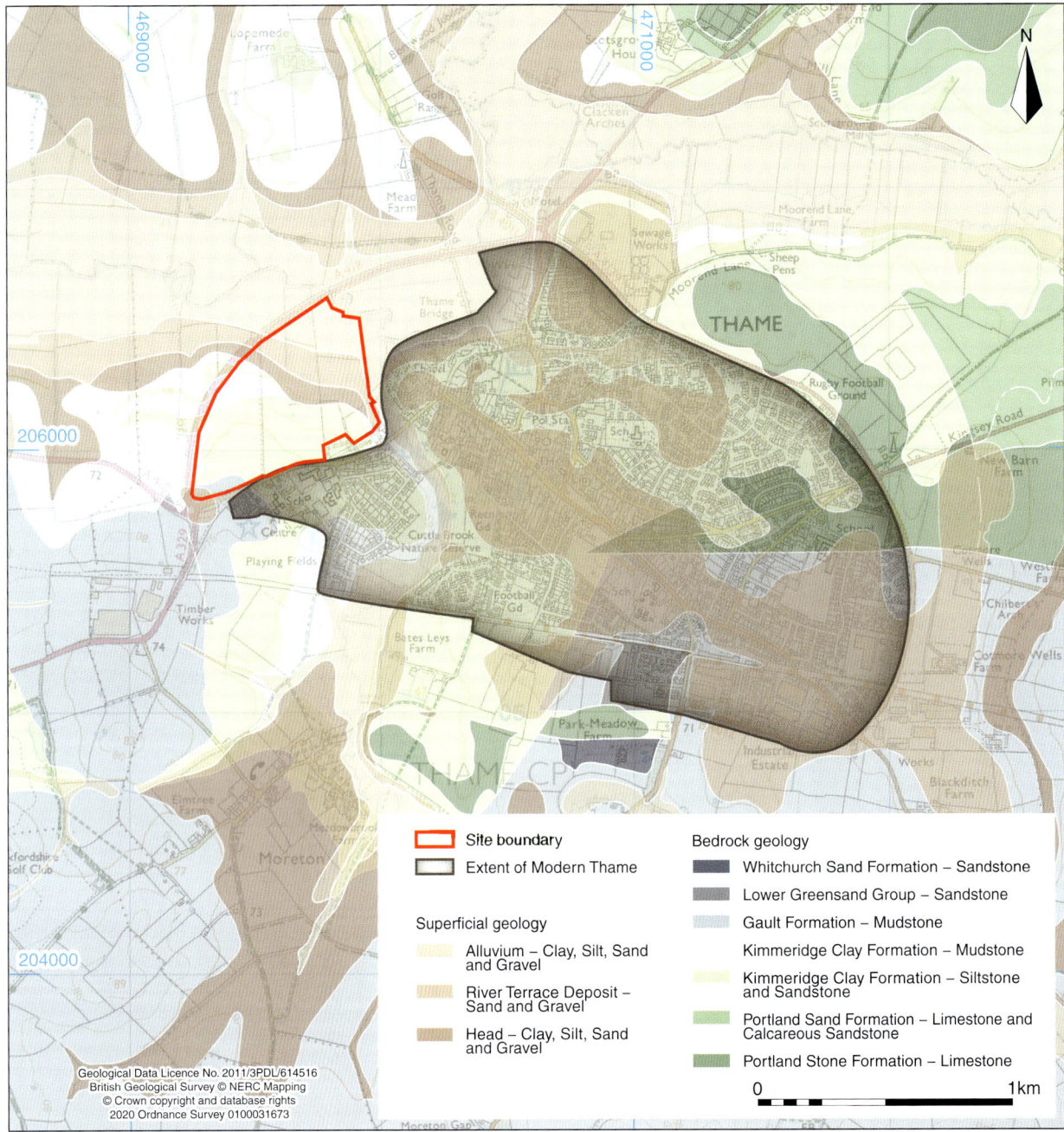

Fig. 1.5   Site geology

the entire excavated area of the site in most periods, so descriptions refer to various parts of the (irregularly shaped) excavation area. The two halves of the site were effectively separated by the 'coombe' area where the site also narrowed. Descriptions of broad location within the site are largely made in relation to the coombe, and this narrow part of the excavated site. The main area of Neolithic activity covered the western half of the site and particularly the north-western corner. Subsequent activity also occurred in the western half, but was focused in the south-western part, as well as in the eastern half of the excavation and the coombe area between them.

The geology

The underlying bedrock geology of the area is mapped as Kimmeridge Clay Formation – Siltstone and Sandstone (BGS 2018), with clay overlain by alluvium to the north-west of the site (Fig. 1.5). The Kimmeridge Clay is overlain by Gault Clay in the south-west. Natural geology was recorded below sandy silt topsoil and subsoil, both with flint inclusions, of 0.7m depth.

On site, where the bedrock is mapped as siltstone and sandstone, it was found to be predominantly characterised by very soft, sterile, fine yellow sand, although granular mudstone outcrops were recorded in the south-east of the western half of the site. The sand occurred to both the east and west of the coombe but was most prevalent on the north-facing sides of both areas. Where spring lines projected from the lower slopes of the excavated area, the natural sand took on a distinctive greenish or bluish, gleyed hue. In places, irregular hollows and irregular curvilinear features within the natural sand were infilled with compacted, very pale pink, fine silty sand and very common rounded flint gravel.

On the higher part of the ridge, the sand was overlain by a natural gravel deposit, although exposures were also noted at the very base of the slope. During excavation of some deeper features, it was observed that the deposit was up to 0.5m thick. It comprised a light orange/brown matrix with silt, sand and clay components containing relatively common flint gravel. It also included abundant dark purple/black ironstone pebbles. In a few locations, irregular columnar and ice-wedge cryoturbation features were evident within this natural gravel, at least 1m deep. These cryoturbation features were filled with a characteristic, very fine, light 'steely' greyish-brown silty sand with sparse calcareous flecks/particles and very rare, sub-rounded flint pebbles, but were otherwise homogenous and sterile. In places the natural gravel overlay calcareous gravels which were also heavily affected by cryoturbation.

In the north-eastern and some central portions of the site there was a natural sandy clay deposit. This deposit comprised a homogenous and sterile light orange/brown fine sandy clay that formed a band between the natural sands and gravels. In the southern central area mudstone rock was recorded only 0.4m below the initial machined surface. It was characterised by a very pale greyish-white, fine granular mudstone with an inherent fine laminar structure which resulted in large tabular blocks (<1.1m in size) up to 0.3m thick. At the interface between the bedrock and the overlying natural sands, a wide band of mid to dark orange iron panning and mineralisation was clearly evident. The bedrock's laminar structure and particular readiness to break into tabular blocks, offered a local resource.

Within the 'coombe' in the centre of the site that ran from the floodplain up onto the ridge, there was a colluvial deposit 0.4–0.6m thick. It extended over 1400m² on the north-east-facing slope of the coombe. It was characterised by a mid to dark greyish-brown fine sand, with very rare, sub-rounded/rounded flint gravel and angular/sub-angular, light yellowish-brown natural sandstone bedrock fragments. The deposit had clearly accumulated at the bottom of the steep slope, and therefore incorporated material that had eroded and washed down from higher ground.

The approach to excavation

The archaeological excavation was undertaken through-

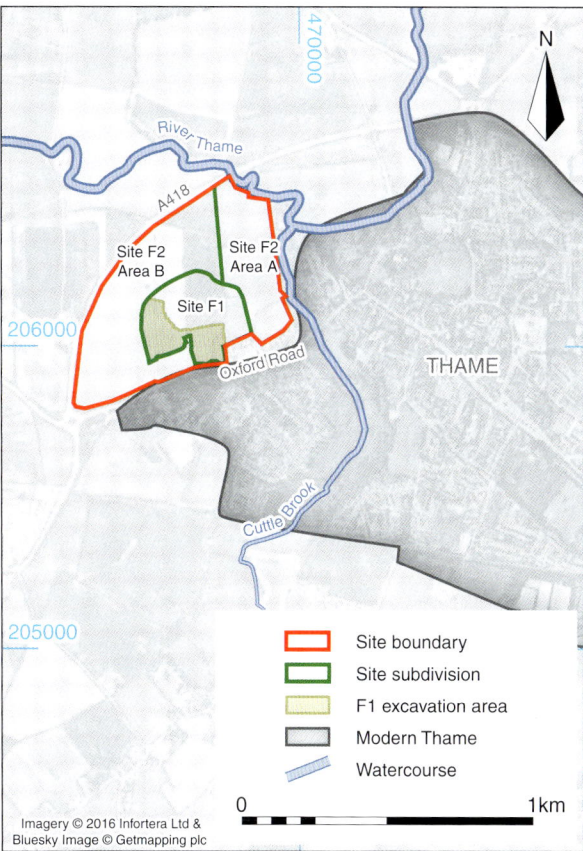

Fig. 1.6   Site Areas

out the areas shown on Figure 1.6. The initial stage of this phase of work involved stripping and recording of the eastern part of the site, followed by the western area. Non-archaeologically significant deposits were removed by machine under archaeological supervision. All machining ceased when the first archaeological horizon or natural geology was revealed. All archaeological features were recorded in plan and a suitable level of sampling agreed with the local authority advisors. Examination of features concentrated on recovering the plan of features and any structural sequences.

Particular emphasis was placed upon retrieving a stratigraphic sequence and upon obtaining details of the phasing of the site. All funerary/ritual activity and domestic/industrial deposits were 100% excavated. All discrete features (postholes, pits) were to be sampled by hand-excavation (average sample unlikely to exceed 50%) unless their common/repetitious nature suggested they were unlikely to yield significant new information. All linear features (ditches, pathways etc.) were sampled to a maximum of 10%. Bulk horizontal deposits were as a minimum 10% (by area) hand-excavated, after which a decision was taken (in conjunction with the local authority advisors) to remove the remainder with machinery. Priority was attached to features which could yield sealed assemblages which had the potential to be related to the chronological sequence of the site.

A strategy for environmental sampling was implemented in order to target specific palaeoenvironmental, geoarchaeological and geochronological questions. Material from the site has the potential to inform about its surrounding and immediate environment, as well as how the area was used and occupied at different periods. Sampling was particularly aimed at addressing these issues in relation to the Neolithic monuments and pits, which are discussed in Volume 1, as well as Roman corndriers and ovens and Saxon sunken-featured buildings discussed in Chapters 3 and 5 in this volume.

A copy of the digital records will be deposited the Archaeology Data Service (ADS) and the artefact and ecofact archive deposited with Oxfordshire County Museum (Museums Resource Centre).

General sequence and chronology

The earliest activity appears to have occurred in the Early Neolithic. Some initial pit digging led to the creation of an extensive scatter of pits, a causewayed enclosure and associated monuments. Later Neolithic activity was limited. The next major phase of activity was in the Early Iron Age. A settlement, enclosure and an extensive zone of pits indicate a period of concentrated use of the south-eastern part of the site. This included burials. There was an apparent hiatus before resumption of use of the area in the Late Iron Age to Early Romano-British period, largely represented by field and enclosure boundaries and trackways. Subsequently the area was used for burial during the post-Roman period before Saxon structures including sunken-featured buildings indicate a further phase of settlement.

Radiocarbon dating and Bayesian modelling

In total, 38 radiocarbon measurements were produced from the excavations, from Neolithic to Saxon features. The methods used are summarised in the Appendix, and the 11 Roman and Saxon results are shown in Table 1.1. Radiocarbon dates are quoted to the 2-sigma calibrated range (95.4%) unless otherwise stated. Samples were selected to consider the use-life of features. These are discussed in more detail in the relevant parts of Volumes 1 and 2 but have informed the overall date ranges for the periods of site use below.

Table 1.1 Radiocarbon dates: Roman and Saxon

Laboratory number	Sample	^{14}C dated material	Context	Radiocarbon age (BP)	δ^{13}C	δ^{15}N	C:N ratio	Calibrated date (95% confidence)	*Highest Posterior Density interval (95% probability)*
SUERC-69136 (GU41780)	666	Charred grain: *Secale cereale*	7274	1119±33	-21.2			cal AD 770–1020	*cal AD 770–1020*
SUERC-69142 (GU41783)	904	Charred grain: *Triticum* sp.	9924	1903±33	-24.3			cal AD 20–220	-
SUERC-69143 (GU41784)	562	Charred grain: *Triticum* sp.	5960	1186±33	-22.1			cal AD 720–960	-
SUERC-80856 (GU48339)	512	Charcoal: *Corylus* sp.	5164	1429±25	-25.6			cal AD 590–660	*cal AD 590–660*
SUERC-80861 (GU48341)	751	Charred grain: *Triticum dicoccum*	8181	1884±25	-21.8			cal AD 60–220	-
SUERC-80862 (GU48342)	903	Charcoal: *Maloideae*	8459	1417±25	-25.2			cal AD 590–660	*cal AD 590–660*
SUERC-80870 (GU48347)	705	Charred grain: *Hordeum* sp.	7453	1327±25	-24.3			cal AD 650–780	*cal AD 650–780*
SUERC-80874 (GU48351)	-	Dog ribs x2	6611	1003±25	-20.5	10.3	3.3	cal AD 990–1160	*cal AD 990–1130*
SUERC-80885 (GU48359)	667	Charcoal *Corylus/Alnus* roundwood	6564	1397±25	-25.1			cal AD 600–670	*cal AD 600–670*
SUERC-80886 (GU48360)	-	Human tibia shaft	1501	1604±25	-20.4	11.0	3.2	cal AD 410–540	*cal AD 420–560*
SUERC-95013 (GU55843)	GENLAB 354	Human molar	1502	1590±29	-20.0	10.8	3.4	cal AD 410–550	*cal AD 420–560*

Chronological summary

The periods of activity can be summarised as:

Period 1 – Neolithic and Bronze Age
    Period 1a: Early–Middle Neolithic (*c.* 4000–3000 BC)   Volume 1
    Period 1b: Late Neolithic (*c.* 3000–2400 BC)   Volume 1
    Period 1c: Neolithic (*c.* 4000–2400 BC)   Volume 1
    Period 1d: Middle Bronze Age (*c.* 1500–1150 BC)   Volume 1

Period 2 – Iron Age
    Period 2a: Early Iron Age (*c.* 400–300 BC)   Volume 1
    Period 2b: Iron Age (*c.* 300–200 BC)   Volume 1
    Period 2c: Prehistoric   Volume 1

Period 3 – Late Iron Age transition and Roman period
    Period 3a: Late Iron Age/Early Roman (*c.* 25 BC–AD 100)   Chapter 2
    Period 3b: Early and Middle Roman (*c.* AD 100–240)   Chapter 2
    Period 3c: Late Roman (*c.* AD 240–410)   Chapter 2
    Period 3d: Roman (AD 43–410)   Chapter 2

Period 4 – Saxon and medieval
    Period 4a: Early–Mid Saxon (*c.* AD 410–850)   Chapter 4
    Period 4b: Late Saxon–early medieval (*c.* AD 850–1399)   Chapter 4

Chapter 2
The Late Iron Age and Romano-British Period

by Alex Davies

After a hiatus in activity on the site after the Early Iron Age which is described in Volume 1, the area was reused in the Late Iron Age, with several phases evident in the final century BC into the 1st century AD. This was succeeded by three main phases of activity which spanned the Romano-British period. The archaeological features and deposits relating to these Late Iron Age/Romano-British and later Roman settlement phases, which generally relate to enclosure and land division, are described in this chapter in terms of the three main phases and a general Roman period where it was not possible to assign features and deposits more closely. To reflect the process of development and change, the three Roman periods are further subdivided below.

Late Iron Age/Early Roman (period 3a; *c.* 25 BC–AD 100)

Three stratigraphic sub-periods could be defined covering the period *c.* 25 BC–AD 100. Pottery groups belonging to the first of these phases were limited, and primarily comprised sherds in grog-tempered 'Belgic' fabrics that date approximately to the first half of this span. The ceramic evidence for the second phase was slightly better, but the third phase was better still and included a few larger groups that belonged to the end of the 1st century AD. It is therefore likely that the first period dates to *c.* 25 BC–AD 50, the second period to *c.* AD 50–70, and the third period to *c.* AD 70–100. However, the relative longevities of the first and second periods remain tentative, as well as the proposed date of the transition between the two periods, although placing this change at approximately the time of the conquest seems reasonable.

Late Iron Age (period 3ai; *c.* 25 BC–AD 50)

The first of three phases of Late Iron Age/Early Roman enclosure and landscape organisation comprised a series of ditches following an east-north-east to west-south-west orientation (Fig. 2.1). They were found mainly in the western part of the excavation area, but related elements were also present in the eastern side of the excavation. The system was more fragmentary and dispersed than the later phases of enclosure.

The most substantial Late Iron Age feature was ditch 202 which ran along the higher ground on the northern edge of the natural coombe leading to the Thame floodplain to the north. Seven recuts of the original ditch were recorded in the south-western intervention (Fig. 2.2), although the ditch was seen to have been recut with less frequency in the other interventions. The first two phases of the ditch were the largest: approximately 2.7m wide and 1.1m deep. The later phases were less substantial and were up to 0.55m deep. One of the later recuts, 7587, was flat-bottomed.

The second phase of the ditch, 7579, contained the base of a fired clay pedestal. An intervention in the ditch adjacent to Early Iron Age pit group J, described in Volume 1, produced a relatively large Early Iron Age pottery assemblage, suggesting that ditch 202 truncated one or more pits in this area.

The upper fills of an intervention further to the north-east, 8796, produced the left humerus, ulna and radius shaft fragments of an adult (Skeleton 510) (see Volume 1), as well as a right humerus shaft and fragment of clavicle from a juvenile. This is within the area of the Early Iron Age cemetery with earlier burials immediately adjacent to the ditch, and it is thought that these human remains were redeposited from Early Iron Age activity. The south-western end of ditch 202 was truncated by Late Roman (period 3cii) ditch 256.

To the south-west of ditch 202, a rectilinear enclosure measuring 42m east to west and at least 26m north to south was discovered. This was formed by ditches 6531, 5403, 5381 and 5030. Ditch 6531 measured 1.1m wide

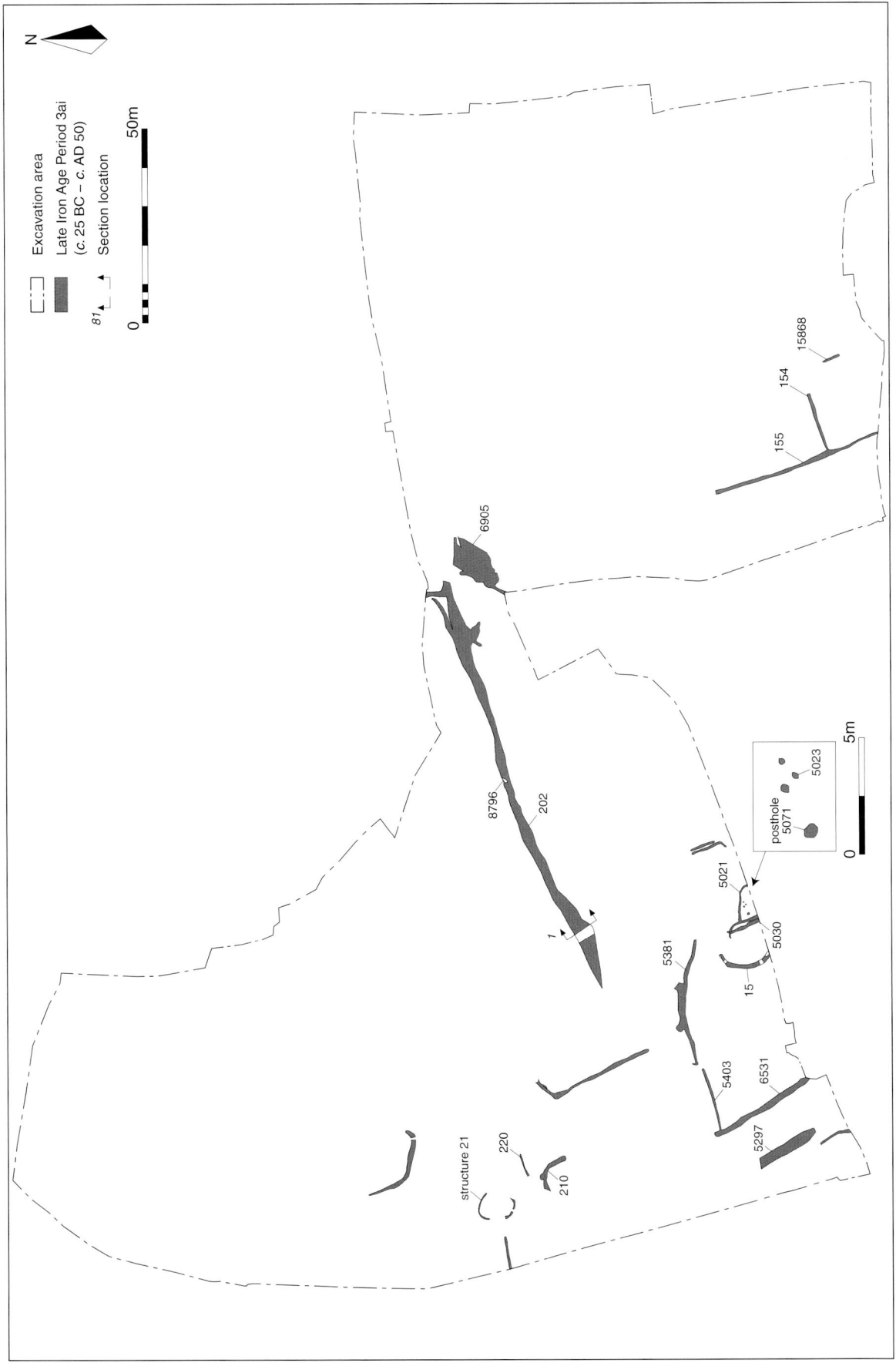

Fig. 2.1   Late Iron Age period 3ai: plan

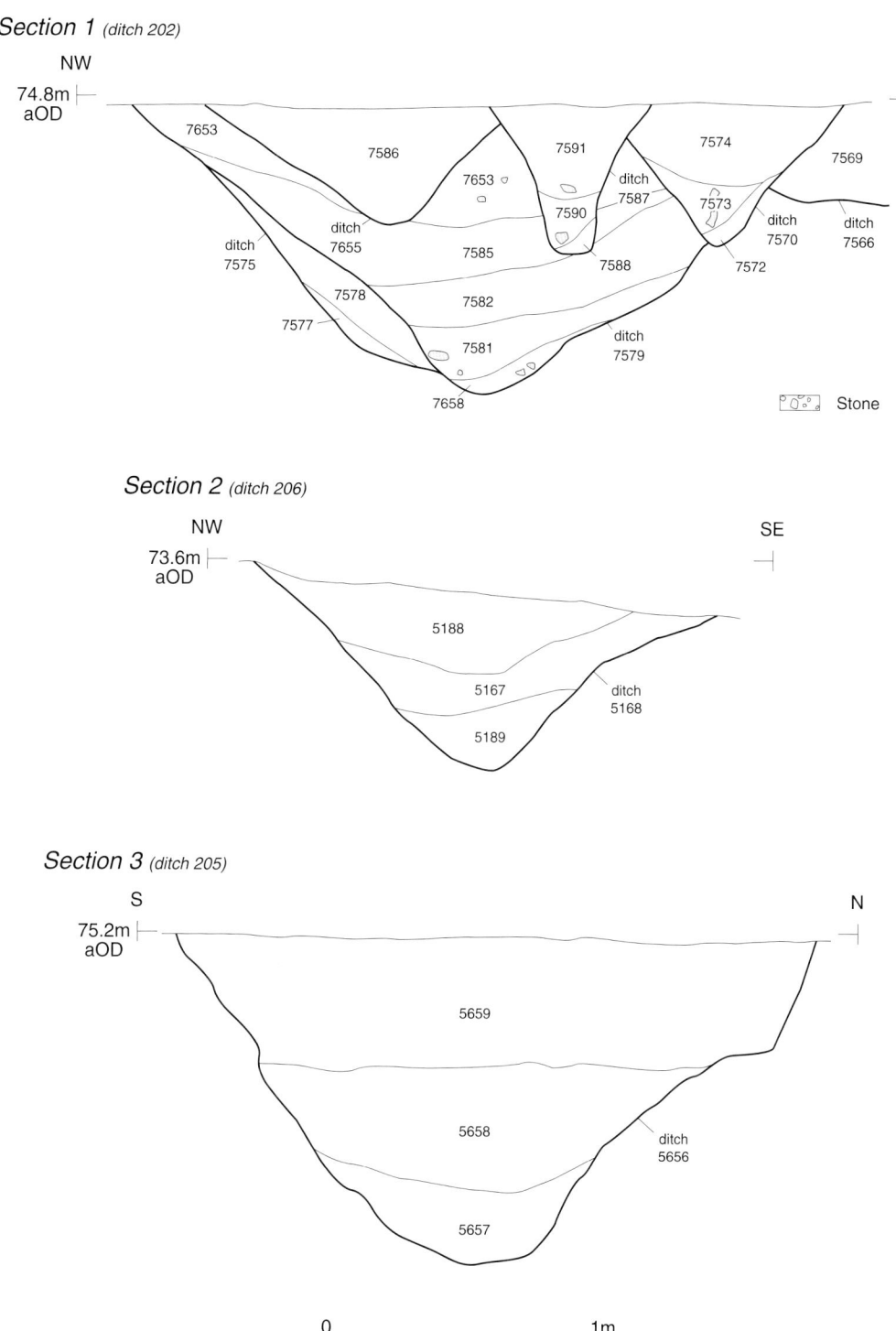

Fig. 2.2 Late Iron Age/Early Roman ditches: sections

and was just 0.08m deep. Ditch 5403 was 0.63m wide and 0.24m deep, ditch 5381 was 1m wide and 0.20m deep, and ditch 5030 was 1.8m wide and 0.6m deep. There was a gap in the enclosure ditches in the north-east corner and a much smaller causeway on the northern side. Curving ditch 15 was found within the enclosure at its entrance and may have functioned to structure movement at the entrance. The southern extent of the enclosure was beyond the excavation area. A fragment of fired clay oven plate (context 6977) and fragments of fired clay oven pedestal (context 7585) were discovered in the ditches creating the enclosure. Ditch 5297 was found 10m to the east of ditch 6531, and together these may have formed a trackway.

An additional smaller rectilinear enclosure defined by ditches 5030 and 5021 was found on the south-eastern side of the larger enclosure, encompassing an area 8m wide. Ditch 5021 was 0.61m wide and 0.13m deep. The length of the enclosure was not ascertained as it was beyond the excavated area. Within this smaller enclosure, four postholes were discovered that are probably related, although they did not form any coherent structure. Posthole 5071 produced a hammerstone (Chapter 3, Worked stone, Ra. 501), and 5023 a small quantity of pottery. While these ditches in the southern area of the western part of the excavation have been phased to the Late Iron Age, dating evidence was sparse and included a few small Roman sherds that are thought to be intrusive.

Three ditches were found to the north of these two enclosures, sharing a similar orientation. A copper alloy awl (Fig. 3.10, 19) was found in ditch 220, along with a small sherd of Late Iron Age pottery.

A penannular ditch that was probably an enclosure around a roundhouse was discovered within this fragmented enclosure system. Structure 21 had a *c.* 3m-wide west-facing entrance, and measured *c.* 7.5m in diameter. The eastern side of the gully had been truncated by ditches dating to periods 3aii and 3aiii. No postholes were found within the gully.

Hollow 6905 was found 10m to the south-east of the eastern end of ditch 202. It was 14m long, 7.5m wide and up to 1.10m deep and near the centre of the natural routeway created by the coombe. It had five fills which suggested it silted naturally.

The Late Iron Age activity in the eastern half of the excavation area comprised ditches 155 and 15868, both running on a north-north-west/south-south-east alignment, as well as perpendicular ditch 154. These ditches created an enclosure that was 22m wide, with gaps in the north-east corner and on the eastern side, and followed the orientation of the ditches in the western part of the excavation area. The length of the enclosure could not be ascertained as it continued to the south beyond the excavated area. Ditch 155 continued beyond the enclosure to the north, forming a further boundary ditch. Ditch 154 cut into the uppermost fill of the Early Iron Age D-shaped enclosure (see Volume 1), demonstrating that this substantial feature had filled completely by the Late Iron Age. These ditches were of modest proportions, being between 0.20 and 0.30m deep.

Late Iron Age/Early Roman transition (period 3aii; *c.* AD 50–70)

Western excavation area – sub-square enclosure

The Late Iron Age (period 3ai) fragmentary but organised series of landscape divisions appears to have soon been abandoned as a major re-orientation of the landscape took place around the period of the conquest (Fig. 2.3). The period 3ai system was replaced by a sub-square enclosure defined by ditch 206, orientated north-east to south-west by north-west to south-east. This was on a distinctly different alignment to the previous system of partial enclosures. The enclosure had a 5m-wide gap on the north-east side and measured 60–80m in length and 65m in width. However, the north-eastern ditch kinked at the entrance, continuing to the east and creating an external spur ditch 20m in length. This had the effect of producing an eastern funnel entrance, leading those approaching the complex through an external area before entering the main enclosure.

Ditch 206 was 1.30–2.25m wide and 0.50–0.90m deep and had a broadly V-shaped profile. Pottery from the ditch was concentrated at the south-western and north-western corners of the enclosure. A fragment of a human skull was found in the middle fill of intervention 5168 on the eastern side of ditch 206 and was probably redeposited from Early Iron Age pit 5281 which the ditch cut. A complete triangular perforated fired clay brick or pedestal was found in the same fill (Fig. 3.17, 8). A spearhead (Fig. 3.11, 24) was found in an upper fill, 3.5m to the north of the skull and pedestal. Fragments of three other blocks/pedestals were found in the ditch, at least one also of triangular form, as well as a flat fired clay oven plate. These objects may have been related to an oven or kiln within the sub-square enclosure, as is also suggested by the material in structures 8847 and 7419 (Fig. 2.6). Fragments from a worn rotary quern were found in the upper fill of ditch 206 in the southern length of the western ditch. Another human skull fragment was found in an upper fill on the southern length of ditch 206 in intervention 5438, some 90m to the south-west of the fragment in the eastern ditch. Most of the contents seem to derive from earlier, disturbed deposits.

Possible house enclosures

Square enclosure 213 and penannular ditch 19 were found in the south-western quadrant of the enclosure defined by ditch 206. These were adjoining, creating two separate, but connecting, enclosures. Square enclosure 213 was open on the eastern side, and measured 8m in length. The ditch was 0.60–0.23m in width and 0.30m deep and contained just two small sherds of Late Iron Age/Early Roman pottery, a redeposited Early Neolithic sherd, and small fragments of animal bone.

Penannular ditch 19 was also open on its eastern side, forming a semicircle. This had an extrapolated diameter of 8.5m and produced a small quantity of Late Iron Age/Early Roman pottery, some redeposited Neolithic sherds and a modest animal bone assemblage. The ditch was 0.3–0.55m wide and 0.3m deep. A truncated posthole, 5358, was found in the southern gully terminal.

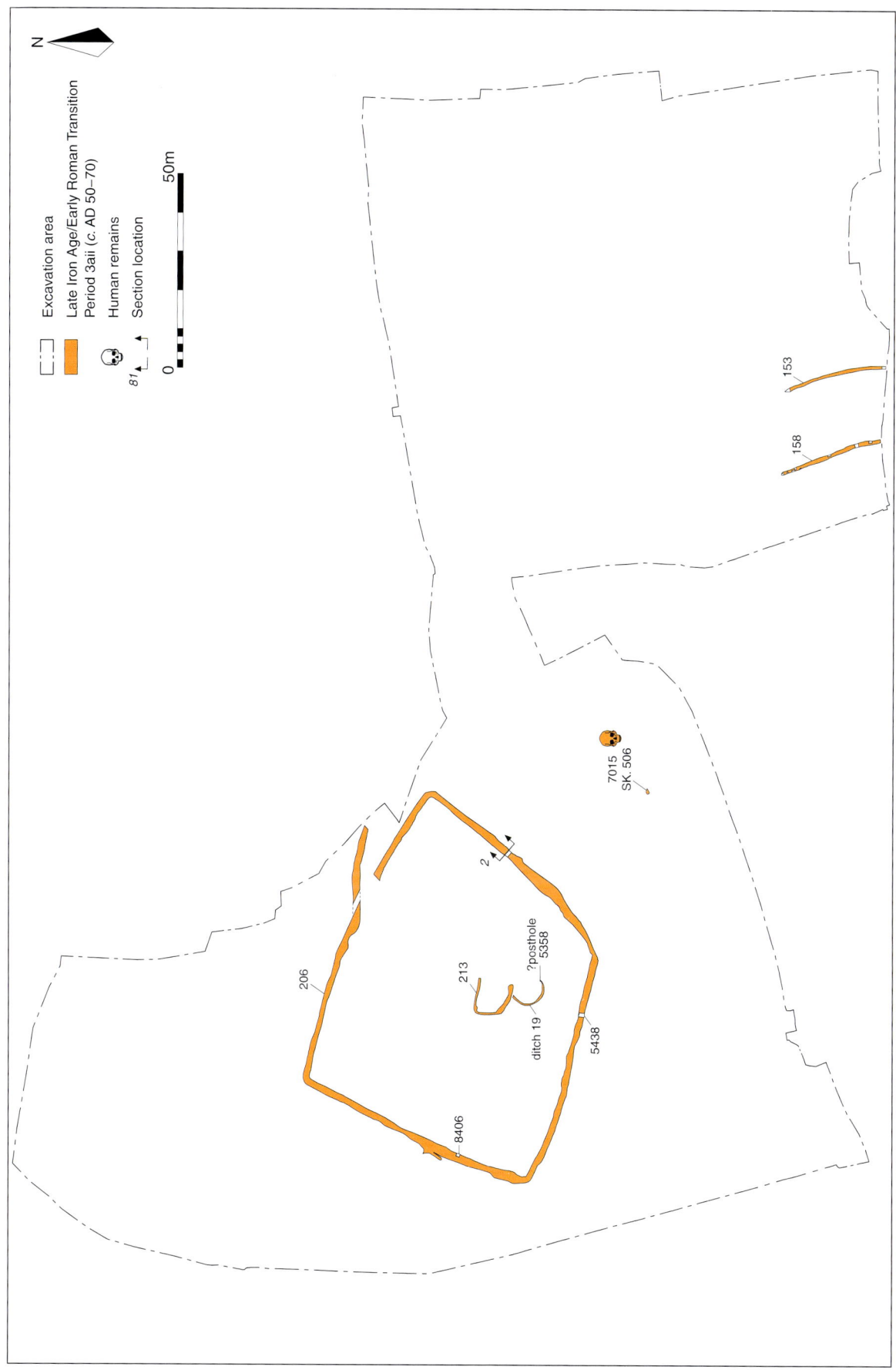

Fig. 2.3 Late Iron Age/Early Roman period 3aii: plan

Skeleton 506

A single inhumation belonging to period 3aii was discovered. Skeleton 506 was probably a female between 18 and 25 years of age, laying extended on her right side with the head to the east in sub-oval grave cut 7015. The grave cut measured approximately 1.60m in length and 0.60m wide and was less than 0.10m deep. The grave was truncated by Early Roman 2 (period 3bi) pit 7173, as well as ditch 234 of the same phase and its Late Roman period 3ci recut, ditch 242. A humerus shaft was found in pit 7173 from another individual, an adult of unknown sex.

Skeleton 506 was 35% complete and was partially exposed during the earlier evaluation of the site (Burial 621; Murray 2014, 14–15). Two near-complete pottery vessels were discovered during the evaluation, placed *c.* 0.5m to the north of the skeleton (Fig. 2.5). These comprised an almost complete intact dish in a black sandy ware, and a small copy of a girth beaker in a fine pink-orange sandy ware, likely to be a product of the early Oxfordshire industry that typologically should date to the pre-Flavian period (Timby 2014, 65).

Eastern excavation area – rectilinear enclosures

The period 3aii features in the south-eastern part of the eastern side of the excavation area included ditches 153 and 158. These followed the line of the period 3ai north-north-east/south-south-west-aligned Late Iron Age ditches. However, the period 3aii enclosure was not re-established in the same position. Ditch 158 was of similar proportions as the earlier ditch, being *c.* 0.20m deep; however, ditch 153 was much more substantial as it was 0.70–0.90m deep.

Early Roman 1 (period 3aiii; *c.* AD 70–100)

Western excavation area – rectilinear enclosures

The first Early Roman period (Fig. 2.4) saw some continuity in elements of the enclosure defined by ditch 206, although the enclosure itself was superseded by six smaller rectilinear enclosures. Ditch 206 was partially recut on its north-eastern and south-eastern sides by ditches 204 and 209, and ditches 211 and 5360 replaced parts of the southern side.

The north-eastern enclosure was square and measured 27m in length. It had a gap on its south-eastern side which could have formed an entrance 8.5m wide, also providing access to the south-eastern enclosure which had a gap on its northern side and may have formed an entrance. The south-eastern enclosure was defined by ditches 209, 211, 205 and 212.

Ditch 209 was 1–1.7m wide and 0.3–0.9m deep. Two skull fragments possibly from a male were found in the eastern part of the ditch, immediately adjacent to Early Iron Age pit 5281. This pit was cut by ditch 209 and also contained human skull fragments, and it is likely that these human remains were redeposited in the ditch fill as the intervention also produced Early Iron Age pottery. A perforated oven plate was also found in ditch 209, and the majority of a medium mouthed jar in a grog-tempered 'Belgic' fabric was found in the basal fill of an intervention in the south-eastern length of the ditch.

Ditch 212 was 1.15m wide and 0.67m deep and had some evidence of recutting. An upper fill of produced 728g of pottery dating to the second half of the 1st century AD. A fired clay oven plate was also found inside the ditch.

The northern enclosure was defined by ditches 203, 204, 205 and 208. The enclosure was 70–90m in length, and 35–45m wide and had a north-eastern entrance. Ditch 203 was 1–1.40m wide and 0.5–0.85m deep. The northern length of ditch 203 corresponded precisely with the prevailing topography at this point, as well as with the course of spring lines. This topographic location continued be defined throughout the Roman period.

Ditch 205 was 1–1.7m wide and 0.6–1.2m deep. Six contexts filling ditch 205 produced more than 500g of pottery. One of these was a basal fill which contained Late Iron Age/Early Roman sherds, and another was a middle fill which produced a group dating to the late 1st or early 2nd century AD. Three of the six contexts, however, were upper fills which contained post-Flavian Early Roman wares, demonstrating that the ditch remained open into at least the later part of the 1st century and into the next stratigraphic phase. Additionally, a Colchester-derivative (Harlow) brooch (fill 5659) (Fig. 3.9, 8) and a one-piece Colchester brooch (fill 8751) (Fig. 3.9, 3) were found in upper fills. These date respectively to the 50–70s AD and the decades around the conquest, both typologically probably a little earlier than the pottery from middle fills, although they need not be residual. Two contexts filling ditch 205 produced fired clay oven plates, one associated with a piece of structural fired clay was also found and near to 'oven' 7419, suggesting contemporaneity.

In the central southern part of the enclosure system, two enclosures were found on the same orientation as the others in the system. The eastern of these was defined by ditches 248, 205 and 5360 and had a gap to the south-east which might have formed an entrance. The enclosure was 35m long and 17m wide and appears to have been subdivided by ditch 7642. Ditch 248 was *c.* 1m wide and 0.45–0.82m deep, whereas the ditch defining the southern side, 5360, was of much more modest proportions than the other enclosure ditches, measuring just 0.18–0.45m wide and 0.15m deep. Ditch 7642 produced a handle of a copper alloy vessel (Fig. 3.10, 14) that is not typologically closely datable.

The western enclosure was L-shaped and appeared to have had a south-western entrance, and was defined by ditches 205, 248, 5360 and 207.

The south-western enclosure was 32m wide and at

Fig. 2.4   Early Roman 1 period 3aiii: plan

least 32m in length and extended beyond the excavated area. The enclosure was defined by ditches 205 and 207. The entrance may have been on the north-western side, although the ditch was obscured in this area. Ditch 207 was 0.45m wide and 0.20m deep at the northern extremity, and 1.37m wide and 0.31m deep along the southern return and produced a copper alloy bell or rattle (Fig. 3.11, 26) that is not closely datable, and an iron strip.

Linear ditches

Four ditches running on east-south-east/west-north-west alignments in the southern area of the western part of the excavation appear to be contemporary with the Early Roman period 3aiii enclosure system. These include ditches 200, 201, 223 and 224. Ditches 200 and 201 formed a partial trackway 3m in width and measured up to 0.55m wide and 0.40m deep, and up to 1.37m wide and 0.88m deep respectively. A fragment of a fired clay oven plate was discovered in ditch 201. Ditch 223 was 1.47m wide and 0.35m deep, and ditch 224 was up to 0.76m wide and 0.38m deep.

Ditch 249 was found running on an east/west alignment 20m to the west of ditch 200 and measured up to 0.83m deep. Ditch 249 was recut in each subsequent Roman phase, meaning its full width was not seen. Ditches 200, 201 and 249 formed an early and more fragmentary version of the major boundary and droveway system in the southern part of the site that was formalised in period 3bi.

Possible house enclosures

Inside the south-eastern enclosure, square enclosure 214 was discovered. This was a replacement of 213 that belonged to the previous phase. The ditch defining 214 was of slighter proportions compared to the earlier enclos-ure, measuring 0.20–0.34m wide and 0.06–0.26m deep.

A penannular ditch, structure 20, was found 12.5m to the south-east. In common with penannular ditch 19, belonging to period 3aii, penannular ditch 20 was semicircular but had a slightly larger diameter of 11m. However, it met ditch 209 on its eastern side, and this might have provided a boundary for any structure that was positioned within the ditches. Penannular ditch 20 was 0.3–0.43m wide and 0.17m deep and contained a small assemblage of residual Neolithic worked flint, deriving from the Early Neolithic pits which were in the same area of the site, one of which the gully truncated.

Pits

Pit 6826 was elongated with an irregular profile and was 0.60m wide, 1.20m long and 0.25–0.40m deep with a single fill that produced a fired clay oven plate. This was cut by the Late Saxon enclosure.

Pit 5344 was 0.35m diameter and 0.34m deep with a single fill and contained an assemblage of pottery weighing 1.6kg dating to the mid–late 1st century AD.

Pit 5006 was located in the south-western part of western half of the excavation area and was 0.90m wide and 0.14m deep. A thin lining of clay was found above the primary fill, and an assemblage of pottery weighing 820g was discovered in the sole fill above this lining.

Skeleton 508

An inhumation was discovered in the ditch 249 in intervention 7772. The ditch in this area was 1.12m wide and 0.82m deep. The skeleton was laid supine with the head to the east across the length of the ditch, within the first of three fills. The skeleton was probably a male aged 26–35 years. Preservation was poor, and the skeleton was only 70% complete. Like period 3aii skeleton 506, skeleton 508 was partially exposed during the earlier evaluation of the site and was also found with a near-intact pottery vessel (Fig. 2.5; Burial 810; Murray 2014, 17). This was a wheel-made necked jar with a shoulder bulge in a white ware which is typical of the early Oxfordshire industry. Although the form is a later Iron Age one, the type persisted into the Roman period and a pre- or early Flavian date seems appropriate (Timby 2014, 65). The vessel was placed adjacent to the feet. Finds from other interventions of ditch 249 also suggest that the feature dates to the latter part of the 1st century AD.

Eastern excavation area – rectilinear enclosures

Ditch 156 represents a recut of ditch 153 and was of similar proportions being 1.30–1.88m wide and 0.45–0.70m deep. Ditch 156 formed the western boundary of a trackway, with the eastern boundary defined by ditch 176. The trackway was 4m wide and its length is not known as it continued beyond the excavation to the south. A complete triangular fired clay pedestal was discovered in ditch 176. Ditch 176 was continued by L-shaped ditch 126 after a gap of 21m to the north.

Ditch 126 was 1.60m wide and 0.30m deep and could be followed some 85m east to the edge of the excavated area. The ditch was recut in Late Roman period 3ci, probably destroying parts of the ditch. This Early Roman ditch provided a major point around which the later Roman landscape was structured.

Ditch 162 ran north/south and was contemporary with L-shaped ditch 163. Together, these ditches formed a square enclosure 9m wide and open on its southern side. Ditch 163 was 2m wide and 0.70m deep, whereas ditch 162 was 0.45m wide and 0.30m deep. A series of postholes were discovered within the square enclosure, although none produced datable material culture and no clear structure could be made from them. As this area also witnessed Early Iron Age activity, the postholes cannot be clearly associated with the Early Roman 1 square enclosure.

Late Iron Age/Early Roman (period 3a; unphased)

A number of features clearly belonged to this transitional

The Late Iron Age and Romano-British Period 21

Skeleton 506 with ancillary vessels as uncovered during the evaluation, looking east (scale 1m)

Skeleton 508 with ancillary vessel as uncovered during the evaluation, looking east (scale 1m)

Fig. 2.5 Late Iron Age/Early Roman inhumations: photographs (used with kind permission from John Moore Heritage Services)

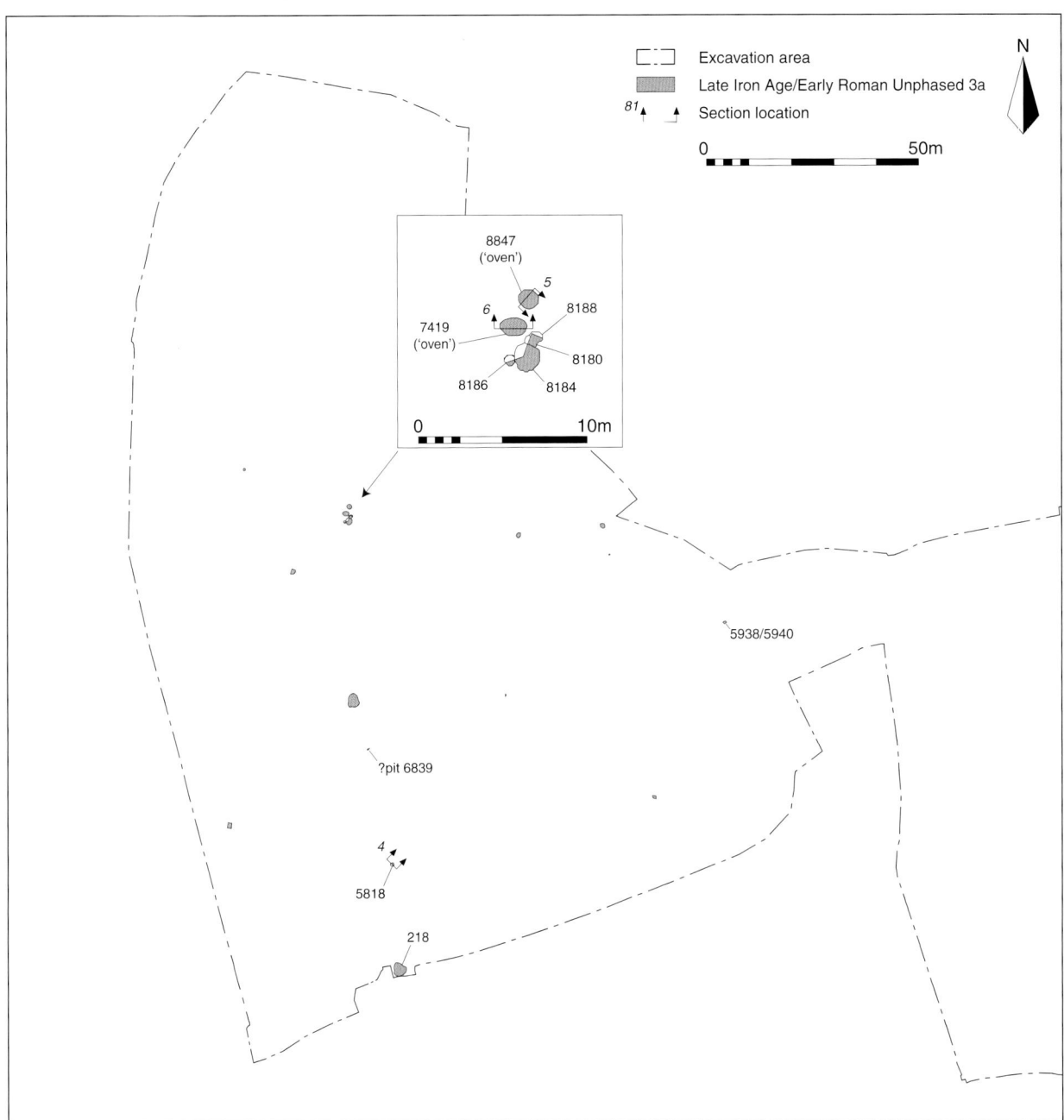

Fig. 2.6   Late Iron Age/Early Roman unphased: plan

phase but could not be assigned more closely to one of the sub-phases (Fig. 2.6).

Cremation deposits 7912 and 5938/5940

Cremation deposits 7912 and 5938/5940 were found 2m apart on the northern side of the coombe very near to the 'cemetery' area dating mainly to the Early Iron Age, and near to the articulated human remains in Late Iron Age (period 3ai) ditch 202. Both were contained in pottery vessels. These were cut into the homogenous colluvial deposit filling the coombe.

Cremation deposit 5938/5940 was in a jar in a grog-tempered 'Belgic' fabric, of which only the base survived. A total of 838g of cremated bone was retrieved from the vessel, representing two individuals including an adult male. Burnt animal bone was also found in the vessel, including chicken bone. A further 15g of cremated bone was found adjacent to the urn, probably from the same deposit.

Cremation deposit 7912 was placed in a carinated jar also in a grog-tempered 'Belgic' fabric, of which only the lower part survived.

Pits

Thirty-two pits dating to period 3a were recorded. The majority could not be placed into sub-periods, although the dating evidence for six pits allow for closer assignment, and these have been discussed above.

Pit 5818 was ovoid, *c.* 0.90m wide and 0.50m deep and contained a very unusual assemblage of finds. A dump of hearth material, 5978, was found in the base, on top of which two layers of pottery were placed in a matrix of stone and clay, including vessels of remarkably different dates (Fig. 2.7, section 4). This included the substantial remains from multiple Early Iron Age vessels, as well as an S-profile jar and a hemispherical bowl of Middle or Late Iron Age date. The Iron Age pottery from layers 5963 and 5943 totalled 336 sherds and weighed over 7.5kg. In addition, ten sherds of pottery dating *c.* AD 50–100 and weighing 252g was found. This was the latest material from the pit and places the deposition in the pit to period 3aii or 3aiii. The upper fill, 5819, also produced ten Neolithic sherds weighing 167g. This unusual combination of components is discussed in Chapter 6.

A small but dense pit cluster, 218, was recorded along the southern edge of the western half of the excavation area. The north/south-aligned, sub-rectangular area of intercutting pits was *c.* 4.9m by 2.7m in extent and truncated a small group of Early Neolithic pits. The pits were sub-oval or sub-circular in shape, with steep, concave or near-vertical sides and concave bases. They varied in size, from *c.* 0.6 to *c.* 2.6m, and 0.23–0.94m (average 0.5m) deep and contained relatively few finds.

'Oven' features

Two adjacent features, 'oven' structures 8847 and 7419, which contained large quantities of fired clay were found in the centre of the western part of the excavation area. It is likely that these belong to period 3aii and/or period 3aiii. During period 3aii, these features would have been located within the enclosure defined by ditch 206, 12m to the east of the western ditch length. These were initially interpreted as oven bases, although it is likely that they represent dumps of material from a nearby kiln or similar feature.

'Oven' structure 8847 took the form of a small oval pit, 1.24m by 1.14m and 0.2m deep, with vertical sides terminating in a flat base (Fig. 2.7, section 5). The cut did not show any sign of *in situ* burning but the basal fill of the pit (8905) contained charcoal, fired clay fragments and burnt stone, including burnt chalk pieces. The latest fill contained a high density of structural fired clay fragments adhering to soil (*c.* 40% of the deposit) including a fired clay pedestal or stokehole arch, two sherds of residual Neolithic pottery, worked flint, animal bone, charcoal, burnt stones, and unburnt clay lumps.

'Oven' structure 7419 was located 0.7m to the south-west of structure 8847. This comprised an east/west-aligned oval pit, measuring 1.74m by 1.02m with a depth of 0.71m, and had near-vertical sides and a shallow concave base. This feature and its finds are described in detail in Chapter 3 (Poole, Fired clay), and it appears to represent a dump from an oven or kiln.

A sequence of four intercutting pits, 8184, 8186, 8180 and 8188, were found immediately to the south of oven 7419. The largest was 8184, and this measured 0.85m in length and was 0.13m deep and had three fills; the other three pits had single fills. The pits contained residual Neolithic pottery, as well as pieces of structural fired clay from an oven. A radiocarbon date was obtained from emmer from upper fill 8181 of pit 8184, returning a date of cal AD 60–220 (SUERC-80861; Table 1.1).

Early and Middle Roman (period 3b; *c.* AD 100–240)

Early Roman 2 (period 3bi; *c.* AD 100–150)

Numerous ditches and enclosures were also established during the Early and Middle Roman period (Fig. 2.8).

Droveways and enclosures

An east/west boundary ran along the southern part of the site, comprising ditches 126, 189, 234 and 230. This formalised a more fragmented boundary that ran along this area in the Early Roman 1 (period 3aiii) period. Ditch 126 was dug in the previous phase and appears to have remained a structuring feature in this part of the site. Ditch 230 represents two recuts of ditch 249, also belonging to the Early Roman 1 (period 3aiii) period. Ditch 230 measured 0.55–0.78m wide and 0.13–0.72m deep. Half of a presumably residual Late Iron Age terret was found in ditch 230, directly associated with 72g of pottery dating to the 2nd century AD or later. These east/west boundary ditches were recut as many as three times during the Early Roman 2 period.

The boundary described above had three southern breaks. One of these breaks, between ditches 126 and 189, led to an apparently open area in the south-eastern part of the excavation area. This southern area was not further enclosed. Another gap in the east/west boundary was found on the far western edge of the eastern part of the excavation area. The ditches here curved to the south-west, leading to an enclosure that was largely outside of the excavated area. This enclosure was 60m in width and defined on its western side by ditch 247 which produced an unusual shale armlet (Chapter 3, Worked stone, Ra. 802). The ditch was also the eastern boundary to another enclosure, 55m in width.

Nearly 3kg of pottery was discovered in an upper fill of ditch 189. This included the majority of a medium mouthed jar in a sand-tempered 'Belgic' fabric, as well as large sherds from a high-shouldered jar in a sandy reduced coarse ware, and most of another medium mouthed jar but in a coarse sandy white fabric. Ditch 189 was around 1.20m in width and 0.20–0.67m deep.

Fifteen metres to the north of the east/west boundary ditches in the eastern part of the excavation area, a

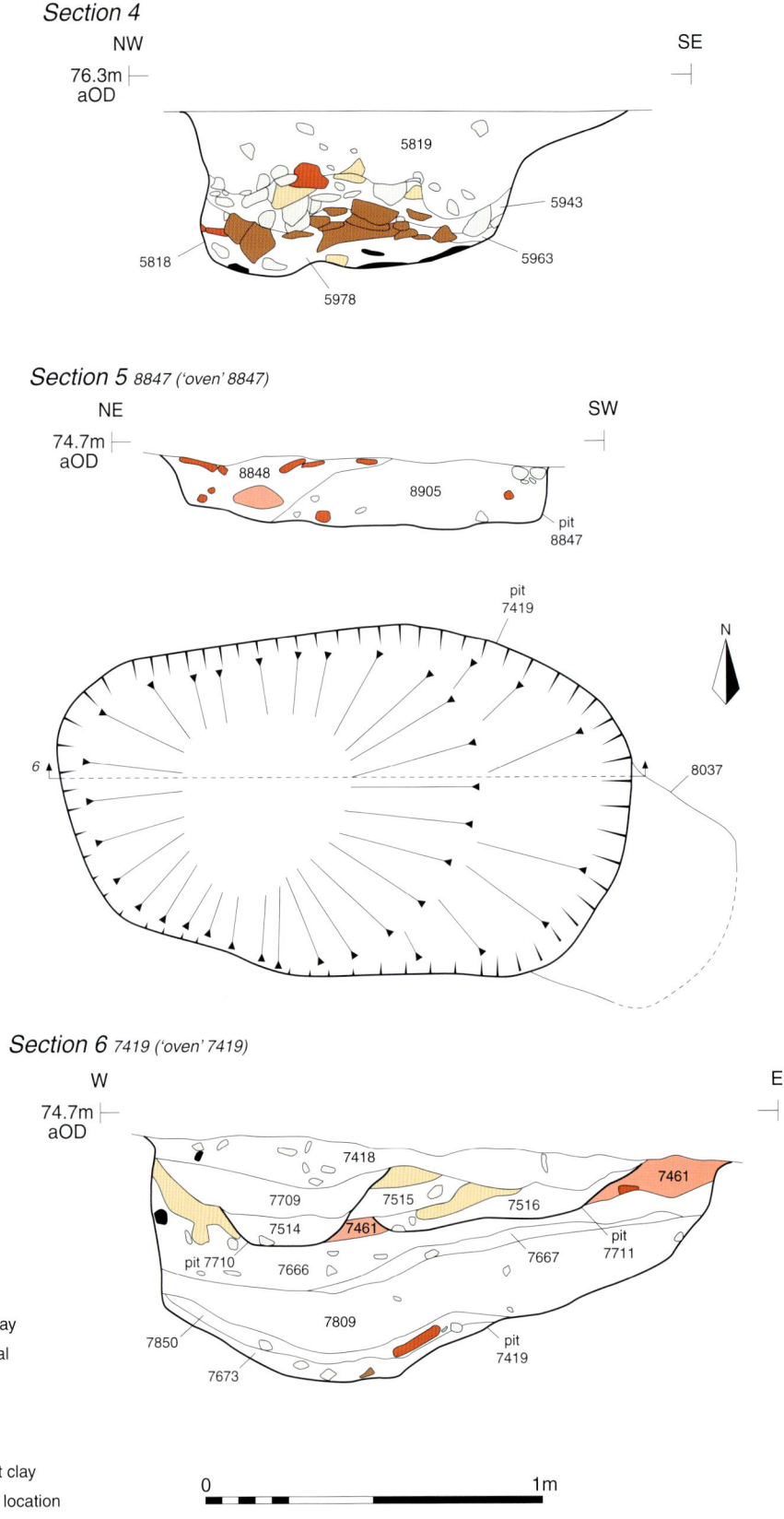

Fig. 2.7 *Late Iron Age/Early Roman unphased pits: plans and sections*

Fig. 2.8 Early Roman 2 period 3bi: plan

series of narrow ditches running north/south or east/west was discovered. These multiple minor recuts of the same L-shaped feature were labelled 190. Immediately to the east a further group of narrow ditches, 193 was found, providing the northern droveway ditch in this area. These were very poorly dated, although they have been tentatively phased to the Early Roman 2 (period 3bi) period due to the similarities to ditch group 190. Additionally, another group of narrow ditches, 191, was found *c.* 35m to the north-west of the L-shaped ditches. These were poorly dated but also appear to belong to the Early Roman 2 (period 3bi) period.

A major north/south fork in the east/west droveway was apparent in the southern part of the western half of the excavation area, defined by ditches 234 and 231. The north/south fork was 13m wide and was seen on the geophysical survey and during the evaluation to the south of the excavated area to curve to the south-west over a distance of 100m, before joining another droveway, aligned north-west/south-east (Fig. 2.9; Bartlett-Clark 2015; OCA 2016). Ditch 234 was 0.66–2.05m wide and 0.26–1.35m deep.

On the western side of the droveway, an enclosure was encountered, the first two phases of which belonged to the Early Roman 2 (period 3bi) period. This was defined by ditch 231 on its northern, eastern and western sides, and ditch 232 on its southern side. The enclosure was 30m in length, and during its first phase it was 25m in width with a *c.* 8.5m-wide gap on the eastern side which could have formed an entrance. During its second phase, the enclosure was 20m in width and had a *c.* 7m-wide entrance on the northern side. To the south of this enclosure, another enclosure was encountered, *c.* 24m wide and defined to the south by ditch 233.

To the west of the north/south droveway, the major east/west droveway continued. This was 13–22m wide and was defined to the north by ditches 229 and 261. Ditch 261 produced a copper alloy drill bit. Ditch 229 was *c.* 1.35m wide and 0.65m deep, and also formed the southern boundary of an enclosure. This enclosure was at least 65m in length and was 35m in width, defined by ditch 205 on its northern and eastern sides, and recut on the eastern side by ditch 257. Ditch 205 was dug during the Early Roman 1 (period 3aiii) period but remained as a boundary into the Early Roman 2 (period 3bi) period. The entrance to the enclosure appears to have been on the south-eastern corner, although the ditches defining this enclosure were much obscured by later ditches. The enclosure was subdivided by a series of narrower ditches, including 235, 236 and 5674. These ditches were less substantial than the main outer enclosure ditches, generally measuring around 0.50m wide and never more than 0.30m deep. Ditches 237 and 5635 were similar in form to ditches 235, 236 and 5674, but positioned outside of this main enclosure.

The north-eastern corner of ditch 205 was replaced by ditch 257 in period 3bi. This ran north/south and could be followed for 60m where it met droveway ditch 225. Ditches 257 and 225 formed boundaries for two enclosures, both measuring approximately 65m in length and 45m in width. The western enclosure was also defined by ditch 205 to the south and had a 10m-wide entrance in the south-western corner. The enclosure may also have had an eastern entrance as ditch 257 appears to have had a causeway halfway along its length. This was, however, obscured by a Late Roman recut. Ditch 257 was 0.32–1m wide and 0.24–0.44m deep. The two other sides of the eastern enclosure were provided by L-shaped ditch 238. This ditch measured 0.60–2.20m wide and 0.20–0.44m deep. There was a 17m-wide gap in the south-western corner of this enclosure, and another 12m-wide gap in the north-east corner. Both gaps could have been entrances. However, L-shaped ditch 228 was just outside the enclosure to the north-east, effectively creating two 5.5m-wide entrances in this corner. Ditch 228 was 0.45–0.86m wide and 0.35m deep.

Another droveway was found running across the northern part of the western half of the excavated area on a curving but generally north-west/south-east alignment. This was correlated with the contour of the ridge along its north face, following the line of earlier ditch 203. The droveway was 5m wide, defined on its northern side by ditch 226, and its southern side by ditch 225. Ditches 225 and 226 were approximately 1m wide and 0.4m deep. The southern droveway ditch, 225, turned to the south in the far north-western part of the western part of the excavation, terminating *c.* 10m to the north of ditch 205. The northern droveway ditch also appeared to turn to follow ditch 225 at the very edge of the excavated area. The geophysical survey appears to show ditches 225 and 226 running parallel to the south immediately to the west of the excavated area (Fig. 2.9).

Ditch 227 on the western side of the coombe was integrated into the droveway system, with its eastern ditch possibly forming the southern end of a droveway with ditch 7143 and/or 217, leading down the coombe towards the Thame floodplain. The upper fill of the south-eastern corner of ditch 227, in intervention 6715, produced one of the largest assemblages of Roman pottery from a single group on the site, comprising 6kg of sherds mostly from reduced coarse ware vessels, but including sherds from a Dressel 20 amphora. This fill was dark suggesting it comprised organic material and it appears to have been a dump of occupation material. Ditch 227 was approximately 1.45m wide and between 0.22–0.49m deep.

Corndriers

Corndrier 25 was T-shaped and aligned east/west, with the stokehole to the west, and was located in the western part of the enclosure defined by ditches 225, 257 and 205 (Fig. 2.10). The structure was 3.4m long and 0.8m

Fig. 2.9   Results of Thame Site F1 Excavation and Site F2 Geophysical survey, showing Roman enclosure and droveway system

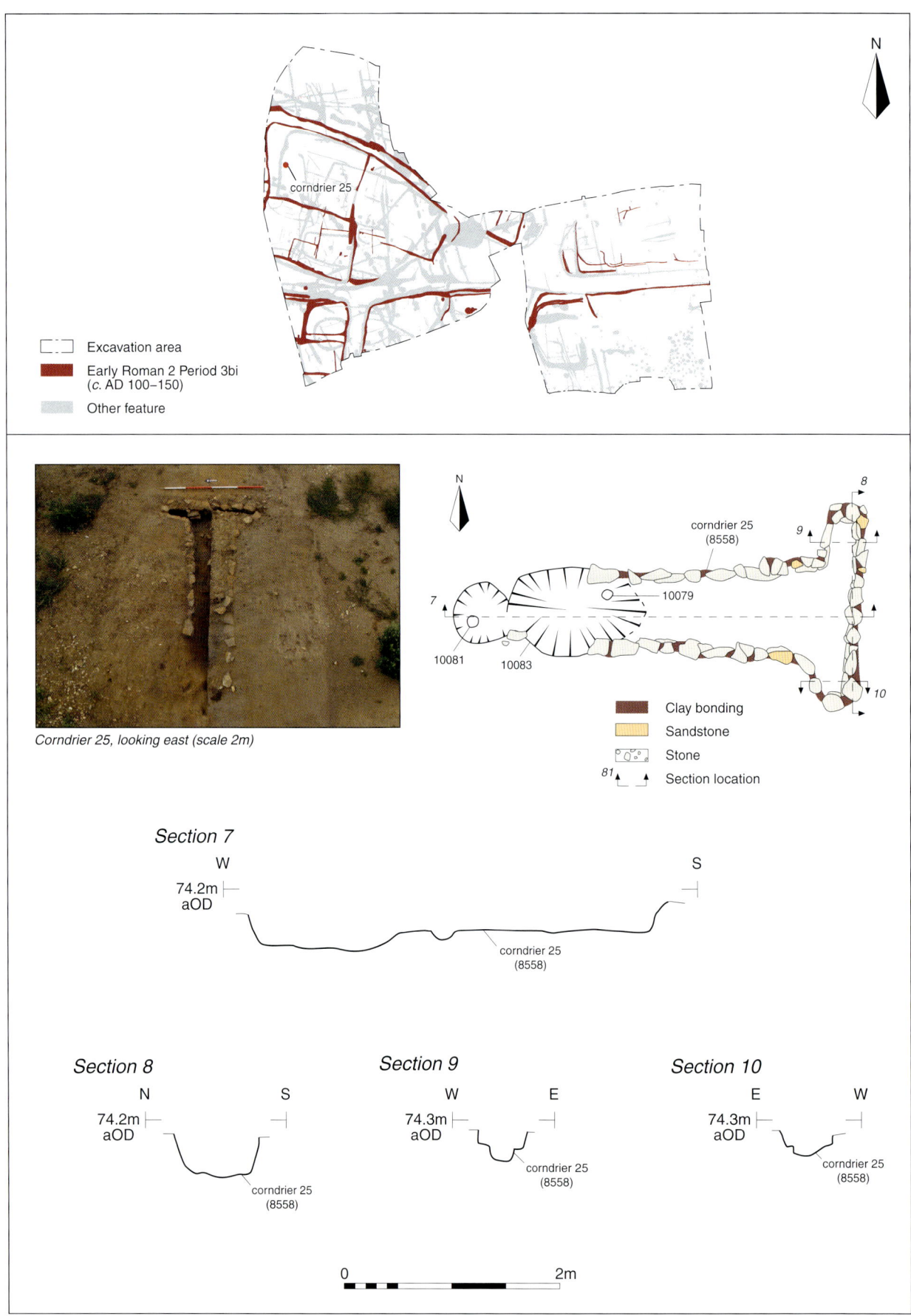

Fig. 2.10 Early Roman 2 period 3bi, corndrier 25: plan, sections and photograph

wide with a 1.8m-long and 0.4m-wide chamber at the east end. The stokehole pit was unlined and was *c.* 2m long and 0.1m deep. Many of the masonry lining blocks showed signs of burning from use of the structure. The masonry was composed of naturally occurring tabular, mudstone blocks, but also included other stone types. These were laid with a silty clay/clay bonding material and survived to between three or four courses. The stones were up to 0.27m long and 0.07m thick. Evidence of a fire-pit at the western end of the structure was marked by the presence of a compact dark red/black heat-affected area, 8653 (not illustrated). Two stakeholes, 10081 and 10079, were recorded mid-structure and near the stokehole and were probably associated with the corndrier superstructure, although very little of the form of this superstructure could be reconstructed. The structure is dated by a single body sherd in a reduced sandy fabric dating to the late 1st century AD or later in upper fill 8651 (not illustrated). A small amount of generally amorphous fired clay was also in fill 8651.

A probable corndrier, 24, was located in the north-western corner of the enclosure defined by ditches 225, 257 and 238. It comprised a stokehole pit at the south end of the structure measuring 1.8m by 0.8m by 0.15m deep, with the main channel of the structure measuring 1.1m long, 0.4m wide and 0.08m deep (Fig. 2.11). Although no superstructure survived, a small number of burnt mudstone blocks and baking/burning of the surrounding natural geology suggest this was a very truncated T-shaped corndrier, perhaps robbed of its masonry, although it may represent a kiln (see Poole, Fired clay, Chapter 3). All of the layers were dark with burnt material, and the natural substrate around the southern stokehole area was less heat-affected. The structure had a north-east/south-west alignment and was dated by a single rim sherd from a jar weighing 59g in a reduced sandy ware fabric probably belonging to the late 1st or the 2nd century. A single stakehole, 9151, was recorded in the base of the stokehole on its south-eastern edge, which may have been a structural component. Similar stakeholes associated with other Roman corndriers and oven structures were recorded on the site.

Possible corndrier or oven 46 (cut 8164) was located within an enclosure in the western part of the western half of the excavation. This east/west-aligned feature had a characteristic 'figure of eight' shape in plan, was 2.5m long, up to 0.97m wide, and 0.17m deep (Fig. 2.11). Both ends of the feature showed clear signs of being heat-affected with *in situ* baking of the natural geology evident.

Just under half of a fired clay oven plate was found next to a burnt millstone fragment of Old Red Sandstone (Chapter 3, Worked stone, Ra. 900), both resting on top of an area of burnt natural on the eastern side of the feature. Above this a 0.03m-thick dark deposit, 8244, was found. Despite the colour, it only contained occasional charcoal flecks, and it is possible this deposit derived from organic matter rather than burning relating to the oven. No datable material culture was found, but the possible corndrier or oven appears to respect the ditches (205, 229, 236 and 5674) which form the enclosure within which it was found, suggesting that the feature was contemporary with them and dates to the Early Roman 2 (period 3bi) period.

The widest part at the western end of the feature suggests that this was the stokehole for a possible corndrier. If this was a corndrier, however, it was almost totally demolished and robbed-out, with only the stokehole and raking-out hollow partially surviving.

Stone-lined well 23 was discovered near the southern baulk of the western side of the excavation, to the immediate east of droveway ditch 234 (Fig. 2.12). The masonry of the lining had been heavily truncated and disturbed by a substantial east/west, Late Roman 2 (period 3cii) ditch, 5123. The area around the well was stepped by machine to facilitate further hand-excavation of the feature itself, although this was discontinued at a depth of 3.05m from the original machined surface before the base of the well was reached. An attempt was made to hand-auger the remaining depth of the well to assess the potential for the survival of waterlogged deposits and to determine the depth of the feature; however, the presence of masonry rubble prevented further exploration.

The well foundation cut was 1.5m in diameter. The stone lining was 0.1–0.2m thick and was composed of unworked mudstone blocks 0.12–0.25m in length and 0.07–0.12m thick. These were very regularly coursed with a silty clay being utilised as a bonding agent, in a very similar fashion to the corndrier structures. The stone lining had an internal diameter of 0.75m, reducing in diameter slightly towards the bottom of the feature as exposed in excavation. Behind the stone lining a series of backfill deposits were recorded, deriving from the construction of the well shaft. Finds from these layers suggest a date for the construction of the well: fills 5227 and 5225 produced a small amount of pottery dating to the late 1st or 2nd century. The well was backfilled in the Middle Roman (period 3bii) period (see below).

Pits

Twenty-nine discrete features have been phased to the Early Roman 2 (period 3bi) period. Many of these are pits, but they also include possible waterholes. A few that have notable finds or those where function can be suggested are discussed below.

Pits 6133 and 6149 were found next to each other in the enclosure defined by ditches 247 and 234 in the south-eastern part of the western half of the excavation area. Pit 6133 was sub-circular and was 2.9m wide. It was excavated to a depth of 1.70m, and further augured to 3.70m, but the base was not reached. The upper fill produced a complete profile of an Oxfordshire white

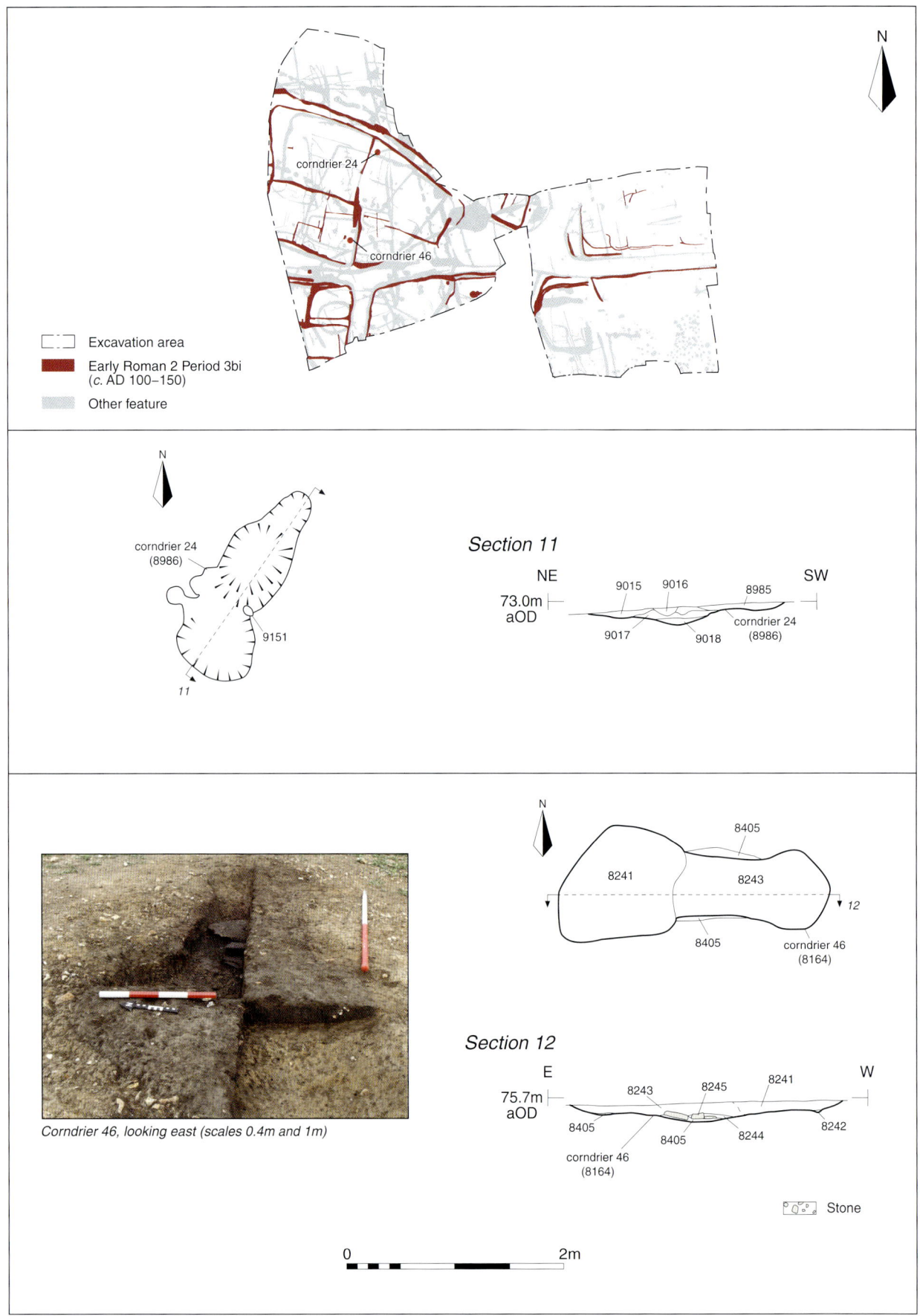

Fig. 2.11 Early Roman 2 period 3bi, corndriers 24 and 46: plans, sections and photograph

The Late Iron Age and Romano-British Period 31

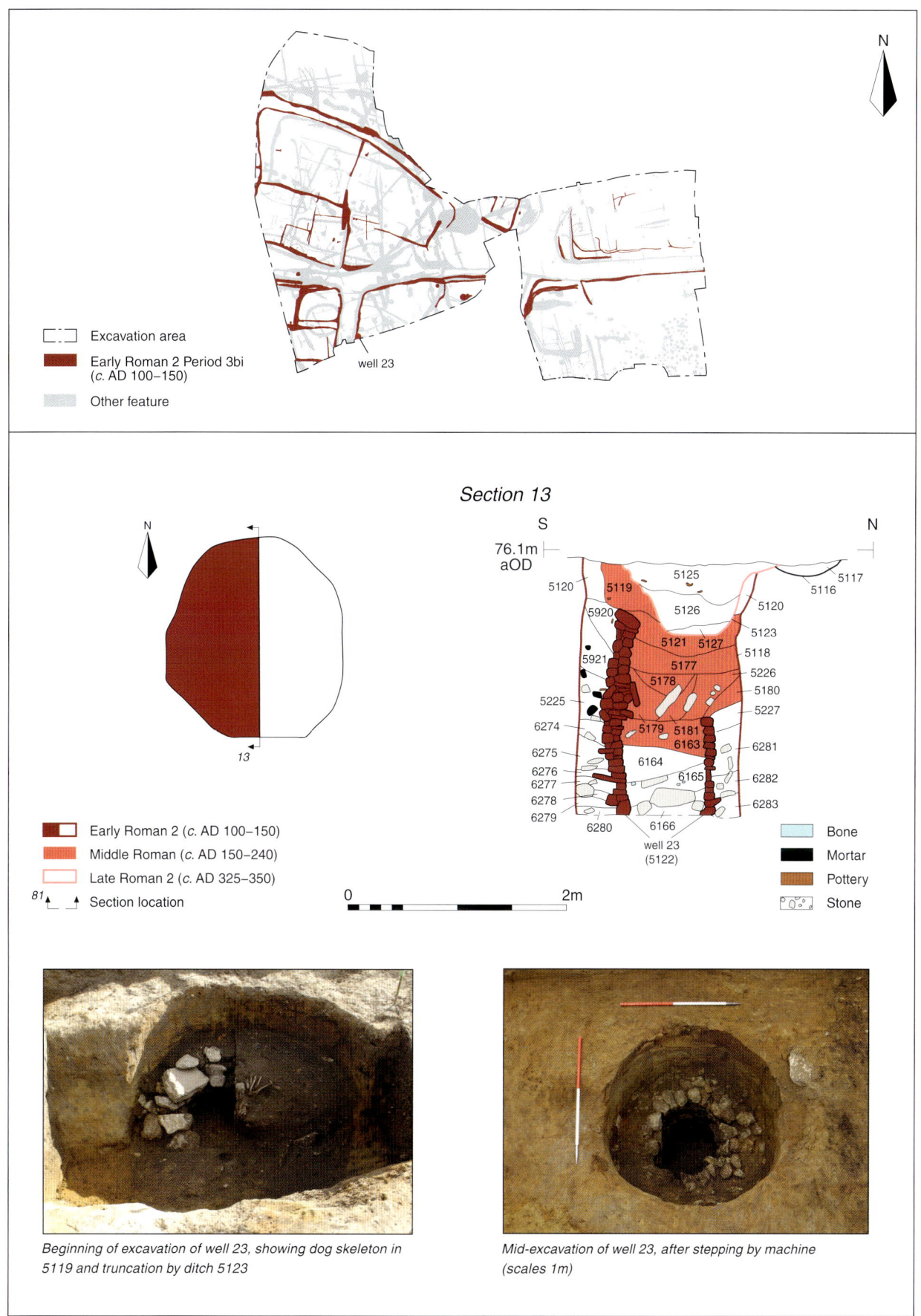

Fig. 2.12 Early Roman 2 (period 3bi) and Middle Roman (period 3bii) well 23: plan, section and photographs

ware mortarium (M2; Young 1977) dated AD 100–170, and sherds of a similar date were found in the lowest exposed fill. Pit 6149 appeared to be a similar feature, although this was only partially excavated. Pit 6120 was found cutting both pits 6133 and 6149. It was 3.5m long and 2.75m wide and was also excavated to a depth of 1.70m, and further augured to 3.70m without the base being reached. It contained pottery that dates to the very end of the Early Roman 2 (period 3bi) period. All three of these features may have been waterholes.

Pit 7866 was located just to the east of ditch 227 and was an undercut 'bell'-shaped pit 1.20m wide and 0.46m deep. All of its three fills contained pottery amounting to 2.3kg and indicating an early 2nd-century date. The middle fill included a large rim sherd of a medium mouthed jar in a coarse grog-tempered fabric, and the upper fill produced a sherd of a jar beaker in a fine Oxfordshire grey ware. This may have been a storage pit, although its fill is presumably rubbish deposited after its primary use.

Pit 8341 was located in the droveway created by ditches 229 and 230. It was sub-square, measuring 2.7m diameter and 0.57m deep, and contained a small amount of pottery probably dating to the Early Roman 2 (period 3bi) period. Its function is uncertain.

Pit 6770 was circular measuring 0.45m in diameter, 0.24m deep with steep sides and a concave base. The pit contained the remains of a near-complete polled sheep with evidence of cut marks, alongside a small amount of Early Roman 2 (period 3bi) pottery. Due to the pit's diminutive size it is likely that it was dug for the purpose of disposing of the remains of the sheep. The pit was located within the enclosure defined by ditches 238, 225 and 257.

Cremation deposits

Four urned cremation deposits could be dated to the Early Roman 2 period. One of these pairs was in the coombe area, the other placed in ditch 234.

Two urned cremation deposits were found within 0.30m of one another in the central part of the coombe, immediately to the east of ditch 227. The cuts that these were placed in could not be discerned due to the homogenous nature of the colluvium filling the coombe. Cremation deposit 16751 comprised 824g of bone probably from an adult female, found inside urn 16752. This was a jar of uncertain form in a fine reduced coarse ware fabric, of which the upper part did not survive.

Cremation deposit 16756 comprised 347g of bone from an adult, deposited in a jar in a coarse-tempered oxidised fabric (16757). The upper part had been truncated. Another jar, 16755, was found placed inside this, containing a further 3g of burnt bone (16754). This was a beaker in a similar fabric as the jar it was within.

Cremation deposit 7104 was found in ditch 234. No separate cut was seen. Some 586g of burnt bone from an adult was retrieved from the lower part of a jar in a sand-tempered 'Belgic' fabric (urn 7103). The upper part of the jar was missing.

Cremation 7541/7542 comprised 30g of burnt bone within and around a pottery vessel (7540). The cut that the vessel was placed in was not seen, suggesting it was quickly backfilled with the material excavated from the feature. The pot went missing before it could be analysed.

Middle Roman (period 3bii; *c.* AD 150–240)

Few features could be dated to the Middle Roman period, *c.* AD 150–240. The only feature that produced ceramic material of certain Middle Roman date was the backfill contexts of Early Roman 2 (period 3bi) well 23.

The construction of well 23 dates to the Early Roman 2 (period 3bi) period (Fig. 2.12, see above). The feature could not be bottomed, although it was excavated to a depth of 3.05m (see above).

A complete dog skeleton was found towards the base of the limit of excavation, in collapse/backfill deposit 6165. Two fills above this in 6163, the complete profile of an M14 Oxfordshire white ware mortarium was discovered (Fig. 3.6, 100), dating to AD 180–240 (Young 1977). The fill pattern above 6163 show some tip-lines from the northern side. Higher up in adjacent fills 5142 and 5121, 439g of probable 3rd-century pottery was found. Another complete dog skeleton was discovered in the uppermost fill, 5119, along with 400g of Early Neolithic pottery, including three rims.

Late Roman (period 3c; *c.* AD 240–410)

The Late Roman period was characterised by the reimposition and redefinition of the enclosure of the landscape which had been undertaken in earlier periods. The major droveways/trackways and some of the enclosures remained very similar in Late Roman phase 1, although the area became more open. There was greater redefinition later in the Late Roman period, although the orientation of the system remained.

Late Roman 1 (period 3ci; *c.* AD 240–325)

Droveways and enclosures

The major east/west boundary crossing the southern part of the site was redefined in period 3ci by ditches 243, 242, 241 and 119 (Fig. 2.13). These ditches tended to be larger than their Early Roman precursors. For example, ditch 241 was 1.48–3.44m wide and 0.86–1.38m deep, ditch 242 was 1.52–3.94m wide and 0.57–1.21m deep, and the east/west length of ditch 243 was *c.* 2.60m wide and *c.* 1m deep, with the north/south return 0.9m wide and 0.64m deep. Three of the contexts belonging to ditch 241 produced assemblages of pottery weighing in excess of 700g.

The Late Iron Age and Romano-British Period 33

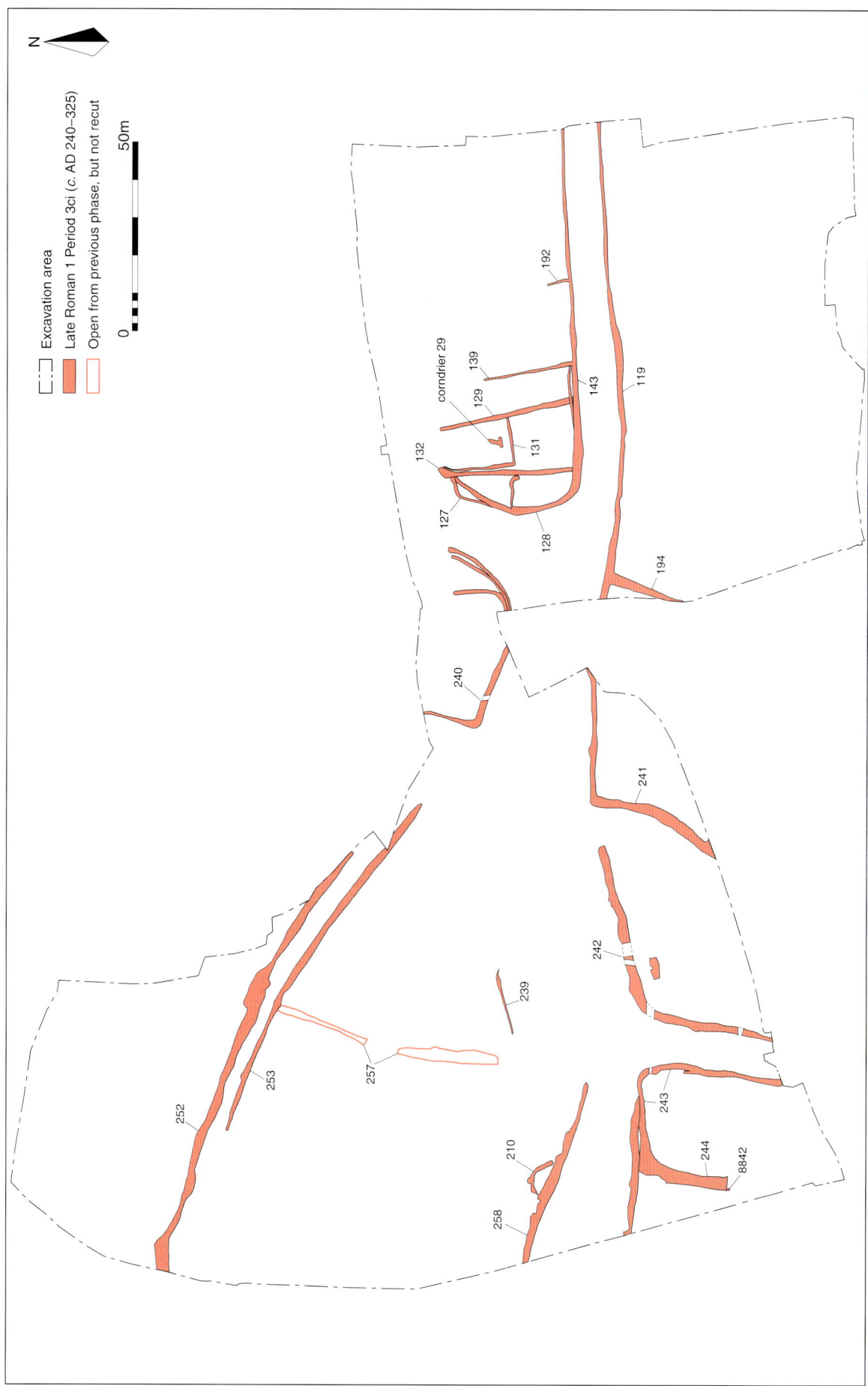

Fig. 2.13 Late Roman 1 period 3ci: plan

The major east/west boundary formed the southern ditch of a droveway that crossed the entire site. In the western part of the western half of the excavated area, ditch 258 was not quite parallel with 243, funnelling the droveway so it had a minimum width of 9m where it met the corner of ditch 243. Ditch 258 was 2.25m wide and 0.96m deep. To the north-east of ditch 258, ditch 257 belonging to the Early Roman 2 (period 3bi) period appears to have remained in use or at least visible through the Late Roman 1 (period 3ci) period since, although this ditch was not recut in this period, a recut is datable to a later Late Roman phase.

In the eastern part of the excavation area, the east/west droveway was 10m wide and defined by slighter ditches in comparison to the western area of the site. The southern side of the droveway was defined by ditch 119 which was 0.60–2.05m wide and 0.18–0.55m deep. The northern side of the droveway was recut in period 3ci and was defined by ditch 192 that had been recut. This was of similar dimensions to ditch 119.

The east/west droveway was joined by two other major droveways as well as a more minor diversion of the track. In the southern part of the western half of the excavation area, the north/south droveway established in the Early Roman 2 period was redefined. In the northern part of the western part of the site, the droveway also established in the Early Roman 2 period, defined by ditches 226 and 225, was redefined by ditches 252 and 253. These ditches were of similar proportions in both periods. However, the southern droveway ditch, 253, did not appear to have been recut along the entirety of the length of the earlier ditch, instead terminating 35m from the western edge of the site. The northern ditch, 252, appeared to continue across all of the eastern part of the site and beyond it to the west.

Another fork in the southern east/west droveway was apparent in the eastern half of the site, defined by ditches 240 and 127/128. This departed the southern droveway on a north-east alignment, and was 15m wide, but did not appear to form another extensive droveway as the flanking ditches terminated 25m and 38m from where they met the southern droveway. This fork formalised a routeway partially defined by ditches 227 and 190 in the Early Roman 2 (period 3bi) period and led down the natural coombe to the Thame floodplain. Ditch 240 effectively replaced ditch 227, and ditch 127/128 replaced 190. Ditch 240 had two recuts and was c. 0.7m wide and 0.3m deep. Ditch 127 produced a redeposited Hod Hill brooch (Fig. 3.9, 5) dating to soon after the conquest, as well as two large sherds from a straight-sided dish dating to the 3rd or 4th century AD.

North/south-aligned ditches 132, 129 and 139 were joined to ditch 143 and created two narrow enclosures. The western of these enclosures was 15m wide and 35m long, and the eastern enclosure was 10m wide and 24m long. Both of the enclosures were open on the northern side, although the western enclosure was subdivided by ditch 131, and corndrier 29 was located within this northern subdivision. Ditch 139 produced a tegula fragment dating to AD 240–380. Two further smaller enclosures, both measuring 14m long and 8m wide, were found to the east of these enclosures. The ditches surrounding this group of enclosures must have derived from more than one phase as together some of the enclosures would not have had entrances.

Four enclosures were seen on the southern side of the main east/west boundary. Each of these had origins in the Early Roman 2 period. In the south-western corner of the western part of the excavation area, ditch 244 defined the boundary between two of these enclosures, which were both otherwise defined by ditch 243. Ditch 244 was 0.92–1.85m wide and c. 0.55m deep, and a northerly intervention produced a decorated copper alloy bracelet probably dating to the 4th century AD (Fig. 3.10, 12).

The eastern of the two enclosures was 28m wide and at least 53m in length. The western enclosure was primarily outside of the excavated area, and the entrances to these enclosures were not discovered. On the other side of the north/south droveway, an enclosure was found that was defined by ditch 242 on its western and northern sides, and ditch 241 on its eastern side. This was up to 55m wide, although the enclosure became narrower towards the southern baulk of the site. An entrance 10m wide was found in the north-west corner of this enclosure. Finally, another enclosure was found to the east, defined by ditch 241 on its western and northern sides, and ditch 194 on its eastern side. This was 55m wide, and the entrance was not exposed as it presumably lay outside the excavated area.

Corndrier 29 has been very tentatively phased to the Late Roman 1 period 3ci. Although no datable material culture was recovered from the feature, the structure was centrally positioned and on the same alignment as the southern end of the enclosure created by ditches 131, 132 and 129, suggesting that they were contemporary. The corndrier was constructed from tabular, local mudstone blocks, set within a yellowish-brown clay mortar. The T-shaped structure had a north/south alignment with a flue orientated at 30° to the chamber and a stokehole at the northern end (Fig. 2.14). The structure had been subject to a significant level of truncation with only part of basal mudstone masonry courses surviving.

A layer of redeposited natural, 16972, comprised the basal fill of the cut of the corndrier. A clay bedding layer, 16541, was placed on this upon which the rest of the structure was built. The flue had an internal width of approximately 0.55m and the chamber of 0.35m and had a total length of 4m. Evidence of plough damage was observed at the southern end with a clear plough-scar mixing silting deposits with the clay lining. Despite the presence of substantial quantities of charcoal within the flue and stokehole, especially in fill 16543, the clay forming the structure showed little to no evidence of being heat-affected. This may be due to the indirect

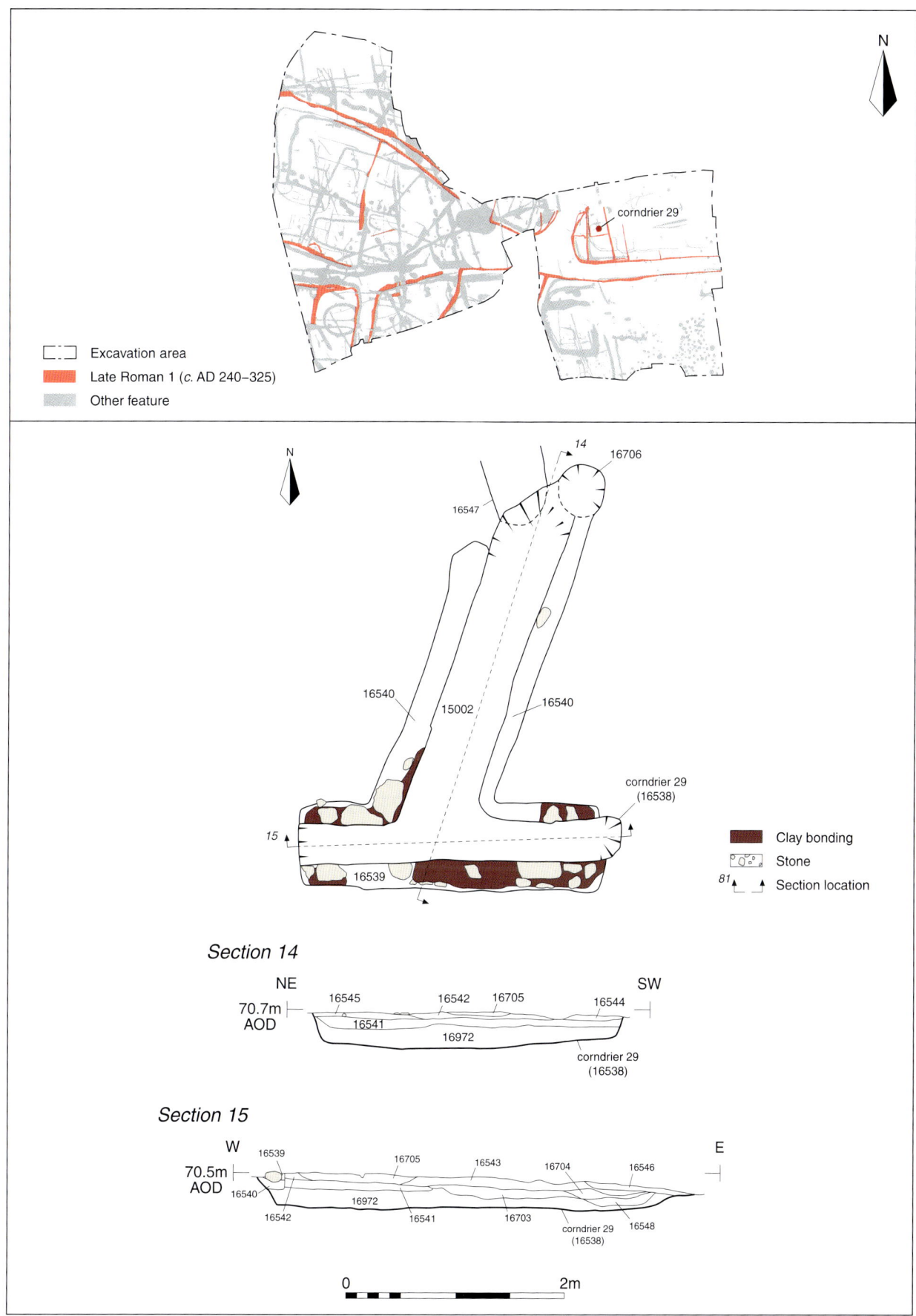

Fig. 2.14 Late Roman 1 period 3ci, corndrier 29: plan and sections

nature of the heat or may suggest minimal use of the structure.

Late Roman 2 (period 3cii; *c.* AD 325–350)

This period was characterised by further ditches defining droveways and enclosures (Fig. 2.15). A major break in the organisation and use of the landscape took place in the Late Roman 2 period, *c.* AD 325–350. The major east/west droveway was significantly altered by ditches 256, 246, 255 and 250, although the south-western ditch belonging to this droveway was partially recut by ditch 260. Together, ditches 260 and 256 formed an east/west droveway than narrowed to just 2.5m at the far western part of the site. The southern boundary of the droveway was taken over by ditch 246 where there was an entrance 6m across, widening the passage in this area to 11m. However, ditch 255 was dug across the path of the droveway, and with the turn of ditch 246 this led the droveway to the south to another narrow opening of just 3.5m. Furthermore, ditch 246 blocked the north/south droveway that had been present since the Early Roman 2 period.

Ditch 256 had been recut twice and was 1.20–1.86m wide and 0.83–1.11m deep. Ditch 246 was 1.44–3m wide and 0.20–0.44m deep, whereas ditch 260 was 2.21–2.96m wide and 0.81–1.13m deep. An easterly intervention of ditch 260 produced an assemblage of 4th-century pottery weighing 817g, a flint sphere and two polishing/processing slabs from saddle querns along with a copper alloy mount or small plate brooch. A residual 1st-century Colchester-derivative (Harlow) brooch (Fig. 3.9, 9) was found in a westerly intervention of ditch 260, along with 338g of pottery probably dating to the 4th century. Three ditches aligned broadly east/west were found to join the western side of ditch 246. One of these, ditch 5123, cut Early Roman 2 well 23 (Fig. 2.12).

Ditch 241 was located to the east of the ditch complex described above. This was not recut in period 3cii, although it appears to have continued as a boundary through this phase since it was recut in period 3ciii, and material culture that could date to period 3cii was found in its fills. Ditch 250 joined the eastern part of ditch 241 in period 3cii. This north/south-aligned feature dramatically altered the layout of the landscape and must indicate significant change to how the site was used, blocking access between the eastern and western halves of the site and between the western portion and the coombe. Indeed, no features could be dated to either periods 3cii or 3ciii in the eastern half, and this area of the site that was previously well integrated with the area to the west appears to have been abandoned. The ditch was 1m wide and 0.5m deep.

Ditches 258 and 257 and the northern droveway, defined by ditches 252 and 253, appear to have remained in use during the Late Roman 2 (period 3cii) period. Although there are no clear cuts that can be assigned to this phase, the ditches were either recut or were more clearly extant in the subsequent Late Roman 3 (period 3ciii) period.

Late Roman 3 (period 3ciii; *c.* AD 350–410)

Numerous elements of the Late Roman 2 (period 3cii) landscape features were re-established in the final Roman phase (Fig. 2.16). L-shaped ditch 246 was replaced by ditch 262. A coin dated AD 364–67 (Chapter 3, Roman coins, no. 16) was found in a western intervention. Ditch 241 was partially replaced by ditch 259. Three contexts belonging to ditch 259 produced good assemblages of pottery. The lower fill of intervention 6516 produced 1.3kg of Late Roman pottery and fragments of brick and tile, with the upper fill producing 3.3kg of pottery post-dating AD 350, as well as a fragmented cattle skull, fragments of a rotary quern and millstone, and brick and tile. The middle fill of intervention 6988 produced nearly 1.5kg of Late Roman pottery, half a fired clay spindle whorl, a stone hone, tile, and a coin dated AD 330–35 (Chapter 3, Roman coins, no. 9). The ditch was recut short of its earlier length and joined ditch 263 that in turn appears to have replaced ditch 250, located *c.* 20m to the west of the earlier ditch. Ditch 263 was a recut and extension of the southern ditch belonging to the northern droveway. This appears to have been recut only to the corner of the large enclosure defined by ditch 251. Two coins dated AD 364–78 (Chapter 3, Roman coins, nos 13 and 19) were found in the latest recut of this ditch during the evaluation (Murray 2014, 32–3, 69).

A large enclosure in the western part of the site was redefined in the Late Roman 3 (period 3ciii) period. The enclosure was 87m long and 60m wide and defined on its western, eastern and southern sides by ditch 251, replacing ditches 257 and 258. The northern side was presumably defined by ditch 252, although no clear recut of this ditch is apparent after the Late Roman 1 (period 3ci) period. The enclosure had a large gap, possibly an entrance, 45m wide on the north-western side. Although Early Roman 2 (period 3b) ditch 225 followed the line of this gap, there is no evidence that this part of the ditch was recut.

The southern length of ditch 251 was 2.12–3.62m wide and 0.8–1.28m deep. The eastern return was slighter: 0.90m wide and 0.22m deep. However, the western length was 2.55m wide and 1.07m deep. A number of large assemblages of late pottery were found in the ditch, with five contexts producing over 500g of pottery of which three could be dated with a degree of certainty to after AD 350, and the others to the Late Roman period. A knife (Fig. 3.11, 20) was found with one of the larger pottery groups. The intervention on the western side of ditch 251 produced two coins, one dated AD 364–78 (Chapter 3, Roman coins, no. 15). A coin with an earlier date of AD 318–24 (no. 8) was found on the surface of pit 5490 immediately to the west of this intervention.

Corndrier 26 was an L-shaped masonry-lined structure lying in the very north of the western half of the excavated area (Fig. 2.17). It was located to the immediate north

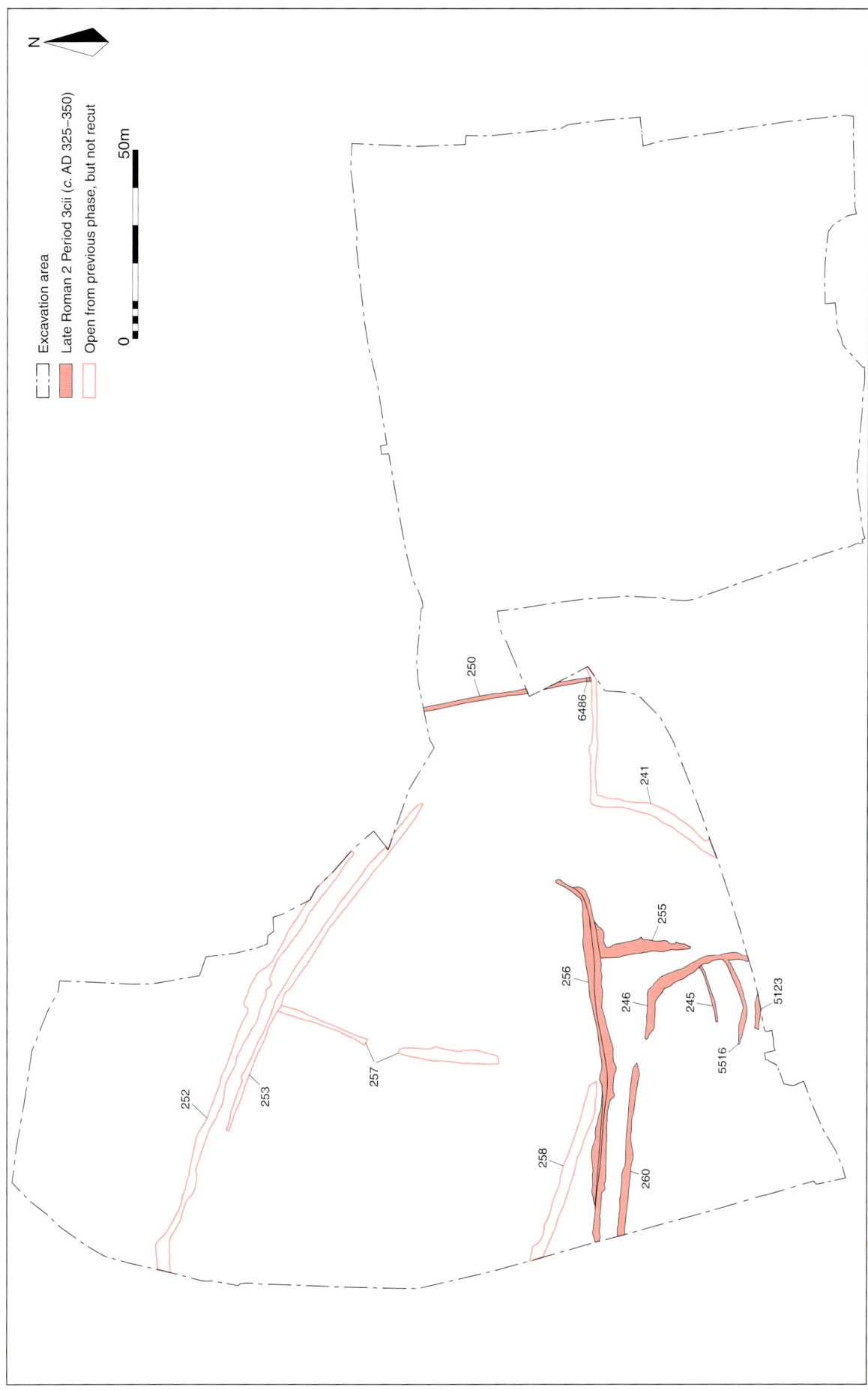

Fig. 2.15 Late Roman 2 period 3cii: plan

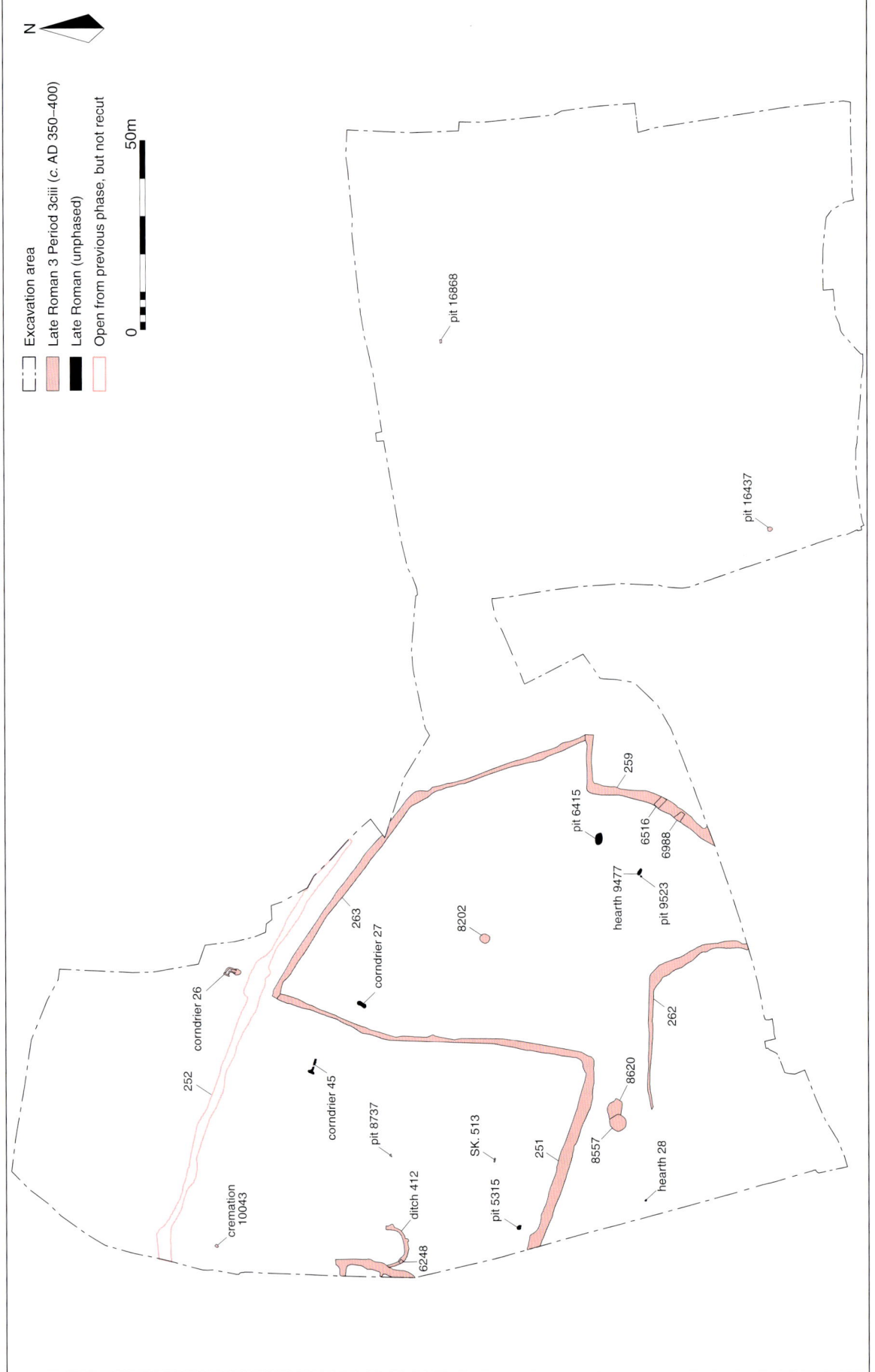

Fig. 2.16 Late Roman 2 period 3ciii and unphased: plan

The Late Iron Age and Romano-British Period 39

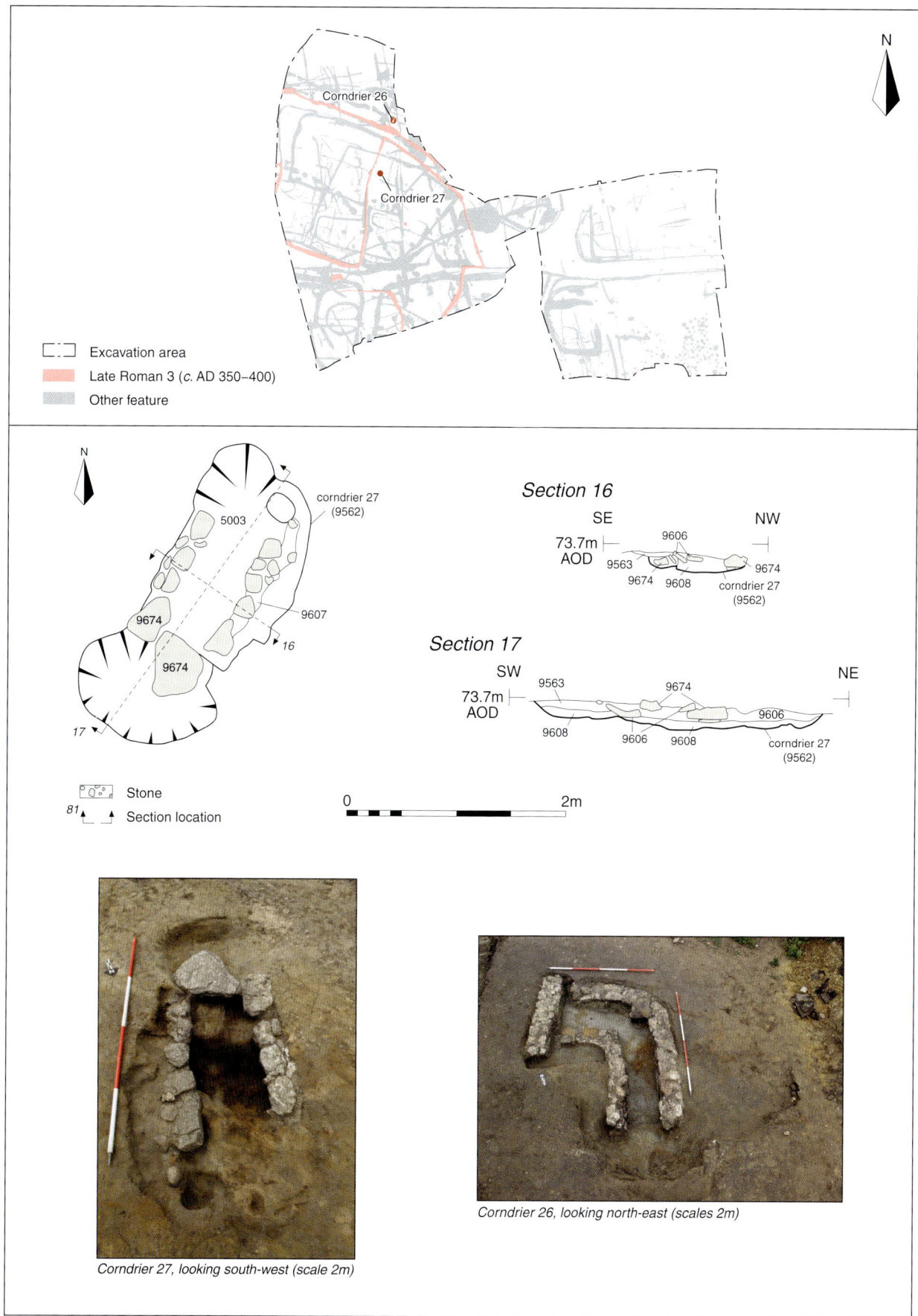

Fig. 2.17 Late Roman 3 corndrier 26 and Late Roman possible corndrier 27: plan, sections and photographs

of the northern 'contour-hugging' droveway which had been in place since the Early Roman 2 period. The structure was north/south-aligned, with the stokehole to the south, and the chamber at the western end of the 90-degree turn. The structure overall was c. 4.6m long and 1.1–1.3m wide, with well-coursed, tabular mudstone blocks comprising the masonry lining. Opposed open flue channels that were both 0.2m wide were preserved in the masonry on the north and south side of the main chamber area. The masonry structure survived to a height of 0.5m within the foundation cut. The stokehole pit, 7670, was 2.65m by 1.74m and c. 0.4m deep, deepening to the north below the masonry. The stone lining was composed of sub-rectangular/sub-square tabular mudstone blocks, 0.2–0.3m in size and c. 70mm thick, bonded in a natural clay mortar. Many of the blocks showed signs of burning/baking. The deposits within the structure, some of which were charcoal-rich, contained deer antler as well as an assemblage of large sherds of pottery, some post-dating AD 340. The largest assemblages of pottery were found in fills 8263, 8503 and 8264.

In the middle of the droveway defined by the southern length of ditch 251 and ditch 262, a large pit, 8620, was discovered. The pit was 5.3m in length and 1.10m deep, and contained 445g of pottery post-dating AD 350. It was cut by another large pit, 8557, that was 4.2m in length and of a similar depth. It contained 178g of pottery as well as fragments of a tegula and box flue. Although these were in the middle of the droveway and may signal the final blocking of this long-lived feature, the droveway was quite wide at this point with a gap of 4–5m between the pits and the flanking ditches, so access around the pits was still possible. Pit 8202 was located in the centre of the western half of the excavated area and was 2.3m wide and 0.45m deep and produced 192g of pottery dating after AD 350, and a nail.

Roman (period 3d; AD 43–410)

Corndrier 27 was a very damaged, stone-lined structure that was probably deliberately dismantled to reuse the stone (Fig. 2.17). The north-east/south-west-aligned structure comprised a stokehole pit at the south-west end, which measured 1.4m by 0.9m and 0.2m deep. The channel of the structure was 2m by 1.2m and 0.18m deep. It contained unworked tabular, mudstone block lining with clear evidence of burning/baking, predominantly along the sides of the structure. Piled on top of the remaining *in situ* elements of the structure, a number of stones were found disturbed from their original positions. In the lower fill of the chamber, 9608, a single small sherd of pottery post-dating AD 240 was found. In the upper fill, 9563, another small sherd post-dating the late 1st century was found. The structure cannot be considered well-dated, although it appears to belong to the Late Roman period.

Unphased Roman east/west-aligned masonry corndrier 45 was a very truncated T-shaped structure located to the north-west of corndrier 27. Its stokehole was at the east end of the structure. The structure's foundation cut (6627) was 4.2m long and 0.7m wide with a 1.9m-long chamber at the west end of the structure. As was encountered on many of the corndriers, the stokehole pit deepened towards the structure proper, in this case to a maximum depth of 0.23m. The masonry lining had been very damaged and survived best at the chamber end and along the sides of the flue. As recorded elsewhere, small, tabular blocks of naturally occurring mudstone had been used to build the superstructure, many of which showed signs of being heat affected and/or charcoal stained. Only residual Early Neolithic worked flint and burnt flint was recorded from the structure, along with fired clay fragments and charcoal-rich fills.

A small hearth, 28, was recorded in the west of the western half of the excavated area, in the northern part of the eastern enclosure defined by period 3ci ditches 243 and 244. It consisted of a 0.77m-diameter, sub-circular pit, which was 0.18m deep and there were clear signs that the natural sand geology had been affected by heat. The single charcoal-rich fill, 6192, contained common animal bone fragments and residual Early Neolithic worked flint, as well as an assemblage of Late Roman pottery.

Possible hearth 9477 was found in the southern part of the western portion of the excavated area. It was oval, measuring 1.83m in length and 0.98m in width, and was 0.22m deep. Its sole fill, 9476, contained fired clay from a hearth floor, and a large piece of burnt sandstone. However, fill 9476 was not particularly charcoal-rich. It contained a large basal sherd of a storage jar in a coarse grog-tempered oxidised fabric, dating to the Late Roman period.

Six pits could be dated to the Late Roman period. Three of these could be placed in the Late Roman 3 period and have been discussed above. The following all contained Late Roman pottery but cannot be more closely phased.

Pit 9523 was adjacent to possible hearth 9477. It was circular and measured 0.55m in diameter and was 0.18m deep and contained a single small sherd of pottery.

Pit 5315 was 1.3m wide and 0.53m deep and located in the south-western corner of the enclosure defined by ditch 251 and contained 206g of pottery. It cut undated pit 5371.

Pit 6415 was sub-rectangular and measured 1.5m in length and 0.49m in width and was 0.49m deep. It contained 182g of pottery. It lay to the immediate east of period 3ci ditch 242, although these two features did not have any stratigraphic relationship.

Chapter 3
The Late Iron Age and Romano-British Finds and Environmental Remains

A variety of artefacts and ecofacts were recovered from Late Iron Age and Romano-British contexts. This included pottery, metal objects and coins, worked stone, fired clay and ceramic building material, industrial residues, human and faunal remains, charcoal and plant macrofossils. Each is described in turn in this chapter.

Late Iron Age and Roman pottery
by Paul Booth

Some 7339 sherds (152,815g, 129.65 Rim Equivalents (REs)) of Late Iron Age and Roman pottery from the excavation were recorded and analysed. These represent all the material readily identified as of these periods on ceramic criteria, but in view of the nature of deposits on the site and the extent of continuities of potting traditions (see below) it is possible that some material of later prehistoric date has been included within these totals. Equally, some Late Iron Age sherds may have been subsumed within the later prehistoric material examined by Lisa Brown (Volume 1, Chapter 5). In either case, however, the scale of this problem and the extent to which it may have compromised the results of these analyses is considered to be very minor. The present assemblage was recorded using the Oxford Archaeology (OA) system for late prehistoric and Roman pottery (Booth 2014), with sherds assigned to subgroups or individual fabrics/wares within major ware groups. Quantification of wares within individual context groups was by sherd count and weight. Vessel types were quantified by rim equivalents (REs) and by a more subjective vessel count (MV) based on rim sherds. Details of decoration were recorded, as well as evidence of use and reuse where identifiable. Methodological issues relating to the recording are discussed further at relevant points below. Notable sherds are illustrated in Figures 3.1–3.8.

The assemblage spans the whole of the Late Iron Age and Roman periods, though pottery of the Middle Roman period (roughly mid 2nd to mid 3rd centuries) seemed to be relatively poorly represented compared to earlier and later material. The pottery was in reasonable condition. The mean sherd weight (20.8g) is quite high for assemblages in this region, though it was clearly boosted by some collections of large sherds from thick-walled vessels and by the presence of a small number of relatively complete vessels associated with burials. Abrasion was not consistently recorded, but heavily worn sherds were scarce.

Fabrics/wares

The excavation produced a wide range of Late Iron Age and Roman fabrics; these are listed in Table 3.1, in order within the series of major ware groups on the basis of significant common characteristics. The ware groups can be combined to constitute two main classes of material: fine and specialist wares on the one hand, and on the other, the rest of the coarse wares (cf Booth 2004). The fine and specialist ware groups (identified by the initial letter of the fabric code) are: samian ware (S); fine wares – colour-coated, lead-glazed, mica-coated etc. – (F); amphorae (A); mortaria (M); white wares – other than mortaria – (W); and white-slipped wares (Q). The remaining ware groups are: 'Belgic type' (broadly in the sense of Thompson 1982, 4–5), usually grog-tempered, fabrics (E); 'Romanised' oxidised coarse wares (O); 'Romanised' reduced coarse wares (R); black-burnished ware (B); and calcareous (particularly shell-tempered) and other wares (C).

Within these classes there are hierarchically arranged subgroups, usually defined on the basis of inclusion type, and individual fabrics/wares are then indicated at a third level of precision, both levels of subdivision being expressed by numeric codes. Thus, R20 is a general code for coarse sandy reduced wares, while R21 is a specific sandy reduced Oxford industry product

Table 3.1 Late Iron Age and Roman pottery fabric codes and descriptions

Ware code	Description	NRFRC code/reference	Source area
Samian ware			
S20	South Gaulish samian ware (general)	incl. **LGF SA**	I
S30	Central Gaulish samian ware (general)	incl. **LEZ SA 2**	I
S32	Les Martres-de-Veyre Central Gaulish samian ware	**LMV SA**	I
S41	Rheinzabern East Gaulish samian ware	**RHZ SA**	
Fine wares			
F20	Uncertain sand-tempered internally glazed ware		?
F30	'Mica-dusted' fabrics	incl. **ROB MD**	?
F35	Lower Farm 'Mica-dusted'	Booth *et al.* 1993, 138	R
F39	London mica-dusted ware (London fabric LOMI)	Davies *et al.* 1994, 136–9	I
F43	Central Gaulish 'Rhenish'	**CNG BS**	I
F44	Trier 'Rhenish' (Moselkeramik)	**MOS BS**	I
F50	Major British colour-coated wares, but usually red-brown colour-coated wares (general). F50 mainly used for probable Oxford wares and related fabrics		R?
F51	Oxford colour-coated ware	**OXF RS**	R
FO	Oxidised probable Oxford fabric (F51) but with no surviving colour coat	cf **OXF RS**	R
F52	Nene Valley colour-coated ware	**LNV CC**	ER
F53	New Forest fabric 1a, white or grey	Fulford 1975, 24–5	ER
F57	New Forest fabric 1b (oxidised reddish-yellow to reddish-brown)	**NFO RS2**	ER
F60	Red/brown colour-coated fabrics (regional?)		R?
F63	Slightly sandy oxidised fabric, grey core and red/brown colour coat. Fairly prominent Fe inclusions		?
Amphorae			
A10	Buff amphora fabrics (general)		I
A11	Dressel 20 Baetican amphorae (Peacock and Williams 1986, 140)	**BAT AM 1** and **BAT AM 2**	I
Mortaria			
M21	Verulamium region white mortaria	**VER WH**	R
M22	Oxford white ware mortaria (Young 1977, 56)	**OXF WH**	R
M31	Oxford white-slipped oxidised ware mortaria, fabric WC. See also Q21, below	**OXF WS**	R
M41	Oxford red colour-coated ware mortaria as fabric F51. Young (1977) forms C97–C100	**OXF RS**	R
White wares			
W10	Fairly fine white fabrics (general)		R/ER
W11	Oxford parchment ware	**OXF PA**	R
W12	Oxford fine white ware	**OXF WH**	R
W20	Coarse sandy white fabrics (general)		R/ER?
W21	Verulamium-region sandy white ware	**VER WH**	R
W22	Oxford sandy white ware	Young 1977, 93	R
W23	Oxford burnt white ware	Young 1977, 113	R
W26	Fine white fabrics (generally thin-walled and few/no obvious inclusions)		?
W35	Hard very fine white, can have pale grey core. Moderate very fine quartz (cf O18)	Timby *et al.* 1997	R
W36	Fine white/creamy-buff, abundant sub-rounded quartz <0.2mm but typically <0.1mm, occasional larger quartz grains. A little less fine and hard than W35 (cf W12)		R

Table 3.1 (cont.) Late Iron Age and Roman pottery fabric codes and descriptions

Ware code	Description	NRFRC code/reference	Source area
W50	Miscellaneous white wares		
White-slipped wares (except mortaria)			
Q20	Fine-moderately sandy oxidised white-slipped fabrics (general)		R?
Q21	Oxford (Young 1977) fabric WC – except mortaria (see fabric M31, above)	OXF WS	R
Q30	Reduced slightly sandy white-slipped fabrics		?
Q40	Coarse sand-tempered oxidised fabrics with white slip		?
'Belgic type' wares			
E10	Organic-tempered 'Belgic type' fabrics		L/R
E20	Fine sand-tempered 'Belgic type' fabrics		L/R
E30	Medium to coarse sand-tempered 'Belgic type' fabrics		L/R
E40	Shell-tempered 'Belgic type' fabrics		L/R
E60	Flint-tempered 'Belgic type' fabrics		L/R
E80	Grog-tempered 'Belgic type' fabrics	SOB GT	L/R
Oxidised 'coarse' wares			
O10	Fine oxidised coarse ware fabrics (general)		R?
O11	Oxford fine oxidised ware	Booth *et al.* 1993, 146; Young 1977, 185, fabric 1	R
O18	Very fine, compact, sandy ware ranging in colour from white to pale brown, pink, orange or grey. The matrix contains very fine quartz sand not macroscopically visible and sparse black fine iron. A slightly coarser sandier variant was noted with a fine pimply interior surface although again the individual grains are not macroscopically visible. Another variant had a white or buff fabric with a purplishbrown 'fumed' exterior (cf W35)	Timby *et al.* 1997	R
O19	Fine oxidised, probably a well-fired variant of O18. A very hard ware with a granular texture and brittle fracture. The matrix contains a moderate to common frequency of well-sorted rounded to sub-angular quartz and sparse brown iron. The interior surface has a distinctive pimply feel. Similar to Silchester Basilica type fabric S16 (Timby 2000). Equivalent to R19	Timby *et al.* 1997	R
O20	Sandy oxidised coarse ware fabrics (general)		L/R?
O24	Sandy oxidised 'Portchester D type' Overwey white/buff ware	OVW WH	ER
O30	Fine/medium-sandy oxidised fabrics		R?
O40	Severn Valley ware	SVW OX 2	ER
O55	Fairly fine oxidised fabric with common clay pellet/grog inclusions		?
O80	Coarse-tempered (usually grog) oxidised fabrics, equivalent to R90		L/R
O81	Pink grogged ware (Booth and Green 1989)	PNK GT	R
Reduced 'coarse' wares			
R10	Fine reduced 'coarse ware' fabrics (general)		R?
R11	Oxford fine grey ware. Young (1977) reduced fabric 4	OXF FR	R
R19	Fine reduced, as O19		R
R20	Sandy reduced coarse ware fabrics (general)		L/R
R201	Coarse sandy reduced fabric, with occasional flint, iron oxides etc. A code for sandy 'storage' jars		L/R
R21	Oxford sandy grey ware. A hard, sandy fabric, usually grey or (characteristically) light grey in colour (5YR 5.5/1, 6.5/1; 7.5YR 6.5/1; 10YR 5.5/1). The principal inclusion is moderate to common rounded quartz up to *c.* 1mm, but typically *c.* 0.5mm in size. Sub-rounded grog up to 2–3mm, iron oxides up to *c.* 1mm and organic fragments also occur sparsely	Booth *et al.* 1993, 149	R

Table 3.1 (cont.) Late Iron Age and Roman pottery fabric codes and descriptions

Ware code	Description	NRFRC code/reference	Source area
R23	Compton? Rounded quartz grains of variable size, often glassy. Sometimes partly oxidised		R
R29	A very hard, sandy fabric, grey (5YR 6/1.5) with a reddish-brown to strong brown core (5YR 5/3 to *c.* 7.5YR 5/6). Contains abundant sub-rounded or rounded quartz, mainly in the range 0.2–0.4mm, with occasional grains from 1–2mm	Booth *et al*. 1993, 149; also Booth 2011b, 153	L/R
R30	Medium/fine sandy reduced coarse ware fabrics (general)		L/R
R37	Reduced fabric with distinctive light grey core and grey-to-black surfaces, generally grey, moderate-abundant fine quartz sand temper 0.2mm and occasional black ?iron ore and organic inclusions. The surface colour varies considerably, from light or mid grey to black. West Oxfordshire	Booth 1997, 114	R
R39	Alice Holt fine sandy grey ware	**ALH RE**	ER
R50	A hard, slightly sandy fabric, usually black (*c.* 5YR 2.5/1) to very dark grey (7.5YR 3/0), often with a reddish-brown or reddish-grey core (5YR 4/3, 4/4, 5/2). Inclusions are sparse to moderate rounded quartz usually in the range *c.* 0.2–0.8mm	Booth *et al*. 1993, 151; cf Young 1977, 203 fabric 5	R
R60	Reduced fabrics with significant organic inclusions (general)		R?
R70	Reduced fabrics with calcareous inclusions (general)		R?
R80	Miscellaneous fairly fine reduced fabrics		
R90	Coarse-tempered (usually grog-tempered) reduced fabrics	e.g. Young 1977, 202 fabric 1	L/R
R95	Savernake ware	**SAV GT**	ER
R96	Reduced, lumpy fabric, grog-tempered with variable amounts of fine quartz sand and occasional organic inclusions. West Oxfordshire (cf Savernake)		R
R97	Late grog-tempered ware, central southern England	Lyne 2015	L/R
Black-burnished wares			
B11	Dorset BB1	**DOR BB 1**	ER
B30	Black-burnished type/imitation fabrics, usually wheel-thrown		R?
Calcareous wares etc.			
C10	Shell-tempered fabrics (general)		L/R
C11	Southern shell-tempered ware. A wheel-made shell-tempered fabric, surfaces commonly rilled, source probably Harrold, Bedfordshire (Brown 1994)	incl. **HAR SH**	ER

See text for explanation of abbreviations

(note that Oxford is used as convenient abbreviation for the major industry studied by Young (1977), since 'Oxfordshire' could refer to other productions in the area which are not part of this industry; note also that references below to Young without further definition are to the 1977 corpus). For the bulk of the present assemblage, fabric identification was at the intermediate level of precision. Much of the material was in fabrics the sources of which are unknown or uncertain, and detailed assignment to specific fabric codes did not seem to be warranted. A particular example is the R30 group of medium-sandy reduced coarse wares, which may have included products of a number of different local and regional centres, including the Oxford industry, but though the latter source was almost certainly the dominant contributor to this group its products are not sufficiently distinctive to allow confident attribution on the basis of relatively superficial examination of fabric. Attribution of sherds to ware groups or to individual fabrics was on the basis of macroscopic inspection, with frequent but not universal use of the binocular microscope at x10 or x20 magnification.

Relatively summary fabric descriptions or labels are given in Table 3.1, although some fabrics recently added to the OA series (but mostly of minor significance) and others added specifically from the present assemblage are described in more detail. More comprehensive descriptions can be found in the project archive and/or in the handbook to the National Roman Fabric Reference Collection (NRFRC) (Tomber and Dore

1998). Fabric codes from the latter are cross referenced in the table in bold.

In addition to fabric codes and descriptions Table 3.1 also gives an estimate of the distance of the source area of a particular fabric from the site. The categories used are I (Continental import), ER (British, extra-regional), R (regional – in a radius of roughly 10–45km from the site) and L (local – up to *c.* 10km distant). The 10km figure for the 'local' range excludes the Oxford industry, although the nearest known component production sites of this industry were only just outside the 10km radius, most falling in a range from *c.* 12–18km distant. Distances are 'as the crow flies' rather than involving calculations of how far a particular product might have had to move to reach the site depending on its mode of distribution. Some wares cannot be assigned confidently to one source category or another, and an L/R group is therefore used. This is particularly the case with the R20 and R30 (sandy and medium-sandy reduced wares) groups. These will have included products of the Oxford industry but also other similar vessels, some of which could have been produced at unknown, more local sites (see further below). Most of the E ware group fabrics are thought most likely to derive from local sources, but there is no definite evidence that this was the case.

Quantification of the fabrics/wares by the three principal measures is presented in Table 3.2. Variation in fabric proportions depending on the measure employed is typical. In many cases, however, percentages based on sherd count lie between the values for weight and REs, and in discussing fabrics are used here as the primary means of quantification. Significant aspects of each ware group are discussed below.

In overall terms the assemblage was dominated by two ware groups: reduced coarse wares, and E ('Belgic type') wares. Together these accounted for 79% of the pottery by sherd count and weight, and slightly less by REs. While reduced wares were more important in terms of sherd count and, particularly, REs, the representation of the two groups in terms of weight was quite similar, though overall the E wares had a slightly higher mean sherd weight than the reduced fabrics (22g and 19.6g respectively). Of the other ware groups, only fine wares produced more than 5% of the total sherds from the site.

The majority of the E ware group consisted of grog-tempered (E80) fabrics. Further definition of the fabric of sherds in this and other E ware subgroups was recorded in some cases, but these data (in archive) are not considered in detail here. The E80 fabrics could be handmade, or wheel thrown, though the latter were in the majority, and the grog inclusions were variable in size and frequency. There was some overlap between the fabrics of the E80 and E30 subgroups – sand occurring as a secondary component of some sherds in the former, and grog as a secondary inclusion type in some of the latter – and organic inclusions were present in a small proportion of sherds in both main E ware subgroups (roughly 9% and 6% of sherds in E80 and E30 respectively).

The E30 ware subgroup is of some interest. These fabrics are characterised by moderate to common, relatively large, sometimes coarse (up to *c.* 1mm) sand grains. Such fabrics can be seen as direct predecessors of the sandy 'Romanised' reduced fabrics of the R20 group (e.g., Booth 2011a, 370–1). R20 fabrics were in turn particularly characteristic of the early stages of development of the Oxford industry and were an important component of the mid 1st to mid 2nd-century assemblage at Thame. Here, however, their importance was retained into the Late Roman period, although fine (R10) and medium (R30) sand-tempered fabrics, most if not all Oxford products, did become more important at this time. The survival of R20 fabrics in some quantity, a characteristic also noted to some extent at Didcot (Booth 2023) but contrasting with the pattern of decline of R20 at other sites in the Oxford region, suggests that much of this material did not originate in the Oxford kilns, and that a more local source or sources might be indicated. That these represented direct continuity of production from the E30 tradition is plausible, but at present there is no local evidence for any of these production sites. Fabrics in an R20 tradition are associated with the production site at Compton, well to the south-west of Thame (see General discussion below) and a very poorly known site at Swan Wood, Nettlebed, some 20km south of Thame, producing a generally almost buff-coloured coarse sand-tempered fabric probably in the 2nd century (pottery in Reading Museum). This site, whose products probably had a very limited distribution, may be representative of other as yet unknown sources for fabrics of broad R20 character.

Fabric R20 sherds accounted for 47.1% of all reduced coarse ware sherds (44.5% by weight), significantly outnumbering the other fine and sand-tempered fabrics R10, R11 and R30, the last of which is usually by a substantial margin the commonest reduced ware subgroup on sites in the region. Apart from R20, however, the great majority of reduced coarse wares were probably from the Oxford industry. Very minor exceptions include a single sherd of Savernake ware (fabric R95) and rather more tentative identifications of a few sherds from the west Oxfordshire industry (fabrics R37 and R96, see e.g., Booth 2018b, 300–1), occurring well beyond their expected range.

The oxidised coarse wares form a similarly heterogeneous group but were collectively much less important than reduced wares. Fabrics O10, O11 and O80 derived largely from the Oxford industry and the coarse sand-tempered O20 subgroup was probably the equivalent of the R20 group and, at least in part, of more local origin. Early Roman 'fine' oxidised fabrics (O18 and O19), perhaps originating in the Abingdon

Table 3.2 Late Iron Age and Roman fabric quantification by sherd count, weight and rim equivalents (REs)

Ware code	No. of sherds	% Nosh	Wt (g)	% Wt	REs	% REs	MSW (g)
S20	7	0.1	27	+			3.9
S30	49	0.7	443	0.3	1.43	1.1	9.0
S32	10	0.1	269	0.2	0.32	0.3	26.9
S41	1	+	34	+			34.0
S subtotal	*67*	*0.9*	*773*	*0.5*	*1.75*	*1.3*	*11.5*
F20	1	+	1	+			1.0
F30	7	0.1	73	0.1	0.17	0.1	10.4
F35	6	0.1	141	0.1			23.5
F39	2	+	83	0.1	0.18	0.1	41.5
F50	4	0.1	58	+	0.07	0.1	14.5
F51	338	4.6	4743	3.1	7.59	5.9	14.0
FO	1	+	10	+			10.0
F52	23	0.3	552	0.4			24.0
F53	1	+	14	+			14.0
F57	1	+	5	+	0.10	0.1	5.0
F60	4	0.1	49	+			12.3
F63	1	+	2	+			2.0
F subtotal	*389*	*5.3*	*5731*	*3.8*	*8.11*	*6.3*	*14.7*
A10	1	+	69	0.1			69.0
A11	4	0.1	485	0.3			121.3
A subtotal	*5*	*0.1*	*554*	*0.4*			*110.8*
M21	7	0.1	454	0.3	0.49	0.4	64.9
M22	29	0.4	2724	1.8	1.26	1.0	93.9
M31	18	0.3	999	0.7	1.15	0.9	55.5
M41	35	0.5	630	0.4	0.46	0.4	18.0
M subtotal	*89*	*1.2*	*4807*	*3.2*	*3.36*	*2.6*	*54.0*
W10	49	0.7	693	0.5	0.59	0.5	14.1
W11	11	0.2	361	0.2	0.36	0.3	32.8
W12	12	0.2	290	0.2	0.71	0.6	24.2
W20	143	2.0	2793	1.8	1.19	0.9	19.5
W21	46	0.6	1332	0.9	1.88	1.5	29.0
W22	33	0.5	782	0.5	0.82	0.6	23.7
W23	6	0.1	143	0.1	0.45	0.4	23.9
W26	3	+	25	+			8.3
W35	5	0.1	15	+	0.21	0.2	3.0
W36	1	+	146	0.1	0.82	0.6	146.0
W50	1	+	15	+			15.0
W subtotal	*310*	*4.2*	*6595*	*4.3*	*7.03*	*5.4*	*21.3*
Q20	7	0.1	53	+	0.14	0.1	7.6
Q21	28	0.4	526	0.3	0.52	0.4	18.8
Q30	4	0.1	28	+	0.07	0.1	7.0
Q40	2	+	15	+	0.04	+	7.5
Q subtotal	*41*	*0.6*	*622*	*0.4*	*0.77*	*0.6*	*15.2*
Fine and specialist ware subtotal	**901**	**12.3**	**19082**	**12.5**	**21.02**	**16.2**	**21.2**
E10	7	0.1	50	+	0.07	0.1	7.1

Ware code	No. of sherds	% Nosh	Wt (g)	% Wt	REs	% REs	MSW (g)
E20	84	1.1	1207	0.8	0.97	0.8	14.4
E30	544	7.4	10626	7.0	6.12	4.7	19.5
E40	11	0.2	54	+			4.9
E60	25	0.3	405	0.3	0.07	0.1	16.2
E80	2095	28.6	47424	31.0	26.93	20.7	22.6
E subtotal	*2766*	*36.4*	*59766*	*39.1*	*34.16*	*26.3*	*22.3*
O10	79	1.1	894	0.6	1.50	1.2	11.3
O11	7	0.1	100	0.1	0.28	0.2	14.3
O18	10	0.1	22	+	0.15	0.1	2.2
O19	17	0.2	43	+	0.12	0.1	2.5
O20	97	1.3	1454	1.0	1.49	1.2	15.0
O24	9	0.1	247	0.2	0.38	0.3	27.4
O30	9	0.1	73	0.1	0.25	0.2	8.1
O40	1	+	40	+			40.0
O55	1	+	3	+			3.0
O80	81	1.1	5683	3.7	0.66	0.5	70.2
O81	37	0.5	1713	1.1	0.25	0.2	46.3
O subtotal	*348*	*4.7*	*10272*	*6.7*	*5.08*	*3.9*	*29.5*
R10	754	10.3	11279	7.4	19.42	15.0	15.0
R11	146	2.0	3087	2.0	6.23	4.4	21.1
R19	1	+	2	+			2.0
R20	1470	20.0	27154	17.8	25.34	19.5	18.5
R201	6	0.1	238	0.2			39.7
R21	3	+	108	0.1	0.28	0.2	36.0
R23	1	+	32	+	0.04	+	32.0
R29	10	0.1	166	0.1	0.22	0.2	16.6
R30	495	6.7	9172	6.0	11.21	8.7	18.5
R37	5	0.1	105	0.1	0.06	0.1	21.0
R39	2	+	19	+			9.5
R50	7	0.1	366	0.2	0.33	0.3	52.3
R60	1	+	35	+			35.0
R70	2	+	34	+			17.0
R80	2	+	40	+	0.14	0.1	20.0
R90	209	2.9	9212	6.0	2.96	2.3	44.1
R95	1	+	23	+			23.0
R96	2	+	60	+			30.0
R97	1	+	15	+	0.08	0.1	15.0
R subtotal	*3118*	*42.4*	*61147*	*40.0*	*66.31*	*51.1*	*19.6*
B11	36	0.5	345	0.2	0.37	0.3	9.6
B30	17	0.2	287	0.2	0.38	0.3	16.9
B subtotal	*53*	*0.7*	*632*	*0.4*	*0.75*	*0.6*	*11.9*
C10	82	1.1	775	0.5	0.25	0.2	9.5
C11	71	1.0	1140	0.8	2.12	1.7	16.1
C subtotal	*153*	*2.1*	*1915*	*1.3*	*2.37*	*1.8*	*12.5*
TOTAL	**7339**		**152815**		**129.69**		**20.8**

Nosh = number of sherds; RE = rim equivalent; MSW = mean sherd weight area, were represented by small sherds. Extra-regional sources were represented by a single sherd of possible Severn Valley ware (O40) and probable sherds of 'Portchester D'/Overwey fabric (O24) while O81, pink grogged ware, derived from a significant regional source at Stowe, Buckinghamshire (Booth 1999).

The other coarse ware groups, black-burnished and calcareous wares, were numerically insignificant. The former comprised Dorset sherds (fabric B11) and a smaller number of wheel-thrown pieces all from later Roman dish forms. The relative paucity of fabric B11 reflects the location of the site towards the eastern margin of distribution of this ware (Allen and Fulford 1996; for a discussion of this in the regional context see e.g., Booth 2017, 468–9). C wares occurred entirely as shell-tempered fabrics. Undiagnostic sherds, most of which were probably of regional origin, were generally recorded as fabric C10, their character indicated by the significantly low mean sherd weight of 9.5g. Late Roman shell-tempered ware (fabric C11, assigned to the production site at Harrold) was identified on the basis of distinctive rim forms and/or the presence of body sherds with rilling, so the attribution is considered fairly secure. It is possible that further small sherds of fabric C11 lacking diagnostic characteristics were recorded as C10.

The combined fine and specialist wares amounted to 12.3% of the total sherds (but 16.2% of the assemblage by REs). Samian ware was quite poorly represented, probably mainly for chronological reasons, consequences of which include an apparent absence of East Gaulish material except for one sherd. The seven small South Gaulish sherds included no rims, and the only sherds attributed to forms were a single decorated piece from a Dragendorff (Drag) 29 bowl and an unspecified cup fragment. Les Martres-de-Veyre vessels included one example each of cup forms 33 and 46 and an unspecified dish fragment, while there were two form 18/31 dishes lacking rims, one stamped by Natalis iii (Table 3.3) and the other with a fragment of the end of an unidentified stamp. Lezoux (S30) material dominated. It included only a single tiny decorated bowl sherd, rims of forms 33, 38, 18/31, 18/31–31 and 31, and further body sherds. One of the dishes was stamped by Cobnertus iii. The only certain East Gaulish product was a Drag 33 base stamped by Dagodubnus ii. The stamps were identified using the NOTS volumes (Hartley and Dickinson 2008; 2010).

Fine wares consisted very largely of Oxford colour-coated ware (fabric F51) supplemented by Nene Valley colour-coated ware (fabric F52), principally in the form of a fine beaker with over-slip white barbotine scroll decoration (Fig. 3.7, 107), and occasional New Forest (fabrics F53 and F57) and possible south-western fine wares (e.g., fabric F63). All these were of Late Roman or probable Late Roman date. Early Roman fine wares, apart from a tiny (and not certainly Roman) glazed fragment, occurred in a range of mica-coated fabrics. These included a variety of beaker and dish forms in unattributed oxidised fabrics (F30) and several fragments probably from the Nuneham Courtenay Lower Farm (Oxford industry) kilns (fabric F35). Most notable were two sherds of a distinctive bowl in London mica-coated ware (fabric F39, Fig. 3.6, 93). Mortarium fabrics and white ware fabrics consisted largely of Oxford and Verulamium-region products. All three main Oxford mortarium fabrics were present, accounting for 85% of all mortaria by REs (92% by sherd count). In the case of white wares there was less certainty of attribution because sandy body sherds from the two main sources cannot be separated easily; consequently, almost half of the white ware sherds were assigned to a general code (W20) for sandy white wares. White-slipped fabrics only formed a minor part of the fine and specialist ware range, with the majority attributed to the Oxford industry (fabric Q21).

Vessel types

The Late Iron Age and Roman vessels amounted to a total of 129.69 rim equivalents (REs). A minimum figure of 1090 vessels based on a count of rim sherds is indicative, but less reliable, and these data are only used occasionally for comparative purposes. Vessels were recorded in terms of a series of major classes arranged approximately in a sequence from narrow mouthed to wide mouthed vessels, defined by letter codes. The classes/codes are amphorae (A), flagons/jugs (B), jars (C), uncertain jars/bowls (D), beakers (E), cups (F), bowls (H), uncertain bowls/dishes (I), dishes (J), mortaria (K), lids (L) and miscellaneous forms (M). 'Intermediate' vessel classes (D and I) are used where insufficient of the rim survives to allow an estimate of the likely ratio of rim diameter to height, the key criterion for definition of the relevant types (Webster

Table 3.3 Samian ware stamps

Potter	Die	Form	Source	Date AD	Context	Site period
Cobnertus iii	1a	31?	Lezoux	155–180	5305	3c
Dagodubnus ii	1a	33	Rheinzabern	160–200	10580	3b
Natalis iii	1a	18/31	Les Martres-de-Veyre	90–120	5398	3b
?	-	18/31?	Les Martres-de-Veyre	100–120?	10204	1a (intrusive)

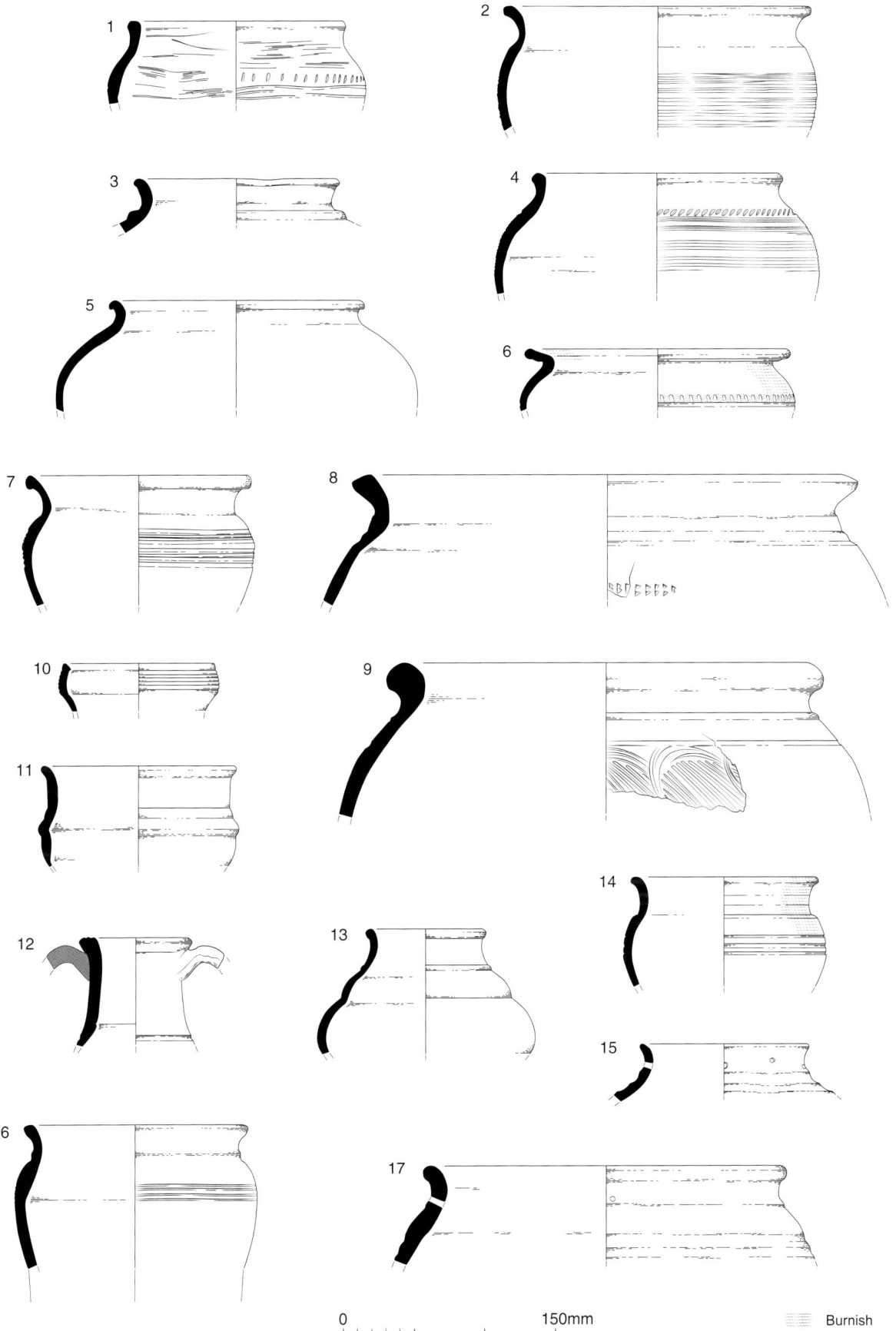

Fig. 3.1 Roman pottery, nos 1–17

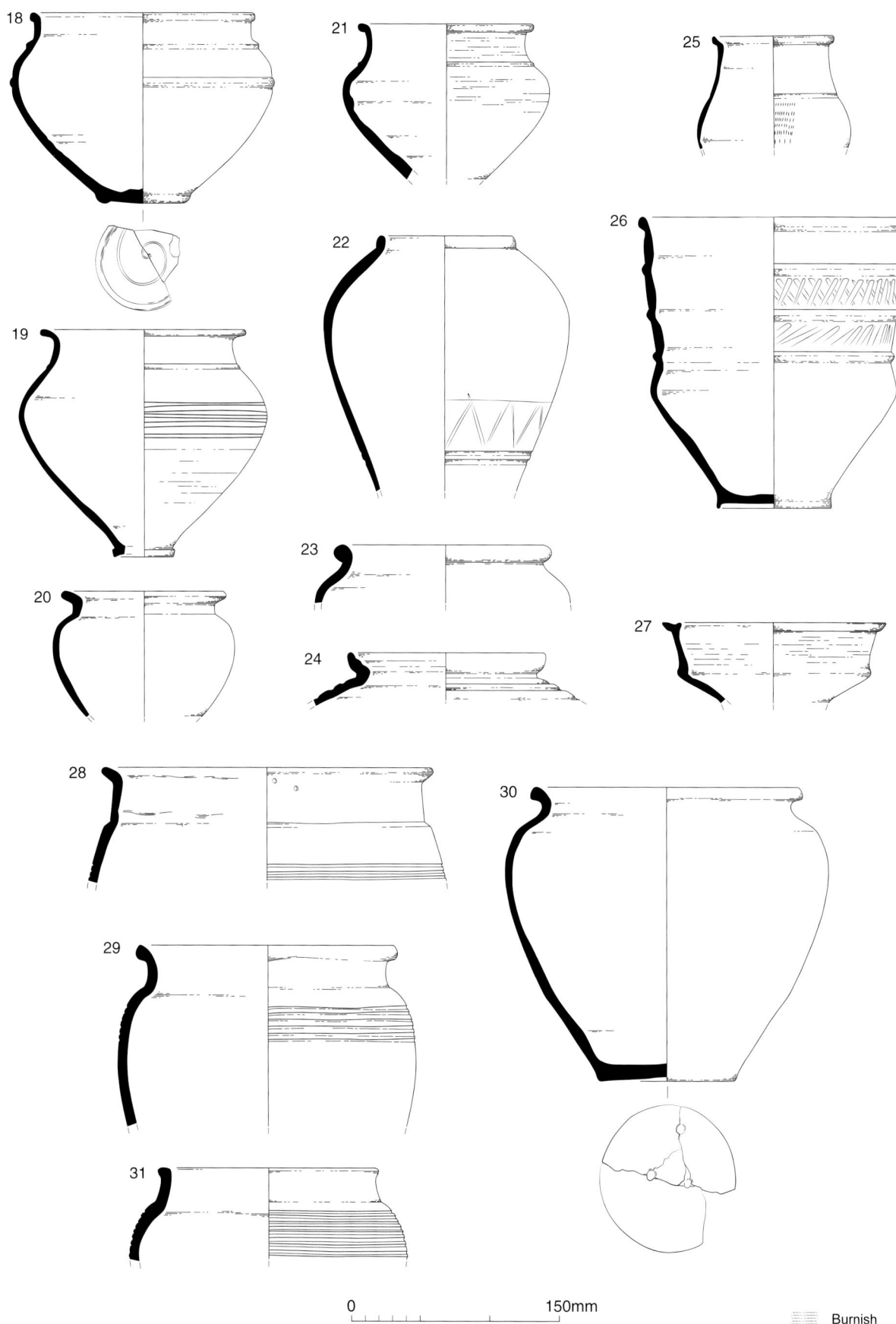

Fig. 3.2   Roman pottery, nos 18–31

The Late Iron Age and Romano-British Finds and Environmental Remains   51

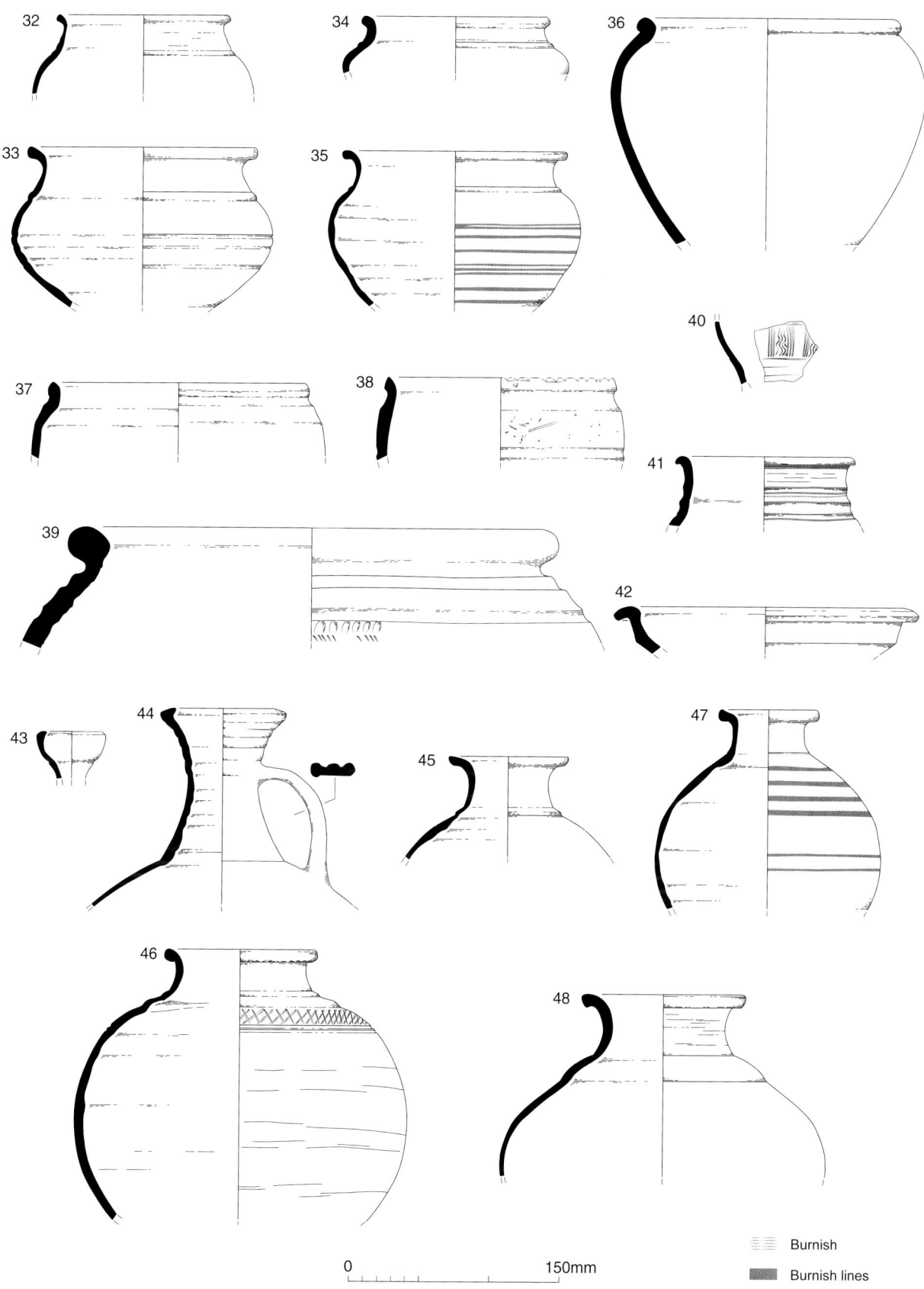

Fig. 3.3   Roman pottery, nos 32–48

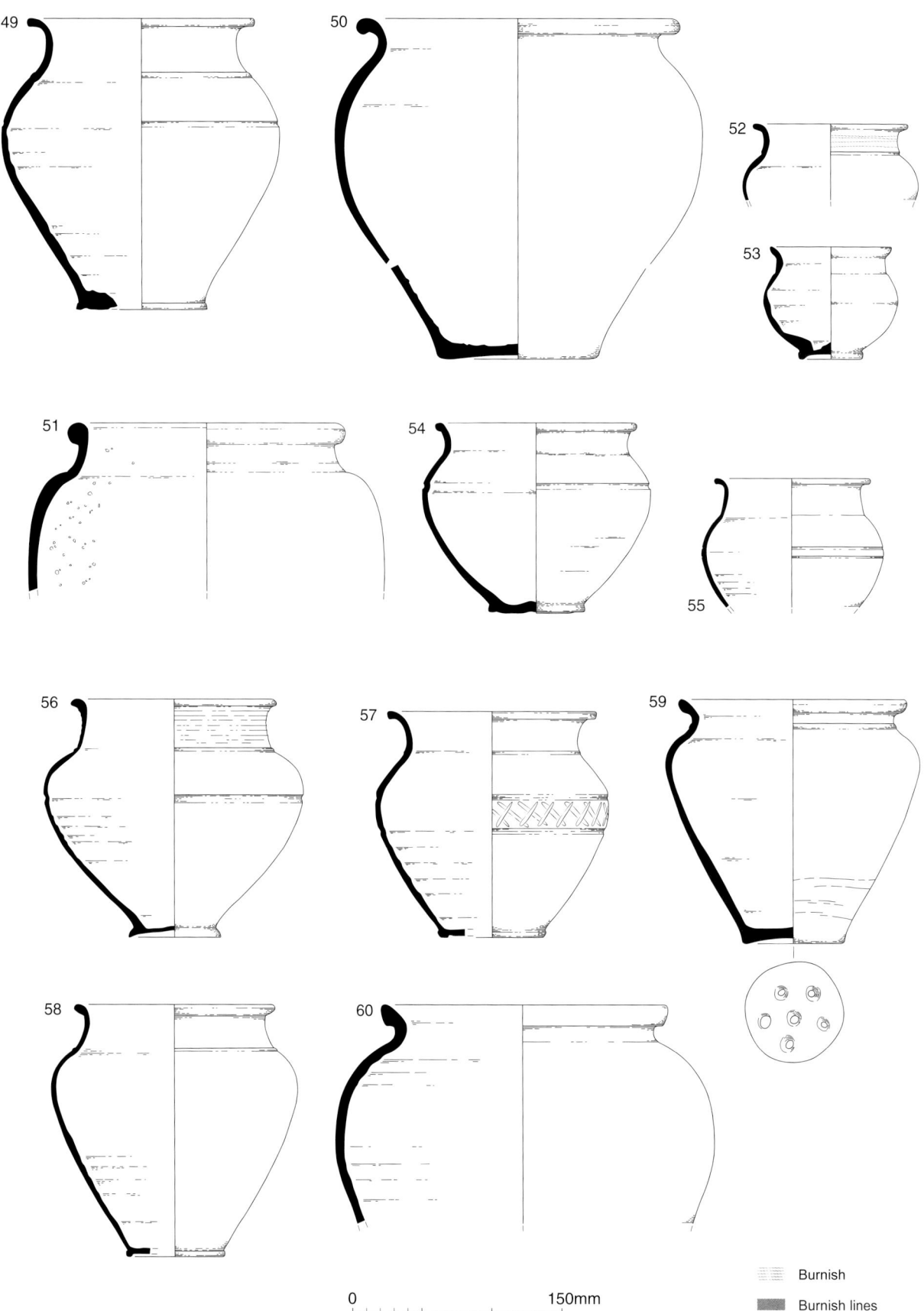

Fig. 3.4   Roman pottery, nos 49–60

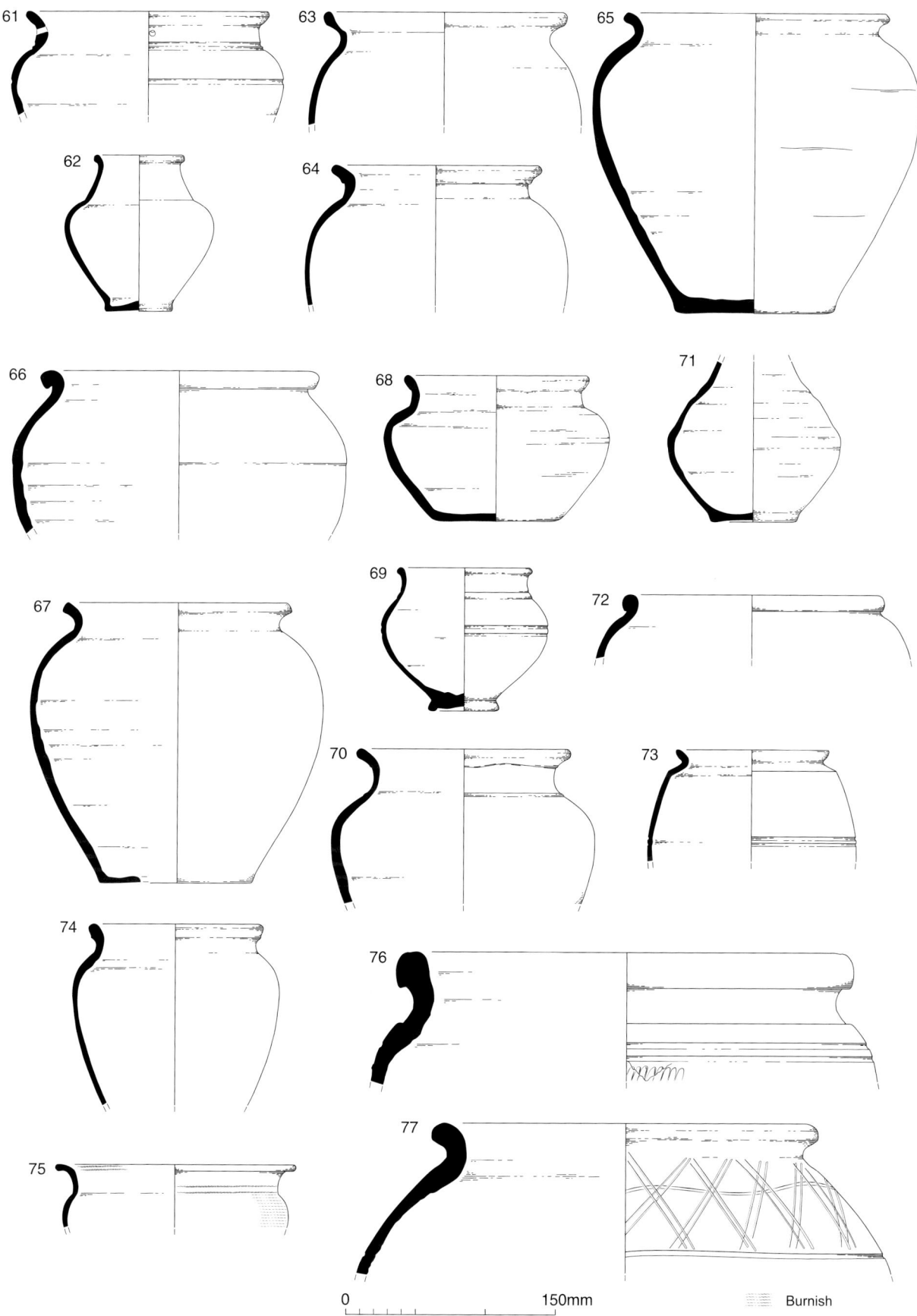

Fig. 3.5 Roman pottery, nos 61–77

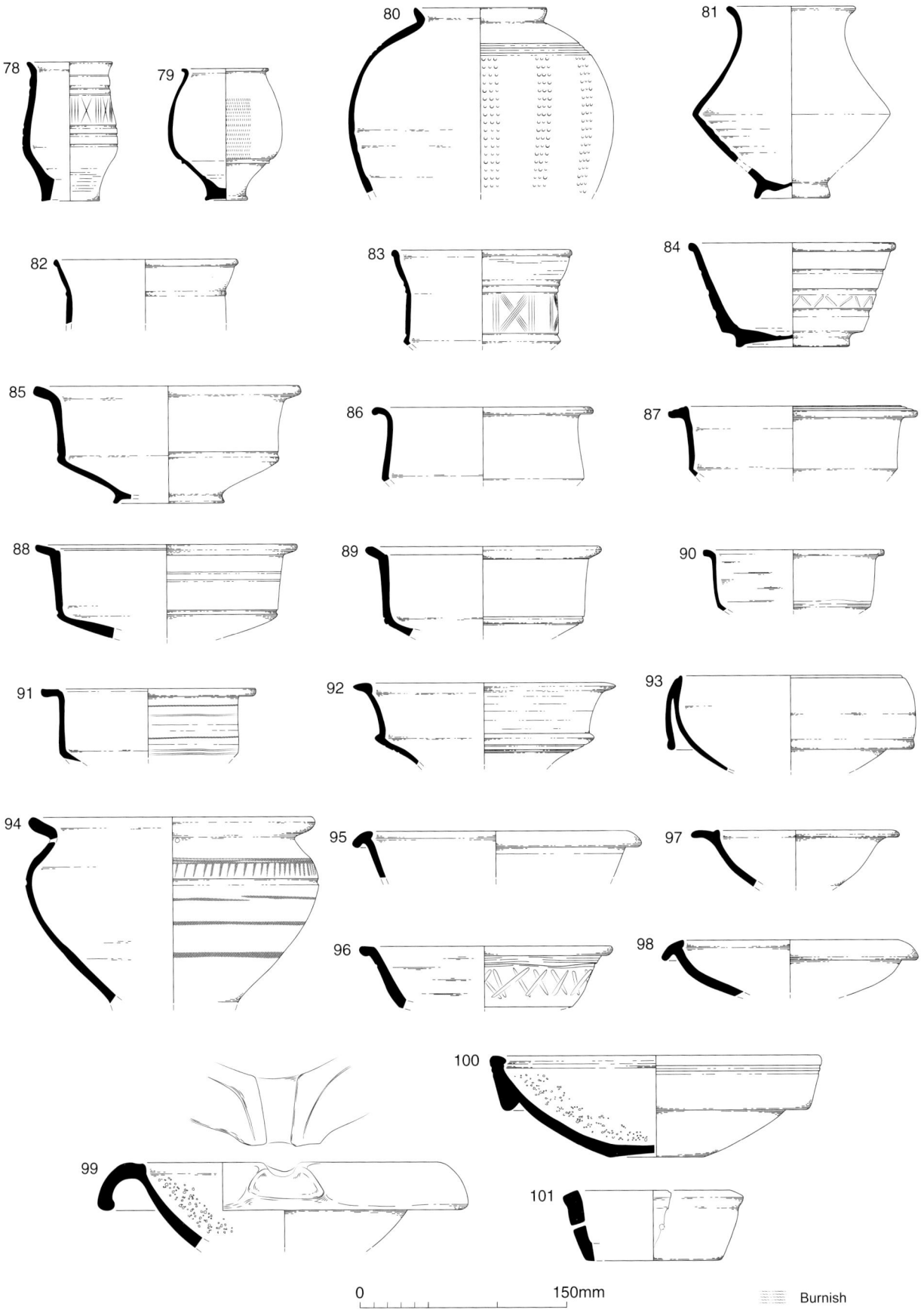

Fig. 3.6   Roman pottery, nos 78–101

The Late Iron Age and Romano-British Finds and Environmental Remains 55

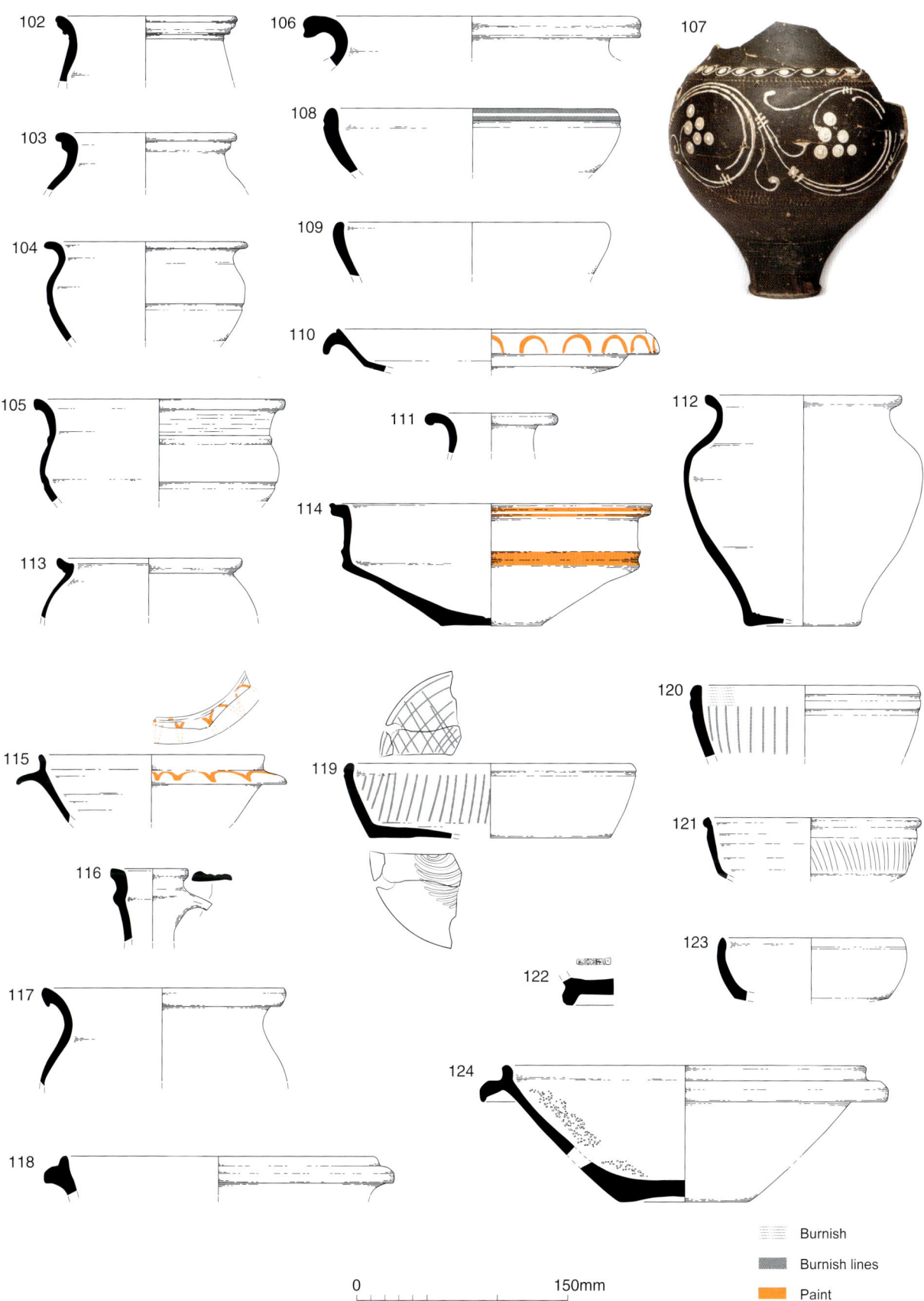

Fig. 3.7   Roman pottery, nos 102–124

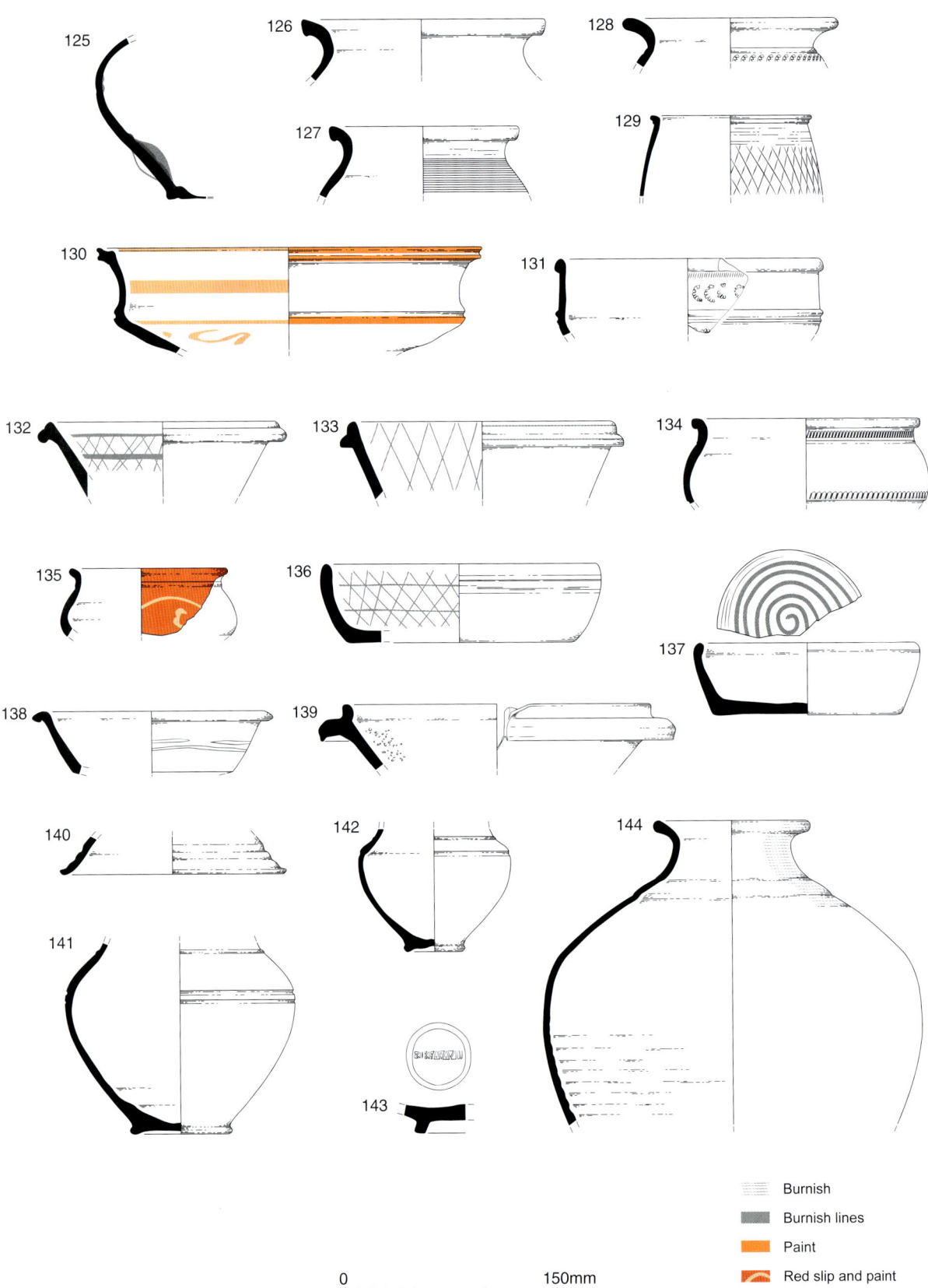

Fig. 3.8   Roman pottery, nos 125–144

1976, 17–19). Vessels of class G (tankards/handled mugs etc.) were not present in this assemblage. The class labels are conventional terms and are not necessarily indicative of specific functions. The vessel classes are divided into broad subgroups, usually with respect to key aspects of form (e.g., a simple division between straight-sided and curving-sided bowls (and dishes)), and in some cases specific typologies were also used in the recording (for example for samian ware and for Oxford fine wares and mortaria – Young's coarse ware typologies were used occasionally but not consistently). Further definition of each vessel is provided by use of a fairly elaborate system of rim codes. This is essentially a descriptive tool but serves as a useful guide to chronology in some cases, for example in distinguishing between the different types of flange on bowls and dishes, which can be of considerable significance for dating. As with the recording of fabrics, discussed above, the hierarchical definition of vessel form is considered to provide an effective approach to the material, revealing broad patterns of assemblage composition very easily, while allowing for more detailed analysis if this appears to be useful. Vessel class and sub-class definitions and overall quantities are given in Table 3.4, and the quantification of the major vessel classes by fabric is presented in Table 3.5, which omits fabrics for which no rim sherds were recorded.

The assemblage was dominated by jars, which amounted to almost 70% of all vessels. Bowls, dishes and beakers accounted for *c.* 10%, 6% and 5% of vessels respectively, with other classes present in very small quantities. A large proportion of the jars were not assigned to sub-classes, usually because insufficient of the profile was present to enable these to be determined. The remaining jars were most commonly of medium mouthed form, with a wide variety of everted rim types (accounting for 34% of all jar REs). Narrow mouthed forms amounted to 10% of all jars and squat high-shouldered vessels (CE, perhaps under-represented) a further 5.3%, while large storage vessels totalled 3.7% of all jar REs. Other sub-classes were numerically insignificant, although they included some types, such as bead rim (CH) and angled everted rim (CI) vessels which, like the CE examples, are particularly characteristic of the Late Iron Age and Early Roman periods. Further early types, such as pedestalled jars, were only represented by their distinctive bases.

Jars were a particularly important part of the E ware repertoire, amounting to 93.3% of all vessels in these fabrics (by REs). They totalled 75% of all reduced coarse ware vessels and totally dominated the small assemblage of shell-tempered wares. By contrast, jars amounted to 52% of oxidised coarse ware vessels (but accounting for all the REs in fabrics O24, O80 and O81), and occurred in much smaller numbers in other ware groups, including examples in fabrics F51 and Q30. They were more common in white wares, particularly the sandy fabrics from both Oxford and Verulamium industries.

Bowls, like jars, occurred in a wide range of fabrics,

Table 3.4 Description and overall quantification of Late Iron Age and Roman vessel classes by rim equivalents (REs)

Class	Description	REs	% of total REs
A	*Amphorae (not subdivided)*	*	
B	Flagons/jugs (not specified)	2.34	1.8
BC	handled jugs/flagons	0.04	+
BE	two-handled flagons	0.90	0.7
B total		3.28	2.5
C	Jars (not specified)	33.94	26.2
CB	barrel-shaped jars	0.13	0.1
CC	narrow mouthed jars (rim diameter less than 2/3 girth)	8.86	6.8
CD	medium mouthed jars (general)	30.39	23.4
CE	squat, high-shouldered (or 'necked') jars	5.28	4.1
CF	carinated jars	*	
CH	bead rim jars	2.68	2.1
CI	angled everted rim jars	1.98	1.5
CK	'cooking pot type' jars (e.g. black-burnished ware jar types)	1.23	0.9
CM	wide mouthed jars (rim diameter greater than girth)	2.12	1.6
CN	storage jars (large, generally thick-walled)	3.29	2.5
CP	pedestal jars	*	
CV	handled jars	0.20	0.2
C total		90.10	69.5

Table 3.4 (cont.) Description and overall quantification of Late Iron Age and Roman vessel classes by rim equivalents (REs)

Class	Description	REs	% of total REs
D	*Uncertain jars/bowls*	*2.20*	*1.7*
E	Beakers (not specified)	2.27	1.8
EA	butt beakers	0.84	0.6
EB	girth beakers	0.83	0.6
EC	bag-shaped beakers	0.90	0.7
ED	globular beakers	*	
EE	indented beakers	*	
EF	poppyhead beakers	0.77	0.6
EG	carinated beakers	0.30	0.2
EH	'jar' beakers, usually small examples of angled everted rim types, cf CI, with small, fine rim	0.93	0.7
E total		*6.84*	*5.3*
F	Cups (not specified)	0.05	+
FA	hemispherical cups	0.08	0.1
FB	campanulate cups (e.g. Drag 27)	*	
FC	conical cups (e.g. Drag 33)	1.30	1.0
F total		*1.43*	*1.1*
H	Bowls (not specified) (diameter:height ratio from *c.* 1:1 to 3:1)	1.02	0.8
HA	carinated bowls	5.18	4.0
HB	straight-sided (usually flat-based) bowls	1.38	1.1
HC	curving-sided bowls	4.31	3.3
HD	necked bowls	0.69	0.5
H total		*12.58*	*9.7*
I	Uncertain bowls/dishes	0.93	0.7
IA	straight-sided bowls/dishes	0.70	0.5
IB	curving-sided bowls/dishes	0.06	+
I total		*1.69*	*1.3*
J	Dishes (unspecified) (diameter:height ratio generally greater than 3:1)	0.31	0.2
JA	straight-sided dishes	4.07	3.1
JB	curving-sided dishes	3.26	2.5
J total		*7.64*	*5.9*
K	Mortaria (not specified)		
KA	hook rimmed/bead and flange mortaria	1.25	1.0
KD	wall-sided mortaria	0.51	0.4
KE	tall bead/stubby or elongated flange mortaria (e.g. Young M17–M22)	1.60	1.2
K total		*3.36*	*2.6*
L	*Lids (not subdivided)*	*0.40*	*0.3*
M	Miscellaneous		
MF	cheese press	0.13	0.1
MG	strainer	*	
TOTAL		**129.65**	

* Type present but not represented by rim sherd(s)

Table 3.5 Quantification of vessel classes by fabric (rim equivalents) (row percent)

| | \multicolumn{12}{c}{Vessel class} | |
	B	C	D	E	F	H	I	J	K	L	M	Total
Ware code												
S30					52.4	14.0		33.6				1.43
S32					90.6			9.4				0.32
S subtotal					*59.4*	*11.4*		*29.1*				*1.75*
F30				29.4				70.6				0.17
F39						100						0.18
F50				85.7		14.3						0.07
F51	4.6	8.4	2.8	1.6		56.3	1.7	24.6				7.59
F57				100								0.10
F subtotal	*4.3*	*7.9*	*2.6*	*4.1*		*55.0*	*1.6*	*24.5*				*8.11*
M21									100			0.49
M22									100			1.26
M31									100			1.15
M41									100			0.46
M subtotal									*100*			*3.36*
W10	20.3	11.9		64.4		3.4						0.59
W11		33.3				66.7						0.36
W12	43.7			28.2				28.2				0.71
W20		95.8		4.2								1.19
W21	58.0	42.0										1.88
W22	100											0.82
W23		100										0.45
W35				100								0.21
W36				100								0.82
W subtotal	*33.3*	*36.6*		*23.6*		*3.7*		*2.8*				*7.03*
Q20	100											0.14
Q21	28.8					71.2						0.52
Q30		100										0.07
Q40						100						0.04
Q subtotal	*37.7*	*9.1*				*53.2*						*0.77*
Fine and specialist ware subtotal	**14.2**	**15.6**	**1.0**	**9.5**	**4.9**	**25.4**	**0.6**	**12.8**	**16.0**			**21.02**
E10		100										0.07
E20		90.7					3.1			6.2		0.97
E30		91.8	1.1			4.4				2.6		6.12
E60		100										0.07
E80		93.8	0.6	3.1		1.5	0.4	0.3		0.4		26.89
E subtotal		*93.3*	*0.7*	*2.4*		*1.9*	*0.4*	*0.3*		*0.9*		*34.12*
O10		38.0	12.7	2.0	12.0	6.7	2.0	26.7				1.50
O11		32.1				67.9						0.28
O18				100								0.15

Table 3.5 (cont.) Quantification of vessel classes by fabric (rim equivalents) (row percent)

	Vessel class											
	B	C	D	E	F	H	I	J	K	L	M	Total
Ware code												
O19				100								0.12
O20		46.3		40.3		7.4	6.0					1.49
O24		100										0.38
O30				48.0		28.0	24.0					0.25
O80		100										0.66
O81		100										0.25
O subtotal		*52.0*	*3.7*	*20.1*	*3.5*	*9.3*	*3.5*	*7.9*				*5.08*
R10	0.2	63.5	3.5	9.0	0.8	15.8	3.3	3.8		*		19.42
R11		70.8		17.2		9.5		2.6				6.23
R20	1.0	83.2	1.1	0.8	0.2	6.0	1.0	6.1			0.5	25.34
R21		100										0.28
R23								100				0.04
R29		63.6						36.4				0.22
R30		77.5	2.7			7.4	3.0	9.4				11.21
R37			100									0.06
R50									100			0.33
R80									100			0.14
R90		96.6	3.4									2.96
R97										100		0.08
R subtotal	*0.5*	*75.1*	*2.2*	*4.5*	*0.3*	*9.0*	*1.9*	*6.2*		*0.1*	*0.2*	*66.31*
B11		37.9				24.3		37.8				0.37
B30								100				0.38
B subtotal		*18.7*				*12.0*		*69.3*				*0.75*
C10		100										0.25
C11		97.6						2.4				2.12
C subtotal		*97.9*						*2.1*				*2.37*
TOTAL	3.28	89.90	2.20	6.84	1.43	12.58	1.69	7.61	3.36	0.40	0.13	129.65
%	2.5	69.3	1.7	5.3	1.1	9.7	1.3	5.9	2.6	0.3	0.1	

though absolute quantities of many of these were small, even in cases where they formed a significant proportion of the REs in the fabrics in question (such as F39, W11, Q21, Q40 and O11). Oxford colour-coated fabric F51 was one of the principal sources of these vessels, most of which were of curving-sided (HC) forms, a category that includes the common Young type C51. Type HB (straight-sided) bowls, including the characteristic black-burnished ware bead and flanged form, were notably rare, with examples occurring almost entirely in reduced coarse ware fabrics. The finer versions of the latter (R10 and R11) contributed the majority of the carinated bowls (type HA) which, unusually, formed the most numerous form group within this vessel class – a consequence in part of the early chronological emphasis of the assemblage as a whole.

Straight-sided (JA) dishes were found mainly in reduced fabrics, with a few examples in black-burnished ware (all the rims in imitation black-burnished ware fabric B30 were of this type) and single vessel in mica-coated fabric F30. Type JB dishes, slightly less common overall, also occurred in reduced fabrics, but more than half (by REs) were Oxford colour-ware types (such as Young type C45), and this group also included samian ware forms and vessels in Oxford fine white ware (fabric W12) and fine oxidised wares (O10). Diverse beaker forms, including examples not assigned to specific subtypes, were found in a comparably wide range of fine and coarse ware fabrics. Fine reduced fabrics R11 and R10, certain and probable Oxford products respectively, accounted for all, or the majority of, examples of type EC, EF, EG and EH beakers. Fine ware beaker sherds were typically well fragmented and thus were assigned entirely to the general vessel class, although indented beakers were recorded as body sherds in fine wares, and a large globular beaker in Nene Valley fabric F52 was represented by a large part of the vessel, but with no rim (Fig. 3.6, 107. A single large girth beaker (Fig. 3.2, 26) was a notable occurrence in fabric E80.

Flagons and mortaria occurred in almost identical (small) quantities overall. The majority of the former were in Oxford and Verulamium white wares, and other Oxford examples were in white-slipped fabric Q21 and colour-coated ware F51, including the common type C8 but also a less common form (Fig. 3.7, 116). Occasional reduced ware examples were also present. Mortaria were entirely from the Verulamium and (principally) Oxford industries. Amongst the other vessel classes the scarcity of lids is notable, and five of the six examples represented by rims were in E wares. There was a single example of a cheese press (Fig. 3.6, 101) in fabric R20, and body sherds of strainers in fabrics E20 and R10, but other 'miscellaneous' forms were absent. Vessels with post-firing holes drilled or knocked in the base and/or lower body wall are sometimes considered to be related to cheese presses, perhaps representing the function before the specialist ceramic type came into production (see also Use, reuse and repair, below).

Phasing and dates

From the perspective of pottery studies in the region the Thame assemblage appears to present a slightly unusual chronological profile, with evidence for activity most pronounced in the Early and Late Roman periods and an apparently significant reduction in the quantities of material that could be clearly assigned to the middle part of the period – particularly from the mid 2nd to mid 3rd centuries. This question has been addressed as far as possible through analysis of the breakdown of the assemblage in terms of the defined periods of site activity. Quantification of fabrics and vessel forms across these periods is presented in Tables 3.6 and 3.7.

The tables demonstrate some of the principal difficulties of the site, in particular the extent to which dense arrays of intercutting features result in the presence of intrusive and (less clearly detected in some cases) residual or redeposited material. Moreover, some of the period groups are too small to sustain reliable conclusions about chronological trends in the supply and use of individual fabrics and vessel forms (and are included in the tables only for completeness). With these caveats in mind, however, some trends are detectable, and the pottery from subdivisions of the Late Iron Age/Early Roman and Late Roman periods, determined principally on stratigraphic criteria, has been quantified to attempt to demonstrate these trends. The totals under the headings '3a all' and '3c all' include the material from those subgroups but also that from contexts assigned to these broad periods but not to any of the subdivisions within them.

The period 3a assemblage, as would be expected, was dominated by E wares, and although the sub-period groups are modest they show a plausible chronological progression of reduction in the percentage of these wares into the later part of the 1st century AD, by which time they should have been residual in terms of production if not of use, though they still formed two-thirds of the period 3aiii assemblage by both sherd count and weight. The same sequence of phases saw a corresponding increase in the occurrence of sandy oxidised and reduced coarse wares (O20 and R20). While the broad trends are clear, the picture is obscured by the presence of intrusive material – such as fabrics S30 and F51 which boost the fine and specialist ware totals unrealistically, particularly in period 3aii, and black-burnished ware. The correlate of the dominance of E wares is that of jars, totalling 84.4% of REs in period 3a (and 100% in period 3ai, but this was a very small group). The second most numerous vessel class comprised beakers, amounting to 7% of the assemblage. This figure was substantially boosted by a single girth beaker in fabric E80 (Fig. 3.2, 26), but beakers overall were quite diverse, including butt beakers in a range of fabrics including O18 (body sherds only), O19, O20 and W35, a 'jar beaker' also in fabric O20 and an unspecified angled everted rim in fine Oxford white ware fabric W12. The representation of all other vessel classes is below 5% of REs, and amongst these, flagons were best represented, at 4.1%, though this was a single vessel in Verulamium white ware (W21 – Fig. 3.1, 12) in a period 3aiii context.

Since the few samian ware sherds in period 3a contexts were intrusive the only contemporary (probable) cup from these contexts was in fabric R20 (Fig. 3.1, 10, possibly imitating Drag 27), while bowls in periods 3aii and 3aiii were in E wares. The single type JB dish in period 3aii was an intrusive piece in fabric F51.

The substantial period 3b assemblage (2222 sherds with a notably high mean sherd weight of 24.6g) broadly continued trends from period 3aiii, but with some apparently significant developments as well. The most obvious point is that the percentage of E wares halved from period 3aiii to period 3b, although, at 33.3% of sherds (31.8% by weight), these remained a substantial component of the assemblage, presumably indicating that contexts of this period contained a significant proportion of residual/redeposited pottery. Reduced wares were now the largest single ware group, at 51.1% nearly double their representation in period 3aiii. The representation of the sandy reduced ware R20

Table 3.6 Fabric by phase (number of sherds – column percent)

Ware code	1a	2a–2c	3ai	3aii	3aiii	3a all	3b	3ci	3cii	3ciii	3c all	3d	4a	4b	post-Med & undated	TOTAL sherds	%
S20							0.1	0.5			0.1				0.5	7	0.1
S30				2.0		0.3	0.6	0.5	1.1	0.3	1.0		1.0		0.5	49	0.7
S32	4.3	1.4					0.2		0.1		0.1					10	0.1
S41							+									1	+
S subtotal	*4.3*	*1.4*		*2.0*		*0.3*	*1.0*	*1.0*	*1.3*	*0.3*	*1.2*		*1.0*		*1.0*	*67*	*0.9*
F20													0.2			1	+
F30							+	0.5	0.1	0.3	0.2		0.2			7	0.1
F35							0.3									6	0.1
F39							0.1									2	+
F50							+	0.2			+		0.3			4	0.1
F51	2.2	1.4		2.0	0.6	0.6	0.3	4.6	8.1	15.6	9.2	1.2	8.7	24.5	8.4	338	4.6
FO							+									1	+
F52								3.4	0.3	0.5	0.8		0.3		0.5	23	0.3
F53									0.1		+					1	+
F57										0.3	+					1	+
F60							+	0.7			0.1					4	0.1
F63								0.2			+					1	+
F subtotal	*2.2*	*1.4*		*2.0*	*0.6*	*0.6*	*0.8*	*9.7*	*8.6*	*16.7*	*10.5*	*1.2*	*9.7*	*24.5*	*8.9*	*389*	*5.3*
A10				0.1	0.1											1	+
A11							0.1				+					4	0.1
A subtotal				*0.1*	*0.1*		*0.1*				*+*					*5*	*0.1*
M21							+	1.2	0.1		0.2					7	0.1
M22							0.3	0.2	1.1	0.5	0.7		0.6			29	0.4
M31									0.4	1.1	0.4		1.0		0.5	18	0.3
M41								1.2	1.1	3.2	1.2		0.6	1.9		35	0.5
M subtotal							*0.4*	*2.7*	*2.8*	*4.8*	*2.6*		*2.3*	*1.9*	*0.5*	*89*	*1.2*
W10						0.2	1.0	0.7	1.3		0.7		0.6		0.5	49	0.7
W11								1.2	0.3		0.4		0.3			11	0.2
W12				0.1	0.1	0.4	0.2			+		0.2		0.5		12	0.2
W20	2.2	1.4		2.0	0.8	0.9	3.8	1.7	1.1	4.2	1.5		0.6		0.5	143	2.0
W21					0.3	0.6	1.4	0.2	0.1		0.2					46	0.6
W22							1.4				+					33	0.5
W23								0.2	0.5	0.3	0.2					6	0.1
W26							0.1									3	+
W35				0.1	0.1				0.5		0.2					5	0.1
W36							+									1	+
W50								0.2			+					1	+
W subtotal	*2.2*	*1.4*		*2.0*	*1.4*	*1.8*	*8.2*	*4.6*	*3.8*	*4.5*	*3.4*		*1.8*		*1.6*	*310*	*4.2*
Q20				0.5	0.1	0.1				0.5	0.2		0.2			7	0.1
Q21					0.1	0.1	0.5	0.7	0.3	0.8	0.3		0.6	0.9	1.0	28	0.4
Q30							0.2									4	0.1
Q40							0.1									2	+
Q subtotal				*0.5*	*0.3*	*0.2*	*0.8*	*0.7*	*0.3*	*1.3*	*0.5*		*0.8*	*0.9*	*1.0*	*41*	*0.6*
Fine and specialist ware subtotal	8.7	4.2		6.5	2.4	3.0	11.3	18.7	16.8	27.6	18.3	1.2	15.5	27.4	13.1	901	12.3

Ware code	1a	2a–2c	3ai	3aii	3aiii	3a all	3b	3ci	3cii	3ciii	3c all	3d	4a	4b	post-Med & undated	TOTAL sherds	%
E10				0.5		0.1	0.1			0.3	0.1				1.0	7	0.1
E20	4.3	1.4		3.0	1.5	2.4	1.0	0.2	1.0	1.3	0.6		1.0		0.5	84	1.1
E30	8.7	9.5	3.2	16.0	10.4	9.4	9.5	2.7	8.1	3.2	4.7	1.2	6.1	4.7	10.5	544	7.4
E40						0.2	0.1		0.8		0.2					11	0.2
E60		4.1		0.5	0.7	0.6	0.1	0.2			0.4		0.2			25	0.3
E80	26.1	35.2	93.6	64.5	54.3	61.9	22.7	7.5	14.5	19.6	17.4	11.1	18.4	10.4	19.4	2095	28.6
E subtotal	*39.1*	*50.2*	*96.8*	*84.5*	*66.9*	*74.5*	*33.5*	*10.6*	*24.4*	*24.4*	*23.3*	*12.3*	*25.7*	*15.1*	*31.4*	*2766*	*37.7*
O10				0.1	0.3	0.8	2.9	0.8	2.9	1.8		2.1	0.9	0.5		79	1.1
O11							0.1		0.1		0.2					7	0.1
O18				0.6	0.3	+				0.1		0.5				10	0.1
O19				2.4	1.1											17	0.2
O20	7.3	1.4		4.6	2.3	0.7	1.4	0.5	2.4	1.2		1.1		2.1		97	1.3
O24							0.5	0.1	0.5	0.3		0.2		0.5		9	0.1
O30	2.2					0.1	0.2		0.3	0.1		0.3				9	0.1
O40							0.2				+					1	+
O55							+									1	+
O80		1.4		1.5	0.4	0.6	1.5	1.0	0.6		0.8	9.9	0.6		3.1	81	1.1
O81						0.1	0.4	0.5	0.5	1.9	0.7		1.3	0.9	1.0	37	0.5
O subtotal	*9.5*	*2.7*		*1.5*	*8.0*	*4.6*	*3.8*	*6.8*	*2.6*	*8.0*	*5.2*	*9.9*	*6.1*	*1.9*	*7.3*	*348*	*4.7*
R10	8.7	13.5		3.0	1.1	1.2	11.4	21.5	11.9	2.7	12.1	44.4	15.8	13.2	14.1	754	10.3
R11	2.2	1.4			0.6	0.4	4.5	1.0	1.6	1.6	1.4			1.9	0.5	146	2.0
R19							+									1	+
R20	28.3	21.6	3.2	1.0	17.9	12.8	24.5	19.1	24.0	17.5	21.2	12.3	20.2	13.2	17.8	1470	20.0
R201							+		0.1		0.2	1.2				6	0.1
R21					0.1	0.1										3	+
R23								0.2			+					1	+
R29							0.1	1.0	0.1		0.3		0.2			10	0.1
R30	2.2	1.4			0.3	0.5	6.3	11.8	11.1	6.6	9.8	8.6	11.0	9.4	12.0	495	6.7
R37							0.1		0.1		+			0.9		5	0.1
R39										0.3	+			0.9		2	+
R50					0.1	0.1		0.7		0.3	0.2					7	0.1
R60							+									1	+
R70									0.1		+			0.9		2	+
R80								0.2			0.1					2	+
R90		1.4		2.5	1.9	1.8	4.0	3.1	3.5	2.1	2.8	1.2	2.4	4.7	1.6	209	2.9
R95					0.1	0.1										1	+
R96					0.1	0.1			0.1		+					2	+
R97											+					1	+
R subtotal	*41.3*	*39.2*	*3.2*	*6.5*	*22.1*	*16.9*	*51.1*	*58.7*	*52.8*	*31.0*	*48.3*	*67.9*	*49.6*	*45.3*	*46.0*	*3118*	*42.4*
B11				0.5	0.1	0.2	0.3	1.7	0.3	1.1	0.7	1.2	0.6	2.8	0.5	36	0.5
B30							+	0.7	0.3	0.3	0.6		0.3			17	0.2
B subtotal				*0.5*	*0.1*	*0.2*	*0.3*	*2.4*	*0.5*	*1.3*	*1.3*	*1.2*	*1.0*	*2.8*	*0.5*	*53*	*0.7*
C10	2.2	2.7		0.5	0.4	0.8	1.8	2.9	1.8	1.1	1.6	1.2	1.1	4.7	1.0	82	1.1
C11		1.4					+		1.1	6.6	2.1	6.2	1.0		0.5	71	1.0
C subtotal	*2.2*	*4.1*		*0.5*	*0.4*	*0.8*	*1.8*	*2.9*	*2.9*	*7.7*	*3.7*	*7.4*	*2.1*	*4.7*	*1.6*	*153*	*2.1*
TOTAL	**46**	**74**	**31**	**200**	**722**	**1545**	**2222**	**414**	**799**	**377**	**2436**	**81**	**619**	**106**	**210**	**7339**	
MSW (g)	14.0	16.5	22.5	28.9	20.2	22.3	24.6	18.7	15.6	17.8	18.5	28.4	14.0	13.0		20.8	

Table 3.7 Vessel type by phase (rim equivalents – column percent)

Type	1a	2a–2c	3ai	3aii	3aiii	3a all	3b	3ci	3cii	3ciii	3c all	3d	4a	4b	post-med & undated	TOTAL REs	%
A																*	
B						0.5	2.6	3.1	1.8	2.0	1.9		1.7			**2.34**	1.8
BC										0.1						**0.04**	+
BE					6.6	3.7										**0.90**	0.7
B total					*6.6*	*4.1*	*2.6*	*3.1*	*1.8*	*2.0*	*2.0*		*1.7*			***3.28***	*2.5*
C	45.8	32.7	34.2	21.3	22.5	23.3	19.4	34.2	43.7	35.2	32.1	23.9	39.0	33.8	35.2	**33.94**	26.2
CB					0.4	0.2	0.1						0.6			**0.13**	0.1
CC			28.9		10.3	6.1	8.7	9.1	3.6		5.5			8.6	21.8	**8.86**	6.8
CD		40.0	36.8	43.2	27.4	33.6	30.6	15.5	7.8	7.6	13.0		14.5	6.6	11.2	**30.39**	23.4
CE				9.5	2.4	6.9	5.3		3.2	7.3	2.2				3.0	**5.28**	4.1
CF																*	
CH				9.1	7.7	0.7			0.9		0.5				6.1	**2.68**	2.1
CI				3.5	2.5	2.0	2.2		1.7		1.1					**1.98**	1.5
CK						1.6	0.5	1.1	1.3		1.1					**1.23**	1.0
CM				6.7		0.9	0.9	7.2			2.0	58.7				**2.12**	1.6
CN				8.6	2.1	3.8	3.5	0.6	0.4	1.0	0.8		3.1	2.6	0.6	**3.29**	2.5
CP						*										*	
CV								2.3	0.1		0.5					**0.20**	0.2
C total	*45.8*	*72.7*	*100*	*92.7*	*76.7*	*84.4*	*72.8*	*69.4*	*61.5*	*53.4*	*58.9*	*82.6*	*57.2*	*51.7*	*77.9*	***90.10***	*69.5*
D		3.6					0.8	2.8	3.9	3.1	3.4	10.1	1.1	11.9		**2.20**	1.7
E	20.8	5.5			1.5	0.8	2.6		1.4	1.3	1.1		3.2			**2.27**	1.8
EA					3.9	2.2			0.9		0.2		2.6			**0.84**	0.6
EB					6.1	3.4										**0.83**	0.6
EC							1.3				0.6					**0.90**	0.7
ED																*	
EE																*	
EF							1.6									**0.77**	0.6
EG							0.6									**0.30**	0.2
EH					1.1	0.6	1.0		2.5		0.7					**0.93**	0.7
E total	*20.8*	*5.5*			*12.6*	*7.0*	*7.2*		*4.8*	*1.3*	*2.6*		*5.8*			***6.84***	*5.3*
F				1.6		0.2										**0.05**	+
FA											1.0	0.2				**0.08**	0.1
FB																*	
FC							1.2		0.6		1.6		0.9			**1.30**	1.0
F total				*1.6*		*0.2*	*1.2*		*0.6*	*1.0*	*1.8*		*0.9*			***1.43***	*1.1*
H					0.4	0.2	0.5	0.5	2.7	1.0	1.4		1.1		2.7	**1.02**	0.8
HA		12.7			2.4	1.9	7.2	1.7	4.6	2.0	2.1		1.5	7.3		**5.18**	4.0
HB							0.5	1.1		4.9	2.3		2.4			**1.38**	1.1
HC				3.8		0.5	1.0		3.0	10.8	6.5		7.9	14.6	4.2	**4.31**	3.3
HD							1.4									**0.69**	0.5
H total		*12.7*		*3.8*	*2.7*	*2.6*	*10.7*	*3.2*	*10.3*	*18.6*	*12.2*		*12.9*	*21.9*	*7.0*	***12.58***	*9.7*
I							0.2	2.3	0.4	1.8	1.3	7.3	2.9			**0.93**	0.7

Type	1a	2a–2c	3ai	3aii	3aiii	3a all	3b	3ci	3cii	3ciii	3c all	3d	4a	4b	post-med & undated	TOTAL REs	%
IA							0.7	1.1	0.4		0.7		0.7			**0.70**	0.5
IB		5.5												2.0		**0.06**	0.1
I total		*5.5*					*0.9*	*3.3*	*0.7*	*1.8*	*1.9*	*7.3*	*3.6*	*2.0*		***1.69***	*1.3*
J							0.1						3.1			**0.31**	0.2
JA	33.3				1.0	0.9	0.5	8.2	5.9	4.9	6.8		4.5	4.0	10.9	**4.07**	3.1
JB				1.9		0.5	1.5	5.1	4.1	4.5	4.9	2.0	6.6		1.2	**3.26**	2.5
J total	*33.3*			*1.9*	*1.0*	*1.5*	*2.1*	*13.2*	*9.9*	*9.3*	*11.7*		*9.5*	*10.6*	*12.1*	***7.64***	*5.9*
K																	
KA							1.1	4.9	2.8		1.7					**1.25**	1.0
KD							0.3		1.5	1.7	0.7		0.7	2.0		**0.51**	0.4
KE									2.1	6.7	2.7		5.9			**1.60**	1.2
K total							*1.4*	*4.9*	*6.3*	*8.4*	*5.1*		*6.7*	*2.0*		***3.36***	*2.6*
L					0.4	0.2	0.1			0.9	0.4		0.5		3.0	**0.40**	0.3
M																	
MF							0.3									**0.13**	0.1
MG				*	*											*	
TOTAL	0.24	0.55	0.38	3.15	13.58	24.60	48.95	8.44	10.87	7.62	41.34	1.09	8.07	1.51	3.30	**129.65**	

fabrics was at its peak at this time (24.5% of sherds), and fabrics R10, R11 and R30, all potentially Oxford products (while a more local source is likely for much of the R20 material, see above), all contributed. By contrast, oxidised wares were poorly represented. Fine and specialist wares now totalled 11.3% of sherds, and while this figure still included intrusive Oxford colour-coated ware (six very small sherds) the remaining components do not appear out of place – the great majority of the material consisting of white wares, supplemented by occasional fine wares, mortaria and white-slipped fabrics as well as a little samian ware (this last amounting to only 1% of the total sherds in this phase).

Progressive trends were also evident in vessel class composition but were more gradual than some of those relating to fabrics. The most significant was the reduction in the percentage of jars, from 84.4% in period 3a (but only 76.7% in contexts specifically assigned to period 3aiii) to 72.8% in period 3b. The proportion of bowls increased significantly; a particularly notable characteristic of this period group was the presence of carinated (type HA) bowls in fabrics R10 and R11, providing the large majority of bowls in this phase. Other vessel classes showed relatively little change from the previous phase. Flagons were slightly less common. The representation of beakers was effectively identical, but this was only because of the presence of a single large girth beaker which had greatly boosted the sub-period 3aiii percentage (see above) and should already have been residual in that phase. Butt beakers were now absent, but the range of beaker types broadened to include EC, EF and EG vessels. Apart from a single small, largely complete beaker (Fig. 3.6, 78) of unusual form in fine white fabric W36, from a burial, and a small fragment from an uncertain beaker type in fabric O30, almost all the beakers of various types were in fine reduced wares R10 and R11, all probable Oxford products.

Other vessel classes were of very minor importance. Dishes still only accounted for 2.1% of vessels. They included a single vessel in fabric O10 (Fig. 3.6, 97) and examples in reduced fabrics. Samian ware contributed three vessels (about one fifth of the total of dish REs in this period), while single examples of forms 33 and 46 totalled just over half of cup REs in this period. Vessels in fabrics O10 and R10 (one each) were probable imitations of Drag 33. Mortaria comprised a mere 1.4% of REs in this period, made up of a Verulamium hook rimmed vessel, three examples of Oxford type M2 (including Fig. 3.6, 99) and a single example of type M14 (Fig. 3.6, 100). The sole cheese press from the site (Fig. 3.6, 101), in fabric R20, was found in this period.

The Late Roman period (3c) produced another relatively substantial assemblage (2436 sherds with a mean weight of 18.5g, 41.34 REs), of which almost exactly 65% (by both sherd count and weight) came from contexts assigned to sub-periods. These allow identification of some trends in assemblage composition within the period, but the individual sub-period totals are not particularly large and interpretation of these trends has to treated with caution. E wares still amounted to 23.3% of the total sherds (20.3% of weight) in this period demonstrating that issues of residuality and redeposition remain. In overall terms the percentage of reduced wares (by sherd count) was rather higher than for period 3b (48.3%) but was lower in terms of weight; this appears to reflect the particularly high representation of substantial sherds in fabrics R10, R11 and R20 in the period 3b group. The period 3c sub-phases showed a decline in the proportion of reduced wares as a whole (particularly marked in sub-period 3ciii) but the overall pattern of the internal trends in this phase (for example, fluctuations in the representation of combined oxidised wares and a markedly low incidence of E wares in sub-period 3ci compared to later) is not completely clear. Taken at face value, however, the sherd count data indicate a substantial decline in the representation of reduced wares by the end of period 3c, compensated for in sub-period 3ciii by rises in the proportion of oxidised wares (of uncertain significance) and shell-tempered wares (particularly the Late Roman Harrold fabric C11) and in fine and specialist wares, mainly represented by Oxford colour-coated ware (F51, but including the equivalent mortarium fabric M41). The sub-period 3ciii fine and specialist wares amounted to 27.6% of sherds, a marked increase on their earlier representation (the overall period 3c figure was 18.3%, see further below) and the corresponding figure for weight was 28.3%, to which Oxford mortaria made a significant contribution. While the breakdown of this sub-period assemblage is credible, it is a small group and distortion of the figures by one or two vessels is possible.

The vessel type data support the view that the period 3ciii group reflects Late Roman characteristics fairly reliably, the most obvious trend being a steady decline in the representation of jars, which is precisely in line with the regional pattern. Here the decline is from 69.4% in sub-period 3ci to 53.4% in sub-period 3ciii, with the overall period 3c figure standing at 58.9%. The expected correlate is a rise in the percentages of bowls and dishes. The former is seen very clearly (though the percentage of bowls in sub-period 3ci (3.2%) is anomalously low) while dishes are particularly well-represented in that sub-period (13.2% of REs) and thereafter are stable at above 9%. The combined representation of these types (including the uncertain 'intermediate' class I vessels) does show a linear trend, from 19.8%, to 20.9%, and then to 29.7% in sub-period 3ciii. As a whole the period 3c assemblage contained very small quantities of flagons, beakers, cups and lids (2%, 2.6%, 1.8% and 0.4% of REs respectively, with values of 2%, 1.3%, 1% and 0.9% respectively in sub-period 3ciii, each represented there by a single example, of which the cup and lid were grossly residual). The relatively high percentage of mortaria in the period 3c assemblage is notable – 5.1% of the period 3c total and 8.4% of REs in sub-period 3ciii, composed entirely of Oxford vessels.

None of the other period groups require comment, except to say that the composition of the Roman material in contexts assigned to the Early Saxon period (4a) does not present any characteristics that suggest systematic selection of pottery, as is sometimes seen in Early Anglo-Saxon settlements. The Late Iron Age and Roman pottery from the period 4a assemblage has a relatively low mean sherd weight (14g) and still retains a remarkably high proportion of E wares (25.7% of sherd count, 32.3% by weight).

Use, reuse and repair

The significance of evidence for these aspects of the assemblage is slightly uncertain. Almost 12% of all sherds had traces of sooting, but it was unclear that this was a direct reflection of use of these vessels for cooking since in at least some cases the soot occurred on the broken edges as well as the surfaces of the sherds, indicating that it related to deposits in which the pottery had occurred post-breakage. It was not possible to distinguish clearly between cases where the occurrence of soot related only to use or was a post-use accretion. Nevertheless, it is notable that the occurrence of soot on E ware fabrics and reduced coarse wares (respectively 43.8% and 47.1% of all instances of sooting) were consistently slightly higher than the representation of these ware groups in the assemblage overall, which might reflect the preferential use of vessels in these fabrics for cooking. It is notable that the coarse sandy fabrics in each group, E30 and R20, were particularly prominent amongst the sooted sherds, these two fabrics alone amounting to 43.7% of such sherds.

Many fewer sherds had internal burnt residues. E wares were very prominent in this respect, and again E30 fabrics were particularly common, accounting for 42 of the 90 sherds. Limescale was recorded on only 11 sherds (including 7 in fabric E30 and 2 in R20) and sooting and limescale combined on just three, all of fabric R20. Despite the problem outlined above, therefore, there does seem to have been a correlation between coarsely sand-tempered fabrics and the use of vessels (jars) in these fabrics for cooking purposes.

Undifferentiated burning was noted on 69 sherds, but the breakdown of these was totally different, including relatively high proportions of Oxford colour-coated ware and white wares, and in many cases is likely to relate to burning after breakage. It is notable, however, that 17 of these sherds were from mortaria (almost one fifth of all mortarium sherds), apparently reflecting an increasingly regularly observed pattern, at least at regional level (e.g., Biddulph 2005a, 163), in which unusually high proportions of mortarium sherds are seen to be burnt, recent examples including Didcot Great Western Park (Booth 2023) and Aylesbury Berryfields (Biddulph 2019).

Secondary use of vessels was indicated in a number

of cases. Much the most common was the occurrence of post-firing drilled holes (see also above). These could have been for rivets for vessel repair but were generally of a diameter (*c.* 4–5mm or larger) considered too large for such use. Commonly found in the bases of jars (17 out of some 36 instances) and/or the lower body wall, drilled holes were also found in vessel shoulders, while the position of others was uncertain. Drilled bases usually had multiple holes, with four or five holes typical where the complete base survived. One such vessel was a sandy white ware jar (Fig. 3.5, 67); and a jar in fabric E30 from the same context was the only example of a vessel with a larger hole knocked, rather than drilled, through its base (Fig. 3.4, 49); two were in fabric R20 and the rest were in E ware fabrics, primarily fabric E80. This chronological aspect to the practice suggests a function that might later on have involved a specialist vessel type and use of these perforated vessels as cheese presses is possible. The function of perforations on vessel shoulders or necks is less clear. Comparable drilled holes in both vessel neck and base locations were noted amongst the Late Iron Age pottery from the Hardwick–Marsh Gibbon pipeline (Wells and Slowikowski 2015, 35). Further instances of vessel modification included two examples of Oxford colour-coated ware Young type C51 bowls, both from context 9745 of ditch 257, which had had the flanges of the rims trimmed off, and a fabric W21 flagon in ditch 234 (context 5210) had the rim broken off and was trimmed just above the lowest ring of the neck. In all three cases the vessels could have continued in use.

The only fairly certain evidence for vessel repair consisted of a single sherd of fabric R20 (period 3b ditch 227, context 6716) with a drilled rivet hole. A hole drilled in a sherd of Central Gaulish samian ware (context 7894, also period 3b) might also have been for a rivet, but this was not certain.

A fragment of South Gaulish samian was one of two examples of sherds reused as spindle whorls (context 7878). This incomplete sherd was only quite roughly trimmed. The other example was a small base sherd in fabric E80, 55mm in diameter and weighing 9g, neatly trimmed and pierced. There were six further instances of trimmed unpierced sherds, two in E80 and one each in fabrics F51, R20, R30 and R90. All were reused bases, so a rounded shape was ready prepared although the trimming was quite roughly done in a couple of cases. Where diameters could be determined they were *c.* 45mm, 75mm and 80mm.

Chronology

The above discussion has attempted to outline the main trends in the development of the pottery assemblage through time, but without discussing specific issues of chronology. As indicated at the head of that section, these are of some importance because of the apparently rather unusual chronological profile of the site in relation to others known from the Upper Thames Valley region. This does beg the question, however, of the extent to which those examples are relevant to Thame, which sits at the eastern margin of the Upper Thames Valley region in an area with few closely adjacent comparably recorded pottery assemblages.

A first question concerns the date of the earliest Late Iron Age pottery. Lying closer to the heartland of the 'Belgic' pottery tradition, it is possible that such material, in the fabrics grouped here as E wares, originated earlier at Thame than in the Upper Thames Valley proper, but there is no way of resolving this issue on present evidence – the chronology of the Late Iron Age–Early Roman phases at Thame relies entirely on the pottery evidence and there is no other material that can be brought to bear on the question. A recent review of Hertfordshire evidence, however, suggests that 'early Late Iron Age ceramic forms and fabric' emerged in the second half of the 1st century BC and only increased significantly in quantity in the late 1st century (Thompson 2015, summary at 131). Moreover, 'native grog-tempered pottery' continued in production into the Flavian period (Thompson 2015, 129). While these trends were not necessarily followed exactly in regions further west, they provide a useful pointer to the development of the assemblage at Thame, and in particular, suggest that the currency of E80 fabrics might have been longer than originally envisaged by a cut-off date of about AD 70. In any case the evidence of sites such as Yarnton and Gravelly Guy in the Upper Thames Valley has been taken to indicate continued use of E wares (though probably not production) into the Flavian period (e.g., Booth 2011a, 373). Identification of such cut-off points, however, remains largely subjective in the absence of clearly defined independent dating.

The ceramic chronology of the 1st century AD is based largely on interpretation of the changing relationship between components of the E and R ware groups. Within the former the grog-tempered (E80) fabrics are considered to be chronologically primary and this is supported by the admittedly tiny sub-period 3ai assemblage which is dominated by these fabrics. The only other numerically significant component of the E ware group consists of the coarse sand-tempered E30 fabrics, which form a relatively significant part of the sub-period 3aii assemblage and in the present context are considered directly ancestral to the sandy reduced wares, R20 and related fabrics. There is, however, no meaningful difference between the form repertoires of fabric E80 compared to E20 and E30 (Table 3.5), so that aspect does not clarify questions of chronological progression within the E ware range. The connection between E30 and R20 fabrics is underlined by the high proportion of jars produced in each (91.8% and 83.2% of REs respectively) and typological similarities between some of the jars in E30 and R20 fabrics though the greater diversity of vessel types in R20 fabrics clearly reflects the continuing use of these fabrics into the 2nd century and perhaps through a large part of the Roman period.

There is very little pottery that helps refine the dating of period 3a, particularly because of the uncertainty about associations arising from the occasional presence of obviously intrusive material in contexts assigned to this period. There is no South Gaulish samian ware from any period 3a context and Gallo-Belgic wares are absent from the site. Verulamium white wares were in production from about the middle of the 1st century but do not certainly occur before sub-period 3aiii, loosely dated to the Flavian period – four small sandy white ware (W20) sherds in period 3aii could have been from this industry but a more local source is also possible. A fine sandy white ware (W35), and probably related fine oxidised wares O18 and O19 (present as tiny sherds from butt beakers) are thought to derive from the Abingdon/Dorchester area (Timby *et al.* 1997) but this production is dated to the pre-Flavian period (and might possibly have originated before the conquest; Timby 2018) and these sherds were probably residual in sub-period 3aiii, although a beaker in fine white Oxford? ware (W12) in the same phase was perhaps contemporary with it. In summary, the chronology of the 3a sub-periods rests on the changing proportions of the principal coarse wares rather than on the identification of particular fabrics and vessel forms with specific closely defined date ranges.

This situation changes somewhat in period 3b, but the date range attached to this phase (mainly AD 100–150 but extending into the second half of the 2nd century) is such that the potential first appearance of fabrics such as Lezoux samian ware and Dorset black-burnished ware, used elsewhere in the region to define the beginning of a 'Middle Roman' phase, falls in the middle of the period and does not help define its inception. The differences in composition between the period 3a and 3b assemblages noted above reflect in part the wider date range of the latter. Had it been possible to subdivide period 3b (for a minor subdivision see below) a sense of more even development of the assemblage might have been obtained. Since this was not the case, interpretation of characteristics such as the continued presence of sub-stantial quantities of E wares, for example, is difficult. Do these simply represent a high degree of residuality/redeposition in contexts of all periods (as is perhaps likely), or is it possible that they represent the character of the assemblage in the earliest part of period 3b, before the impact of (in particular) the fine reduced wares R10 and R11 began to be felt at a significant level?

Samian ware, although scarce, provides some of the best indications of the date range of this period. This must have encompassed the second half of the 2nd century, albeit with activity probably at a rather lower level than seen previously. The relative scarcity of samian ware is itself an indication of this, given that most sites in the region occupied through the Antonine period typically produce more samian ware of that period than is seen here (Booth 2012). Nevertheless, two of the four stamped vessels have date ranges that extend into or lie completely within the second half of the 2nd century (see Table 3.3). An Oxford type M14 white ware mortarium should also date at least to the later 2nd century (context 6163, Fig. 3.6, 100). This was not intrusive (unlike the seven small sherds of F51/FO, with a mean sherd weight of just over 5g) but belongs to a group of contexts forming the upper fills of well group 23, formed after the well had fallen out of use. In total this group of material (defined as sub-period 3bii) comprised 19 sherds weighing 601g with a total RE value of 0.51. In addition to the type M14 sherd it consisted of four sherds of samian ware (three from Lezoux and one from Les Martres-de-Veyre) and reduced coarse wares (fabrics R10, R11, R20 and R30) including a wide mouthed jar in fabric R11 (Fig. 3.5, 75). Although very small, the group is coherent, but is one of very few that clearly extend the date range of the later part of the period 3b assemblage.

Overall, the following Oxford mortarium types (quantified by rim count/REs) were identified: M1 (1/0.20), M2 (3/0.46), M14 (1/0.13), M17 (2+/0.19), M20 (1/0.05), and M22 (3/0.13), plus white-slipped and colour-coated forms WC6/7 (7+/1.15), C97 (7+/0.38) and C100 (1+/0.08), which by definition date to period 3c. This breakdown strongly supports the view that the Middle Roman period, represented only by the M14 vessel (and just in its earlier part by M1 and M2 vessels), saw only a low level of activity. Arguments from absence provide possible, but less certain, support for this view. Nene Valley colour-coated ware does not occur before period 3c, and there were only six sherds of Dorset black-burnished ware. Had there been significant activity at Thame in the Antonine period and the early 3rd century more of this material would surely have been expected, even allowing for the fact that the site lies towards the eastern margin of BB1 distribution.

The beginning of the Late Roman period 3c is defined here, as elsewhere in the region, by the appearance of the suite of Oxford products dated after AD 240 by Young: colour-coated wares, distinctive mortaria, and other white and white-slipped wares – parchment ware (fabric W11), burnt white ware (fabric W23) and oxidised white-slipped ware (fabric Q21), which contributed at least five examples of the jar form WC3. Most of these are present in sub-period 3ci. The Oxford colour-coated ware types present (regardless of phase), quantified by numbers of rims/REs, are as follows: C8 (1/0.20), C18 (1/0.06), C44 (3/0.25), C45 (11+/0.71), C46 (5/0.28), C47 (5/0.42), C48 (1/0.05), C49 (1/0.06), C51 (25+/2.05), C52 (2/0.16), C55 (1/0.08), C61 (1/0.10), C64 (1/0.05), C68? (1/0.05), C75 (7+/0.64), C78 (1/0.12), C81 (2+/0.22), C82, C84 (1/0.03), C85 (1/0.09), C94.1 (1/0.10), C97 (7+/0.38), C100 (1+/0.08), C113 (1/0.12), C114 (1/0.32). Since many

Late Roman Oxford forms have wide date ranges, subdivision of the period can be problematic, but the assemblage provides a few pointers. Three examples of type C47, dated after AD 270 (Young, 158) occur in sub-period 3ci, while a single example of the mortarium type C100 should carry its date range after AD 300. Quantities of black-burnished ware are still very small, but the sole bowl from this sub-period has a bead and flanged rim characteristic of the later 3rd century or after.

Sub-period 3cii is dated from about AD 325 onwards. As noted above, the percentage of Oxford colour-coated ware increases quite substantially in this phase. The vessel types present include C75 and C78, with dates after *c.* AD 325 and AD 340 respectively (Young, 166), alongside a range of other more broadly dated types. It is notable, and perhaps significant, that one of the commonest Oxford colour-coated ware types, C51, only appears now, having been absent in sub-period 3ci. Of the distinct Late Roman coarse wares, fabric C11 is the most important and appears for the first time in this phase. In the Upper Thames Valley, the appearance of this fabric is considered a marker of date after *c.* AD 350, the date suggested for its earliest certain appearance at Cirencester (Cooper 1998, 341; Holbrook 2013, 33) and further north at sites such as Alcester, Warwickshire (e.g., Evans 1994, 146–7). If this fabric came from Harrold, as generally thought, its arrival at sites like Thame rather closer to the source might have commenced rather sooner. In any case the majority appearance of fabric C11 is in sub-period 3ciii, which is dated after *c.* AD 350, though there is an element of circularity in this since the presence of fabric C11 was one of the key markers for features of that sub-period.

The later 4th-century date of sub-period 3ciii is, however, supported by limited evidence from the Oxford types, which include C61, dated after AD 350 (Young, 162) and C113, dated after *c.* AD 340 (Young, 176). Other Late Roman coarse wares, such as the probable Overwey fabric O24, occurred in this period but were also present in sub-periods 3ci and 3cii, though a 4th-century date for all these occurrences is not incompatible with the general dates of these periods. A notable absence, however, was late Alice Holt fabric R39, of which only two sherds were identified at Thame, in sub-period 3ciii. Given the other evidence that activity in this period runs well into the second half of the 4th century, if not right to the end of the century and beyond, this absence is surprising, even in such a relatively small assemblage. Lyne (2008, 188) comments on the relative frequency of Alice Holt grey ware in south Oxfordshire in the Late Roman period, though his early 5th-century dating of some of the contexts that he discusses should be perhaps treated with caution.

General discussion

Thame Site F lies in an area of Oxfordshire that has seen relatively little large-scale examination of Roman settlement sites, in contrast to the situation further west in the Upper Thames Valley (see above). Despite its limitations, the present dataset therefore makes a useful contribution to understanding of patterns of pottery supply and use in the wider region. An arbitrary 20km radius from the site encompasses numerous comparative assemblages in the Bicester area, Oxford and the vicinity of Dorchester-on-Thames, an area also containing all the known major centres of the Oxford pottery industry. To the east and north, assemblages from the Aston Clinton Bypass and Hardwick to Marsh Gibbon Pipeline are unfortunately of limited use because of lack of detailed quantification (and none at all in terms of vessel types). Recently recorded material from Berryfields, Aylesbury, a site associated with the roadside settlement of Fleet Marston, however, provides good data for a Buckinghamshire settlement (Biddulph 2019) – the assemblage is similar in size to the present one in terms of sherd count, although rather smaller by weight.

Variation in chronological profile is a feature of many of the comparative assemblages and few clear patterns emerge. In the Bicester area (Table 3.8), i.e., the hinterland of the 'small town' of Alchester, at a major Roman road junction, there is wide variation including, unusually, two sites with sequences that appear to terminate at about the conquest period, or possibly a little earlier (most Oxfordshire sites with Late Iron Age occupation show continuity of activity into the Early Roman period). Occupation sequences running from the Late Iron Age/Early Roman period through into the 3rd century are quite common, but an equal number of sites have sequences that commence in the mid/late or later 1st century and thus clearly post-date the earliest phases of activity at Alchester and were quite likely established after the end of military occupation there. Of these sites, only at Oxford Road, Thame does occupation cease in the early 2nd century, a pattern which is much more characteristic of sites in the Upper Thames Valley (Booth *et al.* 2007, 43, 50, 52). With this exception, Middle Roman (early/mid 2nd–early/mid 3rd century) occupation is universal. More surprising is the relative paucity of Late Roman occupation in the vicinity of Alchester. Such activity is intensive in the northern extramural settlement area (A421 site; Booth *et al.* 2001) and is likely to have been so within the walled circuit although this area has seen no significant modern excavation, but is largely absent elsewhere, for reasons which are not clear.

A smaller sample of Buckinghamshire sites (Table 3.9) gives a slightly different perspective on settlement chronology. In most of these examples there is evidence for Late Iron Age and Early Roman occupation; these phases are unrepresented only at Weedon Hill. Three of the six sites on this list have intensive 4th-century occupation, a higher proportion than in the Alchester area.

Table 3.8 Broad chronological profiles of quantified Roman assemblages in the Bicester area

Site	Period				Totals		Date range	Reference
	LIR	ERB	MRB	LRB	Nosh	Wt (g)		
North of Oxford Parkway Station		Y	y	y	593	9676	Mostly later 1C–early 3C	Booth 2018b
Charlton, Holts Farm Crossing	y	Y	Y	Y	1595	16188	Mostly early 2C–late 3C/early 4C	Booth 2018b
South of Merton		Y	Y		835	10496	Late 1C–early 3C	Booth 2018b
Langford Lane South		Y	Y		3251	38346	Mid/late 1C–early/mid 3C	Booth 2018b
Langford Lane East	Y	Y	Y		4281	75201	LIA–early/mid 3C	Booth 2018b
Alchester northern extramural (A421B)		Y	Y	Y	36807	546074	Mid/late 1C–late 4C	Evans 2001
Faccenda Chicken Farm		Y	Y		2229	-	Late 1C–2C	Hughes 1984
Whitelands Farm*	Y	Y	Y		3039	33753	LIA–2C**	Brown 2011
Oxford Road	Y	Y			1124	16227	LIA–early 2C	Booth 1996
Bicester Park		Y	Y		2081	19185	Late 1C–3C	Timby 2008
Bicester Fields Farm							LIA	Brown 1999
Slade Farm							EIA–LIA	Woodward and Marley 2000

y = relatively low intensity activity; Y = relatively high intensity activity
EIA = Early Iron Age; LIA = Late Iron Age; LIR = Late Iron Age–Roman; ERB = Early Romano-British;
MRB = Middle Romano-British; LRB = Late Romano-British; Nosh = number of sherds
*Totals include some MIA pottery – usually small amounts
** This figure for the reported pottery accounts for only about 40% of the total

As has been indicated above, the pattern of occupation at Thame suggested by the pottery evidence seems to be different again from those just mentioned. Here, there is good evidence for Late Iron Age–Early Roman activity, and the Late Roman period is well-represented, but the intervening years (after c. AD 150) are not reflected in significant amounts of pottery deposition (subsumed in the period 3b assemblage). For whatever reason, activity through part of the Middle Roman period seems to have been at a relatively low level. A slight suggestion of a similar trend is seen at Didcot Great Western Park Phase 1, where Early and Late Roman material, particularly the latter, was well represented. The Middle Roman phase there produced less pottery in relative terms, but the overall quantity was still fairly substantial (Booth 2023). A similar situation is seen at Aylesbury Berryfields, where the Middle Roman period assemblage was rather smaller than those of earlier and

Table 3.9 Broad chronological profiles of quantified Roman assemblages from selected Buckinghamshire sites

Site	Period				Totals		Reference
	LIR	ERB	MRB	LRB	Nosh	Wt (g)	
Hardwick–Marsh Gibbon Plot 5.03–04	y	y	y	Most	2311	33795	Wells and Slowikowski 2015
Hardwick–Marsh Gibbon Plot 4.02	Y	Y			1148	12779	Wells and Slowikowski 2015
Aylesbury Berryfields	Y	Y	Y	Y	7835	88713	Biddulph 2019
Weedon Hill			Y	Y	2896	33699	Seager Smith 2013
Aston Clinton College Road	Y	Y	y	y	3800	62753	Perrin 2013
Aston Clinton Bypass	Y?	Y			?		Slowikowski 2008

y = relatively low intensity activity; Y = relatively high intensity activity later periods (Biddulph 2019), but it is not clear that this correlated with an identifiable reduction in the intensity of settlement.

The relative dearth of substantial rural settlement excavations in the area just east of Thame makes it difficult to judge the extent to which comparisons with the (ceramically) better known Oxford area are relevant. In terms of broad trends of pottery supply, the picture in the Late Iron Age–Early Roman period appears to be consistent across the wider region. Assemblages are dominated by fabrics in the 'Belgic' tradition (the E ware group), heavily dominated by grog-tempering. On the Bicester–Oxford railway sites small quantities of relatively coarse sand-tempered fabrics were also assigned to this group, though as a whole the E wares were only present in statistically significant quantities at Langford Lane East, where 40.9% of the total sherds were in grog-tempered E80 fabrics, and 2.6% (just under 6% of all E ware sherds) in the coarser sand-tempered E30 (Booth 2018a, 89). At Thame this proportion was considerably higher, with 20% of all the E ware sherds in fabric E30, and at Didcot it was even higher – 31.6% of all E ware sherds were in fabric E30 (Booth 2023). Further west, at Yarnton, the range of fabrics assigned to the E ware group was a little more diverse – here grog-tempered fabrics totalled 73.5% of all E ware sherds, and fabric E30 amounted to 11.6% of E wares (Booth 2011a, 366–7). Together these data suggest that a sand-tempered pottery production within the overall framework of the 'Belgic' tradition (consisting mainly of wheel-thrown vessel forms) was well established in the southern part of the Oxford region by the time of the Roman conquest if not rather earlier. This contrasts with the picture from rather further east, where Thompson characterises the 'Belgic' tradition in Hertfordshire and the Chilterns as 'almost invariably' of grog, but with occasional shell-tempered fabrics, while to the north-west, through the Milton Keynes area and into Northamptonshire, grog, shell and grog-and-shell fabrics predominate (Thompson 1982, 15–16; see also Thompson 2015). Clearly the character of potting traditions additional to the use of grog in the Late Iron Age was variable, but the relative scarcity of Buckinghamshire assemblages makes it impossible to tell if the boundaries between these supplementary traditions as defined in Hertfordshire and the Upper Thames Valley were closely defined. To the south and west the widespread use of flint tempering gives a different character again. In the pre-conquest assemblages from Silchester Insula IX grog-tempered wares accounted for 35.9% of sherds (but only 20.9% by weight) while Silchester flint-tempered ware totalled 39.4% of sherds (58.1% weight). Amongst a wide range of other fabrics, the principal local sandy fabric, amounting to 5.2% of sherds, was attributed to the Alice Holt industry (Timby 2018, 152, 165–9).

Overall, therefore, while grog-tempered pottery is a significant constant in Late Iron Age assemblages across the wider region, from place to place it is supplemented or even outnumbered by other traditions, whether quite unrelated, like Silchester ware, or more closely complementary, like the sand-tempered E30 fabrics seen at Thame. As already indicated, this tradition became even more important in the Early Roman period, and the 'Romanised' sandy R20 fabrics, which are thought to be a direct development from the E30 tradition, accounted for 20% of the entire assemblage (by sherd count), increasing steadily in importance through period 3a (comprising 12.8% of the combined assemblage from that phase) and amounting to 24.5% of sherds in the early–mid 2nd century period 3b and 21.2% in the later Roman period 3c. This was therefore the most numerous 'individual' fabric at Thame from the early 2nd century onwards. While it is clear that heavily sand-tempered fabrics did form a part of the range of the Oxford industry (e.g., Young, 202, fabric 2), especially in the Early Roman period, they were never particularly numerous – in production site assemblages at Nuneham Courtenay Lower Farm and Blackbird Leys, for example, fabric R20 amounted to 1.1% and a mere 0.1% of sherds respectively (Booth et al. 1993, 136; Booth and Edgeley-Long 2003, 248). The proportion of these fabrics normally declined after the 2nd century. Figures of 3.5% of sherds in the Early Roman period and 2.5% in the Late Roman period at Yarnton are fairly characteristic (Booth 2011a, 375). Elsewhere in the region percentages of fabric R20 were higher than at Yarnton. At Tubney Wood, fabric R20 amounted to 6.6% of all sherds, most of which were assigned to an Early Roman phase (Booth 2011b, 154) and was totally absent from the admittedly very small Late Roman phase group there. At Mansfield College, Oxford, fabric R20 amounted to 4.5% of sherds (Booth 2000, 309). Overall percentages of R20 on the Bicester to Oxford railway sites ranged from 2.9% to 9.4% in the four largest assemblages (Booth 2018a, 90) but again the decreasing frequency of this fabric through time was evident in the only one of these that had a significant Late Roman as well as Early and Middle Roman groups (ibid., 123).

Reverting to the south of the region it is unsurprising that at Didcot, where fabric E30 was even more common than at Thame, R20 fabrics were also well represented. Here some attempt was made to subdivide the R20 fabric group, with components of it such as the coarse sand-tempered fabric R23 assigned very tentatively to a later Roman production site at Compton on the Downs, south of Didcot (Hardy 1937; Harris 1935); the fabrics from this site are not very clearly characterised. Overall, the R20 and related fabrics at Didcot totalled 12.2% of sherds in the Early Roman period, 16.4% in the Middle Roman, and then followed the regional trend of reduction in quantity (to 9.3%) in the Late Roman period. The R20 sherds at Thame exhibited some of the same variety seen at Didcot, but time restraints precluded any systematic attempt at more detailed subdivision. This might have produced comparable results, though it is unlikely that Compton products would have travelled as far as Thame. Nevertheless, a single vessel (Fig. 3.7, 108), a slightly curving-sided dish, was identified as of fabric R23. Whether or not a Compton product, this vessel was of a form consistent with that source. Other specifically Late Roman coarse sand-tempered fabrics at Thame included the probable Overwey fabric O24, present as jars (Fig. 3.7, 103 and Fig. 3.8, 126). By contrast, only two sherds of Alice Holt grey ware (fabric R39) were identified.

Reduced coarse wares totalled about half of the period 3b and 3c assemblages, with R20 consistently more numerous than the other main subgroups, fine R10 and medium-sandy R30 fabrics. These would usually be expected to dominate the later Roman assemblages in the region, with the likelihood that most were Oxford products. Both groups were clearly important, and this would surely have been enhanced were it not for the very high proportion of redeposited E wares, still amounting to more than 20% of sherds in period 3c. As noted above, the quantity of clearly residual E wares raises the question of the extent to which R20 sherds might also have been residual in Late Roman contexts – unfortunately there is no clear answer.

Other characteristic components of regional Late Roman assemblages were present at Thame. These included pink grogged ware (fabric O81, for distributions see Taylor 2004; Rippon 2017, 342–4), although this was present from a rather earlier period, and Late Roman shell-tempered ware (fabric C11). The percentage of C11 rose significantly in the final period (3ciii), in line with an expected trend, but this sub-period group was rather small (only 377 sherds) so it is possible that the picture was skewed by sherds from a small number of vessels. Nevertheless, this period group demonstrated another anticipated trend mentioned above, a significant increase in the proportion of Oxford colour-coated ware (F51).

The proportion of 'fine and specialist' wares has been used in the Oxford region as a potential measure of site character (Booth 2004), and significant quantities of comparative data have now been accumulated (e.g., Booth 2018a, 134–7; 2018b, 343–5). These broadly support the original hypothesis, but also indicate the complexity of the issues involved, particularly supporting the view that the correlation between low percentages of fine and specialist wares and low socio-economic status is seen most clearly in the Early Roman period, but that the trend becomes less clear in the Middle and Late periods. The comparative data are not duplicated here, but the relevant figures for Thame can be set beside them, using a broad tripartite chronological framework. Values of fine and specialist wares for the Late Iron Age–Early Roman period (e.g., Booth 2018a, table 3.23) range from 0.2% to 10.7% of sherds. The figure for Thame, 3%, sits comfortably in the middle of this range, in which all 18 sites in the lower part (up to 4.1% fine and specialist wares) are broadly characterised as lower status rural settlements and the eight sites in the upper end of the spectrum are nucleated settlements, villas/proto villas or (in two cases) rural settlements which prefigure development of that character. One of those two sites is Didcot Great Western Park, where the Early Roman fine and specialist ware value is 8.2%, and where Late Iron Age and Early Roman sand-tempered fabrics were particularly important, as at Thame and as discussed above.

The Middle Roman fine and specialist ware value for Thame is 11.3%, or 7.5% if unspecified sandy white ware (W20) sherds are excluded (for this see Booth 2018b, 343). The latter figure again places the Thame assemblage in the middle of the overall range of values for this period (from 2.8% to 19.7%), but alongside a more diverse group of sites: for example, the Middle Roman period assemblage at the villa site of Roughground Farm, Lechlade, also has 7.5% fine and specialist wares, while the northern extramural settlement at Alchester has 7.6%, but other rural settlements in the region also have values of this order. The relevant figure for Didcot is 10.8% (Booth 2018a, table 3.24).

In the Late Roman period the picture becomes even more mixed, and the assemblages available for comparative analysis include fewer from simple rural settlements, reflecting a tendency towards expansion of rural settlement sizes ('complex farmsteads' in the terminology of the Roman Rural Settlement Research Project (Smith *et al.* 2016, 28–33)). The impact of the late Oxford industry, resulting in the ready availability of greatly increased quantities of fine wares (principally fabric F51) means that there is a significant shift in the baseline representation of fine and specialist wares (Booth 2004), the overall range for 20 site assemblages being from 7.2% to 35.8%. The figure for Thame is 18.3%, again in the middle of the range, and again close to values from a variety of site types, including rural settlements such as Old Shifford (17.5%) and perhaps Mansfield College, Oxford (20%), the villa at Claydon Pike (18.5%) and minor nucleated settlements at Gill Mill (Ducklington) and Wantage (19% and 19.4% respectively). The value for Didcot, now more clearly seen as coming from settlement closely associated with the adjacent villa, is 26.4%, and is exceeded only at sites in and very closely adjacent to Dorchester-on-Thames, where ready access to Oxford industry fine wares may have been a determining factor in these high values.

The overall impression from this rapid comparative assessment is that the pottery from Thame reflects a fairly typical rural settlement, but one that involves aspects of complexity consistent with the extensive area of its plan, perhaps particularly in the later Roman period when, as already noted, there seem to have been more agglomerated and fewer simple farmsteads in the regional landscape.

A further aspect of comparison concerns the relative proportions of key vessel classes. Fewer data are available here because fewer assemblages in the region have been recorded using EVEs/REs to quantify vessel types. Nevertheless, there are now sufficient sites from the region recorded in this way to make a brief comparison worthwhile. Again, the comparative data are summarised in Booth (2018a). The analysis defines three principal groups of vessels: jars – almost invariably the most numerous class; bowls and dishes; and vessels related to liquid consumption – flagons, beakers and cups (and tankards when present, which was not the case here). These groupings can be considered to be broadly distinct in functional terms, although there will always have been a degree of overlap between the uses of some of vessels within them. As with changes in the representation of fine and specialist wares, chronological evolution of the varying proportions of these three principal vessel class groupings is evident, but the proportions are also affected by site type, with lower status rural settlement assemblages routinely containing greater numbers of jars compared to the other two vessel categories. The Thame assemblage follows the expected trend across the three main periods of site occupation, with a gradual reduction in the proportion of jars and a corresponding increase in bowls and dishes (Table 3.10).

Table 3.10 Proportions of principal vessel functional groupings by main periods

Vessel class group	Period		
	3a	3b	3c
Jars	84.6%	74.7%	64.7%
Bowls/dishes	4.1%	14.1%	28.4%
Liquid-related	11.3%	11.3%	7.0%
Sum of REs	24.54	47.72	37.65
% of all REs in this period represented by these groups	99.8	97.5	91.1

In terms of comparison with other regional assemblages (see Booth 2018a, 138, table 3.26), using the percentage of jars as a starting point, the Thame assemblage sits roughly in the middle of the range of values (16 assemblages from 93%–63.1%) for the Early Roman period, moves closer to the bottom of the range (18 assemblages from 77.4%–38.8%) in the Middle Roman period and then resumes its central position amongst 11 Late Roman assemblages with values ranging from 78.5% to 43.4%. The breakdown of the Late Roman assemblage at Thame is almost identical to those from the sites at Mansfield College/New Chemistry Laboratory in Oxford and Cotswold Community, much further up the Thames Valley on the Gloucestershire/Wiltshire border. These can be defined as rural settlements, but in both cases there are elements of complexity in the plan which is comparable with the situation at Thame. As was the case with fine and specialist ware figures, comparison with Didcot Great Western Park shows that the latter site consistently had a more diverse (i.e., less jar-dependant) assemblage, which probably reflects the association of that site with an immediately adjacent villa complex, at least from the Middle Roman period.

East of Thame the only local assemblage with comparably quantified data, from Aylesbury Berryfields (Biddulph 2019), shows some interesting differences. Broadly characterised as a roadside settlement, it is unsurprising that the assemblage has greater typological variety than that at Thame. Jars amount to 72.6% of the Early Roman material, and in the Late Roman period the overall vessel profile is very similar to that from the comparable roadside settlement in the northern extramural settlement of Alchester (with jars at roughly 44%). Most remarkable, however, is the situation in the Middle Roman period, when the percentage of jars falls to a mere 31.8% and liquid-related vessels rise to 44.4%. These figures are quite anomalous when compared with contemporary groups, as Biddulph (2019) shows. Unfortunately the Berryfields assemblage for that period is quite small (only 7.52 REs), so the exact significance of these figures is not completely certain, but they suggest an unusual pattern of vessel use perhaps best seen in terms of activities specific to the roadside settlement, such as provision of refreshment to passing travellers, although it is notable that the Middle Roman features from which the majority of the material derived were mostly along a side road away from the line of Akeman Street. Whatever detailed interpretation is placed on the Berryfields Middle Roman evidence, the potential for this analytical method to identify distinct differences in site character is clear.

Catalogue of illustrated vessels (Figs 3.1–3.8)

The vessels are arranged in approximate typological sequence by period.

Period 3aii

1	Fabric E80 type CD jar. Context 5188, ditch 206
2	Fabric E80 type CD jar. Context 7586, ditch 202
3	Fabric E80 type CD jar. Context 5523, ditch 206
4	Fabric E80 type CD jar. Context 6083, ditch 206
5	Fabric E80 type CE jar. Context 6083, ditch 206
6	Fabric E30 type CI jar. Context 5923, ditch 206
7	Fabric E80 type CM jar. Context 15495, ditch 153
8	Fabric E30 type CN jar. Context 7369, ditch 206
9	Fabric E80 type CN jar. Context 5624, ditch 206, and period 3aiii context 5856, ditch 248
10	Fabric R20 type cup. Context 7370, ditch 206
11	Fabric E80 type HC bowl. Context 5623, ditch 206

Period 3aiii

12	Fabric W21 type BE flagon. Context 6235, ditch 204

13   Fabric E80 type CC jar. Context 5658, ditch 205
14   Fabric E80 type CD jar. Context 5087, ditch 201
15   Fabric E80 type CD jar. Context 7010, ditch 209
16   Fabric E80 type CD jar. Context 7201, ditch 205
17   Fabric E80 type CD jar. Context 7010, ditch 209
18   Fabric E80 type CD jar. Context 7992, ditch 209
19   Fabric O20 type CD jar. Context 5363, ditch 248
20   Fabric R20 type CD jar. Context 6235, ditch 204
21   Fabric E30 type CE jar. Context 8332, ditch 205
22   Fabric E80 type CH jar. Context 5815, ditch 205
23   Fabric R90 type CH jar. Context 5612, ditch 248
24   Fabric R20 type CD jar. Context 5685, ditch 209
25   Fabric O20 type EA butt beaker. Context 16272, ditch 162
26   Fabric E80 type EB girth beaker. Context 6176, ditch 6177
27   Fabric E30 type HA carinated bowl. Context 6235, ditch 204

Period 3a unphased
28   Fabric E80 type CD jar. Context 8730, ditch 205
29   Fabric E80 type CD jar. Context 8495, ditch 212
30   Fabric E80 type CD jar. Context 8730, ditch 205
31   Fabric E80 type CD jar. Context 9180, ditch 205
32   Fabric O20 type CD jar. Context 8729, ditch 205
33   Fabric E20 type CE jar. Context 8730, ditch 205
34   Fabric E80 type CE jar. Context 9590, ditch 205
35   Fabric R20 type CE jar. Context 9590, ditch 205
36   Fabric E80 type CH jar. Context 8454, Late Saxon enclosure ditch 8547
37   Fabric E80 type CH jar. Context 8730, ditch 205
38   Fabric C10 type CH jar. Context 8730, ditch 205
39   Fabric E80 type CN jar. Context 7432, ditch 206
40   Fabric W20 beaker body sherd. Context 9539, ditch 203
41   Fabric E80 type HA necked bowl. Context 6075, ditch 203
42   Fabric O10 type JB dish. Context 6422=6376, ditch 221

Period 3b
43   Fabric Q21 flagon. Context 9531, ditch 230
44   Fabric W22 flagon. Context 15192
45   Fabric R10 type CC jar. Context 6716, ditch 227
46   Fabric R20 type CC jar. Context 5640, ditch 249
47   Fabric R30 type CC jar. Context 9531, ditch 230
48   Fabric W21 type CC jar. Context 6716, ditch 227
49   Fabric E30 type CD jar with secondary hole in base. Context 15720, ditch 123
50   Fabric E80 type CD jar. Context 5210, ditch 234
51   Fabric O80 type CD jar. Context 7868, pit 7866
52   Fabric R10 type CD jar. Context 5589, ditch 231
53   Fabric R10 type CD jar. Context 7984, ditch 234
54   Fabric R10 type CD jar. Context 7984, ditch 234
55   Fabric R11 type CD jar. Context 5044, ditch 256
56   Fabric R11 type CD jar. Context 5846, ditch 234
57   Fabric R11 type CD jar. Context 5892, ditch 229
58   Fabric R20 type CD jar. Context 5640, ditch 249
59   Fabric R20 type CD jar with holes drilled in base. Context 5640, ditch 249
60   Fabric R20 type CD jar. Context 5846, ditch 234
61   Fabric R20 type CD jar with holes drilled in neck. Context 6876, ditch 247
62   Fabric R20 type CD jar. Ra. 881. Context 7913, beside cremation burial 7912 (in urn 7911), near ditch 202
63   Fabric R20 type CD jar. Context 15191, ditch 189
64   Fabric R20B type CD jar. Context 6716, ditch 227
65   Fabric R30 type CD jar. Context 5640, ditch 249
66   Fabric R90 type CD jar. Context 5341, pit 5340, cuts ditch 234
67   Fabric W20 type CD jar. Context 15720, ditch 123
68   Fabric E80 type CE jar. Context 9371, ditch 247
69   Fabric R11 type CE jar. Context 6716, ditch 227
70   Fabric R20 type CE jar. Context 15720, ditch 123
71   Fabric E80 type CF jar. Context 5398=6344, 'coombe deposit' colluvium
72   Fabric R90 type CH jar. Context 5208, ditch 234
73   Fabric R11 type CI jar. Context 6716, ditch 227
74   Fabric R30B type CK jar. Context 6716, ditch 227
75   Fabric R11 type CM jar. Context 5121, well 23
76   Fabric O80 type CN jar. Context 5051, ditch 211
77   Fabric R90 type CN jar. Context 6810, ditch 227
78   Fabric W36 small beaker with unusual incised decoration. Auxiliary vessel in burial 16754. Context 5398=6344, 'coombe deposit' colluvium
79   Fabric R10 type EC beaker. Context 6134, pit 6133 beside ditch 223
80   Fabric R11 type EF beaker. Context 6716, ditch 227
81   Fabric R10 type EG beaker. Context 5589, ditch 231
82   Fabric O10 type HA bowl. Context 9334, pit 9333 beside ditch 243
83   Fabric O11 type HA bowl. Context 6716, ditch 227
84   Fabric R10 type HA bowl. Context 6716, ditch 227
85   Fabric R10 type HA bowl. Context 6716, ditch 227
86   Fabric R10 type HA bowl. Context 6716, ditch 227
87   Fabric R10 type HA bowl. Context 6716, ditch 227
88   Fabric R10 type HA bowl. Context 7984, ditch 234
89   Fabric R10 type HA bowl. Context 7984, ditch 234
90   Fabric R11 type HA bowl. Context 5208, ditch 234
91   Fabric R10 type HA bowl. Context 6716, ditch 227
92   Fabric R20 type HA bowl. Context 7984, ditch 234
93   Fabric F39 type HC bowl. Context 8117, ditch 234
94   Fabric R20 type HD bowl with post-firing hole drilled in neck. Context 8369, ditch 230
95   Fabric R10B bowl/dish. Context 8896, ditch 230
96   Fabric R30 type JA dish. Context 5142, well 23
97   Fabric O10 type JB dish. Context 9315, ditch 234
98   Fabric R10 type JB dish. Context 9358, ditch 243
99   Fabric M22 mortarium of Young type M2. Context 6134, pit 6133 beside ditch 223
100 Fabric M22 mortarium of Young type M14. Context 6163, well 23
101 Fabric R20 type MF cheese press. Context 6807, pit 6804 cut by ditch 234

Period 3ci
102 Fabric W23 type CD jar. Context 6620, ditch 240
103 Fabric O24 type CD jar. Context 5434, ditch 243
104 Fabric R10 type CM jar. Context 10006, ditch 253
105 Fabric R10 type CM jar. Context 8434, ditch 253
106 Fabric O81 jar. Context 6646, ditch 240
107 Fabric F52 type ED beaker with elaborate over-slip decoration in white paint. Context 8236, ditch 253
108 Fabric R23 type JA dish. Context 5379, ditch 243
109 Fabric F30 type JB dish. Context 8175, ditch 244
110 Fabric W12 type JB dish. Context 5379, ditch 243

Period 3cii
111 Fabric F51 type CC jar. Context 8288, ditch 241
112 Fabric R20 type CD jar. Context 5034, ditch 241
113 Fabric W10 type EH beaker. Context 5335, ditch 242
114 Fabric Q21 type HA bowl (Young type WC3). Context 6517, ditch 241
115 Fabric W10 type HC bowl. Context 5171, ditch 255

Period 3ciii
116 Fabric F51 flagon. Context 7363, ditch 251
117 Fabric C11 type CD jar. Context 6938, ditch 251
118 Fabric R20 type HB bowl. Context 6938, ditch 251
119 Fabric R20 type JA dish. Context 6939, ditch 251
120 Fabric R20 type JA dish. Context 7814, ditch 251
121 Fabric R30 type JA dish. Context 7211, ditch 251
122 Fabric F51 type JB base with illiterate stamp. Ra. 868. Context 7363, ditch 251
123 Fabric F51 type JB dish (Young type C94.1). Context 7814, ditch 251
124 Fabric M31 mortarium of Young type WC7. Context 6938, ditch 251

Period 3c undifferentiated
125 Fabric F51 flagon. Context 8503, corndrier 26
126 Fabric O24 type CD jar. Context 10276, ditch 251
127 Fabric C11 type CK jar. Context 9852, ditch 243
128 Fabric R20 jar. Context 9745, ditch 257
129 Fabric R10 type EC beaker. Context 9476, fill of hearth 9477
130 Fabric W11 type HA bowl (Young type P24). Context 5316 pit 5315 between ditches 229 and 207
131 Fabric F51 type HA bowl (Young type C84). Context 9745, ditch 257
132 Fabric R30B type HB bowl. Context 9745, ditch 257
133 Fabric R30 type HB bowl. Context 9745, ditch 257
134 Fabric F51 type HC bowl (Young type C79). Context 8264, corndrier 26
135 Fabric F51 type HC bowl (Young type C114). Context 8264, corndrier 26
136 Fabric R10B type JA dish. Context 10276, ditch 251
137 Fabric R20 type JA dish. Context 8263, corndrier 26
138 Fabric R30 type JA dish. Context 5253, fill of 5254
139 Fabric M31 mortarium of Young type WC7. Context 8263, corndrier 26
140 Fabric R97 lid. Context 10276, ditch 251

Period 3b
141 Fabric R10 jar of uncertain form used as cremation urn. Ra. 48. Context 16752, cremation burial 16751
142 Fabric R10 type EH beaker used as auxiliary vessel. Ra. 49. Context 16755, cremation burial 16756
143 Fabric F51 type JB dish with illiterate stamp. Context 17031, ditch 190

Post-medieval
144 Fabric R30 type CC jar. Context 8000, subsoil

Roman metal finds
by E.R. McSloy (with a contribution from Dr Martin Henig)

Of the total of 172 metal artefacts recovered, over half (89) are datable to the Roman period either by form or by stratigraphical association (Table 3.11). All recovered objects, including undated material, are described individually in the archive and a selective catalogue comprising Roman-dated objects of individual interest is presented below.

Some 63 objects were recorded from Roman-phased (period 3) deposits. To this may be added items from Roman objects identified from unstratified finds or among unphased or post-Roman phased deposits (Table 3.11). Approximately half of the metalwork assemblage was recovered using a metal detector, with the remainder hand-excavated or recovered from bulk soil samples. Of the total considered of Roman date, 58 items are iron, 27 are copper alloy and four are lead or lead alloy. Six objects (four of iron; one of lead and one of copper alloy) from the 2014 evaluation are described elsewhere (JMHS 2014).

Table 3.11 Summary of metal finds according to period and functional category

Function	Unph. (Roman)	2a–3d	3	3a	3b	3c	3d	3d–4a	4/post-med.	Totals
Personal adornment/ dress	5	1	1		1	4	2	1		15
Household	3			1	1				1	6
Weights/ measures	2				1	1				4
Tools				1	1	1			2	5
Fasteners and fittings	5			2	3	13			5	28
Agricultural	1									1
Waste/spills					4	2				6
Weaponry				1						1
Indet.				8	7	8				23
Totals	16	1	1	13	18	29	2	1	8	89

The catalogue for the Roman metalwork is set out according to function and subdivided by material. It includes selected finds, illustrated in Figures 3.9–3.11. Functional categories are based on those defined by Crummy (1983). Table 3.11 summarises the 'Roman' assemblage by period and by functional grouping. Most among the copper alloy objects comprise small personalia, mainly brooches and other 'dress' items. Among the ironwork and lead, fixtures/fittings (mostly nails), household items, tools and weights are common. Where dating is possible the focus is on the mid or later 1st century and the 3rd to 4th centuries AD.

Most material probably represents casual loss of items in use or discard/loss of scrap items. Larger iron tools or agricultural implements are uncommon, a possible indication that such items were routinely recycled. The bulk of recovered ironwork consists of iron 'carpentry' nails. Most are 'standard' forms (Manning's (1985) Type 1) with square-sectioned shafts and flattened heads. Where length is measurable these predominantly are in the 40–60mm range, with some larger, conical headed forms measuring 110–130mm. Four nails exhibit T-shaped heads equivalent to Manning's Type 3 and one has an L-shaped head common to Manning's Type 4.

There is some evidence for small-scale crafts activity from the quantities of copper alloy waste/spills from period 3 (Table 3.11). A further 11 examples from subsoil layer 5001 and coombe deposit 5398 may represent further evidence for the casting of objects in this period; however, unfinished items, crucibles or mould fragments were not noted.

Objects of personal adornment/dress (Figs 3.9–3.10)

This category makes up the largest proportion of the catalogued assemblage, a feature common to the majority of Roman assemblages. Items not described in the catalogue comprise hobnails (two) almost certainly deriving from footwear of the type common across the Roman period.

Brooches – Copper alloy

Of ten brooches dating to the Roman period, nine were of copper alloy and one of iron. The latter was a fragmentary unstratified find from the 2014 evaluation (JMHS 2014, 65), which was not examined as part of this analysis. The copper alloy brooches all date to the middle or later decades of the 1st century AD, the peak period of brooch use in Roman Britain. Earliest are the one-piece brooches (nos 1–3) which may slightly pre-date the conquest, although they are as likely to date to the early post-conquest decades. They are fragmentary, precluding full classification according to Mackreth's (2011) scheme. Aucissa brooch no. 4 and Hod Hills nos 5 and 6 also are probably of the 40s to 60s AD. Typologically latest of the Roman brooches are the Colchester derivatives, the use of which extends as late as the 70s AD. Even allowing for the fall-off in brooch use beginning in the late 1st century (Cool and Baxter 2016, 85) the absence of brooches dating to the 2nd century AD would seem to indicate reduced activity from this period.

One piece

1   One-piece brooch (fragment). Only the spring (with four coils and internal chord) and upper portion of the bow survives. The rod-like bow would accord with Mackreth's Drahtfibel class or its derivatives (2011, 21). Wt 1g; L 20.6mm; W 5.3mm at the wings. Periods 3d–4a layer 6688. Ra. 806.

2   Colchester brooch (fragment). Catchplate and pin are absent. The bow is plain, sub-rounded in section and straight – an early feature possibly suggesting a pre-conquest date. The wings are short and undecorated. Wt 5.1g; L 51.1mm; W 13.7mm. Western excavation area – subsoil 5001. Ra. 558.

3   Colchester brooch (fragment). Most of the catchplate and pin are absent. The bow is plain and curved, with a sub-square profile. What remains of the catchplate suggests this was pierced. The short wings are undecorated. Wt 3.5g; L 46.1mm; W 11.7mm. Period 3d ditch 205 (8749) (fill 8751). Ra. 894.

Aucissa and Hod Hill

4   Aucissa brooch (fragment). The foot and hinged pin are missing. The (uninscribed) stepped and curved-overhead bow, which is ridged with a beaded spine, is characteristic of Mackreth's AVCISSA 2b (2011, 90). Wt 6.5g; L 36.8mm; W 18.1mm. Western excavation area – subsoil 5001. Ra. 556.

5   Hod Hill brooch. There is damage to either side of the upper bow and it is unclear whether no. 5 originally had wings. The square upper bow with three ribs and multiple cross mouldings to the foot identify it as of Mackreth's HOD HILL 4.a2 form (2011, 137). An unusual feature is the pronounced central rib, which is deeply grooved. Wt 10.8g; L 53.6mm; W 16.6mm. Period 3c ditch 127 (16088) (fill 16089). Ra. 63.

6   Hod Hill brooch (fragment). Pin, catchplate and one wing are lost and the surfaces poorly preserved. Matches Mackreth's HOD HILL 4.b3 type, defined by a square upper bow with four ribs and multiple cross mouldings below (2011, 138). Wt 3g; L 42.1mm; W 17.7mm. Western excavation area – subsoil 5001. Ra. 532.

Colchester derivatives (Harlow spring system)

7   Colchester-derivative class. Complete brooch of Mackreth's type CD Ha 3a1 – part of his west of England group and probably dating before c. AD 80. Plain bow with cross-cut pseudo hook, wings decorated with perpendicular and oblique grooves, solid catchplate. Wt 18.2g; L 59.3mm; W 27mm at the wings; Th. 17.6mm. Western excavation area – subsoil 5001. Ra. 580.

8   Colchester-derivative class. Complete small brooch corresponding to Mackreth's type Ha1.A3b identical to no. 1176 in Mackreth's catalogue from Harlow, Essex (Mackreth 2011, 52). Probably 50s to 70s AD. Short, wide bow with decorative ribbing to wings and

The Late Iron Age and Romano-British Finds and Environmental Remains 77

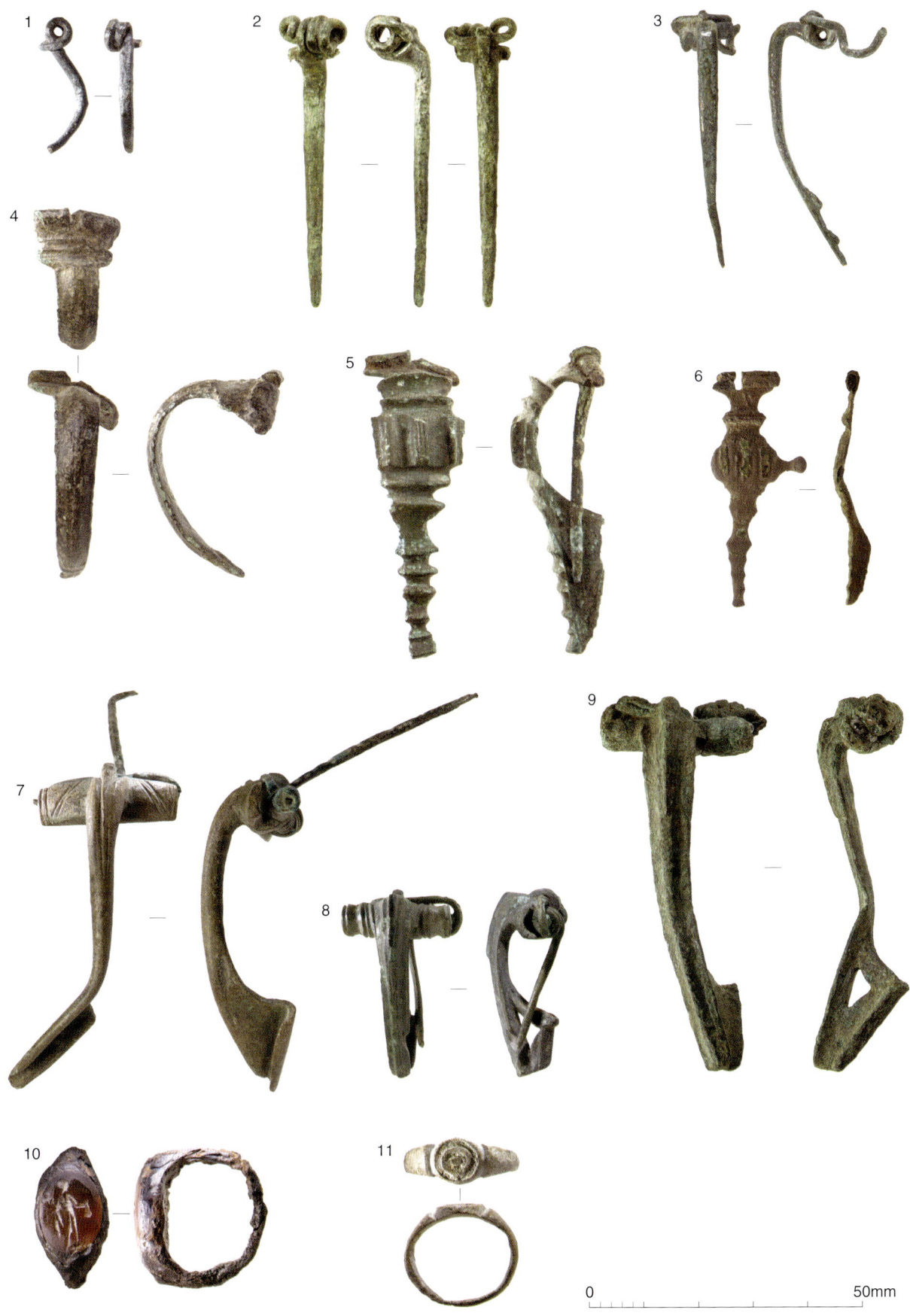

Fig. 3.9 Roman metal objects, nos 1–11

prominent crest at head. Catchplate with triangular piercing and flanged catchplate return. Wt 7.9g; L 31.9mm; W 21.7mm. Period 3bi ditch 205 (5656) (fill 5659). Ra. 686.

9   Colchester-derivative class. Deterioration of the surfaces may have removed the subtle graved decoration which distinguish some of Mackreth's subgroups. It is certainly of his Ha1 grouping, with broad bow and a long spine forming a prominent crest at the upper part of the bow. It features simple ribbed decoration to the wings and triangular-pierced catchplate. Wt 17g; L 69.1mm; W 19mm. Period 3c ditch 260 (5408) (fill 5434). Ra. 529.

Finger rings – Iron (by Dr Martin Henig)

The iron ring is of Type III with a relatively narrow hoop, broadening out at the bezel (Henig 2007, 35–6, fig. 1). The material of the stone is cornelian, a translucent orange chalcedony. The subject is certainly Mercury with his cloak (chlamys) draped over his left fore-arm and holding his caduceus in his left hand; he holds his purse in his outstretched right hand. Of course, right and left would be reversed in impression. For the type see Henig (1991, 241–2, no. 1); likewise, an image of Mercury in an iron ring, dated to Flavian times. The subject is very common in Roman Britain (Henig 2007, 191–2, nos 38–47 and 297–8, nos App. 94 and App. 95; and Johns 1997, 90, nos 174–7 and 95, no. 223). The Thame ring is likely to date from the late 1st century or the first half of the 2nd century.

10   Iron finger ring of Henig Type IIIa (2007, 35–6) with intaglio of cornelian *in situ* (described above). Wt 5.6g; L 23.7mm; W (bezel) 13.2mm. Subsoil 5001. Ra. 58.

Finger rings – Copper alloy

Ring no. 11 was recovered from a deposit containing pottery mainly dating to the later 2nd to 3rd centuries AD and may be of similar date. It falls within a class described by Henig as trinket rings' (2007, 14) of less than robust construction and set with glass paste or enamelled. No. 11 has an enamelled bezel and, in this respect, compares to examples from Colchester (Crummy 1983, 48, nos 1778 and 1785). One amongst the latter comes from a 4th-century grave, although the use of enamel might indicate it was already old when deposited.

A second copper alloy ring of Roman date was a find from evaluation trench 6 (ditch fill 613). It was described by Henig as 'transitional between the form with a keeled hoop and those with hunched, expanded D-shaped shoulders, though it approximates most closely to the latter. It has a raised ovoid bezel octagonally facetted along its sides, containing a setting of glass with a greenish hue, moulded with an intaglio which almost certainly was intended to depict a human figure'. Henig classified it as an example of his Types viii or xb (Henig 1978 and 2007, fig. 1) and more broadly as a low value signet ring or 'Romano-British imitation' and probably dating to the 3rd century AD.

11   Finger ring with enamelled bezel. Sub-circular hoop widening towards angular shoulder and with raised oval bezel. The bezel has an internal raised ring and a central pellet, the areas within filled with (now) yellowish enamel. Wt 2.6g; Diam. 20.7mm; W (bezel) 8.1mm. Unphased coombe deposit 5398 (17162). Ra. 59.

Bracelets/armlets – Copper alloy

Bracelets with 'reversed S' stamp decoration similar to no. 12 appear to date to the 4th century AD and include examples from Colchester (Crummy 1983, 42–3, nos 1679 and 1707) and Alchester, Oxon (Lloyd-Morgan 2001, 224–5, nos 11 and 12). More complete examples from Alchester and from Brockworth, Gloucestershire (Rawes 1981, 45) were fastened by means of a terminal hook and corresponding 'eye'.

12   Two fragments from a strip-form bracelet. It is decorated by a stamped pattern of reversed S motifs within marginal grooves. Wt 3g; W 4.7mm; Th. 1.7mm. Period 3d ditch 244 (9671) (fill 9672). Ra. 1041.

Household utensils – Copper alloy (Fig. 3.10)

No. 13 is of the common Roman form of spoon with its bowl offset, below the handle. Classification dating is usually reliant on the form of the bowl (Crummy 1983, 69), and in its absence dating is broad. The fragmentary nature of no. 15 precludes identification with certainty. The form of moulding and decoration is common to the Roman period, seen for example on toilet implements (Crummy 1983; Eckardt and Crummy 2008, 132). The half-rounded form and size suggests a different function, although in its fragmentary condition the precise form of use is unknown.

13   Handle of spoon of common Roman form with its bowl (missing) offset below the level of the handle, the junction with a U-shaped cut-out. Wt 8.8g; L 106mm. Period 4b Late Saxon enclosure ditch, cut 7117 (fill 7118). Ra. 817.

14   Handle? of unequal bifid form from vessel (flagon?). Wt 8.8g; L 17.6mm; W 17.4mm; Th. 4.7mm. Period 3a ditch 7642 (fill 7643). Ra. 574.

15   Fragment from cast implement or vessel handle; plano-convex in section. The double spool moulding is notched with cordons separating and below, and lipped collar terminal. The tapering shaft features three longitudinal ridges each of which is cabled. Wt 9g; L 43.6mm; W 12.6mm; Th. 4.5–2.8mm. Subsoil 5001. Ra. 517.

Weights and measures – Lead (Fig. 3.10)

Four weights were recorded, three of which are described below (the fourth, from unphased coombe deposit 5398, is incomplete, but probably conical in form). Nos 16 and 17 retain portions of embedded iron loops/hooks for suspension. They are probably steelyard weights of Roman type, with both biconical and cone-shaped forms known (Crummy 1983, 101; Bruce-

The Late Iron Age and Romano-British Finds and Environmental Remains 79

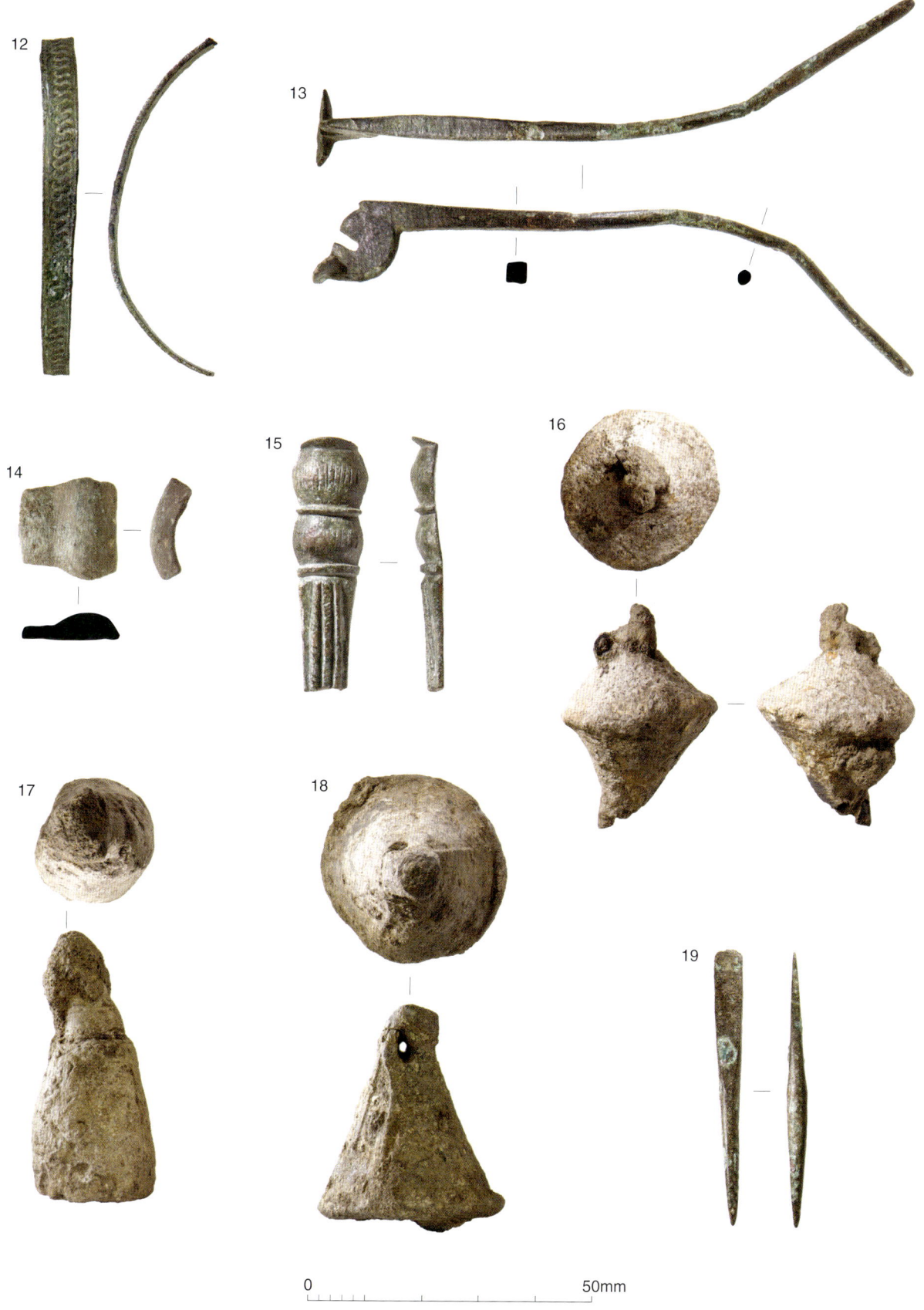

Fig. 3.10 Roman metal objects, nos 12–19

Mitford 1958, 75, fig. 40.11). No. 18 may also have functioned in this way but suspension was by means of a perforation though its apex.

16 Weight of crudely biconical form with (incomplete) iron setting passing through its full length. Wt 70g; L 34mm; Diam. 26.6mm. Unphased coombe deposit 5398. Ra. 568.

17 Weight. Cone-shaped with narrowed 'neck'. Fragmentary iron setting for suspension at apex. Wt 92g; L 46.5mm; Diam. (at base) 22.4mm. Unphased coombe deposit 5398 (17162). Ra. 60.

18 Weight. Cone-shaped transverse perforation at apex. Wt 96g; L 37.5mm; Diam. (at base) 33–34mm. Period 3c ditch 7174 (fill 7175), near ditch 259. Ra. 561.

Tools – Copper alloy (Fig. 3.10)

19 Awl. Circular-sectioned shaft, tapering to a point; spatulate 'handle'. Roman dating is likely for no. 19 and suggested by its context, although an earlier date is also plausible. L 47.6mm; Diam. (max.) 3.9mm; W (terminal) 5.4mm. Period 3a ditch 220 (5510) (fill 5511).

Tools – Iron (Fig. 3.11)

Two knives in the assemblage were considered to be of Roman type. The distinctive form of no. 20 (Manning's Type 24) has Late Iron Age origins, with use continuing well into the Roman period (1985, 118–19). It may however be redeposited in what is a well-dated Late Roman context. No. 21 is certainly residual within its post-medieval-phased deposit. Its blade form would match Manning's (broadly Roman) Type 14 (1985, 115), although essentially similar earlier Anglo-Saxon forms occur, for example from the Dover Buckland cemetery (Evison 1987, 113; Type 4).

20 Knife with S-shaped back, curving up towards the tip (missing) and with a convex edge and long tang level with the back. Manning Type 24 (Manning 1985, 118–19). L (surviving) 122mm; W (max.) 31mm; Th. (blade) 3.9mm–2mm. Period 3c ditch 251 (7962) (fill 7814). Ra. 877.

21 Knife with curving back and straight edge; its tang at shoulder level to the blade. L 96.8mm; W (max.) 16mm; Th. (blade) 3.6mm–0.9mm. Post-medieval ditch 8869 (fill 8870) (not illustrated). Ra. 963.

22 Drill bit. The blade is damaged but flattened and possibly dished – suggesting identification as a spoon bit. This was the most common of drill bits in use by the Roman carpenter (Manning 1985, 26–7). The shaft of the bit is round in section, swelling to a square-sectioned tang, the end of which is missing. L (surviving) 89mm; W (max.) 7mm; Th. (max) 6.8. Period 3b ditch 302 (7677) (fill 7678).

Agricultural – Iron (Fig. 3.11)

23 Rake tine(?). Curved back and, rectangular section (see Manning (1985, 59). Most of the tang is absent. L (surviving) 117mm; W (max.) 10.7mm; Th. 6.8mm–3.7mm. Undated pit 9361 (fill 9365), north of ditch 212, south-east of SFB structure 40. Ra.1036.

Weaponry – Iron (Fig. 3.11)

24 Spearhead no. 24 was recorded from the upper fill of period 3a ditch 206 in association with a small quantity of prehistoric pottery. As a class where form is very much dictated by functionality, spearheads are notoriously difficult to classify and date morphologically. The slender form of no. 24 is unlike the majority of Iron Age spearheads and it lacks the prominent spine seen with some examples, including from Danebury, Hants (Sellwood 1984, 361–6). Spearheads of the Roman period are rare finds from non-military sites but are not unknown – the majority presumed to be used for hunting. Their morphological and size range is wide (Manning 1985) and would accommodate this example. A third possibility, of an earlier Anglo-Saxon date, would necessitate no. 24 being considered an intrusive find (a possibility as the result of the prevailing loose, sand geology on this part of the site). The size and slender, leaf-shaped blade form of this example matches examples of this period of Swanton's C2 class (1973, 50, fig. 11). The absence of a cleft socket however makes an Anglo-Saxon date least likely. Spearhead with blade of slender leaf-shaped form. Closed socket with single rivet hole. The tip is missing and there is damage to the socket terminal. L (surviving) 126.3mm; W (max.) 19.3mm; Th. 6.9mm. Period 3a ditch 206 (9784) (fill 9782). Ra. 1051.

Objects of uncertain function – Copper alloy (Fig. 3.11)

Cruciform object no. 25 may be an untypically small plate brooch of a grouping considered by Mackreth to be of continental origin (2011, 167–79). Although no trace of a pin mechanism remains, the 'elongated lozenge' form and central roundel with provision for a projecting stud are features comparable with Mackreth's type PL CONT 20.1. The dating for such brooches, in the 40s to 60s AD (Mackreth 2011, 176), is in the range shared by the majority of brooches from this site, although if accepted, no. 25 is clearly residual.

In its damaged and distorted state, the original form of no. 26 is unclear, although it is likely to be a bell or rattle. There is some evidence for the use of spherical bells in the Roman period which are similar in form to the 'rumbler' bells of later periods and similar use to alert road users might be imagined (Allason Jones and Miket 1984, 184). In contrast to the medieval and later bells the suspension loop passes through both halves of the 'bell'. In use the two hemispheres may not have been joined, enhancing the jangling effect. Bells or rattles appear also to have been worn in the Roman period as jewellery articles (Crummy 1983, 38–9), or could be part of priestly regalia (Bagnall Smith 1998, 174; fig. 11, no. 16.1).

25 Flat, cruciform or lozenge-like object, the arms concave. Centrally perforated and with ring of corrosion suggesting a stud or boss. Wt 1g; L 20.4mm; W 16.7; Th. 1.7mm. Period 3c ditch 260 (5378) (fill 5379). Ra. 628.

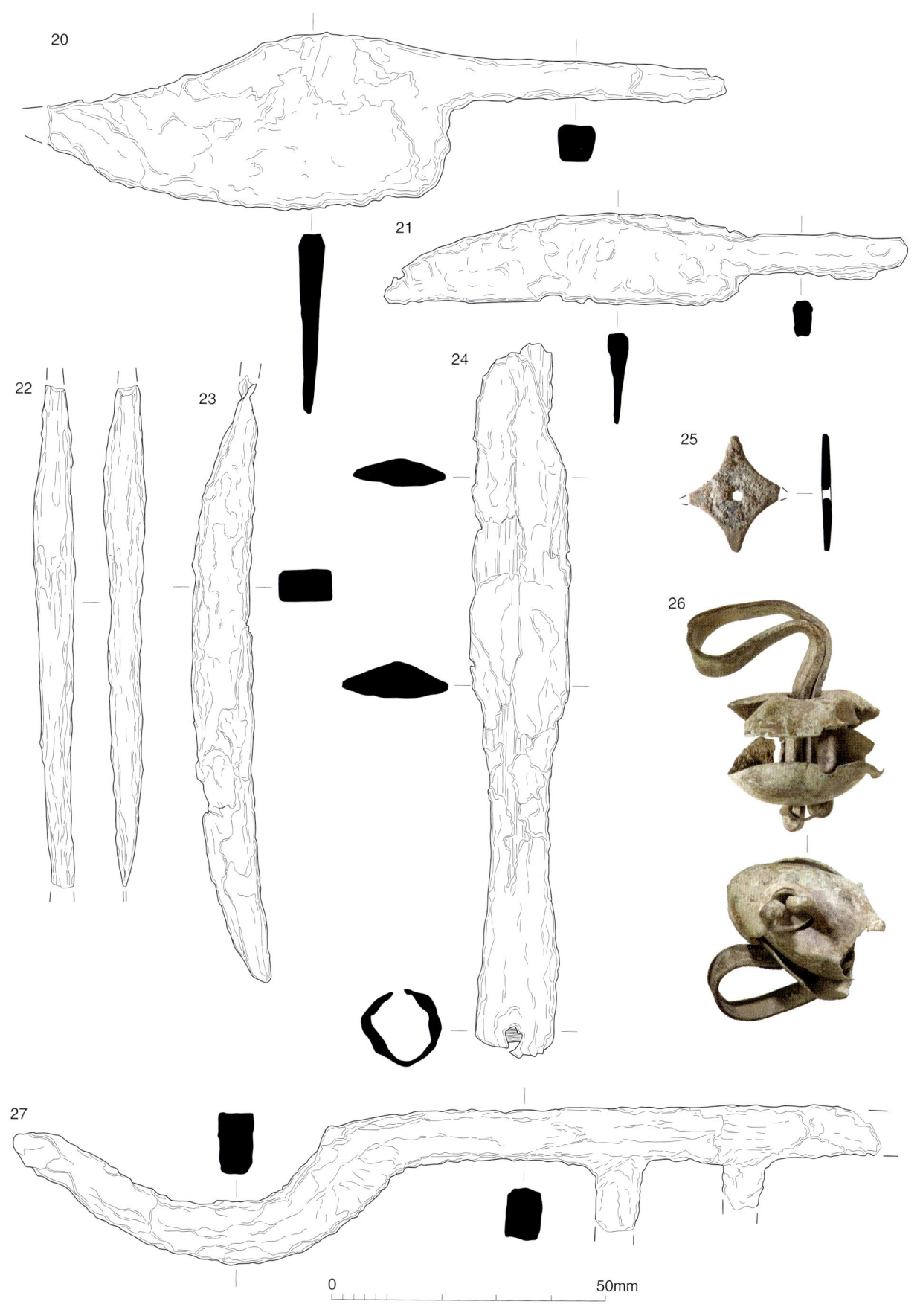

Fig. 3.11 Roman metal objects, nos 20–27

26   Distorted and damaged object, possibly a bell or rattle. The suspension loop is formed from a folded wire, the ends of which are curled outwards. The 'bell' consists of two hemispheres of sheet metal perforated at the apex for suspension but otherwise plain. Wt 10.3g; L 42mm; Diam. 32.6mm. Period 3a ditch 207 (5324) (fill 5325). Ra. 526.

Objects of uncertain function – Iron (Fig. 3.11)

27   Fragmentary object consisting of straight, bar-like shaft object, one end formed into a crescent-like terminal and the other incomplete, but with two projections (also broken). L (surviving) 162mm; W (curved terminal) 30mm; W (shaft) 9.1mm; Th. 17.9mm. Period 3b pit 9969 (fill 9968) between ditches 203 and 206, to the east of ditch 251. Ra. 1043.

Roman coins
by E.R. McSloy

Twenty-four coins of the Roman period were recovered (see Table 3.12), including two (nos 13 and 19) from evaluation trench 19. The large majority of the coins (20) were metal-detector finds, with eight coming from subsoil deposits.

Earliest in the group is a Claudian *as* copy, of a type circulating in the period *c.* AD 48–54 (Reece 1985; Kenyon 1985, 23). There are worn two *sestertii* of the late 2nd century (Reece's issue periods 9–10), four radiates of the later 3rd century (Reece periods 13/14) and the remainder are of the 4th century (Reece's periods 16–19). The 4th-century group includes ten Valentinianic issues (Reece's issue period 19), a number of which were redeposited within Saxon period deposits and one (no. 15) which was perforated for suspension.

In the scarcity of coins from the period before *c.* AD 260, this group compares with the majority from Romano-British rural sites, and the increasing number from after this period is also typical. The elevated numbers of late 3rd-century radiates and *nummi* of the period AD 330–48 correspond to 'spikes' in coin supply/loss which are apparent across lowland rural Britain (Davies and Gregory 1991, 75). Valentinianic issues follow a further, albeit a less-pronounced spike nationally (Reece 1993). The unusually high numbers of Valentinianic coins (and an absence of later issues) is not easily explicable, their distribution seeming not to be suggestive of a dispersed hoard.

Coin list

Abbreviations used: LRBC = Late Roman Bronze Coinage (Carson *et al.* 1960); RIC = Roman Imperial Coinage (10 vols 1926–94); illeg. = illegible; Obv. = obverse; Rev. = reverse

1   *As* copy Claudius I. AD 41–54. Diam. 24.8mm. Rev. SC (Minerva advancing right with spear and shield). Ra. 513. Period 3b ditch 244 (8803; fill 8805).

2   *Sestertius* Commodus. AD 177–92 (*c.* AD 190). Rev. SC (Libertas standing left with sceptre and pileus). Very worn (prob. RIC III, 562). Ra. 578. Subsoil 5001.

3   *Sestertius* Didius Julianus. AD 193. Rev. SC (Fortuna with cornucopia and globe/rudder). Very worn and details unclear. Ra. 512. Period 3b ditch 244 (8803; fill 8805).

4   *Radiate* ?Gallienus AD 253–68. Rev. soldier with globe and spear. Details unclear. Ra. 811. Period 3c ditch 6486 (fill 6484).

5   *Radiate* Tetricus I. AD 270–73. Rev. PAX AVG (Pax). Details unclear. Ra. 544. Period 3b ditch 7634 (fill 7635), between ditches 225 and 226.

6   *Radiate* (copy?). AD 270–90. Diam. 19–20mm. Details unclear. Ra. 53. Period 2a pit 16676 (fill 16678) (see Vol 1).

7   *Radiate* (copy?). AD 270–90. Diam. 19mm. Details unclear. Ra. 64. Subsoil 15001.

8   *Nummus* (AE2) Crispus. AD 318–24. Rev. VIRTVS EXERCIT (trophy with captives). Trier mint (prob. RIC VII, 261). Ra. 634. Period 2c pit 5490 (fill 5491).

9   *Nummus* (AE3) Constantine II. AD 330–35. Rev. GLORIA EXERCITVS (2 standards). Lyons mint (LRBC 203). Ra. 808. Period 3c ditch 259 (6988; fill 6989).

10   *Nummus* (AE3) Constantius II. AD 335–37. Rev. GLORIA EXERCITVS (1 standard). Mint mark illeg. Ra. 566. Unphased coombe deposit 5398.

11   *Nummus* (AE3) Constantius II. AD 335–37. Rev. GLORIA EXERCITVS (1 standard). Mint mark illeg. Ra. 536. Subsoil 5001.

12   *Nummus* (AE3) Constantius II. AD 354–61. Rev. FEL TEMP REPARATIO (soldier spearing fallen horseman). Mint mark illeg. Ra. 527. Subsoil 5002.

13   *Nummus* (AE3) Valentinian I. AD 364–78. Rev. GLORIA ROMANORVM (emperor with captive). Arles mint; (RIC IX prob. Arelate 7 or 16, p. 59). Ra. 1. Evaluation trench 19 ditch 1908 (fill 1911). *Identification by Andrej Čelovský.*

Table 3.12 Coins summary

Reece issue period*	Date range (AD)	No. of coins
2/3	41–54/68	1
9	180–192	1
10	193–222	1
13	260–275	1
13/14	260/275–296	3
16	317–330	1
17	330–348	3
18	348–364	1
19	364–378	10
15–21	C4	2
Total		**24**

* Reece 1993

14 *Nummus* (AE3) Valentinian I. AD 364–67. Rev. GLORIA ROMANORVM (emperor with captive and standard). Arles mint (LRBC 484). Ra. 579. Subsoil 5001.

15 *Nummus* (AE3) Valentinian I or Valens. AD 364–78. Rev. SECURITAS REIPUBLICAE (Victory with wreath advancing left). Siscia mint (LRBC 1433/4). Perforated for suspension and well worn on obv. Ra. 557. Period 3a–3d ditch 251 (5494; fill 5551).

16 *Nummus* (AE3) Valens. AD 364–67. Rev. GLORIA ROMANORVM (emperor with captive). Lyon mint (prob. LRBC 282). Ra. 519. Period 3a–3d ditch 262 (5460; fill 5461). Lost.

17 *Nummus* (AE3) Valens. AD 375–78. Rev. GLORIA ROMANORVM (emperor with captive). Arles mint (LRBC 530). Ra. 571. Period 4a SFB structure 39 (7452; fill 7454).

18 *Nummus* (AE4 minim. copy). Very worn/illeg. Ra. 552. Period 4a/b ditch 8092 (fill 8095).

19 *Nummus* (AE3) Gratian. AD 364–78. Rev. GLORIA ROMANORVM (emperor with standard and shield). Arles mint (RIC IX Arelate 15, type x(b), p. 58, 66). Ra. 3. Evaluation trench 19 ditch 1908 (fill 1911). *Identification by Andrej Čelovský.*

20 *Nummus* (AE3) Gratian. AD 367–78. Rev. GLORIA ROMANORVM (emperor with captive and standard). Details unclear. Ra. 565. Unphased coombe deposit 5398.

21 *Nummus* (AE3) House of Valentinian. AD 364–78. Rev. SECURITAS REIPUBLICAE (Victory with wreath advancing left). Details unclear. Ra. 555. Subsoil 5001.

22 *Nummus* (AE3) House of Valentinian. AD 364–78. Rev. GLORIA ROMANORVM (emperor with captive and standard). Details unclear. Ra. 545. Subsoil 5001.

23 *Nummus* (AE3). Very worn/illeg. Ra. 547. Subsoil 5001.

24 *Nummus* (AE4/copy). Diam. 13mm. Very worn/illeg. Ra. 575. Period 4a SFB structure 38 (6844; fill 6846).

Worked stone
by Ruth Shaffrey

The assemblage of worked stone contains jewellery, tools such as whetstones and hammerstones and most importantly, an assemblage of a significant size for the local region of rotary querns and millstones.

The querns and millstones

Four fragments from Roman contexts have pecked and slightly dished grinding surfaces and are probably from saddle querns, though none are complete. They comprise a substantial piece of Culham Greensand from ditch 128 (Ra. 34) and fragments of sandstone examples (ditches 16667 (Ra. 45), 5123 (Ra. 530) and 227 (Ra. 795)). Two further slabs also have slightly concave grinding surfaces but both have been worn very smooth and are slightly polished (both from ditch 260). It is possible that they are just well used and were due a reworking before being discarded, but maybe they served a different function, resulting in different wear patterns. A fragment of ferruginous sandstone, probably from the Culham Greensand, has slightly worn faces and may also be from a quern (ditch 248, fill 6467, not catalogued) as may a fragment of Old Red Sandstone (ditch 251, fill 8330, not catalogued), but both fragments are too small for the type of quern to be certainly identified.

A total of 43 fragments represent 14 rotary querns. A single fragment of puddingstone (6079, fill of pit 6078, cut by Saxon ditches) and 31 fragments of lava (assumed to be from two querns: fill 15580 of undated pit 15579 between ditches 126 and 193, and fill 8408 of ditch 206, cut 8406) are identified as rotary querns based on material alone (not catalogued). Six other fragments are unarguably from rotary querns or millstones and although they are too small for diameter to be ascertained, experience would suggest that five of these, all of Old Red Sandstone, are from rotary querns (Ras 1077, 1049, 46 and two fragments from 16664). The sixth example is of Millstone Grit and could conceivably be from either a rotary quern or millstone (fill 15861 of pit 15860 which cuts ditch 190, Ra. 28). There are also five items that can be positively identified as rotary querns based on their measurable diameters (Ras 633, 68, 31, 785 and a fragment from 16664). The rotary querns are of standard dimensions for the south of England – between 35 and 48cm diameter – somewhat larger than in other regions at the same time. The Old Red Sandstone querns are of flat-topped type and heavily worn so that there is rotational wear on the grinding surface (Ras. 633 and 68). The only diagnostic lava quern fragment is from a typical kerbed quern (Ra. 31).

The remaining four fragments are from mechanically operated millstones. Two were recovered from period 3b features: one from a fill of oven/corndrier 46 (8164, fill 8245) and the other from the fill of pit 15860 (15861) which cuts ditch 190. The first of these (Ra. 900) measures in excess of 50cm diameter but the eye and circumference do not survive, so it is clearly of millstone size. The latter (Ra. 28, Fig. 3.12, 1) measures over 60cm in diameter and has a fully perforating rynd chase.

Two further millstone fragments were found in period 3c ditches 238 (8498, fill 8497) and 259 (6516). The former of these (Ra. 904, Fig. 3.12, 2) measures at least 52cm (and probably much more) and the latter, three fragments which do not adjoin but appear to be from the same stone, measures in excess of 66cm diameter (Ra. 785, not illustrated).

Catalogue of querns and millstones

Quern fragment, probably saddle quern. Sandstone/sarsen. Measures >170 wide x >120 long x 63mm thick. Roughly worked flat base and edges. Grinding surface is pecked and now a little worn but is concave in one direction. Not enough survives of the other direction to define

Fig. 3.12 Worked stone, nos 1–2

the curvature. Wt 1738g. Ra. 45. Period 3c ditch 16667, fill 16668.

Quern fragment. Culham Greensand. Measures 57mm thick. No edges or centre so not possible to be sure but looks most like a saddle quern fragment. Grinding surface is pecked and slightly concave, other face is rounded and roughly worked. Wt 850g. Ra. 34. Period 3c ditch 128 (16090), fill 16092.

Quern fragment, probably saddle quern. Cream quartzitic sandstone (sarsen-like). Measures 52mm thick. Fragment with flat pecked grinding surface and roughly shaped rounded edge and base. Wt 827g. Ra. 530. Period 3c ditch 5123, fill 5126.

Possible saddle quern fragment. Quartzitic sandstone. Measures 48mm thick. natural rough base. No original edges. One face is pecked and worn slightly concave. Seems most likely to have been a saddle quern. Wt 520g. Ra. 795. Period 3b ditch 227 (6715), fill 6716.

Polishing/processing slab. Quartzitic sandstone. Measures 1–3 x 100 x 90mm. Irregular stone with one flat, very slightly concave grinding surface that has been worn incredibly smooth, slightly polished. Wt 1506g. Period 3c ditch 260 (5378), fill 5379.

Polishing/processing slab. Quartzitic sandstone. Measures 160 x 130 x 65mm. Irregular stone with one slightly concave grinding surface that has been worn incredibly smooth, slightly polished. Wt 2288g. Period 3c ditch 260 (5378), fill 5379.

Upper rotary quern fragment. Old Red Sandstone Quartz Conglomerate, Forest of Dean. Measures approximately 420mm diameter x 38mm thick. Flat-topped type, pecked all over with a very slight lip around the edge of the grinding surface. The grinding surface also has some rotational wear. The eye does not survive. Ra. 633. Unphased ditch 5420, fill 5421. Unphased, but Roman object.

Upper rotary quern fragment. Old Red Sandstone, Forest of Dean. Measures max. 54mm thickness on edge x 400mm diameter. Flat-topped type, with pecked flat top, pecked straight edges and pecked, and grinding surface worn into concentric grooves. Part of shallow basin-shaped hopper approximately 5mm deep. No evidence for handle on this fragment. Wt 2561g. Ra. 68. Unphased coombe deposit 5398=17162, layer in area of cremation burials 7912 and 5939/5940.

Upper rotary quern fragment. Lava. Measures approximately 350mm diameter x 48mm thick on kerb. Rim fragment only. Quite worn but some diagonal tooling survives across the top, including on the kerb which measures 42mm wide x approximately 5mm high. Wt 465g. Ra. 31. Unphased posthole 5016, fill 5017. Unphased, but Roman object.

Upper rotary quern fragment. Old Red Sandstone. Measurements are indeterminate. Small edge fragment with flat grinding surface and steeply sloped upper surface. Pecked all over but worn quite smooth. Wt 134g. Ra. 1077. Unstratified, but Roman object

Rotary quern fragment. Millstone Grit. Measures 38mm thick. Small piece with deep spaced pecking on flat grinding surface in circular pattern and slightly worn. Edges rounded into other face and both worked. Not enough circumference survives to determine diameter and there is no centre. Wt 273g. Ra. 29. Period 3b pit 15860, fill 15861, cuts ditch 190.

Upper rotary quern fragment. Old Red Sandstone. Measures approximately 450mm diameter x 36–45mm thick. Concentric grooves on the grinding surface with straight vertical edges but worn smooth suggesting some reuse for sharpening. The upper face is roughly worked but has also been used as it is worn in some areas towards the circumference. Wt 1203g. Ra. 785. Period 3c second, later, disuse phase of ditch 259 (6516), fill 6517.

Upper rotary quern fragment. Old Red Sandstone Quartz Conglomerate, Forest of Dean. Measures 46mm thick x indeterminate diameter. Small fragment – pecked all over, roughly parallel faces but slightly angled. Centre does not survive. Edges are straight and vertical. Wt 762g. Ra. 1049. Period 3c ditch 203 (7852), fill 7853.

Rotary quern fragment. Old Red Sandstone. Edge fragment with straight vertical edges. Probably from upper stone as pecked upper face and very slightly concave other face is worn smooth. Wt 225g. Period 3c ditch 16662, fill 16664.

Rotary quern fragment. Old Red Sandstone. Measurements are indeterminate. More worn fragment of probable quern with one pecked but worn face. Wt 254g. Period 3c ditch 16662, fill 16664.

Upper rotary quern fragment. Old Red Sandstone. Measures approximately 480mm diameter x 48mm thick on edge. Edge fragment of flat-topped type. Pecked straight edges and flat top and concave grinding surface worn smooth. No centre. Wt 428g. Period 3c ditch 16662, fill 16664.

Lower rotary quern fragment. Old Red Sandstone. Measures 112mm thick. Edge fragment of thick quern – not from a millstone as small part of circumference that survives is too curved. The edges and base are roughly worked and the grinding surface is pecked and slightly sloped/convex. Burnt. Wt 886g. Ra. 46. Period 3c ditch 16667, fill 16668.

Upper millstone fragment (Fig. 3.12, 1). Grit. Approximately 20% upper stone – pecked all over but with rotational wear on grinding surface. Measures approximately 840mm diameter, (600mm survives, no eye) x 29–42mm thick. Small part of rynd chase (cutting right through stone) is apparent towards the middle, but the eye does not survive. Edges are straight, lean in slightly and a little smoothed. Slightly angled disc. Ra. 28. Period 3b pit 15860, fill 15861, cuts ditch 190.

Millstone fragment (Fig. 3.12, 2). Millstone Grit. Measures 140mm thick x indeterminate diameter but >520mm based on wear grooves and probably much more. Fragment of massive millstone. Deep spaced pecking on one flat face. No edges. Centre survives but must be part of curved dovetail. Thick iron deposits on the grinding surface but they are also on the edge so they relate to post-depositional accumulation rather than function. The grinding surface is flat with rotational wear and is worn fairly smooth across most of it. Ra. 904. Period 3c possible boundary ditch 238 (8498), fill 8497.

Upper millstone fragments. Old Red Sandstone or Millstone Grit. Measures >660mm diameter x 46mm maximum thickness. Three fragments, not adjoining but almost certainly from same millstone. There are pronounced, deliberate concentric grooves. The eye does not survive. The edges are straight and vertical. Ra. 785. Period 3c disuse phase of ditch 259 (6516), fill 6517.

Probable millstone fragment. Old Red Sandstone. Measures >500mm diameter x 45mm thick. Flat faces, disc type. No edges or centre, but circular grooves are visible. These suggest a diameter in excess of 500mm. Deep spaced pecking on the other side. Burnt – reddened and blackened. Ra. 900. Period 3b corndrier/oven 46 (8164), fill 8245. Possibly used in structure or fallen in later.

Other worked stone

Roman features produced a small quantity of other types of worked stone. Four of these are tools: a hammerstone with percussion damage and some areas of rubbing (posthole 5071; Ra. 501) and another cobble probably used as a grinding stone or rubber (fill 15158 of ditch 119). A slab has been used as an *ad hoc* hone (fill 6989 of ditch 259) while a square-sectioned whetstone is of more typical form (fill 5335 of ditch 242 (5333)).

Personal belongings are few in number. Two small spheres of flint were probably used recreationally (fill 5379 of ditch 260 (5378); fill 5827 of 5828 (north of ditch 258)). A single piece of shale armlet is the only piece of stone jewellery (Ra. 802; ditch 247, fill 6876). It is of unusual form with an oval section and spiral grooving twisting around the armlet.

Catalogue of other worked stone

Hammerstone. Quartzitic sandstone. Long cobble, rounded/almost pointed at one end and flat/rounded at the other. Pointed end has some percussion damage and flat end some rubbing. Sub-square section. Wt 382g. Ra. 501. Period 3a posthole 5071, fill 5070.

Processor/rubber. Reddish-brown sandstone. Measures >56mm long x 78 x 55mm. Cobble with one flat face, some evidence for wear around the edges of this face so possibly used as a grinding stone/rubber. Wt 368g. Period 3c ditch 119 (15156), fill 15158.

Slab hone. Old Red Sandstone, Brownstones. Thick slab. Both faces worn smooth and slightly concave from sharpening. No grooves. No original edges. Wt 534g. Period 3c ditch 259 (6988), fill 6989.

Whetstone. Fine grained quartzitic sandstone. Measures 51 x >60 long x 41mm. Central fragment of roughly square-sectioned whetstone, very flat and smooth on one face and worn on an additional two faces. Wt 241g. Ra. 605. Period 3c ditch 242 (5333), fill 5335.

Sphere. Flint. Measures 35mm diameter. Almost perfectly spherical stone, slightly damaged on one side. Wt 57g. Period 3c ditch 260 (5378), fill 5379.

Sphere. Ironstone. Measures 34mm diameter. Wt 53g. Ra. 708. Period 3c ditch 5828, fill 5827 (north of ditch 258).

Armlet. Shale. Measures 60mm internal diameter x 14mm thick. Unusual armlet with oval section and spiral groove running around the armlet about 20mm apart. Wt 5g. Ra. 802. Period 3b ditch 247 (6874), fill 6876.

Discussion

Stone sources
Although we have a broad understanding of the chronology of quern material choices in the Upper Thames Valley, almost nothing is known for the region immediately around Thame. In the wider region Culham Greensand was used for saddle querns during the Early Iron Age and disappears from use after the Roman conquest, for example at Didcot (Shaffrey 2023). At Thame, as elsewhere, there is no evidence that it was used for rotary querns, but there are two saddle quern fragments of Culham Greensand from Roman contexts suggesting either considerable residuality, the reuse of much earlier objects, or its continued use for saddle querns only.

Mayen lava querns occur only in a fragmentary state at Thame in broadly Roman and Early Roman contexts. This is typical of the wider north Oxfordshire/West Buckinghamshire region, where lava querns are not common and only survive as very small, non-diagnostic fragments at sites in Aylesbury and Bicester (Holgate and Mann 2007; Shaffrey 2019; Shaffrey in prep). Meanwhile, rotary querns of Old Red Sandstone and Millstone Grit occur at Thame in period 3b and 3c contexts only. These are the most common quern materials to be found on Roman sites in the area, including in Aylesbury but also on the Hardwick to Marsh Gibbon pipeline (Shaffrey 2019; 2008a).

The evidence from Thame indicates a transition away from the exploitation of local stones such as the Culham Greensand for saddle querns to the use of imported stones for rotary querns and millstones during the Roman period, but with an emphasis still on the use of native rock, rather than the lava. The reason for a preference of Millstone Grit and Old Red Sandstone over lava is not clear at present. It is possible that lava querns were not easily available away from the larger urban and military centres but it might also represent an element of choice and a preference for the gritty stones and sandstones that were so similar to rocks exploited by previous generations for saddle querns.

Grain processing
The assemblage at Thame is important, not only for the evidence it provides about the manufacture and supply of the querns themselves, but also because it provides key evidence for the organisation of grain processing on the site. The millstones in particular suggest that this processing was at an intensive and centralised level. Rotary querns were recovered throughout period 3 indicating that crop processing occurred during the Late Iron Age and Roman periods. Millstones are found only in Roman period 3b and 3c contexts, which is in keeping with current knowledge indicating that millstones predominantly come from 2nd-century AD contexts and later (Shaffrey 2015) and that processing was generally only centralised and intensified from this time onwards.

The subject of how mills were powered during the Roman period is problematic, because so few water or animal-powered mills have been excavated. Indeed, no mill structures were identified during excavation at Thame, but water-power was available less than 500m away on the River Thame and possibly the Cuttle Brook and was probably the source of power for the millstones here.

It is increasingly clear that a key organisational tactic in the agricultural economy of southern England was the centralisation of grain processing. The production of flour continued at a low level at the majority of occupation sites, as evidenced by the almost ubiquitous recovery of small numbers of quern fragments from rural farmsteads and other small domestic sites. However, a decision to gather in grain at central points and process it there, for example within a villa estate such as Frocester with its 19 millstones (Price 2000; 2010; Shaffrey 2018), a roadside settlement (Shaffrey 2017a) or a small town (Buckley 2001) was clearly common. This centralised processing could have manifested itself for a number of reasons. Extra grain might have been processed at a roadside settlement to produce surplus flour for baking and malt for brewing in order to feed the travellers passing through and to generate an income (Shaffrey 2017a). Equally, centralisation might occur within a villa estate to allow people time to work in other industries, to meet government taxation requirements or to provide the residents of nearby towns with resources not easily produced within that town (Shaffrey 2018).

The millstones found at Thame are the first in the surrounding region to be recovered. The nearest examples are from Yarnton (Roe 2011, 446), Walton Court, Aylesbury (Farley et al. 1981, 73), Bicester

Park, Bicester (Chapman 2008, 143), Hardwick to Marsh Gibbon (Shaffrey 2008a), and Aston Clinton (Chapman 2013, 11). They provide information about what had previously been a blank space on the map, and they indicate that the settlement at Thame was a key point in the agricultural economy of the region. The range of tools represented – both querns and millstones as well as grinding slabs/saddle querns – suggest that a range of activities were taking place. The rotary querns may represent continued grinding at a domestic household level, whilst the millstones are part of a higher level of intensified processing. However, known watermills always produce querns as well as millstones (Shaffrey 2008b; Spain and Riddler 2010) suggesting that multiple stages of processing occurred, even at mills. Possibly the querns were in use when there was insufficient power to operate the millstones, when water levels were low for example, or they were used either for an extra stage of processing or for processing a different foodstuff altogether (such as legumes). What is also clear is that, at least here at Thame, the distinction was not related to the production of malt. The charred plant remains from Roman features contained only a few sprouted grains and these were not considered enough to have been clear evidence for malting, as seen in the Saxon assemblage (Wyles, this chapter). The querns and millstones at Thame were used to produce flour, and almost certainly a surplus of it.

Fired clay
by Cynthia Poole

A large assemblage of fired clay, which amounted to a total of 1898 fragments weighing 51,359g, was collected during excavation from *in situ* structures and from secondary deposits in features phased to the Roman period. Methods are detailed in the Appendix. The fired clay comprises structural material related to the construction of ovens, corndriers, furnaces or hearths and portable furniture used in conjunction with such structures. The majority of the fired clay found in secondary deposits came from ditch and pit fills, with lesser quantities in postholes, a well and layers, but a significant proportion (42% by weight) was found in primary contexts of ovens and corndriers. Much of the fired clay cannot be intrinsically dated, especially structural material, which changes little in character from the prehistoric to medieval period. Portable oven furniture is more period specific and much of the material in this category is typically Late Iron Age–Early Roman in character. The condition of the material is very variable with everything from tiny fragments to complete or near-complete objects represented. The mean fragment weight (MFW) of 27g, which includes sieved material, is well above average for fired clay and rises to 50g if sieved material is excluded.

Fabrics

The fabrics divide into two main groups of fine clay (fabric group A), often silty or micaceous, and sandy clay (fabric group Q). Fabric Q, used for all the wattle-supported structure from corndrier 45 (6689; Fig. 2.16), exhibited some variations in texture, with some groups recorded as containing variously fine–coarse quartz, mica or glauconite as well as coarser stone grits of flint, ironstone and sandstone. The variations observed in the fabric from what must have been a single structure suggest these reflect variability within the clay source and the variations noted in the archive record are of little significance. Fabric A formed more than half of the assemblage at this period (60%) and a high proportion within this category was chaff-tempered fabric AV, used exclusively for portable furniture, especially kiln plates. Fabric Q was used for much of the structural fired clay, and to a lesser extent for portable furniture, when it frequently included a chaff or finer organic components.

Structural fired clay

The fired clay identified as structural (1464 fragments, 28,907g) was based on intrinsic characteristics such as wattle impressions or its direct association with pyrotechnic structures, which account for the bulk of this (85% count, 58% wt) recovered from five corndriers and an oven. The fabrics used divide roughly equally between fabric groups A and Q.

Much of the material with a single moulded surface is likely to represent oven wall or floor structure or lining. In the absence of diagnostic features, it is not possible to be certain of such an interpretation in all cases but the occurrence of such material either as *in situ* structure or in association with *in situ* structures provides evidence to support such a conclusion. The fragments are usually fired black, grey, yellowish-brown or red at the surface grading to lighter shades of red, orange and yellow in the less fired or heated clay in the core. The range of thickness is predominantly 5–35mm but a few thicker pieces of 47 and 60–95mm were identified as oven or hearth base floor. The thinner example formed the floor of corndrier 45 (6689; layer 6674), whilst the thicker was in fact a block of natural sandy sediment (9476, fill of possible hearth 9477, south of ditch 234) originally burnt *in situ* and found in an irregular hollow, where it is uncertain whether this formed as a result of burning on the base of the hollow or was dumped from elsewhere. Both examples had a flat surface, which was heavily fired and blackened, with the underlying sediment typically grading though grey or brown heated sediment to the unfired yellowish-brown or orange unfired base. Thin fragments of red or black fired surface are likely to have sheared off a largely unfired clay backing structure of walls or floor. The very heavily fired and blackened surfaces usually derive from the wall and floor of the flue or main firing chamber.

A single small fragment from ditch 238 (8498, fill 8496) dating to the Late Roman period was 10mm thick and had a flat smooth undulating surface with reddish patina, below which was a vesicular cindered margin 5mm thick, with a sharp boundary to the buff interior. Even though it was not fully vitrified, this may have formed the lining of a furnace wall or smithing hearth. It is the only piece to indicate industrial activity, but it is possible more furnace structure forms part of the slag assemblage.

Wattle-supported structure

Wattle-supported structure was confined to a single structure, a T-shaped corndrier 45 (cut 6627), apart from a scatter of fragments in a few ditches. The fired clay fragments comprised well-fired blocks ranging from 10–48mm thick with a flat outer surface of variable finish from smooth and flat to quite rough and irregular with finger marks across the surface (Fig. 3.13, 1–2). Some areas of surface had dense chaff impressions and some pieces had an additional render layer or veneer in a light yellowish-brown sandy clay with fine chalk grit. The wattle sizes ranged from 7 to 25mm in diameter, with the main peak in numbers occurring from 15–18mm. The sizes of the wattles are notably larger than those found in either the preceding Iron Age or succeeding Saxon period, suggesting a longer coppice cycle may have been in practice during the Roman period. No vertical sails were identified, but the angles of the rods in relation to each other suggest they formed an interwoven framework. The small number of wattles identified from other features fall within the same range.

Decorated plate

A large broken slab of clay (Ra. 833) found dumped in the top of ditch 251 (7363) was unusual in that the surface had been decorated with impressed circles (Fig. 3.14, 3). The slab measured 40–42mm thick and covered an area of *c.* 0.7m square prior to lifting. It was clear that the structure was in a very fragile condition and therefore only one of the lifted blocks (group 3) was examined. This showed that it formed a large slab of fired clay with a smooth well-finished surface, decorated with small, impressed circles *c.* 50mm diameter, fairly randomly arranged, though some linear alignments are present and some adjacent touching circles occur, though none actually overlap. The decorated surface is lightly fired or burnt grey over a red or orange-red core which grades into the dark grey fired base surface; the grey firing extends to a depth of 12mm before starting to turn red in the core. The surface has a tendency to crack and shear off at a depth of *c.* 3–8mm, suggesting an interface has formed between the fired surface and what is in effect an unfired heat-reddened core. The decorated surface is smooth and well finished but faint shallow finger marks from moulding are visible. This block appears to have formed a large prefabricated plate. Firing on the base suggests it was used as a suspended floor or plate, possibly for use as a drying floor.

Decorated surfaces on fired clay structures are rare, though impressed circles are one of the most common patterns. These have been most commonly found on hearth surfaces and the closest parallels occurred in Iron Age houses at Danebury, Hampshire (Cunliffe and Poole 1991, 57) and Glastonbury, Somerset (Bulleid and Gray 1911, 56, plate VIII). Other examples are known from France including a 6th-century BC example from Castelnau (Roux 2006) and a late 2nd-century BC example from Castellan (Marty 2002), which include additional geometric motifs, and a medieval example with two concentric circles from Le Yaudet, Côtes d'Armor (Cunliffe and Galliou 2007, 115–16). Oven plates or covers decorated with deep fingertip depressions and impressed rectangles or squares have been found in Iron Age contexts at Danebury (Cunliffe and Poole 1991, 149–50) and elsewhere such as Marnhull, Dorset (Williams 1950). A closer parallel comes from a Late Iron Age enclosure ditch at the French site of Trégueux, Côtes d'Armor, which produced not only hearth fragments decorated with circles but also a fragment of a wattle-supported structure, possibly from a drying floor, with an impressed circle (Poole 2012). The occurrence of a decorated plate within Roman deposits at Thame is unusual. It is unlikely to indicate curation of a structure from an earlier period and whilst it could indicate the

Fig. 3.13 Fired clay from wattle-supported structure, nos 1–2

Fig. 3.14 Fired clay decorated plate in situ*, no. 3 (scale 0.4m)*

continuation of earlier traditions in decorating hearths, the concept to decorate the surface need not have recourse to predecessors. It may have originated with the artisan constructing the plate. The inspiration might have arisen from drying pots on a drying floor prior to firing in a kiln.

Portable furniture

This category accounted for 281 fragments (21,623g) of the Late Iron Age–Roman fired clay. The most common forms of portable furniture were oven plates and triangular perforated bricks. A small number of other forms included a firebar, a hand-squeezed lump, pyramidal and rectangular blocks or pedestals and a cylindrical pedestal. Many of the smaller incomplete fragments could not be assigned with certainty to a particular form, but most are likely to derive from the most common varieties of plates and triangular bricks. Most of the portable oven furniture was found discarded in ditches, less commonly pits and rarely postholes. Only a small number were directly associated with ovens.

Triangular perforated bricks
The triangular perforated bricks, totalling eight in number, were confined to Late Iron Age–Early Roman deposits. They are of similar character to those found in the preceding Iron Age period (see Poole, Volume 1). Most examples are fragmentary but one complete brick found in ditch 206 (intervention 5168) measured 75mm thick and the side 190–195mm long (Fig. 3.17, 8). The perforations were oval and tapered ranging in size between 14–17mm x 16–25mm and unusually were encircled by a halo of surplus clay at the surface. One other had an estimated thickness of 80mm and perforations measuring

Fig. 3.15 Fired clay, complete disc in situ, no. 4 (scale 0.3m)

18–19mm wide. Another substantial fragment (8103) measured 94mm thick with an estimated length of 180mm. This had a saddled corner with part of a groove surviving over the exterior. The perforations were on the small side at 8–12mm diameter and again one had a halo of surplus clay ringing its end.

One partial fragment (in unstratified curvilinear ditch 7761) consisting of a corner and two sides with just a hint of the third side came from a very substantial thick example measuring 121mm thick and with a height of about 175mm (sides probably *c.* 180–190mm long) (Fig. 3.17, 9). The triangular surface is rough as though something has been pressed into it, though smoothed areas are present. The edges are roughly moulded with a lot of coarse irregularities including plant impressions and the overall finish is quite crude. The surviving corner is roughly moulded and rounded, pulled out to form a large nib projecting from the triangular face. The apex is broadly hollowed, but not with a distinct finger groove.

As discussed in relation to the Iron Age examples (Poole, Volume 1) evidence increasingly suggests that these objects should be interpreted as oven or hearth furniture rather than loomweights. A common feature of the Roman triangular bricks is the presence of chaff and straw impressions covering the surface or mixed into the fabric: three each were made in fabric AV and QV and two in fabric Q (which both had organic impressions over their surfaces).

Oven plates and discs

These accounted for a large proportion (158 fragments, *c.* 15kg) of the portable furniture. They occur most commonly in Late Iron Age–Early Roman periods, with a notable decline in the Late Roman period 3c when they account for less than 20% by weight (15% fragments, with a MFW 59g) of this category. The quantity in period 3a (53% by weight, 57% count with MFW of 86g) and period 3b (17% of fragments; 21% by weight with a MFW 98g) suggests that the main period of use for these items was the Late Iron Age–Early Roman period and that the material in the Late Roman period may be largely residual.

Circular discs formed only a small element of the group (16 fragments, 237g) being identified in only three instances, except for the fact of a complete disc found in the base of a shallow pit 8842. The broken fragments were made in fabrics AV and QV and were well finished with smooth even surfaces densely coated with chaff impressions. No complete dimensions survived, but thickness was over 25–36mm and one was estimated to have a diameter of 220mm.

The complete disc (Ra. 961; Fig. 3.15, 4) was made in fabric A fired black across the upper half and more lightly fired red across the base with lenses of white clay across the whole plate creating a layer-cake effect. The disc measured 360mm in diameter and 22–23mm thick at the edges increasing to 29mm in the centre. The upper surface was smooth and well finished and the edges smooth and vertical with angular arises. The lower surface was flat and even with a slightly rougher finish than the upper surface.

The plates can be divided into four categories: rectangular, polygonal, curved and flanged rectangular. The majority are straight-sided and rectangular in form, though some show evidence of having slightly bowed curving sides, which could indicate a more oval form or rectangular with the long edges bowed. Some of the rectangular examples tapered slightly to the ends. Two appeared to be polygonal with corners at more than a right angle: one had two straight edges set at an angle of 110°. A significant number have evidence of a flanged edge on the long sides, which appears to reflect the influence of Roman tegulae in their design. Though these could be confused with tegulae, these plates are entirely handmade, the corners are without cutaways, the overall character is that of fired clay, and the patterns of firing and size all indicate these are not crudely made tegulae, but some form of kiln or oven furniture of similar function to the plain plates.

All the plates have smooth surfaces sometimes with evidence of finger marks, and flat perpendicular edges, occasionally knife-trimmed on some flanged examples, rarely curved or bevelled in profile. Overall, the plates are neatly finished. They measured 21–43mm thick. A high proportion of the plain rectangular and polygonal plates were made in chaff-tempered fabrics AV and QV, in contrast to the flanged type which were made predominantly in fabric Q and to a lesser extent A, with no evidence of organic inclusions. The use of chaff found extensively on the oven plates used both as tempering material within the fabric and as a coating to the exterior to prevent the clay sticking to other surfaces during manufacture is particularly common during the Late Iron Age and Roman period and no doubt indicates a ready availability of agricultural by-products.

One near-complete example (Fig. 3.16, 5), found in two parts in pit 7697 ('oven' structure 7419), formed a rectangular plate tapering to both ends. It measured 37–42mm thick, 485mm long and in breadth 180mm across the centre tapering to 160 and 166mm at either end. The ends are poorly fired, possibly having been luted into the supporting structure, and had partly crumbled away. The underside was uniformly fired grey, whilst the top had fired to differently coloured areas: pink-mauve in the centre, grading towards the ends to narrow bands of cerise, orange and finally dark grey at the ends.

The flanged plates (Fig. 3.16, 6–7) were all incomplete: they measured 20–42mm and one complete width of 155mm survived. The maximum surviving length was 155mm. The flanges were usually rectangular in profile, though in some cases they were more triangular in form with a sloping inner edge. The flanges measured 17–27mm wide occasionally tapering to 12mm at the end. The external height of the flange at the edge was 37–66mm, though the internal height was mainly 4–12mm and occasionally up to about 20mm. The example (Ra. 899, Fig. 3.16, 6) with a complete width had a flange on both side edges, but one projecting from the top surface and on the opposite edge projecting from the base. It is uncertain whether this was a standard arrangement or whether most had the flange projecting from the same surface. This plate was found in a figure-of-eight-shaped oven base 8164 (corndrier 46), apparently reused as part of the vaulting over the flue.

The circular discs or plates and polygonal and rectangular plates are a regular component of Late Iron Age and Early Roman fired clay assemblages across the East Midlands from the Thames Valley to Cambridgeshire. They occur both in domestic contexts on settlement sites and associated with pottery production. Although few are found complete, they appear to occur in a variety of sizes: the circular discs and plates from Didcot were estimated to have diameters ranging from 240 to 750mm in diameter (Poole 2023). The thickness from as little as 10–15mm up to 40–50mm (based on multiple sites) also implies a range of sizes were produced. The surface finish often suggests they were fabricated in moulds and other features such as knife trimming and the flanges imply some influence from Roman tile production. Examples of circular discs have been found at Alchester (Booth 2001) from Early Roman contexts and from Watkins Farm (Allen 1990, 53), Farmoor (Lambrick and Robinson 1979, 53–4), Old Shifford (Barclay *et al.* 1995, 138), and Oxford (Biddulph 2005b), where they are all associated with the Roman period. Rectangular plates were associated with pottery production at Didcot (Poole 2023). A circular plate from Water End East, Bedfordshire (Poole 2007a, 274) measured 355mm in diameter and 23–43mm thick was found in an early to mid 2nd-century AD kiln, where it was associated with firebars and a portable pedestal (Poole 2007b, 112–14).

Fig. 3.16 Fired clay, nos 5–7

Miscellaneous furniture

Pedestal

A cylindrical pedestal with a splayed foot (ditch 206, context 5323) was a very well-made and finished object with a splayed smooth flat base tapering to a cylindrical stem with very neatly moulded smooth even sides (Fig. 3.17, 10). It has broken across the point at which two perforations cross piercing the stem horizontally through the long and short axis of the object. A slight lip of clay formed around one end of the perforation through the short axis. The perforations measure 6–9mm wide tapering to the centre. The complete pedestal could originally have been conical or biconical. It measures

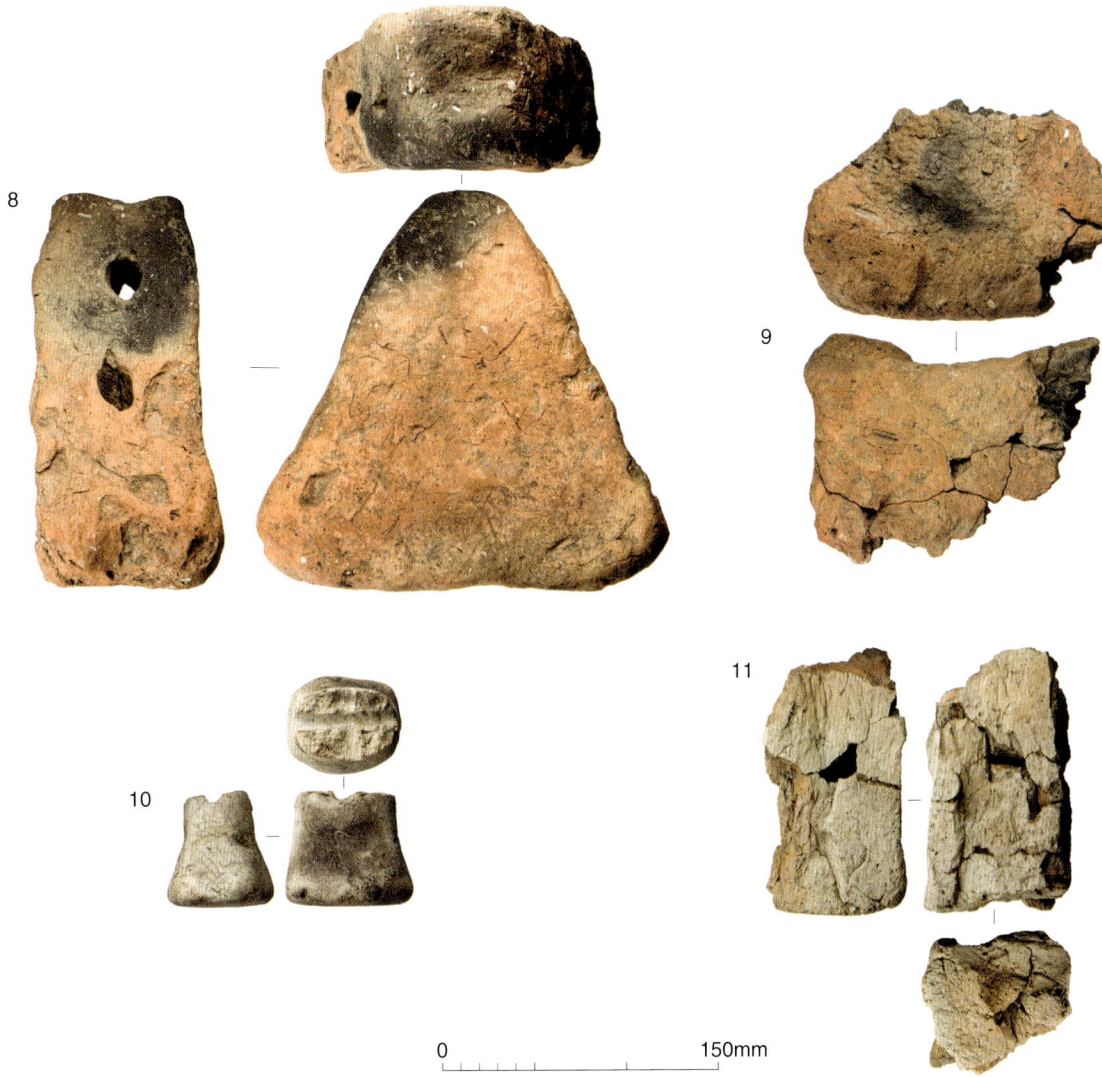

Fig. 3.17 Fired clay, nos 8–11

37–55mm thick, 53–66mm in breadth and is over 58mm high. Its full height may have been *c.* 116mm, if the perforations occurred across a central point. It was made in a grey, fine sandy micaceous clay, black speckled possibly from glauconite and containing occasional quartz sand. Very fine voids are also visible in the fabric probably resulting from fine organic inclusions.

Two objects appear to have a truncated pyramidal form. One (fill 5641 of 5870, ditch 249) appears to be a variant of the standard Iron Age triangular perforated brick forming the central section of a tapered pyramidal block. Both top and bottom are missing but part of one side and one face survives joined by a well-rounded angle. The side is pierced by a perforation *c.* 16mm in diameter. The block measures 95mm wide by *c.* 90mm thick at the perforation widening to one end to over 105mm. It appears to be a truncated pyramidal form tapering to the top and widening to the base. This may be similar to a portable tapered block pedestal measuring 150mm square at the base found in an early–mid 2nd-century kiln at Water End East, Bedfordshire (Poole 2007a, 273–5).

The second takes the form of a tapering square-sectioned block (fill 7585 of 7579, ditch 202) with smooth, well-finished surfaces joined by rounded angles. The main block forms the base or end with two corners surviving and parts of all four side faces as well as the base surface. The block measures 64mm square and over 48mm long. It is widest at the end tapering to the broken end, suggesting this is most likely some sort of pedestal, as although the size is also compatible with firebars, but these normally taper to the ends, unless it was of a form that tapered to one end only.

Firebar

Rectangular firebars are represented by four fragmentary

examples, one from period 3a and the remainder from period 3b. The best-preserved example (Fig. 3.17, 11) formed the square end of rectangular firebar tapering to the ends, very roughly moulded with flat and concave irregular undulating surfaces, but well smoothed, and fired pale grey. It measured 60–75mm thick by over 70mm wide and over 125mm long. The three other examples are all less complete, forming a single corner or edge fragments 50mm (or more) thick, and may be thick plates or rectangular blocks ('Belgic bricks') rather than fire bars.

Hand-squeezed lump
This oblong roughly cylindrical lump of clay found in period 3c Late Roman ditch 241 (cut 6872, fill 6873) had been roughly squeezed to shape, possibly made by rolling up a slab of clay and squeezing the layers together. It is near complete apart from minor damage to one side. It was made in fabric A and had scattered monocot stem/leaf impressions over the surface. It measured 31–35mm thick by 30–46mm wide and 86mm long. Hand-squeezed lumps are more commonly known from salt-working sites but may be associated with any pyrotechnic activity where an *ad hoc* accessory was required to supply an immediate need.

Perforated plaque
A thin lenticular slab of fired clay (12g) had smooth flat moulded surfaces pierced by a small cylindrical perforation 8mm in diameter. It came from period 3a, Late Iron Age/Early Romano-British ditch 6921 (fill 6927; not shown – cut by SFB structure 38). The surface is lightly burnt grey with a barely perceptible thin lamina of red below and the same occurs on the surface of the perforation. The underside is flat but slightly rougher than the top with diffuse organic impressions and slightly reddened but without any grey burnt effect. It measures 7–15mm thick and over 35mm long and was made in a light yellowish-brown fine sandy micaceous clay with organic inclusions.

Structures

The fired clay found in ovens or corndriers is summarised in relation to the structures:

Corndrier 26 (7798), fill 8264 (period 3ciii, Late Roman) (Fig. 2.17): 16 small fragments (14g) of fired clay from a sieved sample, amorphous or with a single moulded surface: these are typical 'rake-out' fragments of lining dislodged in the cinders.

Corndrier 24 (8986), fills 8985, 9015, 9017 (period 3bi, Early Roman) (Fig. 2.11): 12 small fragments (24g) of fired clay from a sieved sample, amorphous or with a single moulded surface: typical 'rake-out' fragments of lining dislodged in the cinders.

Corndrier 45 (6689) (period 3d, Roman) (Fig. 2.16): This typical T-shaped Roman corndrier produced a large quantity of fired clay (1042 fragments, 9442g), nearly all of which consisted of wattle-impressed structure and plain fragments of wall/floor surface or lining. This structure accounted for almost all the wattle-impressed structure from Roman period deposits. It was made exclusively in fabric Q. It is unusual to find wattle and daub structure in Roman corndriers as it was most common to construct the flue with a stone or tile arch, which was then covered with a solid clay, cob or puddled chalk floor. The standard design is now well established, based on well-preserved examples such as those from Grateley (Cunliffe and Poole 2008a, 69–77) and Abbots Ann, Hampshire (Cunliffe and Poole 2008b, 56–9). Here the drying floors were preserved in their entirety (together with the crop) showing the flue was bridged by a tile arch covered by a solid drying floor. The fire was situated close to the flue mouth with the far end of the T left open as a narrow slot, which acted as a chimney to create a draught and with a projecting stone shelf to deflect warm air over the crop. The structures and deposits within corndrier 45 follow this pattern in their entirety except that the drying floor was constructed as a wattle-supported structure across the flue. It is possible the enclosing kerb around the drying floor was also constructed with wattles though a solid clay structure is equally probable. The surviving structure was constructed of stone blocks bedded in and rendered with clay, which accounts for the many fragments with a single flat moulded surface.

Corndrier 25 (8558), fills 8651–3 (period 3bi, Early Roman) (Fig. 2.10): 30 small fragments (108g) of fired clay including sieved samples, most amorphous or rarely with a single moulded surface; one with small stem impression 5mm: 'rake-out' fragments of lining dislodged in the cinders.

Corndrier 46 (8164) (period 3bi, Early Roman) (Fig. 2.11) was a typical dumbbell-shaped feature consisting of a circular chamber on the east 0.65m in diameter, a central linear flue 0.55m wide and an irregular sub-circular stoke hole 0.97m wide at the west end. Most intense burning of the natural (8405) occurred along the sides and base of the central flue together with a smaller patch on the base of the main chamber. A charcoal-rich layer (8244) occurred across the base of the flue and embedded in this were a number of flat tabular stones and a partial oven plate (8245). The slabs have all been reused, apparently lining the floor of the flue. A few additional fragments of fired clay with a curved surface were recovered from the overlying silting deposit (8243) infilling most of the oven and flue. Five fragments (872g) of fired clay: the largest pieces formed a substantial part of a rectangular flanged oven plate (Ra. 899) (Fig. 3.16, 6); fragments from a second object with convex surface from the uppermost fill (8243).

Corndrier 29 (16538; fill 16704, possibly period 3ci Late Roman) (Fig. 2.14): Two small fragments (2g) of fired clay from a sieved sample, amorphous: 'rake-out' fragments of lining dislodged in the cinders.

'Oven' structure 7419 (7697) (period 3a) (Fig. 2.7): A large quantity of fired clay (158 fragments, 11,094kg) was sampled from this feature, which had been heavily disturbed by animal burrowing. Although on site various deposits were recorded as relating to the use of the feature, these could be interpreted equally as erosion, collapse, or dumping. Oven lining (7672) comprised red fired fragments 10–15mm thick with a smooth moulded surface, which appeared to have come away from a backing of heat reddened or unfired yellowish-brown clay 25–35mm thick. The site records indicate this formed the lining of the lower subsurface sides of the feature, but the sample examined appeared to be very disturbed and mixed – it appeared to have been subjected to some degree of weathering or erosion or other disturbance.

The major fired clay artefact found in this feature was a near-complete oven plate that had broken in two and been deposited in two separate episodes of dumping of debris (7673, 7809) separated by a layer of charcoal (7850). The condition of the plate suggests neither piece had been lying around for any length of time at the surface and had been deposited in fairly rapid succession (hours or days, rather than weeks). This implies the layer of charcoal does not represent *in situ* firing of the structure but a tip of cinders cleared out from another structure, as does the further tip overlying 7809 of charcoal (7667), which contained small fragments of fired clay typical of rake-out together with a broken fragment of oven plate. The upper half of the feature was filled with deposits indicative of slower erosion and silting of sediment mixed with finely weathered fired clay debris (7666, 7461).

The upper of these layers was erroneously interpreted as an *in situ* perforated oven plate, rather than in reality, a deposit of naturally accumulated sediment riddled with animal burrows. This view almost certainly clouded subsequent interpretation of the underlying deposits and the function of the feature. There is little evidence to suggest the feature could have successfully functioned as an oven as it is rather deep without a proper flue and stoking area to create a suitable draught to ensure combustion. It is probable that a surface or semi-sunken kiln was located close by and was the source of the tips of burnt debris and fired clay.

Discussion

The fired clay assemblage comprises substantial quantities of both structural material and portable furniture, some of which was directly associated with *in situ* structures, whilst the remainder represented demolished structural material and discarded oven furniture dumped in other features.

The structural material is largely associated with the *in situ* ovens and corndriers and provides evidence for the form of the superstructure. The most significant is the fired clay from corndrier 45 (6689), which produced evidence for a wattle-supported solid clay drying floor. This construction method is not the norm in Roman corndriers which more commonly had the drying floor supported on a vault of tile or stone over the flue. Stone was locally available based on the evidence of the lower wall structure lining the flue, though tile may not have been available if this structure belongs early in the Roman period. The use of wattles as the support for the floor may indicate a recourse to Iron Age practice, perhaps due to a lack of suitable raw materials or skills in constructing the arch over the flue of stone.

The portable furniture is dominated by the oven plates, which together with other less common items such as firebars suggests pottery production was a significant activity on or very close to the site, even though no actual kiln bases were identified during excavation. The main period of use of the plates was during the Late Iron Age and Early Roman period (3a–3b) at a time when kilns were largely surface or only partly subsurface constructions and left little more than a shallow hollow with burning and remnants of charcoal. These are classified by Swan (1984, 55) as La Tène III derived surface or semi-sunken up-draught kilns utilising portable furniture and largely constructed of turves. Examples of Late Belgic or Early Roman date excavated in the Nene Valley by Woods (1974) show that little more than a shallow bowl-like scoop may survive with a little burning *in situ* and no trace of a stoking area. At Greenhouse Farm, Cambridgeshire, kilns in Group 1 (Gibson and Lucas 2002, 97–100) are of more irregular form with an absence of *in situ* burning. It is unsurprising therefore, that kiln bases of 1st-century AD date have not been recognised on site. The site records of all pits producing fragments of oven furniture were rapidly scanned to establish whether any might potentially be kiln bases.

Oven structure 7419 (pit 7697) has been discussed above: rather than representing an actual oven it has probably acted as a repository for debris from an unidentified nearby surface kiln. Corndrier 24 (8986) identified on site as a possible corndrier is a candidate for a kiln: it formed two shallow sub-circular hollows, which could represent the location of the firing chamber and stoking hollow of a kiln. The burnt layers (9015, 9017 and 9018) recorded as fills are in fact likely to be *in situ* burnt natural sand representing the location of the main chamber of the kiln over an area of about 1m in diameter. The southern hollow filled with a dark greyish-brown silty sand containing charcoal and burnt sandstone probably represents the stokehole. This feature produced only a few small scraps of fired clay from the sieved samples identified as possible oven lining. Corndrier 46 described above is one of the more convincing features to be interpreted as a kiln, especially in view of the associated fragment of kiln furniture and comes within Swan's 'semi-sunken' classification.

Pit 8842, which contained the complete circular disc,

formed a shallow sub-circular pit measuring 0.86 by 0.7m wide and 0.2m deep. The site record makes no mention of *in situ* burning but the remains of the sediment attached to the base and edge of the plate exhibited such characteristics. A very thin lens of ash and fine charcoal no more than 1mm thick occurred immediately below the plate overlying a thin layer of grey, burnt sand 10–14mm thick with a few small patches of reddened sand at the surface, and below the grey sand remnants of the yellow sand natural. The characteristics of the plate itself, heavily fired on top, but lightly fired to the base suggest it formed the base floor of the kiln on which a pedestal and other furniture would have rested. A small fragment of chaff-tempered plate was found in the fill 8841 and another fragment from the adjacent ditch fill 8843. A few small scraps of amorphous fired clay were recovered from the sieved samples of the fill.

Although the evidence for pottery kilns from actual features may be considered slight, the array of portable furniture provides convincing evidence for Swan's categories of surface built or semi-sunken kilns with a temporary superstructure (1984, fig. II). The rectangular plates must have formed the suspended floor for the upper chamber with the ends luted into the wall structure. In the centre, they must have rested on some form of portable block pedestal, a function for which the triangular bricks may also have been used. The complete circular plate from pit 8842 certainly appears to have been used as a floor, but some may also have formed part of the suspended floor resting on the pedestal to create a larger central support for the inner ends of the rectangular plates. The walls of any kilns were presumably temporary structures built of turf, possibly with a clay lining, though there is little evidence of lining material associated with the kiln debris.

A final thought is the function of the large plate or drying floor with impressed circles. Although such decoration (if it is indeed decoration) has previously been found on hearth surfaces, this structure from Thame would appear to have formed a large portable plate: the intensity of firing does not indicate high temperature activity, and it has been interpreted as a drying floor. If this is the case were the circles possibly made by a pot rim, and does it actually represent a drying floor for drying pots prior to firing rather than for agricultural produce?

Catalogue of illustrated fired clay (Figs 3.13–3.17)

1   Oven/kiln wall, corndrier 45 (fill 6679 of cut 6627). Id.52. Period 3d Roman.
2   Oven/kiln wall, corndrier 45 (fill 6930). Id.62. Period 3d Roman.
3   Decorated hearth or drying floor, ditch 251 (fill 7363). Id.202, Ra. 833. Period 3c Late Roman.
4   Circular disc, pit 8842 (fill 8841). Ra. 961. Period 3c Late Roman.
5a Rectangular oven plate, oven 7419 (fill 7673). Id.114. Period 3a Late Iron Age–Early Roman. Nos: 3 joining; Wt 2405g.
5b Rectangular oven plate, oven 7419 (fill 7809). Id.120. Period 3a Late Iron Age–Early Roman. Nos: 2 joining; Wt 1424g.
6   Flanged rectangular oven plate, corndrier 46 (fill 8245). Id.899, Ra. 899. Period 3b Early Roman. Nos: 1; Wt 818g.
7   Flanged rectangular oven plate, pit 7316 (fill 7317). Id.234. Period 3b Early Roman. Nos: 1; Wt 657g.
8   Triangular perforated brick, ditch 206 (fill 5167). Id.587, Ra. 587. Period 3a Late Iron Age–Early Roman. Nos: 1; Wt 2875g.
9   Corner of triangular brick, unstratified curvilinear ditch 7761. Id.118. Period 3a Late Iron Age–Roman. Nos: 1; Wt 1590g.
10 Cylindrical pedestal with splayed foot, ditch 206 (fill 5323). Id.615, Ra. 615. Period 3b Early Roman. Nos: 1; Wt 180g.
11 Firebar, ditch 234 (fill 8117). Id.124. Period 3b Early Roman. Nos: 7 joining; Wt 573g.

Roman ceramic building material
by Cynthia Poole

A modest assemblage of Roman tile amounting to 96 fragments weighing 10,098g was limited to the standard forms of tegula, brick, imbrex and flue tile. Methodology is described in the Appendix. The emphasis is on flat varieties of tile, especially brick and tegula that could be easily reused. The assemblage was recovered predominantly from ditch fills (85% by weight) and to a lesser extent pits, postholes, layers and miscellaneous features with a significant proportion found in the Saxon SFBs (12% by weight). The similarity of Roman and post-Roman fabrics meant some of the small indeterminate fragments could not be dated. Approximately 16 fragments (43g) could not be dated or categorised to type. No complete tiles were recovered, and no complete dimensions survived apart from thickness. The largest surviving piece represented over half of a Roman brick. The mean fragment weight (MFW) of 115g is average for Roman material. Abrasion was absent or low on much of the tile, with approximately a quarter of fragments suffering moderate or high abrasion.

Fabrics

The ceramic building material (CBM) fabrics are predominantly sandy containing variable quantities and grades of quartz sand, occasionally occurring in combination with other inclusions. It is probable that the main groups (B, C, D and Q) were produced within the local region.

Fabric B: red, pinkish-red, reddish-brown or orange, coarse sandy clay, sometimes micaceous, containing a high density of medium–coarse quartz sand and dark red/black iron oxide grits up to 0.5mm and occasionally a scatter of angular flint grit *c*. 3mm size.

Fabric C: generally red or orange sometimes with a grey core hard fired, occasionally micaceous, clay containing a low–moderate density of medium–coarse quartz sand *c.* 0.5mm, evenly distributed.

Fabric Q: red or orange, rarely with a grey core, containing a high density of quartz sand, which in most examples was fine–medium less than 0.2mm but some up to 0.5mm–1mm size. One example had in addition leached calcareous inclusions *c.* 1mm and coarse grog or clay lumps up to 21mm in size.

Fabric D: red or orange hard fired very fine sandy clay, occasionally micaceous, generally without additional inclusions.

Eccles?: light brown clay fabric containing evenly distributed, well-sorted, frequent medium–coarse angular–sub-angular quartz sand. Only a single small fragment of this fabric occurred and though it is very similar to that found at Eccles, Kent, it is uncertain whether this was a genuine Eccles tile.

Stowe pink grog-tempered: pinkish brown surface with mid–dark grey core; the colour is similar to the Stowe fabric, but it was difficult to distinguish any grog within the clay fabric. The fabric is similar to that described in the National Roman Fabric Reference Collection (Tomber and Dore 1998).

Forms

Tegulae

Tegula accounted for 15 fragments (2403g) and was made in fabrics C and D. Most pieces had a fairly neat regular finish with fine striations from smoothing visible on the upper surface and the base fairly even and flat, though only two had any evidence of knife or wire trimming of the base. They measured between 16 and 30mm thick. The flange survived on eight fragments and in form most were rectangular (OA type A) and two rounded (OA type D, E). They measured 16–30mm wide and 45–53mm high; two tapered in width being widest at the base edge of the tile. Where a finger groove ran along the base of the flange it was frequently very shallow and fairly flat. Two lower cutaways were present, both of Warry's (2006) type D15, which he dates to AD 240–380.

Imbrex

Only six pieces of imbrex (390g) were found, all fairly flat except one more curved piece, indicating most had a fairly angular profile. Surfaces were regular and even and the exterior often had fine striations from smoothing. Most pieces were mainly made in fabric C with one in fabric D and measured 13–16mm thick, whilst two made in fabric Q were slightly thicker at 18 and 19mm.

Flue tile

A single piece of box flue tile (122g) was identified made in Stowe pink grog-tempered fabric. It had a smooth finely striated exterior surface, a smooth flat edge and evidence of knife trimming on the interior. It measured 16mm thick and over 60mm wide and 125mm long. The full length is estimated to have been in the region of 300mm based on the rectangular vent cut in the side being equidistant from both ends. No keying was present on the surviving surface.

Brick

Brick was the most common form amounting to 11 fragments (4522g) identified on the basis of thickness and general characteristics of finish, when no corner survived. They were made in fabrics B, C, D and Q. Thickness measured from 32 to 42mm and the largest surviving piece was 220mm wide. This had a signature mark, which if placed symmetrically would suggest the complete brick was of pedalis size (*c.* 300mm square). It is probable that all the examples derive from the smaller brick forms of pedalis and bessalis and possibly lydion. Brick was the only type to exhibit any markings in the form of signature marks.

Miscellaneous

The remaining pieces comprised flat tile and indeterminate fragments ranging in thickness from 12mm to 38mm. They were made in all the main fabrics (B, C, D, Q) and one piece was in the Eccles fabric or one closely resembling it. One piece had been deliberately chipped to form a circular disc, possibly shaped from a flue tile. It measured 15mm thick and 102–105mm in diameter and had been lightly burnt around part of the edge on the upper surface.

Markings

Three signature marks were identified on bricks and a single example on a flat tile, possibly also brick. Two comprised curved finger grooves of unidentifiable design and one may be a mark from handling rather than a deliberate signature. The one on the flat tile is incomplete but appears to comprise the crossing tails of a loop (OA type 5.1). The best example covered all the surviving surface and formed an X made with three finger grooves (OA type 14.3).

Discussion

Whilst roof tile (tegula and imbrex) is present, there is no evidence from the quantity or proportions to suggest a building with a tiled roof stood anywhere in the vicinity. Similarly, the single flue tile, whilst originally produced for a heated room, is not evidence of any such structure in the area. All the evidence indicates the tile was obtained from elsewhere for reuse or disposal on the site. There is a clear preference for flat forms, especially tegula and brick, which could be more easily reused in the construction of hearths or ovens.

The numbers with evidence of burning suggest the tile was frequently reused in ovens or kilns on the site. Patterns and intensity of burning suggests tile was built into structures with only edges or part of the tile exposed to heat, as hearth floors with only one surface extensively burnt or as furniture with heavy burning or refiring in evidence on all surfaces and edges. The only pieces of tile to be actually found in association with a burnt structure were three small scraps from a sieved sample from broadly Roman-dated corndrier 45 (6689). This pattern of tile reuse is common on most Roman sites, but on those of lower status is often the only evidence for the utilisation of tile.

No early forms occurred suggesting all the tile is 2nd century AD in date or later. The only pieces more closely datable are two tegula fragments with lower cutaways that are indicative of a mid 3rd to 4th-century AD date.

The quantity of Roman tile found in the Saxon deposits suggests that Roman tile was deliberately being reused in the Saxon period. The largest amount was found in SFB structure 33 (9 fragments, 599g) with single fragments from SFB structures 30 and 37 (see Chapter 4).

Industrial residues
by Lynne Keys

The slag from the site is indicative of very sporadic, small-scale smelting and smithing activity, and there is very little represented during this period. Methodology is described in the Appendix, as well as a technical description of smelting and smithing and the resulting products and waste materials.

Period 3a Late Iron Age/Early Roman. Total = 114g. Nothing of significance.

Period 3b Early and Middle Roman. Total = 3.8659kg. The weight for slag from this period is skewed by the large fragment of furnace slag from ditch 189 (15045), fill 15048 (3.6kg).

Period 3c Late Roman. Total = 1.937kg. Ditch 259 (6988), fill 6989 contained just 417g of slag which consisted of furnace and undiagnostic slags. One smithing hearth bottom was recovered from ditch 240 (17163), fill 17164.

Period 3d Roman. Total = 182g. There is a small quantity of slag from this general phase.

However, it is possible that, given the lack of other evidence of iron making or working during periods 3b and 3c, that this material is redeposited and of Iron Age date.

Human remains
by Lauren McIntyre and Alice Rose, with Louise Loe

The methodology used to record and analyse the human remains can be found in the Appendix.

Period 3a – Late Iron Age/Early Roman (*c*. 25 BC–AD 100)

Human remains dating to period 3a (Table 3.13) comprised two articulated skeletons: a young adult (SK. 506), probably female, in grave cut 7015, and a prime adult, probably male (SK. 508), in ditch 249, as well as two urned cremation deposits (5938 and 5940 inside and around urn 5939, and 7912 in urn 7911).

Articulated inhumations

Skeleton 506 was 35% complete. Fragmentation levels were medium, and bone surface condition was grade 4, meaning that all the bone surfaces were affected by erosion (McKinley 2004a, 16). Overall, the preservation of the skeleton was poor. The mandible and a few fragments of pelvis were present, with indicators which suggested the individual was a probable female. Occlusal wear of the upper and lower dentition indicated a young adult age estimation (18–25yrs). Cranial indices and stature could not be calculated but double calcaneal anterior facets were noted. The maxillary incisors from skeleton 506 had heavy wear, possibly indicating an abnormal bite. Two teeth belonging to this individual had dental enamel hypoplasias. The location of the hypoplastic defects suggest that the growth arrest occurred at approximately 3.5–4.5 years of age (Primeau *et al.* 2015). Dental calculus was present. There were no post-cranial pathological changes.

Skeleton 508 was 70% complete. Fragmentation levels were medium, and bone surface condition was grade 4, meaning that all the bone surfaces were affected by erosion (McKinley 2004a, 16). Overall, the preservation of the skeleton was poor. All the skull and some pelvis elements were present with features which indicated a probable male. Only dental attrition was available for age estimation, signifying a prime adult (26–35yrs).

Cranial indices and stature could not be calculated but some measurements could be taken on the post-cranial elements, including those required for the tibial platycnemic index (indicating an index classification of mesocnemic). Several cranial and post-cranial non-metric traits were observed, including left and right bridged supraorbital foramen and left and right acetabular crease (SK. 508, Table 3.13). The observed traits are relatively common and have genetic and mechanical aetiologies (Veldman 2013).

Skeleton 508 was dentate but had had lost four teeth ante-mortem. There was evidence of dental caries, periodontitis, and dental calculus.

A number of post-cranial pathological changes were observed. Osteoarthritis was present in the articular facets of the thoracic vertebrae. Osteophytes were present on the margins of several extra-spinal joints and osteoarthritis was observed in the left hip and left foot. Healed fractures were observed involving the left clavicle, left intermediate cuneiform (foot) and the left patella (knee). Osteochondritis dissecans was observed in the right talus. Osteochondritis non-dissecans (OND), or pseudo-osteochondritis dissecans (pseudo OD), are small pits or porous lesions located on the concave surfaces of joints (Rogers and Waldron 1995, 29–30).

Table 3.13 Human remains. Period 3a: Late Iron Age/Roman (c. 25 BC–AD 100)

Articulated inhumation burials

SK. no.	Context	Completeness	Condition	Frag.	Sex	Age	Metrics/Non-metrics/Pathology
506	In sub-oval cut (7015) Extended on right side, head at east	26–50%	4	Medium	F?	18–25yrs	*Non-metrics*: L&R calcaneus double anterior facet *Dental pathology*: Calculus, enamel hypoplasia, abnormal bite
508	In Roman boundary ditch 249 (7499) = (7772) Supine, head at east	51–75%	4	Medium	M?	26–35yrs	*Tibial index*: Mesocnemic *Non-metrics*: R lambdoid ossicle, L epipteric bone, L&R mandibular torus, L&R supraorbital foramen, L&R acetabular crease, L&R exostosis in troch-anteric fossa, double anterior facet R calcaneus *Dental pathology*: AMTL, caries, calculus, periodontitis, periapical cavity *Skeletal pathology*: Marginal osteophytes cervical vertebrae and S1 spinal osteoarthritis. Marginal osteophytes L&R shoulder, R elbow, R hip, L&R knee, R foot. Osteoarthritis R acromio-clavicular joint, L hip and L foot. Ante-mortem fractures L clavicle, L intermediate cuneiform and L patella. Osteochondritis dissecans R talus. Osteochondritis non-dissecans L&R navicular, R talus, and L&R intermediate cuneiform. Undiagnosed pathology R humerus

Cremated bone

Context	Feature	Total weight	Colour	MNI	Sex	Age	Non-metrics/Pathology	Pyre goods/debris/grave goods
5938	Fill of cremation urn 5939 (Ra. 723)	838.2g	White 90%, grey 5%, blue 5%, black <5%	2	M?	30–40yrs	Marginal osteophytes, 1x fragment of vertebral body	0.2g unburnt unid. animal bone, 1.3g unid. unburnt mammal bone, 0.5g burnt chicken bone, <0.1g burnt unid. bird bone 5.3g pottery (fragments from urn 5939?) <0.1g charcoal
5940	'Coombe' deposit layer surrounding cremation urn 5939 (Ra. 723)	14.8g	White 95%, grey 5%, brown <5%	1 (belongs to an individual from urn 5939?)	U	Adult >18yrs	Marginal osteophytes, 2x fragments of vertebral body	0.5g burnt unid. animal bone, 0.2g unburnt unid. animal bone
7912	Fill of vessel 7911 (Ra. 880)	12.5g	White 50%, grey 25%, blue 5%, black 5%, brown/orange 15%	1	U	U	-	-

L = left, R = right; MNI = minimum number of individuals; Frag. = fragmentation level; M?/F? = possible male/female; U = unknown; AMTL = ante-mortem tooth loss

Table 3.14 Human remains. Period 3a: Late Iron Age/Roman, summary of bone weights (weight (% of total weight))

Feature	Context	Skeletal element								TOTAL
		Skull	Axial	Upper limb	Lower limb	Unid. long bone	Unid. hand/foot	Unid. joint surface	Unid. other	
7911	7912	2.7g (21.6%)	2.0g (16.0%)	0g (0%)	0g (0%)	1.8g (14.4%)	0g (0%)	0.1g (0.8%)	5.9g (47.2%)	12.5g (100%)
Urn 5939	5938	159.6g	85.0g	73.9g	236.6g	130.0g	4.4g	28.7g	120.0g	838.2g (98.04%)
Surrounding urn 5939	5940	1.1g	3.5g	2.3g	4.4g	2.4g	0g	1.5g	1.6g	16.8g (1.96%)
Urn 5939 and surroundings	Total	160.7g (57.9%)	88.5g (10.38%)	76.2g (8.91%)	241.0g (28.19%)	132.4g (15.49%)	4.4g (0.51%)	30.2g (3.53%)	121.6g (14.22%)	855.0g (100%)

unid. = unidentified

As the name suggests, they may appear like the lesions of osteochondritis dissecans (OD), but their location on concave joint surfaces differentiates them. The aetiology of OND may be circulatory or developmental. OND was observed in the left and right navicular, right talus and left and right intermediate cuneiform.

An undiagnosed pathology was also observed in the right humerus. A rounded, erosive lesion was present on the posterior proximal right humeral neck, on the margin of the proximal articular surface. The lesion was shallow and measured approximately 12x11mm. The margins were quite sharp, and the base comprised dense trabecular bone. It is not clear whether there was a space-occupying lesion present, or if this is an erosive lesion related to some kind of arthropathy or other condition such as tuberculosis. Alternatively, the lesions may be related to the osteophytes, porosity and a possible sub-chondral cyst present in the acromio-clavicular joint.

Cremated bone

Bone weight
Summaries of the bone weights are presented in Table 3.14. Cremation 5938/5940 weighed 855.0g which falls within the weight range cited by McKinley (2013, 154) for cremations which have been recovered archaeologically (600–900g).

Only 12.5g of cremated bone was recovered from context 7912, the fill of urn 7911 (Table 3.14). Considering the small amount of cremated bone present in the vessel, this may represent a token deposit: a small, symbolic quantity of bone (e.g., a deposited memento or cenotaph, commemorating an individual where the bulk of the remains have been deposited elsewhere; McKinley 2013, 154).

Fragmentation
A summary of fragmentation per deposit is presented in Table 3.15. Fragment size ranged from 27.1mm (unidentified: 7912) to 100.7mm (distal left humerus shaft: 5938). In the case of 5938/5940, the largest proportion of bone came from the >10mm sieve fractions, but the smaller fraction (4–2mm) predominated in the smaller deposit (7912). The proportion of bone present in the 2–0.5mm residues are presented in Table 3.16.

Skeletal representation
Summaries of skeletal representation are presented in Table 3.14. Of the identified fragments, bone from the lower limbs was most frequently observed followed by fragments of skull. Much of the bone recovered from the three deposits was unidentified. Smaller proportions of unidentified bone were from the hands or feet and joint surfaces, but most of the unidentified bone was either from the upper or lower limbs or could not be identified to an anatomical region. Small quantities

Table 3.15 Period 3a: Late Iron Age/Roman cremated human bone, summary of fragmentation

Feature	Context	Period	Total weight	>10mm	10–4mm	4–2mm	Max. frag. size and bone
Urn 5939	5938	3a	838.2g	623.1g	171.1g	44.0g	100.7mm, distal left humerus shaft
Surrounding urn 5939	5940	3a	16.8g	11.2g	4.8g	0.8g	30.1mm, unid. long bone
Urn 7911	7912	3a	12.5g	0g	0g	12.5g	27.1mm, unid. other

Table 3.16 Cremated bone: 2–0.5mm fraction proportional bone content (all contexts)

Context	Period	Total 2–0.5mm fraction weight	% cremated bone (based on visual assessment)
5938	3a	86.7g	60%
5940	3a	979.4g	<5%
7104	3b	180.9g	40%
7541	3b	47.5g	20%
7542	3b	104.3g	<10%
16750	3b	508.0g	<5%
16751	3b	111.6g	65%
16754	3b	8.4g	<5%
16756	3b	68.3g	20%

of cranial vault, ribs and vertebrae were identifiable in 7912.

Colour
Most of the bone fragments were white in colour (Table 3.13). This indicates a generally efficient cremation process with most bones being burnt at a temperature more than 600ºC and is a common observation in archaeological cremation burials (McKinley 2006, 84). The remainder of the bone was coloured grey/blue, black, and orange/brown. Only very small quantities of bone from contexts 5940 were orange/brown (indicating that they were minimally affected by heat). The orange/brown fragments could not be identified by skeletal region but may represent areas of the body that were located peripherally on the pyre. Bone fragments from 7912 were predominantly white, but brown/orange, black, and grey/blue fragments were also present, indicating that burning was inconsistent.

MNI, sex, age, and pathology
An MNI (minimum number of individuals) of three adults was present, based upon the number of discrete deposits (contexts 7912 and 5938/5940) and the repetition of observable, identifiable, skeletal elements. There were two left nasal bones and fragments of two left patellae present in 5938 indicating that they had been contributed by at least two individuals (Buikstra and Ubelaker 1994).

No evidence of the sex of the individuals was present in deposit 5940. However, a cranial trait was observed in 5938. One fragment of nuchal crest was robust and possibly indicative of a male individual (Buikstra and Ubelaker 1994, 19). It should be noted that sex estimation methods must be applied to burnt human bone with caution because of the potential for bone shrinkage and warping because of dehydration, which may influence the size and morphology of sexually dimorphic traits.

Osteological indicators of age were very limited. The size and morphology of the identified bone fragments in both deposits were in keeping with those of adults aged over 18 years (Scheuer and Black 2000). Deposit 5938 included one small fragment of a left auricular surface of the pelvis and was consistent with an age of 30–40 years (Lovejoy *et al.* 1985; Buckberry and Chamberlain 2002). No non-metric traits were observed. Pathological evidence was limited to small fragments of vertebral body with marginal osteophytes from 5938 and 5940.

Pyre debris
Small quantities of burnt and unburnt animal bone were recovered from 5938 and 5940 (Table 3.13). Although most of this was unidentified, a small amount of burnt chicken bone was present in 5938.

Period 3b – Early and Middle Roman (*c.* AD 100–240)

Human remains dating to period 3b comprised unburnt disarticulated bone, two urned cremation burials and cremated bone from the fill surrounding one of the urns; and four cremation deposits from the coombe area. Table 3.17 provides an osteological summary per skeleton/context.

Unburnt disarticulated bone
One left humerus shaft was recovered from context 7172 (the fill of pit 7173, which cuts grave 7015, containing skeleton 506) (Table 3.17). As skeleton 506 has a left humerus present, the disarticulated bone represents a second individual, an adult of unknown sex. Additionally, one occipital bone was found in the upper fill 5435 of ditch 206, intervention 5438. This bone derives from an adult individual of indeterminate sex. No non-metric traits, pathology or modification was observed on either of these bones.

Cremated bone from 7541/7542 and 7104
Cremated human bone was recovered from context 7541/7542 and context 7104. A summary of the osteological findings is presented in Table 3.17. Bone from 7542 was assumed to be disturbed remains originally pertaining to 7541 and therefore is treated as one cremation deposit hereon (7541/7542).

Bone weight
A summary of the bone weights is presented in Table 3.18. The weight of deposit 7104 – 585.78g – was just short of the range cited by McKinley (2013, 154) for cremations which have been recovered archaeologically (600–900g). Even when they are combined the deposits from 7541/7542 – 28.35g – were much smaller.

Fragmentation
A summary of fragmentation per deposit is presented in Table 3.19. Fragment size ranged from 70.9mm (humerus shaft) in deposit 7104 to 8.6mm (unidentified fragment: 7542). In the case of deposit 7104, the largest proportion of bone came from the >10mm fraction. In the deposits with lower bone weights (7541/7542), the highest proportions of bone came from the smaller sieve fractions.

Skeletal representation
Of the identified bone, skull and lower limb bones were

Table 3.17 Human remains. Period 3b: Early Roman (c. AD 100–240)

Disarticulated, unburnt bone

Context	Feature type	Condition	Frag.	Elements present	MNI	Sex	Age	Metrics/Non-metrics/Pathology
7172	Fill of pit 7173, cuts grave 7015 (containing SK. 506)	4	Medium	L humerus shaft	1	U	Adult >18yrs	-

Cremated bone

Context	Feature	Total weight	Colour	MNI	Sex	Age	Non-metrics/Pathology	Pyre goods/debris/grave goods
7104	Fill of cremation urn 7103 (Ra. 588)	585.8g*	White 75%, grey 15%, blue 5%, black <5%, orange <5%	1	U	Adult >18yrs	-	-
7541	Fill of cremation urn 7540 (Ra. 867)	26.0g*	White 75%, grey 15%, black 10%	1	U	U	-	<0.1g glass, <0.1g charcoal
7542	Layer surrounding cremation urn 7540 (Ra. 867)	2.35g*	White 60%, grey 30%, black 10%	1 (same as 7541?)	U	U	-	-
16750	Identical to 'coombe deposit' 17162 cut by urned cremation burials 16752 (Ra. 48) and 16757 (RA.50)	17.1g	White 60%, grey 5%, blue 10%, black 25%	1	U	Adult <18yrs	-	-
16751	Fill of cremation urn 16752 (Ra. 48)	823.8g	White 85%, grey 10%, blue 5%, black 5%	1	F?	Adult >18yrs	1x R proximal humeral shaft fragment with exostosis on the medial side of the bicipital groove. Trauma? Or MSM (Lat. Dorsi or T. major?)?	0.1g charcoal

| 16754 | Fill of drinking vessel 16755 (Ra. 49) deposited inside cremation urn 16757 (Ra. 50) | 3.1g | White 50%, blue 50% | 1 | U | U | - | - | - |
| 16756 | Fill of cremation urn 16757 (Ra. 50) | 346.7g | White 50%, grey 30%, blue 15%, black <5%, brown/orange 5% | 1 (same as 16754?) | U | Adult >18yrs | - | - | - |

R = right; L = left; S1 = 1st sacral vertebra; MNI = minimum number of individuals; Frag. = fragmentation level; M? = probable male; ?? = indeterminate sex; U = unknown, AMTL = ante-mortem tooth loss; S1 = 1st sacral vertebra. MSM = musculo-skeletal marker; Lat. Dorsi – latissimus dorsi; T. major – teres major * denotes inclusion of estimated bone weights

the most common (Table 3.18). As mentioned above, a high proportion of skull fragments is a pattern often noted during cremation analysis, as the skull vault is more easily identified than other bones, even within the smaller fractions (McKinley 2004b, 11). The majority of bone, however, was unidentified. Most of this was either from the upper or lower limbs or could not be identified to an anatomical region.

Colour

Most of the bone fragments were white in colour. This indicates a generally efficient cremation process with most bones being burnt at a temperature more than 600ºC and is a common observation in archaeological cremation burials (McKinley 2006, 84). The remainder of the bone was coloured grey/blue, black, and orange/brown. Only very small quantities of bone from context

Table 3.18 Human remains. Period 3b: Early Roman, summary of bone weights (weight (% of total weight))

		Skeletal element								
Feature	Context	Skull	Axial	Upper limb	Lower limb	Unid. long bone	Unid. hand/foot	Unid. joint surface	Unid. other	TOTAL
Urn 7103	7104	42.7g (7.29%)	50.9g (8.69%)	55.0g (9.39%)	77.5g (13.23%)	159.0g (27.14%)	12.2g (2.08%)	42.0g (7.17%)	146.48g* (25.01%)	585.78g * (100%)
Urn 7540	7541	8.9g	0g	0g	0g	0.3g	0g	0g	16.8g*	26.0g* (91.71%)
Surrounding urn 7540	7542	0.3g	0g	0g	0g	0g	0g	0g	2.05g	2.35g (8.29%)
Urn 7540 and surroundings	Total	9.2g (32.45%)	0g (0%)	0g (0%)	0g (0%)	0.3g (1.06%)	0g (0%)	0g (0%)	18.85g* (66.49%)	28.35g* (100%)
	16750)	0g (0%)	0g (0%)	0g (0%)	7.7g (45.03%)	6.7g (39.18%)	0g (0%)	0g (0%)	2.7g (15.79%)	17.1g (100%)
	16751	122.5g (14.87%)	33.2g (4.03%)	69.8g (8.47%)	243.9g (29.61%)	113.6g (13.79%)	10.9g (1.32%)	73.2g (8.89%)	156.6g (19.01%)	823.7g (100%)
	16754	0g (0%)	0g (0%)	0g (0%)	0g (0%)	2.9g (93.55%)	0g (0%)	0g (0%)	0.2g (6.45%)	3.1g (100%)
	16756	49.4g (14.82%)	22.4g (6.72%)	39.2g (11.76%)	27.1g (8.13%)	81.4g (24.42%)	5.8g (1.74%)	30.1g (9.03%)	77.9g (23.37%)	333.3g (100%)

unid. = unidentified* denotes inclusion of estimated bone weights

Table 3.19 Period 3b: Early Roman cremated human bone, summary of fragmentation

Feature	Context	Period	Total weight	>10mm	10–4mm	4–2mm	Max. frag. size and bone
Urn 7103	7104	3b	585.78g*	310.1g	213.2g	62.48g*	70.9mm, humerus shaft
Urn 7540	7541	3b	26.0g*	0.2g	10.6g	15.2g*	18.1mm, unid. other
Surrounding urn 7540	7542	3b	2.35g	0g	0.9g	1.45g	8.6mm, unid. other
Coombe deposit 17162	16750	3d	17.1g	12.8g	3.2g	1.1g	39.1mm, tibia shaft
Urn 16752	16751	3d	823.7g	581.3g	196.0g	46.4g	73.3mm, tibia shaft
Drinking vessel 16755in urn 165757	16754	3d	3.1g	0g	3.0g	0.1g	29.9mm, unid. long bone
Urn 16757	16756	3d	333.3g	205.8g	114.0g	13.9g	53.3mm, cranial vault

7104 were orange/brown (indicating that they were minimally affected by heat). The orange fragments from cremation deposit 7104 were identified as vertebral, which may suggest that the corpse was positioned in a way that meant some of the posterior axial skeleton was subject to less heat (e.g., laid supine), conditions were not totally consistent across the pyre, or burning was not consistent for the entire duration of the cremation process (McKinley 2006, 84).

MNI, sex, age, non-metrics and pathology
A minimum number of two adults was present, based upon the number of discrete deposits and the repetition of observable, identifiable, skeletal elements, and assuming bones from 7541 and 7542 were originally part of the same deposit. No evidence of the sex of the individuals was present, nor were any non-metric or pathological traits observed.

Cremated bone from the coombe deposits
Human remains comprised four deposits of cremated bone (Table 3.17) from the central area of the coombe deposits. Of these, three were contained within ceramic vessels.

Bone weight
A summary of bone weights is presented in Table 3.18. The largest deposit was 16751, weighing 823.8g and thus falling within the expected weight range for archaeologically recovered cremations (600–900g; McKinley 2013, 154). A moderate quantity of bone was present in deposit 16756 (346.7g), but deposits 16750 and 16754 had weights less than 20g. All deposits were truncated to some extent, which is likely to account for the relatively low bone weights, rather than them only representing token deposits or pyre debris.

Fragmentation
Fragment size ranged from 29.9mm (unidentified, one bone: 16754) to 73.3mm (tibial shaft:- 16751; Table 3.19). The largest proportion of bone came from the >10mm fraction in all of the deposits except the smallest (16754) in which the highest proportions of bone came from the 10–4mm sieve fraction. A moderate proportion of bone (c. 65% of the 111.6g of residue) was also present in 2–0.5mm fraction of cremation 16751 (Table 3.16).

Skeletal representation
Of the identified bone, skull and lower limb bones were the most common (Table 3.18). As mentioned above, a high proportion of skull fragments is a pattern often noted during cremation analysis, as the skull vault is more easily identified than other bones, even within the smaller fractions (McKinley 2004b, 11). The majority of bone, however, was unidentified. Most of this was either from the upper or lower limbs or could not be identified to an anatomical region.

Most (at least 50%) of the observed bone fragments were white. The remaining bone was coloured grey/blue, black, and orange/brown, in varying quantities (Table 3.17). Orange/brown bone was only observed in deposit 16756. Deposits 16750, and 16751 seem to have undergone a more efficient cremation process than bone from deposits 16754 and 16756, where colour was more variable.

MNI, sex, age and pathology
A minimum number of four individuals was present, based upon the number of discrete deposits. Bone from 16756 was from a vessel found within urn 16757 (deposit 16754). This bone may also pertain to the same individual, but this cannot be confirmed based solely on the osteological evidence. The small amount of bone from deposit 16750 may originally have belonged to either deposit 16751 or 16756, but this cannot be confirmed so the MNI remains at four. Individuals from 16750, 16751 and 16756 were of adults aged >18 years; the other individual was unaged. Evidence for sex was only present in deposit 16751, where a fragment of orbital margin would be consistent with a female individual. As only one trait was available, the estimation is tentative. No non-metric traits were observed.

Only one example of pathology was noted. One

fragment of proximal left humeral shaft from 16751 exhibited a large, longitudinal exostosis on the medial side of the bicipital groove. It is unclear whether this is indicative of trauma to the soft tissue, or represents an attachment site of a large muscle, e.g., for latissimus dorsi or teres major.

Period 2a–3d Iron Age–Roman (*c.* 700 BC– AD 410)

A single articulated burial (SK. 513) and two disarticulated bones could only be dated as either Iron Age or Roman (Table 3.20). A single cremation burial (10043) which could not be dated is also described here since it seems most likely that it was Roman in date.

Articulated inhumation burial
Inhumation burial 513 was less than 25% complete and highly fragmented. Bone surface condition ranged from grades 3–4 (most or all of the bone surface affected by erosion: McKinley 2004a, 16), and overall preservation was deemed to be poor. A small portion of the right pelvis of the skeleton was present, including the sciatic notch, auricular surface and pre-auricular sulcus, allowing for a sex estimation of possible female and an age estimation of >45 years. It was not possible to calculate stature, cranial or post-cranial indices, and no non-metric traits were observed. The skeleton exhibited osteoarthritis in the facets of two lumbar vertebrae, as well as the right and left wrists.

Unburnt disarticulated bone
A disarticulated left femoral shaft (comprising the proximal, middle and distal thirds, but missing the proximal and distal ends) was recovered from the coombe deposit (5398). The bone was from an adult (>18 years) of unknown sex (Table 3.20). Overall preservation was fair. There was no evidence of pathology or modification.

A right adult (>18 years) parietal was found in pit 8737, fill 8738. Preservation was fair, and there was no evidence of age, sex, pathology or post-mortem modification.

Cremated bone
A single cremation burial (10043) could not be dated to any specific period (Table 3.20). Iron staining was, however, noted on some of the bone fragments and a Roman date seems most likely, and it is, therefore, described here.

Bone weight
Almost 200g of cremated bone was recovered from deposit 10043 (Table 3.21). This falls well below the weight range cited by McKinley (2013, 154) for

Table 3.20 Human remains. Period 2a–3d: Iron Age to Roman (c. 700 BC– AD 410)

Articulated inhumation burials

SK. no.	Context	Completeness	Condition	Frag.	Sex	Age	Metrics/Non-metrics/Pathology
513	In linear E/W grave cut 5472. Position not known	0–25%	4	High	F??	45yrs+	Skeletal pathology: Osteoarthritis left and right wrists

Disarticulated, unburnt bone

Context	Feature type	Condition	Frag.	Elements present	MNI	Sex	Age	Metrics/Non-metrics/Pathology
5398	'Coombe deposit'	4	Medium	L femur shaft	1	U	Adult >18yrs	-
8738	Fill of pit 8737	3	Medium	R parietal	1	U	Adult >18yrs	-

Cremated bone

Context	Feature	Total weight	Colour (% of deposit)	MNI	Sex	Age	Non-metrics/Pathology	Pyre goods/debris/grave goods
10043	Fill of pit 10044 (unurned)	192.78g*	White 90%, grey 5%, blue <1%, black 5%	1	U	U	1x cranial fragment with 'hair on end' lesions	1.4g burnt unid. mammal, 0.1g burnt pig tooth, 2.26g* unburnt animal bone (including pig tooth enamel). Note 1x cranial fragment exhibits iron staining on both the endo-cranial and ecto-cranial sides

MNI = minimum number of individuals; Frag. = fragmentation level; U = unknown; * denotes inclusion of estimated weights

Table 3.21 Human remains, undated, summary of bone weights (weight (% of total weight))

Context	Skeletal element								
	Skull	Axial	Upper limb	Lower limb	Unid. long bone	Unid. hand/ foot	Unid. joint surface	Unid. other	TOTAL
10043 (% of total weight)	14.5g (7.53%)	14.8g (7.69%)	15.2g (7.89%)	4.5g (2.34%)	28.1g (14.59%)	1.4g (0.73%)	4.9g (2.54%)	109.38g* (56.80%)	192.78g* (100%)

Unid = unidentified; * denotes inclusion of estimated weights

Table 3.22 Undated cremated human bone, summary of fragmentation

Feature	Context	Period	Total weight	>10mm	1–4mm	4–2mm	Max. frag. size and bone
10044	10043	2c	192.78g*	49.3g	78.4g	64.91g*	42.2mm, radius shaft

cremations which have been recovered archaeologically (600–900g). It is unclear whether this low rate reflects a genuinely small bone deposit, or whether a significant quantity of bone was lost when the feature was truncated by ploughing.

Fragmentation
The largest fragment from this deposit measured 42.2mm (a fragment of radius shaft), and most bone came from the 10–4mm sieve fraction (49.3g; Table 3.22). The 4–2mm fraction was sizeable and comprised as estimated one third (c. 64.91g) cremated bone, indicating a high degree of fragmentation for the deposit overall. Approximately 10% of material (by volume) from the 2–0.5mm unsorted residue was estimated to be cremated bone. Considering the large total weight of the residue (1301.5g), this has potential to contribute significantly to the total bone weight of 10043: however, it is not possible to qualify the approximate weight of unsorted cremated bone in this fraction, because of weight differences between cremated bone fragments and extraneous material such as sand and small stones.

Skeletal representation
A summary of skeletal representation is presented in Table 3.21. Of the identified fragments, the skull, upper limb and lower limb were all equally represented. Bone from the lower limbs were also present but in smaller proportions. Most of the bone from this deposit was unidentified. This is unsurprising considering the high level of fragmentation.

Colour
Most of the bone fragments were white (90%), with smaller proportions of grey, blue and black bone. This indicates that in this case, the cremation process was efficient.

MNI, sex, age and pathology
There were no osteological indicators of age, sex or non-metric traits. One fragment of cranial vault exhibited possible remodelled porous lesions. Such lesions may be indicative of well-healed porotic hyperostosis (areas of macroscopic pitting and/or porosity on the cranial vault, which may develop as a result of childhood iron deficiency anaemia or vitamin B12 deficiency: Walker *et al.* 2009) or bony changes resulting from chronic irritation/inflammation of the scalp (e.g., caused by head lice, scalp infection).

Pyre debris
A small quantity of burnt and unburnt animal bone was recovered from deposit 10043 (Table 3.20), with fragments identified as pig and unidentified mammal. As only small fragments of animal bone were present, this may indicate that burnt animal remains were selectively excluded here. The unburnt animal remains may be residual. One fragment of human cranial vault exhibited iron staining on both the ecto- and endocranial surfaces. This indicates that this particular fragment must have come into contact with an iron object at some point during or after cremation had occurred. However, no other fragments from this or any of the other deposits containing cremated bone exhibited such staining, and no iron objects were found within the deposit.

Discussion by Lauren McIntyre

The Late Iron Age and Roman burials comprise at least two articulated burials (possibly three if skeleton 513 was Roman) and perhaps as many as eight cremation burials. The range of dental and skeletal pathology observed in the articulated burials falls within the expected pattern for the Roman period, as do the burial types (Pearce 2013). The most common skeletal pathology was joint disease. High rates of dental calculus may be indicative of poor oral hygiene.

The cremated bone deposits, often contained within urns, are also typical of the Roman period, All the observed cremated bone from this period was adult, with at least one probable female represented. Both burnt and unburnt animal bone was found commingled with human bone from deposits 5938 and 5940. This was largely unidentified, except for a single fragment (0.5g) of burnt chicken bone. Domestic fowl are one of the most commonly found species found in association with Romano-British cremation burials (Philpott 1991, 196). The small quantity included within the Thame deposits may indicate that an attempt was made to deliberately exclude animal fragments from the material being selected for burial (ibid.). Deposit 16754 was recovered from a drinking vessel within cinerary urn 16757, deposit 16756. It is unclear whether bone from 16754 was originally from 16756 (i.e., the same individual) or represents a second individual (a cenotaph or 'token' deposit). Urned cremation deposits from the Roman period are frequently accompanied by other ceramic vessels. Of these, drinking vessels are relatively common (ibid., 32, 35).

Animal bone
by Lee G. Broderick

Due to the constraints of the project the entirety of the animal bone which could be assigned to the Romano-British period (9703 specimens) was recorded to assessment level only (Smith and Strid 2017). The contexts from which the Romano-British animal bone assemblage was derived (a range of agricultural rather than settlement features) were not optimal for providing comprehensive evidence concerning animal husbandry and consumption practices. However, several associated bone groups (ABGs) were recovered, which included both articulated skeletons and, where considered to have been deliberately placed, isolated heads or, in one case a mandible; these were recorded in full.

Among the ABGs, the most notable were two dogs recovered from Middle Roman (period 3bii) fill of well 23 (5118). This feature was not fully excavated but a dog skeleton was recovered from the basal limit of the excavation, in collapse or backfill deposit 6165. Further up the well, fill 5119 included much of the post-cranial remains of a small dog together with fragments of distinctive Early Neolithic pottery which may have been placed deliberately alongside. The only complete bones of this animal were not fused so it was not possible to estimate the full adult size of the individual. For the same reasons, however, it was possible to estimate its age at no greater than six months at death (Silver 1969). By contrast, fill 6165 contained a skeletally mature individual standing to between 517mm (Koudelka 1885) and 527mm (Harcourt 1974) at the shoulder based on measurements of the right humerus (Table 3.23), making it a medium-sized dog.

Both dogs had suffered traumatic injury in their lives – the puppy from well 23 context 5119 had a healed fracture in its right 4th metatarsal, while the dog from well 23 context 6165 also has a fractured and healed right 4th metatarsal, as well as a fractured and healed rib and a necrotic right 5th metacarpal. Necrosis can be caused by a fracture disrupting the local blood supply (Bartosiewicz and Gál 2013, 74), so it seems likely that the two injuries to the feet of this individual were related.

ABGs were also recovered from several Early Roman contexts, although for the most part these are less complete and their inclusion as significant items, or ABGs, is therefore less certain. A complete male horse mandible was recovered from ditch 251 fill 6049, as well as a horse cranium (probably female) from fill 6838 of pit 6839 and a domestic cattle frontal with left horncore base from ditch 230 (fill 8893).

The final Early Roman ABG (period 3b) was a near-complete polled sheep found in pit 6770, which was a fairly small circular feature with steep sides and a concave base probably dug for the purpose of disposing of the sheep. Early Roman pottery, burnt bone, and charcoal was also found in the fill. Mandibular tooth wear suggests that this individual was between 3.5 and 5.5 years of age at death (left and right mandibles at stages F and G following Payne (1973), MWS 34–37 and 38–40 following Grant (1982)). Although lesions were observed on the proximal articular surface of the left metacarpal and on the proximal articular surface of the right radius, these are consistent with osteochondrosis and are likely to have not had a serious health outcome and so probably were not noticeable at the time (Sewell

Table 3.23 Measurements taken from the Roman Associated Bone Groups (in mm)

Context	Species	Element	Side	GL	Bp	Bd	SD
6165	Dog	Humerus	Left	152.0	28.5	29.9	11.1
6165	Dog	Humerus	Right	153.5	29.0	30.2	10.7
6165	Dog	Femur	Right	169	35.3	28.3	12.3
6769	Sheep/goat	Radius	Right	152.2	31.7	28.9	16.5
6769	Sheep/goat	Metatarsal	Left	313.2	20.1	24.0	11.6

GL= Greatest Length; Bp = Breadth proximal; Bd = Breadth distal; SD = Shaft diameter

2010). Oblique cut marks were also observed on the posterior of the shaft of the same radius as well as on the medial side of two rib blades which demonstrate that the animal was not a natural fatality. Specimens from this individual also showed signs of having been weathered more than the other bones from this period (stage 4; Behrensmeyer 1978), although the reason for this is unclear.

Dogs are by far the most commonly represented species in ABGs throughout the Roman period in southern England (Morris 2011) and are commonly found in wells (e.g., Maltby 2010; 1993). Such generalisations are tempered, however, by the fact that dog ABGs had been recovered from just nine Middle Roman sites in southern England when Morris undertook his doctoral research (2011, 69). Dog ABGs from this period have commonly been interpreted as culls (where several are present together) or as natural deaths (in the case of individual old or neonatal dogs); some have also been interpreted as ritual deposits (e.g., Woodward and Woodward 2004).

The fact that both individuals here have a matching injury is curious – perhaps especially so since neither can be associated with cause of death, but dogs are prone to injury when fighting or engaged in hunting or herding. Nevertheless, the fact that the older dog had suffered multiple fractured bones in its life and that the puppy had already suffered one suggests that both had led a hard life – either as working animals or as strays. This might be taken to suggest that they would be less worthy sacrifices than animals in better condition. However, referring to Snyder and Moore (2006), Roskams *et al.* (2013) note that there is some evidence for a significant change in the relationship between people and dogs by the Late Roman period with documentary evidence for the keeping of dogs as pets, and they prefer to view the deposition of puppy ABGs in this light.

Recent interpretations of the deposition of dogs in wells have tended to place less emphasis on the ABG as a focus of ritual activity and more on the function of the well itself. The sanctity of water in prehistoric Britain and northern Europe is now widely accepted and the pollution of wells in this way has been seen as a sign of de-consecration (Lepetz and Bourgois 2018). The construction of a well is a significant undertaking and it certainly should normally be assumed that to foul it and decommission it in this way – whether de-consecrating or not – was the result of a conscious decision.

There are now quite a number of Roman sites in Britain where complete dogs have been recovered from shafts or wells. In some cases, the sites have a clear religious focus, but in others the significance is harder to discern, especially where dogs are found in backfilled features together with general rubbish. Key examples include at least 20 dogs recovered from a ritual shaft at the Roman site of Springhead, Kent, a site now considered to be a sanctuary complex. Dating to the last quarter of the 2nd century AD, the feature contained eight puppies, two sub-adult dogs, eight dogs in their prime and two elderly dogs, some with chains, along with other animal ABGs and general butchery waste (Grimm 2007). Twenty dogs were also recovered from a late 2nd-century disused well at Southwark, and dogs have also been found in Roman shafts or wells at Ewell (up to 17 dogs), Keston (19 dogs), Staines (16 dogs) and Yeovilton (six dogs) (ibid.). At Oakridge Well, near Basingstoke, 172 ABGs were recovered from a single well after its abandonment, which included at least 29 dogs of a range of sizes and ages but many of which were immature; at least three were of Middle Roman date (Maltby 1993; Morris 2011, 80–1).

Large numbers of dog ABGs were also recovered from a range of Roman features at Owslebury, near Winchester (Maltby 1987) and Greyhound Yard, Dorchester (Maltby 1993), and these included many puppies: a concentration of neonates was found in 3rd–4th-century cess pits at Owslebury (Morris 2011, 75). It is likely in most or all of these examples that the dogs were disposed of as refuse rather than having any special 'ritual' significance. While the well at Thame was not fully excavated, no other animal remains were recovered from it and the placing of the dogs may have been deliberate, possibly as part of a closing action, although this cannot be established with any certainty.

Most of the other associated bone groups are ABGs in technicality only (in that they consist of bones which are not articulated but appeared to have been deliberately placed, *sensu* Hill 1995). In truth, the crania and paired horse mandibles (which fuse anteriorly) should perhaps be considered as isolated finds rather than ABGs as their significance and placing is equivocal. As ditch fills, and often found in association with other bones (not recorded here), these contexts are far from exceptional.

The Early Roman sheep ABG is, perhaps, more difficult to interpret. Excluding dogs, caprines are the most common ABG in the Early Roman period but we should be cautious in interpreting them as anything other than natural deaths. As argued elsewhere (Broderick 2012), the wider archaeological and taphonomic context should also be considered, which in this case includes evidence of butchery. Many rituals involving animals incorporate feasting or other kinds of ceremonialised butchery (Wilson 1992) so as butchery marks were observed on this animal, the probability of it representing a feasting, possibly ritual, deposit is increased. The butchery marks in this case, on rib blades and on the ventral shaft of a radius would most commonly be found on bone deposited as table waste, so may indicate that the animal was prepared for a communal meal, although the cut radius could relate to skinning. A mix of burnt bone and charcoal was also recovered from the top of the fill, which lends support to the former interpretation. Caution should be sounded, however, by the poor condition of the bones in comparison to the rest of the assemblage, which could represent some time left exposed to the elements, although roasting would also render the remains susceptible to weathering. It seems significant in this regard that the skull was broken, with the occipital missing but with evidence for a post-sized hole through the back of the skull and the nasal bones.

Fish bones
by Rebecca A. Nicholson

Late Iron Age or Roman ditch 206, fill 8115 (sample 749) includes a fragment of a probable cyprinid (*Cyprinidae*) vertebra. Two vertebrae of eel (*Anguilla anguilla* (L.)) came from a Middle Roman fill (5121) of well 23 (cut 5118; sample 505). While fish was evidently eaten by the Roman elite, there is very little evidence that the general Romano-British population did so and it is likely that eating, or not eating, fish was a cultural choice.

Charcoal
by Julia Meen

A total of 89 samples dated to the Romano-British period were processed and assessed. Of these, 11 were assigned to the Late Iron Age/Early Roman transition period, ten as Early Roman, and seven as Late Roman, the remainder assigned a general Romano-British date. Most samples contained very little charcoal and on the basis of the assessment, one sample each from a ditch fill from period 3a, a ditch fill from period 3b, and a corndrier from period 3c were selected for further analysis. In addition, four spatial samples from a second corndrier, 45 (6689), which has not been precisely dated but is also presumed to be Roman, were examined as the assessment suggested variation in wood taxa across the structure. A total of 245 charcoal fragments were identified from features dated to the Romano-British period.

Charcoal identifications for each of the samples analysed are presented in Table 3.24 and the relative proportion of the various wood taxa is illustrated in Figure 3.18. The methodology is detailed in the Appendix.

Period 3a – Late Iron Age/Early Roman (*c.* 25 BC–AD 100)

Ditch 206 (5801)
Charcoal was in excellent condition in the sample from Late Iron Age/Early Roman ditch 206 (5801), with abundant fragments many of which were of a large

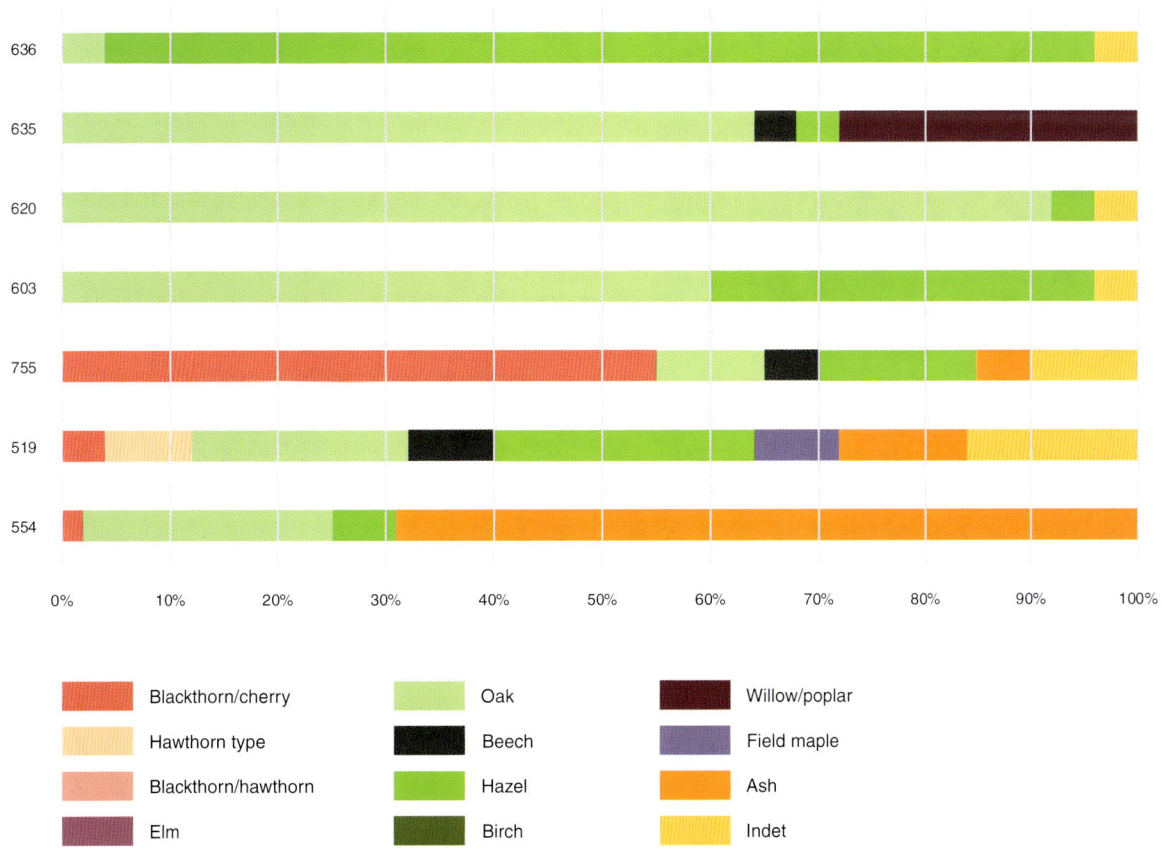

Fig. 3.18 Charcoal taxa, by sample, period 3

Table 3.24 Charcoal from period 3a, 3b, 3c and 3d features

Context number		5803	5323	8264	6628	6628	6674	6952
Feature number		206 (5801)	206 (5288)	26 (7630)	45 (6689)	45 (6689)	45 (6689)	45 (6689)
Sample number (SS)		554	519	755	603	620	635	636
Feature type		Ditch	Ditch	Corndrier	Corndrier	Corndrier	Corndrier	Corndrier
Sample volume processed (l)		8L	40L	10L	16L	10L	10L	10L
Period		3a	3b	3c	3d	3d	3d	3d
Charcoal quantity >4mm		****	**	*	**	***	**	**
Charcoal quantity 2–4mm		*****	***	***	***	****	****	***
Charcoal preservation		Very Good	Moderate	Moderate	Moderate	Moderate	Moderate	Moderate
Family	Species	Common Name						
Rosaceae	*Prunus* spp.	blackthorn/sloe/cherry		1	7 (r)				
	cf *Prunus*	cf blackthorn/sloe/cherry	1 (r)		4				
	cf Maloideae	cf hawthorn type		2					
Fagaceae	*Quercus* spp.	oak	23 (h)	5 (h)	2	15	23 (r)	16	1
	Fagus	beech		1					
	cf Fagus	cf beech		1	1				
Betulaceae	*Corylus avellana* L.	hazel	4	5 (r)		9 (r)	1	1	22 (r)
	cf *Corylus*	cf hazel	2		3 (r)				1
	Alnus/Corylus	alder/hazel		1					
Salicaceae	*Salix/Populus* sp.	willow/poplar		1				6	
	cf *Salix/Populus*	cf willow/poplar		1				1	
Sapindaceae	*Acer campestre* L.	field maple			1				
	cf *Acer*	cf field maple							
Oleaceae	*Fraxinus excelsior* L.	ash	69	3					
		indet diffuse porous		2					
		indet ring porous		1		1			
		indet		1	2	1	1		1
		Total	100	25	20	25	25	25	25

size. It was therefore possible to carry out identification of a full 100 fragments. A high proportion of the assemblage, almost 70%, was ash (*Fraxinus excelsior*), with much of the remainder oak (*Quercus* sp.) and a small number of hazel (*Corylus avellana*) and blackthorn/cherry (*Prunus* sp.) fragments. No other features from this period produced more than a few fragments of identifiable charcoal, but where present the provisional identifications include a similar range of taxa and also include field maple (*Acer campestre*) and beech (*Fagus sylvatica*) (Cobain *et al.* 2017).

Period 3b – Early and Middle Roman (*c.* AD 100–240)

Ditch 206 (5288)
Very few pieces of potentially identifiable charcoal were recovered from this Early Romano-British ditch fill (5323), with most pieces <4mm in size. Only 25 pieces were large enough to attempt identification, and a fifth of these were ultimately indeterminate. However, very few samples from Early Roman features at the site contained charcoal in any significant quantity and therefore identification of these fragments was undertaken to provide some qualitative information for this period. The charcoal comprised a mixture of oak, hazel, blackthorn, ash, field maple and beech; similar taxa to those identified from Period 3a.

Period 3d – Roman (AD 43–410)

Corndrier 45
Assessment of eight samples taken from within corndrier 45 (6689), dated only as broadly Romano-British (Fig. 2.16), indicated spatial variation in wood taxa across the structure (Cobain *et al.* 2017), and further work has aimed to explore and clarify this variation. However, most of the samples from this feature produced limited charcoal and full analysis of an ideal 100 pieces was not possible on any individual sample. It was therefore decided to identify 25 pieces from each of four samples in order to characterise differences in wood taxa in each of these locations within the corndrier.

Although a limited number of charcoal fragments could be identified, the results appear to confirm spatial variation in wood taxa at different locations within the corndrier. Sample 603 was taken from fill 6628, a layer of burnt debris containing much daub and stone that filled the upper part of the corndrier flue close to the entrance and so likely to be a dump of mixed material presumably deposited into the flue after the corndrier had gone out of use. The charcoal from this sample was a mixture of oak and hazel. Although this may be the remains of the main fuels used to fire the corndrier, the hazel could equally be the remains of a wattle-work superstructure forming the upper part of the flue. Fired clay fragments from this corndrier contain impressions of wattles (Poole, this chapter), with rods set at angles that imply they formed an interwoven framework. Although only two of the hazel charcoal fragments were clearly roundwood, hazel coppices readily produce rods ideal for wattle-work so there is a strong possibility that the hazel charcoal in this sample is the remnant of the wattles that formed these impressions.

Sample 620 was also taken from fill 6673, at the junction of the flue and the main chamber of the corndrier. Almost all examined charcoal fragments from this sample were oak, and a scan of the smaller pieces indicated that a high proportion of these were also oak. Samples 635 and 636 were taken from the lower levels of the corndrier, after much of the upper fill had been removed. Sample 635 was taken from fill 6930, from the middle of the flue, and contained a high proportion of oak, but also a number of pieces of willow or poplar (*Salix/Populus*; these taxa are extremely difficult to differentiate using anatomical characteristics). There were also several fragments of bark. Sample 636, taken from the entrance to the main chamber, was almost entirely hazel, including pieces of roundwood, although the number of roundwood pieces may be underestimated as it is more difficult to record curvature for smaller pieces of charcoal. As its composition is so distinct from the other charcoal assemblages from the corndrier, this localised accumulation of hazel charcoal may represent a section of fallen wattle-work superstructure.

Many of the samples from the corndrier contained abundant cereal grain, particularly sample 603, which was especially rich in barley grain. This structure has therefore been interpreted as having been used for the parching of partially processed cereals, with the use of cereal chaff as tinder (Wyles, this chapter). Although there are variations in the wood taxa identified from different parts of the structure, oak occurs throughout and may represent the main fuel. However, as the quantities of charcoal recovered from the feature are relatively low, and mixed with various dumped materials, some doubt inevitably remains that this charcoal represents the remains of fuel used to fire the corndrier.

Period 3c – Late Roman (*c.* AD 240–410)

Corndrier 26
An apparently charcoal-rich burnt layer (8264) from the base of corndrier 26 (7630), dated to the Late Roman period, ultimately produced only 20 pieces of charcoal that could be identified, and unfortunately many of these were still extremely small. The most common taxon was blackthorn/cherry, with oak, cf. beech, hazel and ash also present. A second sample from context 8065 contained only a small quantity of fragmentary charcoal, which was examined during the assessment (Cobain *et al.* 2017). All identifiable pieces from 8065 were oak, although as much of the charcoal was split radially, the number of identifiable pieces was reduced,

and oak tends to be preferentially identified in this type of material. The charcoal from this corndrier, although limited to a small number of identifiable charcoal fragments, corroborates the evidence from corndrier 45 that wood of more than one type was being utilised in these structures. Two out of the three spatial samples from this corndrier were highly abundant in spelt wheat chaff, and this may have been used in conjunction with the wood to light the corndrier.

Woodland in the Romano-British period

The mixed charcoal assemblages from the Romano-British samples hint that diverse woodland resources were being exploited during this period. While hazel charcoal was rare in the prehistoric samples (see Volume 1), this wood is clearly present in Roman times, perhaps reflecting the spread of secondary, more open woodland, although mature oak was certainly still available. Pollen evidence from Mingies Ditch, in the Windrush Valley in west Oxfordshire, suggests that the much of the local landscape had been cleared by the Middle Iron Age (Allen and Robinson 1993), whilst charcoal evidence from Didcot, in south Oxfordshire, suggests that fuel was predominantly being collected from scrubby or secondary woodland by this time (Boardman 2023). At the Roman villa at Mantles Green, Amersham, across the Chilterns from Thame, oak was the most common taxa throughout all periods of activity at the site, from the mid 2nd to the late 4th century. This was followed in abundance by alder (*Alnus glutinosa*) and beech; Miles suggests that a mixed oak-alder-beech woodland was being exploited for fuelwood (1992).

The charcoal assemblage from ditch 206 (5288) shows that beech was being utilised at the site in the Early Roman period, and single fragments of beech were also identified from three contexts dating to period 3a (Cobain *et al.* 2017). Beech pollen was recorded elsewhere on the Thame site, coming from a waterlogged pit sealed by Late Iron Age/Early Roman sediments (Rutherford 2017). No beech charcoal was recovered from either the Early Neolithic samples or from the Early Iron Age features, and no beech pollen was recorded from the enclosure ditch of the causewayed enclosure. Today the Chilterns, only 10km to the east of Thame, are well known for their extensive beech woodlands. Kidd (2014) has suggested that the Chiltern beech woods first developed in the 1st millennium BC, based on finds of both pollen and charcoal from Little Marlow (Richmond *et al.* 2006) and also beech charcoal from prehistoric contexts at Taplow, although subsequent radiocarbon dating has shown that this latter material is probably intrusive (Gale 2011; Warman 2011). Godwin (1984, 276) notes that British pollen diagrams consistently show an increase in beech pollen during the Roman and medieval periods, and he furthermore suggests that it was clearance of the natural oak forests that precipitated this rise, as beech can only outcompete oak during episodes of woodland regeneration (Godwin 1984). It will be seen that beech comes to be of great importance at the site by the Saxon period, particularly as a fuel, and the development of local beech woodlands will be further discussed in Chapter 5.

Plant macrofossils
by Sarah F. Wyles

Roman period plant remains are shown in Tables 3.25–3.26. Methodology is described in the Appendix.

Period 3a – Late Iron Age/Early Romano-British (*c.* 25 BC–AD 100)

Oven 7419
There were four samples examined from oven 7419. The rich assemblage recovered from fill 7667 (sample 731) of section 7419, thought to represent material from the second phase of use, was dominated by the weed seed component. Whereas the smaller assemblages from fills 7418 (sample 695) and 7850 (sample 734) of sections 7419 and 7697 respectively (believed to represent material from the first phase of use of the oven), and deposit 8036 (sample 744) of possible flue 8037 contained cereal remains and weed seeds in roughly equal numbers.

The cereal remains included those of spelt wheat with lower amounts of barley (*Hordeum vulgare*) and possible free-threshing wheat (*Triticum turgidum/aestivum* type). There was also a coleoptile fragment. The weed seeds included those of vetch/wild pea (*Vicia/Lathyrus* sp.), oats and brome grass (*Avena/Bromus* sp.), rye-grass/fescue (*Lolium/Festuca* sp.) and meadow grass/cat's-tails (*Poa/Phleum* sp.).

The assemblage from fill 7667 may be reflective of a mixture of the stored grain being dried debris and tinder used for the firing of the oven. The other assemblages may be representative of remains left in the oven and possible flue after it had been cleaned out after domestic use.

Period 3b – Early and Middle Romano-British (*c.* AD 100–240)

Pit 10268
The moderate assemblage observed from fill 10280 (sample 1006) mainly consisted of grains of barley. It may be indicative of being a dump of domestic settlement waste.

Pit 15860
Fill 15861 (sample 1584) of pit 15860 contained a high number of charred plant remains, in particular those of cereal, with the chaff elements out numbering the grains. The cereal remains included those of spelt wheat, with low numbers of those of barley and free-threshing wheat. There were also a few coleoptile fragments. The weed seeds included those of oats, brome grass, rye-

Table 3.25 Charred plant remains from period 3a and 3b features

Period		3a LIA/ERB				3b ERB		
Feature type		Oven 7419				Pit	Pit	Corn drier/ oven 46
Cut		7419	7697	8037	10268	15860	8164	
Context		7418	7667	7850	8036	10280	15861	8243
Sample		695	731	734	744	1006	1584	758
Vol (L)		10	10	9	8	20	20	10
Flot size		10	10	5	5	25	15	65
%Roots		20	5	20	10	5	10	10
Scanned/ analysed		A	A	A	A	S	A	A
Cereals	**Common Name**							
Hordeum vulgare L. *sl* (grain)	barley	2	1	2	-	46	4	14
Hordeum vulgare L. *sl* (rachis frag)	barley	-	-	1	-	-	2	2
Triticum dicoccum (Schübl) (glume base)	emmer wheat	-	-	-	-	-	-	2
Triticum spelta L. (grain)	spelt wheat	1	-	-	-	-	2	2
Triticum spelta L. (germinated grain)	spelt wheat	-	-	-	-	-	-	9
Triticum spelta L. (glume bases)	spelt wheat	-	2	1	-	-	68	550
Triticum spelta L. (spikelet fork)	spelt wheat	-	-	-	-	-	-	12
Triticum dicoccum/spelta (grain)	emmer/spelt wheat	1	11	2	1	2	30	91
Triticum dicoccum/spelta (germinated grain)	emmer/spelt wheat	-	-	-	-	-	-	15
Triticum dicoccum/spelta (spikelet fork)	emmer/spelt wheat	6	3	-	1	-	12	40
Triticum dicoccum/spelta (glume bases)	emmer/spelt wheat	-	5	1	-	-	93	1015
Triticum turgidum/aestivum (grain)	free-threshing wheat	-	-	cf. 1	-	-	4	2
Triticum turgidum/aestivum (rachis frags)	free-threshing wheat	-	-	-	-	-	2	4
Cereal indet. (grains)	cereal	6	28	3	1	+	60	75
Cereal frag. (est. whole grains)	cereal	4	12	2	1	-	17	40
Cereal frags (rachis frags)	cereal	2	-	-	-	-	-	-
Cereal frags (culm node)	cereal	-	2	-	-	-	1	-
Cereal frags (coleoptile)	cereal	-	1	-	-	-	6	37
Other Species								
Ranunculus sp.	buttercup	-	-	-	-	-	-	2
Urtica urens L.	small nettle	2	-	-	-	-	-	-
Corylus avellana L. (fragments)	hazelnut	2	-	-	-	-	-	-
Chenopodium sp.	goosefoot	-	1	-	-	-	4	1
Chenopodium album L.	fat-hen	1	-	-	-	-	1	1
Montia fontana subsp. *chondrosperma* (Fenzl) Walters	blinks	-	2	-	-	-	-	-
Stellaria sp. L.	stitchworts	-	-	1	-	-	-	5
Persicaria lapathifolia/maculosa (L.) Gray/ Gray	pale persicaria/red-shank	-	-	-	-	1	1	-
Polygonum aviculare L.	knotgrass	-	1	-	-	-	-	-
Rumex sp. L.	docks	-	2	1	1	1	7	6
Rumex acetosella group Raf.	sheep's sorrel	-	2	-	-	-	2	7
Rumex crispus L. Type	curled dock	1	-	-	-	-	4	12
Malva sp. L.	mallow	-	-	1	-	-	-	-
Brassica sp. L.	brassica	-	1	-	-	-	1	1

Table 3.25 (cont.) Charred plant remains from period 3a and 3b features

Period		3a LIA/ERB				3b ERB		
Feature type		Oven 7419				Pit	Pit	Corn drier/ oven 46
Cut		7419	7697		8037	10268	15860	8164
Context		7418	7667	7850	8036	10280	15861	8243
Sample		695	731	734	744	1006	1584	758
Rubus	brambles	1	-	-	-	-	-	-
Prunus spinosa/ Crataegus monogyna (thorns/twigs)	sloe/hawthorn type thorns	1	-	-	-	-	-	-
Vicia L./*Lathyrus* sp. L.	vetch/wild pea	5	76	3	1	3	14	22
Vicia sativa L.	common vetch	-	4	-	-	-	-	2
Lathyrus cf. *nissolia* L.	grass vetchling	-	5	-	-	-	1	2
Medicago/Trifolium sp. L.	medick/clover	-	3	1	-	-	3	8
Odontites vernus (Bellardi) Dumort	red bartsia	-	2	-	-	-	-	2
Galium sp. L.	bedstraw	-	-	-	-	-	-	1
Galium aparine L.	cleavers	-	1	-	-	-	-	-
Valerianella dentata (L.) Pollich	narrow-fruited cornsalad	1	1	-	-	-	-	-
Anthemis cotula L. (seeds)	stinking mayweed	-	-	-	-	-	2	-
Tripleurospermum inodorum (L.) Sch. Bip.	scentless mayweed	1	3	-	-	-	10	25
Lolium/Festuca sp.	rye-grass/fescue	1	6	1	-	-	20	208
Lolium pratensis Huds.	meadow fescue	-	-	-	-	-	-	10
Poa/Phleum sp. L.	meadow grass/ cat's-tails	1	5	1	1	-	1	5
Avena sp. L. (grain)	oat grain	1	6	1	-	-	12	11
Avena sp. L. (spikelet)	oat spikelet	-	-	-	-	-	-	4
Avena sp. L. (floret base)	oat floret	-	-	-	-	-	-	7
Avena sp. L. (awn)	oat awn	-	1	-	-	-	6	23
Avena L./*Bromus* L. sp.	oat/brome grass	2	9	1	-	3	12	8
Bromus sp. L.	brome grass	1	1	-	-	1	4	1
Triangular capsule frag		-	-	-	-	-	-	6
Conglomeration of seed and stem frags		-	-	4	-	-	-	-
Mineralised nodule		-	-	-	-	-	-	2

Key: + = 0–49, ++ = 50–99, +++ - 100+

grass fescue, scentless mayweed (*Tripleurospermum inodorum*) and docks (*Rumex* sp.). This assemblage may be representative of a dump of waste material from the processing of semi-cleaned stored grain or spikelets.

Corndrier 46

A very large charred plant assemblage, dominated by the chaff elements, was recorded from fill 8243 (sample 758) of flue 8164. The cereal remains included those of spelt wheat and smaller numbers of those of barley, emmer wheat and free-threshing wheat. Traces of germination were observed on a relatively small number of the grains and there were a number of coleoptile fragments.

The weed seeds included seeds of rye-grass/fescue, oats, brome grass, scentless mayweed, vetch/wild pea, curled dock (*Rumex crispus*), sheep's sorrel (*Rumex acetosella* group), and clover/medick clover (*Trifolium/Medicago* sp.). There were also oat awn and floret fragments.

This assemblage may be mainly reflective of crop-processing waste derived from the dehusking of hulled grain stored as semi-cleaned grain or in spikelet form (Hillman 1981; 1984). It appears that this kind of crop-processing waste material was used on occasions as tinder within corndriers (van der Veen 1989).

Table 3.26 Charred plant remains from period 3c and 3d features

Period		3c LRB				3d RB					
Feature type		Corndrier 26	Corndrier 24	Corndrier 25	Pit	Corndrier 29		3d RB		Corndrier 45	
Cut		7630	8986	10083	16868	16538			6627		6673
Context		8264	8985	8652	16870	16543	1640	1663	603	612	620
Sample		755	829	846	1654						
Vol (L)		10	10	18	40		10	25	16	7	10
Flot size		110	90	45	150		35	75	150	30	100
%Roots		2	1	20	2		5	5	2	5	2
% 0.5mm fraction analysed		100	100	100	10		100	10	100	100	100
% 0.25mm fraction analysed		100	100	100	100		100	100	100	100	100
Cereals	Common Name										
Hordeum vulgare L. sl (grain)	barley	83	210	18	37		2	3	589	22	232
Hordeum vulgare L. sl (grain still in husk)	barley	3	2	-	-		-	-	2	-	1
Hordeum vulgare L. sl (grain) germinated	barley	3	10	-	-		-	-	11	-	-
Hordeum vulgare L. sl (rachis frag)	barley	160	4	14	e. 23		-	-	6	2	15
Triticum cf. dicoccum (Schübl) (grain)	emmer wheat	7	-	-	-		-	-	-	-	-
Triticum dicoccum (Schübl) (glume base)	emmer wheat	2	2	-	-		-	2	3	-	2
Triticum dicoccum (Schübl) (spikelet fork)	emmer wheat	2	-	-	-		-	-	-	-	4
Triticum spelta L. (grain)	spelt wheat	22	43	8	105		50	30	156	4	45
Triticum spelta L. (germinated grain)	spelt wheat	-	-	1	3		2	2	5	5	-
Triticum spelta L. (grain in spikelet)	spelt wheat	-	-	-	6		-	-	-	2	-
Triticum spelta L. (glume bases)	spelt wheat	870	84	230	1087		255	774	172	17	149
Triticum spelta L. (spikelet fork)	spelt wheat	11	16	10	50		4	14	21	5	23
Triticum dicoccum/spelta (grain)	emmer/spelt wheat	130	74	138	210		41	126	205	32	93
Triticum dicoccum/spelta (germinated grain)	emmer/spelt wheat	3	3	-	3		2	7	12	-	2
Triticum dicoccum/spelta (spikelet fork)	emmer/spelt wheat	135	20	52	e. 255		55	e. 124	36	14	119
Triticum dicoccum/spelta (glume bases)	emmer/spelt wheat	530	168	645	e. 2135		425	e. 1237	104	23	226
Triticum turgidum/aestivum (grain)	free-threshing wheat	14	10	2	33		6	5	26	1	8
Triticum turgidum/aestivum (rachis frags)	free-threshing wheat	20	7	10	e. 28		3	5	15	1	10
Secale cereale (grain)	rye	1	-	-	-		-	-	2	-	-
Cereal indet. (grains)	cereal	60	40	65	145		40	150	60	20	63
Cereal frag. (est. whole grains)	cereal	40	50	40	60		15	55	40	15	57
Cereal frags (rachis frags)	cereal	40	-	15	-		-	-	-	1	2
Cereal frags (culm node)	cereal	-	-	2	-		-	1	3	-	4

Table 3.26 (cont.) Charred plant remains from period 3c and 3d features

Period		3c LRB				3d RB			
Feature type		Corndrier 26	Corndrier 24	Corndrier 25	Pit	Corndrier 29			Corndrier 45
Cut		7630	8986	10083	16868	16538			6627
Context		8264	8985	8652	16870	16543	1663	6628	6679	6673
Sample		755	829	846	1654	1640		603	612	620
Cereal frags (basal culm node)	cereal	-	-	-	-	-	-	-	-	1
Cereal frags (silicified awns)	cereal	-	-	+++	++	+++	+++	-	-	-
Cereal frags (detached embryo)	cereal	3	5	-	-	9	5	4	3	9
Cereal frags (coleoptile)	cereal	10	4	2	14	23	c. 111	4	2	11
Other Species										
Ranunculus sp.	buttercup	-	-	1	1	-	-	-	-	-
Papaver rhoeas L.	common poppy	-	-	-	-	2	-	-	-	-
Urtica dioica L.	common nettle	-	-	-	-	-	-	2	-	1
Corylus avellana L. (fragments)	hazelnut	-	1	-	-	-	-	-	-	-
Chenopodium sp.	goosefoot	10	1	-	-	3	c. 20	-	4	-
Chenopodium album L.	fat-hen	12	-	-	1	5	1	-	-	1
Atriplex sp. L.	oraches	2	-	-	-	2	-	-	-	-
Agrostemma githago L.	corncockle	2	3	-	4	1	5	43	-	16
Silene sp. L.	campions	-	-	-	1	-	-	-	-	-
Persicaria lapathifolia/maculosa (L.) Gray/Gray	pale persicaria/redshank	1	-	-	4	-	-	-	-	-
Persicaria lapathifolia (L.) Gray	pale persicaria	3	-	-	-	1	-	-	-	-
Persicaria maculosa (L.) Gray	redshank	-	-	-	-	1	-	-	-	-
Polygonum aviculare L.	knotgrass	2	-	-	c. 27	2	2	2	1	1
Fallopia convolvulus (L.) À. Löve	black-bindweed	1	-	-	2	1	1	1	-	1
Rumex sp. L.	docks	9	2	9	c. 77	50	-	28	7	14
Rumex acetosella group Raf.	sheep's sorrel	-	2	2	c. 40	10	-	-	4	-
Rumex crispus L. Type	curled dock	20	9	17	c. 165	55	36	30	9	20
Brassica sp. L.	brassica	2	2	-	2	1	2	2	-	3
Raphanus raphanistrum L. capsule	runch	4	-	-	-	-	-	1	-	-
Potentilla sp. L.	cinquefoils	-	-	-	-	-	-	1	-	-
Vicia L./*Lathyrus* sp. L.	vetch/wild pea	3	10	8	20	22	13	23	10	23
Vicia sativa L.	common vetch	-	-	1	1	-	1	3	-	-
Vicia faba L.	Celtic bean	-	-	-	-	1	-	-	-	-
Lathyrus cf. *nissolia* L.	grass vetchling	-	-	-	-	-	-	-	-	-

The Late Iron Age and Romano-British Finds and Environmental Remains 117

Period		3c LRB				3d RB			
Feature type									
Cut	Corndrier 26	Corndrier 24	Corndrier 25	Pit	Corndrier 29		Corndrier 45		
	7630	8986	10083	16868	16538		6628	6627	6673
Context	8264	8985	8652	16870	16543	16543	603	6679	620
Sample	755	829	846	1654	1640	1663	6628	612	6673
Medicago/Trifolium sp. L. — medick/clover	3	2	31	e. 53	11	e. 12	3	3	-
Trifolium sp. L. — clover	-	-	-	-	-	-	4	-	-
Linum usitatissimum L. — flax	-	-	-	-	-	-	-	-	1
Galeopsis cf. *tetrahit* L. — common hemp-nettle	-	-	-	-	-	-	1	-	-
Prunella vulgaris L. — selfheal	-	-	-	-	1	-	-	-	-
Plantago lanceolata L. — ribwort plantain	-	-	-	-	1	2	-	-	-
Odontites vernus (Bellardi) Dumort — red bartsia	-	-	3	e. 20	13	-	-	1	1
Sherardia arvensis L. — field madder	-	-	-	2	-	-	-	-	-
Galium sp. L. — bedstraw	-	1	-	-	-	-	-	1	-
Valerianella dentata (L.) Pollich — narrow-fruited cornsalad	-	1	-	-	-	-	-	1	-
Cardus/Cirsium — thistle	1	-	-	-	-	-	-	-	-
Centaurea cyanus L. — cornflower	2	-	-	3	-	1	-	-	-
Anthemis cotula L. (seeds) — stinking mayweed	10	-	102	-	-	e. 20	18	-	1
Tripleurospermum inodorum (L.) Sch. Bip. — scentless mayweed	-	-	9	e. 146	56	e. 74	5	7	2
Lolium/Festuca sp. — rye-grass/fescue	2	-	3	e. 120	18	e. 110	3	-	2
Lolium pratensis Huds. — meadow fescue	-	-	-	5	-	7	-	-	-
Poa/Phleum sp. L. — meadow grass/cat's-tails	2	1	28	2	4	e. 10	2	4	2
Avena sp. L. (grain) — oat grain	51	9	6	30	15	11	52	5	17
Avena sp. L. (spikelet) — oat spikelet	-	-	-	-	-	-	-	-	-
Avena sp. L. (floret base) — oat floret	9	5	-	-	-	3	1	-	5
Avena sp. L. (awn) — oat awn	32	-	13	e. 90	20	e. 71	-	3	1
Avena L./*Bromus* L. sp. — oat/brome grass	80	5	21	30	26	91	81	3	71
Bromus sp. L. — brome grass	84	3	8	27	45	40	107	12	38
Monocot. stem/rootlet frag	7	-	-	-	-	-	-	-	-
Triangular capsule frag	1	-	2	6	9	10	-	-	2
Mineralised nodule	1	-	-	-	-	-	-	-	-

Period 3c – Late Romano-British (*c.* AD 240–410)

Corndrier 26

Fill 8264 (sample 755), the first layer within the structure of corndrier 26, produced a very large charred plant assemblage, dominated by chaff remains. The cereal remains included those of spelt wheat, which lower numbers of barley, emmer wheat, free-threshing wheat and rye. Traces of germination were observed on a few of the grains and there were a few detached embryos and coleoptile fragments.

The weed seeds included seeds of brome grass, oats, stinking mayweed (*Anthemis cotula*), curled dock and fat-hen (*Chenopodium album*). There were a few oat awn and floret base fragments.

This assemblage may be representative of waste material from the processing of semi-cleaned stored grain or spikelets.

Corndrier 24

The large assemblage recovered from fill 8885 (sample 829) of section 8986 was dominated by cereal remains, in particular those of spelt wheat and barley with smaller amounts of those of free-threshing wheat and emmer wheat. A small number of the grains displayed traces of germination and there were a few detached embryos and coleoptile fragments within the assemblage. The weed seeds included seeds of oats, brome grass, vetch/wild pea and curled dock.

The assemblage may be reflective of a mixture of the stored grain itself being dried and of crop-processing waste derived from the processing of semi-cleaned stored grain or spikelets. The relative abundance of both barley and hulled wheat grains within the assemblage may be indicative of the sampled deposit having derived from a number of different firings of the corndrier rather than two crops being dried simultaneously.

Corndrier 25

Fill 8652 (sample 846) of flue 10083 contained a very high number of charred plant remains. The assemblage was dominated by chaff elements. The cereal remains included those of spelt wheat, with smaller quantities of those of barley and free-threshing wheat. There was a large quantity of silicified awn fragments within the assemblage, which may be indicative of this material having been used as fuel (Wyles 2017). There were also a very few coleoptile and germinated grain fragments. The weed seeds included seeds of stinking mayweed, meadow grass/cat's-tails, oats, brome grass, clover/medick and curled dock.

This assemblage may be representative of waste material from the processing of semi-cleaned stored grain or spikelets being used as fuel within the corndrier.

Period 3d – Romano-British (AD 43–410)

Several features were only dated broadly to the Romano-British period, although corndrier 29 may relate to Late Roman 1 period 3ci, based on its arrangement with adjacent features.

Pit 16868

An extremely large assemblage was recorded from fill 16870 (sample 1654) of pit 16868. This was dominated by chaff elements and the cereal remains included those of spelt wheat and smaller quantities of those of barley and free-threshing wheat. A few of the grains showed traces of germination and there were a small number of coleoptile fragments. There were also silicified awns within the assemblage.

The weed seeds included seeds of curled dock, sheep's sorrel, clover/medick, rye-grass/fescue, scentless mayweed, oat, brome grass, red bartsia, knotgrass (*Polygonum aviculare*) and vetch/wild pea. There were also a number of oat awn fragments.

This assemblage may be reflective of waste material from the processing of semi-cleaned stored grain or spikelets.

Corndrier 29

Both samples (1640 and 1663) from deposit 16543 (thought to represent material from the final firing of the corndrier) of section 16538, produced very large charred plant assemblages, dominated by chaff elements. The cereal remains included those of spelt wheat, with small numbers of those of barley, emmer wheat and free-threshing wheat. There were some detached embryo coleoptile fragments and traces of germination on a few grains. There were also a high number of silicified awns. The weed seeds included seeds of scentless mayweed, rye-grass/fescue, oats, brome grass and curled dock.

Again, these assemblages may be representative of waste material from the processing of semi-cleaned stored grain or spikelets being used as fuel within the corndrier.

Corndrier 45

Fill 6628 (sample 603) of cut 6627 contained a very large grain-rich assemblage. The cereal remains included barley and spelt wheat with smaller quantities of those of free-threshing wheat, emmer wheat and rye. A small number of the grains showed traces of germination and there were a few detached embryos and coleoptile fragments. The weed seeds included seeds of brome grass, oats, stinking mayweed, vetch/wild pea, corncockle and curled dock.

This assemblage may mainly be reflective of stored grain being dried prior to use and it may be indicative of the sampled deposit having derived from a number of different firings of the corndrier rather than two crops being dried simultaneously.

Very high numbers of charred plant remains were recovered from fill 6673 (sample 620) and a large assemblage from fill 6679 (sample 612) of cut 6627. In both cases the assemblages were cereal rich, with roughly equal amounts of grain and chaff remains. The cereal remains included those of barley and spelt wheat with low quantities of free-threshing wheat and emmer wheat. Again, a small number of the grains showed traces of germination and there were a few detached embryos and coleoptile fragments. The weed seeds included seeds of brome grass, oats, vetch/wild pea, curled dock and corncockle.

These assemblages may be a mixture of the crop being dried and the crop-processing waste being used as tinder for the firing of the corndrier.

Probable Romano-British – pit 8184

The moderate assemblage recorded from fill 8181 (sample 751) of pit 8184, part of Early Neolithic pit group 2 (see Volume 1) was dominated by cereal remains. These included those of barley, emmer wheat, spelt wheat and free-threshing wheat. The weed seeds included those of stinking mayweed (*Anthemis cotula*) and blinks (*Montia fontana* subsp. *chondrosperma*). There is no firm indication of the likely date of this deposit from the assemblage, but it is unlikely to be Neolithic. There may be some intrusive material within the assemblage (free-threshing wheat and stinking mayweed are typical of Saxon or later assemblages) and the presence of both emmer and spelt glumes may be indicative of a broadly similar date to the larger assemblage recorded from Early Neolithic pit 5810 (see Volume 1) for this assemblage. Two possible emmer wheat grains were radiocarbon dated to the Roman period and the assemblage would be compatible with this date.

Discussion

Periods 3a and 3b – Late Iron Age/Early Romano-British–Early/Middle Romano-British

Corndriers appear to have been used for a number of different purposes such as drying the crops before storage as semi-processed grain or spikelets, parching the crops after they had been removed from such storage and pounded, or as part of malting process during the brewing process (van der Veen 1989). The oven 7419 and corndrier 46 analysed from these periods appear to have been used for the parched of the processed crops after they had been removed from storage and there is an indication that the crop-processing waste from the dehusking of this stored material was used as tinder. At Whitelands Farm, Bicester (Stevens 2011b) the results from the corndrier were associated with malting rather than drying the crops after storage.

The possible crops included those of spelt wheat, barley and emmer wheat. These species were also recovered in other Late Iron Age and Early Romano-British assemblages in the area such as Yarnton (Stevens 2011a), Ashville Trading Estate (Jones 1978), Whitelands Farm, Bicester (Stevens 2011b) and Gravelly Guy, Stanton Harcourt (Moffett 2004). There appears to be evidence for late-stage crop processing of semi-cleaned stored grain or spikelets during these periods, particularly in the vicinity of pit 15860 and oven 7419 and corndrier 46. The crops may have been harvested low down by sickle. The assemblages from Ashville Trading Estate (Jones 1978) were also glume rich and indicative of waste from late-stage processing, while those assemblages from Yarnton were more typical of remains from the processing of 'grain stored as partially threshed ears or in the sheaf' (Stevens 2011a, 564). The general lack of culm nodes in the assemblages suggests that the initial processing of the crops was done in the fields, removing most of the bulky waste before bringing them into the site.

Again, the weed seed assemblages appear to be generally species typical of grassland, field margins and arable environments and the range of species is indicative of a number of different soil types being utilised, with species favouring lighter drier soils, damper waste rougher ground, heavier clay soils and sandier or heath habitats being present. There is an indication of the exploitation of the scrub/hedgerow/woodland edge environment, as shown by the presence of remains of hazel nut shell, brambles (*Rubus* sp.) and sloe/hawthorn (*Prunus spinosa/Crataegus monogyna*) thorns.

Period 3c Late Romano-British

Corndriers 24, 25 and 26 in the north-west area of the site appear to have been used for the parching of the processed crops after they had been removed from storage and again there is an indication that the crop-processing waste from the dehusking of this stored material was used as tinder. The range of potential crops included spelt wheat, barley, emmer wheat, free-threshing wheat, rye and Celtic bean. Again, the weed seeds are indicative of the utilisation of a number of different soil types such as lighter drier soils, damper waste rougher ground, heavier clay soils and sandier or heath habitats.

Period 3d Romano-British

Corndrier 29 and corndrier 45 from the eastern and western areas of the site respectively, only dated to the broad Romano-British period and appear to have been used for the parched of the processed crops after they had been removed from storage and again there is an indication that the crop-processing waste from the dehusking of this stored material was used as tinder. There is also an indication of the processing of the stored semi-cleaned grain or spikelets in the vicinity of pit 16868. The range of potential crops included spelt wheat, barley, emmer wheat, free-threshing wheat, rye, flax and Celtic bean. Again, the weed seeds are indicative of the utilisation of a number of different soil types such as lighter drier soils, damper waste rougher ground, heavier clay soils and sandier or heath habitats. Once again, the crops may have been harvested low down by sickle.

Chapter 4
The Saxon Period

by Chris Ellis

The evidence from the Thame excavations spans the whole of the Saxon period from the 5th–6th to 10th–11th centuries AD. The earlier evaluation of the Site F1 excavation had recorded just three potsherds that were tentatively identified as Saxon (JMHS 2014, 63). Though most of the occupation occurred in the western area of the excavation, a small but significant number of features were recorded in the eastern part (Figure 4.1). All lay on or above the 75m (aOD) contour occupying the well-drained, higher ground.

The earliest activity which can be assigned to this period were two inhumation burials. Later a settlement characterised by sunken-featured buildings was established. Later still the area was used for processes involving a number of ovens, and an enclosure was created in the Late Saxon period.

Post-Roman/Early Saxon burials

Two heavily truncated inhumation burials were located in the north-west of the western part of the excavation at *c.* 70m aOD (Figs 4.1 and 4.2), a little over 100m to the north-east of a group of Iron Age burials in the coombe area (see Volume 1). Grave cut 16417 was an elongated oval in shape, with moderate concave sides and a flat base, which was north-west/south-east-aligned. The grave was 1.35m long, 0.7m wide and only 0.1m deep, with a single fill 16418. The fill was a dark grey sandy clay with occasional flint (<50mm) which contained skeleton 1501. The burial was supine with the head to the north-west. The adult skeleton was approximately 40% complete, and comprised mostly upper and lower long bones. Its poor condition was probably caused by ploughing during the medieval and post-medieval periods, as well as the relatively waterlogged nature of its location, being on the southern edge of the spring lines.

The burial was accompanied by three metal artefacts (Ra. 40; Fig. 5.5) which were recorded from the abdominal areas of the burial. These included an iron firesteel and iron pin fragment (16417.1 and 16417.3). The firesteel is thought to be of 7th century and later date (Geake 1997, 79–80) and the pin of 6th-century AD date from comparable examples at Dover Buckland (Evison 1987, 230). Comparable examples of the iron knife (16417.2) date to the 5th to 7th/8th centuries AD (Evison 1987, 113). A radiocarbon sample from the left tibia produced a date of cal AD 410–540 (SUERC-80886), modelled as *cal AD 420–560* (see below and Table 1.1), confirming a 5th or 6th-century date.

Skeleton 1502 was found in grave-pit 16629. The pit was very shallow, just 0.05m deep, and the skeleton was fragmentary, but was a prime adult and appeared to have been buried in a supine position. The area was disturbed and when observed in the field was believed to have been truncated by Late Roman (period 3ci) ditch 132. Only one artefact (Ra. 44), apparently associated with the skeleton, was recovered, either representing a grave good or as part of a dressed burial. This pin fragment is consistent with those seen in 5th–6th-century contexts (see McSloy, Chapter 5, Metal finds, 16629.1). A radiocarbon sample from a molar tooth from the skeleton, however, produced a date of cal AD 410–550 (SUERC-95013; Table 1.1), also modelled as *cal AD 420–560* (Griffiths, below). Whilst the relationship with Late Roman ditch 132 is not entirely clear, there is therefore the possibility that this burial suggests a continuance of the field systems in some form, discussed further in Chapter 6.

Sunken-featured buildings

The largest number of features dating to this period constitute a settlement which was located across the western part of the excavation and of which most were sunken-featured buildings (SFBs). Of the 13 SFBs recorded (structures 30–42; Fig. 4.1), all bar one (structure 30) were recorded in the western excavation

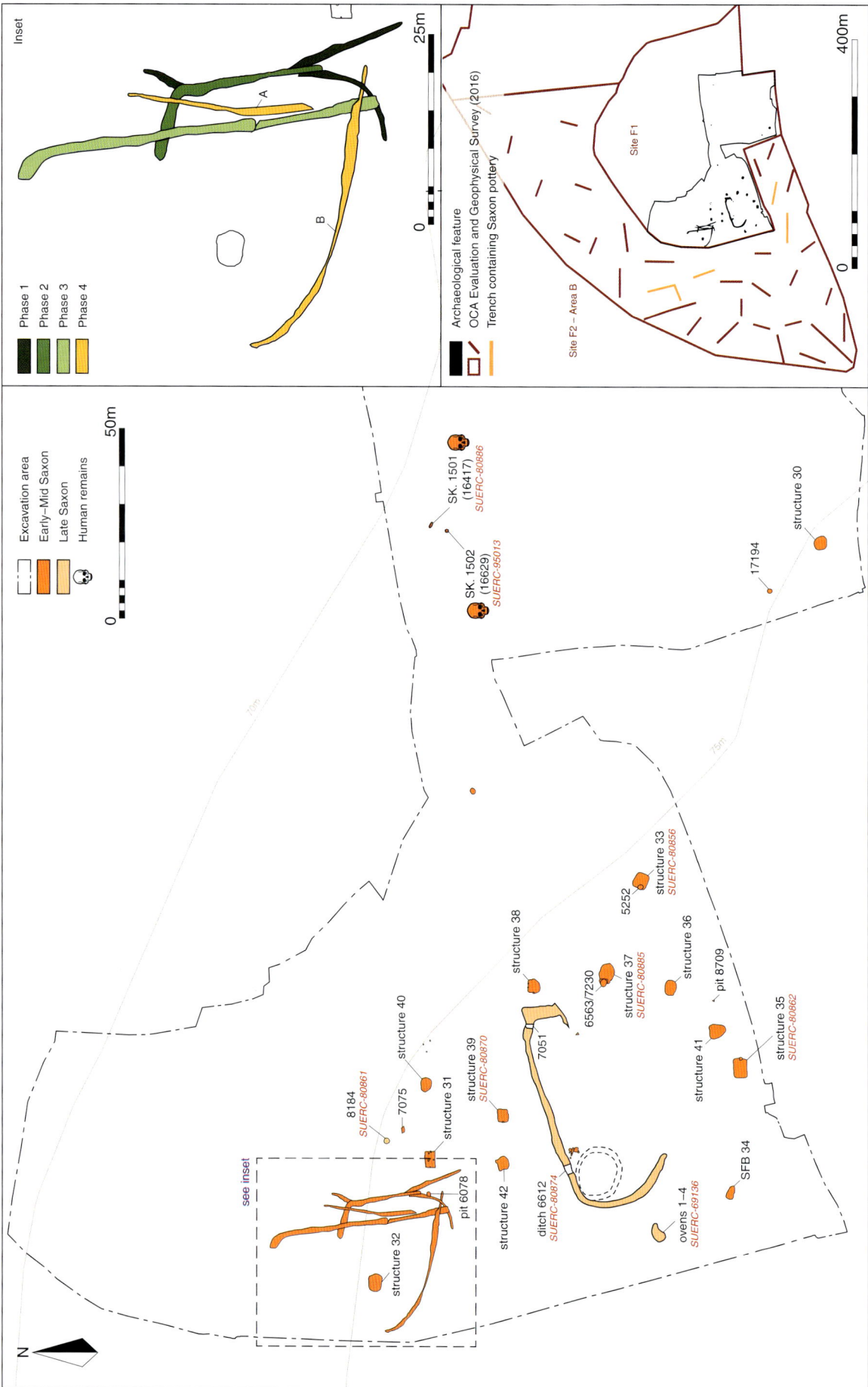

Fig. 4.1 Saxon phase plan

The Saxon Period 123

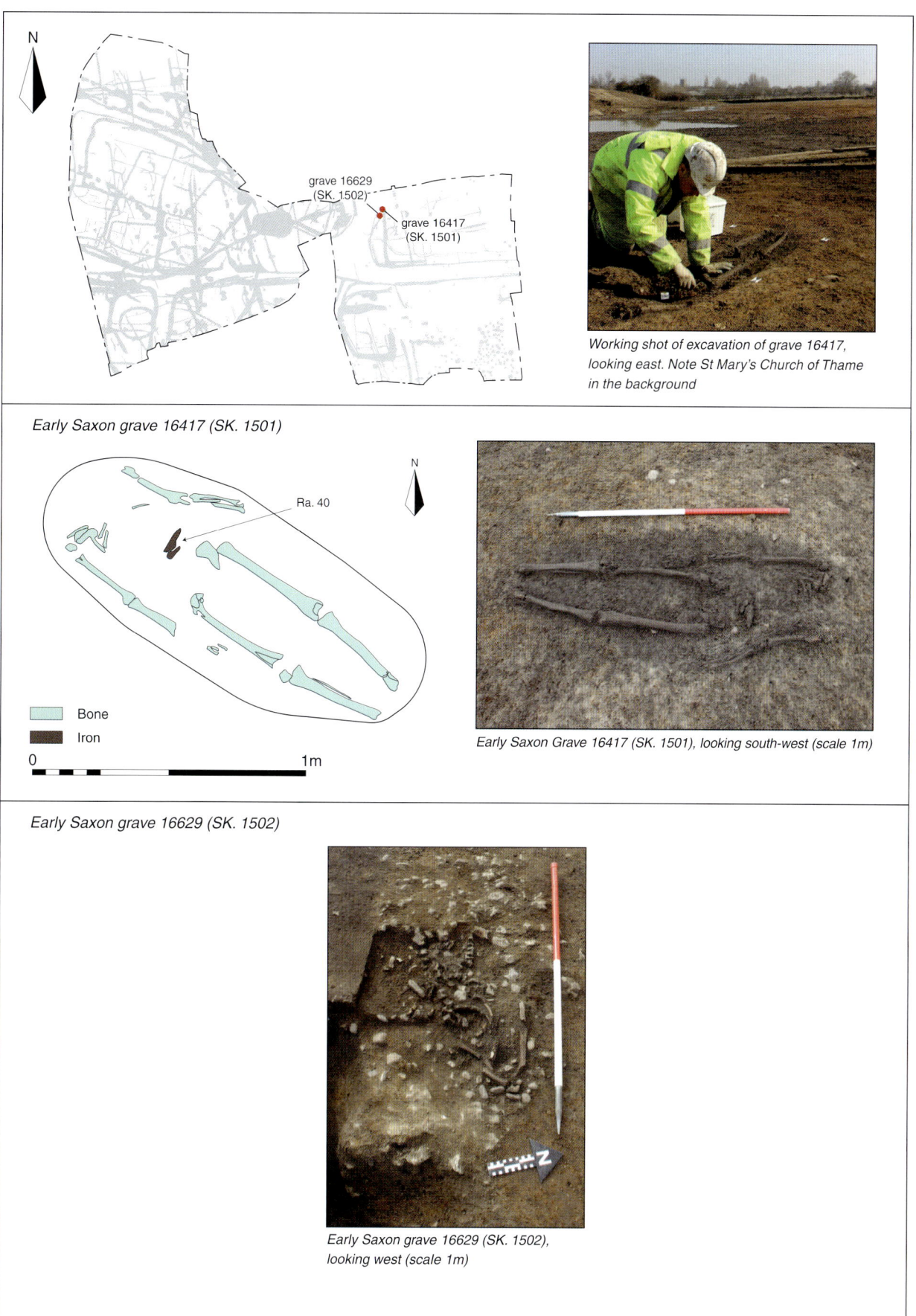

Fig. 4.2 *Grave 16417 (SK. 1501) and grave 16629 (SK. 1502): plan and photographs*

Table 4.1 Summary of SFBs

Str. no.	SFB type (from West 1985)	Pit cut no.	Fills	Fill no.	Posthole cut no.	Posthole fills	Cut shape	Orientation	Comments	Cut length (m)	Cut width (m)	Cut depth (m)
30	A1	15710	15845	5	-	-	Sub-rectangular	E/W	Posthole 15783 in middle of north side. Shallow pit edge to SE and NE of pit. Monolith <1609> through deposits. 72.2% pot SAX, rest PREH & LIR	3.4	3.4	0.54
	-	15710	15846	4	-	-						
	-	15710	15847	3	-	-						
	-	15710	15848	2	-	-						
	-	15710	15849	1	-	-						
	-	15710	-	-	15782	15850, 15851			West gable posthole	0.21	0.21	0.7
	-	15710	-	-	15783	15852			Posthole in mid-north of SFB	0.26	0.26	0.17
	-	15710	-	-	15711	15853			East gable posthole	0.27	0.24	0.49
31	A1	5735	5734	1	-	-	Sub-rectangular	E/W	Cut by two pits 5737 & 5741 in SFB base. Uncertain strat. rel. Cuts Neolithic causewayed enclosure pit C1H. Posthole 5983 in middle of south long side. Replacement of east posthole 5869 with 5867	4.4	3.3	0.35
	A1	5735	5776	1	-	-			Monolith Sample <558> through deposit			
	-	5735	5944	1	-	-			Identical to 5734=5776			
	-	5735	5945	1	-	-			Identical to 5734=5776			
	-	5735	-	-	5867	5866			East gable posthole (earlier)	>0.15	0.27	0.36
	-	5735	-	-	5869	5868			East gable posthole (later)	0.08	0.13	0.4
	-	5735	-	-	5972	5970			West gable posthole	0.18	0.16	0.5
	-	5735	-	-	5983	5982			Posthole in mid-south of SFB	>0.14	0.34	0.07
	-	5735	-	-	5985	5984			Poss. east gable replacement posthole	>0.19	0.28	0.06

32	A1	8577	8578	1	-	-	Rounded sub-rectangle	E/W	Fired clay lumps within pit fill 8578. Spindle whorl (Ra.975) in mid-south. Monolith <789> through deposit	4.7	3.6	0.72
-	-	-	-	-	8246	8247			East gable posthole	0.4	0.4	0.61
-	-	-	-	-	8248	8249			Posthole in NE of SFB	0.58	0.4	0.19
-	-	-	-	-	8462	8463			West gable posthole	0.28	0.28	0.56
-	-	-	-	-	8464	8465			Posthole in SW of SFB	0.34	0.26	0.29
-	-	-	-	-	8466	8467			Posthole in SW of SFB	0.55	0.38	0.16
-	-	-	-	-	8845	8846			Posthole mid-north	0.34	0.34	0.23
-	-	-	-	-	9105	9106			Stakehole in east end of SFB	0.14	0.14	0.31
33*	A1	5166	5163	3	-	-	Sub-rectangular	NW/SE	SFB pit and 'loom pit' 5183 cut mudstone bedrock outcrop and earlier Saxon pit 5252. Cuts causewayed enclosure pit C2AA. Monolith samples <514> & <515> through SFB pit fill 5163	4.1	3.6	0.68
-	-	5166	5164	2	-	-			Sub-square mudstone block seat in NW corner of SFB to north of 'loom pit'. **C14 date: SUERC-80856, cal AD 590–660**			
-	-	5166	5165	1	-	-			Trample layer (80mm thick) in the base of SFB pit. A compacted dark greyish-brown clayey sand with pottery and bone			
-	-	5183	5182	1	-	-	Sub-rectangular	NW/SE	?'Loom pit' running along NE side of SFB. A number of annular unfired/poorly fired loomweights from this pit	3.2	1.2	0.35
-	-	-	-	-	5206	5204			Posthole in centre of SFB pit	0.3	0.24	0.3
-	-	-	-	-	5286	5287			North-west gable posthole. Cuts upper fills of large Saxon pit 5252	0.28	0.24	0.25
-	-	-	-	-	5374	5375			South-east gable posthole	0.24	0.22	0.5

Table 4.1 (cont.) Summary of SFBs

Str. no.	SFB type (from West 1985)	Pit cut no.	Fills	Fill no.	Posthole cut no.	Posthole fills	Cut shape	Orientation	Comments	Cut length (m)	Cut width (m)	Cut depth (m)
34	A	6572	6573	1			Sub-rectangular (incomplete)	WNW/ESE	Cuts penannular ditch and Roman enclosure ditch	3.6	3	0.38
-	-	-	-	-	6642	6573			WNW gable posthole	0.3	0.3	0.32
-	-	-	-	-	6765	6573			ESE gable posthole	0.3	0.3	0.42
-	-	-	-	-	6766	6573			Group of x3 stakeholes to north of SE gable posthole 6765	0.05	0.05	0.24
-	-	-	-	-	6767	6573			Group of x3 stakeholes to north of SE gable posthole 6765	0.05	0.05	0.24
-	-	-	-	-	6768	6573			Group of x3 stakeholes to north of SE gable posthole 6765	0.05	0.05	0.24
35*	A	8461	8459	1	-	-	Sub-rectangular	E/W	Partially burnt down SFB. Largest on excavation. Lots of charred timber & loomweights. Cuts Roman droveway ditches to west. **C14 date: SUERC-80862, cal AD 590–660**	5.68	3.62	0.4
-	-	-	-	-	9570	9571			West gable posthole			
-	-	-	-	-	9516	9517			East gable posthole			
-	-	-	-	-	9465	9466			West/central posthole			
36*	A1	6387	6386	2	-	-	Rounded sub-rectangle	E/W	Fits Ahrens (1966) 'Wall-post house' type	4	3	0.26
		6387	6751	1	-	-			Metalled gravel floor surface in base of SFB pit. Demarcated to north and south by stakeholes running along the long sides of the SFB pit			
-	-	-	-	-	6714	6713			Possible west gable-end posthole	0.37	0.24	0.16
-	-	-	-	-	6389	6388			Posthole in mid-south of SFB	0.4	0.21	0.16
-	-	-	-	-	6391	6390			Small posthole in SE of SFB pit	0.26	0.21	0.1
-	-	-	-	-	6892	6893			Small posthole in NW of SFB pit	0.21	0.14	0.16
-	-	-	-	-	6747	6386			Group No. for stakeholes running along north and south sides of SFB pit	0.1 – 0.15	0.1 – 0.15	0.08 – 0.13

The Saxon Period   127

37	A	6567	6564	3	-	-	Oval	N/S	Identical to 6830. Mudstone bedrock in base of SFB pit. Cuts sequence of large Saxon pits (7230, 6563, 6827) in the west (earlier) Saxon pit. **C14 date: SUERC-80885, cal AD 600–670**	4.6	4	0.34
-	-	6567	6565	2	-	-			Identical to 6830			
-	-	6567	6566	1	-	-			Identical to 6567			
-	-	6830	6897	2	-	-						
-	-	6830	6832	1	-	-						
-	-	-	-	-	6569	6568			North gable posthole	0.45	0.28	0.65
-	-	-	-	-	7447	7395			South gable posthole	0.38	0.36	0.18
-	-	-	-	-	6894	6395, 6396			Possible south gable posthole	0.58	0.46	0.3
-	-	-	-	-	6833	6832, 6834			Possible south gable posthole	0.64	0.6	0.36
38	A1	6844	6846	3	-	-	Sub-square	E/W	Cuts IA tree-throw hole 6855 and Early Roman ditch 6921 in the SE	3.6	3.4	0.25
-	-	6844	6845	2	-	-						
-	-	6844	7013	1	-	-			Small dump of dark organic deposit with pottery and bone in NE of SFB pit below 6845			
-	-	-	-	-	6847	6848			West gable posthole	0.18	0.18	0.53
-	-	-	-	-	6851	6852			East gable posthole	0.2	0.2	0.53
-	-	-	-	-	6849	6850			Posthole in mid-west of SFB pit	0.25	0.25	0.05
-	-	-	-	-	6994	6995			Posthole in mid-west of SFB pit	0.4	0.3	0.08
-	-	-	-	-	6996	6997			Posthole in mid-east of SFB pit	0.4	0.3	0.05
-	-	-	-	-	6853	6854			Posthole in mid-east of SFB pit	0.25	0.15	0.04
39	A1	7452	7454	3	-	-	Sub-rectangular	E/W	Only west gable posthole present	3.4	3	0.2
-	-	7452	7665	2	-	-						
-	-	7452	7453	1	-	-			C14 date: SUERC-80870, cal AD 650–780			
-	-	-	-	-	7455	7456			West gable posthole	0.4	0.3	0.28

Table 4.1 (cont.) Summary of SFBs

Str. no.	SFB type (from West 1985)	Pit cut no.	Fills	Fill no.	Posthole cut no.	Posthole fills	Cut shape	Orientation	Comments	Cut length (m)	Cut width (m)	Cut depth (m)
40	A	7510	7509	1	-	-	Sub-oval			3.6	3	0.33
	-	-	-	-	7699	7698			West gable posthole	0.51	0.47	0.45
	-	-	-	-	7701	7700			East gable posthole	0.44	0.44	0.37
41	A1	9441	9442	1	-	-	Sub-square	N/S	Only north gable posthole present	3.5	3.5	0.6
	-	-	-	-	10004	10003			North gable posthole	0.32	0.2	0.14
42	?C	7595	7596	1	-	-	Sub-square	E/W	Possible four-post structure but only one posthole (NW) present	3.1	3	0.24
	-	-	-	-	7663	7664			Single posthole in NW corner	0.39	0.36	0.06

*denotes structures described in detail in the text

area, located on the higher ground of the ridge and consistently close to, or above the 75m aOD contour. The SFBs in the western excavation area were relatively evenly spaced, being mostly 10–30m apart. These structures have been summarised in Table 4.1. Most of the SFBs were in plan sub-rectangular, or more rarely, square, with round-cornered cuts, the smallest pit being 3.1m long by 3m wide ranging up to 5.68m long, 3.62m wide, although the latter is an outlier and all the others were 4.7m or less in length. The pits ranged in depth from 0.20m to 0.72m with vertical or near-vertical sides and a flattish base. All had at least one associated posthole preserved, generally associated with what is likely to be a gable end. It is likely that most fit within the two-post structural types classed as 'A' or 'A1' by West (1985). Structure 42, with a posthole in one corner may be the sole representative of a four-post construction (a 'Class C' SFB pit structure, cf West 1985), whilst structure 36 may be a 'wall-post type' (cf Ahrens 1966). Structure 30, in the eastern part of the excavation was slightly different in that it had a shallower edge or shelf on one side. Most of the Thame SFBs had one or two fills (Table 4.1) and these were mostly dark greyish-brown sandy silts, suggesting an organic component. Each SFB had pottery and animal bone, as well as other objects in some cases, within their fills. Three SFBs, structures 33, 35 and 36 preserved greater structural complexity or more abundant and/or diverse finds, so these buildings with more significant depositional, morphological or structural aspects will be discussed further in turn below.

Structure 33 (Fig. 4.3)

This north-west/south-east-aligned structure was located in the east of the western excavation area, on the south edge of the coombe, at a point on the site where the mudstone bedrock was very close to the prevailing ground surface (Fig. 4.3). The pit was sub-rectangular, 4.1m by 3.6m and 0.68m deep and cut c. 0.20m into the mudstone bedrock outcrop located in this part of the site. It also cut pit C2AA of the causewayed enclosure (see Volume 1) and a large, backfilled Early Saxon pit 5252. The radiocarbon date from the fill of structure 33 would give a *terminus post quem* date for the pit of cal AD 590–660 (SUERC-80856).

The SFB was a two-post derivative, with a near-central posthole (5206) as well as north-west (5286) and south-east (5374) gable-end postholes which were 3.5m apart. The SFB pit was slightly offset from the posthole alignment. A clearly preserved post-pipe within posthole 5286, the infilling of the extracted post void, indicated that the timber post was at least 0.12m in diameter.

Running along the north-eastern long side, within the SFB pit, was another sub-rectangular pit, 5183. During the excavation this was described as a 'loom pit' because of the distribution of fired and unfired clay loomweights from the structure suggesting an association. The sub-rectangular pit 5183 was 3.2m long, 1.2m wide and 0.35m deep and was wholly cut into the mudstone bedrock. It had irregular concave ends and moderate, concave sides and a very flat base, apparently exploiting the cleavage planes of the mudstone bedrock. This pit contained a single fill 5182, which was identical to the basal 'trample' fill of the SFB pit, 5165, which covered the entire base. Loom pit fill 5182 was characterised by a dark greyish-brown clayey sand with a small assemblage (2/24g) of residual prehistoric and Late Iron Age/Romano-British pottery as well as a shale spindle whorl (Ra. 586).

The SFB pit contained three fills 5163, 5164, and 5165, of which context 5165 not only filled elongated pit 5183 but also covered the base of the SFB pit. This deposit was only 80mm thick and was characterised by a dark greyish-brown clayey sand which was relatively compacted resulting in a 'platy' textural character when trowelled. It contained a moderate pottery assemblage (42/928g) of which only 29% (269g by weight) could be assigned an Early to Mid Saxon date, the remainder being residual prehistoric and Late Iron Age/Romano-British. Two residual worked flints were also recorded. This deposit also contained ten annular, fired clay loomweights (see Shaffrey, Chapter 5, Loomweights). When plotted it is clear that the loomweights were particularly concentrated over the area of the elongated pit or its margins (Fig. 4.3). In the north corner of the SFB, and sat directly on the trample deposit 5165, was a large sub-square natural mudstone block. This was 0.5m long by 0.4m wide and 0.3m high. Its position within the SFB pit and relative to the elongated pit 5182 fits closely that of a similar possible masonry 'seat' proposed for an SFB pit at Bourton-on-the-Water (Dunning 1932, plate LVI).

The overlying fill, 5164, was a 0.24m thick, very mixed light yellowish-brown and mid brown clayey sand. It contained a relatively large pottery assemblage (80/1175g) of which 21.4% by weight (251g) was identified as of Early to Mid Saxon date and the rest (78.6% by weight) was residual earlier pottery. Residual worked flint (4) was also recorded. The fill also contained animal bone (697/6311g) including cattle, sheep/goat, horse, possible cat and domestic fowl. A radiocarbon date from hazel charcoal from the deposit returned a date of cal AD 590–660 (SUERC-80856).

The final pit fill, 5163, was a 0.58m thick deposit of dark greyish-brown sandy clay with a large residual prehistoric and Romano-British pottery and Early to Mid Saxon pottery assemblage (3109g) of which 84.2% by weight (85/2618g) was the latter. This waste deposit also included frequent charcoal, burnt stone, two iron nails, as well as 716g of burnt flint, 92.8% by weight from the SFB. Seven residual worked flints were also recorded. This SFB also contained nine fragments

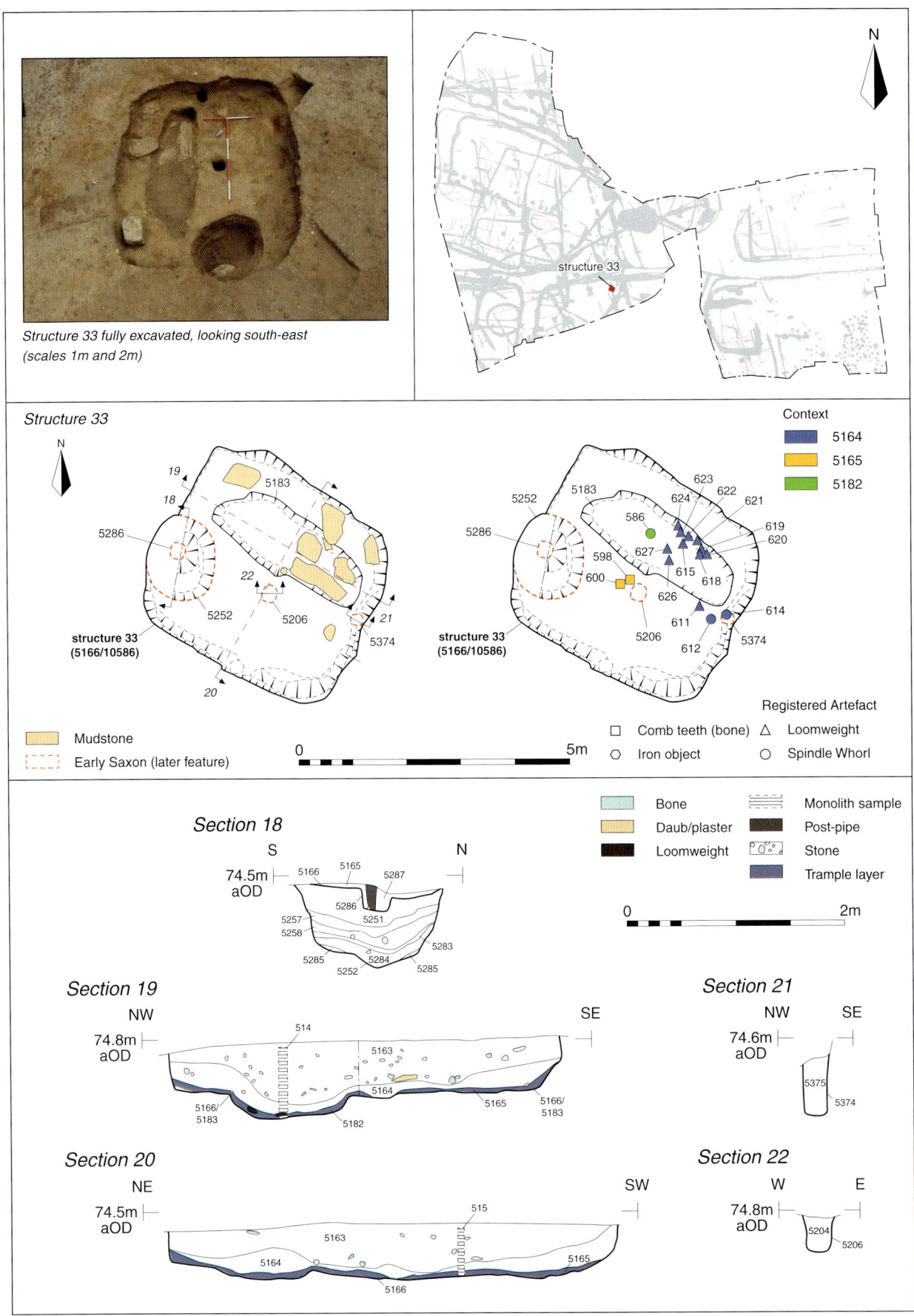

Fig. 4.3   SFB structure 33: plans with the location of finds within the feature, sections and photograph

of Roman ceramic roof tile. The archaeobotanical assemblage included barley, hulled and free-threshing wheat and rye which might represent crop processing as well as settlement waste. The presence of Celtic beans and peas, along with many weed seeds, some mineralised, might indicate dumping of food waste or floor-covering material. A similar archaeobotanical assemblage from structure 37 represented the dumping of crop-processing waste.

Structure 35 (Figs 4.4 and 4.5)

This SFB was an east/west-aligned two-post structure (9570, 9516), which had an additional posthole, 9465, close to a central line through the pit towards the west end. The structure was very close to the southern edge of the eastern excavation area and was the largest and most uniformly-shaped recorded. The SFB pit, 8461, was 5.68m long, 3.62m wide and 0.4m deep, with very straight parallel sides and ends and vertical sides terminating in a flat, rectangular pit base. The west (9570) and east gable (9516) postholes contained single fills, 9571 and 9517 respectively, which were identical, a mid greyish-brown sandy silt with occasional sub-rounded flint and rare charcoal flecks. West gable posthole 9570 was 0.44m diameter and 0.4m deep with vertical sides and shallow, concave base. East gable posthole 9516 was a sub-oval, north/south-aligned cut, being 0.34m long and 0.24m wide and 0.19m deep, with vertical sides and a shallow, concave base. The near-central posthole, 9465, was a sub-oval, east/west cut, and was 0.36m long and 0.31m wide and 0.36m deep, with near-vertical sides terminating in a shallow, concave base. The alignment of the postholes was skewed relative to the pit sides, an aspect already recorded for structure 33.

The pit contained a single fill 8459 which was a relatively homogenous, mid to dark greyish-brown, fine silty sand with occasional rounded flint. This fill included indications of localised scorching which suggested that there had been burning within the pit. The finds assemblage from the fill included 1434g of pottery of which only 32% (by weight, 28/458g) was assigned an Early to Mid Saxon date. The faunal assemblage was one of the largest recorded from the SFBs (796/5594g) and included mainly cattle and sheep/goat but also pig, horse, dog, fowl and goose, although there do not appear to be any associated groups of bone. Finally, the deposit contained 234g of burnt flint, 15 pieces of residual worked flint, and a possible coil-headed iron pin (Ra. 1035). In addition, a large number (59) of annular fired-clay loomweights, in differing states of baking/burning, were recorded from the structure. The loomweights were concentrated in an east–west spread, along the northern long side of the pit. In the north-west of the pit there was a cache of 29 loomweights.

There was also a highly significant concentration of carbonised wood fragments within the fill across the SFB pit. Whilst being excavated, all carbonised timber elements and loomweights were photographed *in situ* and three-dimensionally recorded (Fig. 4.5). All 17 carbonised wood elements collected were given unique Registered Artefact numbers (Ras 910–912, 968, 976, 981, 982, 985–988, 1026–1028, 1032, 1082, 1083) as well as unique sample numbers (Soil Samples 900, 901, 902, 903, 909–918, 967, 968). All 59 complete loomweights or loomweight fragments were also allocated unique Ra. numbers, three-dimensionally recorded and photographed *in situ*. A sequence of pre-excavation, part-excavation (at 0.2m depth) and full-excavation hand-drawn plans and photographs were undertaken. The timber elements included square and sub-square sections as well as roundwood elements of ash, elm, beech and blackthorn (see Meen, Chapter 5, Charcoal).

In the pre-excavation recording it was clearly discernible that several relatively long carbonised timbers which were 0.8–1.6m in length (Ras 911=916, 913, 921=946, 922=947=948=949) had a near-north/south alignment, across the SFB. The relatively small cross-section of the timbers and their cross-section/length ratios would suggest they are probably wall or roofing timbers rather than elements of a suspended timber floor. In the north of the SFB pit fill a 0.7m by 0.42m area of carbonised wattling was recorded (Ra. 988, <903>) which was composed of 10mm diameter roundwood wattles. A radiocarbon date from *Maloideae* charcoal from this wattling returned a date of cal AD 590–660 (SUERC-80862). Along with the charred timbers running across the SFB pit, this small area of wattling may have collapsed from the north wall of the structure or have fallen from the roofing. Another possible structural charred timber was a roundwood ash post segment, not *in situ* (Ra. 968, <909>), which was recorded in the mid-west of the upper part of the pit fill 8459. It lay to the immediate north of posthole 9465 from which it may be derived. The fact that this piece of post does not appear to have been charred *in situ* may suggest that it had been extracted from the posthole prior to the burning. Also potentially of significance was that this post appears to have been sawn off (see Meen, Chapter 5, Charcoal).

Overall, the excavation of structure 35 recorded that greater numbers of the 59 fired clay loomweights from the structure were recorded towards the base of the fill 8459, with many showing signs of burning/scorching. There were two spatial concentrations of loomweights. One comprised the cache of 29 loomweights in the north-west corner (Fig. 4.5) of the pit base. The second was an east/west line (Fig. 4.5) of 30 weights discernible in both the upper and lower plans of the pit excavation but increasing in number towards the pit base. However, given the single fill, and no clear relationships between the charred timbers and the loomweights, it is unclear

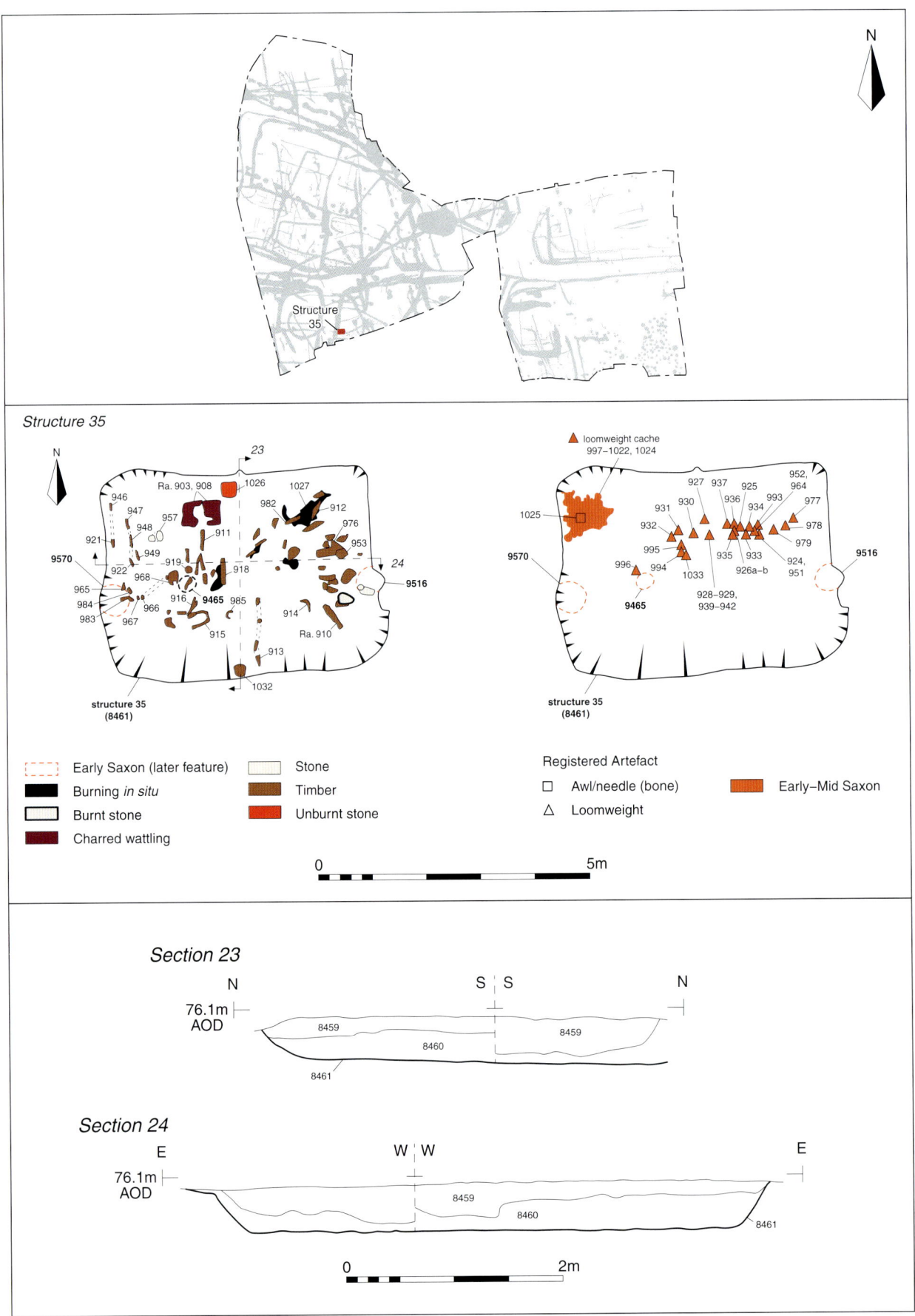

Fig. 4.4   SFB structure 35: plans with the location of finds within the feature and sections

In situ *loomweights and charred timbers in north-east of partially excavated SFB pit, looking north-east (scale 0.2m)*

Excavation and recording of loomweight cache on pit base

Area of charred wattling Ra. 988, looking north-west (scale 0.3m)

Loomweight cache and areas of charred timbers in base of SFB pit, looking north-west (scales 2m)

Fig. 4.5   SFB structure 35: photographs

whether all of the loomweights were within the building at the time of the fire, although their position on the base of the pit, and the fact that many were scorched would seem to support this.

Structure 36 (Fig. 4.6)

This SFB was recorded in the south of the western excavation area and lay equidistant (*c.* 25m) from structures 33 and 35. Structure 36 comprised an east/west-aligned, relatively shallow (0.26m), rounded sub-rectangular pit 6387, which was 4m long and 3m wide and had characteristically outwardly 'bowed' long sides (Fig. 4.6). The pit had a moderate to steep, concave sides and a flat base. The form of the SFB was a two-post structure derivative, with a clear western gable posthole 6714. The sub-oval posthole was north/south-aligned, 0.37m long, 0.24m wide and 0.16m deep. It had vertical sides and a flat base. The other postholes in the west (6892) and south-east (6389, 6891) are of sub-rectangular and oval shapes in plan, and 0.16m, 0.16m and 0.1m deep respectively. Their differing aspects and their positions are difficult to interpret as being integral structural components of the SFB.

However, ranged along both north and south long sides of the SFB pit base were rows of stakeholes (group 6747, Fig. 4.6). The stakeholes in this case were best-preserved along the north edge of the SFB pit and comprised at least two east/west rows 0.2m apart, and also spaced generally at 0.2m intervals (Fig. 4.6). The two rows had a marked outward 'bowing' arrangement, mirroring that of the pit sides, clearly indicating the stakeholes and SFB pit were associated elements of a single structure. The stakeholes were also regularly-sized, being 0.1–0.15m in diameter and 0.1–0.15m deep, with near-vertical/vertical sides and moderate to steep,

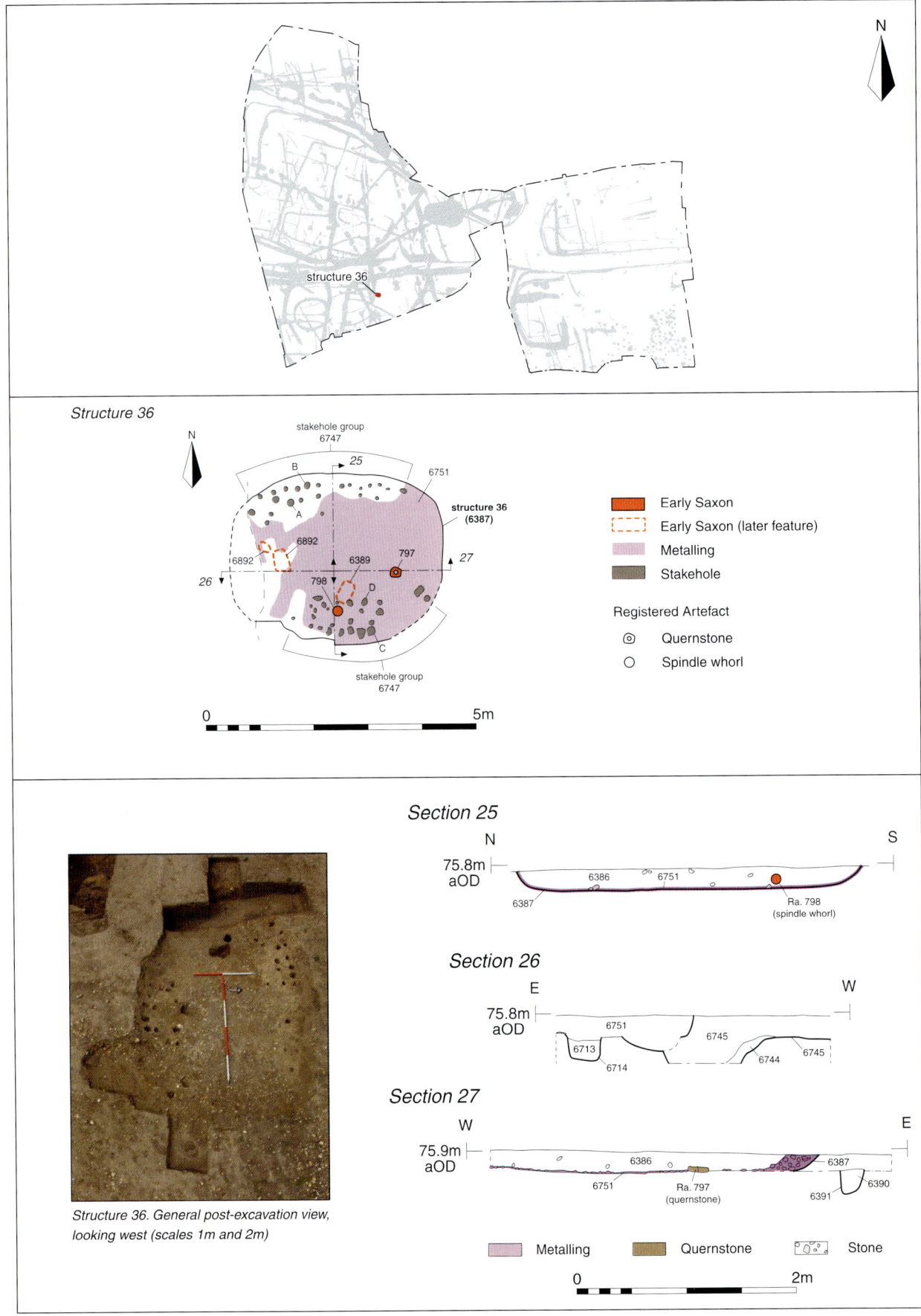

Fig. 4.6 SFB structure 36: plans with the location of finds within the feature, sections and photograph

concave bases. The fills were identical to the SFB pit backfill 6386 (see below). The stakeholes on the south side of the structure formed a more discrete, possibly rectangular group which extended further into the interior of the structure and seem more likely to relate to some interior furnishing. A gravel surface (6751) in the base of this pit would seem to argue against them being required to support a floor.

The single backfill deposit 6386 of SFB structure 36 pit was characterised by a dark greyish-brown fine sandy silt, with occasional small, flint pebbles as well as charcoal flecks and fragments. A moderate finds assemblage was recorded from the structure, all of which derived from the backfill deposit. The assemblage comprised residual prehistoric and Romano-British pottery and Early Saxon pottery (52/762g) of which 85.2% by weight (33/654g) was of Early to Mid Saxon date. The deposit also contained a moderate faunal assemblage (136/1320g) of low identifiable numbers of cattle, sheep/goat, pig and horse. Finally, a very small stone assemblage of burnt flint (3g), residual worked flint (6), a fired clay spindle whorl (Ra. 798) and a rotary quern fragment (Ra. 797) were recorded from the deposit.

Lying on the base of the pit, directly below backfill 6386, a 20mm-thick deposit of mid orange/grey clay (6751) contained frequent sub-rounded and sub-angular gravel. It was markedly compacted, in comparison to the backfill deposit, and respected the 'internal' rows of stakeholes to the north and south. The specific characteristics of this thin basal deposit, including its relative compaction, its gravel inclusions and its demarcation by the stakeholes of the long sides of the SFB, would all strongly suggest that, like structure 33, the floor surface of structure 36 was in the base of the pit. However, rather than the trample as an indirect aspect of the use of the structure's pit base, the 'floor' of structure 36 is a deliberately laid, metalled surface.

Ditches/Gullies

In the north-west of the western excavation area a four-phase sequence of relatively minor curvilinear ditch/gully features was recorded (Fig. 4.1 inset). These were mostly north/south-aligned but also near-east/west-aligned and were uniformly 12–3m distant from SFB structure 32.

Ditch/gully – phase 1

The gullies were north-north-west/south-south-east-aligned and at the north curved eastwards and to the south curved westwards. This possibly indicates two further separate sub-phases. The phase 1 feature extended over at least 35m and was generally 0.5–0.6m wide and 0.2–0.4m deep with a moderate/steep, U-shaped profile. All interventions of this ditch/gully recorded single fills of mid to dark greyish-brown sandy silt, with occasional small angular flint and mudstone inclusions as well as rare to occasional charcoal flecks. The relatively small finds assemblage from this feature included mainly residual prehistoric and Late Iron Age/Romano-British pottery (5/40g) but also a small component assigned to the Early to Mid Saxon period (5/32g). A small animal bone assemblage (34/247g) contained only a few identified cattle and pig elements.

Ditch – phase 2

This was more coherent than phase 1 and was of a scale appropriately described as a ditch. It was near-rectilinear, north/south-aligned and extended overall over a length of approximately 30m. The northernmost 9m curved westwards to a east/west alignment before terminating. The ditch had a maximum width of 1.12m in the east/west segment but was otherwise 0.5–0.85m wide and generally 0.55–0.9m deep. The ditch had a steep, flat or slightly concave sides with a moderate concave base. The ditch contained single fills apart from the east/west segment, which contained multiple fills (four). A slightly larger faunal assemblage was also produced from this part of the ditch. All the fills were characterised by very dark greyish-brown sandy silts with occasional flint and mudstone inclusions and rare to occasional charcoal flecks. A small finds assemblage of pottery, mostly residual prehistoric and Late Iron Age/Romano-British pottery (6/47g) was recorded along with an Early to Mid Saxon component (2/8g). However, a sizeable faunal assemblage was recorded (198/1235g) which of the identified material included mainly cattle and sheep/goat elements, but also pig, horse, and dog, although no associated bone groups were noted. By far the greatest relative quantity of animal bone (106/958g), or 77.6% by weight, was recorded from interventions of the east/west segment of the ditch.

Ditch/gully – phase 3

This ditch was a well-defined, relatively broad and shallow ditch within the sequence. It was near-north/south-aligned and extended over about 50m, with a short segment (4m) in the north which curved westwards to a north-west/south-east alignment, in a similar way to the phase 2 ditch. The ditch was 1.0–1.3m wide and only 0.3m deep with steep sides and a flat base. The single fills of mid greyish-brown sandy silts or silty sands contained rare charcoal flecks. The small finds assemblage included only residual prehistoric and Late Iron Age/Romano-British pottery (11/62g) and worked flint (four) as well as animal bone (194/588g) of cattle, sheep/goat and pig.

Ditch/gully – phase 4

The final phase of ditch/gully features comprised two separate elements (4a, 4b Fig 4.1, inset) that may or may not be contemporary. Ditch 4a was a curvilinear, north-west/south-east ditch that physically cut phase 1 and 3 features. Similar to phase 3, this ditch phase seemed to have been heavily truncated. Ditch 4a was 1.1m wide and <0.2m deep with moderate/steep, concave sides and a flat or shallow concave base. The single fills comprised a mid to dark greyish-brown fine sand, but in places a sandy clay. The finds assemblage included mostly residual prehistoric and Late Iron Age/Romano-British pottery (17/222g) and worked flint (5 fragments). The fills also contained an Early to Mid Saxon component (1/10g) and animal bone (85/368g) of mainly cattle and sheep/goat, but also pig, horse and bird.

Gully phase 4b comprised a near-north/south-aligned feature which was only 0.4–0.5m wide and 0.15m deep. The single fills of mid to dark greyish-brown sandy silt contained a very small assemblage of animal bone (2/21g) of cattle. Although poorly dated the gully clearly cut phase 2 ditch in the north.

Late Saxon ovens and associated features

In the south-west of the western excavation area a sequence of four at least partially superimposed oven structures was recorded (structure 44), associated with two postholes (6443, 6981) and a relatively dense concentration of at least 33 stakeholes (group 8046) (Figs 4.7 and 4.8). The area of the oven sequence was clearly discernible after machine-stripping because of the relatively large area (4.5m by 2.9m) of charcoal spreads, pale pink/red, heat-affected clay deposits and clay superstructure elements, as well as areas of heat-affected natural sand geology. The ovens were located within sub-circular foundation cuts 0.3m deep, which cut Romano-British occupation deposits (6687/6688). These occupation deposits extended over a 196m^2 area in this part of the site but also continued beyond the west edge of the excavation. They contained a large assemblage of Late Roman animal bone and pottery as well as residual Neolithic worked flints. The numerous contexts from the oven sequence contained a small assemblage of residual Neolithic worked and burnt flint, animal bone and Late Roman pottery. However, radiocarbon dating indicates that the ovens date to the 8th–11th century AD, and are therefore possibly associated with the Late Saxon enclosure lying only 9m to the east.

Oven 1

This oven lay on the eastern edge of the area of oven structures and had been heavily truncated to the east, possibly by later ploughing. The oven remnants comprised a north/south-aligned, 1.20m long by 0.3m wide arc of differentially, heat-affected, fired clay. This was up to 25mm thick but flat slabs of fired clay of 10–15mm thick were generally recorded. Some clay fragments were of a white/cream/yellow mottled colouring but some fragments had been heated to a pale pink colouring. The overlying contexts 6576, 6641, 6685, 6837, all comprise fired clay fragments indicative of oven structure demolition, perhaps for reuse in later ovens, as seen in the construction of oven 3 (below). The final oven remains were sealed by the latest charcoal-rich rakings (6574) of ovens 3 and 4 to the immediate west.

Oven 2

This oven survived in a very truncated form in the mid-east of the oven group. It was represented by an *in situ* sub-rectangular area of fired clay oven superstructure which had been truncated by the construction of oven 3 to the north and oven 4 to the west. It comprised a 1.0m by 0.5m area of differentially heat-affected clay (7726), which was up to 70mm thick but was generally 40–50mm thick. A 50mm-thick horizon of heat-affected natural sand geology (7748) was recorded directly below the fired clay. The sand was characterised by a dark reddish-brown/dark red silty sand, some of which still adhered to the underside of the fired clay. The fired clay comprised of flat slabs of varying heat-affectedness, from a white unfired clay to partially heated, pale pink or red clay. The fired clay superstructure represents the *in situ* oven floor remnant. Aside from the fired clay structure itself, no additional material remains or deposits could be ascribed to this oven.

Oven 3

This oven was recorded in the north of the group of ovens. Its construction truncated the northern extent of oven 1 but had itself been markedly truncated by oven 4 to the south. The northern 50% of the structure survived including the foundation structure, oven structure and associated charcoal-rich rakings or accidentally charred plant remains. The incomplete foundation cut 7498 was sub-circular in shape, 1.87m by 1.66m in extent and 0.31m deep, with a moderate, flat side and a very shallow, concave base. Of a number of dark grey sandy silt fills (7303, 7410, 7431, 7436, 7446, 7474, 7486), two (7303, 7474) contained abundant fired clay fragments strongly indicating the reuse of demolished fired clay oven superstructural material. These deposits of compacted fired clay rubble would suggest that the initial oven structure foundation cut was filled with waste material from an earlier oven (perhaps either oven 1 or 2). However, these deposits within cut 7498 could also be interpreted as the very basal foundations of a completely separate earlier oven structure, almost completely overlaid by the construction of an oven, and including the overlying fired clay superstructural contexts 7462 (not illustrated) and 7386 (Fig. 4.7). The partial preservation of oven 3 renders this unclear. Whether part of the same oven, or two separate successive ovens, there can only have been relatively little time between their constructions.

Oven contexts 7462 and 7386 were some of the most

Fig. 4.7 Late Saxon ovens (structure 44): plan and sections

Oven 1, looking north-west (scales 0.3m and 0.4m)

North-west facing sections of ovens 3 and 4, looking south-east (scales 1m and 2m)

Ovens 1, 3 and 4 partially excavated, looking north-west (scales 1m and 2m)

South-facing section of oven 4, looking north-east (scales 1m and 2m)

Fig. 4.8   Late Saxon ovens (structure 44): photographs

significant with regard to the Late Saxon structural characteristics. Similar to other fired clay fragments from the two earlier ovens, these contexts consisted of varying heat-affected clay elements, from unfired white clay, to partially-fired, to a 'cream' or pale pink/red fired colouring. The fired clay also included occasional flint pebbles and sub-angular mudstone fragments (15–70mm), some of which were heat-affected, as well as charcoal flecks and lumps (<20mm). Most of the fired clay fragments were flattish slabs, representing oven wall or lining fragments, <59mm in thickness, but mostly 40–55mm thick. Context 7386 contained a number of fragments with charcoal-stained, wattle impressions. The wattling would have formed the armature for the oven superstructure. One fragment shows that the clay was pierced by a 15mm-diameter wattle rod whilst still soft. Many of the fired clay fragments from both 7462 and 7386 had abundant charred grain adhering to them, with some dense pockets present, probably derived from the overlying charcoal-rich deposits (7248, 7249, and 7274). Also collected with 7462 was a residual iron buckle (Ra. 872; Fig. 5.5, 4) of possibly Early Saxon date (see McSloy, Chapter 5, Metal finds).

The charcoal-rich deposits were characterised by dark grey or brown sandy silts with abundant charcoal, which ranged in thickness from 40mm (7248, 7274) to 0.4m (7249). The charred plant material from these contexts was particularly rich in cereal grains, being over 50% of the assemblage, and including mostly barley and free-threshing wheat, but also oats (21–25%) and rye. Between 12–20% of the grains showed signs of germination which would indicate a malting function for the oven. The assemblage also contained remains of Celtic bean and garden pea, which were also probably crops. A radiocarbon sample from a charred rye grain from 7274 returned a date of cal AD 770–1020 (SUERC-69136).

Oven 4

The latest oven of the sequence was recorded to the immediate south of ovens 2 and 3, both of which were truncated by the construction of oven 4. This was by far the best-preserved structural remains from the sequence, although the superstructural elements survived only in the foundation cut 7151. The sub-circular foundation cut was 1.98m by 1.96m in extent and 0.29m deep, with a moderate, shallow concave sides and a shallow concave base. The superstructure remains 7060 comprised a 0.27m-thick fired clay lining and base with a very similar character to that of oven 3 (7386). A markedly differing aspect of the latest oven was the inclusion of tabular mudstone fragments (20mm thick) into the clay matrix. The base of the oven structure contained charred wattling armature elements of 7–14mm diameter. However, a later demolition deposit (7003) clearly shows that the charred hazel wattling of the oven structure 'rods' were 10–24mm diameter and those of the 'sails' 27mm diameter.

Immediately overlying the superstructure remains were a number of demolition deposits (6570, 6640, 6686, 7002 (not illustrated), 7003). These comprised varying densities of white clay lumps to partially-fired pink/red fired clay fragments, with at least 10mm of dark reddened, heat-affected inner surfaces, set with matrices of dark grey sandy silts and varying quantities of charcoal.

The fragments had a relatively flattish form, <60mm but mostly 20–50mm thick. Notable palaeoenvironmental assemblages were obtained from the demolition deposits, but probably relate to the use of the oven. The assemblages were comprised of between 62–65% cereal grains, consisting mainly of barley and free-threshing wheat, with lower numbers of rye, hulled wheat and cultivated oats. Other potential crops represented were Celtic beans and flax. The assemblages would point to accidental burning of already processed grain and therefore probably used for crop drying in this instance.

Stakeholes group 8046 and postholes 6993, 6981

In the eastern part of the area covered by the group of oven-related features were 33 stakeholes (group 8046) and two postholes (6993, 6981), all of which were undated. They were filled with similar, dark, charcoal-rich sandy silt fills which were identical to charcoal-rich layers from ovens 2–4. Posthole 6993 was sub-oval, 0.17m by 0.1m and 60mm deep with a moderate U-shaped profile. It was filled with single fill 6579, a dark grey sandy silt with abundant charcoal possibly indicating the post was burned *in situ* during use. Posthole 6981 was 3.1m to the north-east of posthole 6993. It was sub-circular in shape, 0.19m by 0.17m in size and only 80mm deep, with moderate, slightly irregular U-shaped profile. It contained two fills, 6982 and 6990. The basal fill 6982 was a dark greyish-brown sandy silt. The later fill 6990 was a dark grey sandy silt with abundant charcoal, but also fired clay fragments, the latter probably from one of the demolished ovens. The posthole fills would indicate the infilling of the feature with oven waste material after post removal.

Lying to the north of the two postholes a tight concentration of 33 stakeholes (group 8046) was recorded covering a 1.8m by 1.4m area. Spatially they were located between oven 1 and ovens 2–4. Three stakeholes on the west edge of the group were located stratigraphically below oven 2. The stakeholes were characterised by circular cuts into the underlying Roman occupation deposits (6687, 6688) which were 40mm diameter and 80mm deep, with vertical sides and deep, concave bases. They were filled with 6718, a mid grey sandy silt with no inclusions.

Aside from posthole 6993, none of the features were observed until the removal of the large charcoal spread 6574, demolition deposit 6576 and oven 2 revealing the underlying heat-affected natural geology, 7748. It is difficult from the limited spatial and stratigraphic evidence to interpret the concentration of the stakeholes further, although this is discussed in Chapter 6 (The Late Saxon settlement).

The Late Saxon enclosure

The ditched enclosure was an incomplete sub-rectangular area with a clear opening to the south, although the

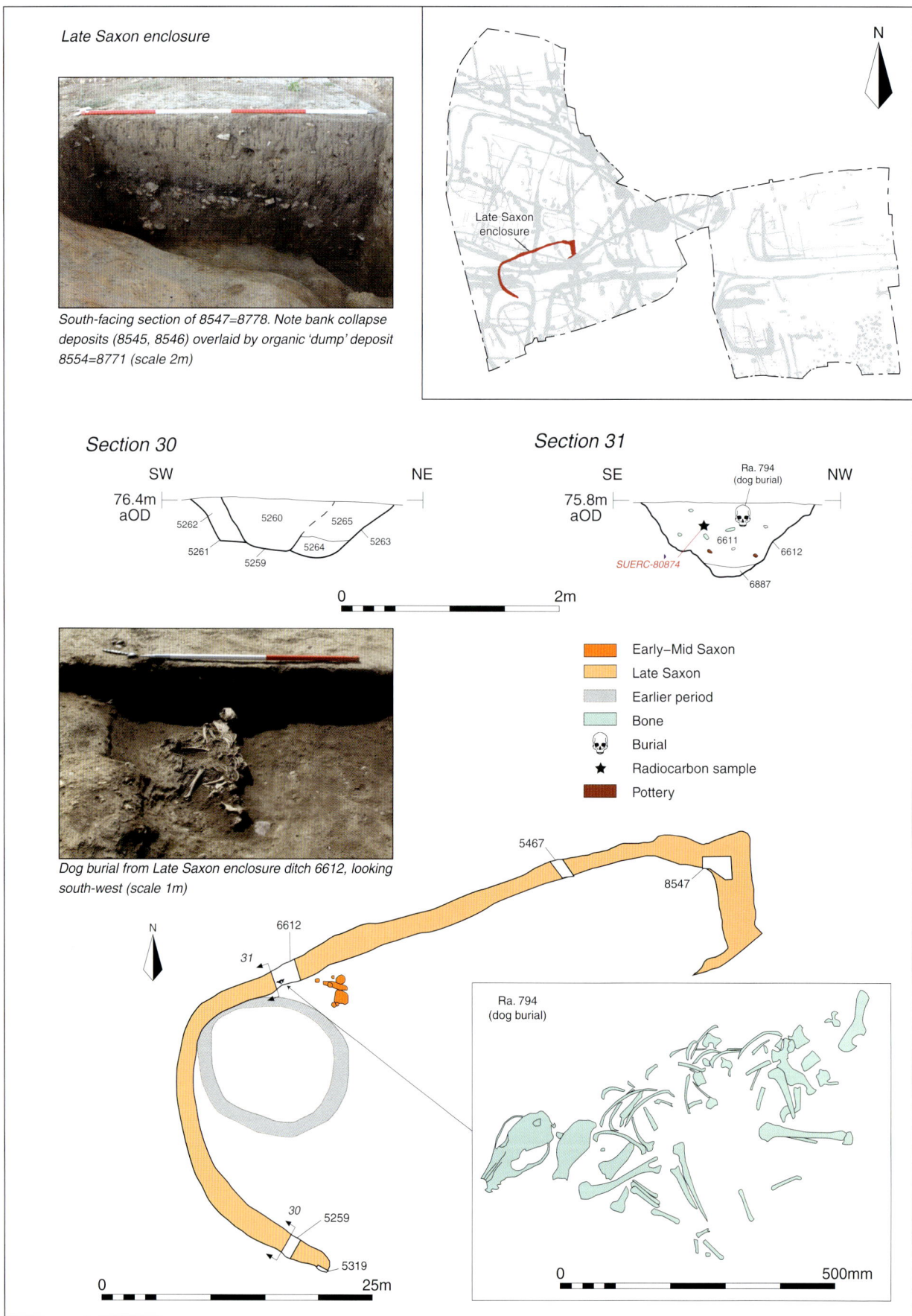

Fig. 4.9   Late Saxon enclosure: plan, sections and photographs

terminal of the south-eastern extent of the enclosure was not discovered (Fig. 4.9). The enclosed space was approximately 50m by 25m with a curving morphology in the west but a ninety degree turn in the north-east. The ditch became steadily more substantial from the western terminal to the north-east corner, where it was at its widest and deepest. In at least two sections (5467, 8547), the ditch displayed an asymmetrical stratigraphic sequence which indicated deposits derived from the collapse of a bank situated on the interior of the ditch. It is worth noting that the north-west corner of the partial enclosure coincided with the location of a Neolithic ring ditch which it encompassed, cutting the ditch of the earlier feature on its northern side. The western extent of the ditch appeared to wrap around its location so that it occupied the corner. There was some indication that there was originally a mound or bank in the interior of this feature (see Volume 1, Chapter 2), but it is unclear whether this would have been extant when the Late Saxon enclosure was established.

In the west of the enclosure, the ditch (5319=5321) was generally 1.3m wide and 0.35m deep with moderate, concave sides and a flat base. The single fill at this point of the enclosure (5320=5322) was a dark greyish-brown sandy silt with no finds. This primary fill was probably derived from the erosion of material from the surrounding ground during initial weathering as well as feature side collapse, which occurred during initial use. In most of the fill sequences recorded there were relatively poorly defined deposit interfaces. This was due to the very similar dark to very dark greyish-brown sandy silt fills encountered. Although primary fills from the collapse of material from the natural sand geology were present to a relatively minor degree, they were not substantial. The products of primary erosion of the ditch were mostly evident as mid yellowish-brown sandy mottling or small lenses of material, within the dark parent contexts. Overall, the relatively few fills (generally between one and four), but mostly one or two fills, in conjunction with their relative dark colouring and overall homogeneity, might suggest a relatively rapid infilling with organic waste derived from activities and occupation within the enclosure. A moderate assemblage of residual prehistoric worked flint, prehistoric, Romano-British, Late Saxon (10th–11th century) pottery and animal bone was recorded. Faunal remains were recorded in most interventions (only 100–300g), and mostly comprised cattle and sheep/goat although pig, horse, dog and fowl were also recorded.

A relatively high concentration of bone was recorded from ditch 6612 (437/2751g) of which 217/598g (21.7% by weight) comprised a near-complete dog burial (Ra. 794) in the upper part of the upper ditch fill 6611. This backfill deposit comprised a dark grey silty sand with common charcoal. It overlaid primary fill 6887, a 0.12m-thick, mid greyish-brown sand. A radiocarbon sample of the dog skeleton returned a date of cal AD 990–1160 (SUERC-80874) modelled as *cal AD 990–1050* (Table 1.1; Fig. 4.10).

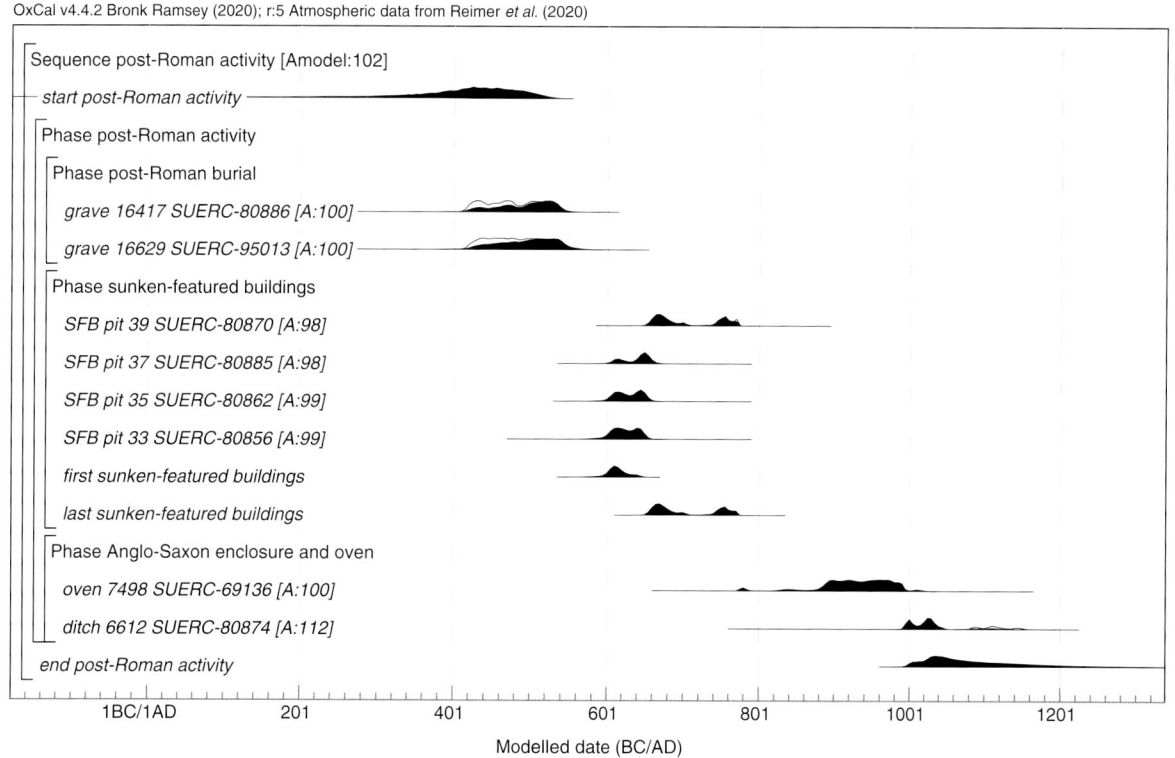

Fig. 4.10 Post-Roman and Saxon features – modelled dates

The radiocarbon dates from the post-Roman features

by Seren Griffiths

A sample each from post-Roman grave 16417 (SUERC-80886; SK. 1501)), Saxon enclosure ditch 6612 (SUERC-80874) and oven 3 (7498) (SUERC-69136) were radiocarbon dated for the purposes of this project and a further date was obtained from post-Roman grave 16629 (SUERC-95013; SK. 1502) as part of an aDNA project. Four samples from pits associated with the sunken-featured buildings (structures 33, 35, 37 and 39; SUERC-80856, -80862, -80885, -80870) were radiocarbon dated as well (Table 1.1). All the post-Roman results are modelled to represent an unordered phase of activity during this period.

The post-Roman activity is estimated to have started in *cal AD 200–500 (95% probability; start post-Roman activity*; Fig. 4.10) and ended in *cal AD 990–1300 (95% probability; end post-Roman activity)*. The individuals buried in the Saxon graves probably died in *cal AD 420–550 or 560 (95% probability; graves 16417 SUERC-80886 and 16629 SUERC-95013)*. This pre-dates the first dated event associated with the sunken-featured buildings, use of which are estimated to have begun in *cal AD 580–650 (95% probability; first sunken-featured buildings)*. The last dated event associated with the use of these buildings occurred in *cal AD 650–780 (81% probability,* or *cal AD 740–770 15% probability; last sunken-featured buildings)*. It is probably only after the current evidence that we have for the sunken-featured buildings that the oven 3 (7498) was in use in *cal AD 860–1000 (90% probability, oven 7498 SUERC-69136)* and that the enclosure ditch was established in *cal AD 990–1050 (88% probability, ditch 6612 SUERC-80874)*.

Chapter 5
Saxon Finds and Environmental Remains

A range of items and materials were recovered from a pair of post-Roman burials, sunken-featured buildings (SFBs) and Late Saxon ovens and an enclosure. These include pottery, metals, worked stone, fired clay and industrial residues, human and faunal remains, charcoal and plant macrofossils, discussed in turn in this chapter.

Saxon pottery
by Paul Booth

Some 783 sherds weighing just over 13kg were assigned to the Early–Mid Saxon period and a further 63 sherds (c. 1.5kg) were assigned to the Late Saxon–early medieval period (broadly 9th–12th centuries). This pottery was fully recorded at the assessment stage of the project in terms of fabric, vessel form and decoration and aspects of use such as evidence of sooting, using codes set out in the OA recording system for Roman pottery (Booth 2014) which incorporates data fields and codes appropriate for later prehistoric and early post-Roman pottery. For the material of both period groups a site-specific fabric series was devised, though in the case of the Late Saxon material this was then correlated with more widely recognised fabric codes where possible. Quantification of the pottery by fabric is given in Tables 5.1 and 5.2. The pottery was in variable but overall, reasonably good condition. The mean sherd weight (17.3g) is quite high but is boosted by the presence of large sherds of a fairly small number of vessels. Some context groups contained only small sherds. Heavily abraded material is, however, rare; surfaces of sherds were reasonably well preserved, although assessment of the extent and survival of surface treatment/decoration (particularly burnishing) was sometimes problematic.

Early–Mid Saxon

Fabrics

The Early–Mid Saxon pottery fabrics were grouped in terms of their principal inclusion type. Five such groupings were defined – A (sand-tempered); CH (chalk-tempered); F (flint-tempered); M (miscellaneous); V ('vegetable'/organic-tempered) – but of these only the first and last were significant, together accounting for 98% of the sherds of this period. A few individual fabrics dominated within these major fabric groups, and a number of fabrics were represented only by single sherds. Fabric descriptions are given below. It should be noted that in a multi-period assemblage 100% accuracy in attribution, particularly of small atypical sherds, to a specific period cannot be guaranteed. At Thame there are distinct similarities between some Early Iron Age fabrics and some Saxon ones, a problem far from unique to this site. Most issues of attribution are thought to have been resolved, but it is inevitable that occasional uncertainties remain.

Almost all the fabrics have a finely micaceous clay matrix, so mica is not mentioned in the individual descriptions. Where size ranges for coarse, medium and fine quartz sand grains are not given they are as in the first quoted use of these terms (in fabrics A1, A2 and A4 respectively).

A. Sand-tempered

A. Sand inclusions not otherwise specified.

A1. Sparse–moderate large sub-rounded glassy quartz sand grains up to c. 1.2mm.
A2. Common medium sub-rounded quartz sand grains typically c. 0.2–0.3mm, with occasional larger grains.
A3. Common–moderate medium quartz sand, occasional larger grains up to c. 1mm; sparse–moderate organic inclus-ions up to c. 3mm.
A4. Common fine sand <0.1mm; sparse–moderate organic inclusions.
A5. Moderate coarse sand grains up to c. 1mm (can be glassy, as fabric A1); sparse–moderate organic inclusions up to c. 6mm.
A6. Moderate sub-rounded–sub-angular coarse sand up to c. 1mm.
A7. Moderate rounded–sub-rounded quartz sand 0.2–0.8mm; moderate organic inclusions up to c. 4mm and occasional angular limestone inclusions up to c. 0.4mm.
A8. Moderate–common sub-rounded medium sand; sparse

Table 5.1 Quantification of Early–Mid Saxon pottery fabrics (+ = <0.1)

FABRIC	Nosh	%	Wt (g)	%	RE	%	No. RIM	%
A	2	0.3	2	+				
A1	9	1.2	93	0.7	0.04	0.8	1	1.6
A2	23	2.9	296	2.3	0.36	7.1	4	6.3
A3	180	23	3130	23.9	1.82	36.1	22	33.0
A4	11	1.4	108	0.8	0.01	0.2	1	1.6
A5	27	3.5	414	3.2	0.21	4.2	5	7.9
A6	7	0.9	94	0.7	0.05	1.0	1	1.6
A7	9	1.2	56	0.4	0.05	1.0	1	1.6
A8	6	0.8	108	0.8				
A9	7	0.9	83	0.6				
A10	1	0.1	13	0.1				
A11	103	13.2	1382	10.6	0.47	9.3	6	7.9
A12	5	0.6	52	0.4				
A13	3	0.4	7	0.1				
A14	17	2.2	373	2.8	0.21	4.2	2	4.8
A15	12	1.5	111	0.8	0.08	1.6	1	1.6
A16	1	0.1	7	0.1				
A17	1	0.1	6	0.1				
A18	1	0.1	7	0.1				
A20	1	0.1	20	0.2				
A subtotal	*426*	*54*	*6362*	*49*	*3.30*	*66*	*44*	*68*
CH1	4	0.5	80	0.6	0.12	2.4	1	1.5
CH2	1	0.1	4	+				
CH subtotal	*5*	*0.6*	*84*	*0.6*	*0.1*	*2.4*	*1*	*1.5*
F1	4	0.5	27	0.2	0.02	0.4	1	1.5
F2	2	0.3	11	0.1				
F3	1	0.1	8	0.1				
F subtotal	*7*	*0.9*	*46*	*0.4*	*0.02*	*0.4*	*1*	*1.5*
M2	1	0.1	13	0.1				
M3	2	0.3	14	0.1	0.03	0.6	1	1.5
M subtotal	*3*	*0.4*	*27*	*0.2*	*0.03*	*0.6*	*1*	*1.5*
V1	203	25.9	4640	35.4	0.74	14.7	6	7.9
V2	10	1.3	317	2.4	0.15	3.0	2	3.2
V3	7	0.9	118	0.9	0.10	2.0	1	1.6
V4	46	5.9	686	5.2	0.12	2.4	1	1.6
V5	32	4.1	293	2.2	0.14	2.8	3	4.8
V6	30	3.8	352	2.7	0.25	5.0	3	4.8
V7	6	0.8	122	0.9				
V8	1	0.1	4	+				
V9	7	0.9	48	0.4	0.07	1.4	2	3.2
V subtotal	*342*	*44*	*6580*	*50*	*1.6*	*31*	*18*	*27.0*
Total	**783**		**13099**		**5.05**		**65**	

Nosh = number of sherds; RE = rim equivalent

Table 5.2 Quantification of Late Saxon pottery fabrics

FABRIC	Tradition	Nosh	%	Wt (g)	%	RE	%	No. RIM
LS1	OXR	22	34.9	381	25.5	0.12	14.6	2
LS2	cf OXBF	9	14.3	268	17.9			
LS3	OXBF	23	36.5	523	34.9	0.21	25.6	3
LS4	cf OXBF	2	3.2	49	3.3	0.12	14.6	1
LS5	cf OXBF	3	4.8	112	7.5	0.15	18.3	1
LS6	cf OXY	1	1.6	17	1.1	0.03	3.7	1
LS7		1	1.6	20	1.3	0.04	4.9	1
LS8		1	1.6	15	1.0			
LS9		1	1.6	112	7.5	0.15	18.3	1
Total		**63**		**1497**		**0.82**		**10**

Nosh = number of sherds; RE = rim equivalent

angular–sub-rounded black-brown lumps up to *c.* 1mm; occasional organic and flint inclusions.

A9. Moderate–common sub-rounded fine to medium sand; occasional rounded–sub-rounded black or brown Fe oxides up to 1.2mm; occasional organic inclusions.

A10. Moderate medium (occasionally coarse) sub-rounded sand grains; sparse organic, flint and Fe oxides and occasional fine chalk inclusions.

A11. Moderate medium–large quartz sand; moderate angular–sub-angular quartz/quartzite lumps up to 2.5mm; very sparse organic inclusions.

A12. Moderate fine quartz sand, sparse medium sand, and occasional large sand grains; sparse organic inclusions and sub-rounded red-brown clay pellets up to *c.* 1.2mm.

A13. Fairly sparse mostly fine sand; sparse organic inclusions.

A14. Sparse variable sand; sparse–moderate ironstone ooliths typically *c.* 0.3mm; occasional organic inclusions.

A15. Moderate medium sand; sparse–moderate organic and shell inclusions up to 2mm.

A16. Common very fine sand <0.1mm and common very fine black ?Fe inclusions.

A17. As A14 but with fewer ooliths, and also sparse fine shell inclusions and occasional clay pellets.

A18. Moderate medium–coarse sub-rounded–sub-angular quartz sand; sparse organic and sparse–moderate sub-rounded–sub-angular chalk inclusions up to 2mm (but most up to *c.* 1mm).

A20. Common–abundant sand, mostly medium but some large glassy grains, rounded brown ?Fe oxides (cf fabric A9).

CH. Chalk-tempered

CH1. Moderate rounded–sub-rounded chalk inclusions typically *c.* 1mm but occasionally up to *c.* 3.5mm; occasional sand, hard fired.

CH2. Sparse–moderate rounded–sub-rounded chalk and voids up to *c.* 2mm; sparse sand and organic inclusions.

F. Flint-tempered

F1. Moderate–common angular calcined flint up to 3mm; sparse medium quartz sand.

F2. Moderate angular white flint up to 1.5mm; moderate fine–medium sand and occasional large sand grains.

F3. Moderate angular calcined flint up to 2mm; moderate or moderate–common medium sand; rounded grey ?chalk and occasional angular brown inclusions. Much more sandy than fabric F1.

M. Miscellaneous temper

M2. Moderate large angular ?quartzite inclusions up to 3.5mm; moderate medium sand; angular platy golden mica etc.

M3. Sparse–moderate angular–sub-angular moderately hard grey-black lumps; sparse sand and organic inclusions.

V. Organic-tempered

V1. Common–abundant linear organic inclusions (grass/straw) up to 5mm; sparse medium sand grains.

V2. Common organic inclusions up to 3–5mm; sparse medium sand; sparse buff-grey sub-rounded grog or clay pellet lumps up to 2mm.

V3. Common organic inclusions; sparse–moderate medium sand; occasional shell inclusions.

V4. Moderate–common organic inclusions up to 6mm; moderate medium sand grains.

V5. Common–abundant organic inclusions up to 4–6mm; no visible sand.

V6. Moderate organic inclusions up to *c.* 4–5mm; sparse–moderate sand grains (occasionally large and glassy); sparse angular/sub-angular black-brown lumps (as in fabric A8) up to 3mm.

V7. Moderate–common organic inclusions up to 4–6mm; sparse sand grains; sparse sub-rounded–sub-angular chalk (cf fabric V3).

V8. Moderate organic inclusions; sparse–moderate medium sand grains; occasional angular flint inclusions up to *c.* 1.5mm.

V9. Moderate–common organic inclusions; sparse–moderate fine sand grains; occasional red-brown clay pellet.

The two principal fabric groups (A and V) were very roughly equivalent in importance, but there are significant differences in their representation. Sand-tempered fabrics were more numerous by sherd count and particularly in terms of quantification of vessels, whether by rim count or by rim equivalents (REs, the estimation of which with relatively fragmented handmade material is inexact, but still provides an important relative measure). These differences emphasise the particular importance of organic-tempered fabrics in a relatively limited number of contexts, for example those associated with SFB structure 33 (5166), the organic-tempered sherds from which amounted to 46% of all V fabric pottery by weight (and just over 30% by sherd count) with a mean sherd weight of 29g.

It is important to note that almost none of the fabrics in the two major groups were tempered solely with the dominant inclusion type. In particular, each included fabrics in which the other was a component. The principal sand-tempered fabrics A3 and A11 both included sparse organic material, and the dominant organic-tempered fabric V1 likewise typically had sparse quartz sand inclusions, though it is debatable if these were a deliberate component of the fabric. The numbers of fabrics assigned, particularly in the sand-tempered group, raise the question of sources – do they represent the importation of pottery from a diverse range of sources, or do they reflect the opportunistic use of local clays of subtly varied heterogeneous character? On balance the latter is more likely, and it is arguable that fabrics in the two main traditions have been over-divided here (cf Blinkhorn 2007, 230–1). A further question raised by the range of fabrics, and the mixing of inclusion types seen in some of them, concerns the relationship between sand-tempering and organic-tempering traditions; in broad terms were they chronologically sequential, or was the distinction driven by social and cultural factors (e.g., Blinkhorn 2007)?

That there were differences is indicated clearly by some of the assemblages from SFBs, albeit that some are not very large (and two SFBs – structure 31 (5735) and structure 39 (7452) – produced no Saxon pottery at all), summarised in Table 5.3. The smaller groups tend to be mixed in terms of fabric composition. The larger groups, however, defined as such either in terms of numbers of sherds or of relatively high mean sherd weight (MSW in Table 5.3) tend to be dominated by one or other of the major fabric groups. Assemblages from three SFBs (structures 33 (5166), 36 (6387) and 35 (8461)) are completely dominated by organic-tempered sherds and one, structure 30 (15710), by sand-tempered sherds. Sand-tempered sherds dominate the assemblage in SFB structure 34 (6572) to a significant but not overwhelming extent, while the case of SFB structure 32 (8577) is less clear cut – here sand-tempered sherds dominate, but organic-tempered ones are well represented. Overall, these figures indicate the clear potential for the question of the significance of the different fabric groups to be addressed here, while bearing in mind the well-known point that SFB assemblages generally reflect disuse deposits rather than representing the use of these features. In relation to the question of possible chronological distinction between groups dominated by sand-tempered or organic-tempered fabric traditions, independent dating is available for three SFB assemblages, from SFBs structures 33, 37 and 35 (5166, 6567/6830 and 8461, respectively). In all of these, the pottery is almost entirely organic-tempered, though structure 37 only contained five sherds. The radiocarbon dates for all these features are firmly centred on the first half of the 7th century.

Table 5.3 Summary of Saxon pottery from SFBs

SFB cut no.	Structure no.	No. sherds	Wt (g)	MSW	% sherds A	% sherds V	% weight A	% weight V	Comment
5166	33	110	3138	28.5	4.5	94.5	2.8	96.3	V dominant. 7th-century radiocarbon date
6387	36	33	654	19.8	9.1	87.9	1.5	97.9	V dominant
6567/ 6830	37	5	66	13.2					V but insignificant. 7th-century radiocarbon date
6572	34	55	1688	30.7	72.7	25.5	79.3	20.1	A dominant
6844	38	3	21	7					V & A, quantities insignificant
7510	40	12	147	12.2	41.7	50.0	59.9	37.4	mixed
7595?	42	1	11	11					V but insignificant
8461	35	28	458	16.4	-	96.4	-	98.7	V dominant. 7th-century radiocarbon date
8577	32	70	866	12.4	61.4	37.1	58.7	41.2	A dominant, but mixed
9441	41	31	292	9.4	32.3	64.5	48.3	50.7	mixed
15710	30	242	3111	12.9	94.2	4.1	94.5	3.1	A dominant
Total		590	10452						

A = sand-tempered, V = organic-tempered

Vessel types, decoration and use

A total of 65 vessels were identified on the basis of rim sherds, counting multiple sherds clearly derived from a single vessel (sometimes occurring in more than one context) as one. Many sherds were insufficiently large to allow detailed characterisation of their forms (a total RE value of 5.05 means that each vessel was represented on average by only 8% of the rim circumference, a very small proportion). Most vessels were therefore defined only in the most general terms as jars or jar/bowls. Within this broad range occasional vessels were defined as barrel shaped or globular in form. A wide variety of rim forms was noted amongst these vessels, but essentially, they amount to variations on simple slightly out-sloping forms and more clearly everted rims, a few everted at a fairly sharp angle and some thickened. In addition, two examples of cauldron-like jars with large raised pierced lugs were present, both in fabric A3, one from SFB structure 30 (15710) (Fig. 5.3, 15) and one from SFB structure 34 (6572) (Fig. 5.1, 4). Notable forms are illustrated in Figures 5.1–5.4.

Five vessels were defined as open forms, comprising three bowls and two indeterminate bowl/dishes. All of these were in sand-tempered fabrics. In addition, there were single examples of small vessels, both with simple out-sloping rims, recorded as a beaker (in fabric A2, Fig. 5.2, 6) and an open cup (in fabric V3, not illustrated).

Vessel bases were mostly characteristic slightly rounded or almost flat forms. The single exception was on a small, slightly carinated jar/bowl in fabric A14 from SFB structure 30 (15710) (Fig. 5.2, 7). This vessel had a recessed/slight footring base, which may be a particular Early Saxon characteristic (cf e.g., Blinkhorn 2004, 269), although these continue into the 7th century (e.g., at Mucking, Hamerow 1993, 41–2). The vessel had small applied horizontally-pierced lugs on the shoulder and was also burnished overall. Burnishing was the only finishing/decorative technique widely encountered in this assemblage. Its application was sometimes rather patchy, and it was frequently difficult to determine if an overall burnished surface was intended or if the observed treatment was just the result of selective smoothing.

Other decoration was very rare. Grooves were present either on the shoulder or in unlocated positions on body sherds in ten cases, all but one in sand-tempered fabrics. In one case (fabric A14; Fig. 5.2, 10) these were combined with impressed rings and small indentations; this was the only example of relatively elaborate decoration in the entire assemblage. Horizontal burnished lines were noted on two sherds, also in sand-tempered fabrics.

Evidence of use consisted of external soot and occasional internal charred deposits, together with occasional instances of limescale. Collectively such deposits were noted on 64 sherds. They were, incidentally, much more common on Late Saxon sherds, though it is possible that the relative scarcity of evidence of sooting on Early Saxon fabrics is in part a consequence of the difficulty of detecting slight traces of soot on the surfaces of (mostly) dark grey-black sherds.

Context, phasing and chronology

These topics have already been touched on in discussing fabrics (above). Early–Mid Saxon pottery was recorded from some 109 contexts, of which only 39 were certainly or probably assigned to the Early–Mid Saxon period of the site, but these contained 85.3% of Early–Mid Saxon sherds (and 90.8% of this material by weight). Thirteen context groups containing Saxon pottery were phased as prehistoric and 30 as Late Iron Age and Roman, so the Saxon pottery in these must have been intrusive. Eight groups dated to the Late Saxon period also contained Early–Mid Saxon sherds, but these were on average quite small (in total 17 sherds with a mean weight of 9.4g) and were presumably redeposited. Four later contexts and 15 groups of uncertain date/phase also contained Early–Mid Saxon sherds.

The great majority (88% by both sherd count and weight) of the Saxon pottery assigned to this period came from SFBs, with small amounts from pits, ditches, and a single layer (5870, not illustrated) which produced 36 sherds weighing 622g. The breakdown of the pottery from SFBs is shown in Table 5.3.

Questions of chronology have also been indicated above. The radiocarbon dates from the SFBs clearly show that organic-tempered fabrics are characteristic of the 7th century, but it is uncertain if these dates define the whole of the span of Early–Mid Saxon occupation at Thame, or if some features could have been earlier still in date. These issues are discussed further below.

Later Saxon/Early medieval

Fabrics and forms

Nine fabrics were initially identified amongst the sherds of this broad period range. These fall into three main groups. The first (fabric LS1) is St Neots type shelly ware (Oxford (Mellor 1994, 54–7) fabric OXR). The second group consists of fabrics LS2–LS5, mainly characterised by coarse sand and flint inclusions, which are thought to be variants of the Kennet Valley 'A' ware tradition (see also Oxford (Mellor 1994, 52–4) fabric OXBF). Together this group accounted for *c.* 59% of the Late Saxon sherds (64% by weight), though these figures are not particularly meaningful given the size of the group overall. The third group (fabrics LS6–LS9) consists of various sand-tempered fabrics, each represented by a single sherd. Of these, fabric LS6 is comparable with, but not necessarily identical to, Oxford Late Saxon–Early medieval fabric OXY (Mellor 1994, 63–71). The others are not assigned to sources at present.

LS1. Abundant shell inclusions. St Neots type ware (fabric OXR, Mellor 1994, 54–7).

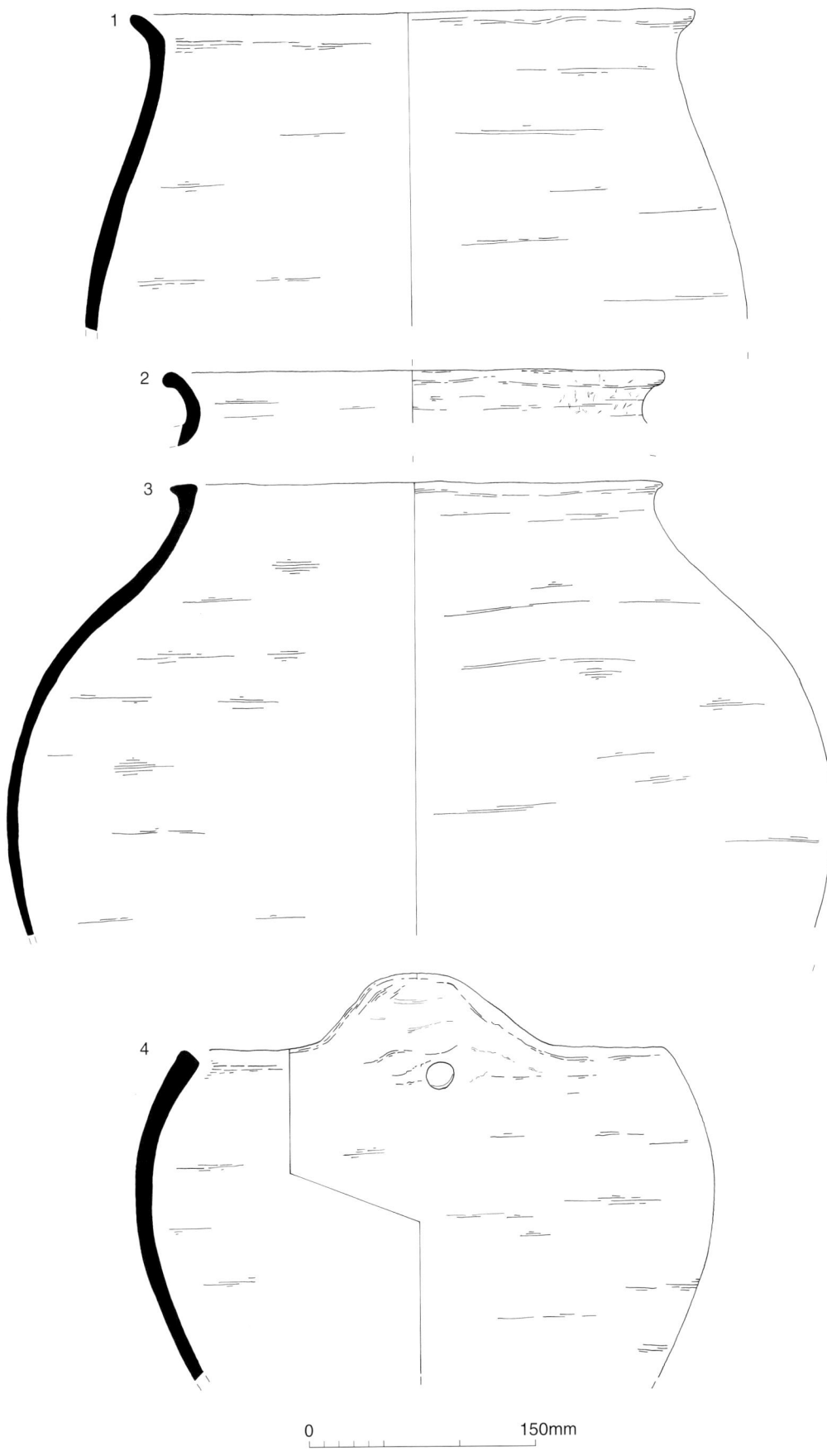

Fig. 5.1   Saxon pottery, nos 1–4

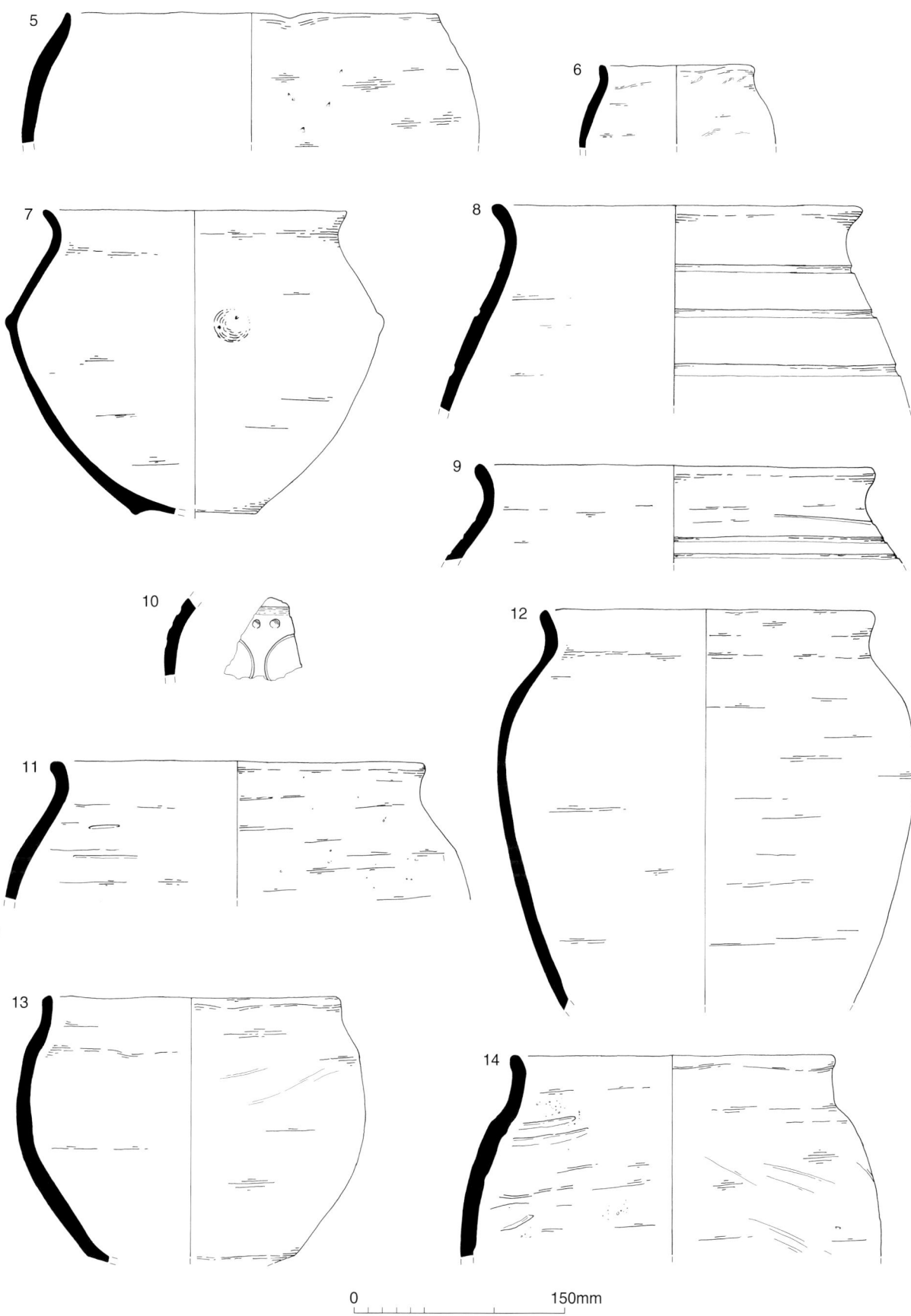

Fig. 5.2   Saxon pottery, nos 5–14

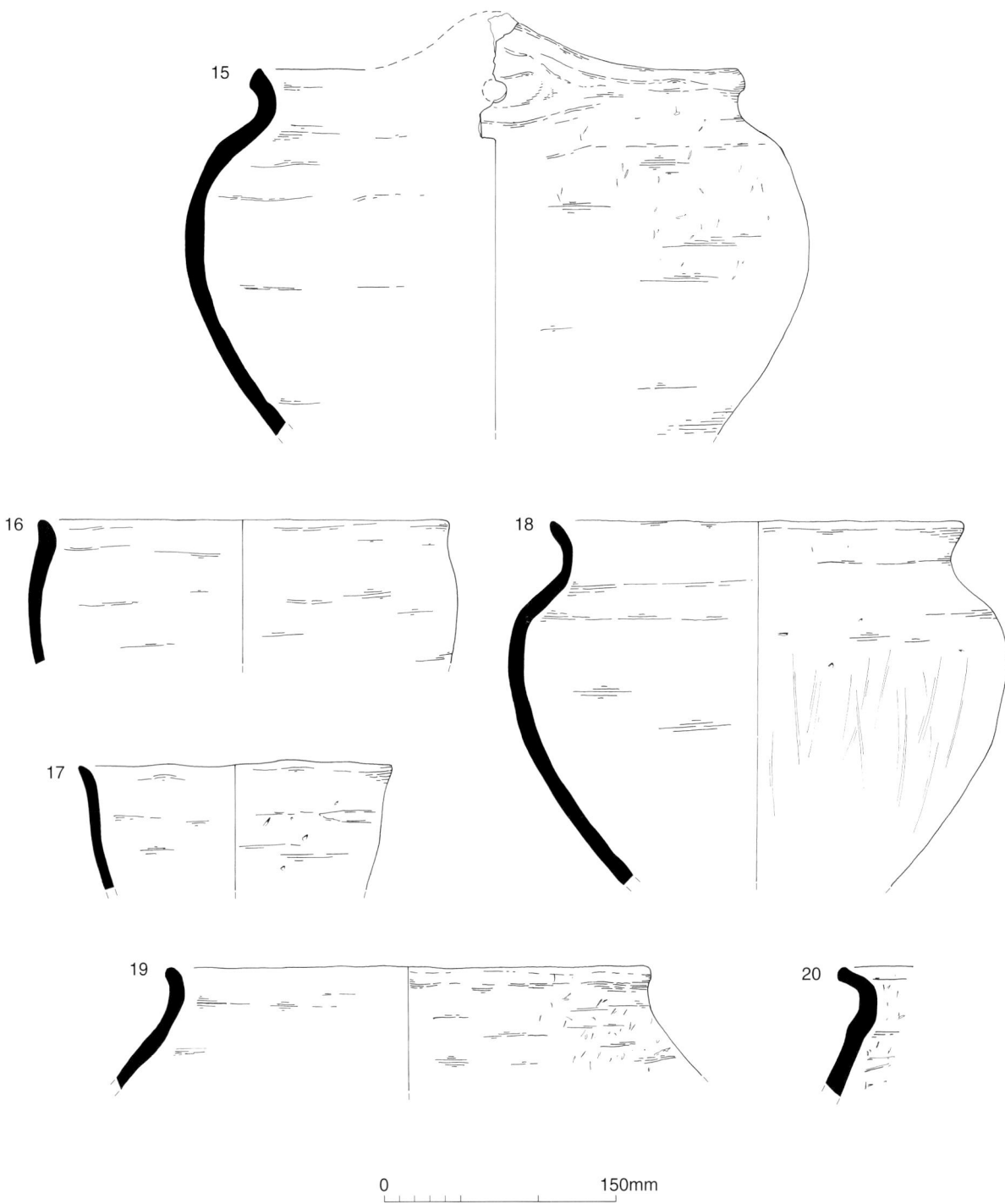

Fig. 5.3 Saxon pottery, nos 15–20

LS2–5. Angular quartz and flint, chalk and sparse sub-rounded soft grey inclusions, occasional shell. Variants of Kennet Valley A ware, equivalent to Oxford fabric OXBF (Mellor 1994, 52–4).

LS6. Common–abundant medium sand. Cf Oxford fabric OXY (Mellor 1994, 63–71).

LS7. Common–abundant medium sand, with occasional larger quartz inclusions; occasional shell and rounded ?grog lumps up to *c.* 2mm.

LS8. Moderate sub-rounded–sub-angular sand up to 1mm; moderate shell up to 1.5mm; occasional organic inclusions and Fe oxides.

LS9. Abundant coarse sand typically up to *c.* 0.7mm but occasionally up to 1.5mm; occasional sub-rounded–sub-rectangular chalk inclusions up to *c.* 2.5mm and occasional flint up to 3mm.

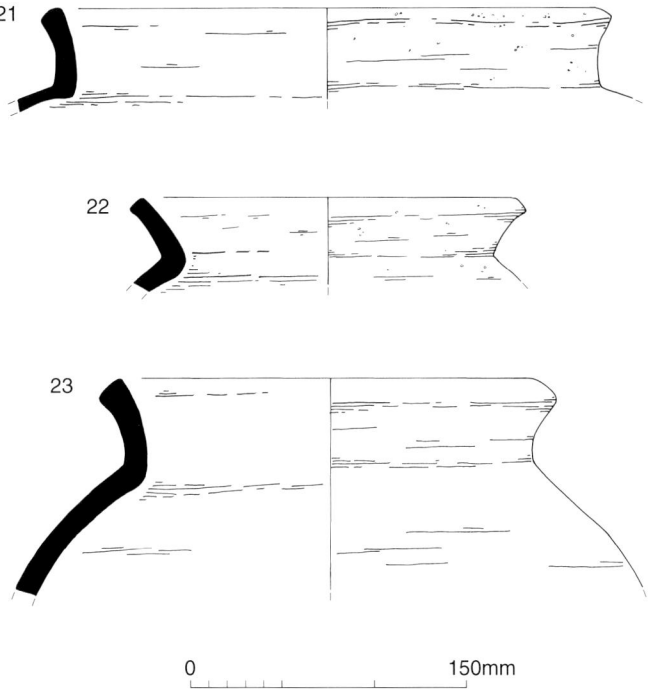

Fig. 5.4   Late Saxon pottery, nos 21–23

Vessel forms present are mostly jars/cooking pots with distinct angled everted rims characteristic of the period (Fig. 5.4, 21–23). The only exception was one of the St Neots (fabric LS1) rims, which was from a typical bowl with angled in-turned rim (cf e.g., Mellor 1994, 56, fig. 15, 3). Thumb impressions were noted on three rims (one each in fabrics LS1, LS3 and LS7) but 'decoration' was otherwise entirely absent.

Context and phasing

Some 87.9% of Early–Mid Saxon sherds and 84.1% of Late Saxon sherds were recovered from contexts phased to the Saxon or Late Saxon periods with varying degrees of certainty (Table 5.2). The number of context groups involved is, however, quite small – only 27 context groups were phased as certainly SAX (i.e., Early–Mid Saxon), with a further 12 as SAX? The corresponding figures for the later Saxon period (LSAX) are 11 and 1. Saxon pottery was recorded from 44 context groups assigned to earlier phases and was therefore presumably considered to be intrusive in these groups. It occurred residually in five groups phased as post-medieval and was present in 13 contexts for which phasing was uncertain or unknown.

The great majority of the Early–Mid Saxon pottery assigned to contexts of that period (SAX and SAX?) came from SFBs (85.6% of sherds and 86.7% by weight). This is a characteristic proportion (cf e.g., Eynsham, where a minimum of *c.* 80% of phased Early Saxon sherds were from SFBs (Blinkhorn 2003, 163); Barton Court Farm, where 77% by weight of the Saxon pottery was from SFBs (Miles *et al.* 1986, fiche 7:F1); and Barrow Hills with 68.1% of the sherd count, 70.8% by weight (Blinkhorn 2007, 234)). Of the remainder, a significant proportion came from layers and a smaller amount from pits. Only one sherd was from a ditch securely assigned to this period, but it is notable that almost all the contexts tentatively phased as Early–Mid Saxon (SAX?) were ditch fills. Ditches are uncommon features in the Early Saxon period in this region, but it is unclear if the uncertainty in phase attribution should be seen as a reflection of this, with a possible implication that ditches belong to the later part of the Early–Mid Saxon period. The quantities of pottery involved (19 sherds/193g, of which 12 sherds/138g are in organic-tempered fabrics) are insufficient to help clarify this question.

The Late Saxon pottery from contexts assigned to that period all derived from ditch fills (from the enclosure). A similar situation was noted for example at Audlett Drive, Abingdon (Underwood-Keevill 1992, 72). A sherd of fabric LS4 (Fig. 5.4, 22) came from SFB structure 33 (5166) and is discussed further below.

Discussion

Chronology remains a major problem for Early–Mid Saxon pottery in this region (for a summary of assemblages from selected sites in the wider Oxford region see Table 5.4). On present evidence close dating of most of the Saxon pottery at Thame is very difficult, and much can only be assigned to the very broad date ranges indicated above. There are few typological characteristics that are clearly chronologically diagnostic, and decoration, which can sometimes be used in this way but is never common on settlement site assemblages in the region (e.g., Blinkhorn 2003, 164–5), is particularly rare here, with only a single sherd (Fig. 5.2, 10) having any decorative elements beyond occasional examples of tooled or burnished horizontal lines (e.g., Fig. 5.2, 8 and 9). The question of the extent to which variations in proportions of major fabric groups, and perhaps of fabric/form combinations can allow refinement of Early–Mid Saxon ceramic chronology remains unresolved but requires the relative dating of sand-tempered and organic-tempered fabrics to be clarified. A view that the sand-tempered tradition is on balance likely to be the earlier of the two in origin (see above) has been quite widely held (e.g., Brown 1976; Berisford 1981; Hamerow 1993), and is implied in a recent review of Early Anglo-Saxon pottery in south-east England, which identifies a 'transition to organic-tempered wares' throughout the 6th century (Jervis *et al.* 2015, 24), but the situation is rarely clear cut, and the nature of most of the relevant sites results in a lack of stratigraphic sequences with which quantified pottery can be associated (Miles *et al.* 1986, fiche 7:F4–F5).

Blinkhorn's (2007, 233–4) analysis of the largest regional assemblage (over 9000 sherds), from Barrow Hills, Radley, suggested that organic-tempered fabrics increased in importance in the 6th century, but he was clear that such fabrics were already present at Barrow Hills and adjacent sites by the later 5th century, and was cautious about pressing the argument for a steady increase in the proportion of organic-tempered sherds through the 6th and 7th centuries too far in relation

Table 5.4 Summary of selected Early–Mid Saxon assemblages from the Oxford region

Site	No. sherds	Wt (g)	Stated date range AD	Comment	Reference
Horcott	2961	34,600	450–850	*c.* 69% of sherds V, 4 sherds Late Saxon	Cotter 2017
Eynsham	6248	53,300	Later 5–7C	More than 50% redeposited in later contexts. Most of the rest in SFBs, of which *c.* 50% of sherds A, 43.5% limestone and 6.5% V	Blinkhorn 2003
Yarnton	106	1700	5–6C	*c.* 60% of sherds A. Plus 11 sherds/492g Middle Saxon	Blinkhorn 2004
Oxford Science Park	925	18,597	6–7C?	50% of sherds A, 36% AV, 9% V	Blinkhorn 2001
Audlett Drive Abingdon	-	6600	Not stated, ?later 5–7C	Exact quantities not specified; 'predominant' fabric 1 (A) is 33.6% of total weight, which includes Roman and Late Saxon material	Underwood-Keevill 1992
Barton Court Farm	-	33,490	5–7C	76% A, 20% V	Miles, Hofdahl and Moore 1986
Barrow Hills, Radley	9131	127,620	5–6C	51.7% sherds A, 35.4% AV, 11.5% V	Blinkhorn 2007
Beech House Hotel Dorchester	380	-	Not stated ?5–7C	*c.* 71% of sherds A, 6% V, *c.* 13% limestone (incl. in combination with sand etc.)	Berisford 1981
Mount Farm Berinsfield	221	3540	Late 5–7C	67.4% of sherds AV	Booth 2010
Benson	356	6438	6–8C	74% of sherds V, 12% A, 10% calcareous	Timby 2003, 154–7
Walton, Aylesbury 1973–4			5–8C		Farley 1976; Brown 1976
Walton Lodge, Aylesbury 1985–6	956	5281	Late 6–8C	62% of sherds V, 19% A, 19% AV. 70% redeposited in later contexts. 66 Middle/Late Saxon sherds not included here	Evans 1989
Walton Road, Aylesbury 1994	378	-	Later 6–8C	Exact fabric quantities not specified, roughly 55% V, 45% A	Timby 2004

A = sand-tempered, V = organic-tempered

to an assemblage in which the majority of the pottery (87% of sherd count) was in primarily sand-tempered fabrics. At Thame the relative percentages of sand-tempered and organic-tempered fabrics are c. 55% and 44% by sherd count, though the representation of these two groups by weight is almost identical. As at Barrow Hills other fabric groups were of minimal importance, a situation that contrasts with the picture at, for example, Dorchester Beech House Hotel, where limestone or shell temper was quite common (Berisford 1981, 39–40) and particularly at Eynsham, where almost 45% of the assemblage (by weight) was in a variety of limestone-tempered fabrics (Blinkhorn 2007, 231; Blinkhorn (2003, 174) gives a figure of 46.5% but calculated in a slightly different way). Fabrics largely or partly tempered with oolitic limestone also formed a significant part of the Horcott assemblage (14.1% of sherds; Cotter 2017, 295) but here were very much subordinate to organic-tempered fabrics. The significance of the strong representation of limestone-tempered fabrics at Eynsham remains uncertain but is likely to reflect the availability of particular calcareous clays associated with the gravel terraces of the Upper Thames (Blinkhorn 2007, 231).

The Thame assemblage makes a small contribution to the discussion of chronology. SFBs with 7th-century radiocarbon dates have associated assemblages (where pottery is present at all) dominated by organic-tempered fabrics. This supports a view that such fabrics are particularly characteristic of the 7th century, but there are possible objections. First, there are no radiocarbon dates for SFB structure 30 (15710) which, with its large assemblage dominated by sand-tempered fabrics and perhaps including typologically early material (see further below) would be expected to pre-date the 7th century. In the absence of radiocarbon dates this view is plausible but unproven. Secondly, the 7th-century radiocarbon dates might be telling the whole story, that this was the principal period of Saxon occupation at Thame, and that pottery thought to be earlier on typological or other grounds was in fact contemporary with the independently dated groups.

The latter possibility, however, is not thought likely. All the characteristics of the structure 30 (15710) assemblage (Figs 5.2–5.3, 6–15) suggest that it should be earlier than the 7th century. These include the dominance of sand-tempered fabrics and the association of these with potentially early forms, particularly the lugged bowl (Fig. 5.2, 7) with vestigial footring, a potentially early feature as mentioned above. Broadly comparable vessels occur at Horcott, Gloucestershire (Cotter 2017, 300, fig. 10.8, 10) and Barrow Hills (Chambers and McAdam 2007, 142, fig. 3.56, 91), though both of these vessels have more rounded profiles than the Thame example. Closer local parallels are found at Sutton Courtenay (Leeds 1927, 67, fig. 5; Myres 1977, fig. 76, 4144) and particularly at Abingdon (Brown 1972, 74, fig. 7,

20; Myres 1977, fig. 75, 4143). Although Myres says that 'the slacker contours of most of the larger English examples suggest that they belong to the 6th century or even later' the implication of his preceding comments is that more angular forms might be of 5th-century date (Myres 1977, 10). The fills of structure 30 also produced a rounded cauldron-like vessel with large upright lugs on the rim (Fig. 5.3, 15), and a second example of this type came from SFB structure 34 (6572), with another assemblage dominated by sand-tempered fabrics (Fig. 5.1, 4). Both vessels were in fabric A3. This form is never common, but is widely paralleled in the region, with examples at Horcott (Cotter 2017, 301, fig. 10.9, 14), Eynsham (Blinkhorn 2003, 166, fig. 7.1, 4, and 170, fig. 7.6, 70), Oxford Science Park (Blinkhorn 2001, 194, fig. 12, 2), Abingdon (Brown 1972, 75, fig. 8, 50) and multiple vessels (at least ten) from Barrow Hills, Radley. Five of the Barrow Hills vessels came from a single feature, SFB 28 (Chambers and McAdam 2007, 163, fig. 3.63, 150, 151, 155, 157 and 158). This type and vessels with longitudinal lugs on the vessel body are described as 'found in features all over the site' (Blinkhorn 2007, 244), but the discussion does not consider the correlation of lugs with fabric (fabric codes are not given against the pottery entries in the SFB catalogue), or their possible chronology. The discussion of SFB 28 (Chambers and McAdam 2007, 162–4) indicates that the associated finds would appear to support a 5th-century date, and the substantial pottery assemblage (over 12kg) consisted almost entirely of sand- and sand and organic-tempered fabrics – the latter, in the majority, was in Blinkhorn's fabric F2, presented as a chaff-tempered fabric in SFB catalogue (Chambers and McAdam 2007, 160). Whatever the significance of this, however, SFB 28 cut an earlier structure (SFB 29), the backfill of which had a 6th-century *terminus post quem*. If this relationship was correctly recorded it suggests either that the material from SFB 28 'conventionally … ascribed to the 5th century' (Chambers and McAdam 2007, 162, a remark confined to the decorated pottery which formed only a small part of a large assemblage) was redeposited, and that at least some of the remaining material should be seen as having a longer date range. It is perhaps more likely that both conditions applied.

While it is likely that a majority of the upright lugged vessels at Barrow Hills were in sand-tempered fabrics, like the two from Thame (and it is notable that the examples from Horcott and Eynsham were all in limestone-tempered fabrics), there is thus no certainty that the fabric associations of this type give a clear indication of their date. On balance, however, a date range encompassing the 6th century (and possibly also earlier and later) appears likely. It is also possible that rather than reflecting a possible chronological aspect, the apparent preference for the use of sand- or calcareous-tempered fabrics for the vessels with upright lugs reflects a functional characteristic. Reverting more broadly to the Thame assemblage, and particularly that from structure 30, it seems most probable that this includes a 6th-century component, with the earliest material perhaps as early as the later 5th century, but this cannot be proven.

A further aspect of chronology at Thame concerns the pottery from SFB structure 33 (5166). Dominated by organic-tempered vessels, the assemblage also included a Late Saxon jar in fabric LS4 (Fig. 5.4, 22) and the organic-tempered jars include two (Fig. 5.1, 2 and 3) with rims that do not seem typical of the Early–Mid Saxon period. It is possible that these are later than the expected date range and more closely associated with the fabric LS4 vessel. However, this SFB is one of those with a 7th-century radiocarbon date, and it is perhaps most likely that Figure 5.4, 22 was indeed intrusive.

The radiocarbon dates have served to demonstrate activity at the site through much of the 7th century and most of the material from SFBs with the relevant determinations can be considered to be broadly contemporary with them. Whether any of the pottery from Thame was later in date than the 7th century is unknown. A general lack of identifiable Mid Saxon (specifically 8th-century) pottery fabrics is considered characteristic of the Upper Thames Valley, demonstrated most clearly at sites such as Yarnton (Blinkhorn 2004). It is uncertain if the same problem applies in south-east Oxfordshire, though it was considered likely to be relevant at Barrow Hills. The date ranges for assemblages from Aylesbury (Walton) are projected into the 8th century (see Table 5.4), but the basis for this is unclear.

The outer ends of the overall date range for the later Saxon/early medieval pottery are quite widely spaced, but in reality the range can probably be narrowed. Date ranges for fabrics OXR and OXBF at Oxford do not extend before about the middle of the 10th century and are supported by the consistent (if limited) evidence of the angled everted rim forms associated with vessels in most of the fabrics present here, including the unassigned fabric LS9. On balance a 10th–11th-century date range is most likely for the majority of the material in the Late Saxon group, though both earlier and later dates may be possible in the case of individual sherds.

Catalogue of illustrated vessels (Figs 5.1–5.4)

SFB structure 33 (5166)
1   Fabric V1, large jar with everted rim. Burnished overall. Context 5163
2   Fabric V2, jar with curving everted rim. Burnish on top of rim. Context 5165
3   Fabric V1, large jar with upright rim expanded at tip. Not burnished. Context 5163

SFB structure 34 (6572)
4   Fabric A3, cauldron with pierced upstanding suspension lug. Burnished overall. Internal limescale deposit. Context 6573

SFB structure 41 (9441)
5   Fabric V1, simple jar with tapered rim. Traces of internal burnish. Context 9442

SFB structure 30 (15710)
6   Fabric A2, small jar or beaker with simple vertical rim. Burnished overall. Context 15847
7   Fabric A14, slightly carinated bowl with everted rim, vestigial footring and small lugs with fine horizontal piercing. Burnished overall. Context 15847
8   Fabric A14, large jar with everted rim. Grooves on upper body and burnish on top of rim and shoulder. Context 15845 and fill 16846 of Roman pit 16844
9   Fabric A14, jar with everted rim. Grooves on shoulder and internal and external burnish. Context 15845
10 Fabric A14, body sherd with horizontal groove, small round indentations and incised circles below. Burnished overall. Context 15847
11 Fabric A15, jar with everted rim. Burnished overall. Context 15845
12 Fabric A11, large jar with slightly everted rim. Not burnished. Context 15845
13 Fabric A11, squat jar with upright rim. Burnished on shoulder and sooted externally. Context 15845 and 15846
14 Fabric CH1, jar with upright rim. Carbonised deposit on interior. Context 15846
15 Fabric A3, rounded cauldron with pierced upstanding suspension lug. Burnished on shoulder and externally sooted. Context 15846 and 15847

Layer group 5870
16 Fabric A3, simple jar with upright rim. Burnished overall. Context 5639
17 Fabric A3, simple bowl. Burnished internally and externally. Context 5639

Pit 16437
18 Fabric V2, rounded bowl with everted rim. Not burnished. Context 16432

Other features
19 Fabric A5, large jar with slightly everted rim. Not burnished. Context 15844, fill of Roman ditch 194 (15843)
20 Fabric V1, jar or bowl of uncertain diameter with sharply everted rim. Context 9145, fill of Iron Age pit 9146 (see Volume 1, Fig. 4.19)

Late Saxon
21 Fabric LS3, angled everted rim jar. Context 8544, Saxon enclosure ditch 8547
22 Fabric LS4, angled everted rim jar. Context 5163, (upper fill) SFB structure 33 (5166)
23 Fabric LS9, angled everted rim jar. Context 5260, Saxon enclosure ditch 5259

Metal finds
by E.R. McSloy

A small number of metal artefacts can be dated to this period, the majority (29 items) from period 4 (earlier Saxon) settlement features and with some items (three) from unphased or unstratified deposits. The recovered material is dominated by objects of iron and includes a group of grave goods from period 4 inhumation 16417. The catalogue presented below is selective, excluding (the majority) fragmentary items where function was indeterminable, as well as modern objects recorded mainly from the subsoil. Selected items are illustrated in Figure 5.5.

Select catalogue

Brooches – Lead alloy

The use of lead and the pin mechanism on Figure 5.5, 1 makes it comparable to early medieval nummular and disc brooches and a similar 10th to 11th/12th-century dating is suggested. Cruciform decoration is a common feature of such brooches although few are of openwork design. An example with a similar, though smaller, open cross device is a metal-detector find from north Lincolnshire (Portable Antiquities Scheme database NLM395).

1   Plate brooch. Disc-like with four sub-triangular perforations making an equal-armed pattée cross design, accentuated by scoring internal to the cross arms and a central lozenge design. The outer edge of the brooch is also notched. The pin mechanism to the back consists of a crudely-cast, perforated square lug and a small L-shaped catch. Traces of an iron pin survive. Wt 15.5g; Diam. 30.6mm. Western excavation area, subsoil 5001; Ra. 511.

Pins – Iron

Three iron pins of earlier or Mid Saxon type were recorded. An example from burial 16417 is described below as part of the grave catalogue. A biconical-headed pin is a type known locally in copper alloy (see MacGregor and Bolick 1993, 186, 31.1–31.3). A large number of iron examples, some like Figure 5.5, 2 with white-metal plating, are known from the Mid Saxon monastic site at Flixborough, Lincs (Rogers 2009, 38–9; Type Fe 3) and on this basis a later 7th or 8th-century date would seem most likely. Another pin (Fig. 5.5, 3) is fragmentary and distorted but is also white-metal-plated – suggesting a decorative function. Its head is loosely coiled and similar loop or curl-headed pins are known from graves in the Butler's Field, Lechlade cemetery (Ross 2011, 32) and in copper alloy from Abingdon, Oxon (MacGregor and Bolick 1993, 188, 31.38). The examples from Butler's Field occurred with 6th and 'later 6th'-century associations (Ross 2011, 32). Dating spanning the 6th or earlier 7th centuries has been suggested for pottery from SFB structure 35 (8461), from which Figure 5.5, 3 was recorded.

2   Pin. White-metal-plated. Biconical head; shaft sub-rounded in section, narrowing towards point (missing). L (surviving) 57.8mm; Diam. (head) 10.3mm; Diam. (shaft) 2.4–1.6mm. Period 3a ditch 6177, recut of ditch 8679–8676 in top of Causewayed enclosure, inner circuit ditch P, fill 6175.

3   Pin. White-metal-plated. Fragmentary and distorted. The head is tapered and loosely coiled. The shaft is round in section and narrows slightly towards point (missing). L (surviving) 58.6mm; Diam. (shaft) 2.9–1.9mm. Period 4a/b SFB structure 35 (8461), fill 8459. Ra. 1035.

Buckle – Iron

4   Buckle. Oval-shaped loop with square buckle plate secured with two rivets. The x-ray shows a narrower axis bar. Pin missing. Matches Marzinzik's (Early Anglo-Saxon) Type Group II.21 (Marzinzik 2003), although a later (medieval) dating is also plausible. L (loop) 37.7mm; W (loop) 28.6mm; L (plate) 27.9mm; W (plate) 31.1mm. Period 4 oven 3 (7498), fill 7462. Ra. 872.

Knives – Iron

Two knives considered of Anglo-Saxon date were recorded, with that from Period 4 grave 16417 described in the grave catalogue (below). The example illustrated in Figure 5.5, 5 comes from a Mid Saxon-phased deposit, although such dating is unsupported by any other artefactual material. Its blade back is insufficiently angled for identification as being of Ottaway type A knives, the use of which spans the Mid Saxon period into the 11th and 12th centuries (Ottaway 2009, 203–31; Ottaway and Rogers 2002, 2751–63). The length, slender proportions and possible provision for a decorative inlay make a medieval dating (c. 12th to 14th centuries) more plausible.

5   Long, whittle-tang knife (tip missing). The back is slightly angled and the edge straight, the tang central to the blade. There is a deep groove running parallel to the blade back, to both sides, perhaps to receive a decorative inlay. L (surviving) 185mm; W (max.) 18.7mm; Th. (blade) 6.5mm–0.6mm. Period 4b enclosure ditch 7641, fill 7640. Ra. 551.

Grave catalogue

Period 4 burial 16417 (SK. 1501)

Three objects (Fig. 5.5) were recorded in association with this heavily truncated adult burial of indeterminate sex, all located seemingly in the area of the pelvis. A radiocarbon determination obtained from a sample of bone returned of a result of cal AD 410–540 (SUERC-80886), implying a date earlier than the SFBs and other occupational features from the site.

16417.1   Iron strike-a-light or firesteel. Triangular form with up-curved ends (incomplete). In section it narrows from the straight back to the apex. Firesteels are relatively common finds from earlier Anglo-Saxon burial contexts. Those of triangular form such as

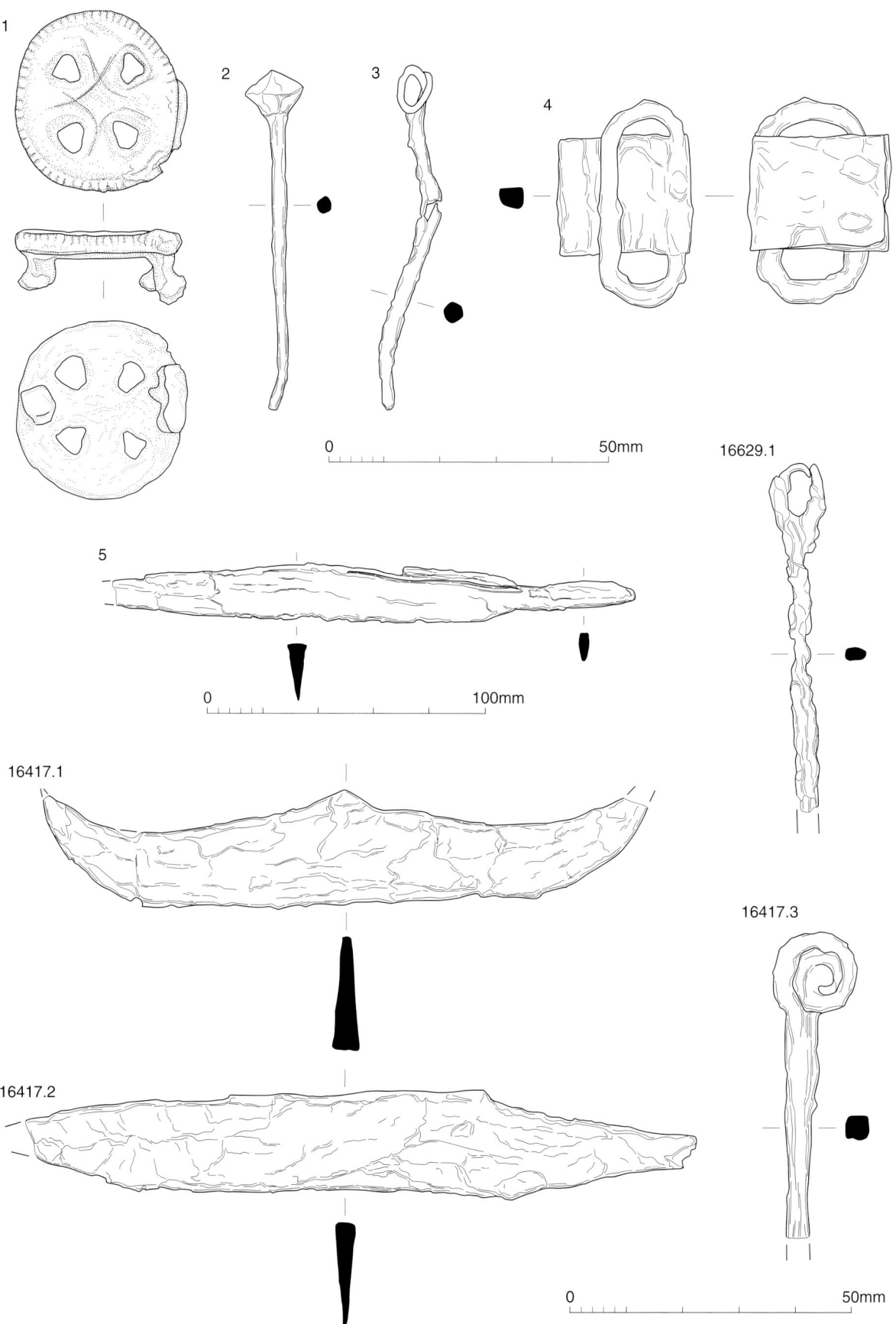

Fig. 5.5   Post-Roman metal objects

this example were considered by Geake to be of 7th century and later date (Geake 1997, 79–80), although the dating for burial 16417 suggests they can occur earlier. Geake's survey recorded examples from both male and female graves (Geake 1997). L 105.5mm; W (at centre) 23.4mm; Th. 4.5–1.9mm. Period 4 grave 16417, fill 16418; Ra. 40.

16417.2 Iron knife. Part of the tang and the tip are missing. The back and cutting edge are straight for the greater part of their length before curving to the tip. The tang is broad and central. The form is closest to Evison's Type 1, which was the most common grouping from Dover Buckland and present in all phases of that cemetery, use of which extends across the later 5th to 7th/8th centuries (Evison 1987, 113). Similar forms were also common at Butler's Field, Lechlade (Boyle *et al.* 2011, 10). L (surviving) 120mm; W (max.) 17.9mm; Th. 4.8–0.8mm. Period 4 grave 16417, fill 16418; Ra. 40.

16417.3 Iron pin(?). Fragment consisting of square/sub-rounded shaft terminating in a coiled terminal. An iron object identified as a pin, with a similar tightly-coiled head, was recorded from a male grave thought to date to the 6th century at Dover Buckland (Evison 1987, 230 and 299; Grave 50). L (surviving) 53mm; Diam. at head (max.) 14.5mm; W (shaft) 6.2–4.2mm; Th. (shaft) 4.9–4mm. Period 4 grave 16417, fill 16418; Ra. 40.

Period 4 burial 16629 (SK. 1502)

Object 16629.1 was associated with a female burial within grave-pit 16629, for which radiocarbon determination of a tooth sample indicated dating *c.* cal AD 410–550 (SUERC-95013). The object is poorly preserved and fragmentary, but likely to be a pin. Simple pins of iron are common from cemetery sites of the period. At Dover Buckland those of iron were the largest group from a total of 45, most of which occurred with female burials and were typically recorded in the area of the neck (Evison 1987, 82–4). A number are similar to 16629.1, the upper shaft turned over to form a crude head (Evison 1987, 84).

16629.1 Pin (?). The head is formed into a loose oval loop. The shaft is probably square in section. L (surviving) 58.9mm. Period 4 grave-pit 16629, fill 16630. Ra. 44.

Worked stone
by Ruth Shaffrey

A moderate assemblage of worked stone was recovered from Saxon contexts and is reported on here, except for a shale spindle whorl, which is included with spindle whorls of fired clay (Shaffrey, below). The worked stone includes fragments from four querns. Three rotary querns include a fragment of flat-topped Old Red Sandstone quern (Ra. 797; Fig. 5.6, 1), a fragment of a very tapered flat-topped Lodsworth Greensand quern with lateral handle socket (Ra. 836; Fig. 5.6, 2) and a fragment of upper stone of Mayen lava (upper fill of ditch 9877). A fourth quern fragment is of classic grain rubber form, that is with a convex pecked grinding surface (fill 7454 of 7452; Fig. 5.6, 3).

Other worked stone includes various types of processing tools. A Greensand cobble has faceting along one long edge, suggesting that, although unusually coarse for such a task, it was used for sharpening (Ra. 791). A further stone has been used along one edge, probably as a hone (Ra. 813) whilst a large cobble has significant percussion damage and rubbed wear suggesting use as a hammerstone and rubber (Ra. 1057). A flint hammerstone was also recovered from context 5284.

Catalogue

Upper rotary quern fragment reused as lower (Fig. 5.6, 1). Old Red Sandstone, pebbly sandstone. Flat-topped type with straight vertical sides. However, it has been reused on the other face as well so that this is now very smooth and slightly concave. Edges are also worn through some reuse. Centre does not survive. Measures 370mm diameter x 38–48mm thick. Wt 1730g. Ra. 797. Period 4a structure 36 (6387), fill 6386.

Upper rotary quern fragment (Fig. 5.6, 2). Lodsworth Greensand. Fragment of steeply tapered upper stone. The faces are pecked but the grinding surface has some rotational wear. It is broken along the lateral handle socket which measures at least 78mm long x 29mm deep. Measures 25–84mm thick. Wt 1708g. Ra. 836. Period 4a structure 39 (7452), fill 7454.

Upper rotary quern fragment. Lava. Fragment without edges or centre but with a pecked concave grinding surface with some rotational wear and pecked upper flat face. Measures 29mm thick. Wt 348g. Period 4b enclosure ditch 9877, upper fill 9879.

Classic grain rubber fragment (Fig. 5.6, 3). Quartz sandstone, sarsen-like. End fragment of pointed rubber fragment with rounded convex pecked but very smooth grinding surface. Measures >54mm thick x >120mm wide x >82mm long. Wt 493g. Period 4a structure 39 (7452), fill 7454.

Cobble hone. Greensand. Cobble, slightly facetted along one long edge. Measures 91 x 26 x 11mm. Wt 45g. Ra. 791. Period 4a structure 34 (6572), fill 6573.

Rubbed stone/hone. Fine grained quartzitic sandstone. One flat face worn very smooth and one edge. Possibly used as hone/multi-functional tool. Wt 752g. Ra. 813. Period 4 7075, fill 7073.

Hammerstone or ballista ball. Flint. Small roughly cuboid stone with percussion damage on all surfaces. Measures 52 x 53 x 55mm. Wt 227g. Period 4a/b pit 5252 (beneath structure 33), fill 5284.

Hammerstone/multi-processor tool. Quartzitic sandstone. Large sub-square hammerstone with percussion damage and rubbed faces. Measures 108 x 81mm. Wt 1349g. Ra. 1057. Period 4b 7051, fill 7056.

Discussion

The Saxon stone assemblage is broadly representative of domestic occupation, with querns, whetstones and

Fig. 5.6   Saxon worked stone

other tools that might have been used around the house or in light industrial activity. The hammerstones, for example, might belong in a household or in a workshop where they could have been used to redress the quern grinding surfaces or to batter other substances.

The rotary querns are all in classic Roman design and the stone types from which they are made are also typical of the Roman period. The Lodsworth Greensand quern seems very unlikely to be of Saxon origin as it was predominantly used for quern manufacture during the Early Roman period. However, there are also querns of lava, which is known to have been extensively imported and used during the Saxon period (e.g., Parkhouse 1997) and Old Red Sandstone, from which querns have been made for more than the last two millennia. These materials could conceivably be either residual from the Roman period or Saxon in origin. If the latter, their form suggests that rotary quern design did not evolve significantly through the Saxon period in this area. Further north at Tamworth, the Saxon millstones include examples with a projecting hopper – a feature not seen on Roman millstones of the Roman south (Wright 1992, fig. 58) and therefore suggesting there were broadly some typological changes. However, large assemblages of Saxon rotary querns and millstones are not common in this region and it is therefore difficult to draw conclusions about quern development based on only a few examples.

Loomweights and spindle whorls
by Ruth Shaffrey

Loomweights

A large assemblage of up to 72 fired clay loomweights were submitted for analysis. Most of the loomweights are soft and friable and few of them survived being lifted intact. However, it has been possible to reconstruct some of them, and these, along with records and photographs of the weights *in situ*, means it is possible to draw some conclusions.

The majority of the loomweights are of rounded 'doughnut' (intermediate) form with moulded surfaces and a cylindrical hole, giving a D-section to the profile of the weights (Ra. 925, Fig. 5.7, 1, and Ra. 927). They are mostly circular, but occasionally oval (Ra. 1010; Fig. 5.7, 2) and there is some subtle variation in the form of the weights. Some are more lenticular in profile (Ra.

Saxon Finds and Environmental Remains 159

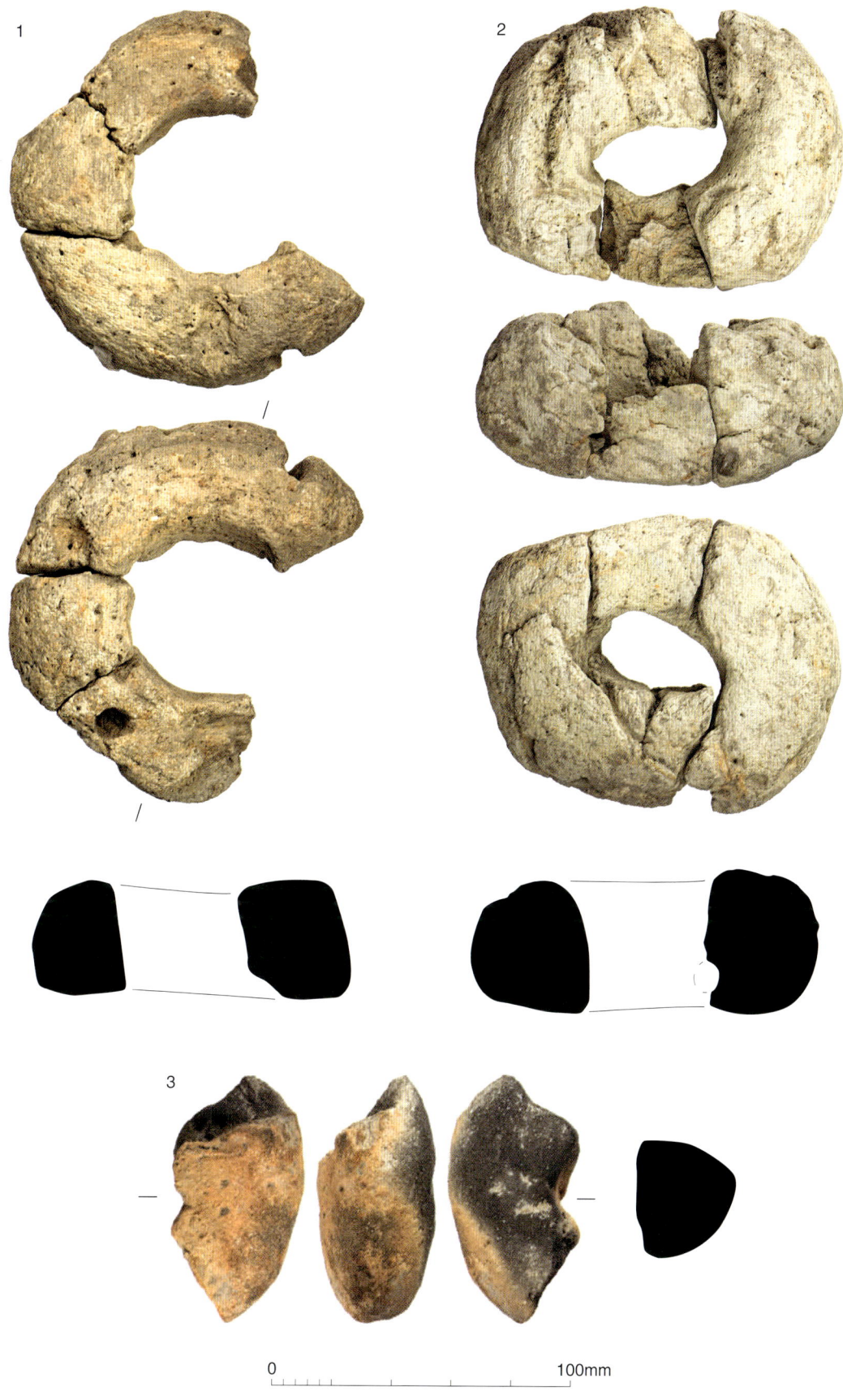

Fig. 5.7   Saxon loomweights, nos 1–3

Fig. 5.8   Saxon loomweights, nos 4–7

834, Fig. 5.7, 3), while others might be better classified as annular because of their wider central hole (Ras 1022 (not illustrated) and 1014, Fig. 5.8, 4).

Few of the weights demonstrate any specific wear marks, except for Ra. 931 (Fig. 5.8, 5) which has some wear from a probable cord. They range in diameter from 100–140mm with a median of 110mm and a mode of 114mm. Only a few loomweights are now complete but extrapolating from the surviving percentage suggests that the weights originally weighed between 393g and 878g, with a mean weight of 597g.

Although showing some minor variation in hole size and overall size and weight, the loomweights from Thame are all circular to sub-circular in shape. Most could not be assigned precisely to a form type by measurement because insufficient survived to measure both the diameter of the hole and the diameter of the weight, but those that can be measured are of doughnut (intermediate) form or of annular form, where the hole measures more than a third of the diameter of the overall weight (Walton Rogers 2007, 30). Occasionally a loomweight verges on the bun (lenticular) shape although without the very narrow hole. The earliest (5th century) form of loomweight is the annular weight. These appeared at Mucking during the 6th century AD and were in common use by the 7th century (Walton Rogers 2007, 30).

Spindle whorls

A total of six fired clay and one pottery spindle whorls were recovered: two from the subsoil 5001, one from ditch 412 (6284), two from SFB structure 33 (5166, fill 5164; Ras 612 and 614), one from SFB structure 32 (8577; Ra. 975) and one from SFB structure 36 (6387; Ra. 798). In addition, a single spindle whorl of shale was found in SFB structure 33 (5166, fill 5182; Ra. 586).

These were assigned to Walton Rogers' types (2007) and a range of forms are represented including bun form (A1: subsoil 5001), rounded disc type (B2: Ra. 612, 5164, Fig. 5.8, 6; 6386, 6823 and possibly the shale whorl Ra. 586, though it is damaged), flat disc type (B1: Ra. 975, 8578, Fig. 5.8, 7), and teardrop (B3: subsoil 5001, 5164). All these can be confidently dated by form to the 5th or 6th centuries, except the B3 example from subsoil 5001, whose narrow perforation suggests a possible Iron Age date. The relatively early dating of the spindle whorl forms is in keeping with the date suggested by the loomweights and the pottery.

Six of the spindle whorls are made from fired clay and one is made from a base of a greyware vessel (Ra. 975). The fired clay spindle whorls have undergone a range of firing. The three complete whorls weigh 26g, 31g and 39g and estimates for the broken examples based on their surviving weight indicate that they originally weighed 38g, 36g and 32g (the seventh example is too small a fragment for an estimate of original weight). These are moderately sized for spindle whorls, not suited to spinning the finest threads, and perhaps better suited to spinning wool.

Catalogue

Loomweight. (Fig. 5.7, 1). Three fragments with rounded edges and flat face in doughnut form with moulded surfaces and oval cylindrical hole. Measures 102–108mm diameter x 39mm thick. Wt 393g. Ra. 925. Structure 35 (8461), fill 8459.

Loomweight. (Fig. 5.7, 2). Oval doughnut-shaped with elongate oval cylindrical hole on same orientation measuring 25 x 44mm diameter. Measures 98–120mm diameter x 44mm thick. Wt 508g. Ra. 1010. Structure 35 (8461), fill 8459.

Loomweight. (Fig. 5.7, 3). Fragment of well-made, smooth well-finished example of lentoid profile, hand moulded. Central conical hole of 11–30mm diameter. Measures approximately 120mm diameter x 37mm thick. Wt 107g. Ra. 834. Subsoil 5001.

Loomweight. (Not illustrated). Approximately 30% survives of annular (ring) loomweight, circular cylindrical hole, D-shaped section with wide central hole of 70mm. Measures 130mm diameter x 43mm thick. Wt 210g. Ra. 1022. Structure 35 (8461), fill 8459.

Loomweight. (Fig. 5.8, 4). Annular with D-shaped section. Three frags adjoin. Oval hole measures 44 x 62mm diameter. Measures 110mm diameter x 40mm thick. Wt 340g. Ra. 1014. Structure 35 (8461), fill 8459.

Loomweight. (Fig. 5.8, 5). Complete well-made example; hand moulded; central perforated finger moulded, irregularly offset. Several grooves in central surface appear to be made pre-firing, but not on both sides. Rounded edges and flat faces in classic doughnut shape. Cord wear in one section out from hole. Perforation measures 28–40mm diameter. Measures 107–112mm diameter x 44mm thick. Wt 520g. Ra. 931. Structure 35 (8461), fill 8459.

Spindle whorl. (Fig. 5.8, 6). Complete. Burnt, less well fired than others and more crudely hand moulded. Circular and cylindrical hole measures 10mm diameter and creates a D-section. Measures 40mm diameter x 17mm thick. Wt 26g. Ra. 612. Structure 33 (5166), fill 5164.

Spindle whorl. (Fig. 5.8, 7). Complete. Flat disc type whorl. Not absolutely circular. Circumference smoothed/worn. Circular and cylindrical hole measures 10mm diameter. Measures 53–56 diameter x 11.5mm thick. Wt 39g. Ra. 975. Structure 32 (8577), fill 8578.

Loomweight. (Not illustrated). Six fragments of doughnut-shaped weight with moulded surfaces. Hole measures 42mm diameter and is cylindrical giving a D-shaped section. Measures 117mm diameter x 30–39mm thick. Wt 389g. Ra. 927. Structure 35 (8461), fill 8459.

Loomweight. (Not illustrated). Five fragments of doughnut-shaped ring with rounded fairly regular moulded surfaces and gently rounded faces. Several worm holes. Hole measures 41mm diameter. Measures 120mm diameter x 40mm thick. Wt 557g. Ra. 979. Structure 35 (8461), fill 8459.

Loomweight. (Not illustrated). 80% survives. Doughnut-shaped with rounded sides and flat faces, an oval and cylindrical hole giving a D-section. Measures 100mm diameter x 43mm thick. Wt 333g. Ra. 996. Structure 35 (8461), fill 8459.

Loomweight. (Not illustrated). Doughnut-shaped with slightly irregular oval hole, D-section measuring 32 x 36mm diameter. Measures 112mm diameter x 42mm thick. Wt 580g. Ra. 1015. Structure 35 (8461), fill 8459.

Spindle whorl. (Not illustrated). Complete. Flat faces but slightly tapered into the edges. Circular and cylindrical hole measures 12mm diameter. Measures 43mm diameter x 11mm thick. Wt 31g. Ra. 614. Structure 33 (5166), fill 5164.

Spindle whorl. (Not illustrated). Approximately 50% of teardrop (B3) type. Damaged, unusual shape compared to others. Measures >33mm diameter x 20mm thick with a 4mm perforation. Wt 19g. Subsoil 5001.

Spindle whorl. (Not illustrated). Approximately 95% of bun-shaped (A1) type – flat-topped, rounded sides, slightly irregular base, probably also flat, but damaged. Cylindrical and circular perforation. Measures 38mm diameter x 21mm thick with a 7mm perforation. Wt 34g. Subsoil 5001.

Spindle whorl. (Not illustrated). Shale. One face is flat with rounded sides; the other face has broken away. It has dried out considerably, so the weight will not be representative of its operational weight. Measures 34mm diameter x >10mm thick 9mm perforation. Wt 9g. Ra. 586. Structure 33 (5166), fill 5182.

Discussion

Few of the loomweights were complete but by extrapolating from surviving percentages, it has been possible to estimate their weights when complete. Anglo-Saxon loomweights ranged in weight from 100–1460g (Walton Rogers 2007, 30), with the vast majority weighing between 150 and 550g. The weights at Thame, ranging from 393g and 878g, with a mean weight of 597g, and with most falling between 480g and 715g, are therefore on the heavy side. As the loomweight mass relates to the type of threads being woven, the heavy weights of these suggests that relatively coarse cloth was being produced. Although it is true that different qualities of cloth could be woven depending on the thickness of the thread and the number of threads attached to each weight (Andersson Strand 2012, 211), the heavier weights could not have been used to produce very fine cloth, because it would not be possible to attach a very great number of threads easily to a single weight. It is useful to note that the spindle whorls were of middle weight range and probably well suited to spinning slightly thicker threads.

Loomweights were recovered from structure 31 (one certain and two possible), structure 32 (three weights and one spindle whorl), structure 33 (ten from a single context plus two spindle whorls), and a single spindle whorl was recovered from structure 36. However, it is clear that weaving was an important activity in structure 35 in particular, where a linear spread of 30 loomweights approximately in two lines was found; these range in weight from 393g to 778g. At one end of the pit was a pile of another 29 loomweights; these weigh between 533g and 878g. These ranges in weights are not typical of a functioning set of loomweights, which ought to be more consistent so that it is easy to create an equal tension. At King William Street and Sherborne Lane, London, the weights varied only by 100g (Pritchard 1984, 65–6). However, most of the original weights at Thame have only been estimated, which might account for some of the variation. Assuming that these represent two sets of loomweights, it suggests a loom that was operated with 15 pairs of weights. The cache of loomweights in one corner of structure 35 also contained 29 weights suggesting that it was a spare set. Storing a spare set of loomweights close to an operating loom has also been observed at Upton and Sparkford (Walton Rogers 2007, 32). The range of weights represented in the cached set suggests a higher average weight (those that can be estimated range from 533g to 878g) and therefore a higher overall weight than those on the loom (which weighed 393g to 778g) but given that only a few weights could be accurately estimated and the difference is slight, it is doubtful whether the difference is significant.

Ideally loomweights should be of equal weight to enable the warp threads to hang vertically and be evenly spaced (Shaffrey 2017b, 240). This was the case at Grimstone End, where the loomweights were equally sized and of an average 500g (the equal size implying an equal weight although without stating it explicitly, Brown *et al.* 1954). However, it is possible to work with weights of different size by attaching a different number of threads to each weight or by the use of a spacing cord. Hoffman records surviving looms that use oblong stones as the weights, necessarily not equally weighted, but with just such a setup (1974, 57). It has proven difficult to find precise Saxon parallels where the weights from a single loom were of a range of weights, because often the range is given only for the weights from the whole site. However the number and general weights of the Thame loomweights appear to have been typical of the period, and they provide another good example of a set of loomweights preserved *in situ* (with another set nearby).

Fired clay
by Cynthia Poole

A large assemblage of fired and unfired structural clay was collected during excavation from *in situ* structures and from secondary deposits in features, amounting to a total of 3312 fragments weighing 89,189g. Methodology is described in the Appendix. The fired clay was derived almost exclusively from a complex of ovens and associated layers (99% by weight) and the amount found in secondary deposits in ditch, pit, SFBs, and posthole fills, was minimal (3% of fragments, 1% by weight) and either indeterminate in form or residual Roman. The condition of the material is very variable ranging from tiny fragments to substantial blocks. The overall mean fragment weight (MFW) of 27g, which includes sieved material, is high for fired clay and rises to 44g if sieved material is excluded.

Fabrics

Fabrics have been characterised on the basis of macroscopic features and with the aid of a x20 hand lens. The fired clay fabrics divide into two main groups. One is a clean white clay (fabric A) with no inclusions, which was found extensively on site in its unfired form associated with the ovens and accounts for the vast majority of fired clay at this period. In its heated or fired form it was typically pink, light red, pale grey or buff in colour. The second major fabric group (fabric Q) was sandy, containing variable grades and densities of quartz sand. This formed a very small proportion of the assemblage at this period (less than 200g) and almost none was associated with the ovens but was found in the other features producing fired clay. Most inclusions, including small fragments of chalk or limestone, flint and ferruginous grits were incidental or naturally occurring within the clay. The exception is the organic-tempered variants of fabric A and Q designated as AQ and AV, which contained chaff or crushed straw, which had been deliberately added as filler, creating a light porous fabric. This fabric is absent from the ovens except for a few small fragments, being recovered instead from other features. Much, if not all of the organic-tempered fabrics is accounted for in this period by residual Roman oven plates. The source of the dominant fabric A in this period is likely to be the Gault, which outcrops a short distance to the south of the site.

Form and function

The fired clay from the Saxon period is dominated by the structural material recovered from the complex of *in situ* oven structures (structure 44, ovens 1–4). A large quantity of clay and fired clay sampled from these structures purportedly came from *in situ* elements, but analysis of much of this suggested it was collapsed superstructure and not *sensu stricto*, *in situ*. Essentially three categories could be identified: oven floor surface; thick flat un/underfired slab; and wattle-supported structure. Indeterminate fragments had either a single flat moulded surface or were amorphous, and which could derive from any of these other structural elements.

Oven floor

The only certain example of this comes from oven 2 (deposit 7726): the fired clay formed an extensive flat slab with a flat undulating upper surface which had been roughly moulded and shaped and had been partly fired hard superficially to black and grey to a depth of 20mm. Some blocks, which preserved the full thickness of 40–70mm, exhibited a gradation through the block from fully and heavily fired at the surface through lightly fired/baked and heat reddened to the yellowish unfired clay at the base. On some pieces, it was possible to expose the even regular bonding surface formed at the back of the slab. Some pieces adhered to a layer of heat-reddened sand (7748) as described in the site records as underlying the clay deposit. However not all the pieces adhered to the burnt sand substrate, but often there was grey charcoaly soil adhering to both the top and base surfaces. This suggests that some of the material recovered included collapsed or demolished oven wall slumped or pushed into the oven base or the floor had been partly constructed over an earlier layer containing burnt debris. The other ovens in the group do not appear to have had a special floor surface with the base of the cut serving as such.

Clay slab

The ovens produced large quantities of flat thick slabs of unfired white or slightly heat-discoloured pink clay. Much of this retained no significant features often not even the original moulded surface survived. It is best exemplified by layer 7386 within oven 3 (7498), where substantial blocks lay flat across the centre of the oven (Fig. 5.9). These ranged between 40mm and 55mm thick, where a complete thickness appeared to be preserved. Thinner fragments with a single moulded flat smooth surface were usually burnt or fired at the surface, which was often blackened grading to red or pink heated clay below. They appear to have sheared off the blocks of unfired slab.

This material was most prevalent in oven 3 (layers 7386 and 7462) and oven 4 (layers 7002–3 and 7060) with smaller quantities from sieved samples found in the burnt layers from both ovens.

Fig. 5.9 Saxon fired clay

Wattle-impressed structure

Wattle-supported structure has been described in Chapter 3 and the basic characteristics of a smooth moulded outer surface forming the exposed face of the structure with wattle impressions in the back remain the same in this period. The fragments ranged in thickness from 6mm to 60mm with 10–35mm the most common. Wattle diameters have been recorded for all contexts and the size range for ovens, and further analysis is included in the archive. The wattle sizes concentrate between 5mm and 21mm diameter with a small number greater than this up to 32mm. The majority of the impressions were of the horizontal interwoven rods, whilst the vertical sails were only occasionally preserved. The sails were on average larger though overlapping in size, measuring from 15–32mm in diameter. The largest deposits of wattle-impressed structure were found in oven 3 (layers 7386 and 7462) and oven 4 (layer 7003). The size range of the wattles is very similar for both ovens.

Portable furniture

There is no evidence that portable oven or hearth furniture was made or used during the Saxon period. A few pieces identified as possible oven plates are all of the Late Iron Age–Roman type described in Chapter 3 and appears to represent residual material in Saxon contexts.

Discussion

Interpretation of the fired clay in relation to the *in situ* oven bases is fraught with problems, not least a lack of detail in the field descriptions, which might have clarified the characteristics, pattern of firing and extent of heating or firing of the structures and adjacent or underlying deposits. There has also been extensive earthworm activity and animal burrowing (probably moles), which in the photos of the ovens can clearly be seen to have damaged and caused some mixing of deposits.

The ovens were constructed in a circular subsurface feature, but it is unclear whether they had any sort of flue or stoking area incorporated into the oven. There is no specific mention in the site descriptions of heavily fired areas relating to ovens 3 and 4, which would enable identification of the area where the actual firing of the structures took place. The latest structure, oven 4, has an array of charcoal-rich layers extending to the north-east side, which probably indicate stoking of the oven was from this side. The only area of a well-fired blackened surface forms the floor (7726) which has been assigned to hypothetical oven 2. However, its location immediately to the east of 7386 and the end of 7462 within a sub-rectangular shallow hollow suggests a more realistic interpretation for this as the base of the flue and the firing area for oven 3.

Oven 3 contained what appeared to be *in situ* floor surface and walls defining a circular chamber, again constructed of solid white underfired clay. However, the floor layer 7386 rests on a thick layer of dark silt (7486; not illustrated) covering the base of the oven cut (7498) and a series of charcoal-rich silts occur around the outer edge of the oven. At this remove it is impossible to establish whether these represent an accumulation from an earlier oven or a build-up of ash and silt during the oven's use below 7386 and around the outside of 7462. If contemporary with the oven's use it would suggest that 7386 in fact represents a suspended drying floor that collapsed and slumped into the underlying hollow and deposits surrounded by the walls or possibly a kerb to the drying floor (7462). The fired clay from these deposits consisted predominantly of slabs of whitish cream and pink underfired clay together with smaller quantities of better fired clay fragments with wattle impressions. It is likely that wattle-impressed fragments were originally attached to the thicker slabs. A wattle framework is more likely to be needed to support a drying floor rather than the lining of a lower chamber. Charred wattles were observed around a section of the interior face of the probable clay wall (7462) and could indicate this had formed a kerb enclosing the drying floor.

The quantity of wattle-impressed fired clay from oven 3 contrasts with the deposit of fired clay (7060) in the base of oven 4 which may combine *in situ* lining of yellow unfired clay overlain by broken more heavily fired reddened lumps of demolished structure. This material exhibited very few wattle impressions in contrast to a dump of fired clay (7003) high in the sequence, which produced the majority of wattle-impressed structure from this oven suggesting a distinction between floor and wall lining of the lower chamber and the structure of the drying floor forming an upper level to the oven.

The low level of firing of the structural clay in general from Thame is unsurprising, as a low level of heat is required in crop processing, which would not fully fire the clay structure except where in direct contact in the firing chamber.

The logical interpretation of the wattle-impressed fired clay from these ovens is that they represent the remains of the drying floor supported on a wattle framework, on which the grain was dried. Where Saxon crop-processing features have been excavated these usually take the form of sub-square, oval or circular features, often quite deep, but unlike Roman corndriers, usually with very little structure surviving apart from the feature itself. Evidence for *in situ* burning of the feature base or sides is generally quite light. Fired clay associated with such features almost uniformly consists of wattle-impressed structure. An example from Springhead, Kent dated to AD 770–900 (Hardy and Andrews 2011, 285–6) was oval with the main chamber 1m deep and the base sloping up to the west end forming the stoking area. Overlying a charcoal layer was a thick deposit of fired clay fragments impressed with wattles that was interpreted as the drying floor of the oven (Poole 2011). The wattles were marginally larger in size than those at Thame and the clay by contrast was well fired. This may indicate a difference in the crop processing in that parching of grain prior to grinding required a higher temperature than malting. If malting only was carried out at Thame this could account for the underfired character of the clay, especially if the activity was intermittent.

Illustrated fired clay (Fig. 5.9)

Oven structure; wattle-impressed structure. Period 4a oven 3, layer 7386.

Medieval and post-medieval ceramic building material
by Cynthia Poole

The post-Roman ceramic building material amounted to a total 44 fragments weighing 1351g and consisted almost entirely of roof tile apart from two pieces of brick. The post-Roman mean fragment weight is exceptionally low at 30g reflecting the small and scrappy character of the assemblage and the predominance of roof tile. The assemblage appears to be broadly of late medieval to post-medieval date (15th to 17th century).

Roof tile

The roof tile (42 fragments, 984g) comprised entirely fragments of flat tile, of which four had evidence of peg holes. Whilst it is likely that the majority of fragments derive from peg tile, it is possible some of the thicker pieces derived from ridge tiles with an angular profile. The tile measured between 11 and 17mm thick, with 13–16mm the commonest. Surfaces were for the most part regular and even, sometimes with fine striations from striking and edges. Two tiles had a narrow, indented border 5–6mm wide along the edge. Peg holes were circular measuring *c*. 13mm in diameter. Another tile had a small circular impression in the surface, 5mm in diameter, made by a tubular object, possibly the tip of the punch used to make peg holes. Two tiles had possible remnants of clear glaze on the surface, hinting that some tiles may be of 13th or 14th-century date.

Fabrics were generally sandy and similar to Oxford fabrics, in particular IIIB and IVA/B in the Oxford tile fabric series. Fabric OX IIIB is a red-orange fabric containing frequent medium–coarse quartz sand and dark red ferruginous grits and was mainly in use during the 13th and 14th centuries, though a variant categorised as IIIB St Giles (Cotter 2008) dates to the 15th–17th centuries. Fabric OX IV was a paler red-orange sandy fabric laminated with cream streaks and containing red and cream argillaceous pellets. It is thought to be produced in the south-east of Oxfordshire in the Chilterns and is similar in character to the fabric used for Penn floor tiles produced in the neighbouring area of Buckinghamshire.

Bricks

Only two fragments of brick (367g) were recovered.

One made in a sandy fabric similar to OX IIIB measured 51mm thick and is probably of 16th–17th-century date. The second piece is probably of later date, 18th–19th century, and was made in a distinctive orange-brown fabric with cream streaks and mottles containing frequent clear fine quartz sand <0.2mm and a high density of rounded black ferruginous grits mostly 1–2mm but some up to 4mm, creating a distinctive black speckled effect.

Discussion

The post-Roman CBM indicates low-level incidental loss probably related to agricultural activity such as manuring or maintenance of trackways, especially that found in furrows and ditch fills. The absence of later post-medieval material may indicate the area was under permanent pasture during this time. Approximately a quarter of the assemblage was recovered from earlier ditch and feature fills suggesting these were not fully silted up until the post-Roman period. The largest individual group of roof tile had been disposed of in a medieval or post-medieval pit (9111; not illustrated).

Industrial residues
by Lynne Keys

The slag present in this period is indicative of very sporadic, small-scale smelting and smithing activity, or represents residual material.

Period 4a/b (Saxon, general). Total = 472g. The iron slag from this period is very likely to be redeposited from earlier phases. SFB structure 32 (8577) contained just 7g of undiagnostic slag; SFB structure 36 (6387) 12g; SFB structure 33 (5166) just 397g of undiagnostic slag. Pit 5252 contained 56g of undiagnostic slag which had copper oxide staining on its surface.

Period 4b (Late Saxon). Total = 474g. The enclosure produced 474g of slag, all possibly redeposited earlier matcrial. Enclosure ditch 6336, fill 633 had a small amount of undiagnostic slag and some vitrified hearth lining; enclosure ditch 6612, fill 6611 just a fragment of furnace slag.

Worked bone
by Leigh Allen

A small number of worked bone objects were recovered from Saxon contexts. The assemblage comprises a comb, comb fragments and textile equipment which were mostly recovered from SFBs. A near-complete comb, Ra. 819/820 (Fig. 5.10, 1), came from the west end of SFB structure 37 (pit 6827; fill 7099). It is a double-sided composite comb of characteristic elongated outline (MacGregor 1985, 92–4) decorated with ring and dot motif on both the end plates and the connecting plates.

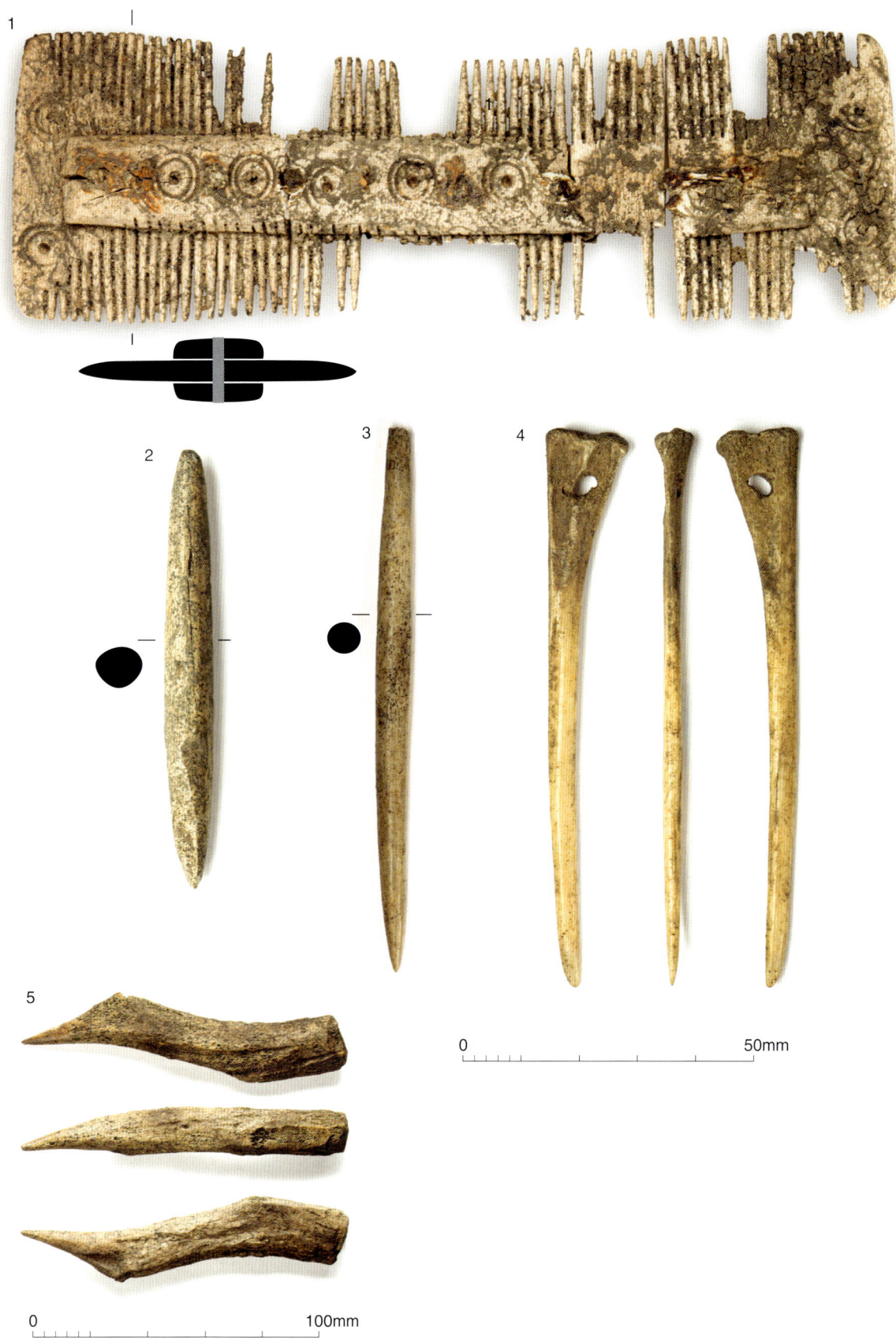

Fig. 5.10 Saxon worked bone

A fragment from a second double-sided composite comb came from SFB structure 32 (8578). It also has ring and dot design on the surviving end-plate. Loose teeth from a comb, Ras 598 and 600, were recovered from SFB structure 33 (5165).

The textile equipment comprises three cigar-shaped double-ended pin beaters of different sizes, two needles and an awl/piercer. Two pin beaters, Ras 906 and 1025 (Fig. 5.10, 2–3), came from SFB structure 35 (8459). They both have circular sections but are different sizes; one is rather stubby with a light polish all over and the other is long and slender with a particularly high polish at the tip. These objects were used to 'strum across the warp to even out threads and to give a preliminary beating-in of the weft' (Walton Rogers 2007, 29). The fact that two pin beaters of different sizes were found together in the same SFB may indicate that they were part of a set of weaving tools (ibid., 33). A third pin beater, Ra. 502, was recovered from subsoil. It has an ovate section and is lightly polished all over. The two needles are both fashioned from pig fibulae; in both cases the proximal end, which forms the head, is unmodified except for a perforation through it. A complete example, Ra. 793 (Fig. 5.10, 4) came from the subsoil and a damaged one came from SFB structure 30 (15847). This type of needle could be used on coarse fabric or for mesh-knitting items such as stocking or shrouds (MacGregor 1985, 193) as the heads are too wide for use on fine fabrics. It has also been suggested that they could have been used with warp weighted looms, 'placed at the selvage to hold the cords which were used to fasten the edges of the woven cloth to the uprights to maintain an even width' (Hoffman 1974, 145–6). An awl/piercer, Ra. 835 (Fig. 5.10, 5), made from roe deer antler came from SFB structure 39 (7454). A length of unmodified antler tine forms the handle and the end is shaped into a slender point, these objects would have been used to pierce soft material such as leather. The Saxon worked bone assemblage with its personal items and simple weaving tools reflects every day, domestic activities which were commonly undertaken in households.

Catalogue

Double-sided composite bone comb (Fig. 5.10, 1) with an elongated outline and rectangular end plates. The teeth on either side show very little difference in size and spacing. The connecting plates are plano-convex and are slightly wider towards the middle; they are attached to the teeth plates by nine iron rivets. The comb is decorated with ring and dot motif on the end plates and along each of the connecting plates. There are notches running along the edges of the connecting plates indicating that they were in place when the teeth were cut/recut. Wear patterns on the teeth take the form of faint striations running transversely across all teeth. L 151mm. Ras 819 and 820. Period 4a 7099 (pit 6827; west end of structure 37).

Double-sided composite comb end-plate fragment with six coarse teeth (complete) surviving on one side and five fine teeth (all broken) on the other. The plate has a circular perforation at the centre for attachment of the connecting plates and is decorated with a row of ring and dot motifs along the edge on both sides. L 43mm. Period 4a 8578 (structure 32).

Two loose teeth from a comb both with flattened oval sections and faint transverse striations running across the teeth as seen on the composite double-sided comb from context 7099 (see above). L 15mm and 24mm. Ras 598 and 600. Period 4a 5165 (structure 33).

Cigar-shaped pin beater (Fig. 5.10, 2) slightly damaged at one end. The beater is short and stubby with a circular section (D: 9mm at widest point) and is lightly polished in places through wear. L 72mm. Ra. 906. Period 4a 8459 (structure 35).

Cigar-shaped pin beater (Fig. 5.10, 3) with one damaged tip. The beater is long and slender with a circular section (D: 6mm at widest point) and is polished all over but the polish is particularly high towards the tip. L 90mm. Ra. 1025. Period 4a 8459 (structure 35).

Cigar-shaped pin beater with a flattened oval section (D: 9mm at widest point) and lightly polished all over. L 84mm. Ra. 502. Subsoil 5073.

Needle (Fig. 5.10, 4) fashioned from a pig fibula (unfused). It has a crude perforation through the proximal end but otherwise the head is unmodified. The shaft tapers to a point and has a light polish from use. L 95mm. Ra. 793. Subsoil 5001.

Needle fashioned from a pig fibula (unfused). It has a crude perforation through the damaged proximal end but otherwise the head is unmodified. The shaft tapers but is incomplete. L 67mm. Period 4a 15847 (structure 30).

Point, bone, incomplete. A point, broken at the top, tapering to a slightly flattened tip. Highly polished in places. L 44mm. Ra. 960. Period 4a 8578 (structure 32).

Awl/piercer (Fig. 5.10, 5) made from a roe deer antler tine. The upper part is unmodified apart from being sawn flat. The other end has been formed into a point with a circular section which is lightly polished through use. L 112mm. Ra. 835. Period 4a 7454 (structure 39).

Human remains
by Lauren McIntyre and Alice Rose, with Louise Loe

Two articulated inhumation burials were dated to period 4a (Table 5.5). The methodology is detailed in the Appendix. Skeleton 1501 was approximately 40% complete and mostly comprised upper and lower long bones. There was medium bone fragmentation and the bone condition was fair (grade 3, McKinley 2004a, 16). The incompleteness and poor preservation of the bone precluded the estimation of sex and age. The skeleton was estimated to be an adult (>18yrs) based on complete epiphyseal fusion and general morphology. All cranial and most post-cranial non-metric traits were not observable. It was only possible to take measurements of a few long bones, such as the left and right femora and the right tibia. This allowed for platymeric (platymeric:

Table 5.5 Human remains. Period 4a: Saxon

Articulated inhumation burials

SK. no.	Context	Completeness	Condition	Frag.	Sex	Age	Metrics/Non-metrics/Pathology
1501	In sub-circular cut 16417. Supine, head at north-west	26–50%	3	Medium	U	Adult >18yrs	Femur/tibia index: Platymeric/eurycnemic Skeletal pathology: Marginal osteophytes R elbow, L hand, R knee, L ankle. Osteoarthritis L hip, L&R knee
1502	In oval cut 16629. Supine, head at west	0–25%	3	High	U	26–35yrs	Dental pathology: Calculus Skeletal pathology: Schmorl's nodes, thoracic and lumbar vertebrae

Frag. = fragmentation level; U = unknown

flattened femoral shaft) and platycnemic (eurycnemic: flattened tibial shaft) indices to be calculated. Stature could not be estimated. Extra-spinal joint disease was present and included osteophytes on the margins of several joints, and osteoarthritis in the left hip and right and left knees.

Skeleton 1502 was approximately 20% complete, comprising part of the right mandible, a partial spine, four left and three right ribs, the upper long bones and part of the right hand. Bone fragmentation was high, and surface condition was scored at grade 3 (McKinley 2004a, 16). Overall bone preservation was poor. Incompleteness of the skeleton meant that it was not possible to determine the sex of the individual. Age was estimated at 26–35 years (prime adult), based upon occlusal wear of the dentition (Miles 1962; Brothwell 1981). All cranial and most post-cranial non-metric traits were not observable, and it was not possible to calculate stature, cranial or post-cranial indices as the relevant bones were either absent or incomplete. Spinal joint disease was present, comprising Schmorl's nodes of three of the thoracic vertebrae and two of the lumbar vertebrae.

Discussion by Lauren McIntyre

Only two articulated skeletons dated to period 4a: a fairly well-preserved adult skeleton of unknown sex, and a poorly preserved prime adult of unknown sex. Although the age of skeleton 1501 could not be narrowed down further than +18 years, the presence of marginal osteophytes and osteoarthritis in the left hip and knees may indicate that the skeleton belongs in one of the older age categories. Typically, osteoarthritis develops progressively with age as a result of multiple, interplaying factors such as general biomechanical stress and repeated microtrauma ensuing from everyday activity (Ortner 2003, 546). Development of osteoarthritis in the hip joints has been linked to factors such as age, occupational activity/mechanical stress, genetic predisposition/ancestry, anatomical influences, body size and body mass (Jurmain 1977; Weiss and Jurmain 2007).

Another form of joint disease, Schmorl's nodes, were present in the spine of prime adult skeleton 1502. These lesions represent sites of herniation in the intervertebral disc material through the vertebral body end plates (Rogers 2000, 169–70), and are likely to form as a result of the combination of activity related stresses placed on the vertebrae and intervertebral disc, and developmental factors associated with vertebral formation and growth in early life (Dar *et al.* 2010, 675). Their presence in the thoracic and lumbar vertebrae of SK. 1502 is consistent with the observation that the condition is most common in these regions (McNaught 2006, 53).

Animal bone
by Lee G. Broderick with Rebecca A. Nicholson

The entire Saxon animal bone assemblage comprised 6790 fragments, of which 5591 fragments were considered securely phased at the time of the assessment (Smith and Strid 2017). For this analysis, in order to focus resources on the most significant and well-dated contexts, only those bones that were recovered from the fills of the Early–Mid Saxon (period 4a) SFBs were included. These comprise 2624 hand-collected and 51 sieved specimens (number of specimens, NSP), of which 2056 hand-collected, and 51 sieved bones were identifiable to taxon or at least to one of large, medium or small/micro mammal (number of identified specimens, NISP). Most of the assemblage was in moderate condition with little sign of post-depositional destruction beyond some gnawing. The fills are likely to represent deliberate backfill deriving from settlement activity. Separately, a single associated bone group (ABG) from ditch fill 6611 (period 4b), which comprised 205 fragments from an articulated dog, is also reported on.

Typically, during the Early and Mid Saxon periods across rural sites in southern England the relative proportions of the main domesticates, cattle, sheep and pig, vary widely, although cattle are generally the most commonly occurring species by NISP followed by sheep/goat then pigs, so in this regard the assemblage from

Thame is consistent with the general picture. In terms of the relative proportion of pigs to other domesticates, however, the assemblage is perhaps more in keeping with sites that are close to wetland or woodland, sheep being more common from sites on chalk downlands and limestone vales (Holmes 2017). Bird bones are relatively frequent for a rural site of this date and include domestic fowl, goose, duck and possibly swan (*Cygnus* sp.), the last indicative of wildfowling.

The assemblage from Thame also includes a piece of worked red deer antler, suggesting some craft activity. A butchered horse bone provides evidence for the consumption of horse meat, which again is seen at other contemporary sites but at a time when a taboo was developing in Britain (Poole 2013).

Taphonomy and spatial distribution

The bone from the Saxon SFBs was moderately well preserved (Fig. 5.11). Just 28 specimens had been gnawed (all by canids) and these were mostly domestic cattle (*Bos taurus taurus*) specimens (NSP=18) with horse (*Equus caballus*), large mammal, and sheep (*Ovis aries*) and/or goat (*Capra hircus*) specimens also gnawed.

Considering only the number of identified fragments (NISP), cattle was the most frequently identified animal, followed by sheep/goat, pig and horse (Table 5.6). Sheep/goat is however proportionately more common when quantified by minimum number of individuals (MNI). However, with a minimum of only eleven sheep/goat, eight cattle and five pigs the use of MNI to calculate relative proportions of animals cannot be considered reliable (cf Hambleton 1999, 39). While sheep was positively identified, there was no unequivocal evidence of goat. A few cat (*Felis catus*) and dog (*Canis domesticus*) bones were also present and may represent pets or, more likely, working animals – the former probably feral but useful to keep vermin in check.

Domestic fowl (*Gallus gallus*) were evidently kept and both goose (*Anser* sp.) and duck (Anatidae) may also have been domesticated, since it is not possible to

Table 5.6 Saxon animal bone. Number of Identified Specimens (NISP) and Number of Specimens (NSP)

	Hand collected	Sieved
Domestic cattle	185	11
Domestic cattle?	2	
Caprine	116	11
Caprine?	1	
Sheep	12	2
Pig	57	4
Pig?	1	
Horse	27	
Dog*	4	
Dog?	1	
Cat	3	3
Red deer	1	
Red deer?	1	
Water vole	2	
Bank/field/common vole		3
Mouse		1
Mouse/vole	2	5
Small mammal	8	
Medium mammal	551	
Large mammal	1060	
Total Mammal	**2034**	**40**
Bird	6	
Swan?	1	
Greylag/domestic goose	7	
Greylag/domestic goose?	1	
Domestic duck/mallard	1	
Domestic fowl	6	5
Small passerine		1
Total Bird	**22**	**6**
Frog/toad		4
Common frog		1
Common toad		
Total Amphibian		**5**
Total NISP	**2056**	**51**
Total NSP	**2624**	**51**

* excludes dog ABG from period 4b enclosure ditch 6612

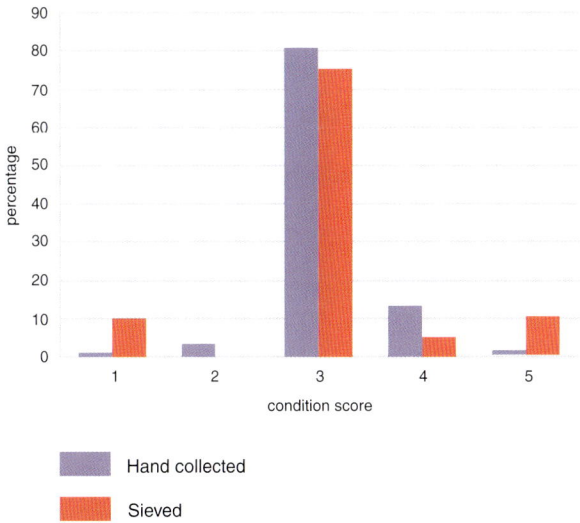

Fig. 5.11 Proportions of identified animal bone fragments by condition category from the SFBs

distinguish between wild and domesticated birds. Bones from greylag goose (*Anser anser*) and domestic goose (*Anser anser domesticus*) cannot be easily separated, but geese have been domesticated in Britain since at least the Roman period (Albarella 2005, 249) so it is likely these were domestic birds which would have provided eggs as well as meat and feathers. Goose and duck remains included a single duck tibiotarsus and several anatomical leg and wing elements in fills from SFB structure 35. Apart from the possibility of mallard (*Anas platyrhynchos*) and greylag, wild birds were represented by possible swan (*Cygnus* sp.) identified from an ulna shaft fragment from SFB structure 33 and a small perching bird in SFB structure 37, again identified from a partial ulna.

The only substantive wild mammal present was red deer (*Cervus elaphus*) which was represented (in SFB structure 30 fill 15845) by a single antler tine, sawn and snapped at the base, clearly the waste from craft activity, as well as by a probable red deer zygomaticus found in SFB structure 33 fill 5164. The presence of a skull fragment may indicate that some antler used on the site was not shed naturally, although the skull may have been part of a 'trophy' head, used for display. It is also possible that deer was butchered on site, as the skull fragment could represent primary butchery waste, which would suggest that animals were hunted. With such a low number of fragments further interpretation is not possible. As well as 11 bones from small mice and voles (*Myodes/Microtus* sp.) found in the fills of several SFBs, water vole (*Arvicola amphibius*) was identified from a mandible found in structure 30 fill 15846 and a loose tooth in SFB structure 37. Amphibian bones including frog (probably most or all *Rana temporaria*) were recovered from the residues of sieved soil samples,

and together with the water vole indicate wet or marshy grassland in the vicinity. It is possible that these small animal remains were deposited in owl pellets from birds perching on an abandoned building, but some small animals may have been pit fall victims or corpses may have been deposited with general domestic refuse.

There was considerable difference in the amount of material collected from each of the SFBs and also large differences in the species proportions between them (Table 5.7; Fig. 5.12). The differences in species proportion cannot be explained by sample size as the four largest SFB assemblages (SFBs structures 30, 33, 35 and 41) exhibited considerable variation. It is important to note, however, that only two of these assemblages have greater than 100 specimens identified to species which although below the threshold suggested for meaningful analysis at site level (Hambleton 1999, 39) is perhaps sufficient to indicate that once the structures had been abandoned they were probably used for episodic disposal of general rubbish. Nevertheless, it is perhaps worth noting the high proportion of caprine specimens from SFB structure 35, the high proportion of cattle from SFBs structures 33 and 41 and the high proportion of pig specimens from SFB structure 30.

Age and sex

The number of both mandibular tooth rows and long bone epiphyses recovered was small, limiting the opportunity for detailed analysis of age profiles. There was no evidence for very young calves but among the 62 loose teeth in the SFB fills, a single loose deciduous cattle premolar at stage b and single loose first molar at stage b indicate the presence of immature animals, while

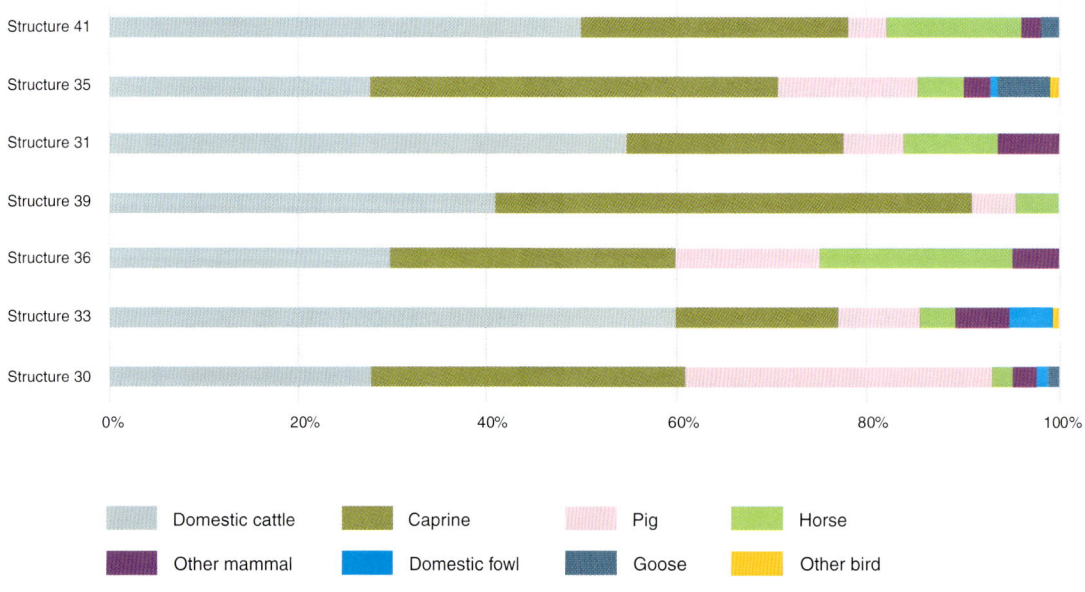

Fig. 5.12 Animal bone species proportions by NISP for each SFB with >20 NISP from hand-collected material

Table 5.7 Saxon animal bone. NISP values per SFB

	Str. 30	Str. 33	Str. 36	Str. 37	Str. 38	Str. 39	Str. 40	Str. 31	Str. 35	Str. 41	Str. 34
Domestic cattle	23	80	6	5	1	9		17	30	25	
Domestic cattle?		1						1			
Caprine	25	20	4	4		11		7	43	11	2
Caprine?										1	
Sheep	2	3	2	1					4	2	
Pig	25	11	3			1	1	2	16	2	
Pig?	1										
Horse	2	5	4			1		3	5	7	
Dog		2							1	1	
Dog?		1									
Cat		3		1					2		
Red deer	1										
Red deer?		1									
Water vole	1			1							
Bank vole/field vole/common vole				2			1				
Mouse nfi				1							
Mouse/vole		1	1	2	2	1					
Small mammal	1	1				2			4		
Medium mammal	239	87	7			18		9	141	50	
Large mammal	186	380	33			22		47	146	246	
Total Mammal	**506**	**596**	**60**	**17**	**3**	**65**	**2**	**86**	**392**	**345**	**2**
Bird		4							2		
Swan?		1									
Greylag/domestic goose									6	1	
Greylag/domestic goose?	1										
Domestic duck/mallard									1		
Domestic fowl	1	6		1				2	1		
Small passerine				1							
Total Bird	**2**	**11**	**0**	**2**	**0**	**0**	**0**	**2**	**10**	**1**	**0**
Frog/toad			1			3					
Common frog				1							
Total Amphibian	**0**	**0**	**1**	**1**	**0**	**3**	**0**	**0**	**0**	**0**	**0**
Total NISP	**508**	**607**	**61**	**20**	**3**	**68**	**2**	**88**	**402**	**346**	**2**
Total NSP	**601**	**883**	**91**	**20**	**3**	**86**	**2**	**97**	**543**	**347**	**2**

two mandibles with tooth rows present demonstrate that cattle were often culled at an optimal age for meat (wear stages D and F). A loose cattle third molar indicates the presence of an older animal, possibly retained for breeding or secondary product such as milk (stage G). There were a greater number of ageable sheep/goat mandibles (12) most of which indicate slaughter at prime meat-bearing age of between 18 months and 3 years (stages D and E) with one example of an older animal (stage H or I) which probably provided wool or milk for several years and at least two lambs. Neonatal caprine bones were also recovered from SFB structure 35 and SFB structure 41, so it is likely that sheep were bred nearby. Seven pig mandibles and loose teeth provide some ageing information, which is consistent with the long bone fusion evidence. As would be expected, as pigs provide no secondary products apart from hide, most animals seem to have been slaughtered as immature or sub-adult animals, prior to the stage at which many of the long bone epiphyses fuse, but a fusing proximal tibia indicates an older, adult, animal. An older animal is also indicated by a third molar from SFB structure 31 at Grant's (1982) wear stage f, perhaps a breeding sow. A maxillary canine tooth in SFB structure 30 is from a female. While most of the tooth-wear data is consistent with the slaughter of pigs at an optimum age for meat, at least one juvenile is also present. Foetal pig long bones were recovered from SFB structures 30 and 33 as well as a neonatal pig bone from SFB structure 35 and it is likely that pigs were stalled and bred at the settlement. All equid long bones, where epiphyses were present, were fused. An equid maxillary canine tooth from SFB structure 41 indicates the presence of a male.

Element representation

Apart from loose teeth, the assemblage from cattle, sheep/goat, pigs and horse includes bones from the head and lower limbs as well as meat-bearing elements including the femur, pelvis, humerus and scapula as well as ribs. The similarity in element distribution between cattle and horse and within the different SFBs suggests that the animals were treated in similar ways after death and that their disarticulated remains were disposed of together with household rubbish, which seems to have included the remains of several cats as well as several disarticulated dog bones.

Butchery

A total of 47 specimens feature butchery marks, roughly evenly split between cut marks (27 specimens) and chop marks (28 specimens) (Table 5.8). Cut marks were mostly oblique marks on the mid-shaft of medium mammal and large mammal ribs, to either or both the medial and lateral aspects, with some butchery marks also present

Table 5.8 Butchery marks recorded from the Saxon animal bone specimens

Species	Element	Side	Quantity	Butchery type	Notes
Cattle	2nd phalanx		1	chop	axial chop through centre
Cattle	humerus	right	1	chop	axial chop through shaft
Cattle	mandible	right	1	cut	oblique cut marks between coronoid and condyle
Cattle	mandible	right	1	cut	oblique cut marks on lingual side of ramus
Cattle	metacarpal	left	1	chop	axial chop through centre
Cattle	metacarpal	right	1	chop	axial chop through proximal end
Cattle	metacarpal	right	1	cut & chop	axial chop through distal end & oblique cut marks on and near posterior end
Cattle	metatarsal	left	1	cut	oblique cut mark on anterior of proximal end
Cattle	metatarsal	right	1	cut	oblique cut marks on distal end
Cattle	pelvis	left	1	chop	oblique chop through pubis
Cattle	pelvis	right	1	chop	chop through pubis from lateral side near acetabulum
Cattle	scapula	left	1	cut	oblique cut on medial aspect of blade
Cattle	tibia	left	1	cut	oblique cut marks on medial side of shaft
Horse	metapodial		1	chop	axial chop through distal end
Large mammal	rib		9	chop	oblique chop through blade from medial side
Large mammal	rib		3	chop	oblique chops through lateral sides of blade
Large mammal	rib		7	cut	oblique cut mark on medial side of blade
Large mammal	rib		2	cut	oblique cut mark on lateral side of blade
Large mammal	vertebra		1	chop	oblique chop through centre
Large mammal	vertebra		1	chop	axial chop through centre
Medium mammal	rib		1	chop	oblique chop through medial side
Medium mammal	rib		4	cut	cut mark on medial side of shaft
Medium mammal	rib		2	cut	oblique cut mark on medial side of shaft, near head
Pig	tibia	left	1	cut	oblique cut mark on anterior of midshaft
Sheep/goat	calcaneum	left	1	cut	oblique cut on medial side of shaft
Sheep/goat	pelvis	left	1	chop	superficial oblique chops on lateral side of pubis

on long bones and a domestic cattle mandible; in this case there were oblique cut marks between the coronoid and condyle. Chop marks were present on 28 specimens (some of them being some of the same specimens that have cut marks), with a more or less equal split between axial and oblique chops through bones. Although cattle bones are the most commonly chopped (27 butchered bones if large mammal ribs are considered as cattle), they are also the most common species in the assemblage so this is not considered particularly significant. Oblique chops would have been made to break up the larger bones into more convenient, 'pot size', chunks, whilst axial chops would have been made to access the bone marrow. Aside from domestic cattle, caprine and horse bones have been chopped through – a caprine pelvis has several superficial chop marks on the lateral side of the pubis indicative of portioning of the carcass, and a horse metapodial is split axially. Just 28 of the specimens show signs of having been gnawed – all by canids, but this indicates that at least a proportion of the bones had been lying around for some time before final deposition, perhaps on a midden, and that dogs may have played a role in both deposition (Wilson 1996) and element destruction (Brain 1981), a factor which may have reduced the numbers of the more readily destroyed bones such as those of immature pigs.

Pathology

Seventeen specimens from the assemblage had pathologies. These were mostly osteochondrosis-type lesions or Baker and Brothwell's type 2 lesions of uncertain aetiology on phalanges, the latter described as 'a narrow slit of variable length between the articular facets' (Baker and Brothwell 1980, 110), both of which are considered to be benign. A horse calcaneum from structure 32 context 8578, however, showed pathologies consistent with early spavin, and a cattle 1st phalanx from structure 30 fill 15845 had extensive exostoses, consistent with what might be expected if the animal had been used for traction (Bartosiewicz et al. 1997; Fabiš 2005). An exostosis on the lateral side of the proximal end of a caprine metacarpal from context 15848 – also in structure 30, as the cattle phalanx just discussed – might suggest penning elbow, an indication perhaps of confinement and poor animal husbandry, although recent study of this pathology has suggested a much wider range of causes (Holmes et al. 2021). Elsewhere, a domestic cattle metacarpal from structure 33 fill 5164 has an osteolytic lesion (which could be caused by a tumour, cyst or chronic inflammation).

A pig mandible from structure 31 context 5945 was missing its first and second molars congenitally. Dental eruption anomalies are fairly common in pigs but this particular disorder is not mentioned in Colyer (Miles and Grigson 1990). Another congenital condition was observed in a mallard-sized duck (*Anas* sp.) tibiotarsus; this is an absent supratendinal bridge. No other archaeological examples of this condition are known to the authors, but it is supposed that the bird would have moved less freely and so may, therefore, be a domestic bird. Possible bird bone pathologies were also reported on in the assessment (Smith and Strid 2017). They include a fractured/misaligned goose humerus from pit fill 8459 (structure 35) and a potential early stage of osteopetrosis in a fowl femur from Late Saxon ditch fill 6611.

Associated Bone Group

A dog ABG was recovered from period 4b enclosure ditch 6612. This was a complete animal, with many of even the smallest bones such as phalanges recovered. Although in moderate surface condition (stage 3, Behrensmeyer 1978), less robust specimens (e.g., ribs) were often broken, contributing to an NSP of 205, including 36 vertebrae and 56 rib fragments. Many of the long bones were still fusing proximally at the time of death, suggesting an age of 18 months or less (Silver 1969). This age estimation is complicated by the fact that the distal ends of all the long bones, some of which normally fuse later than the proximal ends of the relevant elements, were all fused. Both radii were fused at both ends, so it was possible to take a length measurement (see Table 5.9; GL=152.6mm [R]; 152.1mm [L]), giving a withers height of between 483.7mm (Harcourt 1974) and 506.6mm (Koudelka 1885). It was also noted that the sides of all long bone epiphyses were highly porous – which may have contributed to the appearance of proximal ends still fusing. This is probably pathological, although it is difficult to suggest a cause. The anterior wall of the acetabulum of the right pelvis was similarly porous. Many other specimens were recovered from the same context (6611) as the dog, including caprine and domestic cattle teeth, domestic fowl and goose bones, and a horse cranium but these have not been fully recorded and do not form part of this analysis.

Discussion

In keeping with the general picture from faunal assemblages of Anglo-Saxon date, an assemblage of bone from the fills of sunken-featured buildings at Horcott, Gloucestershire, was also numerically dominated by cattle bones, but as at Thame, calculating the proportion of animals using MNI counts enhanced the representation of sheep/goat (Strid 2017). A similar livestock distribution was evident in SFB fills from nearby Lechlade (Maltby 2003). At Horcott it was clear that cattle and sheep/goats were slaughtered at a range of ages, which implies they were used both for their meat and for secondary resources including traction, milk and wool, a pattern typical for a small rural settlement. While the evidence is less clear at Thame due to the small numbers of ageable elements, a similar scenario seems likely. At Lechlade almost all the cattle seem to have

Table 5.9 Measurements taken from the bones recorded from the Saxon period (in mm)

Species	Element	Side	GL	Bp	Bd	SD
Cat	5th metacarpal	right	28.5		4.5	
Cattle	astragalus	right	66.6		42	
Cattle	astragalus	left	63.3		42	
Cattle	humerus	left			72	
Cattle	humerus	right			71	
Cattle	humerus	left			74	
Cattle	metatarsal	left	207	44	50	23.8
Cattle	metatarsal	left			49	
Cattle	tibia	left	318		56	64.4
Cattle	tibia	left			56	
Domestic fowl	coracoid	left	49.5			
Domestic fowl	humerus	right	73.9	19	16	
Domestic fowl	radius	right	57		6.2	2.5
Domestic fowl	tibiotarsus	left	99.3	18	10	5.4
Domestic fowl	tibiotarsus	right			11	
Goose	tibiotarsus	left			17	
Horse	astragalus	left	59.8		50	
Horse	metacarpal	right	208	48	48	34
Horse	radius	right		79	71	37.2
Pig	astragalus	left				
Pig	humerus	left			36	
Sheep	humerus	right			25	
Sheep/goat	metacarpal	left	117	20		122.2
Sheep/goat	metacarpal	left	122	23	24	13.4
Sheep/goat	metatarsal	right	119	19	21	11
Sheep/goat	metatarsal	left			22	
Sheep/goat	radius	left	129	29	28	15.7
Sheep/goat	radius	left	139	29	26	16.5
Sheep/goat	tibia	left			26	
Sheep/goat	tibia	left			23	
Dog	calcaneum		41.1			
Dog	astragalus		25.5			
Dog	calcaneum		41.2			
Dog	astragalus		25.6			
Dog	radius		152.6			10.8
Dog	radius		152.1			10.8

GL= Greatest Length; Bp = Breadth proximal; Bd = Breadth distal; SD = Shaft diameter

been immature, indicating a strategy focused on beef, whilst the sheep/goat assemblage included lambs and adults over four years old (Maltby 2003). Also similar to the Thame livestock assemblage, bones from all body parts were present, suggesting that animals were bred, slaughtered and butchered close by. Small quantities of antler were also present at Horcott, suggestive of small-scale craft working at a farming settlement.

At the Early–Mid Saxon settlement of Pennyland, Buckinghamshire, where a significant proportion of the Saxon faunal assemblage also came from the fills of SFBs, cattle were again the dominant animal by number of identified fragments, with sheep/goat being more common by MNI count, and pigs also relatively frequent as were bones of domestic fowl and goose (Holmes 1993; Ashdown 1993). Other remains in the SFBs included bones of horse, dog, deer, hare, mallard, red kite, raven, pigeon and song thrush. Several horse bones exhibited butchery marks, as did an example from Lechlade, again suggesting that horse meat was eaten. As at Thame, and also from an Anglo-Saxon SFB at Great Western Park, Didcot, Oxfordshire (Strid 2023), livestock bones from the less edible parts of the carcass (heads and lower limbs) formed a significant part of the assemblage, and together with the age profiles again indicate that livestock were reared and butchered at the settlement. Interestingly at Pennyland, biometric analysis of the goose bones provided convincing evidence that most birds were domestic (Ashdown 1993).

Most Saxon animal bone assemblages from the Upper Thames Valley and surrounding areas are, as at Thame, dominated by cattle, but at Barton Court Farm where much of the Saxon assemblage came from a single SFB (Wilson 1986) and Eynsham Abbey (Ayres *et al.* 2003, 343–4) sheep/goat are more frequent, with cattle and pig almost equally represented. A high proportion of pigs is often considered to be indicative of a high-status site (given that it is an animal which is largely used for meat), a feature also indicated by a greater quantity of bones from wild, hunted, animals, but at Barton Court Farm, Wilson has interpreted the material as indicative of a self-contained pastoral economy. A high proportion of pigs was also seen in the Early Saxon assemblage from Broughton, Milton Keynes, most of which derived from the fills of an SFB (Strid 2014). Here, pig bones were second to those of cattle in abundance and it has been argued that in this case it probably relates to the proximity of woodland suitable for pannage.

The most detailed zooarchaeological studies of SFBs are of East Anglian sites, where West Stow (in Suffolk) remains exceptional for having 70 SFBs; excavated in the 1970s, these generally contained two clear layers of deposition, interpreted as a use layer and a post-use layer. It was noted in comparing the faunal data that the post-use data had a lower proportion of pig remains (Crabtree 1990; although the layers associated with the use of the structures had more pig specimens than the later layers). This is interesting in comparison with the SFB structure 30 assemblage at Thame, which had a higher number of pig remains than were recovered from the other SFBs. Most of the pig specimens from this feature came from an upper fill (15845), although pig specimens were also found in 15846, 15847 and 15848. Also excavated in the 1970s, Spong Hill in Norfolk revealed six SFBs (and one further possible SFB), and here the faunal material compared well with the larger West Stow assemblage (Bond 1995). There, 'somewhat surprisingly, an almost identical distribution … covering almost every bone element with no particular bias towards meat-bearing or non-meat-bearing bones' was noted, a feature that can now be seen to extend to the assemblages from Horcott and Thame.

Evidence for the intensive management of land and animals is suggested by the pathologies present on some bones – the horse calcaneum with hints of spavin and the domestic cattle 2nd phalanx with extensive exostoses both suggest the use of animals for traction or as beasts of burden (Bartosiewicz and Gál 2013), while the caprine with possible penning elbow may indicate that those animals were being managed actively, although this pathology may also be age related and/or a result of repeated walking on hard ground (Holmes *et al.* 2021). Such evidence – just three specimens out of more than 2000 – could suggest that the use of animals in these roles was limited, but pathologies like these are typically only found at low frequencies archaeologically. The presence of foetal and neonatal pig and caprine bones, meanwhile, suggests that these animals were being bred on the site.

The identified bird bones demonstrate both the keeping of domestic birds and wildfowling. It has been suggested that the general population of Early and Mid Saxon rural England rarely consumed birds (Holmes 2017, 63), although low numbers of bones from domestic birds are usually present (Homes 2014, 86). At Thame, domestic fowl, goose, duck and possibly swan have been identified within this fairly small assemblage, including bones from juvenile (single examples of domestic fowl and goose) and adult birds and, in the case of domestic fowl and goose, bones from all parts of the wing and leg. Cranial and axial elements were absent but are fragile and less frequently recovered archaeologically.

The worked antler fragment from SFB structure 30 indicates some craft activity, although not a great deal can be inferred from a single specimen. Antler working is thought to have been a specialist craft carried out by itinerant tradesman (Holmes 2014; MacGregor 1989). The axially split horse metapodial is also significant. Splitting a metapodial in this way could either be a preliminary stage in bone working or it could be for accessing marrow. Although horse never made a large contribution to the British diet, evidence suggests that it was frowned upon by the early church. Efforts to discourage hippophagy in Britain and other Germanic areas were supported by Pope Gregory III and the practice declined in England, though not until the 8th and 9th centuries (Poole 2013). Alternatively, this specimen could be evidence for craft working and is, therefore, equivocal. Unlike antler working, bone working is currently understood to be a non-specialised activity at this time, carried out on an *ad hoc* basis (Holmes 2014).

The Late Saxon articulated dog is, of course, a clearly different part of the assemblage. Dogs are the most common ABG found in early medieval British assemblages and frequently consist of complete skeletons (Morris 2010). It has also been noted that burials of complete horses, dogs and their skulls are more commonly found with human inhumations in this period than in domestic contexts (Holmes 2014) and so the association of the dog skeleton with a horse cranium here may be considered to have had some symbolic significance. Articulated bone groups of dogs and horses were also discovered in Late Saxon features from Wallingford (Holmes 2020) and the semi-articulated remains of one young male horse was found in a Saxon sunken-featured building at Horcott, where it appears to represent secondary deposition of a partial carcass. Two SFBs at Horcott also had cattle skulls seemingly deliberately positioned at the base of the feature, possibly as part of a 'closing' ritual (Strid 2017). An articulated dog was also discovered in a Saxon ditch at Pennyland, Buckinghamshire (Holmes 1993), and an adult dog and neonatal pigs were found in SFBs at Broughton, Milton Keynes (Strid 2014). Since dogs and horses are not typically animals used for human food, these deposits may reflect the disposal of companion animals in an area or feature no longer used for domestic activities. However, by drawing on evidence from a wide range of sites Hamerow (2006, 26–7) argues that the placement of dogs and horses in the basal fills of buildings is 'particularly prominent in special deposits in Anglo-Saxon settlements' and can be viewed in the context of termination deposits, whose precise symbolic significance may never be known.

Fish bones
by Rebecca A. Nicholson

Three vertebrae and a cleithrum of eel (*Anguilla anguilla* (L.)) came from Saxon SFB structure 35 (8461, fill 8459; samples 766, 824 and 917). Two eel vertebrae also came from fill 5960 (sample 562) within the Neolithic penannular monument ditch (see Volume 1), a deposit that has been radiocarbon dated to the Saxon period (SUERC-69143; cal AD 720–960). Other fish remains include a tiny cyprinid (Cyprinidae) caudal vertebra from Saxon SFB structure 37 and single small pike (*Esox lucius* L.) vertebrae recovered from Saxon SFB structure 32 (sample 756 from fill 8249 and sample 780 from fill 8578).

Where fish bones occur on inland rural Anglo-Saxon sites they are often eel, although a much wider range of fish are known from ecclesiastical sites, coastal sites and *emporia*. A small collection of fish bones from Anglo-Saxon deposits at the site of Eynsham Abbey near Oxford (Ayres *et al.* 2003, 342) include a few bones from marine species (cod, *Gadus morhua* L., and possibly bullrout *Myoxocephalus scorpius* (L.)) as well as small freshwater taxa (perch, *Perca fluviatilis* L., pike and eel), indicating that transport of sea fish inland as far as Oxfordshire took place by the Mid Saxon period, although most fish available to the rural population would have been those that could be caught or trapped in the local rivers and millponds.

Charcoal
by Julia Meen

A total of 108 samples dated to the Saxon period were processed and assessed. The methodology is detailed in the Appendix. On the basis on this assessment, 12 samples were selected for further work: four samples from SFBs and eight from the oven structures, including three from grab samples of wattle-work thought to derive from the roof of oven 3 (Table 5.10). The assessment showed that a number of charred roundwood fragments had survived from these wattle samples, and analysis of these aimed to record evidence for woodland management.

Sunken-featured buildings

Bulk samples from four of the sunken-featured buildings (SFBs) were selected for charcoal work. The main taxa present were hazel, beech, hawthorn type, field maple and ash, but the proportions of these taxa varied between the structures (Fig. 5.13). In the samples from SFB structures 33 and 37, almost half of the charcoal assemblages consisted of hazel, with between one quarter and one third of the pieces examined clearly roundwood. Hawthorn-type charcoal made up over a quarter of the assemblage from SFB structure 33, with much of the remainder oak (10%) and ash (9%). Field maple, present only rarely in structure 33, was more common in structure 37 (16%), with oak and hawthorn each making up a further 10% of the assemblage.

The bulk sample from SFB structure 35 contained a mixture of charcoal, consisting of, listed in order of decreasing abundance, hawthorn type, elm, beech, hazel and ash. Several of the pieces greater than 10mm in size were large roundwood, with relatively shallow curvature, and it is likely that many of the smaller fragments are also from large roundwood but may be too small a fragment for the curvature to be clear. A further bulk sample was examined from a pit (6824) in structure 37. This contained a fairly even mix of oak, hazel and hawthorn type (29%, 27% and 20% respectively), with a lower proportion (11%) of ash. Many pieces of charcoal in this sample are from roundwood, although these were often fragmented so that not enough of the transverse section was preserved to measure diameter or number of rings, and therefore their value for looking at woodland management practices is limited.

Ovens

Charcoal was recovered from two of the four Saxon ovens. The three sampled deposits from oven 4 are

Saxon Finds and Environmental Remains 177

Table 5.10 Charcoal identifications from Saxon samples

Context number			6564	8459	5163	7099	6574	6670	6686	6640	7249	7386	7386	7386
Feature number			6567	8461	5166	6827		7151	7159	7151	7498	7498	7498	7498
Feature Label			Str. 37	Str. 35	Str. 33	Pit Str. 37	Ovens 1–4 Str. 44	Oven 4	Oven 4	Oven 4	Oven 3	Oven 3	Oven 3	Oven 3
Sample number (SS)			667	779	517	674	593	598	714	640	716	688	689	690
Feature type			SFB	SFB	SFB	Pit	Oven	Oven	Oven	Oven	Oven	Oven	Oven	Oven
Sample volume processed (l)			40L	40L	40L	40L	40L	40L	20L	20L	10L	0.5L	0.5L	0.5L
Period			4a	4a	4a	4a	4a	4a	4a	4a	4a	4a	4a	4a
Charcoal quantity >4mm			***	*****	****	*****	****	*****	****	***	***	***	****	**
Charcoal quantity 2–4mm			*****	*****	*****	*****	*****	*****	*****	****	*****	***	****	***
Charcoal preservation			Good	Good	Good	Good	Good	Good	Good	Good	Good	Good	Good	Good
Family	Species	Common name												
Rosaceae	Prunus spp.	blackthorn/cherry	1	1	3	3 (r)								
	cf Prunus	cf blackthorn/cherry	2	1	2	1								
	Maloideae	hawthorn type	10	39 (r)	21	20 (r)	1							
	Prunus/Maloideae	blackthorn/cherry/hawthorn type			3				2					
Ulmaceae	Ulmus spp.	elm		30 (r)										
Fagaceae	Quercus spp.	oak	7 (r)		10 (h)	29 (h)	5	1	1		1			
	cf Quercus	cf oak												
	Fagus sylvatica L.	beech	3	20 (r)			32 (r)	39 (r)	40	42 (r)	31 (r)	15 (r)	33 (r)	1
Betulaceae	Corylus avellana L.	hazel	43 (r)	8 (r)	41 (r)	27 (r)	1	5 (r)	3r	1r	16 (r)	2 (r)		7 r
	cf Corylus avellana L.	cf hazel	3	2	4							3	1	1
	Alnus/Corylus	alder/hazel		2 (r)										
Salicaceae	Salix/Populus sp.	willow/poplar	2			2								
	cf Salix/Populus	cf willow/poplar	1 r											
Sapindaceae	Acer campestre L.	field maple	15		2	5 (r)	1	2		1	1			
	cf Acer campestre L.	cf field maple	1		1	2 (r)								
Oleaceae	Fraxinus excelsior L.	ash	8 (r)	6	9	11 (r)	9	2	4	4	1			1
	indet. diffuse porous				2									
	indet.		3	1	2		1			2				
		Total	99	110	100	100	50	50	50	50	50	20	34	10

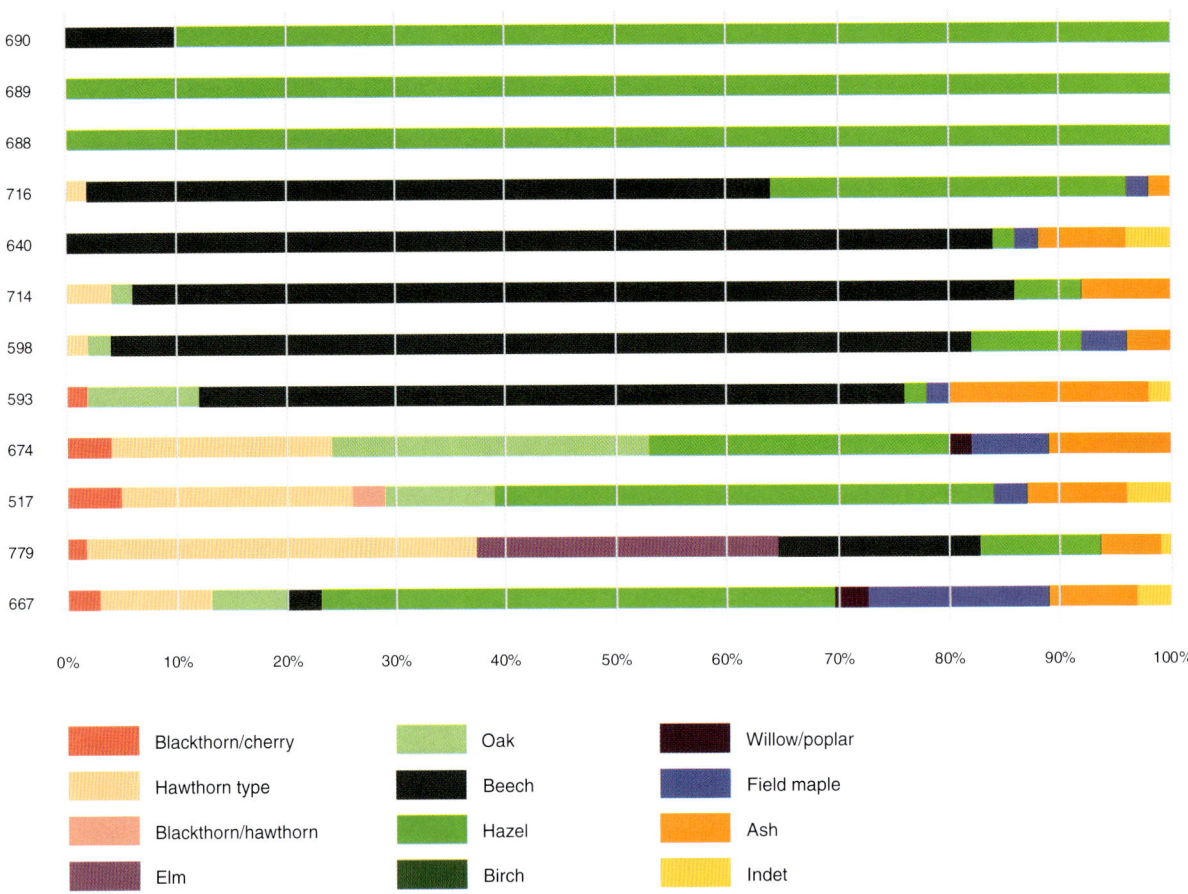

Fig. 5.13 Charcoal taxa, by sample

strongly dominated by beech, a minority of which was roundwood. Other taxa were present consistently albeit at low density, mostly hazel and ash. By contrast, the bulk sample from the charcoal-rich deposit (7249) from oven 3 is a mixture of beech and hazel, with a high proportion of the hazel small roundwood. Three spot samples taken from areas of fallen wattle-work in context 7386 are almost exclusively hazel roundwood. The final charcoal assemblage to be studied was from a charcoal-rich deposit that sealed oven 1, thought to comprise rakings from ovens 3 and 4; this is dominated by beech, but with a little oak and ash.

Discussion

Distribution of charred wood in burnt down SFB structure 35

Structure 35 had apparently been deliberately burned down and frequent charred timbers, many intact and some potentially *in situ*, were found, as well as concentrated areas of *in situ* burning. The bulk sample selected for charcoal identification was from the southeast quadrant of fill 8459, a deliberate backfill which extends throughout the whole structure. In contrast to the hazel-dominated assemblages from SFB structures 33 and 37, hazel charcoal made up only 11% of this assemblage, with the remainder mostly split between hawthorn type (35%), elm (27%) and beech (18%). The results of the assessment from the remaining three quadrants of the backfill, and from species identification of localised finds of charred wood, suggest that proportions of wood taxa vary spatially across the structure, and may therefore relate to different areas of activity, diverse construction materials, and the remnants of domestic fires. SFB structure 35 also contained two clusters of loomweights, apparently the remains of weaving looms abandoned in the buildings before its destruction, and these also imply that other items of furniture or artefacts may have been left *in situ* and could potentially contribute to the charred deposits within the building. Table 5.11 summarises the wood taxa identifications from these spatial samples. Many of the samples contain only one wood taxa, and these may relate to a single, or part of a, piece of wood. Other samples are mixed, containing three or four different taxa. It can be seen from the plans that the mixed samples are often from charcoal spreads and may well represent remains of domestic hearths in which a range of fuelwoods were burnt, including beech, hazel and hawthorn-type wood.

Table 5.11 Wood taxa from spatial samples in SFB structure 35

Sample no.	Ra. no.	Charcoal
794	913	Entirely *Fagus*
795	916	Entirely *Fagus*
796	911	Entirely *Fagus*
797	921	Entirely *Fagus*
798	947	Entirely *Fagus*
799	948	Entirely *Fagus*
801	922	Entirely *Fagus*
803	953	Mostly *Ulmus*, a little *Fagus* and *Corylus*
809	920	Mostly Ulmus, a little *Fagus*
811	965	Entirely *Fagus*
812	966	Mostly *Fagus*, a little *Acer*
815	918	Mostly *Fagus*, a little *Quercus*
817	968	Entirely *Fraxinus* (intact base of post)
818	914	Entirely Maloideae
822	917	Mixture of *Fraxinus* and *Prunus spinosa*
827	976	Mostly *Fagus*, a little *Salix/Populus*
900	910	Entirely *Ulmus*
903	988	Mixture of *Fagus*, *Corylus*, Maloideae
911	981	Mixture of Maloideae, *Fagus* and *Corylus*
912	982	Mostly *Fagus*, a little *Corylus* and *Acer*
913	985	Entirely *Corylus*
914	986	Entirely *Fagus*
915	987	Entirely *Fagus*
916	1026	No charcoal of identifiable size
917	1027	Mostly *Corylus*, a little Maloideae and *Quercus*
918	1032	Mixture of *Fagus* and *Corylus*

The most intact timber was the sawn-off base of a post, found close to a posthole (9465) approximately halfway along the width of the building and about a third of the way from the westernmost wall. The interior of the post had rotted away, but the outer rings have been preserved through charring. The post is made of ash (*Fraxinus excelsior*) wood and is interpreted as part of one of the main structural posts that held up the roof beam of the SFB. A sample from posthole 9516 on the eastern edge of structure 35 was a mixture of ash and blackthorn (*Prunus spinosa*) charcoal, so may well include fragmented charred remains of the post that held the other end of the roof beam (although this fill was recorded as only being flecked with charcoal, rather than indicating anything *in situ*). Spot samples from four north/south-aligned lengths of wood are of beech and are suggested to derive from the roof structure where it has fallen into the building during its destruction. A high number of spot samples from areas of charring also proved to be beech, supporting the case for its use as a construction material; the collapsing of a beech roof would account for this taxon being found spread across the entire building. Where a particular wood forms a substantial part of a structure it would be expected that this wood should be ubiquitous throughout its burnt down remains, and indeed samples from the oak-built SFB reconstruction at West Stow were strongly dominated by oak charcoal (Tipper 2012). Beech is not generally used as a building material, being more commonly exploited as a fuelwood. Roden (1968, 64) notes that medieval accounts relating to trade coming out of the Chilterns show that fuelwood generated a large income and was traded as far away as London, but that these accounts also suggest a shortage of heavy timbers suitable for construction. However, although beech is not weatherproof and cannot be used externally in buildings exposed to wind and rain (Edlin 1949, 35), it is both a strong wood and can bend if required, and it could feasibly form the internal part of a roof structure protected from the elements by a covering of thatch.

Elm formed a large proportion of the charcoal assemblage from the south-eastern bulk sample from the backfill; elm was also recovered from the north-western quadrant and from several spatial samples, including a timber in the south-eastern quadrant and, slightly to the north of this, from the charred spread (Ra. 953). Edlin (1949) observes that elm was one of the main woods used to make chairs up until the 20th century in the Chilterns, and it has also been traditionally used for turned products and for items that need to be durable when damp, such as pipes or tanks. Localised, elm-dominated or pure-elm concentrations of charcoal within the SFB could, therefore, potentially relate to individual elm artefacts or furniture that have become charred.

Ovens

Of the four ovens dated to the Saxon period, only two contained deposits of charcoal that could be sampled, with ovens 1 and 2 preserving only part of the fired clay structure. Preservation was much more extensive in ovens 3 and 4, including abundant fragments of fired clay with impressions of wattle-work which would have supported the upper part of the oven structure (see Poole, this chapter). The distribution of wood taxa through the associated deposits strongly suggests that beech was the main fuel used to fire the ovens, and that hazel rods were used to form the ovens' wattle-work structure. The three bulk samples from oven 4, which come from demolition deposits otherwise rich in charred grain that was presumably accidentally charred whilst being dried in this structure, are strongly dominated by beech charcoal. Similarly, the charcoal-rich layer (7249) from oven 3 has beech as its largest component. Tellingly, the rakings from ovens 3 and 4 (context 6574), are again strongly dominated by beech; the presence of other taxa, especially oak and ash, presumably reflects its being a secondary dump from a mixture of sources. There is almost no hazel amongst these rakings, which supports the idea that the hazel roundwood seen in the ovens, particularly in oven 3, is structural rather than having been used as fuel. The three spot samples that contain almost exclusively hazel roundwood are taken from 7386, a layer rich in fragments of oven 3's fired clay superstructure (Table 5.10). The wattle-work frame that supported the upper structure of the oven is preserved both as clear impressions of rods and sails pressed into the clay, and as the remains of the wattles themselves in the form of these fragments of charred hazel roundwood. That this charred wood formed these impressions is further confirmed in that the measurements of the charcoals match those taken of the fired clay impressions (see below). The relatively high number of hazel fragments in the charcoal layer of oven 3, mixed with the beech fuel, is presumably due to the superstructure collapsing into the oven as it was destroyed.

Reconstruction of local woodlands: importance of beech woodlands and woodland management

The first finds of beech from the site date to the Romano-British period (see Chapter 3), where this taxon is present only in trace amounts, suggesting it was not utilised to a great extent in that period. However, the ubiquity of beech from deposits dated to the Saxon period – both as a fuel and, apparently, as a construction material – indicates that by this time beech was readily available and was an important resource. Beech is an excellent fuelwood and would have been an obvious fuel choice for the Roman corndriers yet is almost absent from those structures. This suggests that either the composition of local woodlands had dramatically changed in the intervening centuries, or that different woodlands, perhaps at a greater distance from the site, were being exploited.

The Chilterns today are famous for their ancient beech woodlands and, although their origins are not fully understood, it has been suggested that human activity was instrumental in the development of beech woodlands across Britain in the Roman and medieval period. Beech does not compete well and struggles to establish itself in existing woodlands but can exploit clearances of oak woodland to colonise (Godwin 1984). However, it has also been suggested that clearance and regeneration of secondary woodland are not requisites to the establishment of beechwoods, and that other human actions can have a dramatic effect on woodland composition. In the Weald, Waller and Schofield attribute a rise in beech pollen recorded from the Mid Saxon period to extensive use of the woodlands as pasture for pigs (2007, 381), and Dark (2017, 245) suggests that a similar process was initiated by grazing of cattle in Epping Forest from the Roman period onwards; both areas contain extensive beech woodlands today. The ground disturbance created by grazing livestock encourages the establishment of beech seeds, and this impact is reinforced as saplings of beech are less palatable to livestock compared to those of other trees (Waller and Schofield 2007, 381). Hughes (1931) notes that the slopes of the Chilterns were described as being forested in the Early Saxon period. The Domesday Book shows that wood pasture was an important part of the economy of the Chilterns by the 11th century. Settlements within and along the edge of its limits, such as West Wycombe and Princes Risborough, consistently record woodland supporting up to 1000 pigs amongst their resources. It can therefore be suggested that it was in the establishment of extensive wood pasture to graze pigs in the Chilterns that the origins of the beech woodlands lie, and this development may account for the high availability of and dependence on beech indicated by the Saxon charcoal assemblages from Thame. Manorial accounts reveal that by the medieval period, the Chilterns included both areas of dense beech wood with little understorey as well as mixed woodlands with beech, oak and ash, and that, while these woodlands underwent large-scale felling in the 11th to 13th centuries, their importance as a resource was subsequently recognised and they were thereafter intensively managed (Roden 1968).

Of the seven samples taken from the charred wattles of oven 3, only sample 689 contained charcoal in sufficient quantity, and with sufficient of the original wood preserved, to be able to study evidence for woodland management. Material from samples 688 and 690 was generally too fragmentary to measure diameter and record growth rings, and the remaining wattle samples contained few pieces of charcoal, possibly only representing single pieces of wood. Therefore, recording of data relating to woodland management practices focused on sample 689. Identification was carried out on 34 pieces, of which morphological data was recorded for 30 pieces (Table 5.12). Figure 5.14 shows a scatterplot of the diameter of the transverse section compared to number of growth rings; blue points indicate fragments in which pith and bark was preserved, allowing measurement of the full diameter and the total number of rings, while orange points represent incomplete fragments, in which measurements are minimum values only. More than half of the complete fragments have four growth rings and are between 10 and 15mm diameter. Most of the remainder have either three or five rings and are within a similar size range or slightly smaller. Most of the incomplete fragments fit the same trend, and for the six samples for which no measurement of diameter was possible, all pieces had between three and six rings preserved. Although 30 fragments is a fairly small sample, limiting the inferences that can be made, it can be seen from the scatterplot of measurements that the fragments fall into more than one size range, with several fragments with six or seven growth rings, so that

Table 5.12 Additional measurements of hazel roundwood from oven 3, layer 7386

Fragment no.	Diameter (mm)	No. rings	Bark	Pith	Cut early?	Other comments
1	6	2	Y	Y		
2	10	4	Y	Y	Y	
3	12	4	Y	Y	Y	
4	11	4	Y	Y	Y	
5	15	4	Y	Y	Y	narrow 1st ring
6	10	4	Y	Y	Y	
7	11	4	Y	Y	Y	
8	13	4	Y	Y	Y	3rd ring much narrower than 1st and 2nd
9	13	5	Y	Y	Y	1st ring very narrow, 2nd and 3rd wider
10	7	3	Y	Y		
11	9	3	Y	Y	Y	
12	12	4	Y	Y		
13	11	4	Y	Y	Y	1st and 2nd rings wide, 3rd narrower
14	14	4	Y	Y		1st ring very narrow
15	10	4	Y	Y	Y	
16	10	5	N	N		
17	14	4	Y	Y		1st ring very narrow
18	12	5	N	Y	Y	
19		4	N	N		
20	10	3	N	N		
21	14	3	N	N		
22		4	N	N		
23		3	N	N		
24	7	3	N	Y		
25		3	N	N		
26	16	7	Y	Y	Y	
27	14	7	Y	N	Y	
28		6	N	N		
29	18	6	N	Y		
30	30	6	N	Y		

a number of different poles must be represented. The incomplete hazel charcoal from the other wattle samples shows a similar picture: the roundwood from samples 688 and 690, as well as the hazel mixed with beech fuel deposit 7249 within the oven, mostly had between two and four growth rings.

The measurements of the impressions left in fired clay from oven 3 also matched the measurements of the wattles in sample 689, with a large number of the rods falling within a 9–15mm size range (see above). The selection of hazel poles would have primarily been dictated by the necessity of the poles being within a limited range of sizes, as rods and sails of the wattle-work structure would need to be of fairly standard size so that they could be easily woven, and this is corroborated by the evidence from the measurements of their charcoal remains. The poles would have reached the required size after only a few years' growth. For a large number of pieces where the bark was preserved, it could be seen that the final ring ended abruptly, evidence that the branch had been cut early in the year, probably in the spring shortly after the new ring started to grow. Some of the roundwood fragments had very narrow first year growth, followed by much wider second and third year growth, after which growth again narrowed; others did not have this narrow first ring but started with wide growth in the first two years followed by slower growth in the following years.

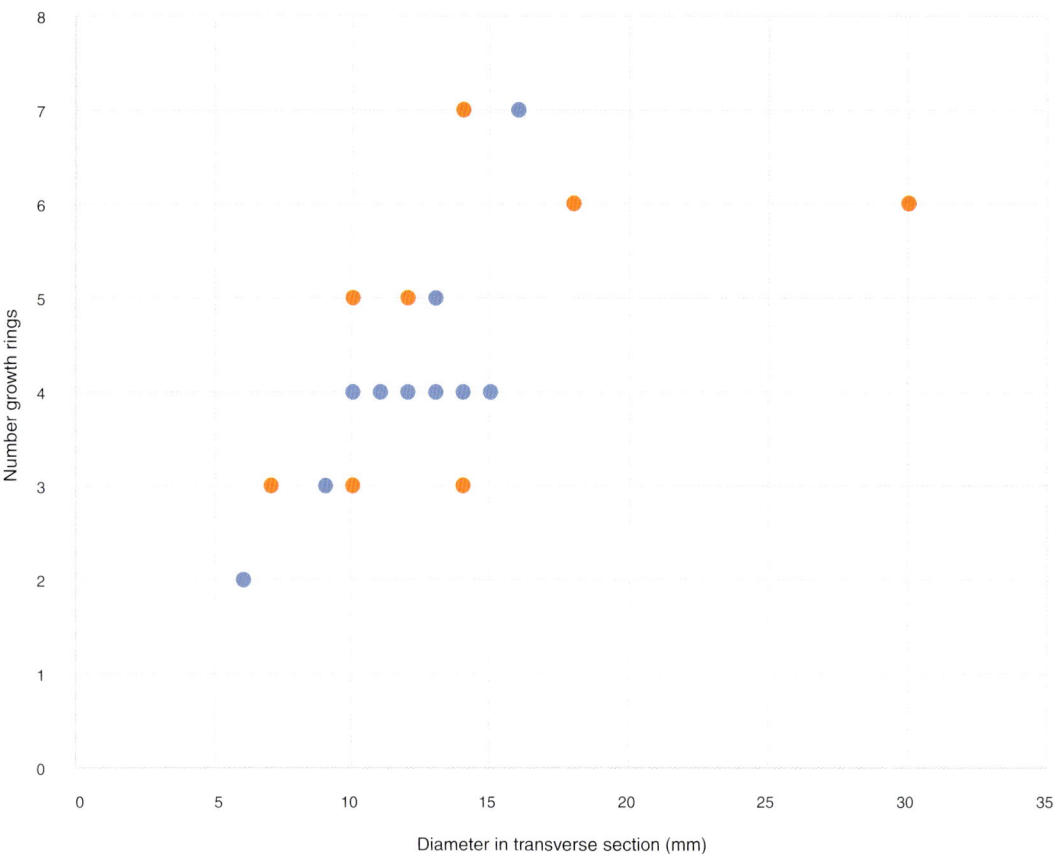

Fig. 5.14 Charcoal growth rings and diameter

Plant macrofossils
by Sarah F. Wyles

Charred plan remains were recovered from a number of SFB contexts, ovens and pits (Table 5.13). Details of methodology are provided in the Appendix.

Period 4a/b Saxon

Structure 44 Ovens 1-4

Fills 7274 (sample 666), 7248 (sample 654) and 7249 (sample 716) of section 7498 of oven 3 in the western part of the group of ovens (1-4) contained extremely high numbers of charred plant remains. A charred rye grain from sample 666 was radiocarbon dated (SUERC-69136, cal AD 770-1020). Cereal remains represented a significant part of all three assemblages, forming over 50% of them. Barley and free-threshing wheat grains were the most numerous, with significant quantities of grains of rye and some hulled wheat. A few of the barley grains were still in the husk and there were only small quantities of chaff elements. Notable quantities of the grains, between 12-20%, showed traces of germination and there were large numbers of detached embryos and coleoptile fragments. Large quantities of oat remains (between 21-25% of the assemblages), comprising mainly grains with some spikelets, floret bases and awn fragments, were noted within these assemblages. These included remains of cultivated oats and some grains with traces of germination. Other potential crops included small number of seeds of Celtic bean (*Vicia faba*) and garden pea (*Pisum sativum*).

The weed seed assemblages included large quantities of corncockle seeds, some of which were germinated. The recovery of geminated corncockle seeds is unusual and it is likely that these seeds germinated together with the grain. Other seeds included those of fat-hen, curled dock, vetch/wild pea, stinking mayweed and brome grass. The weed seeds are mainly those of the larger seeded species or those with seed heads or pods.

The level of germination observed across the range of cereals within these assemblages may indicate that these crops were processed at the same time and that the assemblage is related to malting and the brewing process.

The large assemblage recorded from fill 6640 (sample 640) of cut 7151 of oven 4 in the southern part of structure 44 was dominated by cereal remains, which represented 62% of the assemblage. The cereal remains included those of free-threshing wheat and barley with a few grains of rye and hulled wheat. Very few chaff

Table 5.13 Charred plant remains from period 4a/b features

Feature type		Structure 44 Oven 3		Structure 44 Oven 4		Structure 44 Ovens		SFB Structure 33		SFB Structure 37 Pit	Pit
Cut		7274	7498	7249	7151	6640	6686	6639	6641	5166	5163	6827	8709
Context		666	7248	716		640	714	595	625		5163	517	7099	8711
Sample			654							5163	5163	674	952
Vol (L)		10	10	10		20	20	40	40	40	40	40	25
Flot size		575	275	625		90	250	160	675	80	150	850	20
%Roots		1	1	1		5	2	2	1	10	7	1	5
% 2mm fraction analysed		10	100	100		100	100	100	100	100	100	100	S
% 1mm fraction analysed		10	10	10		100	100	100	100	100	100	100	
% 0.5mm fraction analysed		10	10	10		100	100	100	100	100	100	100	
% 0.25mm fraction analysed		10	10	10		100	100	100	100	100	100	100	
Cereals	Common Name												
Hordeum vulgare L. sl (grain)	barley	c. 1920	459	c. 1030		49	282	17	360	26	56	28	-
Hordeum vulgare L. sl (grain still in husk)	barley	c. 30	4	25		-	5	-	4	-	-	1	-
Hordeum vulgare L. sl (grain) germinated	barley	c. 550	75	c. 395		-	10	-	-	-	2	-	-
Hordeum vulgare L. sl (rachis frag)	barley	c. 20	-	-		1	2	2	2	-	-	-	-
Triticum cf. dicoccum (Schübl) (grain)	emmer wheat	c. 90	8	-		-	-	-	-	-	3	-	-
Triticum cf. dicoccum (Schübl) (germinated grain)	emmer wheat	-	5	-		-	-	-	-	-	3	-	-
Triticum dicoccum (Schübl) (glume base)	emmer wheat	-	-	-		-	-	-	-	1	1	-	-
Triticum dicoccum (Schübl) (spikelet fork)	emmer wheat	-	-	-		-	-	-	-	-	2	-	-
Triticum spelta L. (grain)	spelt wheat	c. 150	-	-		-	-	1	1	3	2	-	-
Triticum spelta L. (glume bases)	spelt wheat	-	-	-		-	-	-	-	1	7	-	-
Triticum dicoccum/spelta (grain)	emmer/spelt wheat	c. 660	c. 81	-		5	10	5	27	3	-	1	-
Triticum dicoccum/spelta (germinated grain)	emmer/spelt wheat	c. 220	-	-		-	-	-	-	3	1	1	-
Triticum dicoccum/spelta (spikelet fork)	emmer/spelt wheat	-	-	-		-	-	1	-	-	-	-	-
Triticum dicoccum/spelta (glume bases)	emmer/spelt wheat	-	-	-		2	3	-	1	10	1	4	-
Triticum turgidum/aestivum (grain)	free-threshing wheat	c. 1670	592	c. 1787		75	290	98	655	5	2	8	1
Triticum turgidum/aestivum (grain) germinated	free-threshing wheat	c. 430	108	155		-	20	-	-	-	-	-	-
Triticum turgidum/aestivum (rachis frags)	free-threshing wheat	-	-	c. 10		10	7	12	21	-	3	1	-
Triticum sp. (grain)	wheat	-	-	-		32	-	11	-	-	-	-	-
Secale cereale (grain)	rye	c. 706	c. 129	c. 293		16	57	15	113	cf. 1	-	-	-
Secale cereale (germinated grain)	rye	c. 160	14	-		1	1	5	3	-	-	-	-
Secale cereale (rachis frag.)	rye	-	-	-		-	-	-	-	-	-	-	-

Saxon Finds and Environmental Remains

Table 5.13 (cont.) Charred plant remains from period 4a/b features

Feature type		Structure 44 Oven 3				Structure 44 Oven 4		Structure 44 Ovens		SFB Structure 33		SFB Structure 37 Pit	Pit
Cut		7274				7151				5166		6827	8709
Context		7498	7248		7249	6640	6686	6639	6641	5163	5163	7099	8711
Sample		666	654	–	716	714		595	625	511	517	674	952
Cereal indet. (grains)	cereal	c. 200	c. 70	–	–	60	165	60	350	12	10	6	+
Cereal frag. (est. whole grains)	cereal	c. 70	65	–	–	45	80	35	190	5	15	4	–
Cereal frags (rachis frags)	cereal	–	–	–	–	3	3	1	–	1	–	–	–
Cereal frags (culm node)	cereal	–	–	c. 10	2	1	2	6	2	3	–	–	–
Cereal frags (detached embryo)	cereal	c. 410	c. 117	–	c. 300	7	5	–	–	–	–	3	–
Cereal frags (coleoptile)	cereal	c. 410	c. 400	–	c. 181	–	15	–	5	–	–	–	–
Other Species													
Ranunculus sp.	buttercup	c. 10	–	–	–	1	–	1	3	1	–	–	–
Papaver rhoeas/dubium L.	common/long-headed poppy	–	–	–	–	–	2	–	–	–	–	–	–
Papaver rhoeas L. stigmatic disc	common poppy	–	–	–	–	–	–	1	–	–	–	–	–
Urtica dioica L.	common nettle	–	–	–	–	–	–	16	–	–	–	–	–
Urtica urens L.	small nettle	–	–	–	–	1	–	–	–	2	–	–	–
Corylus avellana L. (fragments)	hazelnut	c. 10	–	–	–	–	1	–	4	1	–	3	4
Chenopodium sp.	goosefoot	c. 10	c. 40	–	c. 40	4	9	4	14	1	2	–	–
Chenopodium album L.	fat-hen	c. 10	c. 10	–	c. 70	3	5	7	15	–	–	–	–
Atriplex sp. L.	oraches	–	–	–	c. 10	1	3	4	3	1	–	–	–
Stellaria media L.	common chickweed	–	–	–	–	–	1	1	–	1	–	–	–
Stellaria sp. L.	stitchworts	–	–	–	–	–	2	–	–	–	1	–	–
Agrostemma githago L.	corncockle	c. 482	c. 213	–	c. 435	11	45	1	35	1	–	–	–
Agrostemma githago L. (germinated)	corncockle	c. 80	c. 28	–	5	–	5	–	–	–	–	–	–
Agrostemma githago L. (capsule)	corncockle	–	–	2	–	–	–	–	–	–	–	–	–
Silene sp. L.	campions	–	–	–	–	–	–	–	2	–	–	–	–
Persicaria lapathifolia/maculosa (L.) Gray/Gray	pale persicaria/redshank	–	–	–	–	–	–	–	1	–	–	–	–
Persicaria lapathifolia (L.) Gray	pale persicaria	–	–	–	–	–	–	–	–	1	–	–	–
Polygonum aviculare L.	knotgrass	c. 10	c. 13	–	c. 10	1	3	3	3	1	1	–	–
Fallopia convolvulus (L.) À. Löve	black-bindweed	–	–	–	1	–	–	1	2	–	–	–	–
Rumex sp. L.	docks	c. 20	–	–	c. 50	12	12	7	11	8	88	–	–
Rumex acetosella group Raf.	sheep's sorrel	–	–	–	–	2	2	3	4	2	5	–	–
Rumex crispus L. Type	curled dock	c. 50	–	–	c. 70	4	8	1	17	2	70	2	–
Malva sp. L.	mallow	c. 30	1	–	c. 30	1	1	3	3	–	–	–	–

Saxon Finds and Environmental Remains 185

Feature type		Structure 44 Oven 3			Structure 44 Oven 4		Structure 44 Ovens		SFB Structure 33		SFB Structure 37 Pit	Pit
Cut		7274	7498	7249	7151				5166		6827	8709
Context		666	7248	716	6640	6686	6639	6641	5163	5163	7099	8711
Sample		e. 20	654	e. 21	640	714	595	625	511	517	674	952
Brassica sp. L.	brassica	-	1	-	2	3	4	1	2	2	1 + 1 (min)	-
Prunus spinosa L.	sloe stone	-	1	-	-	-	-	1	-	-	-	-
Prunus spinosa L.	sloe fruit frag	-	-	-	-	-	1	-	-	-	-	-
Prunus spinosa/Crataegus monogyna (thorns/twigs)	sloe/hawthorn type thorns	-	-	-	-	-	-	-	-	-	2	-
Vicia L./*Lathyrus* sp. L.	vetch/wild pea	e. 80	e. 17	e. 51	8	6	3	8	3	9	2	2
Vicia sativa L.	common vetch	-	4	2	-	-	-	-	-	4	-	-
Vicia faba L.	Celtic bean	-	2	2	-	2	-	-	-	1	1	-
Vicia faba/Pisum	Celtic bean/pea	-	-	5	-	2	-	-	-	-	1	-
Lathyrus cf. *nisolia* L.	grass vetchling	-	-	-	-	-	-	-	2	-	-	-
Pisum sativum L.	pea	e. 20	-	-	-	-	-	-	-	cf.2	-	-
Medicago/Trifolium sp. L.	medick/clover	e. 40	e. 20	e. 10	20	12	23	12	2	14	-	-
Medicago sp. L.	medick	-	-	-	4	3	-	-	-	2	-	-
Trifolium sp. L	clover	-	e. 20	-	5	7	-	-	-	8	-	-
Linum usitatissimum L.	flax	-	-	-	-	1	-	-	-	1	-	-
Pimpinella sp. L.	burnet-saxifrage	-	-	-	1	-	1	1	-	-	-	-
Torilis sp. Adans	hedge-parsley	-	-	e. 10	-	-	1	-	-	-	-	-
Solanum dulcamara L.	bittersweet	-	-	-	-	cf. 1	-	-	-	-	-	-
Galeopsis cf. *tetrahit* L.	common hemp-nettle	e. 10	-	-	-	-	-	-	-	-	-	-
Prunella vulgaris L.	selfheal	-	-	-	-	1	-	2	-	-	-	-
Plantago lanceolata L.	ribwort plantain	e. 10	e. 20	-	1	1	1	-	1	-	-	-
Odontites vernus (Bellardi) Dumort	red bartsia	e. 20	e. 10	-	2	2	2	2	-	3	-	-
Sherardia arvensis L.	field madder	-	e. 11	-	1	-	-	1	1	-	-	-
Galium sp. L.	bedstraw	e. 10	-	1	2	3	1	-	-	-	-	-
Galium aparine L.	cleavers	e. 10	11	7	1	10	-	5	2	-	-	-
Valerianella dentata (L.) Pollich	narrow-fruited cornsalad	-	-	-	-	1	3	-	1	-	-	-
Cardus/Cirsium	thistle	-	-	-	-	-	-	-	-	2	-	-
Centaurea cyanus L.	cornflower	-	1	-	1	-	-	-	1	-	-	-
Anthemis cotula L. (seeds)	stinking mayweed	e. 60	e. 40	c. 40	15	15	30	21	2	-	-	-
Tripleurospermum inodorum (L.) Sch. Bip.	scentless mayweed	e. 10	e. 10	-	-	3	-	1	1	1	-	-
Isolepis setacea (L.) R. Br.	bristle club-rush	-	-	-	-	-	-	-	-	1	-	-
Carex sp. L. trigonous	sedge trigonous seed	-	-	-	-	-	-	-	-	4	-	-

Table 5.13 (cont.) Charred plant remains from period 4a/b features

Feature type		Structure 44 Oven 3			Structure 44 Oven 4		Structure 44 Ovens			SFB Structure 33			SFB Structure 37 Pit	Pit
Cut		7274			7151				6641		5166		6827	8709
Context		7498	7248	7249	6640	6686	6639		6641	5163	5163	5163	7099	8711
Sample		666	654	716	640	714	595		625	511	517	517	674	952
Carex sp. L. flat	sedge flat seed	-	-	-	-	-	-	-	-	-	-	-	-
Lolium/Festuca sp.	rye-grass/fescue	e. 20	1	-	-	-	3	4	-	-	-	-	-
Poa/Phleum sp. L.	meadow grass/cat's-tails	e. 20	e. 20	e. 10	14	3	10	10	8	-	31	-	-
Poa sp. L.	meadow grass	-	-	-	-	-	-	-	-	-	20	-	-
Arrhenatherum elatius Var. *bulbosum* (Willd)	false oat-grass	-	-	-	-	-	-	-	-	-	-	1	-
Avena sp. L. (grain)	oat grain	c 1850	c. 750	c. 1950	13	140	21	210	-	12	9	4	-
Avena sativa. L. (grain cf. cultivated)	oat grain	e. 320	e. 49	40	-	30	-	-	1	-	-	-	-
Avena sp. L. (grain) germinated	oat grain	e. 300	e. 102	e. 405	1	5	-	10	8	-	-	-	-
Avena sp. L. (spikelet)	oat spikelet	-	-	-	-	2	-	-	-	-	-	-	-
Avena sativa. L. (spikelet cf. cultivated)	oat spikelet	e. 30	3	4	-	3	-	2	-	-	-	1	-
Avena sativa. L. (floret base cf. cultivated)	oat floret	e. 30	e. 23	e. 435	-	1	-	3	-	-	-	1	-
Avena sp. L. (floret base)	oat floret	e. 40	e. 90	e. 31	-	1	1	-	-	-	-	-	-
Avena sp. L. (awn)	oat awn	-	-	e. 10	-	-	-	-	-	-	-	-	-
Avena L./*Bromus* L. sp.	oat/brome grass	e. 450	e. 270	e. 1000	35	127	28	130	6	5	14	-	-
Bromus sp. L.	brome grass	e. 640	e. 280	e. 226	10	40	7	20	1	1	6	-	-
Monocot. Stem/rootlet frag		-	-	-	4	4	-	-	-	-	-	-	-
Parenchyma/Tuber		-	-	-	3	-	-	-	1	12	-	1	-
Triangular capsule frag.		-	-	-	-	-	-	-	1	-	-	1	-
Conglomeration of seed and stem frags		-	-	-	2	1	-	-	-	-	15	-	-
Tuber/Rhizomes		-	-	-	-	-	1	-	-	-	-	-	-
Mineralised nodule		-	-	-	-	-	-	1	2	3	-	4	-

Key: + = 0–49, ++ = 50–99, +++ = 100+, c. = estimated

fragments were recovered and there were a few detached embryos noted. The weed seeds included seeds of oat, brome grass, clover, medick, stinking mayweed, meadow grass/cat's-tails, corncockle, curled docks and sheep's sorrel. This assemblage may be representative of the remains from the accidental burning of a crop, which had already been fully processed by threshing, winnowing and sieving, during the parching process.

Fill 6686 (sample 714) of section cut 7151 of oven 4 contained a very large quantity of charred plant remains, 65% of which were those of cereals. These included high numbers of remains of free-threshing wheat and barley with lower numbers of rye and hulled wheat. The mixture of grains may be indicative of crops grown together in a maslin. A few of the grains showed traces of germination and there was also a small quantity of detached embryos. There were also a large number of oat remains, some of which were those of the cultivated variety (*Avena sativa*). Other potential crop remains were those of Celtic beans and flax. The weed seeds included seeds of corncockle, brome grass, stinking mayweed, clover, medick, curled dock and fat-hen. This assemblage may be reflective of material from the drying of the crops.

The large assemblage recovered from fill 6639 (sample 595) within the eastern part of structure 44 comprised 58% cereal remains, whereas the very high number of plant remains recorded from fill 6641 (sample 625) comprised 75% cereal remains. Those of free-threshing wheat were predominant together with significant amounts of barley and rye and a small quantity of hulled wheat. There were a few coleoptile fragments. There were a large number of oat remains, including a number of the cultivated variety. The weed seeds included seeds of corncockle, fat-hen, curled dock, clover/medick, stinking mayweed and brome grass. These assemblages may be representative of the remains from the accidental burning of the crops, which had already been fully processed by threshing, winnowing and sieving, during the parching process.

SFB structure 33
Deposit 5163 (sample 511) produced a moderately large mixed assemblage of cereals and weeds in broadly equal quantities. The cereal remains included those of barley, hulled wheat, free-threshing wheat and rye and there was a moderate amount of chaff elements. The weed seeds included seeds of oats, brome grass, meadow grass/cat's-tails, vetch/wild pea and docks. There were also a few mineralised remains. The assemblage may be reflective of a mixture of crop processing and domestic settlement waste material.

The high number of charred remains recorded from another part of the same deposit (sample 517) was dominated by the weed seed element which represented 67% of the assemblage. The cereal remains were predominantly those of barley, with smaller amounts of those of emmer wheat and free-threshing wheat. There were few fragments of chaff and Celtic beans and peas. The weed seeds included those of meadow grass/cat's-tails, curled docks, sedge, clover, medick, oats and brome grass. There were also a few mineralised remains and some conglomerations of charred seeds and stems. This assemblage may be representative of a mixture of food waste material and possibly floor-covering material. There appears to be some spatial variation in the composition of the assemblages within this SFB.

SFB structure 37
Fill 7099 (sample 674) of pit 6827 within structure 37 produced a moderate charred plant assemblage. The cereal remains were predominant and included those mainly of barley with some of free-threshing wheat and hulled wheat. The weed seeds included seeds of oats and brome grass and there were a small number of mineralised remains. This assemblage may be representative of a dump of processed grain waste.

Pit 8709
The small assemblage recovered from fill 8711 (sample 952) of pit 8709 included free-threshing wheat grain and hazelnut shell fragments. It is likely to represent food waste material.

Discussion

The assemblages from ovens 1–4 appear to be reflective of malting, with the brewing process indicated in cut 7498 of oven 3. Crop drying, generally once the crops had been fully processed, is reflected within cut 7151 of oven 4. The eastern part of the structure also appears to have been used for drying the fully processed crop. The assemblages from the Saxon corndrier at Springhead were also indicative of the corndrier being used for drying the fully processed crop (Stevens 2011c). The other assemblages from SFB structures 33 and 37 seem to be indicative of mixtures of crop-processing waste, food waste and possible floor-covering material.

The potential crops include free-threshing wheat, barley, rye, spelt wheat, emmer wheat, cultivated oats, Celtic beans, peas, and flax. Free-threshing wheat is the predominant wheat in southern Britain during this period and rye is also typical of assemblages of this date (Greig 1991). A similar range of species was recovered from Saxon deposits at Yarnton (Stevens 2004), Springhead (Stevens 2011c) and Northfleet (Smith 2011). The predominant grain within the samples from the SFBs was barley and this was also the case from other assemblages from SFBs at Yarnton (Stevens 2004), Abbot's Barton (Wyles and Stevens 2015) and Abbot's Worthy (Carruthers 1991). Significant quantities of oats have been recovered from other Saxon ovens such as at Pinbrook, Exeter (Wyles 2019) and Stafford (Moffett 1994). Again, the composition of the cereal remains within the assemblages suggests that the initial processing of all the crops was done in the fields, removing most of the bulky waste before transporting them on to site.

A number of the weed seeds are typical of assemblages of this date such as stinking mayweed, corncockle and cornflower. Corncockle and cornflower are weeds very closely associated with the rye crop (Godwin 1984, 350, 479) and are typically recorded in assemblages of Saxon and medieval date. Corncockle is thought to have been introduced as a grain contaminant to southern Britain during the Roman period. Stinking mayweed becomes more common in assemblages of Saxon and medieval date (Greig 1991) and this is thought to be linked with the increased cultivation of heavier clay soils (Green 1984) associated with the change to mouldboard ploughs from ards (Jones 1981; Stevens with Robinson 2004; Stevens 2009). Corncockle and stinking mayweed were also noted in Saxon assemblages from Yarnton (Stevens 2004). Finds of charred germinated corncockle are unusual and have been recorded elsewhere from an assemblage associated with malting from a 10th-century oven or kiln from Lawrence Street, York (Kenward *et al.* 2004) and from a Late Saxon pit assemblage from Sussex Street, Winchester (Green 2009).

The range of weed seed species within the assemblages are indicative of a number of different soil types being exploited for crop production. Species such as corncockle, field madder, narrow-fruited cornsalad, ribwort plantain, clover and medick favour lighter drier soils, whereas stinking mayweed and red bartsia are typical of heavier clay soils, sheep's sorrel of sandier or heath habitats and mallow (*Malva* sp.) and curled dock of damper rough waste. Again, oraches and fat-hen can be indicative of nitrogen-rich soils. There is an indication of wetter habitats being utilised in the vicinity with the presence of seeds of sedge and bristle club-rush (*Isolepis setacea*) in one of the assemblages from SFB structure 33.

Chapter 6
Discussion

by Alex Davies and Chris Ellis

The Late Iron Age and Roman periods
by Alex Davies

Excavations revealed activity throughout the Late Iron Age and Roman periods, albeit of reduced scale between *c.* AD 150–240. Enclosure ditches dominated the cut features throughout, with corndriers and other pyrotechnical features appearing in numerous sub-periods. One of the most significant periods of change in the layout of the landscape was the transformation of the initial Late Iron Age enclosure system with a single settlement enclosure around the period of the Roman conquest. This is quite rare evidence of discontinuity in rural settlement and landscape use during this period in the region, and the establishment of land enclosure cannot be directly related to the political upheavals related to the conquest. The orientation of the land division was maintained when the site developed into a more significant enclosure system in the Early Roman period. Millstones attest to industrial activities during the early 2nd century, and pottery and other material culture suggest settlement that is otherwise not clearly evidenced archaeologically. Activity greatly reduced in the Middle Roman period, although the enclosures must have remained visible, since some of them were recut in the Late Roman period. Settlement and any industrial activity probably moved away from the area, with the site probably remaining in agricultural use in the Middle Roman period. More visible activity resumed in the Late Roman period with more recutting of enclosures and greater amounts of material culture.

Based on the ceramic and stratigraphic evidence, the main Late Iron Age and Roman archaeological periods could in many cases be subdivided into sometimes quite precisely defined site phases. However, significant amounts of recutting took place during the Roman period. Some of the main structuring elements established in the Early Roman period were redefined numerous times up to the late 4th century. This led to a large amount of redeposition of material culture, which is seen most clearly in the pottery but also in the metalwork. There was very little direct evidence of Middle Roman activity, although there was a general continuity in the structure of the landscape.

The Late Iron Age/Early Romano-British period

The very limited Middle Iron Age activity in the western part of the site (see Volume 1) appears to have directly preceded the Late Iron Age evidence, following a period of apparent abandonment during the earlier part of the Middle Iron Age. The Late Iron Age (period 3a) archaeology comprised features which divided up the land combined with ephemeral settlement evidence. The initial Late Iron Age phase was evidenced by ditches and enclosures associated with a handful of roundhouses. This was superseded by a single settlement enclosure with further houses and a burial around the period of the conquest, which was in turn superseded by a larger enclosure system. Numerous pits, some with concentrations of material culture, were cut and a couple of ovens were constructed.

The pre-conquest Late Iron Age (period 3ai) plan is fragmentary, and it is difficult to fully understand the layout of the settlement. This is largely because the western part of the site witnessed a significant amount of activity, with many, mainly Roman, ditches cutting and confusing earlier evidence. Nevertheless, a gridded enclosure system with at least one partial trackway appears to have been present, within which a possible roundhouse was located. This pattern is reasonably typical of Late Iron Age settlement patterns in the Thames Valley (Lambrick with Robinson 2009, 88–90).

The features from this first period included a substantial boundary ditch with multiple recuts. While this was clearly integrated within a wider system, the function of the ditch, its excessive size compared to other contemporary features, and the reason for so many successive recuts are unclear. The ditch does not obviously form a major boundary. Contemporaneous features that were similar to one another were present on either side of it. The ditch does, however, appear to lead to a natural routeway to the lower ground to the north-east of the site that was also exploited, apparently independently, during the 2nd to early 4th centuries. The field system was significantly altered around the conquest period (period 3aii). The rectilinear enclosures were replaced by a single sub-square enclosure that surrounded possibly two visible houses.

Pits may have fulfilled a number of functions including storage and ultimately refuse disposal in the Late Iron Age settlement as they had in the Early Iron Age (see Volume 1). Pit cluster 218 was located in one of the few locations on the western half of the excavation area where calcareous gravels were recorded. The relative lack of finds from this group indicates the pits were not used to discard refuse. This evidence, in conjunction with the geological location of the cluster, may suggest they were quarry pits for the extraction of the calcareous gravels. If they belonged to period 3ai, they would have been adjacent to the settlement area, but if they date from periods 3aii or 3aiii they would have been some way from the settlement.

The contents of pit 5818 should be considered against this backdrop. There were few notable concentrations of material culture or ABGs in these pits. Pit 5818, in contrast, stands out as it contained material in some quantity which related to the previous phases of occupation at Thame. The layers of Iron Age pottery of mixed dates in layers 5963 and 5943 must have been deliberately placed in the pit. They include substantial sherds dating to the Early, Middle/Late Iron Age, and smaller amounts of Neolithic and Early Roman pottery were also found in the pit. While material of Late Iron Age date may have been curated over the intervening decades, the Early Iron Age vessels must have been discovered in the Late Iron Age/Early Roman period. The fabrics are consistent with those found in Early Iron Age contexts on the site, and the vessels may have been discovered during the course of the construction of the later boundary ditches. The Neolithic pottery in pit 5818 may also have been discovered and deliberately deposited, although given the smaller sizes of the sherds it is more difficult to be certain.

The deliberate deposition of multiple older pots with Middle or Late Iron Age vessels (which themselves were either also discoveries or pots that had been circulating for perhaps over a century) demonstrates that a degree of value was placed on these already ancient artefacts. This practice of deliberately depositing ancient, discovered artefacts during the Roman period has been noted multiple times with regard to Bronze Age metalwork, most spectacularly at the temple site at Ashwell, Hertfordshire. There, numerous deposits of Bronze Age metalwork representing multiple discoveries of earlier material were made in the Early, Middle and possibly also Late Roman periods (Burleigh 2018, 159–62; Wilkin 2018). Other sites where this has been noted include Hengistbury Head, Dorset (Hingley 2009, 149), Wanborough, Surrey (O'Connell and Bird 1994), and Hayling Island, Hampshire, where earlier prehistoric flint as well as a Middle Bronze Age spearhead appear to have been deliberately deposited in the Late Iron Age (King and Soffe 1998, 41). The purposeful deposition of material in pits might be a continuation of this practice that was widespread in the Iron Age (see Volume 1). The deposits in pit 5818 sit within a tradition in the area but clearly incorporate new practices of recovery and curation of material.

The Early and Middle Roman period

The evidence for period 3b (*c*. AD 100–240) largely comprises landscape boundaries with a few pits as well as corndriers. The amount and type of cultural material within these features indicates that it was not far removed from a focus of settlement, although the location of this is not entirely clear.

The re-organisation of the site that took place in the latter decades of the 1st century AD (period 3aiii) was clearly influenced by the previous enclosure. The layout of the site was altered from a single consolidated settlement enclosure to a series of subdivided enclosures, one containing evidence for possible houses (structure 20 and the adjacent enclosure 214). Linear ditches were present outside of these enclosures, although how they relate to the wider structuring of the landscape is unclear, again partly due to the density of later ditches many of which directly recut predecessors, obscuring the exact layout during this phase. The area also became appropriate for burial; SK. 508 dates to this phase.

The Early Roman 2 (period 3bi) period witnessed the greatest level of archaeologically visible activity compared to any of the other Late Iron Age or Roman sub-periods. It produced the largest number of features, with cremation burials, and a significant pottery assemblage. The enclosure system developed further in the first half of the 2nd century (period 3bi), with occupation in this period being the most intensive. Activity expanded from the still reasonably consolidated set of subdivided enclosures in the previous phase to more clearly being part of a much wider enclosed landscape. Further elements of this landscape can be seen to the south and west on the surrounding geophysical survey, although some of this must belong to the later Roman period (Fig. 2.9). The axial east/west-aligned droveway extending across the whole of the excavated area was formalised with two additional forks leading to the north and south. A further droveway leading to the north-west was also developed. If the line of the east/

west droveway continued beyond the excavated area to the east, it would have crossed the Cuttle Brook at a known historical crossing point. The northern fork of the droveway led down to the River Thame floodplain, exploiting the natural coombe feature in the centre of the site. The southern fork of the droveway is known from the geophysical survey to have curved to the south-west.

The enclosed landscape that appears at its height to date to the first half of the 2nd century was clearly influenced by the prevailing topography. The trackway bounding the northern part of the enclosure system follows the *c.* 74m aOD contour line, representing the northern edge of a plateau where the rest of the system was located. To the north beyond this, the land slopes down to the Thame floodplain, with the enclosure system not appearing to be present in this area (JMHS 2014; Fig. 2.9).

The greater investment in the spatial structuring of settlement and agricultural activities is also evident in the construction of two stone-lined corndriers (25 and 24), an oven or possible corndrier (46) and a stone-lined well (23). The discovery of millstones at the site dating to the same period is possibly significant since these objects also indicate a degree of centralisation in the processing of arable products (Shaffrey 2015). As is discussed further below, the millstones indicate that the site was an important focus for the agricultural economy of the region with the objects suggesting an intensive level of processing, with grain from the surrounding area being made into flour to be redistributed. Millstones are rarely found prior to the 2nd century (Shaffrey 2015, 63), and these objects and the trackways possibly both indicate more centralisation and intensification of agricultural production from the 2nd century onwards.

The Middle Roman period

A significant decline in activity took place during the Roman period in the middle of the 2nd century (period 3bii; *c.* AD 150–240). Very little activity or cultural material can be dated to the Middle Roman period. However, the site was not abandoned. The major droveways established during the Early Roman 2 (period 3bi) period were recut in the Late Roman period, demonstrating that these were probably still in existence and in some use in the intervening century. The only contexts that produced ceramic material of certain Middle Roman date were the backfills of Early Roman 2 (period 3bi) features. Whilst it is possible that the site was genuinely abandoned between *c.* AD 150–240, and the recutting in the Late Roman period represented a reoccupation of the landscape and re-establishment of relict enclosures, the likelihood that the focus of activity simply shifted location outside of the excavated area, rather than the landscape being completely abandoned, is suggested by the remarkable continuity of the enclosure system between the Early and Late Roman periods, and a continued agricultural use is perhaps likely in the Middle Roman period.

The backfilling of a well was the only clear event belonging to the Middle Roman period. The incorporation of distinctive earlier sherds with an articulated dog in well 23 may have been deliberate. The well was backfilled in the first half of the 3rd century. The burial of a dog in both the middle or lower part of the shaft in addition to one at the top indicates that the well was still a remembered and recognised feature when it was almost entirely filled. The filling therefore may have taken place over a relatively restricted time period. Dog burials in Roman wells are a recurring feature (Roskams *et al.* 2013), and the examples from Thame may have been deposited deliberately to mark the termination of the well's use.

The Late Roman period

As outlined above, despite a clear reduction of activity and deposition during the Middle Roman period the landscape was probably not abandoned, demonstrating the continuity of use of the landscape during the period *c.* AD 150–240. While activity in the Late Roman period (period 3c, *c.* AD 240–410) was much more visible than it was in the Middle Roman period, activity was never as intensive as had been the early 2nd century. Most of the ditches belonging to the first Late Roman period, *c.* AD 240–325 (period 3ci), were direct recuts of those dating to the first half of the 2nd century. These again show the distinct influence of the prevailing topography, enclosing the plateau and providing ditched routeways to the Thame floodplain to the north and Cuttle Brook to the east. Again, there was no direct evidence for houses and settlement, although the quantity of material culture and the presence of at least one corndrier shows domestic and potentially small-scale industrial activity.

The Late Roman period (period 3cii), *c.* AD 325–350, marks a distinct decline in the use of the site. The eastern area appears to have been abandoned and a ditch cut off the western part from this area. The long-established northern route to the Thame floodplain and the eastern route to the Cuttle Brook appears also to have fallen into disuse. The ditches of the major east/west droveway remained but were significantly altered, in some places widening and in others blocking parts of the system. The northern trackway and western enclosure also continued in use. Many elements of this scheme were again re-established in the final Late Roman period (period 3ciii; *c.* AD 350–410) as elements of the ditch system were recut.

The site further developed in the last half of the 4th century, with activity defined by a series of larger adjacent enclosures again restricted to the western part of the site, recutting some elements of the earlier system with minor changes in the overall layout. The Late

Roman features were more specifically associated with controlling movement through the landscape rather than a wider range of types of activity represented by a larger number of enclosures in the Early Roman period. The latest dated material culture comprised pottery post-dating AD 350, and coins dated AD 364–78. While the coins in part reflect a wider chronological pattern of coin losses (McSloy, Chapter 3; Reece 1993, table 1; Walton 2015, fig. 3; 2022), the large number of Valentinianic issues (AD 364–78; ten out of 24 coins overall), is unusual and needs some additional explanation. These include examples from the evaluation, a subsoil find and one in a Saxon context, with the finds not appearing to be from a hoard. A peak in Valentinianic coins is a noted feature of Late Roman temple sites, and the assemblage from Thame might reflect a votive function of coins during this period on rural settlements (Walton 2015, 116–17), especially as one of them was perforated (McSloy, Chapter 3).

The development of Late Iron Age and Roman occupation at Thame in context

Transformations and continuities

Although there are strong elements of continuity between some of the periods of development at Thame, there were also a number of marked transformations. This section attempts to trace these developments, relate them to wider developments in the areas around Thame, and provide some account of their causes.

The character of the Late Iron Age (period 3ai, *c.* 25 BC–AD 50) occupation is poorly defined, and although the possible roundhouse might have lain within a field system, it could be characterised as open in the terms of Smith *et al.* (2016, 21–3). The subsequent simple enclosed settlement (period 3aii, *c.* AD 50–70) was more clearly defined, although the presence of a trackway in the south-east of the site does suggest that the wider landscape was partially enclosed.

The next striking transformation of the site is marked by the elaboration of this enclosure in period 3aiii (*c.* AD 70–100) into a subdivided complex farmstead (again in the terms of Smith *et al.* 2016, 28–33). This complex farmstead was further elaborated in the next phase (period 3bi, *c.* AD 100–150) which also provides the first indications of linear development (Smith *et al.* 2016, 32) along the trackway in the eastern part of the site. Otherwise, period 3bi does not appear to have marked a major change in the structure of the site, although as is discussed further below, it may have been associated with significant changes in the way in which the site was used. The next period (3bii, *c.* AD 150–240) seems to be characterised by a decline in activity on the site (as judged by the relative quantities of pottery). As noted above, the site may, nonetheless, have remained in use as agricultural land.

The basic structure of the landscape established in the Early Roman period appears to have persisted throughout most of the Late Roman period. This was, however, marked by a gradual simplification of the landscape – especially in the area of the subdivided complex farmstead in the west of the site in the first Late Roman period (3ci, *c.* AD 240–325) – and then in later periods (3cii, *c.* AD 325–350 and 3ciii, *c.* AD 350–410), a gradual contraction of the areas which were enclosed.

Despite the marked transformations of the site, from a simple enclosure in period 3aii to a subdivided complex farmstead in period 3aiii, and the apparent Middle Roman decline in period 3bii, there was considerable continuity in the organisation of the landscape. Although the Early Roman (period 3aii) enclosure did not obviously follow the alignment of the preceding Late Iron Age (period 3ai) boundaries, the trackway in the south-east of the site did follow the alignment of earlier boundaries. Furthermore, the northern and southern sides of the enclosure established boundaries which were followed (with modifications) throughout much of the rest of the Roman occupation of the site. In later phases (e.g., period 3bi; Fig. 2.8) these boundaries were followed by trackways, and it is possible that trackways, not so clearly marked by parallel ditches, were already present in period 3aii. By period 3aii the broad structure of the area which persisted throughout most of the Roman occupation at Thame – marked by the northern and southern edges of the enclosure (206) and the south-eastern trackway – had been established. The only major element of this structure which was not yet clearly marked was the east/west-aligned trackway in the eastern part of the site (marked by ditch 126 in period 3aiii and more clearly as a trackway in period 3bi), and the fact that even this boundary was marked by the end of the south-eastern trackway, suggests that it too may have been marked in an archaeologically invisible way in preceding periods.

The Late Iron Age to Early Roman transformation

It is tempting to see the shift from the Late Iron Age (period 3ai) to the Early Roman period (period 3aii), which involved the replacement of open settlement perhaps set within a field system by a single settlement enclosure, as a direct result of the threat posed by the conquest and a desire to live within a defended structure. The discovery of a spearhead in the enclosure ditch might support such an interpretation. However, because of the general scarcity of metalwork on settlements in this period, it is difficult to directly associate any such metalwork with specific activities or with the functions of features in this period. More generally, no assemblage of Iron Age metalwork can be seen as representative of the assemblage that was in use at the time, making it difficult to interpret differences between the finds from different sites with any confidence or to infer the function of sites and features from such finds. Very similar sub-square settlement enclosures in fact form a continuous tradition in the region from at least the Middle Iron Age (Davies 2018, 190–5). Late Iron Age examples are known at Barton Court Farm (Miles 1986, 4–8), and Bicester Fields Farm (Cromarty *et al.* 1999). These could also, of course, have been built in part for defensive purposes, but the linking of structures to specific historical events in such a period where so few events are known can only ever be highly speculative unless there is specific evidence in its favour.

The Late Iron Age to Early Roman period is one primarily of continuity on a rural site upon which the Roman conquest left very few marks which are perceptible in the archaeological record (Booth *et al.* 2007, 42–3). In more general terms, the development at Thame is similar to that on some other sites in the Upper Thames. The desire to live within enclosures can also be seen in social terms, as having been related to the use of enclosures to define communities which were physically separate from those who did not belong (Bowden and McOmish 1987; Sharples 2010, 295; Davies 2018, 174). This social interpretation is not incompatible with the use of the enclosure for defence.

Certain elements of the later sequence of development at Thame can also be paralleled more widely. The development of a simple enclosure into a more complex farmstead can, for example, be paralleled at sites such as Barton Court Farm (Miles 1986) and Great Western Park (Hayden *et al.* 2023; Davies *et al.* forthcoming) which, as is discussed further below, share other features with Thame.

The Middle Roman decline and transformation: from settlement to agricultural production

The Middle Roman (*c.* AD 150–240) decline in activity, in contrast, is one of the more unusual features of the sequence. Booth *et al.* (2007, 43–52) have noted a widespread dislocation in settlement, often marked by the abandonment of sites early in the 2nd century (*c.* AD 120–150), slightly earlier than, but perhaps related to the decline at Thame. A parallel for the decline can be found at Great Western Park, Didcot (Hayden *et al.* 2023) where both Early and Late Roman activity were better represented than Middle Roman. The sequence of development at Great Western Park was also notably similar to that at Thame, beginning with a Late Iron Age simple enclosure associated with a roundhouse, followed by the development of a more complex landscape, including both subdivision and linear development along trackways. These earlier phases can also be paralleled at Barton Court Farm (Miles 1986) where an enclosure developed into a more complex farmstead. At both of these two sites, the later phases of development were associated with villas. Both thus underwent a transformation from smaller scale activity, possibly centred on one or two domestic structures, to larger scale agricultural activities centred on and coordinated by villas. This transformation may help explain the developments at Thame, and the apparent decline in activity in the Middle Roman period in particular.

The Middle Roman decline at Thame is particularly striking because of the apparent continuity in the structure of the landscape. As noted above, it is possible that the area was temporarily abandoned and that when it was reoccupied in the Late Roman period enough of the preceding structure survived to be revived. It is, however, more plausible to think that the landscape remained in use, and that the apparent decline in activity, marked above all by more limited ceramic evidence, was related to a shift in the location of settlement away from the site, leading to reduced deposition.

This shift was broadly associated with changes in the kinds of structures on the site and its use for burial, both of which suggest a marked change in use. The most obvious is the disappearance of evidence for roundhouses and other possibly domestic structures. The Late Iron Age open settlement (period 3ai) was associated with a single penannular gully (structure 21) the diameter of which (7.5m) is consistent with it having been related to a roundhouse. The subsequent Early Roman enclosure settlement (period 3aii) contained a pair of features: a slightly larger (8.5m diameter) semicircular gully (19, perhaps the truncated remains of a penannular gully) and a square enclosure (213), 8m long, which could have been related to another structure or to a small animal pen. The same pairing recurs in the first phase (period 3aiii) of the succeeding complex farmstead. In this case the penannular gully (structure 20) was notably larger (11m diameter) but the square enclosure (214) was similar in size. In all three phases, the structures lay in roughly the same area.

No similar evidence is found in later phases which did, however, see the construction of corndriers. The first of these was constructed in period 3bi (*c.* AD 100–150), but further examples were constructed in period 3ci (*c.* AD 240–325) and period 3ciii (*c.* AD 350–410). The site thus appears to have changed from being a centre of small-scale settlement, presumably related to similarly small-scale agricultural production, perhaps largely supplying the settlement itself, to a site focused on perhaps more specialised agricultural production.

The interpretation of this contrast is, unfortunately, complicated in two ways which make this suggestion less certain than it might appear. It is, firstly, impossible to demonstrate that the penannular gullies were related to roundhouses. The later examples, in fact, only consist of semicircular gullies. It has been assumed that these were the truncated remains of penannular features, but it is possible that they were related to small animal pens or structures which were not used as houses. Since the gullies would have lain outside any associated roundhouses, the artefacts recovered from them need not have been related to the use of any such structures. Similar arguments could apply to the square enclosures. The character of any structures associated with the square enclosures is unclear, and their pairing with penannular gullies suggests, in fact, that the two were used in different ways. Secondly, many Roman structures, and houses in particular, may be archaeologically invisible. Booth *et al.* (2007, 35–6) suggest that cob, or a similar technique of mass-wall construction, may have been used which has left very little trace in the archaeological record. The absence of evidence for structures after period 3aiii does not, therefore, necessarily indicate an absence of occupation. If the quantities of ceramic evidence are used as an indication of settlement, the increasing quantities of pottery in the Late Roman period (period 3c) would suggest that the site was reoccupied then.

There are, however, further aspects of the evidence of Thame which indicate that a marked change in use occurred at roughly the transition between periods 3aiii and 3bi (*c.* AD 100). All of the burials date from before this point. The dating evidence for the burials is often limited, but the interpretation put forward above suggests that they occurred during period 3a (*c.* 25 BC–AD 100). Given that the later period (3bi) was much shorter than the earlier (3a) this might be taken to indicate an increase in the population over this period. This would be consistent with the development from a simple enclosure to a complex farmstead. The numbers of burials are, however, small, and the reasons why some individuals were buried on the site and others not, and for the differences in burial practices, are unknown. Although it is therefore difficult to make any inferences about population from the numbers of burials, their absence from the later phases is consistent with occupation having moved away from the site.

Equally, the appearance of fragments of millstones in periods 3b and 3c, suggesting the construction of a mill – possibly a watermill on the Thame or the Cuttle Brook – is consistent with a focus on agricultural production, and implies more specialisation in certain aspects of production than is likely to have existed in the earlier Roman period. As Shaffrey (2015, 65) argues, although fragments of millstone are likely to have been reused and might have been moved away from the location of the associated mill, they are not likely to have moved far.

Overall, the disappearance of domestic structures and the end of burial during the earlier phases contrast with the construction of corndriers and the evidence for the existence of a mill in the later phases. These changes suggest a shift from a small-scale, perhaps household-based, agricultural regime to a more intensive regime, perhaps based in some respects on coordination between groups larger than households.

This contrast does not coincide in a neat way with the wider development of the site. Although burial continued into period 3bi (albeit of cremation deposits not inhumations), the main transition can be placed between period 3aiii and 3bi (*c.* AD 100). The major transformation of the site – from a simple enclosed settlement to a complex farmstead – had occurred earlier, between period 3aii and 3aiii (*c.* AD 70). The transformation thus appears to have been gradual. Rather than being the result of the site having been abandoned, the apparent Middle Roman decline in activity which occurred in period 3bii (*c.* 150–240) could be better explained by the fact that settlement had shifted to another location, presumably not far away, but not within the limits of the excavation. This need not imply the existence of a villa, as at Great Western Park or Barton Court Farm. Although there is no obvious reason for their absence, no villas are known around Thame (Smith *et al.* 2016, fig. 5.19), and the pottery from Thame does not suggest the existence of a high-status site.

Late Roman agricultural intensification

The landscape associated with the enclosed Early Roman (period 3aii) settlement appears to have been quite open and suggests a relatively extensive agricultural regime (in the sense of van den Veen and O'Connor 1998, 128). The crop-drying ovens, the putative construction of a mill, and the increasingly complex structuring of the landscape – as the enclosure expanded and was subdivided and the linear development along the eastern trackway proceeded – suggest a much greater investment in agricultural 'capital' in the later Roman phases at Thame than in the preceding period. The general aim of such 'investment' is to increase productivity. In the case of Thame, much of this investment was related to the processing of crops and whilst it may have increased the output of certain products, it may not have had much effect on the overall agricultural yield of the site (except insofar as more productive crop processing released labour for other agricultural tasks). This suggests that the transformation of the site may have been related more to the demand for certain products than it was to the need to increase the supply of food for consumption on the site. It is more likely, in fact, that the equation between the increased productivity of some crop-processing tasks and overall agricultural production should be reversed. Rather than leading to increased arable production, efforts to increase the productivity of crop processing may have been made because arable production had been increased (Booth *et al.* 2007, 298).

Corndriers
The most obvious signs of such 'capital' investment are the corndriers. The way in which these structures were used has been debated (e.g., Allen *et al.* 2017, 57–61). On the basis of their experiments, Reynolds

and Langley (1979, 40–1) suggested that corndriers were not an efficient means of drying crops, especially given that they can be dried perfectly well in stacks. They might, though, have increased the productivity of malt production much more significantly since this would have been a much more labour-intensive process in the absence of large-scale ovens. It is equally possible that they were used to parch hulled grain before it was pounded. This latter process would help explain the common presence of chaff (glume bases) in corndriers (although chaff would also have been a by-product of malting; van der Veen 1989).

This late stage of processing is usually regarded as having been carried our piecemeal, as grain was required, at a household level (e.g., Stevens 2003, 64; Hillman 1984, 13). The possibility that it was carried out on a larger scale, in ovens, thus suggests that production was aimed at either a wider market or at recipients elsewhere (such as absentee owners if the site did form part of a villa estate; Allen *et al.* 2017, 61). The distribution of corndriers in Britain suggests that the presence of a market was a more important factor in their construction than the climate (as might be expected if their major role was in drying crops before storage). They were most common in Allen *et al.*'s (2017, 58, fig. 2.45) Central Belt (which includes Oxfordshire) and the South (where population was concentrated) than in wetter areas in the North and Central West – exactly the opposite of what might be expected if their role was related to the climate.

Usually only one or two corndriers have been found on sites in the Upper Thames (Booth *et al.* 2007, 291). Although the presence of five at Thame thus suggests a particularly high level of production, the figure needs to be assessed against the longevity of the site. This suggests that two ovens might have been in use at any one time and is comfortably exceeded by sites such as Great Western Park where larger numbers of ovens were found (albeit spread over a much larger area; Davies *et al.* forthcoming).

Mill
The probable presence of a mill has implications similar to the corndriers. Like the corndriers, it could have been involved in the production of both malt and flour (Shaffrey 2015, 70; Allen *et al.* 2017, 72). Allen *et al.* (2017, 72) found evidence for malting at a much higher proportion of sites with millstones (16%) than at those without (3%), although the overall proportion is still low. Whatever its precise use, a mill would have increased the productivity of flour production rather than of primary agriculture production, and thus like the corndriers may have been aimed at a wider market or recipients elsewhere. The presence of rotary querns alongside the millstones suggests that the production of flour for local use may have been carried out separately at a household level (Shaffrey 2015, 73; Allen *et al.* 2017, 72) and thus supports the idea that efforts to increase productivity were directed more to an external market than to increased local use. In contrast to the rotary querns, the millstone fragments suggest production on a large scale, implying a large enough market in which the flour could be used (given that flour will only keep for a few months).

This raises a series of questions concerning who the recipients of the flour were, who constructed the mill, and who benefitted from its operation. Given the costs of transport, the market or recipients are unlikely to have been very distant (cf however, Allen *et al.* 2017, 83). Obvious candidates are the towns at Dorchester (17km away as the crow flies) or Alchester (21km). It could also have been a less distant settlement, but many roadside settlements and villages were clearly also involved in such large-scale agricultural evidence.

The question of who constructed the mill and benefitted from its operation is more difficult to answer, but some clues are offered by the contexts in which millstones have been found. Although Shaffrey (2015, fig. 2) has shown that mills were much more widespread than had been thought, it is unlikely that they were very common. Allen *et al.* (2017, 72) found records of millstones on only 5% of the sites they examined. Amongst these sites, they were most common on roadside settlements (18% of sites), villages (16%) and villas (15%), although the figure for complex farmsteads (14%) is only just lower. Although it is noticeable that millstones were found at both Great Western Park (Hayden *et al.* 2023, 501) and Barton Court Farm (Miles 1986, microfiche 5A13) where they were associated with villas, it is, nonetheless, clear that they were not confined to villas where the estate owner would provide an obvious source of the 'capital' needed to construct the mill and an obvious recipient for any 'rent' generated. The capital needed may have been quite substantial, especially if it was a watermill (Wilson 2002, 12). Although not directly relevant to Thame, some idea of the cost is given by Diocletian's *Edict of maximum prices* (15.52–5) which gives the cost of a millstone for a watermill as 2000 denarii (Wilson 2002, 6, note 23). Even if the site at Thame did not form part of a villa estate, the most likely source of the capital for a mill is the local landed elite, presumably someone with wider interests in the area.

The structuring of the landscape
In contrast to the corndriers and mill, the last indications of intensification – the increasing scale and elaboration of the boundaries marked by ditches – is likely to have been more directly related to improving the productivity of primary agricultural production. In this respect the site developed in two ways. The first involves the subdivision of the area where the original Early Roman (period 3aii, *c.* AD 50–70) enclosure had been situated. This area was first elaborated into a subdivided enclosure in period 3aiii (*c.* AD 70–100), which was then further

enlarged, modified and elaborated in period 3bi (*c.* AD 100–150), before being simplified, and finally reverting to an open area in later phases. The second involves the linear development of enclosures along the east/west-aligned trackway on the eastern side of the site. This second development was marked most clearly in period 3bi (*c.* AD 100–150) but may have begun in period 3aii (*c.* AD 70–100), and in contrast to the area of the enclosure, was elaborated further in period 3ci (*c.* AD 240–325), after which this area was also left open.

The specific ways in which the areas defined by ditches were used is usually unclear. In the area of the original enclosure, the possibly domestic structures lay within an enclosure in an area that appears to have been the location of such structures from the Late Iron Age (period 3ai, *c.* 25 BC–AD 50) to period 3aiii (*c.* AD 70–100). In the Early Roman phases, this area was surrounded by some of the smallest enclosures at Thame, and it seems likely that this area would have had the character of a farmyard, presumably used in a variety of ways, perhaps for milking, temporarily keeping animals, and for processing and storing agricultural produce. The earliest corndriers were situated in this area, suggesting that in later phases, these enclosures were used for crop processing. A similar range of activities were probably also carried out in the simple Early Roman (period 3aii, *c.* AD 50–70) enclosure where they were centred on the domestic structures. The subsequent enlargement and subdivision of the area reflects the greater scale of production and the resulting need to organise it into more discrete, specialised processes, more akin to a production-line.

In contrast, the enclosures established in a linear fashion along the east/west-aligned trackway are more likely to have been used as fields, which can be more obviously related to increases in productivity. As well as potentially improving drainage and providing shelter, both of which might have increased crop yields, such enclosures would have decreased the labour needed to manage livestock, would have facilitated the management of pasture, and allowed animals to be folded overnight, thus allowing the distribution of manure to be managed.

If the corndriers and mill did involve surplus produce, transport would also have been an important consideration. The subdivided enclosure at Thame lay in an area where trackways leading in various directions converged. It would thus have been well placed to receive the produce of the surrounding areas. The trackways would also have facilitated the movement of livestock and were presumably also used to transport the produce to the wider marker. The closest Roman road, which ran from Dorchester-on-Thames to *Magiovinium*, lay on the other side of the Thame (Viatores 1964, road no. 173).

The post-Roman and Saxon period
by Chris Ellis

The earliest activity that can be assigned to this period was represented by two inhumation burials which were associated with the final phases of the Roman land division. Taking into account the inexactitude of the dating, provided mainly from the pottery, there may have then been a hiatus before a settlement which comprised 13 sunken-featured buildings was established. After what appears to have been a further gap, a sequence of ovens to the west of the settlement suggest that the area was again used for agricultural processing. These may have just pre-dated, or overlapped with, an enclosure which was created in the Late Saxon period.

The post-Roman period

During the immediate post-Roman period it appears that the area was used for burial, reviving a practice from the earlier Roman period, but given the passage of time, unlikely to be directly associated with it.

The two adult graves, situated in an area covered by Late Roman field ditches in the eastern part of the site, were shallow and the skeletons fragmentary and in poor condition, but both were observably extended, supine burials. SK. 1501 (grave 16417; Figs 4.1–4.2), was accompanied by an iron firesteel with 7th-century comparanda, an iron pin fragment comparable to 6th-century examples and an iron knife with 5th to 7th/8th-century AD comparisons. A radiocarbon date, modelled as *cal AD 420–560* (Table 1.1) confirms a 5th or 6th-century date. SK. 1502 (grave 16629; Figs 4.1–4.2) was accompanied by a fragmentary pin of a type seen at Dover Buckland (Evison 1987, 84), either as a grave good or as part of the clothing. In this case a radiocarbon date was also modelled as *cal AD 420–560* (Table 1.1), with which the pin would be compatible.

In the case of SK. 1502, during excavation the burial appeared to be truncated by Late Roman (period 3ci) ditch 132. This raises the prospect that the Late Roman ditches may in fact have continued in use into the post-Roman period. It is possible that the pottery which they contained was all effectively residual. However, it must be noted that the remaining cut of grave 16629 was only 0.05m deep, and the relationships difficult to interpret. It seems more likely that the burial was positioned to mark a point in the Late Roman field system which was most likely out of use but still perhaps discernible during the immediate post-Roman period. Nevertheless, there is an indication that there may have been little chronological break between the Roman fields becoming disused and the use of the area for burial.

These two apparently isolated interments fit with a pattern of single burials or burial artefacts (Dickinson 1976; Blair 2018; Hamerow *et al.* 2013) across the region. Continuity or reuse of Late Roman sites is known elsewhere. At Barton Court Farm villa (Miles

1986) and Yarnton (Hey 2004) mid to late 5th-century evidence overlaid Late Roman occupation. However, there are few burials or settlements of this date in the immediate vicinity of the Thame site, with the main distributions especially in the Abingdon to Dorchester-on-Thames part of the Upper Thames Valley (Figs 6.1–6.2). Aside from Saxon pottery recorded from Crendon Industrial Estate about 2.5km to the north-east (JMHS 2014, fig. 16), there is no evidence of occupation close to Thame. This therefore is an important addition to our understanding of activity of this early date in this part of the Thames catchment.

The Early–Mid Saxon settlement

The most substantial activity of this period comprised a settlement made up of 13 sunken-featured buildings, arranged in a loose scatter across the western part of the site. It is possible that the area of occupation was more extensive; pottery of Saxon date also came from evaluation trenches to the south and west of the excavation area (OCA 2016; Fig. 4.1 inset). It should also be noted that charred grain from the ditch of a Neolithic penannular feature gave a radiocarbon date of cal AD 720–960 (SUERC-69143; see Volume 1). While this was clearly intrusive within the prehistoric feature, it suggests that there was also activity to the north of the area of the SFBs and fits with a widespread practice of revisiting earlier monuments. It is perhaps significant that the structures were some distance away from the two post-Roman burials described above. Radiocarbon determinations from four SFBs suggest a later 6th/early 7th-century AD beginning to occupation (Table 1.1), with the activity estimated to have begun in *cal AD 580–650 (95% probability)*, with the latest use of the SFBs modelled at *cal AD 650–780 (81% probability)* (Griffiths, Chapter 4; Fig. 4.10). The chronology of the pottery of the region is still poorly understood and could in general only be assigned to the Early–Mid Saxon period. However, there are components of the assemblage which strongly suggest a 6th-century element, with some aspects possibly as early as the 5th century (see Booth, Chapter 5) so the settlement activity may have commenced slightly earlier than suggested by the radiocarbon dates (although these dates do assist with clarifying the regional position). However, taken on their own, the modelling of the radiocarbon dates suggests that the inhumation burials pre-dated the commencement of the earliest SFB by up to one hundred years. Nevertheless, it remains unclear whether there was continuity or a hiatus between the burials and the establishment of the settlement.

In general, the Thame SFBs are relatively standard examples of a widespread type (cf Tipper 2004). The structures were square or more typically sub-rectangular in plan with rounded corners and were between 3.1 and 5.68m long, 2–4m in width and 0.2–0.72m deep, with vertical or near-vertical sides and a flattish base. The majority were around a very typical 4m by 3m; the possibility of chronological differences between the buildings of different sizes has not been teased out (cf Hamerow 2012, 54). As noted in Chapter 4, most of the SFBs were two-post structural types classed as 'A' or 'A1' by West (1985). This was supplemented by a single example of a possible four-posted, 'Class C' SFB pit structure (structure 42, cf West 1985). A single SFB, structure 36, is analogous to a 'wall-post type' (cf Ahrens' 1966), while structure 30 had a 'shelf' around the southern long side of the pit, comparable examples of which have been recorded by Tipper (2004).

Their fills all contained finds in varying degrees of abundance and diversity. The limited number of fills in the Thame SFBs also follows a widespread pattern for these structures (Tipper 2004, 99–111). These are generally interpreted as 'primary' fills associated with the use-life of the building, and 'secondary' fills derived from the deliberate deposition of material into the demolished/disused structure. This may derive from waste material from nearby settlement, as well as possible 'special deposits' (Hamerow 2006; Morris and Jervis 2011; Semple 2013, 77–84). Finally, 'tertiary fills' are derived from elsewhere within the settlement context. These can give important information regarding macro-scale occupation activities but less so regarding intra-site spatial patterning. However, the 'tertiary' fills are probably derived from midden deposits containing material which may well have had a very complex pre-depositional history of use, reuse and attrition (Foreman *et al.* 2002, 62 and fig. 5.3). Tipper has argued that this broad-brush stratigraphic sequence recorded for many SFBs may be a post-depositional, geoarchaeological process and that backfilling may have been a single stratigraphic event, or the material was derived from the same source (Tipper 2004, 107). However, as Hamerow explains (2012, 61), there are examples where it is clear that the fills within SFB pits are very evidently derived from the immediate vicinity (i.e., where it is possible to demonstrate that human remains come from an earlier burial disturbed by construction). The Thame SFBs with their indications of a high degree of residuality and redeposition of Neolithic and Iron Age pottery (in some cases significantly outnumbering the Early or Mid Saxon pottery) support this tendency, and it seems likely that the SFB pits were backfilled at least in part with material that had been disturbed during their construction, with the addition of contemporary refuse. This of course introduces problems with interpreting the faunal remains and other non-inherently datable materials from within the SFBs.

Many of the SFB fills recorded at Thame appear to represent post-structure 'secondary' deposits following the disuse and dismantling of the SFB and the subsequent reuse of the pit as a convenient feature for settlement waste from continuing occupation. Only five SFBs at

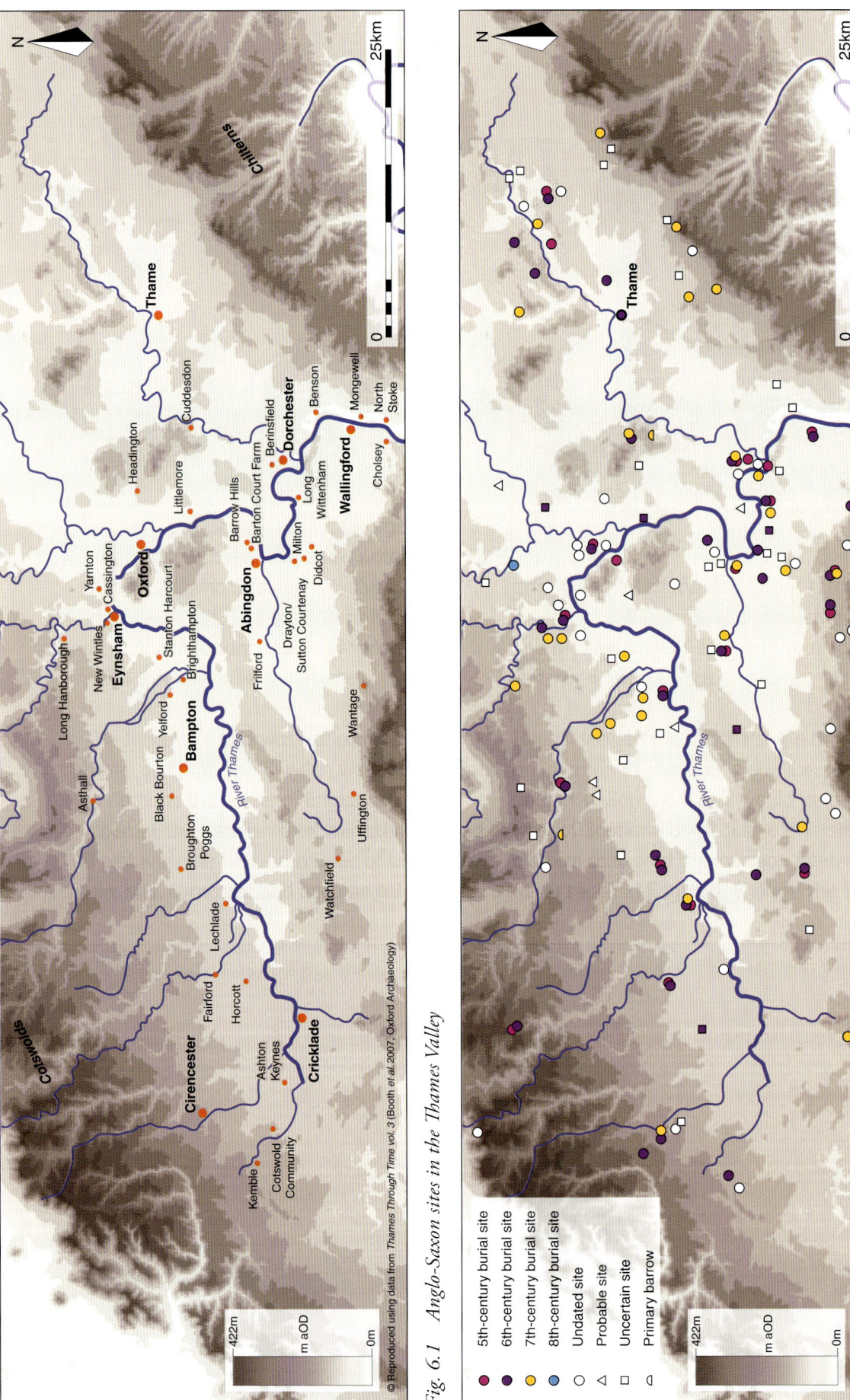

Fig. 6.1 Anglo-Saxon sites in the Thames Valley

Fig. 6.2 Early Anglo-Saxon cemeteries in the Upper Thames Valley

Thame contained greater than two fills (structures 30, 33, 37, 38, 39) with the greatest number of fills (five) recorded from structure 30, one of the deeper SFB pits (0.54m). The SFB pit fills were characterised by relatively dark deposits, possibly reflecting the organic-rich discarded settlement waste, while the finds probably comprised material from the disuse of the SFB as well as a possible component from the structure's life-use.

The SFB assemblages included Early/Mid Saxon (and residual Late Iron Age/Romano-British) pottery, animal bone, fired clay loomweights, quernstone fragments, fired clay lumps, spindle whorls, iron and copper alloy artefacts (including residual 4th-century coins), burnt flint and a small assemblage of residual worked flint and residual Roman roof tile (in structures 30, 33 and 37). Some of the SFBs were relatively finds-rich (structures 30, 32, 33, 35) whilst two SFBs (structures 31, 39) contained no Saxon pottery at all. The proportion of Saxon material of the pottery assemblage from each structure varied widely, from 1.7% (structure 40) to 91.3% (structure 34). In fact, most of the pottery from the SFB pits was residual Late Iron Age and Romano-British material, presumably largely a function of the density of earlier features in this part of the site rather than anything intentional.

Aside from pottery, the largest component of the assemblages comprised animal bone, with a maximum of 8520g (structure 33) and between 2000–5000g (structures 31, 32, 35, 41, 42). As usual with Early to Mid Saxon assemblages (Banham and Faith 2014, 75–10) they mainly comprised cattle and sheep/goat, along with pig and smaller amounts of horse, dog, cat as well as domesticated fowl and a few goose and duck bones. The plant remains suggest the growing of predominantly barley, but also hulled wheat, free-threshing wheat, and rye, as well as beans and peas. The evidence also points to the exploitation of the heavier, clayey soils of the Thame Valley as well as the lighter, drier soils of the higher ground, as part of a mixed arable/pastoral economy. Quernstone fragments in two of the SFBs (structures 36, 39) are inconclusive indicators of the buildings' function although they may have provided ancillary agricultural/settlement storage (cf Hamerow 2012, 60–4). However, the plant remains did not occur in sufficient quantities to indicate crop storage or processing. The presence of sedge and rush, along with the wildfowl, points to exploitation of nearby wild riverside flora and fauna.

Several of the SFBs provided indications as to their above ground construction or interior features. Structure 36 was slightly different in plan to the other buildings, having an outward bowing to the long sides of the 4m by 3m structure. Within the SFB pit were numerous stakeholes, one set of which ran along the north side following the bowing of the north pit edge, suggesting contemporaneity. The group on the south side seem more likely to relate to some internal structure.

Stakeholes have been recorded from a number of SFB pit bases, particularly pit edges and have been interpreted as possible revetments for the pit sides (Hamerow 1993) although Tipper (2004, 87–8) dismisses all recorded examples as being incorrectly identified bioturbation features. This is highly unlikely to be true, and clear examples with stakeholes within the building but no adjacent evidence of disturbance (e.g., Riverdene, Hants; Hall-Torrance and Weaver 2003), supports the view that stakeholes with a clear relationship to the original structure can be present. The stakeholes could be interpreted as a supporting structure for the pit walls or constituting evidence of wattle and daub walls to the SFB (cf Tipper 2004, 87). This is pertinent in relation to the evidence from structure 35 which is explored below. Another interpretation is that they may represent stakehole supports for a suspended floor as proposed for most SFBs (Tipper 2004, 84) and as recorded for Marlowe Car Park, Canterbury, Structure 10 (Blockley *et al.* 1995, 349), although a gravel metalling surface in the base of the SFB pit would suggest this is not the case. Clay or chalk 'floors' in SFB pit bases have been recorded at Upton, Northants (Jackson *et al.* 1969, 206–10), Yeavering, Northumberland (Hope-Taylor 1977, 103–5), Mucking, Essex (Hamerow 1993, 11) and Canterbury (Blockley *et al.* 1995), which suggests that this was a regular occurrence.

In a few examples (structures 32, 33, and 35), the finds indicate their use for textile manufacture or the storage of textile-related equipment. The concentrations of loomweights in several of the SFBs, particularly structures 33 and 35, suggest that textile production was an important element of settlement activity. This may link to the relatively high abundance of sheep/goat within the faunal assemblage. Concentrations of fired clay loomweights commonly occur in excavated SFBs, and the caching of loomweights has been used to interpret SFBs as ancillary storage or textile production structures (Tipper 2004, 168; Hamerow 2012, 63). Both linear and aggregated concentrations are well-known aspects of the spatial patterning of fired clay loomweights (Tipper 2004). Alignments of loomweights can be interpreted as indicating the position of the vertical loom from which they are thought to have been cut during the dismantling of the loom and SFB structural timbers for reuse elsewhere (Hamerow 2012, 62). Others interpret alignments of loomweights as possible storage on long wooden rods or placed on shelves (Tipper 2004, 167). On the other hand, deposition of loomweights in SFBs has been interpreted as possibly some sort of ritually significant 'closure' deposit (Gibson and Murray 2003, 210–11).

Internal features such as 'seats' or postholes for loom frames have been proposed for Bourton-on-the-Water (Tipper 2004) or Upton (Jackson *et al.* 1969), although Tipper (2004, 169–70) argues that the form of upright looms that could have been used in some SFBs would not require these features. However, this sort of requirement may explain an elongated pit, parallel with the north-eastern, long, side of the SFB pit of structure 33, which was cut into the mudstone bedrock and obviously an integral part of the construction and function of the SFB (Fig. 4.3). The initial fill of both the elongated pit and the SFB pit was identified in excavation as probably resulting from trampling. Also, in this case the loomweight distribution clearly shows a marked elongated concentration within or close to the elongated pit indicating a possible functional association. Lastly, a mudstone block was placed upon the trample layer in the base of the SFB pit, positioned on the edge of the elongated pit. These relationships strongly indicate a functional association related to textile production and *contra* Tipper, suggest that in certain circumstances structural embellishments were made to incorporate a loom within the SFB, as with German examples (Hamerow 2002).

Structure 35, which also contained a substantial group of loomweights, provided some significant information about the construction. This SFB contained a concentration of carbonised wood, whilst the loomweights in the deposit showed signs of burning/baking, and the fill itself was in places scorched. Discernibly lying across the SFB pit, the charred timbers appear to relate to the superstructure, rather than a collapsed floor, whilst a charred wattling fragment may have related to the infilling of the wall, roof or an interior structure. The long transverse timbers were of beech wood, and whilst not usual for construction due to its lack of weather resistance, it is strong and would be suitable for the interior of a roof (see Meen, Chapter 5). A sawn-off section of an ash post was recovered from close to an internal posthole. It is possible that it was the charred remains of a post which already had been extracted from the posthole, suggesting that the building was dismantled prior to burning. The woods represented aside from ash and beech included elm and blackthorn, representing a degree of diversity of materials, and probably reflecting the availability in nearby woodlands as much as structural choices.

Structure 35 is one of the few examples of an SFB that has been subject to partial or full burning, such as Yeavering (Hope-Taylor 1977, fig. 37), Upton (Jackson *et al.* 1969) and West Stow (West 1985). However, the number of charred timbers preserved in the structure 35 pit is far less than one would expect for a single, intact building, when compared to the quantity of timber used in SFB reconstructions where the frame timber alone weighed 4.8 tonnes (Tipper 2012, 28). The 17 carbonised timber components from structure 35 clearly represent a fraction of the original building. Other material from the fill suggests that after the burning the pit was used, as many of the others on the site were, for the deposition of a variety of refuse, although structure 35 contained a substantial faunal assemblage. Notably, there was a lack of burnt bone in this material indicating that its deposition was a separate event. It seems, however, that the two large groups of loomweights were probably in the building at the time the burning took place due to their location on the base of the pit and the variable scorching to which they had been subjected. However, it is possible that some of them could have been placed in the building afterwards, as at Cardinal Park, Godmanchester (Gibson and Murray 2003).

As with a majority of Early Saxon settlements, and few Mid Saxon examples (Reynolds 2003; Hamerow 2012), the settlement at Thame displayed limited evidence of a planned layout. However, the SFBs, whilst not all contemporary, are quite regularly spaced at about 15–30m apart, as recorded at Hurst Park in the Middle Thames Valley (Andrews 1996). Regarding the cluster of buildings in the western part of the excavation and taking into account that there may have been further contemporary activity to the south and west as mentioned above, there appears to have been an area about 65m in diameter area which contained no buildings, and which the SFBs in this area surround. This sub-circular, 'central' zone may have been an open, possibly communal area; it is possible that there were contemporary post-built structures subsequently removed by truncation, but this is speculative. The series of ditches or gullies to the north-west of the area covered by the SFBs is somewhat enigmatic, particularly as they do not appear to describe or enclose a definable area, other than having a broad relationship with SFB structure 32, which they might be regarded as surrounding. Their longevity, being reconstituted four or five times during the same period as the occupation of the SFBs does however suggest that they had lasting purpose and significance.

For Early Saxon settlements, spatial structuring through ditched or fenced areas is rare (Booth *et al.* 2007, 83), and paddocks, enclosures, and droveways are recorded from the 7th century onwards (Reynolds 2003, 104; Hamerow 2012, 98–9). An example of division of Early Saxon date occurred at Hurst Park, Surrey (Andrews 1996) and some spatial divisions occur on Middle Saxon sites of the Middle and Upper Thames Valley. Examples dating to the 7th century have been recorded at the North Site of New Wintles, Eynsham (Hawkes 1986). The practical management of the various livestock within the settlement is likely to have required segregation of functionally distinct areas. However, this could have been accomplished with relatively ephemeral hurdle fencing, with which to protect livestock, settlement structures and horticultural/agricultural crops, but which has left no archaeological traces. At Thame, the proximity of SFB structure 32 and other contemporary features may indicate a functional or social association. Alternatively, the ditch/gully features may be components of a rectilinear settlement pattern (Reynolds 2003, 119) which is otherwise beyond the limits of the present excavation to the west. However, given the limited understanding of the chronology it is difficult to consider which elements of settlement and land division existed alongside each other and how they functioned.

The Late Saxon settlement

The Late Saxon occupation consists of a series of 'ovens' and an incomplete sub-rectangular enclosure. Both were located broadly within the area which had been covered by the earlier Saxon settlement. The dating suggests that whilst the series of ovens and the fills of the enclosure ditch may have been contemporary, the ovens may have been slightly earlier, although the date of the cutting of the enclosure ditch has not been established. Oven 3 has been modelled as being in use *cal AD 860–1000 (90% probability)* whilst the enclosure ditch has been modelled as being in existence *cal AD 990–1050 (88% probability)* (Griffths, Chapter 4).

The sequence of ovens, 1–4, provides an insight into the Late Saxon settlement in the area and its economy. Similar Saxon sub-circular ovens have been found within 'kitchen' structures (Wade-Martins 1980) as well as free-standing (Moffett 1994). No structural features were associated with the Thame ovens apart from ephemeral post and hurdling fencing. The spatial and stratigraphic position of the postholes associated with the group of ovens, with at least some earlier than oven 2, would suggest they are associated with oven 1 and may represent a relatively minor hurdle windbreak for the oven, repeatedly re-erected/rebuilt in slightly differing positions during its use-life. However, the stakeholes could possibly represent remnants of earlier ovens' superstructural 'sails' which otherwise have no record. Although the lack of wattling 'sails' of the surviving oven structures piercing below the level of the respective oven foundation cuts might negate this interpretation, it seems that a relatively ephemeral hurdle windbreak associated with oven 1 is the most plausible interpretation of the available evidence. The unfired and differentially-fired clay from superstructural elements, as well as the partial baking of the surface on which the ovens stood, suggests that the temperature of the ovens was not particularly intense. This would be consistent with their use in malting and drying grain which require only a gentle heat. Experimental work (Moffett 1994, 61) and archaeological evidence (Wade-Martins 1980, 72) has demonstrated that unfired and unaffected superstructure clay can survive from both malting and drying structures.

The archaeobotanical evidence from the Thame ovens points to the processing of cereal crops, particularly barley and free-threshing wheat, in conjunction with other crops which might suggest the drying of a maslin. Other deposits show levels of germination which would indicate malting and brewing, so these appear to have been multi-purpose ovens (see Wyles, Chapter 5). The Thame ovens are smaller than the malting oven seen at Higham Ferrers, Northants, which contained sprouted barley (Hardy *et al.* 2007) but the reconstruction on the same spot may have masked this to an extent. The relatively high percentage of germinated grain is comparable with proportions (30%) noted for the ovens at West Cotton and Raunds, Northants (Campbell 1994, 69), and suggests a similar, combined malting and drying function for the Thame ovens. Similarly-sized Late Saxon ovens recorded at Stafford, Staffordshire, were thought too small to be for drying a whole year's harvest and were interpreted as serving a large establishment such as a high-status residence or a military or religious community, rather than just a single household (Moffett 1994, 61–2).

The location of the partial enclosure is interesting – it not only occupies the 'blank' area amongst the SFBs but appears to reference a Neolithic ring ditch (which had some indications of an internal bank or a mound) in the location and form of its north-western corner. This implies that this feature was still visible during this period, and indeed during the preceding one, which may explain the 'gap' between the earlier buildings. There are many regional sites where Saxon settlement and burial have been associated with prehistoric monuments such as recorded at Stanton Harcourt, Barrow Hills, Radley and Sutton Courtenay (Semple 2013). If this area had been of significance in the earlier settlement, either because it contained post-built buildings now lost or it was a communal space, incorporating the mound, the partial enclosure might be seen as formalising this space in the Late Saxon period. This would be intriguing given that the dating suggests a hiatus of up to three hundred years between the existence of the SFBs and the enclosure, although it may have been considerably less than this. The datable material and radiocarbon dates from the fills indicate that the enclosure ditch was filling between the 10th and 12th centuries.

The function of this enclosure is also largely obscure, especially as the ovens lay outside it, although this may have been a practical consideration, separating a high temperature activity from whatever went on within the enclosure. If this was domestic, and any structures were ephemeral, there may be an echo from the function of the ditches and gullies in the previous period which appear to have encompassed the SFB structure 32. The 10th–12th-century lead-alloy disc brooch (Ra. 511) found to the south of the ovens suggests the presence of people of a degree of means. The size of the Thame enclosure at approximately 50m by 25m fits examples of other Late Saxon enclosures less than 60m across, which have been shown to contain manorial accommodation (Reynolds 2003, 110), but the Thame example lacks both evidence of buildings or proximity to an early church. Whilst no contemporary structures were recorded within the Thame Late Saxon enclosure, the scale of investment of the enclosure's construction and number of ovens (if broadly contemporary) might suggest the occupation of a larger or higher status group beyond that of a single farming household. However, the apparent multiple function of the ovens and the length of time over which they may have been in use may argue against this.

The articulated dog skeleton in the Late Saxon enclosure ditch raises questions around the meaning of this type of deposit on a site of this date. The presence of 'special deposits' within Saxon settlement contexts has been widely recorded (Hamerow 2006; Morris and Jervis 2011) for both the pre- and post-conversion periods and points to continued informal ritual practices despite probable church prohibitions. Although dog remains make up 19% of 'placed deposits' from Saxon settlements, they comprise a disproportionate number in comparison to the faunal assemblages overall (Hamerow 2006, 8), a well-established pattern recognised in deposits from the Iron Age onward (Hill 1995; Grant 1984; Wait 1985). Hill suggested that the degree of domestication/training and socialisation of horses and dogs within their communities affected their treatment (Hill 1995, 107–8). The study of 'special deposits' in Saxon settlements undertaken by Hamerow (2006) recorded 42 deposits. However, only two at Friars Oak, West Sussex (Butler 2000) were comparable in date to the dog burial at Thame. Whilst dog burials occur frequently as part of closure deposits in SFBs during the Early and Mid Saxon period, in the Late Saxon period this shifts to pits and ditches, albeit often in an urban context. The practice however continues into the medieval period (Holmes 2018, 191). The status of the dog in life, either working or purely as a companion remains obscure, but this is an example of a widespread treatment. The deposition of this animal in the ditch may have been one of practicality, careful burial of a companion animal, or an echo of the practices of the past, marking the boundary.

The Saxon settlements in context

The Thame site is significant in that it demonstrates the capacity for sites along the Thames Valley and its tributaries to contain previously unrecorded settlements of this period. Dickinson's research (1976) on the distributions of Saxon cemeteries and burials and Benson and Miles' research on aerial photographic evidence from the Thames Valley (1974) both showed that extensive Saxon settlement and cemeteries were present in the Upper Thames Valley by the 6th century. The latter research highlighted numerous settlement sites from cropmarks and so presciently cautioned that we should anticipate Saxon occupation throughout the Upper Thames Valley, even where Saxon evidence was currently lacking, and as has been demonstrated at Thame.

In the later Mid Saxon period Thame lay on the frontier of the competing kingdoms of Mercia and Wessex. The regional lands of the earlier *Gewisse* had become divided into several Mercian-controlled provinces following Mercian success and expansion under first Penda and then Wulfhere. The Bishopric of Dorchester-on-Thames was re-established by Wulfhere between AD 675 and 685, with extensive estates granted to the Bishopric which included Thame as an episcopalian vill. Thame is known to have had an episcopal residence, perhaps within the prebendal enclosure, as Bishop Oscytel died at the residence at Thame in AD 971 (Garmonsway 1953, 119). The region during the 7th century also saw the establishment and expanding influence, both ecclesiastical, political and commercial, of minster churches and their communities, which were to have a dramatic effect on the patterns of occupation and trade across the region.

It was within this wider historical context that the Early to Mid Saxon occupation of the site at Oxford Road occurred. As is generally encountered elsewhere for the early 7th century, the settlement at Thame was relatively unstructured, whilst the buildings are largely typical of the period and region, albeit adding some useful detail with respect to their construction and use. The faunal assemblage clearly shows a typical mixed farming economy (cf Banham and Faith 2014), with mainly cattle and sheep/goat, supplemented with domestic and wild fowl. The arable economy is also fairly typical with cereals including barley, hulled and free-threshing wheat and rye cultivated and Celtic beans and peas grown. The reasonably diverse wood suggests exploitation of mixed deciduous woodland but hints at the beginnings of the association of the Chilterns and their hinterland with beech woods; wood was clearly managed for harvesting.

The typicality of these various aspects of the Thame settlement and the later Saxon occupation is difficult to consider in its local context as there is little contemporary evidence in the immediate area. This is probably due to the relative lack of modern development and archaeological investigation in the area to date rather than a genuine lack of settlement. Only a few small-scale watching briefs and evaluations (JMHS 2014; TVAS 1994; 1995; 1997; 2001) and the Church Farm excavations (TVAS 2012) to the north-east of the town have been carried out.

This also means that it remains unclear what relationships the Early to Mid Saxon occupants of the Oxford Road site would have had within the regional power-politics from the 7th century onwards. Thame itself, from historical sources, was a centre of growing political and commercial importance, as a strategically-placed religious centre and episcopalian vill. Although on lower ground, the Priestend area of 'Old Thame' directly overlooks the River Thame and its crossing with the junction of London–Oxford road (Thame High Street) and Aylesbury/Quarrendon–Dorchester-on-

Thames roads. It is also positioned on the north-western edge of the north-west/south-east-aligned gravel ridge that 'New Thame' was eventually built upon. This area and the minster church would have had a commanding position over the river crossing and commercial traffic moving east/west or north/south.

By the early 10th century, the kingdom of Wessex expanded back into areas north of the Thames and Midlands previously held by the Mercians, or from the later 9th century by the Vikings. The Wessex expansion led to the construction of a number of defensive *burhs* along the Thames Valley at Cookham, Wallingford, Oxford and Cricklade (Booth *et al.* 2007, 396). By the 11th century Thame was a location of considerable importance (Blair 1988) and this might suggest similar significance in earlier centuries. It was within this milieu that the Thame Late Saxon settlement with its enclosure and ovens came into being. Whilst the evidence is limited, the Thame enclosure might have supported an arrangement greater than a single domestic household, with the processing of arable crops and possible beer production. It may have been part of a pattern of contemporary holdings which may have supported a wider ecclesiastical or other series of estates in the region.

The Late Saxon settlement completed a period of around five thousand years of use of the land at Thame. It is therefore interesting to ponder whether one of the final phases of activity on the site was actually influenced by one of the first. The possible association of the Late Saxon enclosure with the Neolithic ring ditch indicates how the actions of the earliest inhabitants ultimately affected the choices of the last. As with the dog burial from the enclosure ditch, the motivations and dispositions of the individuals constructing the enclosure are unknowable, and we are left wondering, as for the earliest prehistoric archaeology, what comprises a secular act, or whether concepts of memory, genealogy, land ownership and territoriality (cf Semple 2013, 99) were still exerting their influence in the early medieval period.

Appendix
Methods Employed in Analysis

Radiocarbon dates methodology
by Seren Griffiths and Alex Davies

Thirty-two radiocarbon measurements in total were produced as part of this project on short-life samples from the Neolithic monuments and post-Roman features. A further seven dates were obtained from Iron Age and post-Roman burials by Prof. Ian Armit as part of a project to investigate aDNA (Reich *et al.* in prep.) which was funded by the European Research Council (ERC) under the European Union's Horizon 2020 research and innovation programme under grant agreement No. 834087. An eighth sample taken as part that project failed to produce a date due to insufficient carbon. The dates from the Neolithic and post-Roman features were modelled by Seren Griffiths; the Iron Age dates by Alex Davies.

Samples from Neolithic and post-Roman features were selected in order to try and understand the use-life of these features, though in some cases small ecofactual assemblages meant that there were possibilities that samples could represent residual or intrusive materials. A couple of results appear to represent later activity that has become incorporated into the fills of features that morphologically were expected to be significantly earlier.

Samples were pre-treated, graphitised and measured by accelerator mass spectrometry at the Scottish Universities Environmental Research Centre (SUERC) Radiocarbon Laboratory according to the method outlined in Dunbar *et al.* (2016). The results are conventional radiocarbon ages (Stuiver and Polach 1977), quoted according to the international standard set at the Trondheim Convention (Stuiver and Kra 1986). The results have been calibrated using IntCal13 (Reimer *et al.* 2013), and OxCal v4.3 (Bronk Ramsey 1995; 1998; 2001; 2009) for the Neolithic dates and using IntCal20 (Reimer *et al.* 2020) for the post-Roman and Iron Age dates. The date ranges (Table 1.1) have been calculated using the maximum intercept method (Stuiver and Reimer 1986), and have the endpoints rounded outward to 10 years. The probability distributions shown in the figures were obtained by the probability method (Stuiver and Reimer 1993). In this volume radiocarbon dates are quoted to the 2-sigma calibrated range (95.4%) unless otherwise stated.

Fired clay methodology
by Cynthia Poole

Fired clay was recorded by context, form, fabric, fragment count, weight, condition, size, impressions, a general description and where possible a spot date. This was recorded into an Excel spreadsheet catalogue which is available in the archive. Dating fired clay is only possible in relation to certain diagnostic forms which can be assigned to broad periods, whilst non-diagnostic material can show little variation in form and character throughout the time fired clay was in use. The only diagnostic fired clay forms during the Saxon period are the loomweights, which are separately reported.

Large quantities of material were collected from Saxon period deposits during excavation as samples of *in situ* structure and were sorted, recorded and large quantities immediately discarded. The notes made during this process were recorded in a Word document which forms part of the archive, and a summary of the data was incorporated in the Excel file that forms the complete catalogue of the fired clay. Some samples were found to consist solely of soil lumps and were discarded without record; burnt stone mixed with the fired clay was either passed to the relevant specialist or a brief record made on an Excel file and then discarded.

Ceramic building material methodology
by Cynthia Poole

The assemblage has been fully recorded on an Excel spreadsheet in accordance with guidelines set out by the Archaeological Ceramic Building Materials Group (ACBMG 2007). The record includes quantification, fabric type, form, surface finish, forms of flanges, cutaways and vents, markings and evidence of use/reuse (mortar, burning etc.). The terminology for Roman tile follows Brodribb (1987); coding for markings, tegula flanges, etc. follows that established by OA for the recording of CBM, and tegula cutaway types follow Warry (2006). Fabrics were characterised with the aid of a x20 hand lens.

The industrial residues methodology
by Lynne Keys

For this report the assemblage was examined by eye and tested with a magnet. The material was categorised on the basis of morphology; a magnet was used to test for iron-rich material and detect smithing micro-slags in the soil adhering to slags. Each slag or other material type in each context was weighed except for smithing hearth bottoms, which were individually weighed and measured for statistical purposes. Quantification data and details are given in the archive.

Activities involving iron can take two forms, smelting or smithing.

Smelting is the manufacture of iron from ore and fuel in a smelting furnace. The products are a spongy mass called an unconsolidated bloom consisting of iron with a considerable amount of slag still trapped inside, and slag (waste). The slag produced varies depending on the technology used in different periods: furnace slags (including slag blocks and furnace bottom cakes), run slag, tap slag, dense slag or, in later periods, blast furnace slag.

Furnace slag is a general term used for slag which can be recognised as having been produced by smelting but which is incomplete or has no particular morphology which can identify the furnace type or technological method used. Much of the Thame smelting material had to be assigned to the furnace slag category because of its fragmentary nature. It appears to have undergone redeposition and damage over time.

Run slag is what its name suggests and was produced by smelting; it can be produced by smelting in slag pit furnaces or tapping furnaces. If tap slag is very fragmentary it can be hard to identify as such and the term 'run slag' has been used in these instances. Very little was present in the assemblage. There was no tap slag, and no run slag that might have come from tap slag. Tap slag is flowing slag (resembling lava flows) produced by the technology and methods introduced and used by the Romans during their occupation.

Smithing involves the hot working (using a hammer) of the bloom to remove excess slag (primary smithing) or, more commonly, the hot working of one or more pieces of iron to create or to repair an object (secondary smithing). As well as bulk slags, including the smithing hearth bottom (a plano-convex slag cake which builds up under the tuyère hole – hottest part – where the air from the bellows enters the hearth), smithing generates micro-slags; these can be hammerscale flakes from ordinary hot working of a piece of iron (making or repairing an object) and/or tiny spheres from bloom smithing or high temperature welding used to join or fuse two pieces of iron. Hammerscale, because of its tiny size, is usually only recovered by taking soil samples from fills and deposits but it is very magnetic and its presence can be detected using a magnet; it is most prevalent (thickest) in archaeological contexts in the immediate area of smithing, i.e. in the vicinity of the anvil and between it and the smithing hearth.

The human remains methodology
by Lauren McIntyre and Alice Rose, with Louise Loe

All human remains were analysed and recorded with reference to Brickley and McKinley (2004) and Mays (2002).

Unburnt skeletons

Unburnt skeletons were assessed for their condition (Grade 0–5+, after McKinley 2004a, 16), completeness (0–25%, 26–50%, 51–75%, 76–100%) and fragmentation ('low', <25% of the skeleton fragmented, 'medium', 25–75% of the skeleton fragmented, or 'high', >75% fragmented). The minimum number of individuals represented by the disarticulated bones was estimated per context based on the repetition of bones, whilst factoring in age and sex (Buikstra and Ubelaker 1994).

Sex and age were estimated using relevant standards (Miles 1962; Moorrees *et al.* 1963; Phenice 1969; Brothwell 1981; Lovejoy *et al.* 1985; Brooks and Suchey 1990; Buikstra and Ubelaker 1994; Miles 2001; Buckberry and Chamberlain 2002; Scheuer and Black 2003). Skeletons were estimated to be probable or possible males or females to reflect the degree reliability of the estimation: some sexually dimorphic traits can be ambiguous, poorly preserved, or only a small number present for observation (Buikstra and Ubelaker 1994, 16). Standard metrical analysis was carried out and stature was calculated for discrete articulated skeletons with suitably intact long bones, using regression equations devised by Trotter and Gleser (1952; 1958) and revised by Trotter (1970). Non-metric traits were routinely scored for discrete articulated adults following the guidelines set out by Berry and Berry (1967) and Finnegan (1978). Pathology was described and differential diagnoses explored, with reference to standard texts (e.g., Aufderheide and Rodríguez-Martín 1998; Galloway 1999; Ortner 2003).

Cremations

Urned cremation burials were block lifted, then excavated by hand, in 2cm spits. Each spit was photographed and recorded using Oxford Archaeology pro-forma recording sheets. Unurned cremations were recovered in bulk and washed through a sieve stack to sort them into >10mm, 10–4mm, 4–2mm and 2–0.5mm fractions.

Analysis of each deposit involved recording its colour, weight (in grams) and maximum fragment size. These observations can provide information on factors such as the effectiveness of cremation (i.e., how well burnt the body was), relative quantity of fuel used, attained temperature within the pyre, length of time over which the cremation took place, degree of bone oxidation, and how well collected the burnt remains were from the pyre site (McKinley 2004b, 10–11). Evidence for the presence of pyre goods was also recorded where relevant. The weight, and presence or absence of charcoal fuel waste was also considered in order to explore deposit type, i.e., whether the deposit represented a formal burial or pyre debris.

Each deposit was examined for identifiable bone elements and the minimum number of individuals (MNI) was estimated by employing the methods given above. Where possible, sex and age were estimated and pathology described and diagnosed, as above.

Where the 4–2mm fraction weighed more than 20g, a 20g sample was sorted. An estimation of the total bone weight was calculated for the entire fraction, based on the proportion of cremated bone present in the 20g sample. The estimated weights are included in the total weights presented. The smallest fraction sizes (2–0.5mm) were not sorted but were rapidly scanned for identifiable skeletal remains and artefacts. Estimations of the proportions of bone present within the 2–0.5mm fractions were made and recorded in the archive. These are presented below but were not included in the total bone weights.

Charcoal methodology
by Julia Meen

The soil samples, ranging in size from 0.1 to 40 litres, were processed for charred plant remains and charcoal by mechanical flotation in a modified Siraf-type machine, with the sample held on a 500µm mesh and the flot collected on a 250µm mesh. Where sample volumes were small (less than 5L) they were floated by hand using the 'wash-over' technique. The flots were then air-dried and a brief assessment was carried out. The flots (or in the case of larger flots, a sample of material) were rapidly scanned under a stereo microscope at x10–x40 magnification. Any seeds or chaff noted were provisionally identified and an estimate of abundance made, the presence of molluscs and insects was also noted. The heavy residue fractions from the samples were also air-dried and scanned for abundance of charred material and artefacts. Preliminary identifications of plant macrofossils and charcoal are noted following the nomenclature of Stace (1997; 2010) for wild plants and trees and traditional nomenclature as provided by Zohary *et al.* (2012) for cereals.

Charcoal > 2mm was considered potentially identifiable and quantified. A random selection of representative charcoal fragments from each sample was examined to provide a provisional species identification. This most commonly involved examining the transverse section at x10–x40 magnification. While this provides a reliable method of the identification for ring porous taxa (e.g., *Quercus* sp.), identifications are tentative for the semi- to diffuse-porous taxa (Maloideae/Pomoideae, *Prunus* etc.). Selections of the more unusual items were checked on the radial and tangential sections using a Brunel Metallurgical SP-400BD microscope at up to x400 magnification. Items were identified with reference to keys, images and descriptions in Schweingruber (1990), Hather (2000), Gale and Cutler (2000), Schoch *et al.* (2004) and Wheeler *et al.* (1989).

Plant macrofossils methodology
by Sarah F. Wyles

The bulk samples were processed following standard flotation methods, using a 250µm sieve for the recovery of the flot and a 0.5mm sieve for the collection of the residue. All identifiable charred plant remains in the analysed samples were identified following nomenclature of Stace (1997) for wild plants, and traditional nomenclature, as provided by Zohary *et al.* (2012) for cereals. Where assemblages were very rich, some of the fractions were sub-sampled and the results multiplied up and marked with 'e.' in the tables to show that these figures are estimates. Where the samples were scanned in detail rather than analysed, the charred plant remains were recorded by a mixture of absolute accounts and a scale of abundance. These samples have been marked with an S.

References

Journal abbreviations follow those of the Council for British Archaeology, April 1991 in *Signposts for archaeological publication* (3rd edn), 59–70

ACBMG 2007 *Ceramic building material: minimum standards for recovery, curation, analysis and publication*. Archaeological Ceramics Building Materials Group https://www.archaeologicalceramics.com/uploads/1/1/9/3/11935072/ceramic_building_material_guidelines.pdf (accessed 10 October 2023)

Ahrens, C. 1966 'Vorgechichte des Kreises Pinneberg und der Insel Helgoland. Die vor – und frühgeschichtlichen Denkmäler und Funde in Schleswig-Holstein 7', in K. Kersten (ed.) *Verroffentlichung des Landesamtes fur Vor – und Frühgeschichte in Schleswig*. Neumünster, Karl Wachholtz, 205–32

Albarella, U. 2005 'The role of domestic ducks and geese from Roman to medieval times in Britain', in G. Grupe and J. Peters (eds) *Feathers, grit and symbolism: birds and humans in the ancient Old and New Worlds*. Oxford, Verlag Marie Leidorf, 249–58

Allason Jones, L. and Miket, R. 1984 *The catalogue of small finds from South Shields Roman Fort*. Newcastle, The Society of Antiquaries of Newcastle upon Tyne Monogr **2**

Allen, J.R.L. and Fulford, M.G. 1996 'The distribution of south-east Dorset Black Burnished category 1 pottery in south-west Britain', *Britannia* **27**, 223–82

Allen, M., Brindle, T., Lodwick, L., Fulford, M. and Smith, A.T. 2017 *New visions of the countryside of Roman Britain, Volume 2: The rural economy of Roman Britain*. London, Britannia Monogr Ser **30**

Allen, T.G. 1990 *An Iron Age and Romano-British enclosed settlement at Watkins Farm, Northmoor, Oxon*. Oxford, Oxford University Committee for Archaeology, Thames Valley Landscapes: the Windrush Valley Volume **1**

Allen, T.G. and Robinson, M.A. 1993 *The prehistoric landscape and Iron Age enclosed settlement at Mingies Ditch, Hardwick with Yelford, Oxon*. Oxford, Oxford Archaeology, Thames Valley Landscapes Monogr **2**

Andersson Strand, E. 2012 'From spindle whorls and loom weights to fabrics in the Bronze Age Aegean and Eastern Mediterranean', in M.-L. Nosch and R. Laffineur (eds) *Kosmos: jewellery, adornment and textiles in the Aegean Bronze Age, Proceedings of the 13th International Aegean Conference*. University of Copenhagen, Danish National Research Foundation's Centre for Textile Research, 207–15

Andrews, P. 1996 'Prospect Park and Hurst Park: the settlements and the landscape', in P. Andrews and A. Crockett, *Three excavations along the Thames and its tributaries, 1994*. Salisbury, Wessex Archaeol Rep **10**, 108–11

Andrews, P., Mepham, L., Schuster, J. and Stevens, C. 2011 *Settling the Ebbsfleet Valley, High Speed 1 excavations at Springhead and Northfleet, Kent. The Late Iron Age, Roman, and medieval landscape, Volume 4: Saxon and later finds and environmental reports*. Oxford and Salisbury, Oxford Wessex Archaeology

Ashdown, R.R. 1993 'The avian bones', in R.J. Williams, *Pennylands, Hartigans: two Iron Age and Saxon sites in Milton Keynes*. Aylesbury, Buckinghamshire Archaeological Society Monogr **4**, 154–8

Astill, G.G., Lobb, S.J., Coy, J., Hinton, D., Jones, G., McDonnell, G., Clark, A.J., Digby, N., Farwell, D., Richards J. and Hawkes J. 1989 'Excavation of prehistoric, Roman, and Saxon deposits at Wraysbury', *Berkshire Archaeol J* **146**, 68–134

Aufderheide, A.C. and Rodríguez-Martín, C. 1998 *The Cambridge encyclopedia of human paleopathology*. Cambridge, Cambridge University Press

Ayres, W.R., Ingrem, K., Light, C., Locker, A., Mulville, J. and Serjeantson, D. 2003 'Mammal bones, bird, fish remains and oysters', in A. Hardy, A. Dodd, and G.D. Keevill, *Aelfric's Abbey: excavations at Eynsham Abbey, Oxfordshire, 1989–92*. Oxford, Oxford Archaeology, Thames Valley Landscapes Monogr **16**, 341–432

Bagnall-Smith, J. 1998 'More votive finds from Woodeaton, Oxfordshire', *Oxoniensia* **63**, 147–85

Baker, J.R. and Brothwell, D.R. 1980 *Animal diseases in archaeology*. London, Academic Press Inc.

Banham, D. and Faith, R. 2014 *Anglo-Saxon farms and farming*. Oxford, Oxford University Press

Barclay, A., Glass, H. and Hey, G. 1995 'Fired clay', in G. Hey, 'Iron Age and Roman settlement at Old Shifford Farm, Standlake', *Oxoniensia* **66**, 136–8

Bartlett-Clark Consultancy, 2015 *Site F2 Oxford Road Thame*. Unpublished report, Oxfordshire

Bartosiewicz, L. and Gál, E. 2013 *Shuffling nags, lame ducks: the archaeology of animal disease*. Oxford, Oxbow Books

Bartosiewicz, L., Van Neer, W., Lentacker, A. and Fabiš, M. 1997 *Draught cattle: their osteological identification and history*. Tervuren, Belgium, Annales Musée Royal de l'Afrique Centrale – Serie in 8° – Sciences Zoologiques **281**

Behrensmeyer, A.K. 1978 'Taphonomic and ecologic information from bone weathering', *Paleobiology* **4**, 150–62

Benson, D. and Miles, D. 1974 *The Upper Thames Valley: an archaeological survey of the river gravels*. Oxford, Oxford Archaeological Unit Survey **2**

Berisford, F. 1981 'The Anglo-Saxon pottery', in T. Rowley and L. Brown, 'Excavations at Beech House Hotel, Dorchester-on-Thames 1972', *Oxoniensia* **46**, 39–43

Berry, A.C. and Berry, A.J. 1967 'Epigenetic variation in the human cranium', *J Anatomy* **101**, 361–79

BGS (British Geological Survey) 2018 *Geology of Britain viewer*. http://www.bgs.ac.uk/discoveringGeology/geologyOfBritain/viewer.html (accessed March 2018)

Biddulph, E. 2005a 'Roman pottery', in P. Bradley, B. Charles, A. Hardy and D. Poore, 'Prehistoric and Roman activity and a Civil War ditch: excavations at the Chemistry Research Laboratory, 2–4 South Parks Road, Oxford', *Oxoniensia* **70**, 155–67

Biddulph, E. 2005b 'Fired clay', in P. Bradley, B. Charles, A. Hardy and D. Poore, 'Prehistoric and Roman activity and a Civil War ditch: excavations at the Chemistry Research Laboratory, 2–4 South Parks Road, Oxford', *Oxoniensia* **70**, 167–9

Biddulph, E. 2019 'Late Iron Age and Roman pottery', in Biddulph *et al.* 2019, 55–80

Biddulph, E., Brady, K., Simmonds, A. and Foreman, S. 2019 *Berryfields: Iron Age settlement and a Roman bridge, field system and settlement along Akeman Street near Fleet Marston, Buckinghamshire*. Oxford, Oxford Archaeology Monogr **30**

Blair, J. 1988 *Anglo-Saxon Oxfordshire*. Oxford, Oxfordshire Books

Blair, J. 1996 'The minsters of the Thames', in J. Blair and B. Golding, *The cloisters and the world: essays in medieval history in honour of Barbara Harvey*. Oxford, Clarendon Press, 5–28

Blair, J. 2018 *Building Anglo-Saxon England*. Princeton, NJ, Princeton University Press

Blinkhorn, P. 2001 'Anglo-Saxon pottery', in J. Moore, 'Excavations at Oxford Science Park, Littlemore, Oxford', *Oxoniensia* **66**, 189–97

Blinkhorn, P.W. 2003 'Early and middle Saxon pottery', in A. Hardy, A. Dodd and G.D. Keevill, *Aelfric's Abbey: excavations at Eynsham Abbey, Oxfordshire, 1989–92*. Oxford Archaeology, Thames Valley Landscapes Monogr **16**, 161–75

Blinkhorn, P. 2004 'Early and middle Saxon pottery', in Hey 2004, 267–73

Blinkhorn, P. 2007 'Anglo-Saxon pottery', in Chambers and McAdam, 229–47

Blockley, K., Blockley, M., Blockley, P., Frere, S.S. and Stow, S. 1995 *The archaeology of Canterbury, Volume 5: Excavations in the Marlowe Car Park and surrounding areas*. Canterbury, Canterbury Archaeological Trust

Boardman, S. 2023 'Report on the charred plant remains and charcoal from Didcot Great Western Park', in Hayden *et al.* 2023,

Bond, J.M. 1995 'Animal bone from Early Anglo-Saxon sunken-featured buildings and pits', in R. Rickett, *The Anglo-Saxon cemetery at Spong Hill, North Elmham, Part VII: The Iron Age, Roman and Early Saxon settlement*. Ipswich, East Anglian Archaeol Rep **73**, 142–7

Booth, P. 1996 'Pottery and other ceramic finds', in C. Mould, 'An archaeological excavation at Oxford Road, Bicester, Oxfordshire', *Oxoniensia* **61**, 75–89

Booth, P. 1997 *Asthall, Oxfordshire, excavations in a Roman 'small town'*. Oxford, Oxford Archaeological Unit, Thames Valley Landscapes Monogr **9**

Booth, P. 1999 'Pink grogged ware again', *Study Group for Roman Pottery Newsletter* **27**, 2–3

Booth, P. 2000 'Roman pottery', in P. Booth and C. Hayden, 'A Roman settlement at Mansfield College, Oxford', *Oxoniensia* **65**, 307–17

Booth, P. 2001 'Fired clay', in P. Booth, J. Evans, and J. Hillier, *Excavations in the extramural settlement of Roman Alchester, Oxfordshire 1991*. Oxford, Oxford Archaeology Monogr **1**, 260–1

Booth, P. 2004 'Quantifying status: some pottery data from the Upper Thames Valley', *J Roman Pottery Stud* **11**, 39–52

Booth, P. 2010 'Appendix 7: Anglo-Saxon pottery', in G. Lambrick, *Neolithic to Saxon social and environmental change at Mount Farm, Berinsfield, Dorchester-on-Thames*, Oxford, Oxford Archaeology Occasional Paper **19**, digital archive (http://library.thehumanjourney.net/)

Booth, P. 2011a 'The Iron Age and Roman pottery', in Hey *et al.* 2011, 345–411

Booth, P. 2011b 'Iron-Age and Roman pottery', in A. Simmonds, H. Anderson-Whymark and A. Norton, 'Excavations at Tubney Wood Quarry, Oxfordshire, 2001–2009', *Oxoniensia* **76**, 148–64

Booth, P. 2012 'The occurrence and use of samian ware in rural settlements in the Upper Thames Valley', in D.G. Bird (ed.) *Dating and interpreting the past in the western Roman Empire: essays in honour of Brenda Dickinson*. Oxford, Oxbow, 254–65

Booth, P. 2014 *Oxford Archaeology Roman pottery recording system: an introduction*. Unpublished document, Oxford Archaeology

Booth, P. 2017 'Pottery [from Arkells Land]', in C. Hayden, R. Early, E. Biddulph, P. Booth, A. Dodd, A. Smith, G. Laws and K. Welsh, *Horcott Quarry, Fairford and Arkell's Land, Kempsford: Prehistoric, Roman and Anglo-Saxon settlement and burial in the Upper Thames Valley in Gloucestershire*. Oxford, Oxford Archaeology, Thames Valley Landscapes Monogr **40**, 451–77

Booth, P. 2018a 'Pottery', in A. Simmonds and S. Lawrence, *Footprints from the past: the south-eastern extramural settlement of Roman Alchester and rural occupation in its hinterland. The archaeology of East West Rail Phase 1.* Oxford, Oxford Archaeology Monogr **28**, 81–138

Booth, P. 2018b 'Pottery', in P. Booth and A. Simmonds, *Later prehistoric landscape and a Roman nucleated settlement in the lower Windrush Valley at Gill Mill, near Witney, Oxfordshire.* Oxford, Oxford Archaeology, Thames Valley Landscapes Monogr **42**, 259–395

Booth, P. 2023 'Late Iron Age and Roman pottery', in Hayden *et al.* 2023, 429–475

Booth, P. and Edgeley-Long, G. 2003 'Prehistoric settlement and Roman pottery production at Blackbird Leys, Oxford', *Oxoniensia* **68**, 201–62

Booth, P. and Green, S. 1989 'The nature and distribution of certain pink, grog tempered vessels', *J Roman Pottery Stud* **2**, 77–84

Booth, P., Boyle, A. and Keevill, G.D. 1993 'A Romano-British kiln site at Lower Farm, Nuneham Courtenay, and other sites on the Didcot to Oxford and Wootton to Abingdon water mains, Oxfordshire', *Oxoniensia* **58**, 87–217

Booth, P., Evans, J. and Hiller, J. 2001 *Excavations in the extramural settlement of Roman Alchester, Oxfordshire, 1991.* Oxford, Oxford Archaeology Monogr **1**

Booth, P., Dodd, A., Robinson, M. and Smith, A. 2007 *The Thames through time: the archaeology of the gravel terraces of the Upper and Middle Thames: the early historical period AD 1–1000.* Oxford, Oxford Archaeology, Thames Valley Landscapes Monogr **27**

Bowden, M. and McOmish, D. 1987 'The required barrier', *Scott Archaeol Rev* **4**, 76–84

Boyle, A., Jennings, D., Miles, D. and Palmer, S. 2011 *The Anglo-Saxon cemetery at Butler's Field, Lechlade, Gloucestershire. Volume 2: The Anglo-Saxon grave goods specialist reports, phasing and discussion.* Oxford, Oxford Archaeology, Thames Valley Landscapes Monogr **33**

Brain, C.K. 1981 *The hunters or the hunted?: an introduction to African cave taphonomy.* Chicago, IL, University of Chicago Press

Brennan, N. and Hamerow, H. 2015 'An Anglo-Saxon great hall complex at Sutton Courtenay/Drayton, Oxfordshire: a royal centre of early Wessex?', *Archaeol J* **172(2)**, 325–50

Brickley, M. and McKinley, J. 2004 *Guidelines to the standards for recording human remains.* IFA Paper No. 7, British Association for Biological Anthropology and Osteoarchaeology and the Institute of Field Archaeologists

Broderick, L.G. 2012 'Ritualisation (or The Four Fully-Articulated Ungulates of The Apocalypse)', in A. Pluskowski (ed.) *The ritual killing and burial of animals: European perspectives.* Oxford, Oxbow Books, 22–32

Brodribb, G. 1987 *Roman brick and tile.* Gloucester, Alan Sutton

Bronk Ramsey, C. 1995 'Radiocarbon calibration and analysis of stratigraphy: the OxCal program', *Radiocarbon* **37(2)**, 425–30

Bronk Ramsey, C. 1998 'Probability and dating', *Radiocarbon* **40(1)**, 461–74

Bronk Ramsey, C. 2001 'Development of the radiocarbon calibration program OxCal', *Radiocarbon* **43(2A)**, 355–63

Bronk Ramsey, C. 2009 'Bayesian analysis of radiocarbon dates', *Radiocarbon* **51(1)**, 337–60

Brooks, S.T. and Suchey, J.M. 1990 'Skeletal age determination based on the os pubis: a comparison of the Acsádi-Nemeskéri and Suchey-Brooks methods', *Human Evolution* **5**, 227–8

Brothwell, D.R. 1981 *Digging up bones.* Oxford, Oxford University Press

Brown, A. 1994 'A Romano-British shell-gritted pottery and tile manufacturing site at Harrold, Beds', *Bedfordshire Archaeol* **21**, 19–107

Brown, B., Knocker, G.M., Smedley, M. and West, S.E. 1954 'Excavations at Grimstone End, Pakenham', *Suffolk Archaeol* **26**, 186–207

Brown, K. 1999 'The pottery', in Cromarty *et al.* 1999, 182–95

Brown, K. 2011 'Late prehistoric and Romano-British pottery', in J. Martin, 'Prehistoric, Romano-British and Anglo-Saxon activity at Whitelands Farm, Bicester', *Oxoniensia* **76**, 201–10

Brown, P.D.C. 1972 'The pottery, and other finds', in M. Avery and D. Brown, 'Saxon features at Abingdon', *Oxoniensia* **37**, 69–81

Brown, P.D.C. 1976 'Some notes on grass-tempered pottery', in Farley 1976, 191–3

Bruce-Mitford, R.L.S. 1958 *Antiquities of Roman Britain.* London, Trustees of the British Museum

Buckberry, J. and Chamberlain, A. 2002 'Age estimation from the auricular surface of the ilium: a revised method', *Amer J Phys Anthropol* **119**, 231–9

Buckley, D. 2001 'Querns and millstones', in A.S. Anderson, J.S. Wacher and A.P. Fitzpatrick, *The Romano-British 'Small Town' at Wanborough, Wiltshire.* London, Britannia Monogr Ser **19**, 156–60

Buikstra, J.E. and Ubelaker, D.H. (eds) 1994 *Standards for data collection from human skeletal remains.* Arkansas, AR, Arkansas Archaeological Survey Research Series **44**

Bulleid, H. and Gray, H. St. G. 1911 *The Glastonbury Lake Village, Volume 1.* Glastonbury

Burleigh, G. 2018 'The excavations at Ashwell, 2003–2006', in R. Jackson and G. Burleigh, *Dea Senuna: treasure, cult and ritual at Ashwell, Hertfordshire.* London, Brit Mus Res Publ **194**, 157–211

Butler, C. 2000 *Saxon settlement and earlier remains at Friars Oak, Hassocks, West Sussex.* Oxford, BAR Brit Ser **295**

Campbell, G. 1994 'The preliminary archaeobotanical results from Anglo-Saxon West Cotton and Raunds', in J. Rackham (ed.) *Environment and economy in Anglo-Saxon England.* York, CBA Res Rep **89**, 65–82

Carruthers, W. 1991 'The mineralised plant remains', in Fasham and Whinney (eds) 1991, 67–75

Carson, R.A.G., Hill, P.V. and Kent, J.P.C. 1960 *The Late Roman bronze coinage A.D. 324–498*. London, Spink and Son Ltd

Chambers, R. and McAdam, E. 2007 *Excavations at Barrow Hills, Radley, Oxfordshire, 1983–5, Volume 2: The Romano-British cemetery and Anglo-Saxon settlement.* Oxford, Oxford Archaeology, Thames Valley Landscapes Monogr **25**

Chapman, A. 2008 'The querns and millstones', in A. Westgarth and S. Carlyle, 'A Roman settlement at Bicester Park, Bicester, Oxfordshire', *Oxoniensia* **73**, 143

Chapman, A. 2013 'The querns and millstones', in C. Simmonds and C. Walker, *Archaeological excavation on land at College Road, Aston Clinton, Buckinghamshire: assessment report and updated project design*. Unpublished report, Northamptonshire Archaeology ref. **13/56**, 46

Cobain, S. Meen, J. and Wyles, S. 2017 'Appendix 17: charred plant remains and charcoal', in OCAJV (Oxford Cotswold Archaeology Joint Venture), *Site F1, Oxford Road, Thame, Oxfordshire: post-excavation assessment and updated project design: Volume 2: Appendices*. Unpublished report, Oxford and Kemble, 239–366

Cool, H.E.M. and Baxter, M.J. 2016 'Brooches and Britannia', *Britannia* **47**, 71–98

Cooper, N.J. 1998 'The supply of pottery to Roman Cirencester', in N. Holbrook (ed.) *Cirencester: the Roman town defences, public buildings and shops*. Cirencester, Cirencester Excavations **5**, 324–50

Cotter, J.P. 2008 'Ceramic building materials', in A. Norton and G. Cockin, 'Excavations at the Classics Centre, 65–67 St Giles, Oxford', *Oxoniensia* **73**, 161–94

Cotter, J. 2017 'Anglo-Saxon pottery', in C. Hayden, R. Early, E. Biddulph, P. Booth, A. Dodd, A. Smith, G. Laws and K. Welsh, *Horcott Quarry, Fairford and Arkell's Land, Kempsford: Prehistoric, Roman and Anglo-Saxon settlement and burial in the Upper Thames Valley in Gloucestershire*. Oxford, Oxford Archaeology, Thames Valley Landscapes Monogr **40**, 294–302

Crabtree, P.J. 1990 *West Stow: early Anglo-Saxon animal husbandry*. Ipswich, East Anglian Archaeol Rep **47**

Cromarty, A.M., Foreman, S. and Murray, P. 1999 'The excavation of a late Iron Age enclosed settlement at Bicester Fields Farm, Bicester, Oxon', *Oxoniensia* **64**, 153–234

Crummy, N. 1983 *The Roman small finds from excavations in Colchester*. Colchester, Colchester Archaeological Trust, Colchester Archaeol Rep **2**

Cunliffe, B. 1984 *Danebury: an Iron Age hillfort in Hampshire, Volume 2: The excavations 1969–1978: the finds*. London, CBA Res Rep **52**

Cunliffe, B. and Galliou, P. 2007 *Les fouilles du Yaudet en Ploulec'h, Côtes-d'Armor, Volume 3 : Du quatrième siècle apr : J.-C. à aujourd'hui*. Oxford, Oxford University School of Archaeology Monogr **65**

Cunliffe, B. and Poole, C. 1991 *Danebury: an Iron Age hillfort in Hampshire, Volume 4: The excavations 1979–1988: the site*. London, CBA Res Rep **73**

Cunliffe, B. and Poole, C. 2008a *The Danebury Environs Roman Programme: a Wessex landscape during the Roman era, Volume 2, part 2: Grateley South, Grateley, Hants, 1998 and 1999*. Oxford, English Heritage and Oxford University School of Archaeology Monogr **71**

Cunliffe, B. and Poole, C. 2008b *The Danebury Environs Roman Programme: a Wessex landscape during the Roman era, Volume 2, part 7: Dunkirt Barn, Abbotts Ann, Hants, 2005 and 2006*. Oxford, English Heritage and Oxford University School of Archaeology Monogr **71**

Dar, G., Masharawi, Y., Peleg, S., Steinberg, N., May, H., Medlej, B. and Hershkovitz, I. 2010 'Schmorl's nodes distribution in the human spine and its possible etiology', *European Spine Journal* **19(4)**, 670–75

Dark, P. 2017 'The environment of southern Roman Britain', in D. Bird (ed.) *Agriculture and industry in south-eastern Britain*. Oxford, Oxbow Books, 15–34

Davies, A. 2018 *Creating society and constructing the past: social change in the Thames Valley from the Late Bronze Age to the Middle Iron Age*. BAR Brit Ser **637**

Davies, A., Allen, M., Hayden, C., Lawrence, S. and Masefield, R. forthcoming *Great Western Park, Didcot, Oxon: phase 2 excavations, 2015–2016*. Oxford, Oxford Archaeology Thames Valley Landscapes Monogr

Davies, B., Richardson, B. and Tomber, R. 1994 *A dated corpus of early Roman pottery from the City of London*. London, CBA Res Rep **98**

Davies, J.A. and Gregory, T. 1991 'Coinage from a civitas: a survey of the Roman coins found in Norfolk and their contribution to the archaeology of the civitas Icenorum', *Britannia* **22**, 65–102

Dickinson, T.M. 1976 *The Anglo-Saxon burial sites of the Upper Thames Region and their bearing on the history of Wessex, circa AD 400–700*. Unpublished D. Phil. thesis, University of Oxford

Dunbar, E., Cook, G., Naysmith, P., Tripney, B. and Xu, S. 2016 'AMS 14C dating at the Scottish Universities Environmental Research Centre (SUERC) Radiocarbon Dating Laboratory', *Radiocarbon* **58(1)**, 9–23

Dunning, G.C. 1932 'Bronze Age settlements and a Saxon hut near Bourton-on-the-Water, Gloucestershire', *Antiq J* **12**, 279–92

Eckardt, H. and Crummy, N. 2008 *Styling the body in Late Iron Age and Roman Britain: a contextual approach to toilet instruments*. Montagnac, France, Monographies Instrumentum **36**

Edlin, H.L. 1949 *Woodland crafts in Britain*. Newton Abbot, Country Book Club

Esmonde Cleary, A.S. 2000 *The ending of Roman Britain*. London, Routledge

Evans, D.H. and Loveluck, C. 2009 *Life and economy at early medieval Flixborough, c. AD 600–1000: the artefact evidence*. Oxford, Oxbow Books

Evans, J. 1989 'The Saxon pottery', in H. Dalwood, J. Dillon, J. Evans and A. Hawkins, 'Excavations in Walton, Aylesbury, 1985–86', *Rec Buckinghamshire* **31**, 160–5

Evans, J. 1994 'Discussion of the pottery in the context of Roman Alcester', in S. Cracknell and C. Mahany (eds) *Roman Alcester: southern extramural area: 1964–1966 excavations, part 2*. York, CBA Res Rep **97**, 144–9

Evans, J. 2001 'Iron, Roman and Anglo-Saxon pottery', in Booth *et al.* 2001, 263–383

Evans, J., Thompson A. and Leeds, E.T. 1941 'A hoard of gold rings and silver groats found near Thame, Oxfordshire', *Antiq J* **21**, 197–202

Evison, V.I. 1987 *Dover: Buckland Anglo-Saxon cemetery*. London, Hist Build Monuments Comm Engl Archaeol Rep **3**

Fabiš, M. 2005 'Pathological alteration of cattle skeletons – evidence for the draught exploitation of animals?', in J.J. Davies, M. Fabiš, I.L. Mainland, M.P. Richards and R.M. Thomas (eds) *Diet and health in past animal populations: current research and future directions*. Oxford, Oxbow Books, 58–62

Farley, M.E. 1976 'Saxon and medieval Walton, Aylesbury: excavations 1973–4', *Rec Buckinghamshire* **20**, 163–290

Farley, M.E., Nash, D. and White, R.F. 1981 'A late Iron Age and Roman site at Walton Court, Aylesbury', *Rec Buckinghamshire* **23**, 51–75

Fasham, P.J. and Whinney, R.J.B. (eds) 1991 *Archaeology and the M3*. Salisbury, Trust for Wessex Archaeology, Hampshire Fld Club Archaeol Soc Monogr **7**

Finnegan, M. 1978 'Non-metric variation of the infracranial skeleton', *J Anatomy* **125**, 23–37

Foreman, S., Hiller, J. and Petts, D. 2002 *Gathering the people, settling the land: the archaeology of the Middle Thames landscape: Anglo-Saxon to post-medieval*. Oxford, Oxford Archaeological Unit

Fulford, M. 1975 *New Forest Roman pottery*. Oxford, BAR Brit Ser **17**

Gale, R. 2011 'The charcoal', in J. Hart, E.R. McSloy and A. Mudd, 'A late prehistoric hilltop settlement and other excavations along the Taplow to Dorney Water Pipeline, 2003–04', *Rec Buckinghamshire* **51**, 36–7

Gale, R. and Cutler, D.F. 2000 *Plants in archaeology: identification manual of artefacts of plant origin from Europe and the Mediterranean*. Otley, Westbury and Kew, the Royal Botanic Gardens

Galloway, A. 1999 *Broken bones: anthropological analysis of blunt force trauma*. Springfield, IL, Charles C Thomas

Garmonsway, G.N. 1953 *The Anglo-Saxon Chronicle*. London, Everyman Press

Geake, H. 1997 *The use of grave-goods in conversion-period England, c. 600–c. 850 AD*. Oxford, BAR Brit Ser **261**

Gibson, C. and Murray, J. 2003 'An Anglo-Saxon settlement at Godmanchester, Cambridgeshire', *Anglo-Saxon Stud Archaeol Hist* **12**, 137–217

Gibson, D. and Lucas, G. 2002 'Pre-Flavian kilns at Greenhouse Farm and the social context of early Roman pottery production in Cambridgeshire', *Britannia* **33**, 95–127

Godwin, H. 1984 *History of the British flora* (2nd edn). Cambridge, Cambridge University Press

Grant, A. 1982 'The use of tooth wear as a guide to the age of domestic ungulates', in B. Wilson, C. Grigson and S. Payne (eds) *Ageing and sexing animal bones from archaeological sites*. Oxford, BAR Brit Ser **109**, 91–108

Grant, A. 1984 'Animal husbandry', in Cunliffe (ed.) 1984, 496–547

Green, F.J. 1984 'The archaeological and documentary evidence for plants from the medieval period in England', in van Zeist and Casparie (eds) 1984, 99–144

Green, F.J. 2009 'Late Saxon, medieval and post-medieval plant remains', in D. Serjeantson and H. Rees (eds) *Food, craft and status in medieval Winchester: the plant and animal remains from the suburbs and city defences*. Winchester, Winchester Museum Service, 14–26

Greig, J. 1991 'The British Isles', in van Zeist *et al.* (eds) 1991, 229–334

Grimm, J. 2007 'A dog's life: animal bone from a Romano-British ritual shaft at Springhead, Kent (UK)', in N. Benecke (ed.) *Beiträge zur Archäozoologie und Prähistorischen Anthropologie* **6**, 54–75

Ground Investigation Services 2011 *Site F, land adjacent to A418, Town Farm, Thame: geotechnical and geo-environmental site investigation report*. Unpublished report, ref. **S3924**

Hall-Torrance, M. and Weaver, S. 2003 'The excavation of a Saxon settlement at Riverdene Basingstoke, Hants. 1995', *Proc Hants Fld Club Archaeol Soc* **58**, 63–105

Hambleton, E. 1999 *Animal husbandry regimes in Iron Age Britain: a comparative study of faunal assemblages from British Iron Age sites*, Oxford, Archaeopress, BAR Brit Ser **282**

Hamerow, H. 1993 *Excavations at Mucking, Volume 2: the Anglo-Saxon Settlement*. London. Engl Heritage Archaeol Rep **21**

Hamerow, H. 2002 *Early medieval settlements: the archaeology of rural communities in north-west Europe 400–900*. Oxford, Oxford University Press

Hamerow, H. 2006 ' "Special deposits" in Anglo-Saxon settlements', *Medieval Archaeol* **50**, 1–30

Hamerow, H. 2012 *Rural settlements and society in Anglo-Saxon England*. Oxford, Oxford University Press

Hamerow, H., Hayden, C. and Hey, G. 2007 'Anglo-Saxon and earlier settlement near Drayton Road, Sutton Courtenay, Berkshire', *Archaeol J* **164**, 109–96

Hamerow, H., Ferguson, C. and Naylor, J. 2013 'The Origins of Wessex pilot project', *Oxoniensia* **78**, 49–69

Harcourt, R.A. 1974 'The dog in prehistoric and early historic Britain', *J Archaeol Sci* **1**, 151–75. doi:10.1016/0305-4403(74)90040-5

Hardy, A. and Andrews, P. 2011 'Saxon, medieval, and post-medieval landscape', in P. Andrews, E. Biddulph, A. Hardy and R. Brown, *Settling the Ebbsfleet Valley High Speed 1 excavations at Springhead and Northfleet, Kent: the Late Iron Age, Roman, Saxon, and medieval landscape, Volume 1: The sites*, Oxford and Salisbury, Oxford Wessex Archaeology, 249–305

Hardy, A., Charles, B. and Williams, R. 2007 *Death and taxes: the archaeology of a Middle Saxon estate centre at Higham Ferrers, Northamptonshire*. Oxford, Oxford Archaeology

Hardy, W.K. 1937 'Romano-British pottery kilns between Compton and Aldworth, Berkshire', *Trans Newbury Dist Fld Club* **7**, 211–16

Harris, W.E. 1935 'The later Romano-British kiln in Compton, Berkshire', *Berkshire Archaeol J* **39**, 93–5

Hartley, B.R. and Dickinson, B.M. 2008 *Names on terra sigillata: an index of makers' stamps and signatures in Gallo-Roman terra sigillata (samian ware), Volume 3: CERTIANUS to EXSOBANO*. University of London, Bull Inst Class Stud Suppl **102–03**

Hartley, B.R. and Dickinson, B.M. 2010 *Names on terra sigillata: An index of makers' stamps and signatures in Gallo-Roman terra sigillata (samian ware), Volume 6: MASCLUS I-BALBUS to OXITTUS*. University of London, Bull Inst Class Stud Suppl **102–06**

Hather, J. 2000 *The identification of northern European woods*. Walnut Creek, CA, Left Coast Press

Hawkes, S.C. 1986 'The early Saxon period', in G. Briggs, J. Cook and T. Rowley (eds) *The archaeology of the Oxford region*. Oxford University Department of External Studies, 64–108

Hayden, C., Simmonds, A., Lawrence, S. and Masefield, R. 2023 *Great Western Park, Didcot, Oxfordshire: Phase 1 excavations, 2010–2012*. Oxford, Oxford Archaeology, Thames Valley Landscapes

Henig, M. 1978 *A corpus of Roman engraved gemstones from British sites*. Oxford, BAR Brit Ser **8**

Henig, M. 1991 'Intaglios', in Holbrook and Bidwell 1991, 241–2

Henig, M. 2007 *A corpus of Roman engraved gemstones from British sites* (2nd edn). Oxford, BAR Brit Ser **8**

Henig, M. and Booth P. 2000 *Roman Oxfordshire*. Stroud, Sutton Publishing

Hey, G. 2004 *Yarnton: Saxon and medieval settlement and landscape: results of excavations 1990–96*. Oxford, Oxford Archaeology, Thames Valley Landscapes Monogr **20**

Hey, G., Booth, P. and Timby, J. 2011 *Yarnton: Iron Age and Romano-British settlement and landscape*. Oxford, Oxford Archaeology, Thames Valley Landscapes Monogr **35**

Hill, J.D. 1995. *Ritual and rubbish in the Iron Age of Wessex: a study of formation of a specific archaeological record*. Oxford, BAR Brit Ser **242**

Hillman, G.C. 1981 'Reconstructing crop husbandry practices from charred remains of crops', in Mercer (ed.) 1981, 123–62

Hillman, G.C. 1984 'Interpretation of archaeological plant remains: the application of ethnographic models from Turkey', in van Zeist and Casparie (eds) 1984, 1–41

Hingley, R. 2009 'Esoteric knowledge? Ancient bronze artefacts from Iron Age contexts', *Proc Prehist Soc* **75**, 143–65

Hoffman, M. 1974 *The warp-weighted loom*. Oslo, Maper

Holbrook, N. 2013 'Interpreting the archaeology of late Roman and early post-Roman Cirencester', in H. Eckardt and S. Rippon (eds) *Living and working in the Roman world: essays in honour of Michael Fulford on his 65th birthday*. Portsmouth, Rhode Island, J Roman Archaeol Suppl Ser **95**, 31–46

Holbrook, N. and Bidwell, P. 1991 *Roman finds from Exeter*. Exeter, University of Exeter and Exeter City Council, Exeter Archaeological Reports **4**

Holgate, C. and Mann, J. 2007 *Registered finds in Steppingly to Aylesbury: archaeological watching brief 1997, Volume 2: Appendices*. Lincoln, Network Archaeology Limited Report **234**

Holmes, J.M. 1993 'The animal bones', in R.J. Williams, *Pennylands, Hartigans. Two Iron Age and Saxon sites in Milton Keynes*. Aylesbury, Buckinghamshire Archaeol Soc Monogr Ser **4**, 133–54

Holmes, M.A. 2014 *Animals in Saxon and Scandinavian England: backbones of economy and society*. Leiden, Sidestone Press

Holmes, M. 2017 *Southern England: a review of animal remains from Saxon, medieval and post-medieval archaeological sites*. Swindon, Historic England Res Rep **8/2017**

Holmes, M. 2018 'Beyond food: placing animals in the framework of social change in post-Roman England', *Archaeol J* **175(1)**, 184–213

Holmes, M. 2020, *The animal bone from Wallingford Police Station*. Unpublished report for Oxford Archaeology

Holmes, M., Thomas, R. and Hamerow, H. 2021 'Lesions in sheep elbows: insights from a large-scale study', *Int J Paleopathology* **34**, 50–62

Hope-Taylor, B. 1977 *Yeavering: an Anglo-British centre of early Northumbria*. London, Department Environment Archaeol Rep **7**

Hughes, J. 1984 'The pottery', in M. Foreman and S. Rahtz, 'Excavations at Faccenda Chicken Farm, near Alchester, 1983', *Oxoniensia* **49**, 31–4

Hughes, M.W. 1931 'Grimsditch and Cuthwulf's expedition to the Chilterns in AD 571', *Antiquity* **5(19)**, 291–314

Hurst, H.R. 1985 *Kingsholm: excavations at Kingsholm Close and other sites with a discussion of the archaeology of the area*. Gloucester, Archaeological Publications Ltd

Hydrock 2014 *Site F, Oxford Road, Thame: desk study and ground investigation*. Unpublished report, Hydrock ref. **14223/001**

Jackson, D.A., Harding, D.W. and Myres, J.N.L. 1969 'The Iron Age and Anglo-Saxon site at Upton, Northants', *Antiq J* **49**, 202–21

Jervis, B., Barber, L., Blackmore, L., Cotter, J., Jarrett, C., Jones, P., Mepham, L. and Sudds, B. 2015 'Early Anglo-Saxon pottery in south-east England: recent work and a research framework for the future', *Medieval Ceram* **36**, 17–29

JMHS (John Moore Heritage Services) 2010 *Desk-based assessment on land adjacent to A418, Thame, Oxfordshire*. Unpublished report, Beckley. doi:org/10.5284/1009102

JMHS 2014 *Heritage assessment of land adjacent to A418, Thame, Oxfordshire (Site F)*, NGR SP 6962 0620. Unpublished report, Beckley

Johns, C. 1997 *The Snettisham Roman jeweller's hoard*. London, British Museum

Jones, M.K. 1978 'The plant remains', in M. Parrington (ed.) *The excavation of an Iron Age settlement, Bronze Age ring ditches and Roman features at Ashville Trading Estate (Oxon) 1974–6*. London, CBA Res Rep **28**, 93–110

Jones, M.K. 1981 'The development of crop husbandry', in M.K. Jones and G. Dimbleby (eds) *The environment of man: the Iron Age to the Anglo-Saxon period*. Oxford, BAR Brit Ser **87**, 95–127

Jurmain, R.D. 1977 'Stress and the etiology of osteoarthritis', *Amer J Phys Anthropol* **46**, 353–66

Kenward, H., Hall, A., Jaques, D., Johnson, K. and Carrott, J. 2004 *Technical report: biological remains from excavations at the former D. C. Cook site, off Lawrence Street, York (site code: YORYM 2001.9444)*. Palaeoecology Research Services Report **2004/04**

Kenyon, R. 1985 'The Claudian copy coins', in Hurst 1985, 23–6

Kidd, S. 2014 'Buckinghamshire Late Bronze Age and Iron Age historic environment resource assessment', in G. Lambrick (ed.) 'The Late Bronze Age and Iron Age: resource assessment', in G. Hey, and J. Hind (eds) *Solent-Thames research framework for the historic environment: resource assessments and research agenda*. Oxford Wessex Monogr **6**, 115–47

King, A. and Soffe, G. 1998 'Internal organisation and deposition at the Iron Age temple on Hayling Island', *Proc Hampshire Fld Club Archaeol Soc* **53**, 35–47

Koudelka, F. 1885 'Das Verhältnis der Ossa longa zur Skeletthöhe bei den Säugetieren', *Verhandlungen Naturforsch Vereines in Brünn* **24**, 127–53

Lambrick, G. and Allen, T. 2004 *Gravelly Guy, Stanton Harcourt: the development of a prehistoric and Romano-British community*. Oxford, Oxford Archaeology Thames Valley Landscape Monogr **21**

Lambrick, G. and Robinson, M. 1979 *Iron Age and Roman riverside settlements at Farmoor, Oxfordshire*. Oxford and London, Oxford Archaeological Unit Report **2**, CBA Res Rep **32**

Lambrick, G. with Robinson, M. 2009 *The Thames through time: the archaeology of the grave terraces of the Upper and Middle Thames: the Thames Valley in late prehistory, 1500 BC–AD 50*. Oxford, Oxford Archaeology, Thames Valley Landscapes Monogr **29**

Leeds, E.T. 1927 'A Saxon village at Sutton Courtenay, Berkshire, second report', *Archaeologia* **76**, 59–80

Lepetz, S. and Bourgois, A. 2018 'Were sanctuary wells in Roman Gaul intentionally contaminated using animal carcasses (3rd–4th C. AD)?', *Gallia* **75**, 173–88. doi:10.4000/gallia.2946

Lloyd-Morgan, G. 2001 'Objects of copper-alloy, bone, antler, jet and shale', in Booth *et al.* 2001, 221–42

Lovejoy, C.O., Meindl, R.S., Pryzbeck, T.R. and Mensforth, R.P. 1985 'Chronological metamorphosis of the auricular surface of the ilium: a new method for the determination of adult skeletal age at death', *Amer J Phys Anthropol* **68**, 15–28

Lyne, M. 2008 'Late Iron Age and Roman pottery tradition [at Site 11]', in T. Wilson, *A narrow view across the Upper Thames Valley in later prehistoric and Roman times: archaeological excavations along the Chalgrove to East Ilsley gas pipeline*. Oxford, BAR Brit Ser **467**, 188–9

Lyne, M. 2015 *Late Roman handmade grog-tempered ware producing industries in South East Britain*. Oxford, Archaeopress, Roman Archaeol **12**

MacGregor, A. 1985 *Bone, antler, ivory and horn: the technology of skeletal materials since the Roman period*. London, Routledge

MacGregor, A. 1989 'Bone, antler and horn industries in the urban context', in D. Serjeantson, and T. Waldron (eds) *Diet and crafts in towns: the evidence of animal remains from the roman to the post-medieval periods*. Oxford, BAR Brit Ser **199**, 107–28

MacGregor, A. and Bolick, E. 1993 *Ashmolean Museum, Oxford: a summary catalogue of the Anglo-Saxon collections (non-ferrous metals)*. Oxford, BAR Brit Ser **230**

Mackreth, D.F. 2011 *Brooches of Late Iron Age and Roman Britain*. Oxford, Oxbow Books

Maltby. J.M. 1987 *The animal bones from the excavations at Owslebury, Hants: an Iron Age and Early Romano-British settlement*. English Heritage, Ancient Monuments Lab Rep (New Series) **6/1987**

Maltby, J.M. 1993 'Animal bones', in P.J. Woodward, S.M. Davies and A.H. Graham (eds) *Excavations at the Old Methodist Chapel and Greyhound Yard, Dorchester, 1981–1984*. Dorchester, Dorset Natur Hist Archaeol Soc Monogr **12**, 313–40

Maltby, J.M. 2010 *Feeding a Roman town: environmental evidence from excavations in Winchester, 1972–1985*. Winchester, Winchester Museums

Manning, W.H. 1985 *Catalogue of the Romano-British iron tools, fittings and weapons in the British Museum*. London, British Museum Publications Ltd

Martin, J. 2011 'Prehistoric, Romano-British and Anglo-Saxon activity at Whitelands Farm, Bicester', *Oxoniensia* **76**, 173–240

Marty, F. 2002 'L'habitat de hauteur du Castellan (Istres, B.-du-Rh.) à l'âge du Fer', *Documents d'Archéologie Méridionale* **25**, 129–69

Marzinzik, S. 2003 *Early Anglo-Saxon belt buckles (late 5th to early 8th centuries AD): their classification and context*. Oxford, BAR Brit Ser **357**

Mays, S. 2002 *Human bones from archaeological sites: guidelines for producing assessment documents and analytical reports*. London, English Heritage

McBride, A., Hamerow, H. and Harrison, J. 2022 'A seventh-century high-status settlement at Long Wittenham, Oxfordshire', *Anglo-Saxon Stud Archaeol Hist* **22**, 23–49

McKinley, J.I. 2004a 'Compiling a skeletal inventory: disarticulated and co-mingled remains', in M. Brickley and J.I. McKinley (eds) *Guidelines to the standards for recording human remains*. IFA Paper No. 7, Southampton and Reading, British Association for Biological Anthropology and Osteoarchaeology and the Institute of Field Archaeologists, 14–17

McKinley, J.I. 2004b 'Compiling a skeletal inventory: cremated human bone', in M. Brickley and J.I. McKinley (eds) *Guidelines to the standards for recording human remains*, IFA Paper No. 7, Southampton and Reading Biological Anthropology and Osteoarchaeology and the Institute of Field Archaeologists, 9–13

McKinley, J.I. 2006 'Cremation...the cheap option?', in C. Knüsel and R. Gowland (eds) *The social archaeology of funerary remains*. Oxford, Oxbow Books, 81–8

McKinley, J.I. 2013 'Cremation: excavation and analysis', in S. Tarlow and L. Nilsson Stutz (eds) *The Oxford handbook of the archaeology of death and burial*. Oxford, Oxford University Press, 147–72

McNaught, J.M. 2006 *A clinical and archaeological study of Schmorl's Nodes: using clinical data to understand the past*. Unpublished PhD thesis, University of Durham

Mellor, M. 1994 'Oxfordshire pottery: a synthesis of middle and late Saxon, medieval and early post-medieval pottery in the Oxford region', *Oxoniensia* **59**, 17–217

Mercer, R. (ed.) 1981 *Farming practice in British prehistory*. Edinburgh, Edinburgh University Press

Miles, A. 1962 'Assessment of age of a population of Anglo-Saxons from their dentition', *Proc Royal Soc Medicine* **55**, 881–6

Miles, A. 1992 'The charcoal', in P.A. Yeoman, and I.J. Stewart, 'A Romano-British villa estate at Mantles Green, Amersham, Buckinghamshire', *Rec Buckinghamshire* **34**, 175

Miles, A.E.W. 2001 'The Miles method of assessing age from tooth wear revisited', *J Archaeol Sci* **28**, 973–82

Miles, A.E.W. and Grigson, C. 1990 *Colyer's variations and diseases of the teeth of animals*. Cambridge, Cambridge University Press

Miles, D. (ed.) 1986 *Archaeology at Barton Court Farm, Abingdon, Oxon: an investigation of late Neolithic, Iron Age, Romano-British and Saxon settlements*. Oxford and London, Oxford Archaeological Unit Report **3**, CBA Res Rep **50**

Miles, D. Hofdahl, D. and Moore, J. 1986 'The Saxon pottery', in Miles (ed.) 1986, fiche 7:F1–7:G6

Moffett, L. 1994 'Charred cereals from the ovens/kilns in late Saxon Stafford and the botanical evidence for the pre-burh economy', in J. Rackham (ed.) *Environment and economy in Anglo-Saxon England*. York, CBA Res Rep **89**, 55–64

Moffett, L. 2004 'The evidence for crop-processing products from the Iron Age and Romano-British periods and some earlier prehistoric plant remains', in Lambrick and Allen 2004, 421–45

Moorrees, C.F.A., Fanning, E.A. and Hunt, E.E. 1963 'Age variation of formation stages for ten permanent teeth', *J Dental Res* **42**, 1490–502

Morris, J.T. 2010 'Associated Bone Groups: beyond the Iron Age', in J.T. Morris and J.M. Maltby (eds) *Integrating social and environmental archaeologies: reconsidering deposition*. Oxford, Archaeopress, BAR Brit Ser **2077**, 12–23

Morris, J.T. 2011 *Investigating animal burials: ritual, mundane and beyond*. Oxford, Archaeopress, BAR Brit Ser **535**

Morris, J. and Jervis, B. 2011 'What's so special? A reinterpretation of Anglo-Saxon "Special Deposits" ', *Medieval Archaeol* **55**, 66–81

Murray, P. 2014 *An archaeological evaluation at Site F, Oxford Road, Thame, Oxfordshire*. Unpublished report, John Moore Heritage Services, Beckley

Myres, J.N.L. 1977 *A corpus of Anglo-Saxon pottery of the pagan period*. Cambridge, Cambridge University Press

OCA (Oxford-Cotswold Archaeology) 2016 *Site F2, Area B, Oxford Road, Thame Oxfordshire: Archaeological evaluation*. Unpublished OCA typescript report, Oxford and Kemble

O'Connell, M.G. and Bird, J. 1994 'The Roman temple at Wanborough, excavation 1985–1986', *Surrey Archaeol Collect* **82**, 1–168

Ortner, D.J. 2003 *Identification of pathological conditions in human skeletal remains*. London, Academic Press

Ottaway, P. 2009 'The knives', in Evans and Loveluck 2009, 203–31

Ottaway, P. and Rogers, N. 2002 *Craft, industry and everyday life: finds from medieval York*. York, York Archaeological Trust/Council for British Archaeology, The Archaeology of York: The Small Finds **17/15**

Parkhouse, J. 1997 'The distribution and exchange of Mayen Lava quernstones in early medieval northwestern Europe', in G. De Boe and F. Verhaeghe (eds) *Exchange and trade in medieval Europe: papers of the 'Medieval Europe Brugge 1997' conference, Volume 3*, 97–106

Payne, S. 1973 'Kill-off patterns in sheep and goats: the mandibles from Aşvan Kale', *Anatolian Studies* **23**, 281–303. doi:10.2307/3642547

Peacock, D.P.S. and Williams, D.F. 1986 *Amphorae and the Roman economy*. London, Longman

Pearce, J. 2013 *Contextual archaeology of burial practice: case studies from Roman Britain*. Oxford, Archaeopress

Perrin, R. 2013 'Iron Age and Roman pottery', in C. Simmonds and C. Walker, *Archaeological excavation on land at College Road, Aston Clinton, Buckinghamshire: assessment report and updated project design*. Northampton Archaeol Rep **13/56**, 38–43

Phenice, T.W. 1969 'A newly developed visual method of sexing the os pubis', *Amer J Phys Anthropol* **30**, 297–301

Philpott, R. 1991 *Burial practices in Roman Britain: a survey of grave treatment and furnishing, AD 43–410*. Oxford, BAR Brit Ser **219**

Poole, C. 2007a 'Structural clay and ceramic building material', in Timby *et al.* 2007, 265–78

Poole, C. 2007b 'The Roman sites: archaeological descriptions', in Timby *et al.* 2007, 67–144

Poole, C. 2011 'Fired clay and daub from Springhead', in P. Andrews, L. Mepham, J. Schuster and C.J. Stevens, *Settling the Ebbsfleet Valley: High Speed 1 excavations at Springhead and Northfleet, Kent: the Late Iron Age, Roman, Saxon, and medieval landscape, Volume 4: Saxon and later finds and environmental reports*. Oxford and Salisbury, Oxford Wessex Archaeology, 40–1

Poole, C. 2012 'La terre cuite structurale et le petit mobilier d'argile', in T. Allen, M. Dodd, M. Donnelly, B. Gourlin and C. Poole, *Rocade d'agglomération briochine (Trégueux – Côtes-d'Armor – Bretagne). Enclos défensif, bâtiment public et habitat nucléé de La Tène 2, et leurs développements à la période gallo-romaine et à l'époque médiévale*. Unpublished report, Oxford Archaeology

Poole, C. 2023 'Fired clay', in Hayden *et al.* 2023, 491–501

Poole, K. 2013 'Horses for courses? Religious change and dietary shifts in Anglo-Saxon England', *Oxford J Archaeol* **32**, 319–33. doi:10.1111/ojoa.12017

Price, E. 2000 *Frocester: a Romano-British settlement, its antecedents and successors, Volume 2: The finds*. Stonehouse, Gloucester and District Archaeological Research Group

Price, E. 2010 *Frocester: a Romano-British settlement, its antecedents and successors, Volume 3: The supplement: excavations 1995–2009*. Stonehouse, Gloucester and District Archaeological Research Group

Primeau, C., Arge, S.O., Boyer, C. and Lynnerup, N. 2015 'A test of inter-and intra-observer error for an atlas method of combined histological data for the evaluation of enamel hypoplasia', *J Archaeol Sci Reports* **2**, 384–8

Pritchard, F.A. 1984. 'Late Saxon textiles from the City of London', *Medieval Archaeol* **28**, 46–76

Rawes, B. 1981 'The Romano-British site at Brockworth, Glos.', *Britannia* **12**, 45–78

Reece, R. 1985 'Coins', in Hurst 1985, 22–3

Reece, R. 1993 'British sites and their Roman coins', *Antiquity* **67(257)**, 863–9

Reich, D. Armit, I. Patterson, N. Isakov, M. Booth, T. Büster, L. and Fischer, C.-E. in prep. 'Previously unknown migration into Britain in the context of a peak of mobility in late Bronze Age Europe'

Reimer, P., Bard, E., Bayliss, A., Beck, J., Blackwell, P., Bronk Ramsey, C., Grootes P., Guilderson, T., Haflidason, H., Hajdas, I., Hatté, C., Heaton, T., Hoffmann, D., Hogg A., Hughen, K., Kaiser, K., Kromer, B., Manning, S., Niu, M., Reimer, R., Richards, D., Scott, E., Southon, J., Staff, R., Turney C. and van der Plicht J. 2013 'IntCal13 and Marine13 Radiocarbon Age calibration curves 0–50,000 years cal BP', *Radiocarbon* **55(4)**, 1869–87

Reimer, P.J., Austin, W.E.N., Bard, E., Bayliss, A., Blackwell, P.G., Bronk Ramsey, C., Butzin, M., Cheng, H., Edwards, R.L., Friedrich, M., Grootes, P.M., Guilderson, T.P., Hajdas, I., Heaton, T.J., Hogg, A.G., Hughen, K.A., Kromer, B., Manning, S.W., Muscheler, R., Palmer, J.G., Pearson, C., van der Plicht, J., Reimer, R.W., Richards, D.A., Scott, E.M., Southon, J.R., Turney, C.S.M., Wacker, L., Adolphi, F., Büntgen, U., Capano, M., Fahrni, S.M., Fogtmann-Schulz, A., Friedrich, R., Köhler, P., Kudsk, S., Miyake, F., Olsen, J., Reinig, F., Sakamoto, M., Sookdeo, A. and Talamo, S. 2020 'The IntCal20 Northern Hemisphere Radiocarbon Age calibration curve (0–55 cal kBP)', *Radiocarbon* **62**, 725–57

Reynolds, A. 2003 'Boundaries and settlements in later sixth to eleventh-century England', in D. Griffiths, A. Reynolds and S. Semple (eds) 'Boundaries in early medieval Britain', *Anglo-Saxon Stud Archaeol Hist* **12**, 98–136

Reynolds, P.J. and Langley, J.K. 1979 'Romano-British corn-drying oven: an experiment', *Archaeol J* **136**, 27–42

RIC = Roman Imperial Coinage 1926–94 10 vols., some revised. London, Spink and Son Ltd

Richmond, A., Rackham, J. and Scaife, R. 2006 'Excavations of a prehistoric stream-side site at Little Marlow, Buckinghamshire', *Rec Buckinghamshire* **46**, 65–102

Rippon, S. 2017 'Romano-British coarse ware industries and socio-economic interaction in Eastern England', in M. Allen, L. Lodwick, T. Brindle, M. Fulford and A. Smith, *New visions of the countryside of Roman Britain, Volume 2: The rural economy of Roman Britain*. London, Britannia Monogr Ser **30**, London, 336–52

Roden, D. 1968 'Woodland and its management in the medieval Chilterns'. *Forestry* **41(1)**, 59–71

Roe, F. 2011 'Worked stone', in Hey *et al.* 2011, 439–47

Rogers, J. 2000 'The palaeopathology of joint disease', in M. Cox and S. Mays (eds) *Human osteology in archaeology and forensic science*. London, Greenwich Medical Media, 163–82

Rogers, N. 2009 '1.8: The pins', in Evans and Loveluck 2009, 30–72

Rogers, J. and Waldron, T. 1995 *A field guide to joint disease in archaeology*. Chichester, John Wiley & Sons

Roskams, S., Neal, C., Richardson, J. and Leary, R. 2013 'A late Roman well at Heslington East, York: ritual or routine practices?' *Internet Archaeol* **34**. doi:10.11141/ia.34.5

Ross, S. 2011 'Pins', in Boyle *et al.* 2011, 29–34

Roux, J.-C. 2006 'Relecture du foyer décoré de cercles de Substantion, Castelnau-le-lez, Hérault (2ème moitié du VIe s. av. n. è.)', *Documents d'archéologie méridionale* **28**. http://dam.revues.org/document550.html (accessed 7 May 2009)

Rutherford, M. 2017 'Appendix 19: palaeoenvironmental report', in OCAJV (Oxford Cotswold Archaeology Joint Venture), *Site F1, Oxford Road, Thame, Oxfordshire: post-excavation assessment and updated project design, Volume 2: Appendices*. Unpublished report, Oxford and Kemble, 372–84

Scheuer, L. and Black, S. 2000 *Developmental juvenile osteology*. Oxford, Elsevier Academic Press

Schoch, W., Heller, I., Schweingruber, F.H. and Kienast, F. 2004 *Wood anatomy of Central European species*. www.woodanatomy.ch

Schweingruber, F. 1990 *Microscopic wood anatomy* (3rd edn). Birmensdor, Swiss Federal Institute for Forest, Snow and Landscape Research

Seager Smith, R. 2013 'Pottery', in G. Wakeham and P. Bradley, 'A Romano-British malt house and other remains at Weedon Hill, Aylesbury, Buckinghamshire', *Rec Buckinghamshire* **53**, 12–17

Sellwood, L. 1984 'Objects of iron', in Cunliffe 1984, 346–71

Semple, S. 2013 *Perceptions of the prehistoric in Anglo-Saxon England: religion, ritual and rulership in the landscape*. Oxford, Oxford University Press

Sewell, L. 2010 *Osteochondrosis in sheep and cattle: differential diagnosis and estimating prevalence*. York, University of York

Shaffrey, R. 2008a 'The worked stone', in C. Thatcher, *Romano-British activity at Grendon Underwood: excavations on the Hardwick to Marsh Gibbon Gas Pipeline, Buckinghamshire. Post-excavation assessment and updated project design*. Bar Hill, Cambridgeshire, Oxford Archaeology East, 80–4

Shaffrey, R. 2008b 'The millstones', in B. Cunliffe and C. Poole, *The Danebury Environs Roman programme: a Wessex landscape during the Roman era, Volume 2, part 3: Fullerton, Hants, 2000 and 2001*. Oxford, English Heritage and Oxford University School of Archaeology Monogr **71**, 124–30

Shaffrey, R. 2014 'Stone', in Oxford Archaeology, *Bicester Eco Development Bicester Oxfordshire, Archaeological Evaluation Report Volume 1: Main Report and Appendices*, 69

Shaffrey, R. 2015 'Intensive milling practices in the Romano-British landscape of southern England. Using newly established criteria for distinguishing millstones from rotary querns', *Britannia* **46**, 55–92

Shaffrey, R. 2017a 'Roman Ewell: a review of the querns and millstones and implications for understanding the organisation of grain processing', *Surrey Archaeol Collect* **100**, 259–69

Shaffrey, R. 2017b 'A re-investigation of British stone loomweights', in R. Shaffrey (ed.) *Written in stone: papers on the function, form, and provenancing of prehistoric stone objects in memory of Fiona Roe*. St Andrews, Highfield Press, 229–48

Shaffrey, R. 2018 'Grain processing in and around Roman Cirencester. What can querns and millstones tell us about supply to the Roman town?', *Trans Bristol and Gloucestershire Archaeol Soc* **136**, 161–170

Shaffrey, R. 2019 'Worked stone', in Biddulph *et al.* 2019, 86–9

Shaffrey, R. 2023 'The worked stone', in Hayden *et al.* 2023

Sharples, N. 2010 *Social relations in later prehistory*. Oxford, Oxford University Press

Silver, I.A. 1969 'The ageing of domestic animals', in D.R. Brothwell and E.S. Higgs (eds) *Science in archaeology: a survey of progress and research*. London, Thames & Hudson, 283–302

Slowikowski, A.M. 2008 'The pottery from the Aston Clinton bypass', in R. Masefield, *Prehistoric and later settlement and landscape from Chiltern Scarp to Aylesbury Vale: the archaeology of the Aston Clinton bypass, Buckinghamshire*. Oxford, BAR Brit Ser **473**, 78–118

Smith, A., Allen, M., Brindle, T. and Fulford, M. 2016 *New visions of the countryside in Roman Britain, Volume 1: The rural settlement of Roman Britain*. London, Britannia Monogr Ser **29**

Smith, I. and Strid, L. 2017 'Appendix 14: Animal bone', in OCAJV, *Site F1, Oxford Road, Thame, Oxfordshire: post-excavation assessment and updated project design: Volume 2: Appendices*. Unpublished report, Oxford and Kemble, 231–51

Smith, W. 2011 'Charred plant remains from Northfleet', in Andrews *et al.* 2011, 100–5

Snyder, L. and Moore, E. (eds) 2006 *Dogs and people in social, working, economic and symbolic interaction, Proceedings of the 9th ICAZ Conference, Durham 2002*. Oxford, Oxbow Books

Spain, R. and Riddler, I. 2010 'The millstones', in P. Bennett, I. Riddler, and C. Sparey-Green, *The Roman watermills and settlement at Ickham, Kent*. Canterbury, The Archaeology of Canterbury (New Series) **5**, 277–85

Stace, C. 1997 *New flora of the British Isles* (2nd edn). Cambridge, Cambridge University Press

Stace, C. 2010 *New flora of the British Isles* (3rd edn). Cambridge, Cambridge University Press

Stevens, C. 2003 'An investigation of agricultural consumption and production models for prehistoric and Roman Britain', *Environmental Archaeol* **8**, 61–76

Stevens, C.J. 2004 'Charred plant remains', in Hey 2004, 351–64

Stevens, C.J. 2009 'Charred plant remains', in P. Andrews, K. Egging Dinwiddy, C. Ellis, A. Hutcheson, C. Phillpotts, A. Powell and J. Schuster, *Kentish sites and sites of Kent: a miscellany of four archaeological excavations*. Salisbury, Wessex Archaeol Rep **24**, 41–7

Stevens, C.J. 2011a 'Crop-husbandry as seen from the charred botanical samples from Yarnton', in Hey *et al.* 2011, 534–68

Stevens, C.J. 2011b 'Charred plant remains', in Martin 2011, 226–33

Stevens, C.J. 2011c 'Charred plant remains from Springhead', in Andrews *et al.* 2011, 95–9

Stevens, C.J. with Robinson, M. 2004 'Production and consumption: plant cultivation', in Hey 2004, 81–2

Strid, L. 2014 'Animal bone', in R. Atkins, E. Popescu, G. Rees and D. Stansbie, *Broughton, Milton Keynes, Buckinghamshire: the evolution of a South Midlands landscape*. Oxford, Oxford Archaeol Monogr **22**, 409–12

Strid, L. 2017 'Animal bone', in C. Hayden, R. Early, E. Biddulph, P. Booth, A. Dodd, A. Smith, G. Laws and K. Welsh, *Horcott Quarry, Fairford and Arkell's Land, Kempsford. Prehistoric, Roman and Anglo-Saxon settlement and burial in the Upper Thames Valley in Gloucestershire*. Oxford, Oxford Archaeology, Thames Valley Landscapes Monogr **40**, 339–45

Strid, L. 2023 'Animal bone', in Hayden *et al.* 2023

Stuiver, M. and Kra, R.S. 1986 'Editorial comment', *Radiocarbon* **28**, 2B, ii

Stuiver, M. and Polach, H.A. 1977 'Reporting of ^{14}C data', *Radiocarbon* **19**, 355–63

Stuiver, M. and Reimer, P.J. 1986 'A computer program for radiocarbon age calculation', *Radiocarbon* **28**, 1022–30

Stuiver, M. and Reimer, P.J. 1993 'Extended ^{14}C data base and revised CALIB 3.0 ^{14}C age calibration program', *Radiocarbon* **35**, 215–30

Swan, V. 1984 *The pottery kilns of Roman Britain*. London, HMSO and Roy Comm Hist Monuments Suppl Ser **5**

Swanton, M.J. 1973 *The spearheads of the Anglo-Saxon settlements*. London, Royal Archaeological Institute

Taylor, A. 2012 'Excavation of late Neolithic pits, an early Bronze Age ring-ditch, and an early Iron-Age pit alignment at Church Farm, Thame', *Oxoniensia* **77**, 153–98

Taylor, J. 2004 'The distribution and exchange of pink, grog-tempered pottery in the East Midlands: an update', *J Roman Pottery Stud* **11**, 60–6

Thompson, I. 1982 *Grog-tempered 'Belgic' pottery of South-eastern England*. Oxford, BAR Brit Ser **108**

Thompson, I. 2015 'When was the Roman conquest in Hertfordshire?', in K. Lockyear (ed.) *Archaeology in Hertfordshire: recent research*. Hatfield, Hertfordshire Publications, 117–34

Timby, J.R. 2000 'The pottery', in M. Fulford and J. Timby, *Late Iron Age and Roman Silchester: excavations on the site of the forum-basilica 1977, 1980–86*. London, Britannia Monogr Ser **15**, 180–312

Timby, J. 2003 'The pottery', in J. Pine and S. Ford, 'Excavation of Neolithic, late Bronze Age, early Iron Age and early Saxon features at St Helen's Avenue, Benson, Oxfordshire', *Oxoniensia* **68**, 144–57

Timby, J. 2004 'Pottery', in S. Ford, I. Howell and K. Taylor, *The archaeology of the Aylesbury-Chalgrove Gas Pipeline, and the Orchard, Walton Road, Aylesbury*. Reading, Thames Valley Archaeological Services Monogr **5**, 74–81

Timby, J. 2008 'The Roman pottery', in A. Westgarth and S. Carlyle, 'A Roman settlement at Bicester Park, Bicester, Oxfordshire', *Oxoniensia* **73**, 136–41

Timby, J. 2014, 'Pottery', in JMHS 2014, 61–5

Timby, J. 2018 'The pottery', in M. Fulford, A. Clarke, E. Durham and N. Pankhurst, *Late Iron Age Calleva: the pre-conquest occupation at Silchester Insula IX*. London, Britannia Monogr Ser **32**, 150–213

Timby, J.R., Booth, P. and Allen, T.G. 1997 *A new Early Roman fineware industry in the Upper Thames Valley*. Unpublished report, Oxford Archaeological Unit

Timby, J., Brown, R., Hardy, A., Leach, S., Poole, C. and Webley, L. 2007 *Settlement on the Bedfordshire Claylands Archaeology along the A421 Great Barford Bypass*. Oxford, Bedfordshire Archaeol Monogr **8**

Tipper, J. 2004 *The Grubenhaus in Anglo-Saxon England*. Yedingham, Landscape Research Centre

Tipper, J. 2012 *Experimental archaeology and fire: the investigation of a burnt reconstruction at West Stow Anglo-Saxon Village*. Ipswich, East Anglian Archaeol Rep **146**

Tomber, R. and Dore, J. 1998 *The national Roman fabric reference collection: a handbook*. London, Museum London Archaeol Services Monogr **2**

Trotter, M. 1970 'Estimation of stature from intact long bones', in T.D. Stewart (ed.) *Personal identification in mass disasters*. Washington D.C., Smithsonian Institution Press, 71–83

Trotter, M. and Gleser, G. 1952 'Estimation of stature from long-bones of American whites and negroes', *Amer J Phys Anthropol* **9**, 427–40

Trotter, M. and Gleser, G. 1958 'A re-evaluation of estimation of stature based on measurements of stature taken during life and of long bones after death', *Amer J Phys Anthropol* **16**, 79–123

TVAS (Thames Valley Archaeological Services) 1994 *Southern Road, Thame, Oxfordshire: an archaeological evaluation*. Unpublished typescript report, Reading (February 1994)

TVAS 1995 *Corner Close, Thame, Oxfordshire: an archaeological watching brief*. Unpublished typescript report, Reading (June 1995)

TVAS 1997 *13 Bell Lane, Thame, Oxfordshire: an archaeological watching brief*. Unpublished typescript report, Reading (December 1997)

TVAS 2001 *12a Bell Lane, Thame, Oxfordshire: an archaeological watching brief*. Unpublished typescript report, Reading (June 2001)

TVAS 2012 'Church Farm excavation of Late-Neolithic pits, an Early Bronze-Age ring ditch and an Early Iron-Age pit alignment at Church Farm, Thame', *Oxoniensia* **77**, 153–98

Underwood-Keevill, C. 1992 'The pottery', in G.D. Keevill, 'An Anglo-Saxon site at Audlett Drive, Abingdon, Oxfordshire', *Oxoniensia* **57**, 67–73

van der Veen, M. 1989 'Charred grain assemblages from Roman-period corn driers in Britain', *Archaeol J* **146**, 302–19

van der Veen, M. and O'Connor, T. 1998 'The expansion of agricultural production in late Iron Age and Roman Britain', in J. Bayley (ed.) *Science in archaeology: an agenda for the future*. London, English Heritage, 127–43

van Zeist, W. and Casparie, W.A. (ed.) 1984 *Plants and ancient man: studies in palaeoethnobotany*. Rotterdam, Balkema

van Zeist, W., Wasylikowa, K. and Behre, K.-E. (eds) 1991 *Progress in Old World Palaeoethnobotany*. Rotterdam, Balkema

VCH (Victoria County History) 1962a 'Thame: topography, manors and estates', in M. Lobel (ed.) *A history of the county of Oxford, Volume 7: Dorchester and Thame Hundreds*. London, VCH, 160–78

VCH 1962b 'Thame: churches, schools and charities', in M. Lobel (ed.) *A history of the county of Oxford, Volume 7: Dorchester and Thame Hundreds.* London, VCH, 199–219

VCH 1962c 'Thame: trade, industry and agriculture', in M. Lobel (ed.) *A history of the county of Oxford, Volume 7: Dorchester and Thame Hundreds.* London, VCH, 178–93

Veldman, J.K. 2013 *Non-metric traits. an assessment of cranial and post-cranial non-metric traits in the skeletal assemblage from the 17th–19th century churchyard of Middenbeemster, the Netherlands.* Unpublished Masters thesis, University of Leiden

Viatores 1964 *Roman roads in the south-east Midlands.* London, Gollancz

Wade-Martins, P. 1980 *Excavations in North Elmham Park 1967–72, Volume 1.* Ipswich, East Anglian Archaeol Rep **9**

Wait, G. 1985 *Ritual and religion in Iron Age Britain.* Oxford, BAR Brit Ser **149**

Walker, P.L., Bathurst, R.R., Richman, R., Gjerdrum, T. and Andrushko, V.A. 2009 'The causes of porotic hyperostosis and cribra orbitalia: A reappraisal of the iron-deficiency-anemia hypothesis', *Amer J Phys Anthropol* **139(2)**, 109–25

Waller, M.P. and Schofield, J.E. 2007 'Mid to late Holocene vegetation and land use history in the Weald of south-eastern England: multiple pollen profiles from the Rye area', *Vegetation History and Archaeobotany* **16**, 367–84

Walton, P.J. 2015 'From barbarism to civilisation? Rethinking the monetisation of Roman Britain', *Revue Belge de Numismatique et de Sigillographie* **160**, 105–20

Walton, P. 2022 'Where, when and what for? Coin use in the Romano-British Countryside', in M. Henig, G. Soffe, K. Adcock and A. King (eds) *Villas, sanctuaries and settlement in the Romano-British countryside.* Oxford, Archaeopress, 14–24

Walton Rogers, P. 2007 *Cloth and clothing in Early Anglo-Saxon England, AD 450–700.* York, CBA Res Rep **145**

Warman, S. 2011 'Radiocarbon dating', in J. Hart, E.R. McSloy, and A. Mudd, 'A late prehistoric hilltop settlement and other excavations along the Taplow to Dorney Water Pipeline, 2003–04', *Rec Buckinghamshire* **51**, 33–4

Warry, P. 2006 *Tegulae manufacture, typology and use in Roman Britain.* Oxford, BAR Brit Ser **417**

Webster, G. (ed.) 1976 *Romano-British coarse pottery: a student's guide.* London, CBA Res Rep **6**

Weiss, E. and Jurmain, R.D. 2007 'Osteoarthritis revisited: a contemporary review of aetiology', *Int J Osteoarchaeol* **17(5)**, 437–50

Wells, J. and Slowikowski, A. 2015 'Iron Age and Romano-British pottery', in C. Thatcher, E. Popescu and D. Hounsell, 'Excavations along the Hardwick to Marsh Gibbon Pipeline: an Iron Age to Roman Landscape', *Rec Buckinghamshire* **54**, 34–43

West, S.E. 1985 *West Stow: the Anglo-Saxon village.* Ipswich, East Anglian Archaeol Rep **24**

Wheeler, E.A., Baas, P. and Gasson, P.E. 1989 'IAWA list of microscopic features for hardwood identification', *IAWA Bulletin* **10(3)**, 219–332

Wilkin, N. 2018 'Bronze Age metalwork', in R. Jackson and G. Burleigh, *Dea Senuna: treasure, cult and ritual at Ashwell, Hertfordshire.* London, Brit Mus Res Publ **194**, 300–13

Williams, A. 1950 'Excavations at Allard's Quarry, Marnhull, Dorset', *Proc Dorset Natur Hist Archaeol Soc* **72**, 20–75

Wilson, A.E. 2002 'Machines, power and the ancient economy', *J Roman Stud* **92**, 1–32

Wilson, A. 2012 'Water, power and culture in the Roman and Byzantine worlds: an introduction', *Water History* **4**, 1–9

Wilson, B. 1986 'Faunal remains: animal bones and marine shells', in Miles (ed.) 1986, fiche 8:A1–8:G14

Wilson, B. 1992 'Considerations for the identification of ritual deposits of animal bones in Iron Age pits', *Int J Osteoarchaeol* **2**, 341–9. doi:10.1002/oa.1390020411

Wilson, B. 1996 *Spatial patterning among animal bones in settlement archaeology: an English regional exploration.* Oxford, BAR Brit Ser **251**

Woods, P.J. 1974 'Types of Late Belgic and Early Romano-British pottery kilns in the Nene Valley', *Britannia* **5**, 262–81

Woodward, A. and Marley, J. 2000 'The Iron Age pottery', in P. Ellis, G. Hughes and L. Jones, 'An Iron Age boundary and settlement features at Slade Farm, Bicester, Oxfordshire: a report on excavations, 1996', *Oxoniensia* **65**, 233–48

Woodward, P. and Woodward, A. 2004 'Dedicating the town: urban foundation deposits in Roman Britain', *World Archaeol* **36**, 68–86. doi:10.1080/0043824042000192650

Wright, S.M. 1992 'Millstones', in P. Rahtz and R. Meeson, *An Anglo-Saxon watermill at Tamworth: excavations in the Bolebridge Street area of Tamworth, Staffordshire, in 1971 and 1978.* London, CBA Res Rep **83**, 70–9

Wyles, S.F. 2017 'Charred plant remains', in L. Higbee and L. Mepham, *Living on the Edge: archaeological investigations at Steart Point, Somerset.* Salisbury, Wessex Archaeol Occas Pap, 59–67

Wyles, S.F. 2019 ' Charred plant remains', in N. Garland, 'Prehistoric settlement and burial, early medieval crop processing and a possible early medieval cemetery along the Clyst Valley: investigations south of the Pin Brook, Broadclyst, near Exeter, 2015–2016', *Proc Devon Arch Soc* **77**, 127–33

Wyles, S.F. and Stevens, C.J. 2015 'Charred plant remains', in A.B. Powell, 'Early–Middle Anglo-Saxon settlement beside the Winchester to Silchester Roman road at Abbotts Barton, Winchester', *Proc Hampshire Fld Club Archaeol Soc* **70**, 90–1

Young, C.J. 1977 *The Roman pottery industry of the Oxford region.* Oxford, BAR Brit Ser **43**

Zohary, D., Hopf, M. and Weiss, E. 2012 *Domestication of plants in the Old World: the origin and spread of cultivated plants in West Asia, Europe, and the Nile Valley* (4th edn). Oxford, Clarendon Press

Index

Illustrations are indicated by page numbers in *italics* or by *illus* where figures are scattered throughout the text. Places are in Oxfordshire unless indicated otherwise.

Abbots Ann (Hants), fired clay 94
Abbot's Barton (Hants), plant macrofossils 187
Abbot's Worthy (Hants), plant macrofossils 187
Abingdon, pottery 45–8, 151, 152, 153; *see also* Barton Court Farm
agriculture
   Late Roman 194–6
   Saxon 202
   see also animal bone; crop processing; plant macrofossils
Alcester (Warks), pottery 69
Alchester
   fired clay 91
   pottery 69, 70, 72, 73, 91
   town 3, 195
animal bone
   Roman 107–9
   Saxon
      age and sex 170–2
      assemblage 168–9
      associated bone group 173
      butchery 172–3
      discussion 173–6, 199, 202
      element representation 172
      pathology 173
      taphonomy and spatial distribution 169–70, *169*, *170*
antler/antler working, Saxon 169, 170, 175
armlets *see* bracelets/armlets
Ashville Trading Estate, plant macrofossils 119
Ashwell (Herts), metalwork deposits 190
Aston Clinton (Bucks)
   millstones 87
   pottery 69, 70
awl, Roman, copper alloy 16, *79*, 80
awl/piercer, Saxon, bone *166*, 167
axes, Neolithic 5
Aylesbury (Bucks)
   pottery
      Roman 66, 69, 70, 73
      Saxon 152, 154
   querns/millstones 86

ballista ball 157
barley (*Hordeum vulgare*)
   Roman 112, 114, 118, 119
   Saxon 182, 187
Barrow Hills
   pottery 151, 152–3, 154

   Saxon settlement 201
Barton Court Farm
   animal bone 175
   enclosure 193
   millstones 195
   pottery 151, 152
   villa 3, 193, 194, 196–7
beech woodland 112, 180, 202
bell/rattle, Roman 20, 80, *81*, 82
Benson, pottery 152
Berinsfield
   cemetery 3
   pottery 152
Bicester
   corndrier 119
   enclosures 193
   millstones 87
   pottery 70
   querns 86
   see also Slade Farm; Whitelands Farm
Bishopstone (Bucks), burials 3
bone working 175
Bourton-on-the-Water (Glos), SFB 129, 199
bracelets/armlets, Roman
   copper alloy 34, 78, *79*
   shale 23, 85, 86
brambles (*Rubus* sp) 119
brewing
   Roman 86, 119
   Saxon 182, 187, 201, 203
bricks
   Late Iron Age–Roman 16, 89–90, *93*, 97
   medieval–post-medieval 165
brooches
   Roman
      Aucissa and Hod Hill 34, 76, *77*
      Colchester derivatives 18, 36, 76–8, *77*
      one-piece 18, 76, *77*
      plate 80, *81*
   Saxon 155, *156*, 201
Broughton (Bucks), animal bone 175, 176
buckle, Saxon 139, 155, *156*
burials *see* cremation deposits; dog burials; inhumations; sheep burial
butchery
   Roman 108
   Saxon 172–3

Canterbury (Kent), SFB 199
Castellan (France), fired clay 88
Castelnau (France), fired clay 88
Celtic beans (*Vicia faba*)
  Roman 119
  Saxon 131, 139, 182, 187, 202
cemeteries
  Roman 3
  Saxon 3
ceramic building material
  methodology 205–6
  Roman
    assemblage 96
    discussion 97–8
    fabrics 96–7
    forms 97
  medieval–post-medieval 165
charcoal
  methodology 207
  Roman
    assemblage 109, *109*
    description 109–12
    discussion 112
  Saxon
    discussion 178–81, *182*
    ovens 176–8
    samples 176
    sunken-featured buildings 176
Charlton, pottery 70
Chilterns, beech woodland 112, 180, 202
Cirencester (Glos), pottery 69
Claydon Pike (Glos), pottery 72
coins, Roman 36, 82–3, 192
combs, Saxon 165–7, *166*
Compton (Berks), pottery 45, 71–2
Cookham (Berks), *burh* 203
coombe 7, 8, 9
corndriers
  charcoal 110, 111–12
  discussion 191, 193, 194–5, 196
  excavation evidence
    period 3b *25*, 26–9, *28*, *30*
    period 3c 34–6, *35*, 36–40, *39*
    period 3d *39*, 40
  fired clay 88, *88*, 94, 95
  plant macrofossils 113–19
Cotswold Community (Glos/Wilts), pottery 73
cremation deposits
  discussion 190, 194
  excavation evidence 22, 32
  human bone 99, 100–1, 101–5, 105–6, 106–7
  methodology 206–7
Cricklade (Wilts), *burh* 203
crop processing
  Roman 86–7, 111, 191, 194–5, 196
  Saxon 164–5, 187, 201, 203
  see also plant macrofossils
Cuttle Brook 7, 86, 191, 194

Danebury (Hants), fired clay 88
decorated plate, fired clay 88–9, *89*, 96
Didcot
  animal bone 175
  charcoal 112
  corndriers 195
  farmstead 193
  fired clay 91
  Middle Roman decline 193
  pottery 45, 66, 70, 71, 72, 73
  villa 193, 194
  worked stone 86, 195
Dinton (Bucks), burials 3
ditches
  Late Iron Age 13–16, *14*, *15*
  Late Iron Age/Early Roman
    charcoal 109–11
    discussion 189–90, 192
    excavation evidence 16, *17*, 18–20, *19*
  Early–Middle Roman
    charcoal 110, 111
    discussion 190–1
    excavation evidence 23–6, *25*, *27*
  Late Roman
    discussion 191–2, 195–6
    excavation evidence 32–4, *33*, *36*, *37*, *38*
  Saxon *140*, 141
ditches/gullies, Saxon *122*, 135–6
Ditchley, enclosures 3
dog burials
  Roman 32, 107, 108, 191
  Saxon
    bone 173, 175–6
    discussion 202, 203
    excavation evidence *140*, 141
Dorchester (Dorset)
  dog burials 108
  pottery 152, 153
Dorchester-on-Thames
  bishopric 3, 202
  Roman town 3, 195
Dorney (Bucks), pottery 3
Drayton, enclosures 5
drill bits, Roman 26, 80, *81*
droveways
  Early Roman 23–6, *25*, *27*, 190–1
  Late Roman
    discussion 191
    excavation evidence 32–4, *33*, *36*, *37*, *38*, 40
Ducklington, pottery 72

enclosures
  Late Iron Age–Early Roman
    discussion 189, 190, 192–3
    excavation evidence 13–16, *14*, *15*, *17*, 18–20, *19*
  Early–Middle Roman
    discussion 190, 191
    excavation evidence 23–6, *25*
  Late Roman
    discussion 191–2, 192, 194, 195–6
    excavation evidence 32–4, *33*, *36*, *37*, *38*
  Saxon 139–41, *140*, 201–2, 203
Ewell (Surrey), dog burials 108
Exeter (Devon), plant macrofossils 187
Eynsham
  animal bone 175
  pottery 151, 152, 153
  Saxon settlement 200

Farmoor, fired clay 91
field systems 190, 192; *see also* enclosures

finger rings, Roman 77, 78
firebar, Roman 89, 93–4, *93*, 95
fired clay
  Roman
    assemblage 87
    discussion 95–6
    fabrics 87
    methodology 205
    portable furniture 89
      miscellaneous 92–4, *93*
      oven plates and discs 90–1, *90*, *92*
      triangular perforated bricks 89–90, *93*
    structural 87–8
      decorated plate 88–9, *89*
      wattle-supported structure 88, *88*
    structures 94–5
  Saxon
    assemblage 162–3
    discussion 164–5
    fabrics 163
    form and function 163
      oven floor 163
      portable furniture 164
      slab 163, *163*
      wattle-impressed structure 163–4
    loomweights and spindle whorls 158–62
    methodology 205
    ovens, excavation evidence 136, 138–9
firesteel, Saxon 121, 155–7, *156*, 196
fish bone
  Roman 109
  Saxon 176
flax (*Linum usitatissimum*) 119, 139, 187
Fleet Marston (Bucks), pottery 69; *see also* Aylesbury
Friars Oak (Sussex), special deposits 202
Frocester (Glos), millstones 86
fuel
  Roman 111, 112
  Saxon 178, 179–80

Gewisse 202
Glastonbury (Som), fired clay 88
Godmanchester (Cambs), SFB 200
Grateley (Hants), fired clay 94
Gravelly Guy
  plant macrofossils 119
  pottery 67
Greenhouse Farm (Cambs), kilns 95
Gregory III 175
Grimstone End (Suffolk), loomweights 162
grinding stone/rubber, Roman 85–6
gullies *see* ditches/gullies

hammerstones
  Iron Age–Roman 16, 85
  Saxon 157, 158
handles *see* vessel handles
Hardwick–Marsh Gibbon pipeline (Bucks)
  pottery 67, 69, 70
  querns/millstones 86, 87
hawthorn *see* sloe/hawthorn
Hayling Island (Hants), structured deposition 190
hazelnut shells 119, 187
hearths, Roman 40
Hengistbury Head (Dorset), structured deposition 190

Higham Ferrers (Northants), ovens 201
hippophagy 175
hoard, medieval 5
hollow, Late Iron Age 16
hones
  Roman 36, 85, 86
  Saxon 157
Horcott (Glos)
  animal bone 173–4, 175, 176
  pottery 152, 153
house enclosures, Late Iron Age–Roman
  discussion 190, 193–4, 196
  excavation evidence 16, *17*, *19*, 20
human bone
  methodology 206–7
  Roman
    articulated/disarticulated 98–100, 101, 102, 105
    cremated 99, 100–1, 101–5, 105–6
    discussion 106–7
  Saxon 167–8
Hurst Park (Surrey), settlement 200

industrial residues 98, 165, 206
inhumations
  Iron Age–Roman
    Early Iron Age 13, 16, 18
    Late Iron Age–Early Roman
      discussion 190, 194
      excavation evidence 18, 20, *21*
      human bone 98–100, 105, 106
  post-Roman/Early Saxon
    discussion 196–7, *198*
    excavation evidence 121, *122–3*
    grave catalogue 155–7
    human bone 167–8
intaglio, Roman *77*, 78

Keston (London), dog burials 108
kilns 29, 95–6
Kingsey (Bucks), burials 3
knives
  Roman 36, 80, *81*
  Saxon 121, 155, *156*, 157, 196

Langford Lane East, pottery 70, 71
Langford Lane South, pottery 70
Lechlade (Glos), animal bone 173–4, 175
Little Marlow (Bucks), charcoal 112
London
  dog burials 108
  loomweights 162
Long Wittenham, settlement and burials 3
loomweights, Saxon
  catalogue 161–2
  description/discussion 158–61, *159–60*, 162, 199–200
  excavation evidence 129, 131–3, *133*
Lot's Hole (Bucks), ditches 3
lump, fired clay, hand-squeezed 94

malting
  Roman 86, 119, 195
  Saxon 139, 165, 182, 187, 201
Mantles Green villa (Bucks) 112
Marnhull (Dorset), fired clay 88
Mercia 202

Mercury, depiction of *77*, 78
Merton, south of, pottery 70
metal finds
   Roman 75–6
      agricultural 80, *81*
      household utensils 78, *79*
      personal adornment 76–8, *77*, *79*
      uncertain function 80–2, *81*
      weaponry 80, *81*
      weights and measures 78–80, *79*
   Saxon 155–7, *156*
mill 194, 195, 196
millstones, Roman
   description 83, *84*, 85
   discussion 86, 191, 194, 195
   excavation evidence 29, 36
Mingies Ditch, pollen analysis 112
mount, Roman 36
Mucking (Essex)
   loomweights 161
   pottery 147
   SFB 199

needles, Saxon *166*, 167
Nettlebed, Swan Wood, pottery 45
Northfleet (Kent), plant macrofossils 187
Nuneham Courtenay Lower Farm, pottery 48, 71

Oakridge (Hants), dog burials 108
oats (*Avena sativa*), Saxon 182, 187
Old Shifford
   fired clay 91
   pottery 72
Oscytel, Bishop 202
oven disc 90–1, *90*, 95–6
oven plates 90–1, *92*, 94, 95, 96
ovens
   Late Iron Age–Early Roman
      discussion 189, 191
      excavation evidence 20, *22*, 23, *24*, 30
      fired clay 95
      plant macrofossils 112, 113–14, 119
   Saxon
      charcoal 176–8, 179–80, *180–1*
      discussion 201–2, 203
      excavation evidence 136, *137*
         Oven 1 136, *137*, *138*
         Oven 2 136, *137*
         Oven 3 136–9, *137*, *138*
         Oven 4 *137*, *138*, 139
      fired clay 163–5, *163*
      plant macrofossils 182–7
Owslebury (Hants), dog burials 108
Oxford
   Blackbird Leys, pottery 71
   burh 203
   Mansfield College, pottery 71, 72, 73
   New Chemistry Lab
      fired clay 91
      pottery 73
   Oxford Parkway Station, north of, pottery 70
   Oxford Science Park, pottery 152, 153
Oxford Road, excavations (Thame)
   archaeological background 1–5, *4*
   background, location, topography and geology 1, *2*, 5–9, *7*, *8*

chronology 10–11
discussion
   Late Iron Age–Roman periods 189
      agriculture 194–6
      Late Iron Age–Early Roman 189–90
      Early–Middle Roman 190–1
      Middle Roman 191
      Late Roman 191–2
      occupation history, transformations and continuities 192–4
   post-Roman–Saxon periods 196, *198*
      post-Roman 196–7, *198*
      Early–Mid Saxon settlement 197–201
      Late Saxon settlement 201–2
      settlements in context 202–3
excavation evidence (*illus*)
   period 3a (Late Iron Age–Early Roman c.25 BC–AD 100) 13–23
   period 3b (Early–Middle Roman c.AD 100–240) 23–32
   period 3c (Late Roman AD 240–410) 32–40
   period 3d (Roman AD 43–410) 40
   period 4 (Saxon c.AD 410–1399) 121
      ditches/gullies 135–6
      enclosure 139–41
      ovens and associated features 136–9
      post-Roman/Early Saxon burials 121, *122–3*
      sunken-featured buildings 121–35
excavation methodology 9–10, *9*
finds *see* animal bone; ceramic building material; charcoal; coins; fired clay; fish bone; human bone; industrial residues; metal finds; plant macrofossils; pottery; worked bone; worked stone
previous work 5, *6*
project aims 5

peas (*Pisum sativum*), Saxon 131, 139, 182, 187, 202
pedestals, clay
   description/discussion 89, 92–3, *93*, 96
   excavation evidence 15, 16, 20, 23
Penda 202
Pennyland (Bucks), animal bone 174–5, 176
piercer *see* awl/piercer
pin fragments, Saxon 121, 131, 155, *156*, 157, 196
pin-beaters, Saxon *166*, 167
pits
   Late Iron Age–Roman
      discussion 189, 190
      excavation evidence *19*, 20, 22–3, *22*, *24*, 29–32, 40
      plant macrofossils 112–14, 115–17, 118, 119
   Saxon, plant macrofossils 183–6, 187
   see also sunken-featured buildings
plant macrofossils
   methodology 207
   Roman
      description
         period 3a 112, 113–14
         period 3b 112–14
         period 3c 115–17, 118
         period 3d 115–17, 118–19
      discussion 119
   Saxon
      discussion 187–8
      ovens 182–7
      pit 183–6, 187
      SFBs 183–6, 187

plaque, perforated, fired clay 94
point, bone, Saxon 167
polishing/processing slabs, Roman 84
postholes
    Late Iron Age–Roman 16, 20
    Saxon 129, 131, 133, 139, 179, 201
pottery
    Late Iron Age–Roman
        assemblage 41
        chronology 67–9
        discussion 69–73
        fabrics 41–8
        illustrated vessels *49–56*, 73–5
        in inhumations 18, 20, *21*
        phasing and dates 61–6
        use, reuse and repair 66–7
        vessel types 48–61
    Saxon
        assemblage 143
        discussion 151–4, 199
        Early–Mid Saxon
            context, phasing and chronology 147
            fabrics 143–6
            vessel types, decoration and use 147, *148–50*
        Later Saxon–medieval
            context and phasing 151
            fabrics and forms 147–51, *151*
pottery production 95–6
pottery stamps, Roman 48, *56*
Princes Risborough (Bucks), woodland 180

quern fragments
    Roman
        discussion 86–7, 195
        excavation evidence 16, 36
        rotary 83, 84–5
        saddle 83–4
    Saxon 135, 157, 158, *158*, 199

radiocarbon dates 10, *141*, 142, 205
rake tine, Roman 80, *81*
rattle *see* bell/rattle
Raunds (Northants), ovens 201
ring ditch, Neolithic 141, 201, 203
Riverdene (Hants), SFBs 199
roads, Roman 3, 196
Roughground Farm (Glos), pottery 72
roundhouses, Late Iron Age 16, 189, 192, 193
rubber *see* grinding stone/rubber
rye (*Secale cereale*)
    Roman 118, 119
    Saxon 182, 187

settlements, Anglo-Saxon, regional 3
sheep burial, Early Roman 32, 107–8, 108–9
Silchester (Hants), pottery 71
Slade Farm, pottery 70
slag *see* industrial residues
sloe/hawthorn (*Prunus spinosa/Crataegus monogyna*) 119
Sparkford (Som), loomweights 162
spearhead, Roman 16, 80, *81*, 192
spheres
    flint 36, 85, 86
    ironstone 86

spindle whorls
    Roman 36
    Saxon
        discussion 199
        fired clay 135, 161, 162
        pottery 161, 162
        shale 129, 161, 162
Spong Hill (Norfolk), animal bone 175
spoon, Roman 78, *79*
Springhead (Kent)
    dog burials 108
    fired clay 164
    oven 187
    plant macrofossils 187
Stafford (Staffs), ovens 187, 201
Staines (London), dog burials 108
stakeholes
    Roman 29
    Saxon 133–5, 136, 139, 199, 201
Stanton Harcourt, Saxon settlement 201
Stowe (Bucks), pottery 48
structured deposition
    Late Iron Age–Roman 108, 190, 191, 192
    Saxon 176, 199, 202
sunken-featured buildings 121–9, *122*
    charcoal 176, 177, 178–9
    discussion 197–200
    plant macrofossils 183–6, 187
    Structure 30
        discussion 129, 197, 199
        pottery 146, 147, *149–50*, 153, 154
        summary 124
    Structure 31
        discussion 199
        loomweights 162
        summary 124
    Structure 32
        discussion 199, 200, 201
        loomweights 162
        pottery 146
        summary 125
    Structure 33
        charcoal 176
        discussion 199, 200
        excavation evidence 129–31, *130*
        loomweights 162
        plant macrofossils 187
        pottery 146, *148*, 154
        summary 125
    Structure 34
        discussion 199
        pottery 146, 147, *148*, 153, 154
        summary 126
    Structure 35
        charcoal 176, 178–9
        discussion 199, 200
        excavation evidence 129, 131–3, *132*, *133*
        loomweights 162
        pottery 146
        summary 126
    Structure 36
        discussion 197, 199
        excavation evidence 129, 133–5, *133*
        pottery 146
        summary 126

sunken-featured buildings (cont.)
  Structure 37
    charcoal 176
    discussion 199
    plant macrofossils 187
    pottery 146
    summary 127
  Structure 38 127, 199
  Structure 39 127, 199
  Structure 40 128, 199
  Structure 41 128, *149*, 154, 199
  Structure 42 128, 129, 199
  Sutton Courtenay
  pottery 153
  Saxon settlement 3, 201

Taplow (Bucks), charcoal 112
terret, Iron Age 23
Thame
  church 3
  Church Farm 5, 202
  Crendon Industrial Estate 5, 197
  manor 3
  medieval settlement 3, 5
  Oxford Road excavations *see* Oxford Road excavations (Thame)
Thame, River 7, 194, 202–3
tiles
  Roman 97–8
  medieval–post-medieval 165
timbers, charred, Saxon 131, *133*, 176, 178–9, 200
tools, Roman *79*, 80, *81*
trackways
  Late Iron Age 16, 189
  Early Roman *19*, 20, 191, 192
  Late Roman 191, 196
Trégueux (France), fired clay 88
triangular perforated bricks 89–90, *93*
Tubney Wood Quarry, pottery 71

Upton (Northants)
  loomweights 162
  SFB 199, 200

vessel handles, Roman, copper alloy 18, 78, *79*
villas, Roman 3

Wallingford
  animal bone 176
  burh 203
Wanborough (Surrey), structured deposition 190
Wantage, pottery 72
Water End East (Beds), fired clay 91, 93
waterholes, Roman 32
Watkins Farm, fired clay 91
Weedon Hill (Bucks), pottery 69, 70
weights, Roman, lead 78–80, *79*
well, Roman
  discussion 191
  dog burials 107, 108
  excavation evidence 29, *31*, 32
Wessex 202, 203
West Cotton (Northants), ovens 201
West Stow (Suffolk)
  animal bone 175
  charcoal 179
  SFB 200
West Wycombe (Bucks), woodland 180
whetstones
  Roman 85, 86
  Saxon 157
Whitelands Farm, pottery 70
Winchendon (Bucks), burials 3
Winchester (Hants), plant macrofossils 188
woodland
  Romano-British 112
  Saxon 180–1, 202
worked bone, Saxon 165–7, *166*
worked stone
  Roman 83–7, *84*
  Saxon 157–8, *158*
Wraysbury (Bucks), enclosure 5
Wulfhere 3, 5, 202

Yarnton
  millstones 86
  plant macrofossils 119, 187, 188
  pottery 67, 71, 152, 154
  settlement, post-Roman 3, 197
Le Yaudet (France), fired clay 88
Yeavering (Northumb), SFB 199, 200
Yeovilton (Som), dog burials 108
York (N. Yorks), plant macrofossils 188